# KEY PAPERS
# in
# INFORMATION SCIENCE

edited by
Belver C. Griffith

Published for the
American Society for Information Science
by
Knowledge Industry Publications, Inc.
White Plains, New York

# KEY PAPERS IN INFORMATION SCIENCE

edited by Belver C. Griffith

**Library of Congress Cataloging in Publication Data**
Main entry under title:

Key papers in information science.

Includes index.
1. Information—Addresses, essays, lectures.
I. Griffith, Belver C. II. American Society for Information Science.
Z699.K422 029 79-24288
ISBN 0-313257-77-9

Distributed by
Greenwood Press, Inc.
Westport, CT 06881
ISBN Prefix 0-313

P



**In order to keep this title in print and available to the academic community, this edition was produced using digital reprint technology in a relatively short print run. This would not have been attainable using traditional methods. Although the cover has been changed from its original appearance, the text remains the same and all materials and methods used still conform to the highest book-making standards.**

# TABLE OF CONTENTS

**Part III - The Structure of Literature and Documents**



**Part IV - Information Retrieval and Analysis**

**Part V - Tools and Ideas: The Interface of Information Science and Librarianship**

# FRONTISPIECE

## A Map of Some Major Information Science Writers

Citations of earlier published works have been used to map the position of documents, as in the paper by Small included in this collection. White's recent work on combining authors to retrieve from the *Science Citation Index* (SCI) and the *Social Science Citation Index* (SSCI) now permits the mapping of authors.

Howard White and the editor generated this figure based upon the co-citations of the entire work of some major writers in information science. Distances between pairs of authors were estimated through a procedure which starts with counts of co-citations of the entire published work of pairs of authors by any citing paper covered in seven years (1971-1978) of SSCI. Raw co-citations across the matrix of 39 authors were then subjected to Pearson product-moment correlation procedure correlating pairs of authors (after a suitable transform was employed to create diagonal scores). The resulting correlation coefficients were subjected to Kruskal's MDSCAL method of non-metric multidimensional scaling. All normal criteria for this procedure indicate that the spatial model fits the data well.

The author list was taken from this volume after first eliminating persons who were too rarely cited to generate reliable results. To that was added a list of well-known writers, including some precursors (e.g. Luhn) whose work is not included herein. While certainly not complete, the list and resulting map tell us where most "missing" persons would go.

The regions were delineated through another clustering procedure, the labels coming from the mappers' imagination. The origin is set by procedure; most generalists, as for example, Brookes and Kochen, lie nearby. The axes are arbitrary, being set to run horizontally between the centers of the scientific communication group and the information retrieval group. The vertical axis seems to represent different variables on the left, center and right sectors of the figure. At the left, lower writers use only behavioral measures to study scientific communication; higher writers, only citation measures. In the center, there is some broad opposition of theory (Shannon and Zipf) and practice (Sandison and those persons involved in system design and evaluation): At the far right, persons who evaluate retrieval seem to oppose persons who develop methods of document analysis.

The figure is a unique attempt of a field to display itself using its own methods.

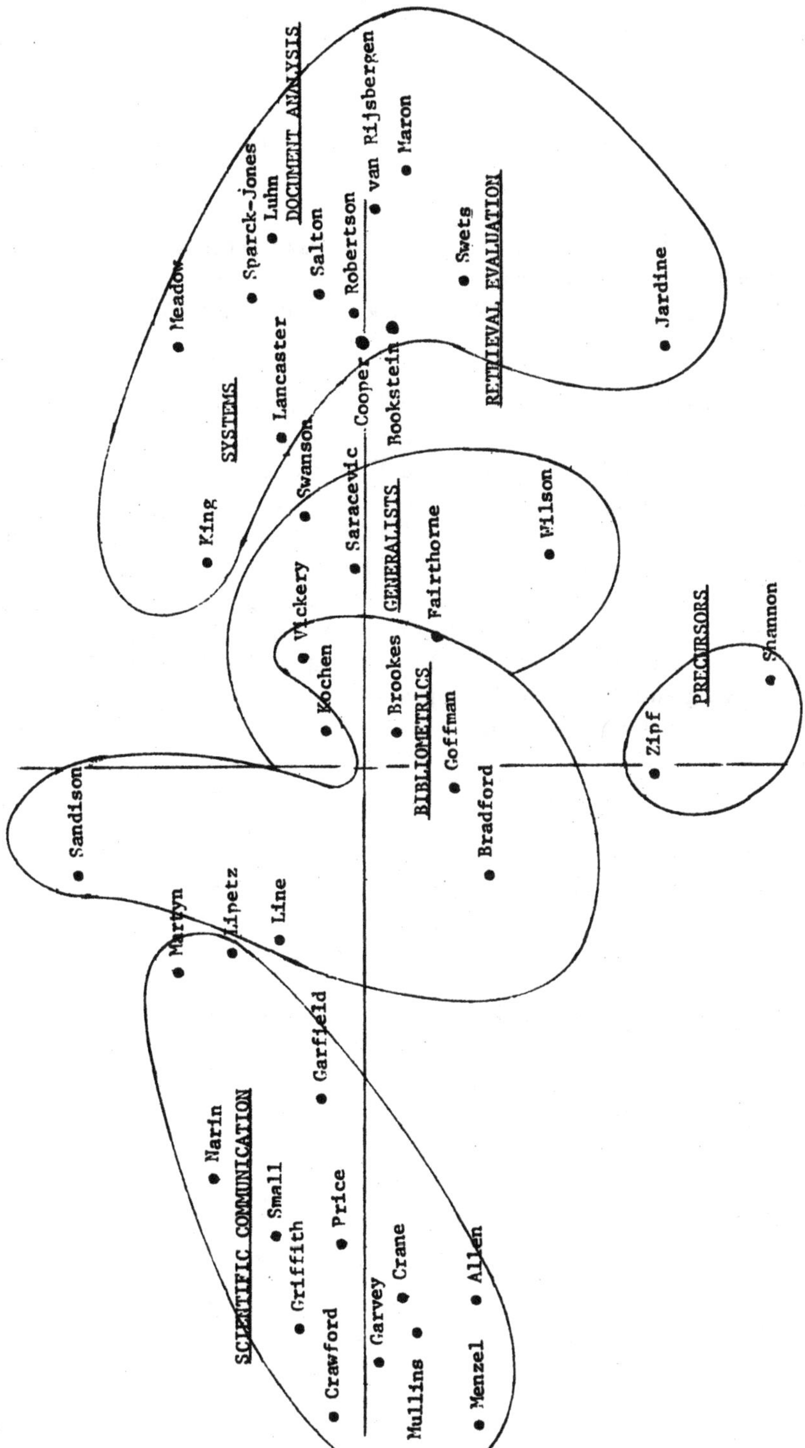
SCIENTIFIC COMMUNICATION
Crawford
Griffith
Small
Narin
Price
Garfield
Garvey
Mullins
Crane
Allen
Menzel
Martyn
Lipetz
Line
Sandison
BIBLIOMETRICS
Bradford
Goffman
Brookes
Kochen
Vickery
GENERALISTS
Fairthorne
Saracevic
Wilson
Swanson
SYSTEMS
King
Lancaster
Meadow
Cooper
Bookstein
DOCUMENT ANALYSIS
Sparck-Jones
Luhn
Salton
Robertson
van Rijsbergen
Maron
RETRIEVAL EVALUATION
Swets
Jardine
PRECURSORS
Zipf
Shannon

# ACKNOWLEDGEMENTS

My principal acknowledgement is to the researchers and scholars whose efforts justify this volume and whose products are herein embalmed. The dreadful logistics of permissions, originals, etc. were ably managed by Lynn A. Deglin in a several months' orgy of tactfulness, intelligence and attention to detail. A chance debate with Gerard Salton revealed that we had similar views on the value of literature on information retrieval; he very kindly reviewed my selections and made helpful additional suggestions; M. Carl Drott and Michael E.D. Koenig contributed to the introduction to that section. Howard D. White contributed the seminal ideas leading to the development of the technique used in creating maps of authors, as in the frontispiece; we shared the technical work. The idea of an appendix listing works citing the Key Papers was suggested by Roger Needham of the University of Cambridge Computer Laboratory and kindly transmitted by his wife, Karen Sparck Jones; Patricia N. Servi assisted in creating the appendix. Portions of the work, especially those exemplifying and displaying techniques developed by coworkers, Henry Small, M. Carl Drott, Howard White and myself, were funded by PHS Grant #ROI LM00911 07 from the National Library of Medicine.

Belver C. Griffith

# DEDICATION

To those persons who have, over the period covered by this volume, instructed most of the rest of us — especially,

Bertram C. Brookes
Robert A. Fairthorne
Manfred Kochen
Derek J. de Solla Price

# INTRODUCTION

Our community of researchers and scholars has offered several efforts aimed at identifying "key" contributions to information science. This, the newest, comes at a time when there have been significant achievements in understanding the major aspects of information processing and handling. There are now important parallels among our ideals, as professionals, regarding the requirements the field must meet, the principal areas of intensive research activities and the important accomplishments.

I am pleased to have had the opportunity to bring together this volume because the process closed off a lengthy debate in my own mind as to what sort of science information science should be. At this point, I would like to discuss the problem at some depth. Despite various cries to the contrary, there is much sound empirical work. The chief difficulty, to my mind, lies in our expectations for the field.

To state what any science "should be" requires a difficult prior step, namely the acceptance of some framework, or even some fragmented ideas, to characterize a science. The intellectual resources available for discussing science are primitive — but not negligible — and have been amplified, in fact, by information science. Among such resources are Merton's work on scientific norms; Price's continua of hardness and softness in science and his attempts to distinguish among science, technology and nonscience; Ben-David's ideas on institutionalization and internal direction if disciplines; Ziman's concept of scientific consensus; and Ravetz's concept of scientific craft. These tools are being variously used to describe earlier states in other sciences, and can be used here to consider information science.

Early on, I concluded that the most important dimension of information science is that it must be regarded as a "soft" as opposed to a "hard" science. There is no particularly clear definition of soft and hard, but most people feel comfortable with contrasting the social soft science with the physical hard science. Within disciplines there are degrees of softness: experimental psychology is hard for psychology; molecular genetics is hard for biology; pyschoanalysis is soft for medicine; and, perhaps, user studies are soft for information science.

Softness is attributed to fields that permit multiple approaches and multiple answers. The subject matter in these fields is elusive and complex, and differences in points of view are necessary and expected. It is difficult to assess work in a soft field; there is no way in which many persons could independently evaluate a discovery. Thus, there are no brilliant outbursts of activity, as would follow major findings in physics.

On consideration, several features of information science that might suggest some degree of hardness include:

- *A dependence on hard technology*. This seems to me a relationship that does affect the internal structure of information science. At the principal interface, computer science, the principal commodity exchanged is hardware.

- *The training and background of "pioneers."* This is superficial, a historical accident like the fact that Gestalt psychology was founded by three persons holding doctorates in physics.

- *The use of analytical tools, quantification.* This reflects the field's inability to avoid large numbers, a point to which I shall return.

- *The "cleaning up" of a point in theory or data.* The most telling of these arguments is the fact that occasionally one can, regarding a particular issue, do a clearly better job than the next fellow, that is, collect better data, clarify a relationship, etc.

Information science is soft because people with all their glorious flexibility and petty fickleness are intrinsic to the systems we study, whether as users, producers, operators, decision makers or as the ultimate, apparently unanalyzable, language processing devices. Immediately, this introduces the possibility of a variety of approaches: theories are not clearly right or wrong; results are rarely the final answer. Both research problems and concepts linger on, as the literature of many social sciences makes clear.

Living with a soft science is a difficult art at best and has been particularly difficult recently for information science and its research personnel. In the United Kingdom and the United States, the beginnings of information science were marked in the 1950s by the migration of a number of natural scientists, behavioral scientists, and applied mathematicians into problem areas dealing with information. The vast majority were, however, natural scientists, and despite the great contributions of these pioneers, major mismatches of approaches and subject matter resulted.

Saracevic's excellent review of research on document relevance shows the way in which an apparently simple problem is gradually recognized to be a very complex one. Why shouldn't it be a simple problem is gradually recognized to be a very complex one. Why shouldn't it be a simple matter to partition a collection into relevant and irrelevant documents and determine how many of each are retrieved? Because the concept of relevance involves all the complexities of human judgment and behavior. Rather than furnishing simple answers, as apparently anticipated, the research ultimately showed that the problem was more like the experimental analysis of aesthetics. More recently, the science policy area has stumbled upon an issue held in common with us, namely, assessing the quality of documents and authors. This issue will ultimately make such items as employee rating scales seem straightforward, but it is at present in the hands of hard scientists who have yet to recognize this complex judgment as a problem in itself. The mismatch of the insensitive investigator and the elusive subject matter is, fortunately, self-correcting and limited to particular research problems. The larger problem is that information scientists have consistently had the wrong expectation for information science.

A decade ago, a senior statesman talked privately of how he felt he had oversold the field. He had promised, from a position of influence, that better techniques would move more and better information that would generate more and better science and technology. Analyzed from a rough epistemology, he, a hard science type, dealt with science policy people, who were nearly all hard science types. He expected to deliver, and they expected to receive, clear, simple answers; he didn't and they didn't. Techniques, systems, hardware and software flourished, but the end product was disappointing. Similar views have recently been expressed by Brookes and by Zunde and Gehl.

From my perspective, this has not been failure but a symptom of the painful recognition that information science is soft. In terms of examining the effects of information on people, their use and interaction with information in a wide variety of situations, the first, very approximate answers came in the period 1958-1970. However, the problems remain, and although they look exceedingly difficult and complex, now finally we have made some major steps toward making them more manageable.

Information science seems to have had, as a science, only one source of fundamental research problems, scientific and technical information. Hopefully, we will see more research and new applications in management information systems. All researchable questions — whether an organization, structure, language, cognition, and so on — seem likely to appear in their purest or most difficult forms in these areas. Each feeds into systems that output and feedback, features essential to assessing the quality of research results. Principles and techniques developed in these areas may be applied broadly to the entire world of information and documents, but they are never severely tested outside these areas.

There is a final critical feature, namely that the field is as wedded to the large data processing devices and the large file as to the human being. The evident progress and excitement surrounding statistical studies of language and documents is not an accident. A probabilistic approach and large numbers are inherent to the field — a matter which should not be entirely forgotten by either an investigator or a subspecialty. Perhaps this aspect of information science explains the low practical impact of retrieval research. Another, perhaps equally important problem, seems to be the low marginal benefit of most suggested improvements.[1]

When we combine the machine, the file and the human being in a statistically based science, we generate a series of problems dealing with structure, language and cognition that relate to, but differ in several important respects from, similar problems in linguistics, psychology, sociology and even epistemology.[2] The disciplinary pressures in these other fields must force them to the simple problem, the "pure" example, the uncontaminated result, pressures which must be counterproductive in our field.

Kuhn wrote an immensely valuable essay for understanding certain transitions in physics. In softer areas of knowledge, this seems to turn into a potentially dangerous weapon, sending many of the untutored around looking for revolutions in softer areas — including ours. We should simply be patient; information science is and should be non-Paradigmatic, my own counter-Kuhnian term for fields that flourish on new facts and techniques rather than new conceptualization. Much of good science can be understood better as the unravelling or wresting of new facts from a recalcitrant nature than as a series of revolutions. Biochemistry hit upon

---

[1]Another unfortunate aspect is that the very difficult problems of retrieval (see Swets and Swanson in the present volume) have been regarded, unreasonably, as central to the field when many distinctive achievements lie elsewhere.

[2]In the above I have deliberately ignored the distinctive economic and organizational problems of information. While information scientists may work on these problems — and they are certainly important — the work will either be congruent with, meet the standards and follow the directions of the economic and decision disciplines or be highly applied and lie mainly in the area of evaluation. These topics are not included in this collection.

the broad relationship between genetic information and biological function and structure a good time ago, probably prior to World War I, and this has set the stage for a continuing series of patiently achieved triumphs in research.

The only candidate for a revolution in the softer sciences is transformational grammar and now that is beginning to look like the reevaluation of a European school of thought that had not originally been allowed to grow through adolescence. In social and behavioral sciences, there is a continuing intellectual dither but little replacement of concepts or vocabulary for at least 30 to 40 years. Why should not we, in information science, also expect to struggle with a single, but highly interesting set of problems for decades?

To summarize, information science is, and should be, messy, diverse and difficult. We should recognize these conditions and live with them. When we look, though, at the actual directions of current research and the nature of recent achievements, we find them to be quite on target.

The ideals we develop as a profession, while less specific and controversial than the above, have much the same direction and force. The American Society for Information Science attempts to represent the field and, in that process, articulates its goals and boundaries. One such statement (ASIS, ca. 1975) follows: "Information Science is concerned with the *generation, collection, organization, interpretation, storage, retrieval, dissemination, transformation* and *use* of information, with particular emphasis on the applications of modern technologies in these areas. As a discipline, it seeks to create and structure a body of *scientific, technological,* and *systems* knowledge related to the transfer of information. It has both *pure science (theoretical)* components, which inquire into the subject without regard to application, and *applied science (practical)* components, which develop services and products." I supplied the emphasis; in current activities we see each aspect emerge as an important area of scholarship.

The contents of this particular volume are the end result of several selection processes undertaken to insure that it reflects current research. Two starting points were chosen. First, I examined citations received by all articles appearing in the several research-oriented information and library science journals. Second, I examined the citations of articles written by authors who had been frequently mentioned in the first seven volumes of the *Annual Review of Information Science and Technology* (ARIST). These were considered complementary starting points, and persons who were discovered as publishing well-cited articles in specialized journals were also searched in the author listing. In this way I identified about 60% of the final selections and all the principal topics.

Evidently, authors in library and information science and technologies cite works in seven principal areas. These areas nearly completely capture the principal processes involving information.

1) Retrieval theory, methods and evaluation: the retrieval, interpretation, "transformation" and analysis of information.
2) Statistical studies of literature: the organization of information.
3) Communication and information exchange in, principally, science: the generation, dissemination and use of information.
4) The impact of information and communication on technology: the use of information.
5) Design and evaluation of information systems and products: the applied science of information services and products.
6) Specific information products and services.
7) Oddments and miscellaneous: apparently, one-paper fields generated by the specific application of theory or method of analysis to a particular problem.

Several additional facts emerged from this process about the research world of library and information science. Actual levels of citation were disappointingly low: 15 citations over 10 years, or three citations per year for recent material, eliminated all but a workable handful relative to each topic. In truth, the community of active scholars is small. Books and chapters in *ARIST* were rather well-cited, but clearly inappropriate to this purpose. I sought mainly original and important empirical contributions. Also, it quickly became clear that Saracevic's 1971 *Introduction to Information Science* did an excellent job, especially on topics 1, 2, and 5 above and on material published through 1970; Saracevic had nicely harvested the well-cited and classic papers generated by the excellent research fundings of the late 1960s.

These facts and the companion volume, Donald King's *Key Papers in the Design and Evaluation of Information Systems,* set the context for making the final selections. Papers on system evaluation, including economic aspects, were eliminated, and no papers reporting on specific services seemed sufficiently general or resistant to aging to be included. But the major topics, and the period 1970 to the present, were set.

The recognition of the various limits on subject matter and on temporal coverage introduced new criteria for selection: coherence, the representation of major techniques and research, and currency. In this last, more difficult process, I attempted thorough selection to show these topics in terms of major research developments from the late 1960s through 1978. In becoming less empirical, I hope I managed, at least, a form of intellectual fairness both to fellow researchers and to readers.

The contents accurately reflect the ideals of the profession. There are major contributions, however, in every area. The studies of retrieval amount to a subdiscipline with well-developed techniques and standards. Despite its low current level of application, it offers many possibilities for future information systems with more internal partitioning and storage than those presently existing. An immensely clever retrieval system, DOSZKOCS, utilizes several of the basic principles on the Medline files of the National Library of Medicine. I suspect that in the future we will be using the techniques of Sparck Jones and Salton on our personal pocket-sized stores of the world's literature. Studies of the literature have generated a great deal of theory as well as clever techniques and findings. The theory arises naturally as the observed structure of the literature must reflect something of the nature of science and the perceptions of the user. Needless to say, the actual analyses which detect and display structure have required much effort and ingenuity. The recent appearance of powerful and general theories, when combined with numerous technical improvements and innovative methods, promises to generate much exciting research.

It is generally unfortunate that we have not placed greater emphasis, within the discipline, on studies of the use, application and communication of scientific and technical information. While less quantitative than studies of document retrieval and of literature, they have furnished a conceptual framework for the understanding of information handling. Their greatest potential lies in pointing to the processing of information that occurs in the application of information and in the processes of assimilation, criticism, and synthesis which are intrinsic to the creation and transmission of knowledge. Future information science needs to define and develop major roles in those processes. Finally, we can expect clever people to appear, attack an information problem and obtain some definitive answers, as in the last section of the book. This will continue, and some will found the specialties of the future.

There are many ideas, some brilliance and even touches of humor in the papers which follow. If this work is regarded not against particle physics, but against a vintage decade of operations research or behavioral science, it is quite good, even though the community of researchers still remains so small.

*References*

Ben-David, Joseph. *The Scientist's Role in Society; a Comparative Study.* Englewood Cliffs, New Jersey: Prentice-Hall, 1971.

Brookes, Bertram C. (Informal communication.) London, 1975.

Kuhn, Thomas S. *The Structure of Scientific Revolutions.* 2nd ed. Chicago: University of Chicago Press, 1970.

Merton, Robert King. *The Sociology of Science; Theoretical and Empirical Investigations.* Chicago: University of Chicago Press, 1973.

Price, Derek de Solla. "Citation Measures of Hard Science, Soft Science, Technology and Nonscience." In C.E. Nelson and D.K. Pollack, *Communication Among Scientists and Engineers.* Lexington, Mass.: Heath, 1970.

Ravetz, Jerome R. *Scientific Knowledge and its Social Problem.* New York: Oxford University Press, 1971.

Saracevic, Tefko. "On the Concept of Relevance in Information Science." Ph.D. dissertation, School of Library Science, Case Western Reserve University, June 1970.

Ziman, John M. *Public Knowledge; the Social Dimension of Science.* Cambridge, England: University Press, 1968.

Zunde, Pranas an Gehl, John. "Empirical Foundations of Information Science." In *Annual Review of Information Science and Technology.* Volume 14. White Plains, New York: Knowledge Industry Publications, Inc., 1979.

# PART I: The Structure and Dynamics of Science Information Flow

Information science and the offering of information services have reached their highest development in handling scientific information. We are all aware that the technologies and theories we use can be readily applied to fields with less structure and fewer resources, such as the humanities; there is a general understanding of the potential of business applications, despite proprietary problems and traditions of not making the background and bases of decisions fully explicit. But granted that, most of the research contained within this volume, and nearly all sophisticated systems development, has been done in the area of science information, and the institutions which serve the information needs of scientists are the sites of most of our sophisticated practitioners.

Information science has an ambivalent approach to science as the activity which generates and structures its finer raw material, and perhaps that can be corrected with better understanding. The selections in this division of the book look first at the general principles which control scientific communication (Menzel); then at the formal structure of information flow within scientific disciplines (Garvey and Griffith) and finally, at informal communication and evaluation processes in science (Crane, Crawford, Griffith and Mullins). These papers were selected as bringing forth the inherent structure of scientific disciplines as powerful mechanisms for processing information. In particular, these papers emphasize and contrast formal and informal aspects of these mechanisms and discuss the underlying driving forces.

Reprinted from American Sociological Review,
Vol. 34, No. 3, June, 1969

# SOCIAL STRUCTURE IN A GROUP OF SCIENTISTS: A TEST OF THE "INVISIBLE COLLEGE" HYPOTHESIS *

DIANA CRANE
*Johns Hopkins University*

***The existence of social organization within a research area may be inferred (a) if scientists who have published in the area have more social ties with one another than with scientists who have not published, and (b) if scientists who have published in the area can be differentiated by degree of social participation within the area. Using a mail questionnaire, sociometric data on different types of scientific relationships were obtained from scientists, all of whom had published in a particular problem area. Respondents chose scientists who had not published in the area as often as they chose scientists within the area. Analysis of direct and indirect ties, using Coleman's method for analysis of sociometric connectedness, revealed that a tie with one or more of the highly productive scientists brought other scientists of less productivity into a large network of influence and communication. Similarities between this type of social organization and that of the "social circle" are discussed.***

ONE type of social group which has received relatively little attention from sociologists is the group comprised of scientists who work on similar research problems. This neglect is probably due to the amorphous character of this type of group. Its members are highly individualistic and widely separated geographically. Participation is voluntary. Turnover is very high; the majority of scientists have only one or two publications in any research area (Price, 1963). Even the boundaries of research areas are difficult to define since most scientific work can be classified in numerous ways, and, often, agreement among scientists regarding the categorization of certain work is far from unanimous. It can thus justifiably be asked whether anything resembling social organization exists in a research area.

Studies of informal communication among scientists indicate that scientists working on similar problems are usually aware of each other and in some cases attempt to systematize their contacts by exchanging reprints with one another (Libbey and Zaltman, 1967; Menzel, 1960; Paisley, 1965). Price has stated that some but not all scientists in a particular research area maintain a high level of informal communication and that information received in this manner is essential for the conduct of effective research (Price, 1963). The amount of material published in some fields is so large that it cannot be monitored effectively by any other means. Kuhn (1962) has argued that groups of scientists develop shared definitions of their work, paradigms which interpret findings and guide new research. In other words, scientists adjust to the problems of dealing with knowledge in their fields by forming social organizations of various kinds, based upon shared communication and shared interpretations of the situation.

However, the existence of "invisible colleges" has been difficult to prove. Scientists have many contacts with other scientists in their own research areas and in other fields, some fleeting, some lasting. If social organization exists in a research area, it is of a highly elusive and relatively unstructured variety. The present research was designed to discover if anything resembling social organization could be observed in a research area. For this purpose, a sociometric analysis of a group of scientists with common research interests was required.[1] The existence of so-

* This research was supported by Grant GN-527 from the National Science Foundation. I am grateful to Derek Price for support and advice and to David Vachon, Edwin Olson and Erik Steiner for developing a computer program for Coleman's method of tracing sociometric connectedness.

[1] Although there have been a number of studies of informal communication among scientists, a sociometric study of communication patterns among scientists who are doing research in the same area had not been attempted before. Nicholas Mullins (1966) did a sociometric analysis of informal communication but did not focus upon a particular field. Several sociometric studies are currently in

cial organization could be inferred (a) if scientists who had published in a particular research area had more social ties with one another than with scientists who had not published in the area, and (b) if scientists who had published in the area could be differentiated in terms of degrees of social participation within the area, suggesting the existence of leadership in the field.

### THE MEASUREMENT OF SOCIAL TIES

If social organization exists in a research area, it is likely to be based on a number of different types of social ties. Informal communication regarding research findings, research-in-progress, and research techniques represents one way in which members of a problem area can be linked to one another. In the present study, information about informal communication was obtained only from those currently engaged in research in the field, a subsample of 52 members from a total of 147 respondents.

In addition to informal communication, several other types of ties between scientists exist. Collaboration occurs in several ways. In the case of formal collaboration (as indicated by bylines on research publications), communication between two or more scientists about their research was so important that it received formal recognition in the publication itself. However, collaboration among scientists may occur before research reaches the stage of formal publication. Another form of collaboration takes place when a student writes a thesis under the direction of one or more teachers; other teachers not formally directing the thesis may play a role in the development of the thesis, and this relationship also represents a kind of collaboration.

Finally, there are intellectual linkages represented by the influence of one scientist's work upon that of another. Citation references in journal articles are direct indications of such influences, and studies of citations have been made (Garfield, 1964; Kessler, 1965; Weinstein, undated). This type of relationship can also be measured by asking scientists to name others who have influenced them in their selection of problems and techniques. Questions of this sort do not elicit data identical to that obtained using linkages among citations. The latter method is more precise and provides more complete information. In addition, the question used in the present study deliberately restricted the scope of the information requested in order to simplify the task of the respondent. Respondents were asked about influences on the selection of problems and techniques but not about influences upon the course of the research. However, many articles include numerous citations, but the relative importance of each citation may vary considerably from a reference to a scientist whose work has had a very strong influence on the author to a scientist whose work is relevant only in connection with a minor point. The use of a questionnaire to elicit some of this information probably has the advantage of obtaining the most important influences, rather than a complete list of major and minor influences.[2]

---

progress, for example, Lingwood (1968), APA Project on Scientific Information Exchange in Psychology (1968), and a dissertation by David Vachon (1969), who was the first to use the Coleman Sociometric Connectedness Program with this type of data. For analysis of problem areas using different techniques, see Fisher, 1966 and 1967, Mullins, 1968 and Russett, 1969. For analyses of scientific literature which relate to this problem, see Cole (1962 and 1963), Kessler (1965), Kessler and Heart (1962), McGrath and Altman (1966), Meadows (1967), Parker et al. (1967), Price and Beaver (1966), Stevens (1953), Stoddart (1967) and Weinstein (undated).

[2] A copy of the questionnaire which was used to elicit information concerning social ties in the area will be sent upon request. The question requesting names of scientists who had influenced the respondents' selection of research problems was not answered by 41% of the group. A similar question requesting names of scientists who had influenced their selections of research techniques was not answered by 59%. This was partly because these questions were not asked of respondents who had written a thesis in the area and nothing more (34 or 23% of the sample), although six of these respondents answered these questions anyway. Failure to respond to these questions was related to low productivity and lack of commitment to the area. A few scientists indicated that the research topic had been assigned to them. Other respondents claimed that these questions were difficult. The degree of perceived difficulty seemed to depend on whether the respondent thought that he was being asked to list every possible influence or only those which had been especially important (the latter was what was requested). In the lengthy career of a scientist influences on the development of re-

Each of these several different types of ties among scientists produces a somewhat different picture of the relationships within the problem area and between members of the area and outsiders. But the juxtaposition of these various indicators of linkage may provide an approximate picture of the degree of the relationship of each with every other. Combining several indicators into a composite index supplies further information about the group. Some members may be related to other members through influences on the selection of problems or techniques, others through some type of collaboration or through informal communication, but, if social organization does exist in a research area, most members should be related to others in at least one of these ways.[3]

As has been indicated previously, these measures are essentially sociometric, involving ties between one scientist and another. Some can be meaningfully looked at in terms of the degree of reciprocity involved; others cannot. Analysis of this type of data, especially for large groups, has always been somewhat problematical for sociologists. For the purpose of this study, it seemed preferable to rely on three methods. The first was simply an overall quantitative statement of the number of choices of various kinds directed both within and without the problem area.

The second was a method of assessing the extent of direct and indirect[4] relationships between members of the problem area. For example, a scientist who communicates with another scientist may obtain indirectly information which was transmitted to the second scientist by a third. A scientist (A) collaborating with another (B), who has in turn collaborated with others (C and D), may benefit indirectly from the work of C and D. Similarly, students, through the mediating efforts of their thesis director, may be in contact with one another even if they are in different settings.

When scientists in an area are linked by ties based on influences regarding the selection of research problems and techniques, their publications in the field build upon ideas expressed in previous works and are closely related. Price (1965) has argued that this is the case in fields where new knowledge is developing rapidly.

All techniques for assessing indirect relationships in groups other than analysis by manual procedures, which are impractical with large groups, are approximate (Coleman, 1964:447). The technique which was used here was a modification of one which was devised by James Coleman (1964:444–455).[5] The choices of members of a group are arranged in matrix form where one axis represents choices made by a member of the group; the other axis, choices received by a member. Continuous multiplication of the matrix by itself provides a means of locating the indirect relationships between the individuals represented in the matrix.[6] This analysis provides figures indicating the total number of persons to whom a particular scientist's choices directly or indirectly lead and the total number of persons choosing him directly or indirectly. In addition, it is possible to construct a measure of connectivity for a group as a whole. This is done by dividing the number of connections which occur (either from or toward individuals) by the total number of connections which could possibly occur.

search can be numerous, but it is quite possible that only a relatively small number of names are very significant in any particular problem area. Some respondents seemed to have difficulty or were unwilling to make the effort to distinguish such influences.

[3] A more difficult problem is that of evaluating the degree of cohesion which occurs. One solution is to define cohesion by means of probability considerations. The probability of each possible structure occurring by chance could be used in assessing the actual outcome, but such probabilities are difficult to construct when the number of choices permitted to each individual is unlimited. An alternative approach is to compare many groups of the same type. If data were available for scientists in many problem areas, one would then be able to evaluate a particular set of data according to such standards. However, in this study, data are presented in which choices within and without the group are compared, and choices by members of different subgroups are also compared.

[4] An indirect relationship is one in which A is linked to C because both are in communication with B.

[5] The program which was used here is a substantial revision and correction of the program which Coleman outlines in his book (Coleman, 1964:466–468).

[6] It is theoretically possible to find all the indirect ties. The algorithm used to solve the problem is not complete. However, it does obtain the vast majority of all the different connections among individuals.

Finally, direct and indirect relationships among members of different subgroups within the problem area were analyzed. For this purpose, members of the problem area were divided into five groups on the basis of productivity in and commitment to the area. The latter was measured in terms of continuity of interest in the area. Using three levels of productivity and two of continuity, it was possible to form six groups, of which five actually occurred in this problem area. Members of three subgroups indicated in response to an item on the questionnaire that they had continued to do research in the area: (1) eight High Producers, each of whom had published more than ten papers in the area; (2) eleven Moderate Producers, who had published four to ten papers in the area; (3) 33 Aspirants, who had published fewer than four papers in the area. Members of two subgroups indicated that they had not continued to do research in the area: (1) nine Defectors, each of whom had published four to ten papers in the area; (2) 86 Transients, each of whom had published fewer than four papers in the area. Every one with more than ten papers continued with his research in the area.

## DESIGN OF STUDY

The selection of a suitable group of scientists was complicated by the fact that scientific fields can be defined as broadly as a discipline or as narrowly as a problem area (a cluster of closely related problems) and by the fact that the precise boundaries of research areas are usually difficult to define.

Among the different types of groups to which scientists belong, the problem area appeared to be the most suitable for an exploratory study, both because it is likely to be fairly small and because the bases for the relationships between members of the group (the scientists' immediate research interests) are fairly specific. An intensive case study of a particular problem area was used to develop techniques and hypotheses which could later be applied to a larger sample of problem areas.

Since scientists frequently work in more than one problem area at a time and often shift areas of interest and, in addition, tend to define the relevance of their work in different ways, it is difficult to locate all the scientists who have worked in a particular problem area. At least four methods of locating members of a problem area are possible: the use of bibliographies, abstracting services, citation networks and sociometric data. Each of these methods has limitations in terms of locating a complete list of members. Lists of abstracts and bibliographies reflect the evaluations of relevance made by the compilers; citations reflect the evaluations of relevance of authors as do sociometric questions. In each case, some references or some names are likely to be omitted.

Although these problems cannot be solved completely, the availability of a bibliography, designed especially for maximum completeness and compiled by a highly productive member of a problem area, provided one means of dealing with the problem outlined above. Use of such a list made it likely that a very high proportion of members of the relevant group would be located.[7]

The problem area selected for this study, the diffusion of agricultural innovations,[8] was part of the research specialty—rural sociology. Since the "invisible college" hypothesis was developed from observations of the be-

[7] Use of such a bibliography entailed accepting the judgment of its compiler regarding the scope of the field and relevant publications. (It is recognized that other authors would supply equally acceptable but somewhat different bibliographies.) The validity of his judgment was borne out by the finding that two-thirds of the respondents placed their publications (on the list) within the area of "diffusion of agricultural innovations" or some variation of this label. Over four-fifths of the more productive members defined the field in this way. The author of the bibliography has stated that "In our continued searchings we now find very few studies that are over one year old. Our confidence is further bolstered when we receive few additional publications or suggestions for inclusion from the leading researchers to whom we send copies of an annual bibliography on diffusion (Rogers and Bettinghaus, 1966)."

[8] The diffusion of innovations has been studied in several academic disciplines (anthropology, economics, geography, psychology), in another research specialty within sociology (medical sociology), and in several applied fields (journalism, communication, consumer behavior, and industrial engineering) (Rogers, 1962; Rogers and Stanfield, 1966). The existence of research on a similar topic in a variety of disciplines is not uncommon. For example, the study of science as an institution and the study of formal organizations exhibit similar patterns.

havior of scientists in fast-moving specialties within physics, the selection of a research area in the social sciences might seem inappropriate. However, an analysis of the 403 papers published in the area between 1941 and mid-1966 revealed that it possessed several of the characteristics which have been found in the literature in the natural sciences (Price, 1961): (1) Growth of the field (number of papers published per year) had progressed through the first three of the four stages which Price has described as being characteristic of scientific literature, (2) the number of new authors entering the field per year showed the same series of stages of growth, (3) A few authors in the area had been highly productive and a majority had produced one or two papers. Although the field contained a larger proportion of single author publications (61%) than would be expected for a research area in the natural sciences, so many factors are believed to influence the amount of collaboration in a research area, and these factors are so imperfectly understood that this characteristic did not seem important enough to disqualify the area for a study of this type.

A second aspect of this problem area which might be considered to limit its usefulness for a case study of this sort is the type of situation in which research in this field has been conducted. For reasons related to the history of rural sociology, research in the diffusion problem area has often been financed and conducted in agricultural experiment stations (Kaufman, 1956). As a result, much of the research has had an applied character. However, this research is not carried out under the conditions of restricted communication which usually characterize applied research in industry. Rural sociologists studying diffusion have been in excellent communication with one another.[9] Thus, the applied character of some of the research does not appear to have inhibited the development of informal social organization in the field.

Using the most recent bibliography compiled for the area (Rogers, 1966), questionnaires were sent to 172 of the 221 scientists listed,[10] both junior and senior authors; 147 replies were received. Each respondent was sent a letter which included references to his publications as listed in the bibliography and was requested to respond to the questionnaire with respect to those publications only (rather than with respect to any other publications he might have produced).[11]

The aim of the study was to obtain some information regarding the circumstances surrounding publication in the area from every scientist who had ever published in it. Since publications in the area began to appear in 1941, some respondents were describing events which had taken place many years ago. The majority of the publications in the area have appeared in the last ten years. An alternative plan would have been to focus upon only those scientists who had published within the last five years. This would, however, have reduced the size of an already small sample. In addition, it would not have

[9] Rogers describes these activities as follows: "The Rural Sociological Society annually devotes several sessions of papers to diffusion, and many studies are published in the Society's journal, *Rural Sociology*. Semiannual meetings of Midwestern rural sociologists studying diffusion are sponsored by the Farm Foundation, and out of these conferences have grown several summary publications and bibliographies." (Rogers, 1962:38)

[10] Due to an oversight, questionnaires were not sent to 15 junior authors, each of whom had one collaborative publication. The considerable period of time which had elapsed since some of the publications had appeared made it difficult to locate a number of members of the group. Addresses were traced by writing to university alumni offices and by searching relevant biographical directories but were unavailable for 34 members of the group; 79% of the remaining members of the group responded. The overall response rate was 67%. Telephone interviews were conducted with 17 members who did not return the questionnaire. Obtaining responses was complicated by the fact that about a quarter of the sample was residing abroad. Since the investigation was viewed as a case study for developing techniques for studying problems of this kind, the questionnaire was not extensively pretested but was tested principally in interviews with colleagues. In addition, ten pretest versions were sent to members of the problem area of which four were returned.

[11] Publications included theses, papers presented at professional meetings, and agricultural experiment station bulletins and reports, as well as journal articles and two books. Data regarding scientific communication should specify precisely which particular research by each scientist should be the referent for his response. Since scientists are often involved in research in more than one area, failure to specify precisely the relevant research can lead to the collection of many irrelevant names.

TABLE 1. NUMBER OF CHOICES RECEIVED BY MEMBERS OF PROBLEM AREA AND OUTSIDERS[a]

| Number of Choices Received | Affiliation of Scientist Chosen: | |
|---|---|---|
| | Problem Area | Outsiders |
| 0 | 46 | .... |
| 1 | 23 | 63.7 |
| 2 | 9 | 20.5 |
| 3– 5 | 10 | 12.5 |
| 6–10 | 5 | 3.0 |
| 11–20 | 4 | 0.3 |
| 21–50 | 2 | 0 |
| Over 50 | 1 | 0 |
| Total | 100 | 100 |
| N | (221) | (389) |

[a] Choices were made by members of the problem area with respect to informal communication, current collaboration, theses directors, thesis influence and influences on the selection of problems and techniques. A scientist could be chosen more than once by the same respondent with respect of different categories as listed above.

provided an overall picture of the development of the problem area. Even though information about publications written many years ago may not be as precise as information about recent publications, it seemed preferable to have information about both types of publications in order to understand the social organization of the area.

### CHOICES WITHIN AND OUTSIDE THE AREA: THE GROUP AND OUTSIDERS

On every measure examined, respondents were about as likely to choose a scientist who had not published in the area as they were to choose one who had. Out of a total 1351 choices made by all respondents on all the different types of ties, outsiders were named 684 times (51%) and problem area members 667 times (49%). Does this suggest that a social group within the area did not exist? There are three reasons for arguing that these figures do not imply the absence of social organization within the problem area.

First, the majority of "outsiders" were selected only once; 84% were chosen no more than twice; twelve, or 3%, were named more than five times. Within the problem area, about half the members were never named;[12] 78% were chosen twice or less. Most of these scientists had been relatively. unproductive; many had only a brief contact with the problem area. On the other hand, 26, or 12%, were named more than five times. Fifteen, or 7%, were named more than ten times. Thus, the social organization of the problem area appeared to be centered around a small and relatively productive proportion of the total membership.

Since only one outsider was named more than ten times, there did not appear to be a group of outsiders whose influence had similar weight. The twelve outsiders who received

[12] In a sample of high energy physicists who were asked to name the two persons with whom they most frequently exchanged information, the proportion of physicists not named was slightly more than a third (Libbey and Zaltman, 1967:31–32).

TABLE 2. NUMBERS OF CHOICES RECEIVED BY SUBGROUPS OF THE DIFFUSION PROBLEM AREA

| Number of Choices Received | Subgroup Affiliation of Scientist Chosen | | | | | |
|---|---|---|---|---|---|---|
| | High Producers | Moderate Producers | Defectors | Aspirants | Transients | Total Group |
| 0 | 0 | 0 | 0 | 24 | 43 | 31 |
| 1 | 0 | 0 | 11 | 39 | 34 | 29 |
| 2– 5 | 0 | 73 | 33 | 27 | 16 | 23 |
| 6–10 | 0 | 27 | 22 | 9 | 5 | 8 |
| 11–20 | 38 | 0 | 22 | 0 | 2 | 5 |
| 21–50 | 38 | 0 | 11 | 0 | 0 | 3 |
| Over 50 | 25 | 0 | 0 | 0 | 0 | 1 |
| Total[a] | 101 | 100 | 99 | 99 | 100 | 100 |
| N | (8) | (11) | (9) | (33) | (86) | (147) |

$\tau_{yx}$=.39 (See Footnote b)

[a] Percentages in this and subsequent tables do not always total 100 due to rounding error.

[b] For computation of tau, the categories of the dependent variable were combined as follows: 0–10, over 10. Goodman and Kruskal's tau indicates the proportion of errors saved in predicting the dependent variable if the independent variable is known (Blalock, 1960:232–234).

more than 5 choices could be characterized in three ways. One was a scientist working in the problem area who had not yet published at the time the questionnaires were mailed but who published during the following year. Two others had published numerous articles in an adjacent problem area, the study of the diffusion of medical innovations. Most of the remaining frequently-chosen outsiders had achieved a high degree of eminence. Seven out of nine had been president of the American Sociological Association or the Rural Sociological Society. Thus these scientists were well known in the discipline as a whole.

There was some indication that the relationships between respondents and members of the problem area were different from their relationships with scientists who had not published in the area. Respondents were asked to indicate if they had any personal acquaintance with the scientists whom they mentioned as having influenced their selection of problems in the area. Of 246 choices of problem area members, 76% were designated as personal acquaintances; of 256 choices of outsiders, 57% were indicated to be personal acquaintances. This outcome suggests that to some extent the influence of outsiders was exerted through publications, while that of insiders was exerted through personal contact.

The problem area which included 221 scientists was able to compete with respect to choices with members of a very much larger population, the former receiving 49% of the total 1351 choices. The outsiders were drawn from several disciplines (unfortunately, this information was not available for many of the outsiders) which altogether include more than twenty thousand scientists.[13] Similar distributions of choices have been found in the analysis of citation references (Swanson, 1966). About half the articles on a particular subject tend to be concentrated in a dozen or so journals; the remainder are widely scattered. Something analogous to the phenomenon of "reference scattering" seems to occur in relation to these measures of scientific relationships.

### CHARACTERISTICS OF MEMBERS OF SUBGROUPS IN THE DIFFUSION PROBLEM AREA

*Selection of Group Members versus Outsiders.*—The five subgroups differentiated on the basis of productivity and commitment to the area were expected to exhibit varying degrees of linkage both with the members of the group and with those who had not published in the area. When all types of ties were considered together, one subgroup of highly productive members appeared to be equally strongly linked to the area and to outsiders.[14] Another subgroup (one which was relatively unproductive) appeared to have a relatively peripheral relationship to the area as well as to outsiders. The other three subgroups ranged between these two in degree of linkage to the area and to outsiders. This suggests that both types of ties are characteristic of productive scientists in a research area.

*Direct and Indirect Ties by Subgroups.*—When direct and indirect choices of the members of the various subgroups were measured using the Sociometric Connectedness Program, the differences between the subgroups emerged more definitively. Among the subgroups currently doing research in the area, informal communication choices by the High and Moderate Producers linked them to more members of the group than did the choices of the Aspirants. In addition, a high proportion of choices by others led to the High Producers, placing them in the center of a fairly sizeable communication network. (Table 4 shows how frequently a scientist is

[13] Eighty-one percent of the members of the problem area who returned the questionnaire (147 scientists) were sociologists (defined as having received a doctorate in the area or, in the absence of a doctorate, a master's degree). A few of these individuals were also identified with other disciplines as well (i.e. had received degrees in joint programs). Thirteen percent were in anthropology, agricultural economics, economics, agricultural extension, or psychology; 5% were in a number of other fields. Thirty-eight percent of the outsiders were sociologists; 22% were in anthropology, agricultural economics, economics, agricultural extension, or psychology; 7% were in several other fields. No information was available for 32% of the outsiders.

[14] In this table, and the tables which follow, percentages are frequently based on very small figures. However, the percentage differences between High Producers and the other subgroups are in most cases large and are so consistently in the same direction that the data, when considered as a whole, provides substantial evidence for the hypothesis being examined here.

TABLE 3. PERCENTAGES OF SUBGROUPS IN THE PROBLEM AREA HAVING AT LEAST ONE TIE[a] WITH OTHER MEMBERS OF THE AREA AND WITH OUTSIDERS

| | Subgroup | | | | | |
|---|---|---|---|---|---|---|
| Percentages of Subgroup Having | High Producers | Moderate Producers | Defectors | Aspirants | Transients | Total Group |
| One or more ties with members of problem area | 100 | 91 | 89 | 88 | 66 | 76 |
| One or more ties with outsiders | 100 | 91 | 78 | 94 | 58 | 72 |
| No ties | 0 | 0 | 0 | 6 | 22 | 14 |
| N | (8) | (11) | (9) | (33) | (86) | (147) |

[a] The following types of ties were included: informal communication, current collaboration, thesis directors, thesis influence, and influences on the selection of problems and techniques. Reciprocal communication and published collaboration were excluded since choices of outsiders were not relevant to those categories.

TABLE 4. DIRECT AND INDIRECT CHOICES OF MEMBERS OF SUBGROUPS BY MEMBERS OF SUBGROUPS IN THE DIFFUSION PROBLEM AREA AS MEASURED BY THE COLEMAN SOCIOMETRIC CONNECTEDNESS PROGRAM

1. Type of Choice: Informal Communication[a]

| Number of Times Members of Subgroups Are Chosen Directly or Indirectly | Subgroup Affiliation | | | | | | |
|---|---|---|---|---|---|---|---|
| | High Producers | Moderate Producers | Defectors | Aspirants | Transients | Non-respondents | Total Group |
| 0* | 0 | 27 | .. | 68 | .. | .. | 50 |
| 1–10* | 0 | 27 | .. | 23 | .. | .. | 21 |
| 11–20 | 0 | 0 | .. | 0 | .. | .. | 0 |
| Over 20 | 100 | 46 | .. | 9 | .. | .. | 29 |
| Total | 100 | 100 | .. | 100 | .. | .. | 100 |
| N | (8) | (11) | .. | (33) | .. | .. | (52) |

$r_{yx}=.57$

2. Type of Choice: Most Important Communication[a] [a]

| Number of Times Members of Subgroups Are Chosen Directly or Indirectly | Subgroup Affiliation | | | | | | |
|---|---|---|---|---|---|---|---|
| | High Producers | Moderate Producers | Defectors | Aspirants | Transients | Non-respondents | Total Group |
| 0 | 0 | 46 | .. | 79 | .. | .. | 62 |
| 1–10* | 86 | 45 | .. | 18 | .. | .. | 32 |
| Over 10* | 14 | 9 | .. | 3 | .. | .. | 6 |
| Total | 100 | 100 | .. | 100 | .. | .. | 100 |
| N | (8) | (11) | .. | (33) | .. | .. | (52) |

$r_{yx}=.38$

3. Type of Choice: Reciprocal Communication[a]

| Number of Times Members of Subgroups Are Chosen Directly or Indirectly | Subgroup Affiliation | | | | | | |
|---|---|---|---|---|---|---|---|
| | High Producers | Moderate Producers | Defectors | Aspirants | Transients | Non-respondents | Total Group |
| 0 | 25 | 64 | .. | 85 | .. | .. | 71 |
| 1–5* | 12 | 18 | .. | 9 | .. | .. | 12 |
| Over 5* | 63 | 18 | .. | 6 | .. | .. | 17 |
| Total | 100 | 100 | .. | 100 | .. | .. | 100 |
| N | (8) | (11) | .. | (33) | .. | .. | (52) |

$r_{yx}=.22$

4. Type of Choice: Published Collaboration

| Number of Times Members of Subgroups Are Chosen Directly or Indirectly | Subgroup Affiliation | | | | | | |
|---|---|---|---|---|---|---|---|
| | High Producers | Moderate Producers | Defectors | Aspirants | Transients | Non-respondents | Total Group |
| 0* | 0 | 18 | 0 | 43 | 45 | 27 | 34 |
| 1–10* | 12 | 55 | 78 | 45 | 40 | 62 | 50 |
| 11–20 | 25 | 0 | 11 | 3 | 5 | 5 | 5 |
| Over 20 | 63 | 27 | 11 | 9 | 10 | 5 | 11 |
| Total | 100 | 100 | 100 | 100 | 100 | 99 | 100 |
| N | (8) | (11) | (9) | (33) | (86) | (74) | (221) |

$\tau_{yx}=.15$

5. Type of Choice: Influences on Problem Selection [d]

| Number of Times Members of Subgroups Are Chosen Directly or Indirectly | Subgroup Affiliation | | | | | | |
|---|---|---|---|---|---|---|---|
| | High Producers | Moderate Producers | Defectors | Aspirants | Transients | Non-respondents | Total Group |
| 0* | 0 | 9 | 11 | 73 | 78 | .. | 63 |
| 1–10* | 12 | 82 | 44 | 24 | 19 | .. | 26 |
| 11–20 | 0 | 0 | 0 | 0 | 0 | .. | 0 |
| Over 20 | 88 | 9 | 44 | 3 | 3 | .. | 11 |
| Total | 100 | 100 | 99 | 100 | 100 | .. | 100 |
| N | (8) | (11) | (9) | (33) | (86) | .. | (147) |

$\tau_{yx}=.45$

6. Type of Choice: Thesis Directors [d]

| Number of Times Members of Subgroups Are Chosen Directly or Indirectly | Subgroup Affiliation | | | | | | |
|---|---|---|---|---|---|---|---|
| | High Producers | Moderate Producers | Defectors | Aspirants | Transients | Non-respondents | Total Group |
| 0 | 12 | 46 | 45 | 52 | 60 | .. | 54 |
| 1–10* | 38 | 18 | 55 | 39 | 26 | .. | 31 |
| 11–20* | 0 | 0 | 0 | 0 | 0 | .. | 0 |
| Over 20* | 50 | 36 | 0 | 9 | 14 | .. | 16 |
| Total | 100 | 100 | 100 | 100 | 100 | .. | 101 |
| N | (8) | (11) | (9) | (33) | (86) | .. | (147) |

$\tau_{yx}=.05$

7. Type of Choice: Total Ties [d e]

| Number of Times Members of Subgroups Are Chosen Directly or Indirectly | Subgroup Affiliation | | | | | | |
|---|---|---|---|---|---|---|---|
| | High Producers | Moderate Producers | Defectors | Aspirants | Transients | Non-respondents | Total Group |
| 0* | 0 | 0 | 0 | 21 | 24 | .. | 19 |
| 1–100 [f]* | 0 | 36 | 0 | 30 | 8 | .. | 14 |
| Over 100 | 100 | 64 | 100 | 49 | 68 | .. | 67 |
| Total | 100 | 100 | 100 | 100 | 100 | .. | 100 |
| N | (8) | (11) | (9) | (33) | (86) | .. | (147) |

$\tau_{yx}=.14$

[a] Only choices of those members of the problem area currently engaged in research in the field are included in these computations.

[b] Asterisks indicate that categories were combined for computation of tau.

[c] Respondents were asked to rate from 1 to 5 the importance of each communication tie for their research. Those ties which were rated 4 or 5 were considered as the most important ties.

[d] Only choice of respondents (not non-respondents) were included in these computations.

[e] Total ties included informal communication, current collaboration, published collaboration, thesis directors, thesis influence, influence on the selection of problems and influence on the selection of techniques.

[f] All these scores were between 1 and 5.

linked to others by their choices of him; it does not show his choices of others.)

High Producers were more likely to be linked to others through communication ties which they considered to be very important for their research; moreover, a high proportion of choices of this type by others also led to them. The communication choices of the High Producers were more frequently reciprocated than were those of the other groups, again suggesting their central position in the group.

The High Producers were also linked through published collaboration to a large number of other members of the area, suggesting that much of the collaboration in the area had been conducted in association with High Producers. In addition, the High Producers had played an important role in the area as thesis directors.[15]

The High Producers were not predominantly linked to others in the area through their own choices of influences on the selection of problems; however, they did receive a much higher number of direct and indirect choices with respect to this type of influence. They had apparently played an important role for many members of the area in the selection of research problems. The Defectors were the only other group that had played a significant role in this respect. However, comparisons of direct and indirect choices suggested that their role had been largely indirect. They had influenced the High Producers, who, in turn, had influenced many of the other members of the group. The role of the High Producers as influences on the selection of research techniques was less pronounced, although choices of members of the area were also more likely to lead to them than to members of other subgroups.

When all types of links were examined together, the High Producers, the Moderate Producers and the Defectors were linked to many members of the area through their own choices. The Aspirants were linked to fewer members and the Transients to even fewer. The High Producers and the Defectors also dominated on the receipt of choices. One hundred percent of the High Producers and of the Defectors had very high scores, much higher than any of the remaining groups. Thus, the High Producers, sometimes in company with the Moderate Producers, sometimes along with the Defectors, provided orientation for the other members of the area.

The group connectivity scores show the extent to which members of each subgroup had activated their potential relationships with each other and with members of other subgroups. This measure can be computed in two ways: (a) the number of choices of members of the entire group made by a subgroup in relation to the total number of possible choices and (b) the number of choices of a particular subgroup made by its members and members of other subgroups in relation to the total number of possible choices. The first measures how often members of a subgroup choose other members; the second measures how often members of a subgroup are chosen by members of the entire group. The High Producers' choices tended to relate them to more members of the area than did the choices of other subgroups. However, with respect to certain ties, they were chosen by members of other subgroups more frequently than they chose members of these subgroups. For example, 21% of the possible links between High Producers and other members of the area currently active in research were realized on the basis of the High Producers' own choices with respect to informal communication. Through the choices of others, 47% of the potential ties with members of the area were realized. With respect to influences on the selection of problems, only 4% of their potential links with other members of the area were filled as a result of their choices. On the basis of the choices by others in the area, 21% of these relationships were filled. A similar type of difference appears when all types of ties were considered simultaneously.

This set of tables suggests that differences between the subgroups within the problem area existed. One subgroup, the most productive one, appeared to have more ties with the entire group than the other subgroups, although on certain measures the Moderate Producers and the Defectors exhibited a similar degree of linkage. Since the High Producers were more frequently linked to the

[15] The High Producers also were more likely to be chosen with respect to the influence of teachers (other than thesis directors) upon the thesis.

TABLE 5. PROPORTION OF POSSIBLE TIES ACTIVATED AMONG SUBGROUPS OF THE DIFFUSION PROBLEM AREA AS MEASURED BY COLEMAN'S GROUP CONNECTIVITY SCORES[a]

| Proportion of Possible Ties Activated re | Subgroup Affiliation | | | | | |
|---|---|---|---|---|---|---|
| | High Producers | Moderate Producers | Aspirants | Defectors | Transients | Total Group[b] |
| Informal communication | | | | | | |
| Choosing[c] | .205 | .237 | .124 | .... | .... | .161 |
| Chosen | .468 | .283 | .039 | .... | .... | .161 |
| Most important communication | | | | | | |
| Choosing | .154 | .089 | .025 | .... | .... | .049 |
| Chosen | .122 | .069 | .011 | .... | .... | .049 |
| Reciprocal communication | | | | | | |
| Choosing[b] | .115 | .021 | .010 | .... | .... | .029 |
| Current collaboration | | | | | | |
| Choosing | .032 | .014 | .004 | .... | .... | .010 |
| Chosen | .026 | .014 | .005 | .... | .... | .010 |
| Published collaboration | | | | | | |
| Choosing[b] | .093 | .038 | .017 | .033 | .019 | .022 |
| Thesis directors | | | | | | |
| Choosing[d] | .079 | .056 | .017 | .012 | .026 | .028 |
| Influences on problem selection | | | | | | |
| Choosing | .039 | .080 | .041 | .039 | .021 | .032 |
| Chosen | .214 | .023 | .007 | .127 | .015 | .032 |
| Influences on technique selection | | | | | | |
| Choosing | .018 | .030 | .013 | .001 | .005 | .009 |
| Chosen | .059 | .008 | .005 | .027 | .004 | .009 |
| Thesis influence | | | | | | |
| Choosing | .005 | .010 | .005 | .001 | .003 | .004 |
| Chosen | .031 | .003 | .001 | .016 | .001 | .004 |
| Total ties[e] | | | | | | |
| Choosing | .664 | .673 | .590 | .664 | .474 | .536 |
| Chosen | .801 | .518 | .392 | .802 | .542 | .536 |

[a] The number of possible ties is obtained by multiplying the number of cases in the group by the number of cases minus one (to eliminate self-choices). The sum of all the individual scores representing the number of direct and indirect relationships with other members gives the number of relationships which actually occur. The group connectivity score represents the proportion of possible ties which actually occur. The number of possible ties for a subgroup is obtained by multiplying the number of cases in the subgroup by the number of cases in the total group minus one. Only respondents currently engaged in research in the area are included in the first four measures. The remaining measures include all respondents (N=147). Published collaboration also includes non-respondents (N=221); the non-respondents' score was .015.

[b] These scores are the same for "Choosing" and "Chosen."

[c] "Choosing" represents a score based on respondents' own choices; "Chosen" represents a score based on choices by others of the respondents.

[d] These scores are the same for "Choosing" and "Chosen" since the relationship between thesis director and student was assumed to be a reciprocal one.

[e] Total ties included informal communication, current collaboration, published collaboration, thesis directors, thesis influence, influence on the selection of problems and influence on the selection of techniques.

group as a whole by the choices of others than by their own choices, it would seem that they had a high degree of visibility in the problem area. Many others looked to them for orientation. Thus the connectivity which developed in this area appeared to be at least partially the result of a large number of choices directed toward a few members. Anyone choosing even one of these individuals was brought into contact with a large network of individuals. This is a reasonable outcome in science where students or collaborators of very productive scientists are brought into contact, directly or indirectly, with many other scientists in the field. However, for some members, this contact had been very brief. Many of the Transients appeared to have had only peripheral contact with the area. In some cases, they seemed to have been drawn almost involuntarily into the activities of the area and to have detached themselves as quickly as possible. Comments on the questionnaires implied that some members of this group were unaware of any "tradition" of research in the area.

### CHANGES IN THE NETWORK OF SOCIAL TIES OVER TIME

So far, the group has been described without reference to the fact that members belonged to the group at different times and for different lengths of time. This approach is justified by the fact that, in a research area, scientists who are no longer working in a field continue in a sense to be the colleagues of those who are presently working in the field since their publications provide the basis for future research. However, as was described earlier, the amount of activity in the area steadily increased during the 25-year period examined. During the first ten years of activity in the area, only 5% of the members were active. Between 1948 and 1958, the number of authors entering the area doubled every three years. After 1958, the number of authors entering the field doubled every five years; the increase per year stabilized at approximately 17 authors per year. The trend for the number of publications was similar. Between 1951 and 1960, 49% of the authors entered the field, most of this increase occurring during the latter part of the decade. Another 46% entered between 1961 and 1966.

Since, as we have seen, the High Producers were very influential in the area, tracing the development of their interest in the field would help to explain the growth of the area. Two High Producers entered the field in the first decade, apparently influenced by the publications of a Defector and a Transient who had been active during that period. In the middle of the second decade, each of these High Producers had a student who also became a High Producer. Another thesis director and his student, both High Producers, entered the field at the same time along with a collaborator who also became a High Producer. By 1957, all of the High Producers had entered the field. Although almost two-thirds of the Aspirants and more than one-third of the Transients entered after 1960, only 11% of the more productive scientists (those with more than three publications in the area) entered the field in that period. Since at that time interest in the field was beginning to diminish relative to its earlier rate of exponential growth, this suggests that productive scientists may be especially sensitive to the potentialities for growth in a field in making their selection of research problems.

The influence of members who had published in the area steadily increased relative to those who had not published. Before 1956, about 25% of the theses written in the field were directed by members of the area. From 1956 to 1966, close to two-thirds of the theses in the area were directed by members of the area. The number of scientists mentioning only outsiders as influences on their selection of research problems in the area decreased from 38% among scientists entering the field before 1951 to 9% among scientists entering after 1956.[16] Examination of the total number of choices by members of the group with respect to influences on the selection of problems in various periods revealed that, among scientists entering the area prior to 1951, 42% of the choices were for members. Between 1951 and 1955, the figure was 38%. Among scientists entering between 1956 and 1960, 57% of the choices were for members. Among scientists entering after 1960, the comparable figure was 48%. The proportion of collaborative publications also increased from 22% before 1951 to 30% in 1951 to 1955, 41% in 1956 to 1960, and

[16] The date of a scientist's first publication in the field was used as the date of his entry into the field.

37% after 1960. These last two distributions suggest that the field was somewhat more integrated from 1956 to 1960 (the second half decade of rapid exponential growth) than at other periods. A slight decline in integration parallels the shift from exponential to linear growth.

The influence of the High Producers also increased over time. None of the theses written in the area by scientists entering the field before 1956 were directed by High Producers. After 1956, 38% of the theses in the area were directed by High Producers, a subgroup representing 8 individuals. Twenty-seven percent of the theses were directed by members of the four remaining subgroups representing 139 respondents. Similarly, the proportion of scientists in the group mentioning High Producers as having influenced their selection of research problems increased from 25% among scientists entering prior to 1951 to 39% among scientists entering after that date, more than twice as high as the proportion naming any of the other subgroups. More than 50% of the total number of choices of this type by scientists entering the field after 1950 were for High Producers.

Another development reveals the changes which were taking place in the field. On the basis of collaboration and student-thesis director relationships, members of the area were assigned to distinct subgroups of varying sizes (see Crane, 1968a; Price and Beaver, 1966). A scientist was assigned to a particular group of collaborators if he had a published collaboration with at least one of its members or had been the student or thesis director of at least one of its members. Before 1956, the group consisted of small groups of collaborators and student-teacher pairs and a number of isolates. After 1956, when the group as a whole increased in size, some of these small groups expanded. Two large groups emerged, with 27 and 32 members respectively, as well as several medium-size groups with five to 13 members.[17] A number of new small groups with 2 to 4 members and numerous isolates appeared. Few of the small groups lasted more than a couple of years.[18] Turnover among the isolates was also high. Medium-size groups, especially the relatively larger ones, were more durable. Four had lasted more than ten years. One of the two large groups had lasted more than ten years; the other had lasted eight years.

Six of the eight High Producers were members of the two large groups. The remaining two belonged to the largest of the medium-

[17] These sizes represent the number of members each collaboration group had during the entire period, 1941 to mid-1966.

[18] The duration of a collaboration group was measured inclusively by finding the number of years from the date of the earliest publication by one of its members to the date of the most recent publication by a member.

TABLE 6. FREQUENCY TOTAL AND AVERAGE DURATION FOR GROUPS BY SIZE[a]

| Number of Authors in Group | Frequency | Total Number of Authors in Group | Average Duration of Group (in Years)[b] |
|---|---|---|---|
| 1 | 47 | 47 | 1.3 |
| 2 | 9 | 18 | 1.1 |
| 3 | 5 | 15 | 1.6 |
| 4 | 3 | 12 | 5.0 |
| 5 | 1 | 5 | 1.0 |
| 6 | 4 | 24 | 9.0 |
| 7 | 1 | 7 | 7.0 |
| 9 | 1 | 9 | 22.0 |
| 12 | 1 | 12 | 11.0 |
| 13 | 1 | 13 | 12.0 |
| 27 | 1 | 27 | 8.0 |
| 32 | 1 | 32 | 14.0 |
| Total | 75 | 221 | Mean 2.9 |

[a] Includes non-respondents although student-teacher relationships were unknown for them.

[b] Duration of a collaboration group was measured inclusively by finding the number of years from the date of the earliest publication by one of its members to the date of the most recent publication by a member.

sized groups. The large groups of collaborators appeared to reflect the way in which the High Producers exerted their influence upon the field, i.e., by surrounding themselves with students and collaborators among whom turnover was frequently high. Thus, these large groups of collaborators, under the direction of High Producers, provided continuity and structure in a situation which would otherwise have been amorphous due to the continual arrivals and departures of less committed scientists.

It seems plausible that these large groups could have exercised control over the direction of research in the area. Since their approach to the field was so visible due to the large number of publications produced by these groups, scientists outside these groups who had other types of approaches might have found it difficult to exert a comparable influence. A content analysis of publications in the area by the compiler of the bibliography which lists them (Rogers, 1966) made it possible to determine (a) the collaboration group affiliation of the first users of all dependent and independent variables appearing in empirical studies in the area, and (b) the number of times each variable was used. Variables appearing for the first time in publications by scientists who were not members of the large groups were not less frequently used than variables appearing for the first time in publications by members of large groups. On the other hand, more than half the variables ever used first appeared in publications by members of large groups and by members of two of the medium-sized groups (Crane, 1968b).

## CONCLUSION

As predicted, the social group which was described here was not one which was tightly knit or closed to external influences. "Outsiders" played an important role in influencing the activities of members of the group. That a social group within the problem area existed was principally apparent from the number of choices received by a relatively small number of members of the group. It appeared that members of the area were not so much linked to one another directly but were linked to each other indirectly through these highly influential members. The importance of these scientists was not obvious, except in terms of productivity, unless one examined their many and varied influences on the remaining members of their field, each of whom might be affected in only one or two ways and for short periods of time.

A question which remains to be discussed is how a group of this kind can best be conceptualized theoretically. Price has popularized the term "invisible college" which refers to an elite of mutually interacting and productive scientists within a research area. However, this conceptualization does not comprehend two aspects of the social organization of research areas which have emerged from the analysis presented here: (a) the interaction between the most active and influential members of the area and the "rank and file" and (b) the role of "outsiders" in the organization of the area.

Of the various types of social organization which have been identified by sociologists, the social circle would appear to be the one which best describes the social organization of a research area (Kadushin, 1966). The social circle is not well instituted, compared to the bureaucracy or even to less formalized entities such as the tribe or the family. Members come together on the basis of their interests rather than propinquity or ascribed statuses. Indirect interaction, interaction mediated through intervening parties, is an important aspect of the social circle. It is not necessary to know a particular member of a social circle in order to be influenced by him. Certain characteristics are more common to members of a particular social circle than to non-members, but members do not necessarily share all or even most of these defining characteristics. Each member is usually aware of some but not all other members. The exact boundaries of the social circle are difficult to locate.

While something comparable to a social circle may at times develop in a research area, it seems unlikely that it would exist at all times in all research areas. In some areas, nothing of the sort may develop. In areas in which social circles do develop, their size and importance to their members are likely to change from one period to another. There is some indication that absence of continuity of personnel in a research area is associated with lack of productivity in the area and the failure of knowledge to disseminate and to cumulate (Fisher, 1966, 1967). In some cases the same research problems tend to be treated again and again (Barton and Wilder, 1964). This suggests that the presence of scientists whose productivity is sufficient to make them visible to most of those who enter the field, even briefly, produces a social circle which in turn plays an important role in the normal growth of the research area.

The diffusion problem area studied here is the only problem area devoted to the study of diffusion in which a sizeable number of papers have been published. Each of the other areas has remained quite small (Rogers and Stanfield, 1966:5). It can be argued that an important factor in the growth of this area was that a few individuals developed a high degree of commitment to it and as a result were able both to direct the activities of others in the field and to make it visible as a research area. Since all research areas in a research specialty (and to a lesser extent in science as a whole) are potentially related to one another, one group becomes separated from others only when certain scientists develop a strong interest in the field and assert its independence, even temporarily, from its context.

On the other hand, since ties between members of the area and "outsiders" were numerous, it can also be asked whether it is meaningful to speak of specialties or problem areas at all. Mullins (1966) has argued that it is not. It was suggested above that choices of "outsiders" were analogous to the phenomenon of "reference scattering"; about half the articles on a subject tend to appear in a few "core" journals, the rest being widely scattered. Perhaps the importance of both "core" and "scatter" can best be understood by assuming that each was the exclusive mode of organization of scientific activity. For example, if there was no "scatter," scientists would be divided into small groups, sharing the same interests, speaking only to each other, and reading and citing only each other's work. If this were the case, problem areas would have the characteristics of what sociologists in other contexts refer to as "sects." Religious sects break away from the church and build separate organizations, emphasizing aspects of doctrine or policy which they believe have been ignored or misinterpreted by the church. The religious sect is a relatively closed system, resisting external influences rather than attempting to adapt to them. Members who deviate from orthodox views on any issue are quickly expelled (see, for example, Coser, 1954; Johnson, 1963; Yinger, 1957:144–155). If scientific problem areas had these characteristics, science would consist of hundreds of disparate groups, none of which would have any communication with or relevance for each other.

Science is actually organized in exactly the opposite fashion. Emotional neutrality is one of the norms of science (Barber, 1962: 125–127); psychological overinvestment in one's scientific ideas is frowned upon. Groups which attempt to advocate particular points of view to the exclusion of others without adequate empirical substantiation are often referred to as "schools" of thought and are considered unscientific. Most problem areas are open to influences from other fields. The desire for originality motivates scientists to maintain contacts with scientists and scientific work in areas different from their own in order to enhance their ability to develop new ideas in their own areas. Scientists in problem areas are usually committed more to the solution of the problem than to the group itself. The problem area can best be understood as a temporary unit which deals with special problems and then dissolves after one or several decades when the problems have either been solved or been determined to be unsolvable.[19]

On the other hand, if there was only "scatter" in science and no "core," scientific knowledge would not cumulate. A high proportion of ideas would be lost. Swanson (1966) claims that an important proportion of the scientific literature is so scattered as to defy the efforts of any individual to bring all of it together. If all the literature on a particular subject was so scattered, it would be impossible for scientists to build on each other's work. Each scientist would be working by himself and with perhaps a few other scientists whom he accidently discovered. The existence of a "core" of journals in the literature, and of scientists in the problem

[19] Bennis (1966) has argued that this type of organization is the prototype of an organization designed to produce innovation.

area, provides a kind of repetitiveness in scientific communication, insuring that certain ideas will be repeated sufficiently so that the relevant scientists may be assured of receiving at least some of the currently important findings. There are integrating factors in science as well as disintegrating factors.[20] Both are necessary, the former to permit scientific knowledge to cumulate and grow, the latter to prevent it from becoming a completely subjective, sect-like phenomenon.

Future studies will be needed to perfect the methods for studying groups of this kind.[21] For example, it would be useful to compare the results of different techniques for locating groups of scientists, such as the use of comprehensive bibliographies, abstracting services, citations, and sociometric data with "snowball" samples (Goodman, 1961; Mullins, 1966). In order to obtain a complete picture of activities in a problem area, information regarding scientists who have made very many or very few contributions is needed. While comprehensive bibliographies cannot be expected to be 100% complete, they are likely to provide a high proportion of both types of participants. If an adequate list of authors can be compiled from the scientific literature or other sources, the use of sociometric data obtained from "snowball" samples is probably less appropriate for locating members of a particular area since a high proportion of members in other areas tend to be mentioned. Kessler (1965) has shown that scientific publications form groups on the basis of common citation references but no attempt has yet been made to explore the social ties among authors drawn together in this fashion. Cluster analysis (Bailey, 1969) is being used to locate groups of scientists with similar interests on the basis of thematic similarities in the contents of research grant applications. This technique which could also be used to analyze the contents of abstracting services will be combined with analysis of social relationships among members of such groups.

Evaluation of different methods for analyzing this type of data is needed. The present study used Coleman's Sociometric Connectedness Program to examine the relationships between members of an entire group. Sociometric techniques for determining non-intersecting cliques are still inadequate (Lingwood, 1968:20). However, if a group is actually a social circle, one would not expect to find distinct cliques based on sociometric ties. A true social circle should consist of a complex and undivided network of relationships. If such a group is to be meaningfully partitioned, it ought to be done on the basis of criteria other than social relationships. In the present paper, productivity and commitment to the area were used. Price and Beaver (1966) have suggested a method of locating cliques which utilizes ties based on published collaborations. Communication and influence ties between units formed on this basis have been examined (Crane, 1968a). Russett (1969) relied upon factor analysis to identify within a problem area subgroups who tended to cite each other's publications.

Finally, the points of intersection between problem areas should be examined. If science actually consists of hundreds of groups of scientists, each of which concentrates upon a cluster of related problems, future studies should trace the movement of communication and influence from one area to another. Here sociometric data obtained from snowball samples would be useful. Starting from lists compiled from the scientific literature and other sources of scientists from several areas in the same discipline, interviews with successive waves of respondents would pinpoint the nature of their relationships to different social circles.

[20] Mullins (1966) has argued that the integrating factor in science is a set of orientations toward which research can be directed. For example, research can emphasize chemical or physical aspects of nature, structure or process, control or energy. Such dimensions, however, would appear to incorporate such disparate kinds of work as to be unlikely to play a role comparable to that attributed here to the core members and core journals of the problem area.

[21] For a discussion of methods of studying social circles consisting of political leaders, see Kadushin, 1968.

## REFERENCES

Allen, T. J. and S. I. Cohen.
1966 Information flow in an R and D laboratory. Unpublished manuscript.

APA Project on Scientific Information Exchange in Psychology.
1968 "Networks of informal communication among scientifically productive psychologists." Unpublished manuscript.

Bailey, D.
1969 "Cluster analysis of physiological psychology grant requests and descriptors." Unpublished manuscript, University of Colorado.

Barber, B.
1962 Science and the Social Order. New York: Collier Books.

Barton, A. H. and D. E. Wilder.
1964 "Research and practice in the teaching of reading: a progress report," pp. 361–398 in Matthew B. Miles (ed.), Innovation in Education. New York: Bureau of Publications, Teachers College, Columbia University.

Bennis, W. G.
1966 Changing Organizations. New York: McGraw-Hill, Chapter 3.

Blalock, H. M.
1960 Social Statistics. New York: McGraw-Hill, pp. 232–234.

Cole, P. F.
1962 "A new look at reference scattering." Journal of Documentation 18 (June):58–64.
1963 "Journal usage versus age of journal." Journal of Documentation 19 (March):1–11.

Coleman, J. S.
1964 Introduction to Mathematical Sociology. New York: The Free Press of Glencoe: 447–455.

Coser, L.
1954 "Sects and sectarians." Dissent 1:360–369.

Crane, D.
1968a "Communication, collaboration, and influence: a study of formal and informal collaboration among scientists." Unpublished manuscript.
1968b "The diffusion of innovations in science: a case study." Unpublished manuscript.

Fisher, C. S.
1966 "The death of a mathematical theory: a study in the sociology of knowledge." Archives for History of Exact Sciences 111:137–1959.
1967 "The last invariant theorists: a sociological study of the collective biographies of mathematical specialists." European Journal of Sociology VIII:216–244.

Garfield, E.
1964 The Use of Citation Data in Writing the History of Science. Philadelphia: Institute for Scientific Information.

Goodman, L. A.
1961 "Snowball sampling." Annals of Mathematical Statistics 32:148–170.

Johnson, B.
1963 "On church and sect." American Sociological Review 28 (August):539–549.

Kadushin, C.
1966 "The friends and supporters of psychotherapy: on social circles in urban life." American Sociological Review 31 (December):786–802.
1968 "Power, influence and social circles: a new methodology for studying opinion makers." American Sociological Review 33 (October):685–699.

Kaufman, H. F.
1956 "Rural Sociology, 1945–55." pp. 104–105 in Hans L. Zetterberg (ed.), Sociology in the United States of America. Paris: UNESCO.

Kessler, M. M.
1965 "Comparison of the results of bibliographic coupling and analytic subject indexing." American Documentation 16 (July):223–233.

Kessler, M. M. and F. E. Heart.
1962 "Concerning the probability that a given paper will be cited." Unpublished paper.

Kuhn, T. S.
1962 The Structure of Scientific Revolutions. Chicago: University of Chicago Press.

Libbey, M. and G. Zaltman.
1967 The Role and Distribution of Written Informal Communication in Theoretical High Energy Physics. New York: American Institute of Physics.

Lingwood, D. A.
1968 "Interpersonal communication, scientific productivity, and invisible colleges: studies of two behavioral science research areas." Paper read at the colloquium: Improving the Social and Communication Mechanisms of Educational Research, sponsored by American Educational Research Association, Washington, D.C.

McGrath, J. E. and I. A. Altman.
1966 Small Group Research: A Synthesis and Critique of the Field. New York: Holt, Rinehart and Winston.

Meadows, A. J.
1967 "The citation characteristics of astronomical research literature." Journal of Documentation 23 (March):28–33.

Menzel, H.
1960 Review of Studies in the Flow of Information Among Scientists. New York: Columbia University, Bureau of Applied Social Research, 2 Volumes (Mimeo).

Mullins, N. C.
1966 "Social Networks Among Biological Scientists." Unpublished Ph.D. dissertation, Harvard University.
1968 "Social origins of an invisible college: The phage group." Unpublished paper read at the meeting of the American Sociological Association, Boston, 1968.

Paisley, W. J.
1965 The Flow of (Behavioral) Science Information: A Review of the Research Literature. Palo Alto: Institute for Communication Research, Stanford University.

Parker, E. B., W. J. Paisley and R. Garrett.
1967 Bibliographic Citations as Unobtrusive

Measures of Scientific Communication. Palo Alto: Institute for Communication Research, Stanford University.

Price, D. J. de S.
1961 Science Since Babylon. New Haven: Yale University Press, Chapter 5.
1963 Little Science, Big Science. New York: Columbia University Press, Chapter 2.
1965 "Networks of scientific papers," Science 149 (July 30):510–515.

Price, D. J. and D. de B. Beaver.
1966 "Collaboration in an invisible college." American Psychologist 21 (November): 1011–1018.

Rogers, E. M.
1962 Diffusion of Innovations. New York: Free Press.
1966 Bibliography on the Diffusion of Innovations. Diffusion of Innovations Research Report, No. 4. East Lansing: Michigan State University.

Rogers, E. M. and E. P. Bettinghaus.
1966 "Comparison of generalizations from diffusion research on agricultural and family planning innovations." Paper presented at the American Sociological Association, Miami Beach, August 30, 1966.

Rogers, E. M. and J. D. Stanfield.
1966 "Adoption and diffusion of new products: emerging generalizations and hypotheses," unpublished paper presented at the Conference on the Application of Sciences to Marketing Management, Purdue University.

Russett, B. M.
1969 "Methodological and theoretical schools in international relations." Unpublished manuscript, Yale University.

Stevens, R. E.
1953 "Characteristics of subject literatures." ACRL Monographs, No. 6:10–21.

Stoddart, D. R.
1967 "Growth and structure of geography." Transactions and Papers of the Institute of British Geographers, Publication No. 41:1–19.

Swanson, D. R.
1966 "Scientific journals and information services of the future." American Psychologist 21 (November):1008.

Vachon, D.
1969 "Differential Productivity of Colleague Groups at Two Research Frontiers." Unpublished Ph.D. dissertation, Georgetown University.

Weinstein, N.
undated "The development of theoretical cosmology, 1963–1965; or 'Que sçais-je?' " Unpublished manuscript.

Yinger, J. M.
1957 Religion, Society and the Individual. New York: Macmillan.

Reprinted from the Journal of the American Society for Information Science, Vol. 22, No. 5, 1971. 

# Informal Communication Among Scientists in Sleep Research*

**At the frontiers of an active area of science, social structure based upon communication is demonstrated. Using sociometric techniques, an informal communication network was identified which included 73% of the scientists. Within the network was a core group of scientists who were the focus of a disproportionately large number of contacts and who were differentiated from others by greater productivity, higher citation record and wider readership. Information transferred to these scientists is so situated that it could be transmitted to 95% of the network scientists through one intermediary scientist or less.**

**SUSAN CRAWFORD**

*Director, Archive-Library*
*American Medical Association*

The interval between inception of projects in psychology and the publication of formal results was recently investigated by the American Psychological Association (APA) (*1*). If the sequence is started at the time an investigator initiates a project, it is their estimate that approximately eighteen months elapse before the first preliminary report, which is usually to the granting agency. Thirty months after initiation of the project, a manuscript is submitted to a journal, but it will be another six months before the article is published, and still an additional year before entry into Psychological Abstracts. Another eighteen months elapse before the article is mentioned in the Annual Review. Thus, between initiation of a project and its mention in the Annual Review, more than five years have elapsed.

Is this delay excessive, especially at the frontiers of fast-moving areas of science? There is now much evidence that scientists have made attempts to bypass the publications gap in order to get the current information they needed. Derek Price hypothesized the existence of "new invisible colleges" in each really active area of science whose "whole raison d'être was to substitute personal contact for formal communications" (*2*). For a brief period during the 1960's Information Exchange Groups flourished under support of the National Institutes of Health (*3*). One of the latest ventures, reported in Science (February 1970), is the APA's new and controversial "early dissemination scheme" for distributing manuscripts before they are accepted or edited for journals (*4*).

This paper reports an investigation of how scientists at the frontiers of an active field of science communicate with each other informally concerning their work. Informal communication is distinguished from formal or organized methods of communication which include the scientific literature and its abstracting-indexing services as well as papers read at formally established meetings. Informal communication entails a person-to-person relation in which a scientist selects out of the population other scientists to communicate with on aspects of his work. Information exchange through informal comunication has been the focus of a number of recent investigations (Crane, Gaston, Griffith, Mullins) (*5–8*).

## • Scientists at the Frontiers of Sleep Research

The area we chose for investigation was the psychophysiological study of sleep—one with relatively well-defined boundaries and a comparatively young field. A tabulation of articles, exclusive of those on interpretation of dream content from the clinical viewpoint, is shown in Table 1. From 1951–1955, the average number of articles published each year was less than four; by 1961–1965, the average per year was over 170, an increase by a factor of over forty-seven. The growth in number of articles clearly indicated that sleep research was an active field of

* This article is based upon a paper presented at the Annual Meeting of the Association for Psychophysiological Study of Sleep, Santa Fe, New Mexico, 1970.

TABLE 1. Articles published in the psychophysiological study of sleep to 1966. Data to 1965 were derived from a comprehensive bibliography compiled by A. Rechtschaffen, University of Chicago, Department of Psychology. Data for 1966 were derived from the Index Medicus and Psychological Abstracts. These data may be regarded as close approximation to the universe of substantive articles in sleep research to 1966

| Period Covered | Number of Articles | Average per Year |
|---|---|---|
| Before 1950 | 26 | ... |
| 1951–55 | 18 | 3.6 |
| 1956–60 | 165 | 33.0 |
| 1961–65 | 852 | 170.4 |
| 1966 | 426 | 426.0 |
| Total | 1,487 | |

science which had not yet peaked and declined in interest (*9*).

We proceeded to identify all scientists working at the research front in the problem area, that is, those participating in current research projects. An attempt was first made to determine, as completely as possible, all scientists who had written in the field, held membership in the Association for Psychophysiological Study of Sleep, or received grants for sleep research during the four years preceding this investigation (1964–67). A total of 618 scientists in the United States were identified, and to derive the subset of scientists presently active in the field, we asked them to indicate their current projects in sleep research. Responses were received from 427 scientists (69% of the scientists queried). Of these, only 218 (51% of the respondents) indicated that they were still participating in projects in sleep research; 197 indicated that they were no longer active in the field and that sleep research was of "peripheral interest." Only about a half of the scientists associated with sleep research during the four years preceding this investigation now indicated that they were still active in the field.

The 218 active scientists are distributed over thirty states. There are five research centers (*10*) with large clusters of scientists: New York (38), Los Angeles (28), San Francisco-Palo Alto (26), Boston (14), and Chicago (13). Outside these great centers, there are twelve with 3–5 scientists, ten with two scientists, and nineteen scientists who work alone.

The orientation of the group is toward research rather than its application. Of the 218 active scientists, only 13% indicated that their primary function was patient care rather than research. The work is done on animal or human subjects, and a number of specialties are often involved; psychology, neurology, electroencephalography, and physiology are examples. Equipment, special experimental conditions as well as allied specialists require considerable financial outlay for most research problems in sleep. This university-based research is sustained mainly by Federal support through the National Institutes of Health. The reward system is monitored in large part by peer control over both recognition and grant funding.

The measurement of psychological and physiological correlates of sleep is a night-time endeavor, disruptive to the usual daily cycle of human activities. The sleep scientist collects his data during lonely hours, and is often isolated for consecutive nights, weeks and even months. The work environment often places a strain on personal and social activity as well as physical endurance.

A typical project takes place in a university laboratory or hospital where student subjects are paid a small sum to sleep in the laboratory. Brain waves, eye movements, penile erections or other physiological characteristics are measured through wires attached to the subject's head or other mechanisms. A well-known experiment concerned an attempt to shift the circadian rhythm, the 24-hour cycle in which the body temperature rises and falls (*11*). In 1938, Kleitman and a student descended into Mammoth Cave, Kentucky, into a dark environment with constant conditions, illuminated by an electric light. There, they set up living quarters and attempted to live a 21-hour day and a 28-hour day. On the effect of the unique working environment of scientists in sleep and dream research, one senior investigator commented: "This isolation draws us (the scientists) closer together."

As far as communication of information is concerned, there appears to be some dissatisfaction with present provisions among the sleep scientists, as evidenced by a recent meeting to consider initiation of other methods. The group does not have its own journal, and the literature is scattered mainly in psychological and psychiatric publications. The Association for Psychophysiological Study of Sleep (APSS) was founded a few years ago for the major purpose of scientific communication. A four-day annual session is held by APSS members, devoted almost entirely to presentation of papers. It is within this context that we have investigated informal communication among scientists.

## • Incidence of Informal Communication

The sleep scientists were first asked to name *all* persons they contacted at least three times during the past year concerning their work. These included sleep scientists as well as specialists in other areas. We found that, on the average, they were in contact with 3.3 persons concerning their work. As indicated in Table 2, scientists in sleep research were contacted slightly, but not significantly more often (58% of the total persons named). Scientists in other specialties were also found to be important (42% of persons named).

When we examined informal communication among the scientists' own colleagues in sleep research, an interesting pattern was observed. Sleep scientists contacted an average of 1.9 scientists in their own research area, but there were great individual differences in both contacts initiated and received. As Table 3 indicates, ninety-nine scientists

TABLE 2. Total persons inside or outside their research centers contacted by sleep scientists, subdivided by those who are in sleep research and those in other areas of specialization.

| Research Area | Scientists Contacted Within Same Research Center | Scientists Contacted In Other Centers | Average Number of Contacts | Total Contacts |
|---|---|---|---|---|
| Sleep Research | 272 (56%) | 149 (62%) | 1.9 | 421 (58%)* |
| Other Areas of Specialization | 217 (44%) | 90 (38%) | 1.4 | 307 (42%)* |
| Total | 489 (100%) | 239 (100%) | 3.3 | 728 (100%) |

* $X^2 = 1.52$, not significant at $P < .05$

(45%) were contacted by no one, and twenty-three scientists (11%) received 54% of all choices made. Thirty-three scientists initiated or received contacts from six or more scientists; on the average, they were in contact with five times as many sleep scientists as others in their research area. They were designated in this study as "central scientists." As the focus of a disproportionately large number of contacts, these scientists are in a position to interpret and monitor information to a large number of scientists.

In a related study (*12*), we investigated indicators of the quality and quantity of an investigator's work and related these to incidence of informal communication. We worked with the widely accepted, but by no means infallible notion that the number of times an article is cited in the published literature is a reasonable indicator of the quality of a piece of work, particularly when taken over time. We found the citation record highly correlated with amount of communication made ($r = .71$) and received ($r = .60$) by the scientists. When we examined readership and papers produced, we found that those who were consulted most also tended to write the most papers ($r = .62$) and were most widely read by their fellow scientists ($r = .80$). Scientists who are the focus of the most communications therefore tend also to be cited the most, to produce the most papers, and to be read most by those in their research area.

TABLE 3. Number of colleagues in sleep research contacted by sleep scientists three times or more during the past year concerning their work. The number of colleagues from whom contacts are received as well as the number of colleagues contacted are tabulated

| Contacts Made | | Contacts Received | |
|---|---|---|---|
| Number of Colleagues Contacted By Scientists | Distribution of Scientists Contacting | Number of Scientists Contacting Colleagues | Distribution of Colleagues Contacted |
| 0 | 71 | 0 | 99 |
| 1 | 42 | 1 | 38 |
| 2 | 35 | 2 | 32 |
| 3 | 26 | 3 | 13 |
| 4 | 18 | 4 | 9 |
| 5 | 13 | 5 | 4 |
| 6 | 4 | 6 | 7 |
| 7 | 4 | 7 | 1 |
| 8 | 3 | 8 | 3 |
| 9 | 2 | 9 | 3 |
| 10 | — | 10 | 3 |
| 11 | — | ≥11 | 6 |
| $\sigma = 10.3$ | | $\sigma = 3.3$ | |

Contacts made or received: $\bar{x} = 1.9$

## • Social Organization in Informal Communication

To what extent can information be transferred through informal communication among scientists in sleep research? Can we identify some type of social organization among scientists based upon their interpersonal contacts for communicating information? One approach is to view informal communication of information as a process of diffusion through a social structure, as in the flow of influence, ideas, or of contagion. Coleman, in his study of the flow of drug information among physicians concluded: "It may well be that an epidemiological approach is required to understand what happens when a new drug comes to the medical profession. For the profession is not a mere aggregate of individual physicians. Doctors constitute communities, more or less tightly interconnected; stimuli that impinge upon any member of the community are likely to set in motion processes that will with varying degrees of speed and thoroughness, pervade the rest of the community." Coleman further observed that the process of adopting a new drug resembled the step-by-step chain reaction of an infectious disease. The adoption curve indicated a snowball effect in which the proportion of unconverted doctors who would adopt the new drug decreased in proportion to the number who had already been converted (*13*).

At least two aspects of the organization of members in a population are important, if we are concerned with how a structure would function, given a process or contagion which flows through it. First, we are interested in the routes by which the information may travel, or the "connectedness" of the members. We want to know which investigators in sleep research communicate with each other so that messages may be transferred from one to the other. We also want to know if a message may be transferred no further, should it reach particular scientists. Second, we are interested in identifying any subgroups which may be of special consequence in informal communication. The "invisible college" hypothesized by Price is in part an intuitive notion of the "connectedness" of scientists in communicating information at the frontiers of an active field of science.

By the end of 1968, at least six investigators were known to be studying the structure of interpersonal relations in informal communication. N. Mullins selected an initial sample of fifty from 10,000 biological scientists listed in the American Men of Science and attempted to identify groups of scientists who communicated intensively among themselves. As a result of using such a small sample from a large base population, he was not able to identify clusters of intercommunicating scientists cut off from each other. He concluded that the "invisible college" remained invisible, that social organization consisted of "loosely-knit networks," rather than neatly delineated groups, and that the "invisible college" was made up of one's own personal contacts and was different for each scientist (*14*).

From Mullins' observation that no two scientists have the same circle of colleagues, N. Storer (*15*) suggested the possibility that "the concept of invisible college may be no more than the reification of what might be more realistically thought of as custom-made reference groups." Storer further stated that "any attempt to identify the boundaries of a single invisible college is apparently doomed to failure, because no such entity really exists in a form capable of delineation."

D. Crane (*16*) focused upon a small group of scientists concerned with the diffusion of agricultural innovations. Crane tested "the hypothesis of the invisible college" which was interpreted as social organization based upon influence and communication relations. Using seven indicators of "social ties," Crane identified a core group which received the largest number of direct and indirect choices from the members. The existence of this subgroup, Crane argued, indicated that the group as a whole was "meaningful" to scientists in the research area. In general, she concluded, social organization among scientists in the same research area resembled the "social circle," an unstructured type of group whose boundaries are difficult to locate and whose members are largely influenced by those outside the group.

J. Gaston (*17*), in a study of high energy physics scientists (HEP), used Crane's adaptation of Coleman's Sociometric Connectedness Program. Gaston also found that a small subset received a large number of direct and indirect communication choices and that members of this subset communicated more among themselves than with other HEP scientists. He concluded that "there appears to be ample evidence that an invisible college exists."

In these five papers, all recently issued, we find the current thinking concerning social organization of scientists for communicating information through interpersonal contact. The studies do not address themselves to precisely the same questions and therefore pose problems in comparative analysis.

In our investigation, we relied heavily upon Coleman's conceptualizations (*18*). We collected data which indicated among which of the scientists in sleep research there is frequent personal interaction, i.e., three times or more each year, for the purpose of communicating information. Considering these relations between scientists as potential paths for the flow of information, we then (1) looked at the total population to see how "connected" are the members; (2) investigated the occurrence of subgroups in which members communicated intensively among themselves.

Two assumptions concerning the communication relation are at the base of the methodology we developed. First, that in informal person-to-person communication, information may be transmitted in two ways, from the scientist who initiates the contact to the persons contacted, or the reverse. Second, that information may be transmitted stepwise through both direct and indirect contacts. A direct contact is one in which scientist i interacts with scientist j in one step, as denoted in the relation $i \rightarrow j$. An indirect contact is one in which there is at least one intermediary, as in the chain $i \rightarrow k \rightarrow j$. To determine which scientists are connected directly and indirectly by the communication relation, we devised an algorithm for identification of networks or groups of connected scientists (*19*).

## • Communication Network Among Scientists in Sleep Research

The 218 active scientists in sleep research were found to be divided into one large network of 160 connected members, one group of three members, another group of

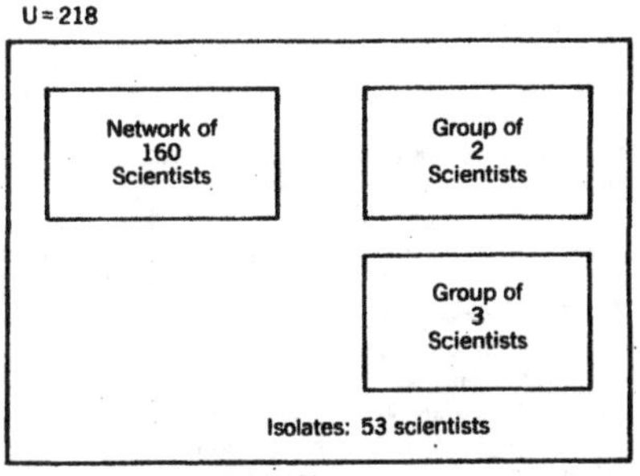


FIG. 1. Connectedness of scientists. The 218 scientists are divided into three disconnected groups and isolates: (1) group of 160 scientists who make up one large communication network; (2) small group of 3 scientists; (3) small group of 2 scientists; (4) 53 isolates

two members, and 53 persons who are connected with no one (Fig. 1). Seventy-three percent of sleep scientists were directly or indirectly connected in a large network through informal communication.

Any scientist located within the large network is in contact with at least one other scientist directly, and with all others in the network indirectly. It should be cautioned, however, that isolates and subgroups are only relatively isolated, for even though they are not connected through informal communication, they may be in touch through other channels of communication. Coleman found, in his study of diffusion of drug information, that isolates were not unaffected by the communication network, but rather that the effect upon them came considerably later. When doctors integrated within the network were compared with non-integrated ones, differences in time-of-adoption curves led Coleman to conclude that the network had an important effect on early adoption of drugs (*20*). At the frontiers of a fast-moving competitive field, a scientist integrated within a communication network is therefore at a greater advantage than his non-integrated colleagues in receiving new information.

In a related study, we found that this large network contained all the scientists who were cited the most, read the most, contacted the most and who produced the most papers (*21*). The isolates are the less active participants in the research area, and in likelihood comprise the group which Price observed as "a floating population of people who appear to collaborate with (extremely active researchers) in one or two multiple-authorship papers and then disappear not to be heard from again (*22*)." It should be noted, however, that research areas are not closed social systems, and these isolates may belong to other research areas and other communication networks.

### • Communication Relations Within the Network of Scientists

The network thus tells us which scientists are in contact with each other directly or indirectly, and there is evidence that membership in a network has an important effect on information transfer. Having identified this network, we proceeded to investigate organization within it for more sensitive indicators, for example, any clustering of scientists in which there is high incidence of interaction.

There is presently no completely satisfactory method for representing distance between points in a network of sociometric relations and measuring its significance. Analysis of relations by manual techniques as well as matrix multiplication are compromises; each has its shortcomings (*23*). Our population of 160 network scientists is a relatively small one, and we began by mapping the communication relations among the scientists. In the sociogram of Fig. 2 the numbers represent scientists and the lines between them represent communication relations. From this sociogram it is obvious that some scientists are the focus of a great number of contacts. The lines of communication appear to converge on them like spokes in a wheel. These are the "central scientists" whom we earlier identified as those who initiated or received contacts from six or more scientists. One scientist (number 37) was the focus of such a disproportionately large number of contacts that we decided to omit him in the sociogram in order that the clusters of communicating scientists may be more clearly visualized. Addition of 37 would (1) not alter the basic pattern of the relation clusters; (2) have the effect of superimposing a great "gatekeeper" with connections to eleven research centers and a total of 31 contacts.

As indicated in Table 2, sleep scientists communicated with almost twice as many sleep scientists who are working inside their research centers in comparison with those who are outside. The sociogram reflects this relationship, and scientists in the same research center tend to be clustered together in the network, as they tend to communicate with each other. The frequency of communication among those in the same center is such that the communication network can be divided into clusters of scientists who communicate with each other and who also belong to the same research center. These clusters we have enclosed in broken lines in the sociogram of Fig. 2.

From Fig. 2, it is also apparent that the central scientists are unevenly distributed among the research centers. The largest centers tend to have more central scientists, although there is variation among the centers in ratio between central and non-central scientists. Los Angeles, with 26 scientists, has nine central scientists, the highest number of all research centers. Five small centers did not have an investigator who is in contact with at least six persons, but each had a central scientist relative to its own members.

Of the total pair relations *within* the research centers, 75% entailed at least one central scientist. Of the relations *between* centers, an even greater number (83%) entailed central scientists. To illustrate the importance of these central scientists in communication, we removed all relations with them in the sociogram of Fig. 3. The original configuration dissolves into local clusters and a half of the scientists are either isolated (27%) of paired with only one person (23%). Without the sociometrically central scientists the rest of the scientists are relatively isolated within their research centers and interpersonal communication between centers is infrequent.

In Fig. 4, we have isolated the central scientists and mapped their relations with each other. All central scientists are in direct contact with at least one other central scientist, with the exception of two scientists who are one step removed. The thirty-three central scientists initiated a total of 150 contacts, of which eighty-eight were directed among themselves and sixty-two were directed to the remaining 185 non-central scientists. On the average, each central scientist was contacted by eight times

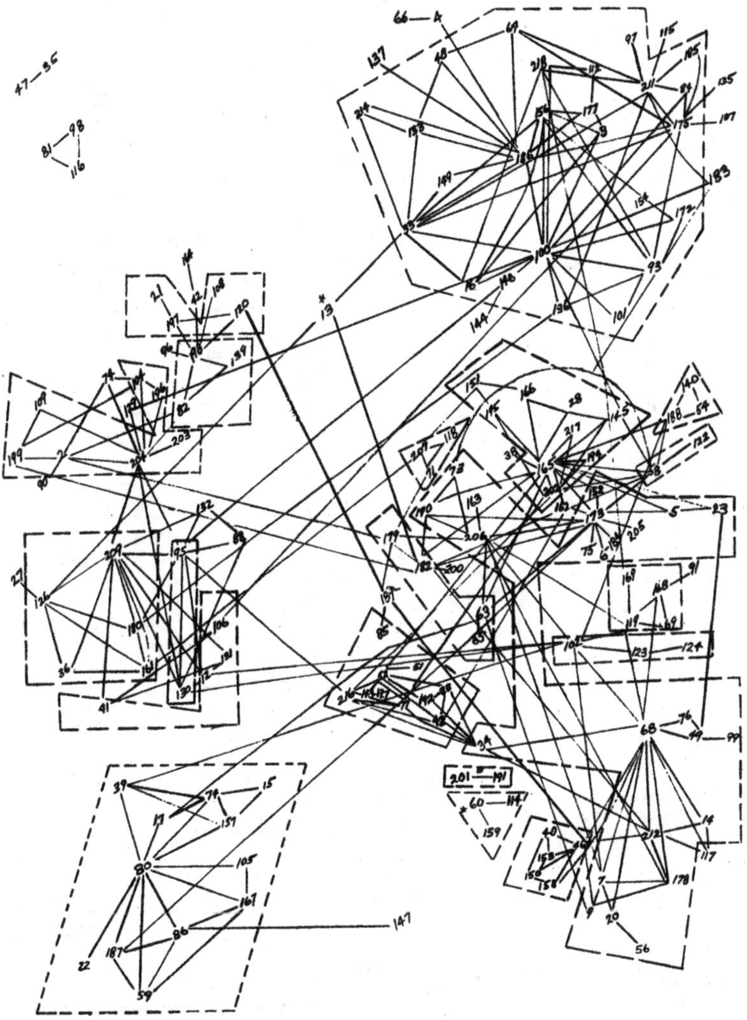

FIG. 2. Communication network of 160 scientists. Each scientist is numbered; the solid lines indicate communication between scientists. Broken lines enclose scientists who work in the same research center.

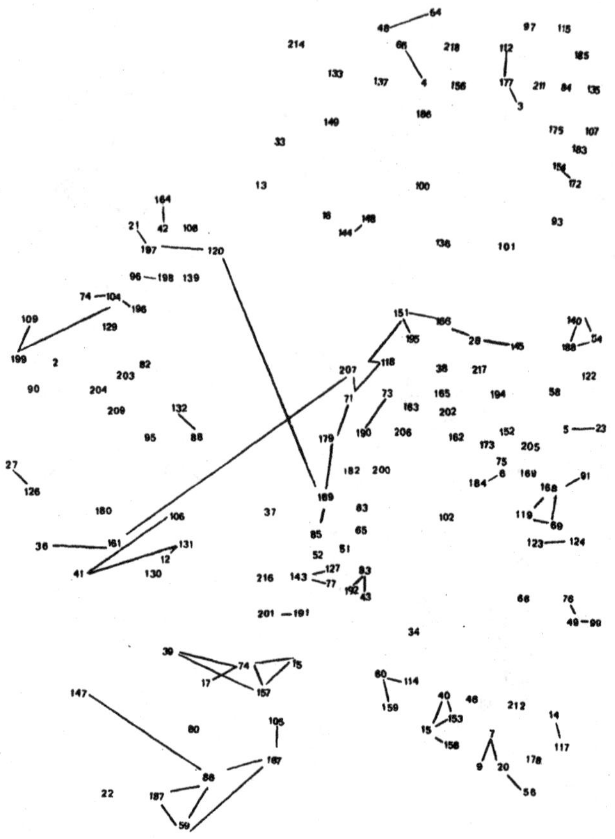

FIG. 3. Communication network of 160 scientists. The network is depicted after removal of all communication relations with sociometrically central scientists

as many other central scientists as the non-central scientists.

When the number of communication steps between scientists was examined, it was found that no investigator was more than three steps removed from a central scientist. Ninety-five percent of the scientists were two steps or less from a central scientist and 61% were in direct contact with the latter, as indicated in Table 4.

How does this affect the flow of information among sleep scientists at the research front? We have identified thirty-three scientists, distributed among the research centers, who are the focus of a large number of communications and who are also the most productive as indicated by the number of papers they produce, the number of scientists who cite them and who also read their work. Information transmitted to these thirty-three sociometrically central scientists would be so situated that it could be transmitted through informal communication to 95% of the network scientists through one intermediary scientist or less.

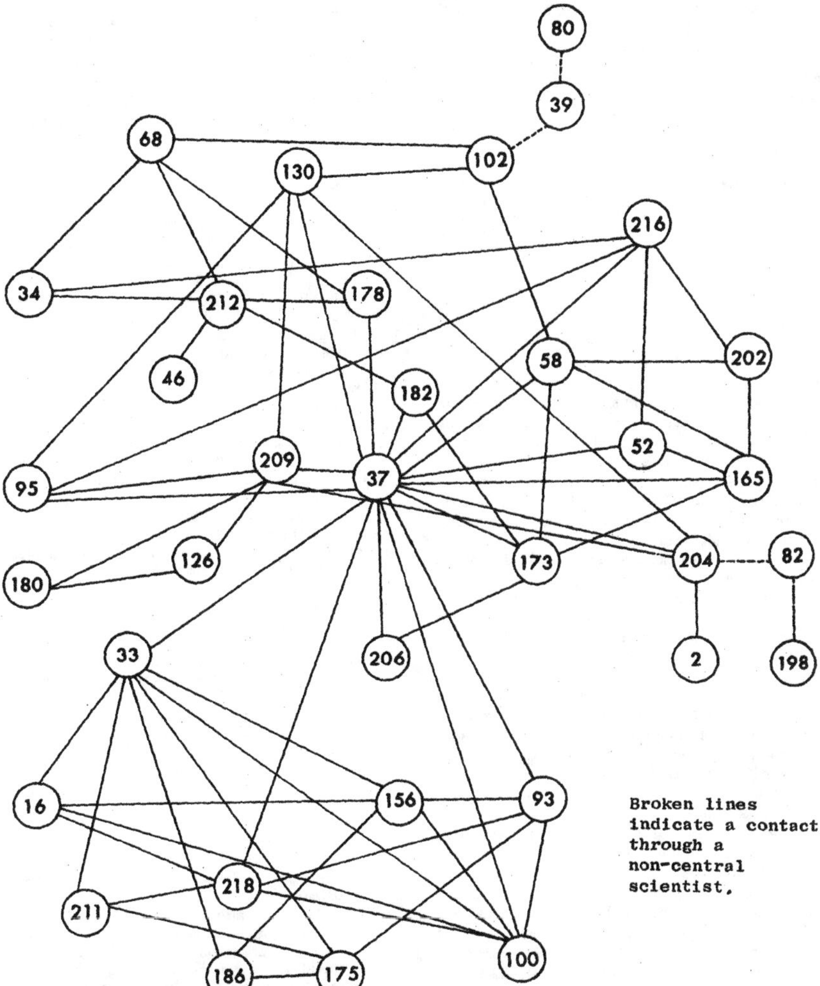


FIG. 4. Map of communication relations between sociometrically central scientists (SCS). All SCS are in direct contact with at least one other SCS, with the exception of two scientists (80 and 198) who are in contact through a non-central scientist

TABLE 4. Shows communication-wise, how far removed non-central scientists in the network are from sociometrically central scientists (SCS). Over 60% of non-central scientists in the network are in direct contact with at least one SCS, and 95% are in contact through only one intermediary scientist

| Number of intermediary scientists between non-central scientists and closest central scientist | Number of non-central scientists | Percentage of non-central scientists |
|---|---|---|
| 0 (Direct contact) | 78 | 60.5 |
| 1 | 45 | 34.8 |
| 2 | 6 | 4.6 |
| Total | 129 | 99.9 |

## • Conclusions

This paper reported investigation of informal communication among scientists at the research front in the psychophysiological study of sleep. Using sociometric techniques, an informal communication network was identified, which included 73% of the active scientists. Within the network was a core group of thirty-three "central scientists" who were the focus of a disproportionately large number of contacts and who were differentiated from others by greater productivity, higher citation record and wider readership.

These central scientists are distributed in research centers over thirty states. The rest of the scientists are organized around them. They are stationed in their laboratories, work with or under them, and go to them for advice and information. From the viewpoint of communication, these key scientists are nodal points for the dissemination of information. On the average, they are in contact with five times as many scientists as the others and account for 83% of the contacts between research centers. Information transmitted to the central scientists is so situated that it could be transmitted to 95% of the scientists in the network through one intermediary scientist or less.

This investigation opens a number of questions and leads us to new areas for further investigation. First, given limited time or funds in scientific endeavors, one can determine the points of entry through which information can most effectively disseminate. Second, this demonstration of the existence of social structure among scientists is silent on the effect of such structures on the direction in which a field develops. It appears that the central scientists identified in this study are highly influential in the field—they are in a position to monitor new information and in likelihood exert strong control over type of research and funding. This question deserves further exploration. Finally, through investigations of the type reported here, we can better discover the functions of our present communication media.

## • Acknowledgments

This work was supported by the University of Chicago Biomedical Communication Research Project under Don R. Swanson. The author expresses appreciation to Allan Rechtschaffen, Director of the Sleep Laboratory and Fred Strodtbeck, Director of the Social Psychology Laboratory, University of Chicago; Derek Price, Yale University; and scientists in sleep research who made this investigation possible.

## References

1. GARVEY, W. D., N. LIN, and C. E. Nelson, Communication in the Physical and the Social Sciences: The Processes of Disseminating and Assimilating Information Differ in These Two Groups of Sciences, Science, 170: 1166–1173 (1970).
2. PRICE, D., The Scientific Foundations of Science Policy, Nature CCVI: 843 (1966).
3. CONFREY, E. A., Information Exchange Groups to be Discontinued, Science, 154: 843 (1966).
4. Boffey, P. M., Psychology: Apprehension over a New Communications System, Science, 167: 1228–1230 (1970).
5. Crane, D., Social Structure in a Group of Scientists: A Test of the 'Invisible College' Hypothesis, American Sociological Review 34: 335–352 (1969).
6. GASTON, J., Big Science in Britain: A Sociological Study of the High Energy Physics Community, unpublished doctoral dissertation, Yale University, 1969.
7. GRIFFITH, B., Networks of Informal Communication, American Psychological Association, Washington, 1963.
8. MULLINS, N., Social Networks Among Biological Scientists, unpublished doctoral dissertation, Harvard University, 1966.
9. D. Price has found that, in general, the growth rate of branches of science proceeds in a logistic curve. Exponential growth inevitably reached a period of saturation when a breakdown begins, followed by an interval of restraint which may lead to escalation or fluctuation. Little Science, Big Science. Columbia University, New York, 1963.
10. A number of problems were encountered in defining physical distance. At first, the laboratory or institutional affiliation was chosen as a starting point from which to measure distance. However, a scientist may be affiliated or hold appointments with a number of institutions within a community. He may also collaborate with other scientists in a proximate geographic area which does not conform with political boundaries of city or state. The requirement for this study is identification of centers in which scientists, located with a reasonable distance from each other, may function as a single community for scientific purposes.

    When the geographic locations of the sleep scientists were examined, we found that they were distributed singly or in clusters in areas where a diameter $\leq 80$ miles included all scientists in any community. We therefore defined a "research center" to designate an

area where there is at least one scientist, and where no scientist is more than 80 miles from another scientist.
11. Kleitman, N., Sleep and Wakefulness; University of Chicago Press, Chicago, 1963.
12. Crawford, S., Communication Centrality and Performance, Proceedings of the American Society for Information Science (Philadelphia, Pennsylvania, October 1970), 1970, pp. 45–48.
13. Coleman, J., E. Katz and H. Menzel, Medical Innovation: a Diffusion Study, Bobbs-Merrill, New York, 1966.
14. Mullins, N., Ibid., considered the following groups in his study: (1) pair relations between scientists; (2) strong units: largest collection of direct relations in which all members can reach each other; (3) neighborhood groups: a cluster of short-distance choices in which there are fewer connections than the maximum $n(n-1)$, but more relations than a chain, because of feedback to members previously chosen.
15. Storer, N., Modes and Processes of Communication Among Scientists, Columbia University, New York, 1968. Mimeo.
16. Crane, D., Ibid.
17. Gaston, J., Ibid.
18. Coleman, J., An Introduction to Mathematical Sociology, Free Press of Glencoe, New York, 1964.
19. The objective is to identify (1) all persons who are connected by the communication relation measured in this study; (2) all disconnected subgroups and the composition of each subgroup. The choices of the 218 scientists are represented in a matrix. The rows indicate choices made and the columns indicate choices received, with a 1 denoting contact and an 0 denoting no contact. The matrix is read into the computer, and all values in the central diagonal are converted to 0.

The algorithm indicates a matching process in which, beginning with cell $A_{11}$, all cells are systematically searched. Cells with a 1 indicate that the scientists are in contact, and the scientist contacted is added to the chain. The rest of the cells are searched for contacts made by each scientist added to the chain. When the end of a chain is reached, an "uncommitted" scientist is chosen and matched against remaining members. The process is continued until all scientists are "used up."

Instructions for execution of this algorithm are available on request from the author.
20. Coleman, J., et al., Ibid.
21. Crawford, S., Ibid.
22. Price, D., and D. Beaver, Collaboration in an Invisible College, American Psychologist 21: 1011–1018, (1966).
23. Coleman, J., Introduction to Mathematical Sociology, Chap.14.

# SCIENTIFIC COMMUNICATION:

## ITS ROLE IN THE CONDUCT OF RESEARCH AND CREATION OF KNOWLEDGE

WILLIAM D. GARVEY AND BELVER C. GRIFFITH

*Johns Hopkins University* — *Drexel University*

From its inception, the Board of Scientific Affairs has devoted special attention to the role of scientific communication in the development of psychological science. In a 1959 issue of the *American Psychologist* (14, pp. 267–271), Dorwin Cartwright and Arthur Melton, the first two Chairmen of the Board, stated that "BSA considers the problem of efficient and effective communication of scientific information to be perhaps the most critical problem faced by scientific psychology today [p. 270]." The Board called for careful studies of the processes of scientific communication, urging that researchers explore the role of formal and informal channels, collect data on the natural history of scientific information transmission, review the problems of information retrieval, and examine the applicability of available technologists to the communication problems in psychology.

In 1960, the National Science Foundation granted funds to the APA for a program of research on scientific information exchange in psychology. William D. Garvey and Belver C. Griffith were asked by the Central Office to develop and undertake this program of research. The work of these researchers over the last decade has given psychologists a rare resource—a series of empirical studies of the nature of scientific communication within their own field.

APA is now engaged in a large-scale revision of its system of communications. Many innovations are being explored, and many traditional institutions are being reexamined. It is not surprising that scientists' emotions run high in such circumstances, and it is scarcely news that the communication program has been ardently praised and vigorously criticized. It is regrettable, however, that in the midst of such great interest, there is sometimes so little information. The Board of Scientific Affairs feels that one of its responsibilities to the Association is to call members' attention to the pioneering research done under APA's auspices which ought to be central to the current discussion of our communication system.

On the assumption that sound decisions are most likely to be made with the benefit of accurate information, the Board asked Drs. Garvey and Griffith to prepare a summary of some of their major findings for presentation at the 1970 meeting of the Association. While this assignment required heroic selection and condensation, a coherent and comprehensible picture of scientific communication emerged. The paper is of such interest and importance to psychologists that the Board urged the authors to submit it for publication. We hope this article will give the benefit of the authors' hard-won knowledge and deep insight to a wide audience. And we hope that the members of APA will give serious thought to these findings as they make decisions affecting the communication structures available for scientific information exchange.

JAMES J. JENKINS
*Board of Scientific Affairs*

THERE is considerable apprehension today within the scientific community over the communication crisis in science. The present article, which attempts to clarify certain aspects of the problem, overviews the data collected by the APA Project on Scientific Information Exchange in Psychology,[1, 2] together with data which we have more recently obtained relative to other disciplines. Such a reexamination of the data should help to clarify APA's relationship to the many information media involved in the communication process which begins with research and ends with the incorporation of research findings into psychological knowledge.

## Productive Scientist within the Context of His Discipline

Figure 1 shows the growth of the population of psychologists and of scientific and technical information. The solid curve is a plot of the growth of APA membership. Disregarding the drop in production of psychologists during the two war periods, the number of psychologists has been increasing exponentially for the past century.[3] The overall rate of manpower growth in psychology has been remarkably steady, doubling every 10–12 years, until 1959. From that point, the growth rate appears to have slowed down, doubling every 12–15 years. This is similar to most estimates of the growth rate of scientific manpower in general.[4]

The broken curve in the figure shows a crude measure of the growth of information output of APA—in this instance it is the number of pages published annually in APA journals, plus the number of presentations programmed annually at APA conventions. Initially, psychologists accumulated information at a rate roughly equivalent to the manpower growth in psychology. From 1910 to the present, however, the information production rate slowed down to a rather steady rate, doubling every 15–20 years. (Information growth has been measured in several ways—number of "abstracts" published, number of new journals established, etc. All measures confirmed this rate.)

The growth rates of these two products of American psychology—psychologists and information—indicate the nature of certain scientific communication problems in the field. Note that American psychology produces psychologists faster than it produces information. As long as this trend persists, there will be an increasingly larger proportion of psychologists to process a steadily increasing amount of scientific information—that is, the proportion of total consumers to total new information will continue to increase. It would appear, then, that the major information problem facing psychology is not so much that psychology is producing more information than its total manpower can assimilate, but rather that the individual scientist is being overloaded with scientific information. Perhaps the alarm over an "information crisis" arose because sometime in the last information-doubling period, the *individual* psychologist became overburdened and could no longer keep up with and assimilate all the information being produced that was related to his primary speciality.[5]

Initially, the Project concentrated on studying the producers, and an unmistakable conclusion was

[1] Requests for reprints should be sent to William D. Garvey, Center for Research in Scientific Communication, The Milton Eisenhower Library, Johns Hopkins University, Baltimore, Maryland 21218.

[2] The history of the APA Project on Scientific Information Exchange in Psychology begins with a report by the Board of Scientific Affairs, prepared under the consecutive chairmanships of Dorwin Cartwright and Arthur Melton (*American Psychologist*, 1959, **14**, 267–271). Two years later, the National Science Foundation granted funds to APA for a program of *research* on *scientific* information exchange in psychology. The authors were hired to plan and execute the program from the attic of the old APA building. An indispensable force behind the initiation of this program was John G. Darley, then the Executive Officer of APA.

The advisory panel contributed immeasurably to the success of the Project and also to the pleasure of being part of it. The group consisted for much of the Project of Raymond A. Bauer, Charles W. Bray, Dorwin Cartwright, Kenneth E. Clark, John G. Darley, Quinn McNemar, Charles E. Osgood, and Donald W. Taylor.

The data reported here are described in detail in the three volumes of the Project's reports (APA, 1963, 1965, 1969), and direct citation to these reports will not be made in the text.

[3] This exponential growth of APA membership was no surprise. As early as 1951, E. G. Boring had pointed out that the rate of increase in the number of psychologists greatly exceeded the rate of increase in the United States population, in general, and had concluded, with tongue in cheek, that before the end of the twenty-first century, every man, woman, and child in the United States would be a member of the APA.

[4] See Price's (1963) discussion of the general growth of science and its information products.

[5] For a thorough description of this problem, see J. C. R. Licklider's (1966) excellent analysis.

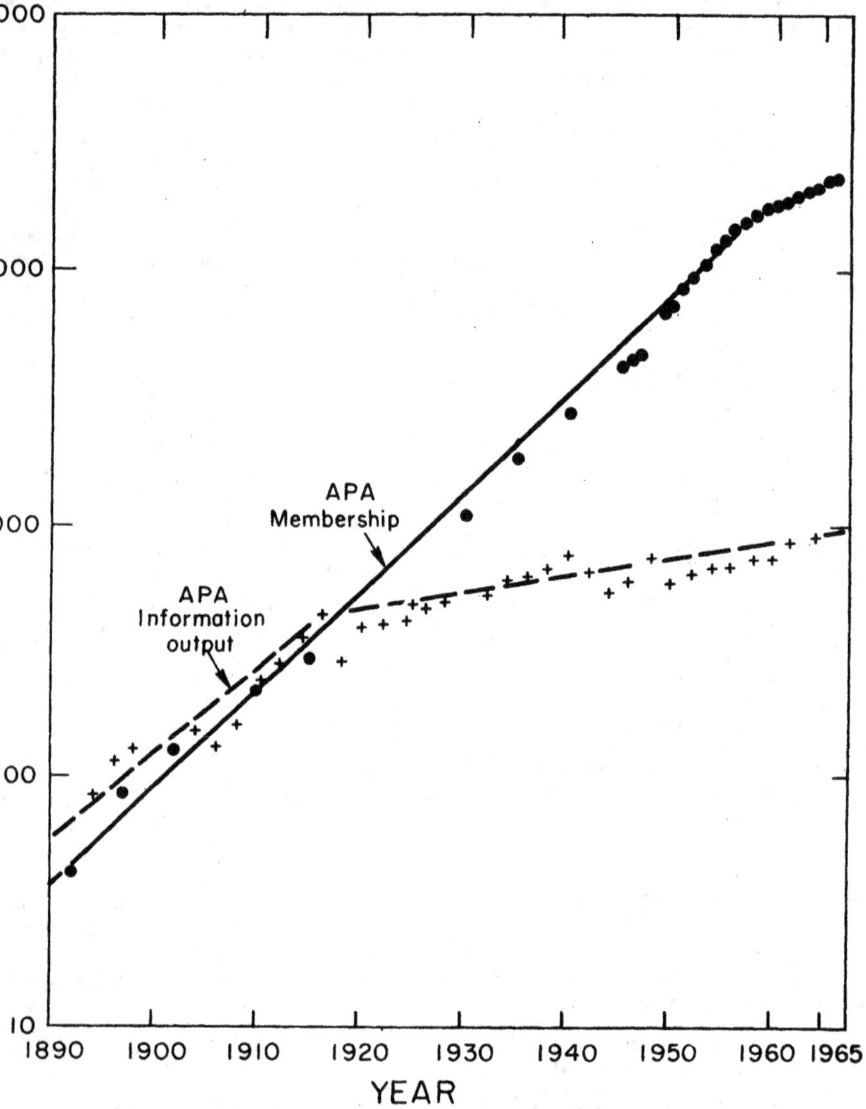


**Fig. 1. The growth of APA membership and APA information output. (The broken line actually represents one-tenth of the annual information output, that is, the number of article pages published plus the number of convention presentations programmed annually by the APA divided by 10.)**

that the significant producers of scientific information in psychology are, indeed, a small minority; curves in Figure 1 suggest that since the early 1900s an ever-decreasing proportion of the APA membership remains in activities productive of scientific information. Figure 2 plots the number of events (such as published articles or review citations) over a five-year period, against the per-

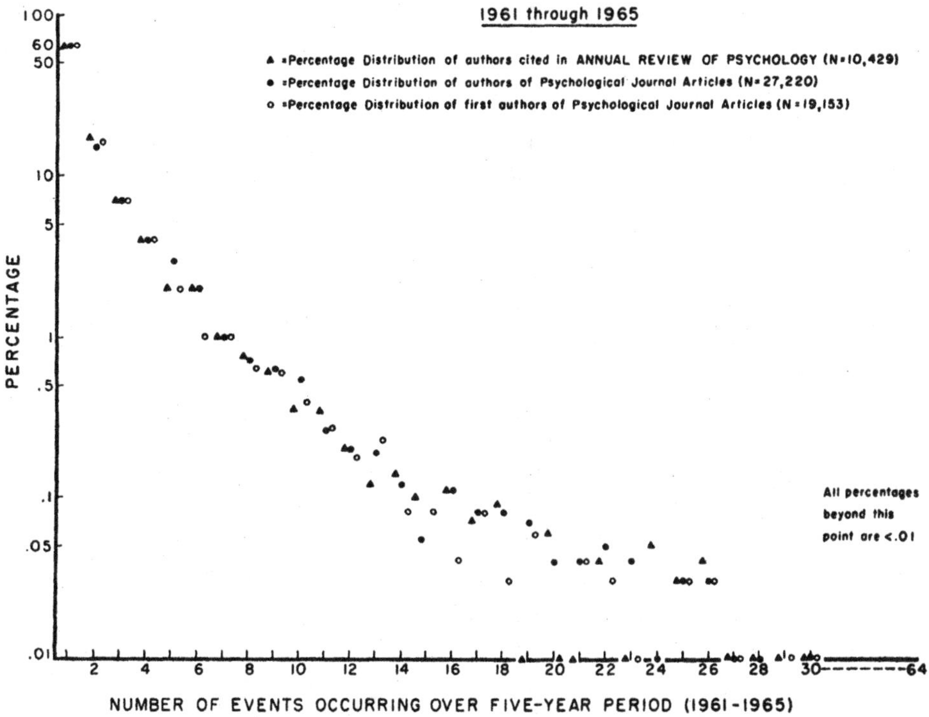


FIG. 2. Percentage distribution of journal-article productivity of those psychologists who contributed to at least one psychological article published during the five-year period, 1961–1965.

centage of scientists associated with given numbers of such events. Three distributions are shown. The solid dots represent the percentage of articles to which a scientist contributed, that is, the number for which he was listed among the authors. A total of 19,153 articles was produced by 27,220 authors during this five-year period, and of these authors, 65% contributed to only one article during this period. Using the somewhat arbitrary criterion that a productive psychologist is one who contributes at least one article per year, we find that only 10% of these authors can be considered productive. The distribution represented by the open dots resulted when all of the authors except those who were single or first-listed authors were eliminated.

Next, we examined the distribution of authorships after the journal literature had been culled and integrated into a scholarly review. Over this five-year period, the works of 10,429 authors were cited in the *Annual Review of Psychology*. The distribution represented by the triangles in Figure 2 shows that 65% of the authors were cited only once, and only 10% were cited on an average of once a year.

All of these data suggest that the "significant" producers of scientific information may be reduced to a small group (probably about 2,000 APA members in the early 1960s). These same 2,000 psychologists were encountered repeatedly in the Project's studies. They produced most of the material that required or warranted scientific information-exchange activities in psychology, and it was their work that kept psychology going as a scientific discipline. They regularly published journal articles, made formal presentations at annual meetings, and produced treatises and books on psychological subjects. They held major research grants and often served as reviewers or advisers on other research grants or programs. They also

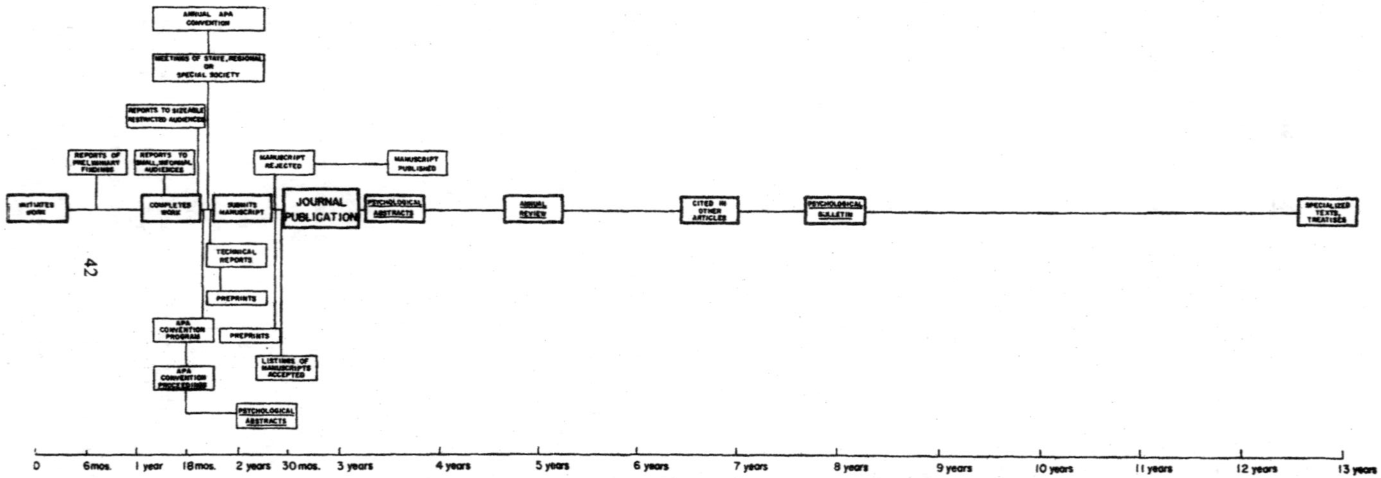


FIG. 3. The dissemination process from the time the research scientist initiates his work until his findings become integrated into the fund of scientific knowledge. (The abscissa gives the median time, after initiation of work, of each form of dissemination shown in the figure.)

monitored the processing of scientific information (i.e., were editors and referees).

The data in this figure also indicated that psychology was training a large number of psychologists who would graduate, publish their theses, or dissertations, or first research studies in the real world, and then pass on to fields in which they would cease to be producers. They would be, instead, the major source of those "piecemeal" reports which editors seek to consolidate into more substantial publications. The problem is more complicated than originally thought because a majority of these reports of "first steps" of research, being the final step of doctoral training, are never followed up by their authors. Consequently, the integrated series of studies, with general conclusions, must often await further research and review by other scholars.

In this section, we have sought to segregate the minority of individuals who carry on that mission of generating knowledge in the name of the discipline as a whole. In the next three sections, we are concerned with their activities, largely to the exclusion of other members of the discipline. That these persons are a very small minority is critical to the nature of their activities, the manner in which they conduct them, and the entire problem of creating significant scientific achievements. For most of these men, the process discussed in the next three sections constitutes their continuing daily activities as highly productive scientists.

## Planning of Research and Informal Exchanges

The left portion of Figure 3 presents the various dissemination events that occur between the time the scientist begins his research and the time he publishes it in a journal. Most of the statistics are medians related to the "average" author of a journal article, of a presentation at a scientific meeting, etc. On the left in this figure, we show at Time Zero the initiation of work that will be published some three years later.

How the scientist gets his ideas for research in the present-day world of "big science" is not altogether clear. It is clear, however, that the productive scientist cannot be an isolated scholar who devotes years to reading scientific literature related to the phenomenon he wishes to research. Usually he cannot afford this, except perhaps during graduate training, since the quantity of material and the rapidity of movement at the research front usually prohibit exhaustive searching and reading. Nor is he the recluse, more or less ignored by society, who can privately pursue his own intuition. The cost of research and the problem of acquiring funds to support it, the responsible role society now expects science to play, and the relative rapidity of communication do not allow him to divorce himself from influences outside his laboratory. In other words, research ideas and problem development can be primarily influenced by the published channels of scientific information exchange. In a study of over 200 research efforts in psychology, we found that ideas for less than one out of seven originated from sources such as journal articles, presentations at national meetings, etc. Instead, the scientist relies heavily on informal networks of information exchange to keep abreast of current activities and of the current views of the community on the value and relevance of specific research problems.

Early Project findings clearly demonstrated the great importance of informal contacts. Consequently, we made several attempts to determine in what way the communication network connecting various groups of psychologists might be organized. We found no clear-cut network or group of networks which transfer scientific information among groups of active scientists; nor are there media that present in a comprehensive and coherent way the materials being developed within even one specialty. Psychology is not, however, completely fragmented into isolated subdisciplines, nor is there an absence of coherence for the individual specialties. At the grossest level, there is a rather elaborate structure of societies which serve the widely ranging interests of APA members and which exist largely outside of APA.

Figure 4 presents Wood's (1966) sociometric diagram of memberships held by APA members in various professional societies; the diagrams suggest considerable structure among these groups in terms of overlapping membership and some interesting straddling, by individuals, of subject-matter boundaries. It is now becoming evident that this type of organization within disciplines is one of the internal forces which saves any one scientific specialty from proceeding too independently down a wrong path; that is, scientific progress in one field

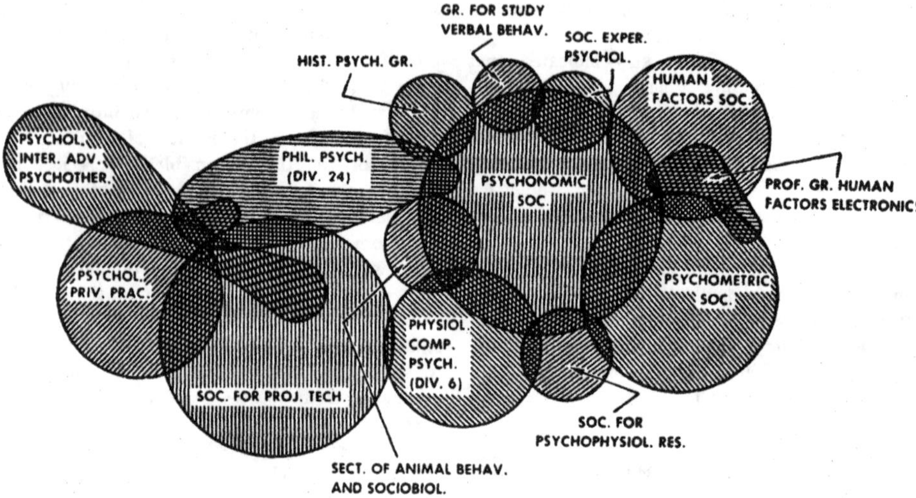


FIG. 4. Relative sizes and major overlaps of memberships of psychological organizations. [The figure is reprinted from an article by Paul J. Woods published in the August 1964 issue of the *American Psychologist* (1964, 19, 663–669).]

cannot be isolated from the criticism of particularly well-informed and experienced researchers who straddle several fields or who are in immediately adjacent specialties.

At a more molecular level of analysis, that is, that of the individual research specialties, there is considerable organization and communication among the small minority of productive researchers within psychology. In one of the last studies (Griffith & Miller, 1970) conducted by the Project, it became evident that this minority is highly organized into small clusters of researchers who maintain continual contact with one another's work. The degree of organization within these clusters varies greatly and appears to depend partially on size, partially on the chance occurrences which brought the specialty into existence, and very largely on the nature of the intellectual development within the specialty and the relationship of such developments to other specialties.

### Early Dissemination of Research Findings

When the scientist is clear enough about his research question to plan his investigation, he interacts with his immediate colleagues, usually to formulate his research problem more precisely and obtain specific information relative to methodology, apparatus, anticipated data analysis, etc. One interesting aspect of information feedback to the researcher at this stage is its stimulating and encouraging influence on his planned research. Interest expressed by a colleague is encouragement to go ahead with one's plans. Without such interest or encouragement, there is a tendency to delay the research or to abandon it altogether.

During the first 12–18 months—from the time the work begins until the researcher believes he can give a complete and defensible report of it to colleagues working in the same subject-matter area—the scientist is relatively uncommunicative about his work. Exceptions, of course, are the casual, but often fruitful, discussions with immediate colleagues.

Very shortly after the researcher feels he can report his work, he begins to disseminate his findings, a process that continues for many months, usually until he has submitted a manuscript reporting his findings to a journal. Usually the first reports are informal ones, presented to small, relatively sympathetic audiences at gatherings such as colloquia within the scientist's own institution. Next, the researcher launches out into broader territory, perhaps responding to a request that he present his work at a conference sponsored by the agency funding his research. Or, if he is recognized by his peers as being among the top researchers in his field, he may be invited to speak at a small conference of specialists working in the same field.

Up to this point, the scientist's dissemination of information on his work is minor and primarily concerns persons who are already aware of the areas or problems he is working on and who may need only the briefest communication to understand what he has accomplished. If all has gone well, the scientist, having tested his findings and their interpretation on fellow workers, is now ready to disseminate his work to larger and larger segments of the scientific community.

Within a few months, about one productive scientist in four will report his work to a fairly large audience at a meeting of a state, regional, or national professional society. There is a hierarchy of psychological societies within the framework of American psychology. At the base, there are perhaps 50 state associations that hold meetings attended by 25–1,000 or more persons. There are seven regional meetings with 50–3,000 or more attendants. And at the national level, there is the APA convention which encompasses the entire discipline of psychology. In addition, there are the numerous societies (the Psychonomic Society, the Psychometric Society, etc.) that hold their own meetings.

The APA convention was found to be an especially important medium in the dissemination process.[6] The meeting occurs 15–18 months prior to journal publication of the contents of most of the papers presented there, and includes a sizable proportion of the annual scientific information output of American psychology. (About one-fifth of the journal articles published in the main psychological journals, for example, are based on material previously presented at an APA convention.)

The published programs of these meetings often constitute the first genuinely public announcement of the completion of a particular research effort. Consequently, almost all persons who present papers at APA conventions (and also at the major regional meetings) receive requests for copies of their presentations. These requests sometimes number more than 100. The majority of these requests come from persons who did not attend the meeting at which the paper was presented. The typical requester is a very young researcher. He exerts considerable effort to gain access to recent research findings through such early-alerting media as published programs, probably because he is unlikely to have received this information earlier through the special, restricted informal networks which the author first uses to disseminate his work.

The Project's studies of information exchange at meetings revealed that the presentation author is the focus of a particular communication process. He is spotlighted at the session and thereafter associated with the topic of his presentation. About one meeting-presentation attendant in six will contact this author about his presentation, and about half of these contacts will be made at the meeting. They will seldom be made during the session itself, however. The author can expect that most attendants who contact him will want to discuss an aspect of the work not mentioned in his presentation. The typical author finds such interest valuable to his own research since attendants will be likely to apprise him of the existence and availability of related work.

Of the various groups who participate in meetings, the authors of presentations undoubtedly benefit the most. For one thing, convention presentations are viewed by authors as interim reports of their work—about three-fourths of those who contribute papers will seek journal publication of their papers during the three- to four-year period following the convention. The dissemination of information about their research at the meeting usually affords them an opportunity to seek critical feedback before submitting that manuscript to the journal editorial process. For another thing, most authors have already initiated new work in the same subject-matter areas as their presentations, and are seeking information that is relevant to this new work.

During this period in the information flow process, about 1 author in 10 will also produce and distribute a technical report. We studied over 1,000 technical reports that were produced by psychologists in 1962 and found that the main content of one-third of these had been published in a scientific journal by 1965. There were no substantial differences between the technical report and the journal article in almost half of these 337

[6] In light of these findings about the APA convention, an experimental trial of preconvention publication of contributed papers was initiated in 1960. For a description of the rationale leading to the design of this innovation, see Garvey and Griffith (1966).

cases; most of the remaining studies were reported at more length in the technical reports than in the journal articles, although the corresponding journal articles were typically better written and better related to other work in the same subject-matter areas.

Two-thirds of the technical reports produced in 1962 had not achieved journal publication by 1965, and, apparently, the contents of the vast majority of these reports were never submitted for journal publication. Many authors of such reports indicated that "no further dissemination of the information was deemed necessary." The fate of the majority of the material in psychology which appears in technical reports and does not later appear in journals is unknown. This raises some questions about the ultimate value of the information in these reports and its relevance to the established body of scientific knowledge. Thus, whether or not archival status is bestowed on this corpus of literature is a matter of some concern to the experienced scientist who is deeply involved in the advance of scientific understanding of his research subject.

The problem is complicated in some respects because the recognized researcher generally receives a majority of the technical reports of research related to his own work, and, for each useful technical report he receives, he receives many irrelevant or useless ones. The impression which results is that the bulk of this type of informal literature is worthless. Yet, the individual researcher often finds it easier to reproduce or follow up an experiment described in a technical report than one described in a journal article. This, of course, is because the former frequently includes wiring diagrams, pictures of apparatus, more detailed descriptions of the procedures, and, in social science areas, full reports of the data and questionnaires or interview schedules. In technical reports, the authors tend to speculate more in discussing their research. Such speculation can be tolerated and may even be productive in the *informal* literature, but it can play havoc later on in the formal literature where the process is directed at separating scientific fact from conjecture.

The scientist continues to disseminate information about his research up until he submits his manuscript to a journal. From the time he completes his work until he submits his manuscript, many a new stew may be made from the same old bones, and one might conclude that the scientist is trying to wring every bit of recognition he can from this single piece of work. But the situation does not appear to be so simple, for the various forms used to disseminate the material are dictated by a number of factors, some of which are beyond the control of the scientist himself. A variety of audiences for information require a variety of reports. There are also reports which the scientist is required to make or which he feels he owes it to scientific or academic tradition to produce. Institutional pressures, both implicit (the dean's annual request for a list of publications) and explicit (the payment of expenses to attend a scientific meeting may be contingent upon the making of a presentation there), may force reports that serve little, if any, communication function. However, the multiple reports which the scientist makes in order to encourage critical feedback from others do serve important functions in his work.

A growing informal dissemination medium is the preprint (a prepublication draft of the manuscript which is submitted to a journal). In 1963, for example, about half of the authors of articles published in major psychology journals distributed an average of 10 preprints. Authors distribute preprints on several of the occasions relative to journal submission and acceptance of their manuscripts. Prior to manuscript submission, the authors primarily seek comment and criticism; after submission or notification of journal acceptance, authors distributed preprints as a means of rapidly and selectively disseminating their findings to other workers in the subject-matter areas. Earlier disseminations of findings may determine the selection of preprint recipients. Almost a quarter of the authors who distributed preprints did so to persons who had become familiar with the work through the author's earlier reports of it and who had, as a consequence, asked to receive a copy of the manuscript when available.

Preprint distribution appears to serve both the recipient and the author. Over 60% of those authors who distributed preprints received feedback that prompted them to modify their manuscripts. These modifications were not simply a matter of improvement in the grammar and style of the manuscript but, instead, involved significant modifications such as reanalysis of data, redefinition of concepts, etc. Consequently, preprint distribution is, for many authors, an effective means of obtaining independent evaluation of the scientific worth of their work.

## Journal Publication

Thus, the author of a journal-article manuscript is likely to have disseminated his findings on several occasions prior to submitting it to a journal. He probably started with small groups, testing his findings and interpretation on relatively friendly audiences, and then seeking progressively larger and less intimate groups. On each occasion, he gave careful thought to the feedback he received, and where appropriate he incorporated changes in the manuscript he was preparing for a journal. Having tested his findings and interpretation on his peers, he was then ready to submit his manuscript to the rigorous journal editorial process. But in most instances he hesitated here for one last "ally" review and to distribute preprints. Having revised his manuscript on the basis of feedback from preprint recipients, he had little left to do but submit his manuscript to a journal and then to wait for editorial action.

Once a manuscript is submitted to a journal, the information contained in the manuscript is effectively obscured from the scientific public until journal publication. The author, having submitted his manuscript, has no further personal need to disseminate its content. For the typical scientist, research is an ongoing process. Once the manuscript goes to a journal, the research cycle is, in effect, complete; the active researcher then begins the cycle anew, concentrating on information exchange associated with new work. Seventy percent of the authors studied had, in fact, started new work in the same areas as their articles by the time their articles were published. This new work had progressed well; 60% of the authors had completed this new work, and over a quarter had reported it in either oral or written form, prior to the publication of their previous work.

An average lag of nine months exists between manuscript submission and journal publication. Approximately one-fifth of the articles published in the main psychology journals have been previously rejected by one or more journals. The most frequent reason given for rejection is inappropriateness of subject matter for the journal; this may be, however, a socially acceptable way of stating that the manuscript is of poor quality. In psychology, there is apparently a hierarchy of journals to which authors submit their manuscripts. At the top are the most prestigeful, with high rejection rates and long publication lags. These publish the core of the discipline's literature. At the next level, the journals are usually less prestigeful, have lower rejection rates, and are less central to the literature in the field. At the lower level, the journals share few of the characteristics of the main or core journals and may be unrefereed.

An interesting point here is that authors know the structure of the hierarchy. If they fail with a journal in the upper level, they will resubmit to a journal at a lower level; seldom do they submit a manuscript rejected by a lower-level journal to a journal on a level above. Moreover, as the years go by, many authors discover their ecological niche in this hierarchy, and seldom venture beyond it.

Sometimes an author must resubmit his manuscript two or more times before achieving journal publication, but a persistent author will seldom fail to get his manuscript published eventually. Often the critical feedback from referees helps him to improve his manuscript so that it becomes an acceptable piece of work for publication in the next journal of submission. In any event, it is quite clear from the Project's studies that rejection may keep a manuscript from appearing in a particular scientific journal, and it adds 10–12 months to the journal publication process, but it rarely prevents the manuscript's eventual appearance in the public journal literature of a scientific discipline.

The most crucial point in the process of dissemination of *scientific* information is the transfer of information from the informal to the formal domain, which occurs with the journal publication of the article. During the two months after publication, the audience for most articles is very small. About half of the research reports in core psychology journals are likely to be read (partially or entirely) by 1% or less of a random sample of psychologists. No research report is likely to be read during this period by more than 7% of a random sample of psychologists. When we extrapolate this to the population studied (approximately 20,000 psychologists), we find that half the articles have a total of 200 or fewer readers. This is well within the range of some other forms of distribution (copies of meeting presentations, technical reports, reprints) which, since they are distributed mainly to interested persons, may have very high rates of readership.

Though to conclude from the results of this study of *immediate* readership of journal articles that psychology journals are not read by psychologists is to misinterpret the findings, it was quite clear in 1962 that the journal article in psychology was no longer the medium for disseminating *current* scientific findings to researchers active on the research front. It should become clear later in this article that while "current" journal reading is relevant to the assimilation of research findings, this is only a minor portion of the use to which journal articles are ultimately put.

### Transfer of Information from the Informal to the Formal Domain

The article, now part of the primary literature of science, becomes a permanent record of completed research; that is, it becomes part of the "archives" of science. Next begins the procedure by which the article is assimilated into the established scientific literature of the field, and the flow from here on is slow but steady. Related findings, repetition, and further research, plus continued informal and formal evaluation (e.g., in reviews, etc.), eventually establish the scientific credibility and originality of the work. (An insignificant or poor piece of research will usually fade away through inattention, and will do no more harm than clutter up the archives.)

The information in the article moves into secondary sources where scientific "information" is processed into "knowledge." Separate items of information from separate journal articles are interrelated, and these clusters in turn become compounded into a self-consistent, meaningful body of knowledge which eventually represents the most acceptable and coherent scientific understanding of a subject matter at that time.[7] Each of the secondary sources shown in Figure 3 serves a different function in this integrative process. About seven to eight months after an article is published, it will be abstracted in *Psychological Abstracts.* The abstract places the article in a public secondary source along with other contemporary works on the same subject. No item of scientific information is likely to proceed efficiently through the remainder of this process without going through this comprehensive cataloging, without which most articles would be randomly stored, to be discovered by chance.

Evidence that this integrative and evaluative process is in motion usually appears some two to three years after the article is published when it is cited by another author. Here the scientific information in the article is built upon, evaluated in the light of new information, and linked to new information which has been generated since its publication. Because of publication delay encountered by the *citing* article, the general scientific public is not aware of this integrative step until some months later (and by then it is three years after the *cited* article's publication).

Some two or three years after publication, the article, if it shows evidence of potential scientific importance, reappears in a subject-matter chapter of the *Annual Review of Psychology.* (If a published work was initially trivial or found to be incorrect but has done no harm, it is likely to perish before this stage.) Another major source of reviews in psychology is the *Psychological Bulletin.* Because this journal once depended solely on voluntary reviews, the average age of an article cited in the *Bulletin* was over five years old. The current editor of the *Bulletin,* James E. Deese, has initiated steps to speed the reviewing process for certain rapidly developing fields.[8]

Reviews synthesize and evaluate recent progress in an area. Good reviews are explicit accounts of what the vast majority of experienced scientists in a field consider to be the acceptable facts and the significant relationships among these facts. Good reviews precisely identify, but do not necessarily exclude, that which is still regarded as speculation and may provide other experienced researchers in the field with strong indications of what is ripe for scientific inquiry. Reviews are an essential part of the continuous reassessment of the current stage of scientific knowledge in a field, and such reassessment is not simply a matter of retrieving and synthesizing piecemeal, discrete facts. The impor-

[7] For an excellent, novel essay on the consensus process and the role of universally accepted knowledge in science, see Ziman (1968).

[8] With Deese, the second author conducted a survey of productive psychologists to determine (*a*) what areas were especially "hot" and ripe for review and (*b*) who might be the best persons to perform these reviews. Editor Deese has now solicited and published such reviews along with the submitted reviews traditionally published in the *Bulletin.*

tant thing to be noted here is that analysis, evaluation, and synthesis have been proceeding ever since the work first appeared in the journal literature, in a process so central to science as to be virtually indistinguishable from it. By this process, high critical standards, earlier embodied in the judgment of editors and referees, now become reinforced through the even higher standards imposed by the collective "integrative" activity of all productive researchers and scholars in a field.

The researcher who has been following the progress of his own work may get the impression that little happens to it after it is cited in a review. Earlier in the process, his article may have been cited by the author of another article, but henceforth the review article will usually serve as an appropriate reference to his contribution.[9] If his work has survived the process up to now, however, and if it subsequently proves to be an important contribution to his field, then a decade or more after he has published it, he might find reference to his article in a treatise or specialized text.

During the last half of the first decade after an article has been published, near the end of that process by which scientific "information" is transformed into scientific "knowledge," lies the final goal of all the accumulation of research data and of all the scientific communication that we have encountered up to now, that is, the synthesis of existing scientific information into erudite, general accounts of the current scientific understanding of a subject-matter area. The treatise or specialized text are major media (in Figure 3) used during this final stage. But there are others, the most interesting of which is the presidential address.

For the experienced psychologist who is actively involved in research in a particular area, a treatise or specialized text may serve only to reinforce or to reorganize his own conceptional framework of the subject matter. Information disseminated through such media is more generally understandable, and now, after years of critical evaluation and synthesis, scientific knowledge may be readied for dissemination beyond the active research community—to the nonexpert, to the inexperienced student, to the applied worker, to the practitioner, etc. The major dissemination events through which the work of the accomplished research psychologist evolves, from the time the work is initiated until it is deposited in the great archival reservoir of scientific knowledge, typically occur over a 12- to 15-year period in psychology. This picture of the long, slow, cautious process of creating, evaluating, reevaluating, integrating, synthesizing, and transforming scientific information into scientific knowledge, creates considerable sympathy for the dedicated professional scientist and scholar who has devoted his career to an area of psychology. His concern over the current emphasis on developing mechanisms to speed up the flow of informal scientific information and distending this flow into the formal domain, thus increasing the flow of unevaluated information, is understandable—such mechanisms would change the norms governing these processes and confuse the mechanisms concerned with evaluating and integrating knowledge.

## Contrasts between Formal and Informal Domains

A misunderstanding of the values and the specific functions of scientific communication may be at the root of much of the current conflict about developing an information system in psychology. The flow of information through the informal channels is relatively free of filtering or monitoring; the individual researcher is free to select both the communication media and the audience. The general procedure in the informal domain is to allow all work that reaches even minimum scientific standards to be disseminated there—the disseminator is the initial judge of the quality of the work.[10] Conversely, before information can be transferred to the formal domain, it must be evaluated thoroughly by its author's peers. Throughout the informal process, the typical research scientist is aiming for journal publication of his research and is seeking prevenient evaluation of his work. Most authors' manuscripts are shaped and reshaped as the work is repeatedly reported. The informal information-exchange process transforms a preliminary report into a finished scientific product. In *science,* the journal-article manuscript is clearly a special product which is developed through the informal information-exchange process.

The information that flows through the informal domain is not meant to have the same attributes

[9] Clear examples of the replacement of citations of original articles by citations of reviews are presented by Price (1965).

[10] See Allen (1970), Garvey and Griffith (1967), Griffith and Miller (1970), and Menzel (1967) for detailed discussion of the processes involved in informal communication.

as that published in the reputable journal literature. In the informal domain, the information may be unfinished. ("Doe, a reputable scientist, has only run two subjects but in both cases he finds this very interesting thing.") No claim is made or substantiated here, but the information may be assimilated and stored by the experienced, professional scientist in the particular field of research, for he knows the current state of knowledge in the research area and has good insight about what problems are now ripe for attempted solution. Also, he knows which findings fit into existing paradigms and which do not. Should Doe's findings, based on only two subjects, be surprising, important, and, at the same time, interpretable in the existing conceptual framework (or should they at least not render this framework obsolete), the scientist may "use" this "unfinished" information in thinking about his own work. If he is experienced in the field, he will, however, treat the findings as "unreliable" information, and not as established scientific knowledge, a judgment which requires not just methodological and statistical sophistication but primarily an appreciation of the current activity on the research front and a comprehension of the current state of scientific knowledge in the field. With these abilities, the scientist may immediately perceive a perfectly conducted piece of research as trivial, he can recognize an irregular finding, and he can withhold acceptance of it, pending closer examination. The end result of such judgments is that major findings, which challenge the current state of scientific knowledge in a field, can be held in abeyance, until they have been exposed to objective criticism, evaluation, or, perhaps, repetition.

Information flowing through the informal domain is commonly abstracted, usually colloquial, frequently incomplete, and often vague. The communicator here is not seeking to report a finished scientific work. He often knows, in fact, that the person with whom he is communicating needs only a minimal communication of an idea to understand fully its meaning and importance for their common subject of research. The recipient embodies integrated knowledge; therefore, the message need not, in itself, be integrated.

Such loose communication cannot, of course, be tolerated in the journal literature of science where a more universal audience exists. Here the author is required to prepare a manuscript of sufficient clarity and completeness to make certain that the scientific information in the article receives the widest exposure to critical evaluation and that the full implication of the scientific information is examined within the broadest possible context of science.

Finally, information flowing through the informal domain may turn out to be completely false, but as long as it is contained in the informal domain it rarely does any harm to science. The examples of the "Piltdown Man" or the Lysenko Era in Soviet biology, however, do show how the inclusion of a false finding or the creation of dogma in the acceptable body of scientific knowledge can damage a field of science.

### Custodianship of Information-Exchange Media

These particular differences between informal and formal information exchange seem to be related directly to problems encountered in developing information systems in science. The information flowing through the informal domain, though not genuinely public, is amenable to considerable promiscuousness which does not affect the scientific importance of the work or the discipline's state of knowledge. Efforts to formalize this process—the centralization and public dissemination of preprints, for example—may destroy those special attributes which sustain the informal communication system for the producer of scientific information. For example, in almost all instances where such efforts have been made, some monitoring and filtering have been introduced. These have tended to take the selection of the disseminating event and the audience out of the hands of the researcher. The critical feedback which an author seeks at this stage is not improved upon by this change and may, in fact, be lost entirely. This change also requires a more finished product than is usually acceptable in the informal domain. In other words, much of the laxness, gamble, interplay, mutual accord, etc., are formalized out of the informal exchanges of preprints. Consequently, regardless of efforts to keep these reports from taking on the status of a formal communication, the receiver gets the impression that the reported findings are reliable, the work has been evaluated, the conclusions are sound, and the discovery is original. This conclusion may be reached simply because the reports no longer have the characteristics of *informal* communication and come to resemble the formal journal article.

We do not mean to imply that nothing can or should be done to facilitate informal information exchange, and important moves have been made in this direction at APA. There is the risk, however, whenever we formalize an informal channel, that we are eliminating those very attributes of informal communication which, even without our good intentions, scientists feel are slipping from their grasp. Systems developers who treat this matter lightly are almost certain to receive very negative feedback from active scientists.

In addition, accelerating the flow of scientific information in the informal domain and expanding its dissemination is a problem precisely because it occurs in systems that obscure the boundary between the informal and formal domains. This boundary is one that science has deliberately erected to curtail, temporarily, the flow of information until the information has been examined against the current state of knowledge in a discipline. Nonscientists view procedure of curtailment as ultraconservative; experienced, practicing scientists perceive it as the essential feature of science. The scientist knows that at some point in this process, a research result, if it is ever to have relevance to science, must become eligible for status as a scientific finding, and a scientific finding, in turn, becomes genuine only if it can contribute to the understanding of a previously unexplained phenomenon. The long judicious procedure by which this conversion is made is unique to science. To reorganize it for the sake of speed, or for open communication with other spheres of intellectual endeavor, would almost certainly dismantle the institution of science as we know it today.

## REFERENCES


ALLEN, T. J. Roles in technical communication networks. In C. E. Nelson & D. K. Pollock (Eds.), *Communication among scientists and engineers.* Lexington, Mass.: Heath Lexington Books, 1970.

AMERICAN PSYCHOLOGICAL ASSOCIATION. *Reports of the American Psychological Association's Project on Scientific Information Exchange in Psychology.* Vol. 1. Washington, D. C.: APA, 1963.

AMERICAN PSYCHOLOGICAL ASSOCIATION. *Reports of the American Psychological Association's Project on Scientific Information Exchange in Psychology.* Vol. 2. Washington, D. C.: APA, 1965.

AMERICAN PSYCHOLOGICAL ASSOCIATION. *Reports of the American Psychological Association's Project on Scientific Information Exchange in Psychology.* Vol. 3. Washington, D. C.: APA, 1969.

GARVEY, W. D., & GRIFFITH, B. C. Studies of social innovations in scientific communication in psychology. *American Psychologist,* 1966, 21, 1019–1036.

GARVEY, W. D., & GRIFFITH, B. C. Scientific communication as a social system. *Science,* 1967, 157, 1011–1016.

GRIFFITH, B. C., & MILLER, A. J. Networks of informal communication among scientifically productive scientists. In C. E. Nelson & D. K. Pollock (Eds.), *Communication among scientists and engineers.* Lexington, Mass.: Heath Lexington Books, 1970.

LICKLIDER, J. C. R. A crux in scientific and technical communication. *American Psychologist,* 1966, 21, 1044–1051.

MENZEL, H. Planning the consequences of unplanned action in scientific communication. In A. De Reuck & J. Knight (Eds.), *Communication in science.* London: J. & A. Churchill, 1967.

PRICE, D. J. *Little science, big science.* New York: Columbia University Press, 1963.

PRICE, D. J. Networks of scientific papers. *Science,* 1965, 149, 510–515.

WOODS, P. J. Psychological organizations: Their nature and membership. *American Psychologist,* 1964, 19, 663–669.

ZIMAN, M. *Public knowledge.* Cambridge, England: Cambridge University Press, 1968.

# Coherent Social Groups in Scientific Change

"Invisible colleges" may be consistent throughout science.

Belver C. Griffith and Nicholas C. Mullins

Recent studies have revealed a great deal about the communication and organizational patterns that underlie major advances and changes of direction in science. An important feature of these patterns is their consistency throughout a variety of disciplines, periods of time, and types of research. Biologists on Long Island in the 1940's, ethnomethodologists in southern California in the 1960's, physicists in Copenhagen in the 1920's, and mathematicians in Göttingen in the 1900's acted in very similar ways when, armed with insights radical for their times and disciplines, they faced important scientific problems. Our data on these and other such groups suggest that a single set of social mechanisms evolves in response to the challenge posed by new and major scientific problems. When challenged, some members of a scientific specialty become organized to work toward certain objectives, voluntarily and self-consciously, as a coherent and activist group. This article examines findings from surveys, individual interviews, and biographical essays, and discusses the similarities among contemporary groups that developed into small, coherent, activist groups and that subsequently had major impacts on their "home" disciplines.

## Low Levels of Organization and Communication

Communication and some degree of voluntary association are intrinsic in science, and the important question therefore becomes not whether scientists organize, but rather how, why, and to what degree? As a background to understanding high degrees of communication and organization, the first section of this article examines the processes entailed in the "loose" networks, the level of communication and organization that appears normal for science. This level has been repeatedly demonstrated by different methodologies for specialties in various disciplines.

Three groups of psychological researchers studied by Griffith and Miller exhibited this effective, loose communication network (*1*). The workers in these groups had considerable knowledge of the activities of other major researchers, and it is clear that individuals sought out, and interacted very effectively with, one another on the basis of their current research interests. Mullins' data on biologists and Crane's on rural sociologists also show this kind of loose communication network. In both of these studies, respondents named more persons outside their specialty than inside as having had significant effects on their work, thereby suggesting that scientists work in and influence more than one specialty, an apparently normal condition for highly active scientific researchers (*2*). In addition, the Crane study showed that productive scientists were more frequently named as the object of contact, indicating, as expected, that communication is more intense around productive researchers. This finding was later quantified by Griffith *et al.* (*3*).

The Griffith and Miller study (*1*) focused upon persons who were comparatively productive, each of whom headed a team of students and junior colleagues. These respondents employed several special strategies to facilitate information exchange within their specialty. For example, one area, speech perception, was small enough that few communication problems developed, even though the area exhibited low levels of social organization. Of the other specialties studied, those that exhibited loose networks employed, for varying periods of time, mechanisms that are used in highly coherent groups (for example, conference series and exchanges of papers before publication). However, the adoption of a pattern of communication within these specialties was in response to a current scientific problem and to the inadequacy of formal meetings and journals for answering communications needs created by these problems. For example, psycholinguists seemed to develop different patterns of organization depending upon whether they were in the process of applying psychological theories and methodology to studies of language (as they did in the early 1950's) or modifying linguistic theories so they could be used in experimental psychology (as they did after the development of generative grammar). By contrast, research-

Dr. Griffith is professor of library science, Drexel University, Philadelphia, Pennsylvania 19104. Dr. Mullins is associate professor of sociology, Indiana University, Bloomington 47401.

ers in the effects of drugs on behavior formed a small specialty in which communication patterns reflected the activities of individual researchers, and the membership of groups in close communication changed continually in response to changes in research interests. This group was particularly well served by journals; thus informal contacts were not supplementing or replacing publications.

Crawford's sociometric analysis of data on sleep researchers revealed a network of research centers, each organized around one or more key researchers. The operation and effectiveness of such networks is illustrated by the finding that nearly 95 percent of all researchers lay within two sociometric links of such a key researcher (that is, across only two continuing, person-to-person contacts) (*4*).

These findings seem no more than would be expected because of the substantial size and efficiency of circles of acquaintanceship that exist throughout science. These circles are encouraged and developed within science by mechanisms such as meetings and conferences. Their efficiency as a basis for communication is partly a result of science's institutionalization into academic disciplines and scientific societies and partly a function of the comparatively small size of the scientific community.

To obtain a more precise idea of the effectiveness of such patterns of acquaintanceship, the active researcher might try the following experiment: first, consider how many persons he knows personally who are doing work in any way related to his own. Second, try to use organization figures to generate the total number of persons working in his discipline, then the fraction of those doing related work, and, finally, the minority who are extremely active and who contribute most to the literature. We believe most researchers, whether in the center of a highly active specialty or in a backwater, know not only their immediate competitors and collaborators, but also a vast peripheral group of other researchers (perhaps, for a mature scientist, 600 to 1000). The overlap of these many circles of acquaintanceship offers a basis for rapidly developing loose networks as temporary mechanisms for the transmission of findings and ideas (*5*).

We can regard such loose networks of researchers as resulting from "normal" scientific activities and as conforming generally to scientific norms of objectivity and emotional neutrality. A disciple of Kuhn might regard the groups that have been studied and that meet this description as working to fill out existing paradigms. If one conceptualizes the scientific community as linked by acquaintanceships, extending in all directions from individual specialties, loose networks meet researchers' needs for information and feedback by temporarily focusing communication on current research activities.

### High Levels of Organization and Communication

The highest levels of communication and organization are achieved by groups that are in the process of formulating a radical conceptual reorganization within their field. Members of each of the six groups discussed in this article appeared to be convinced that they were achieving the overthrow of a major position within their discipline or making a major revision in methodology. The groups that have been studied and that exhibit such characteristics are the phage workers in molecular biology, the Skinnerian psychologists, the quantum physics group in Copenhagen, the Göttingen mathematicians, the audition researchers in psychology, and the ethnomethodologists in sociology (*6–9*). Each offered a distinctively different theory or a new or modified research methodology in opposition to a clearly established position; each maintained its beliefs over a protracted period; and each ultimately demonstrated substantial achievements (*10*). In the process, none of these groups consistently observed the attitude of disinterested objectivity that is regarded as a norm of science; indeed, these groups often ventured actively into the politics of science in order to obtain or protect appointments and research support. Most important, each of these groups operated through close and continual interaction on scientific issues; for example, when an audition researcher was asked whether he and others in his field exchanged preprints (prepublication copies of papers), he said that such exchange was usually unnecessary because they followed one another's work so closely that often a single, newly found constant sufficed to inform others of an important advance (*11*).

Table 1 shows some of the common features of these six groups. Among these features are the presence of an acknowledged intellectual and organizational leader or leaders, a geographical center, and a brief period of comparatively intense activity. As might be expected, the degree of organization was not uniform throughout these groups. The more highly organized groups were truly "revolutionary": they saw themselves as opposed to a definite outgroup that was better established than they were within universities and recognized disciplines. The three groups best described as "revolutionary" were the Skinnerians, the phage workers, and the ethnomethodologists. In operation, the three revolutionary groups differed somewhat from the remaining groups, which were recognized as being of central importance to their respective disciplines even while they were developing (usually within major universities) and while their interests and patterns were diverging from those of other research workers. The contrast between these two groupings of the six specialties is broadly analogous to that between revolutionary cabals and self-conscious elites.

### Theoretical Break

An announced or evident break in a given theoretical framework can be an important social mechanism, particularly for the revolutionary groups, because it erects a barrier between those who accept it and everyone else. It provides the basis for separating groups into ingroups and outgroups and helps ingroups to develop high morale, which assists them in opposing formidable outgroups. For the phage group, biochemists were the outgroup; for operant conditioning, it was Hullian learning theorists. The histories of biochemists' references to molecular biologists, sociologists' to ethnomethodologists, and learning theorists' to operant conditioners show similar and considerable acrimony.

In addition to sounding a battle cry, a theoretical break provides personal motivation for fellow scientists. For example, Delbrück's 1938 paper "The one-step growth process in *E. coli*" (*12*) had major effects on many persons, such as Anderson, Luria, and Weigle, who later made important contributions to phage genetics. Skinner's *The Behavior of Organisms*, first published in 1938 (*13*), constituted a striking break with stimulus-response learning theory and was, for many years, a doctrinaire support for operant conditioning. A parlor game among adherents in the late 1940's was to furnish, on request, the page number of brief, recited passages (*14*). Skinner's other works both extended his approach and set forth a utopian version of his approach as applied to human society.

### Leadership Roles

Highly coherent groups organize themselves consciously, usually under the leadership of a person who is actively emulated (that is, a person who serves as the scientific model). While many of the persons occupying this role have had exceptional intellectual and personal skills that seem to explain their special position within the group, the existence of such a leader may not be necessary for creating a highly coherent group. The reservoir of talent within a dedicated group of productive scientists may be great enough that leadership will appear in response to the needs of particular situations. Independently of whether a single person serves as a scientific model, two different leadership roles, intellectual and organizational, can be identified in the formation and maintenance of these groups and these roles may or may not be filled by the same individual.

The intellectual leader (or leaders) (i) lays the original conceptual foundations for work, (ii) makes public statements on theory and research, which normally result in an acknowledged theoretical break, and (iii) approves and validates others' work. Moreover, an intellectual leader frequently functions as the central communicator within the group, although this role, which is partially a social one, may be dispersed among members of the group. The phage group most clearly exemplified this pattern of leadership, although there was an identifiable intellectual leader for some period in all of the groups studied. In the phage group, Delbrück performed all leadership functions, strongly suppressing some lines of research while pushing other work forward. His opinions were widely sought within the group; he established research priorities, and he standardized techniques and quantitative models. His own original research was superior and among the first efforts in the new area (Table 1).

The organizational leader arranges times, funds, and facilities for research and means for communicating findings and ideas. He arranges appointments in such a way that specific scientists obtain jobs in specific locations, organizes research programs and obtains funds, and guides the organization of meetings (Table 1). In all cases, the organizational leader, if different from the intellectual leader, was a respected researcher in his own right.

Findings generally reveal a conscious effort to direct the group's work toward a specified series of problems, from a particular perspective, with a stated goal. Such an effort may begin after a few discoveries or ideas and may be largely triggered by individual genius or other isolated events (that is, events that would resist deliberate programming). Nevertheless, a conscious effort on the part of a leader or cadre of students seems to be required for an activist group to develop and continue for any length of time. The organizational leader largely directs and implements these efforts.

The focusing of the group's attention on a single series of phenomena and the development of a distinctive scientific style resulted, in most of the groups studied, in considerable restriction of the range of information regarded as relevant, with corresponding changes in the input of information. If we think of the highly coherent group in terms of a network, we can regard these groups as an extreme thickening in the network, with a resultant loss of some links to the remainder of the network (if we assume that individuals have some upper limit to their communication activities). Needless to say, if the highly active, coherent group is working on basic problems pursued by many others within the discipline, their general indifference to the work of other researchers can generate considerable antagonism. The revolutionary groups (the Skinnerians, phage workers, and ethnomethodologists) have, of course, been extreme in terms of isolating themselves from the remainder of their home disciplines.

Table 1. Common features of coherent activist groups. Mode of group operation describes relation to home discipline: revolutionary groups are in opposition to a better established group, while elite groups are divergent but recognized as central to the discipline.

| Group | Intellectual leader | Organizational leader | Place(s) | Approximate dates (inclusive) | Field | Mode of operation |
|---|---|---|---|---|---|---|
| Quantum mechanics (Copenhagen) | Bohr | Bohr | Copenhagen | 1920–1934 | Physics | Elite |
| Phage | Delbrück | Delbrück | Cold Spring Harbor, California Institute of Technology | 1947–1958 | Biology | Revolutionary |
| Algebraists (Göttingen) | Hilbert, Minkowski | Klein | Göttingen | 1896–1910 | Mathematics | Elite |
| Operant conditioning (Skinnerians) | Skinner | Cadre of students and postdoctoral fellows (Harvard) | Columbia, Harvard | 1947–1960 | Psychology | Revolutionary |
| Audition research | Stevens | Stevens | Harvard | 1940–1950 | Psychology | Elite |
| Ethnomethodology | Garfinkel | Cicourel | University of California at Los Angeles, Santa Barbara | 1965–1971 | Sociology | Revolutionary |

### Geographical Center

Speculations that it is important to have a "critical mass" of research at a single location seem to be borne out by these data; a factor in the development of highly coherent specialties is a geographical center or centers—usually one, but no more than three. For every specialty studied there is a specific place or places at which its first work was done and at which the group worked exclusively for an extended period of time. For instance, the phage group showed a specific, stable migration pattern involving two locations: the California Institute of Technology was the winter location, Cold Spring Harbor, New York, the summer one.

For that part of quantum mechanics described as the Copenhagen School, the center was Bohr's institute in Copenhagen. This center has literally been immortalized in song and story as the birthplace of much of modern physics. The mathematics group's center was the Göttingen mathematics department, an imposing group assembled in 1899 around Klein, the department chairman, and including Minkowski and Hilbert. These three became the nucleus of a walking seminar that met on Thursday afternoons and in which the outlines of much of what is now regarded as modern mathematics were thrashed out. Operant conditioners developed at Harvard, Columbia, and (on the postdoctoral level) the animal behavior laboratories at Walter Reed Hospital in Washington, D.C., with orderly migration among these centers. Audition research was concentrated in Cambridge, Massachusetts—first within Harvard, then spreading to the Massachusetts Institute of Technology, industry, and other institutions; separate centers developed later around Harvard Ph.D.'s in the Midwest. Ethnomethodologists until recently were concentrated in Southern California at the University of California at Los Angeles and at Santa Barbara.

### Recruitment

Recruitment of able new members is a major activity of these groups; because mature investigators outside the group have other commitments, recruitment generally proceeds among the young—mostly among graduate students in the groups studied. The more revolutionary groups emphasized the encouragement of younger researchers, easy access to leaders, and democratic procedures within the group. For example, the operant conditioning researchers confined the choice of an editor for a new journal to younger persons outside the central cadre.

The importance of these activities is clear: groups without students die. Fisher makes this clear in his analyses of the mathematical specialty of invariant theory; this group disappeared because its members had no access to students for training in the specialty (*15*). The problems did not die; they still exist, but they have been reshuffled and have become problems in other, living areas (for example, linear algebra). It is interesting to note that Hilbert, a leader at Göttingen, was once a major figure in invariant theory, but his 69 students were all trained at Göttingen after his work in invariant theory was over.

Delbrück was a noteworthy innovator at recruiting students. Most academic scientists seek settings with graduate students and teach those who come their way. In turn, their students teach other students, each new (student) generation being somewhat larger than the previous (teaching) generation, thus setting up the necessary and sufficient conditions for exponential growth. Although the length of the generation is very short in terms of years, initial growth is slow and a period of nearly 15 years is required to develop "explosive" rates of growth. [Because of limits on the population available to be drawn into any specialty, as well as other factors, the actual pattern of growth conforms generally to epidemiological models (*16*).] Delbrück short-circuited the initial slow growth period by instituting the summer phage course at Cold Spring Harbor directed at scientists who already had students. As a result, 35 people were already working on phage problems by 1950, as compared to four in 1945. Had they relied on normal student recruitment, they would have taken until 1960 to generate this level of activity.

### Intellectual Processes and Dynamics

Several of the groups studied revealed the importance in the group's continued existence and development of a single, definitive program statement. This statement delineates a specific problem and a direction for the group; it defines research goals and identifies the basic steps toward that goal. Schrödinger's *What Is Life?* (1944) (*17*) was clearly phage work's first such programmatic statement. Delbrück's 1948 address to the Connecticut Academy of Sciences, "A physicist looks at biology," constituted a second (*12*). In both cases, the statements indicated that phage workers wanted to understand how biological information was transmitted from generation to generation. Mathematics found a complete, sparse, direct presentation of a program in Hilbert's 1900 speech in Paris. Hilbert stated the 23 problems in mathematics that needed to be solved and how these problems fell into groups, thereby providing a focal point not only for the Göttingen group, but also for a great deal of mathematics from that time on (*18*). Skinner's *The Behavior of Organisms* (*13*) laid down the structure of a new approach to behavior and immediately attracted wide attention. However, the development of the Skinnerian group was apparently delayed both by the war and by the absence at that time of appropriate organizational leaders.

During an initial period in the development of each group, significant communication within the group was verbal; such free, unmonitored exchanges of information about unpublished results and ideas required powerful norms to protect the individual's priority of discovery. While certain precautions are implicitly observed throughout science, highly coherent groups exhibit particularly strong controls. Production of reports and articles was controlled in ethnomethodology from 1966 to 1970, becoming virtually independent of current research activity. The research front can come to exist in the private exchanges of group members. One significant phage paper was not published for years to protect priority; among audition researchers, a creative nonwriter was pushed into being the senior author of a paper that others wrote to present his theory. With much of the group's activity consisting of the review and evaluation of research and theory, individuals may rapidly develop different public and in-group reputations as a result of the controls over research and publication and the general group involvement in evaluation. In view of the strength of the tensions within activist scientific groups and the degree of members' involvement, it is not surprising that these groups generate "tribal folklore" and customs, including distinctive life-styles, mock ceremonies and awards, special ingroup roles, and even, on occasion, a group sport (for example, camping for the phage group and rock climbing and Ping-Pong for quantum mechanics).

## Discussion

Communication and the exchange of information are intrinsic in the normal operation of science as an endeavor that produces and processes information. In our examination of highly coherent groups, we see two additional factors as basic to science: first, the radical revision of scientific theory and method (and the consequent reexamination and reinterpretation of data); second, the rarity of high levels of personal creativity. Our understanding of these factors has been extended recently through the analyses of science made by Kuhn (*19*) and Price (*20*). Kuhn has emphasized, following Butterfield (*21*) and Koyré (*22*), the conceptual reorganization required in major scientific advances (*23*). His central concept of the paradigm, the base from which "normal" science is pursued, contains elements of both scientific theory and methodology, as well as large attitudinal components—for example, untested assumptions as to the outcome of alternative lines of research. As Ziman has pointed out, even accepted scientific findings and theories rest in part on faith, given the near universal absence of logical proofs in science (*24*). Price proceeds differently, regarding science from a distance and seeking to describe the structure of science in terms of aggregates of people, monies, and results. In his analyses, elites of persons, institutions, and nations have clearly emerged.

Of these two approaches, Kuhn's is the more attractive. He is reassuring in his picture of all scientists as workers in the vineyard, filling in missing bits according to paradigm or, alternatively, finding chinks in an existing system. Price's ideas are rather harder to live with; the discrepancy he noted between the incredibly high activity level of the most creative scientist, as opposed to that of journeymen, has become, in his latest papers, a direct concern with elites and elitism and the difficulties they create in science (*25*). The bridge between these approaches may be found in the fact that coherent activist groups are, in many cases, the producers of change in science and the social location of creative scientists.

The aforementioned factors contribute in several ways to the creation of coherent groups. The difficulties of the conceptual reorganization required by major advances preclude mass conversion to any new points of view. An idea must gradually recruit adherents, such recruitment usually being expedited by active proselytizing; this process requires high degrees of communication and social organization to succeed. The work of the minority of highly active, highly creative scientists attracts other researchers; this process affords a natural basis for intellectual leadership within groups, a focus for communication, and a natural starting point for the coherent activist group. All of these factors reinforce the basic and direct role of communication of findings and ideas in science; given their presence, the conscious development of a distinctive scientific approach marks the takeoff point for the coherent group.

All groups we regard as coherent had a distinctive approach with broad theoretical implications (*26*). Thus, a key factor in determining success or failure may well be whether a group is proceeding only empirically (that is, simply moving from problem to problem within the context of the established theoretical framework) or whether its program proceeds from an innovative theoretical base. For example, an overemphasis on strict empirical procedure in biochemistry prepared an area for the innovations of molecular biology; similarly, crystallography followed empirical leads, never making a break with its past comparable to the break that originally established it as a field.

One necessity for the development and continuance of a coherent group is simply the practical one of acquiring sufficient resources to sustain a sizable group of researchers at the geographical center. Prior to the heavy governmental support of basic research, Klein in the 1900's and Stevens in the 1940's were adroit at raising research funds; the group in Copenhagen was largely supported by a special award to Bohr from the Carlsberg Breweries. Unfortunately, much of science has been done in situations that would prohibit maintaining such critical masses of researchers at single locations. Molecular biology had not only theoretical orientation and financial support, both in extreme degrees, but also other characteristics that create conditions in which a highly coherent grouping could develop in its most exaggerated form. These include the maverick nature of its leadership, the continued existence of major scientific challenges (and consequent intense competition), and the capacity to perform experiments in astonishingly brief periods of time.

There probably exist, at all times, groups within the network of science that experimentally attempt and then retreat from this role of the coherent activist group for a brief period. This retreat may be occasioned by a variety of factors, the chief of these probably being low scientific vitality or low distinctiveness of the group's interests and its work, as compared to the remainder of the discipline. However, even successful groups seem to have a comparatively limited life span; 10 to 15 years is typical, and many last for shorter periods. Some groups, as, for example, the audition researchers, largely succeed in obtaining the scientific goals they have pursued; however, even the most expansive groups must ultimately grow so large as to dilute personal ties and influence. Institutionalization (for example, creating a department of molecular biology or a departmental slot for an operant conditioner) reduces levels of antagonism and group identity and generally marks the successful group's return to the normal, loose networks of science (*27*). Thus, the penalty of success, whether success is measured in specific goals or in the conversion of a discipline to new points of view, is the death of the group as a distinct social and intellectual entity.

### References and Notes


1. B. C. Griffith and A. J. Miller, in *Communication among Scientists and Engineers*, C. Nelson and D. Pollock, Eds. (Heath, Lexington, Mass., 1970), p. 125.
2. N. C. Mullins, *Amer. Sociol. Rev.* **33**, 786 (1968); D. Crane, *ibid.* **34**, 335 (1969).
3. B. C. Griffith, M. J. Jahn, A. J. Miller, *Science* **173**, 164 (1971).
4. S. Crawford, *J. Amer. Soc. Inf. Sci.* **22**, 301 (1971).
5. See S. Milgram [*Psychol. Today* **1** (No. 1), 60 (1967)] for a review and analysis of the analogous problem of patterns of social acquaintanceship within the general population. Although Milgram's discussion suggests that circles of social acquaintanceship include about 500 persons, a figure in line with our speculations, acquaintanceship circles in science may be far more powerful. A scientist is categorized by field and specialty into a conceptual schema with which most of his fellows are conversant; therefore, although a particular person may be unknown, a mutual acquaintance might be identified purely on the basis of subject matter interests. As a result, the circle of acquaintanceship may be

readily extended in new directions, as desired by the researcher.

6. The principal sources of data on these groups are: N. C. Mullins (*7*); D. Krantz, *J. Hist. Behav. Sci.* **8**, 86 (January 1972); *J. Appl. Behav. Anal.* 4, 61 (1971); numerous personal communications between Krantz and B.C.G. (in his work on operant conditioning, Krantz is continuing the most thorough study ever made of a single specialty); J. Cairns, G. S. Stent, J. D. Watson (*8*); G. Gamow, *Thirty Years That Shook Physics* (Doubleday, Garden City, N.Y., 1966); R. Moore, *Niels Bohr* (Knopf, New York, 1966) (note that Copenhagen may be only the putative home for this specialty; several other centers, particularly Manchester, are of great importance in the development of quantum physics); C. Reid (*9*); *Reports of the Project on Scientific Information Exchange in Psychology* (American Psychological Association, Washington, D.C., 1969); N. C. Mullins, *Theory and Theory Groups in Contemporary American Sociology* (Harper & Row, New York, in press).
7. N. C. Mullins, *Minerva* **10**, 51 (January 1972).
8. J. Cairns, G. S. Stent, J. D. Watson, Eds. *Phage and the Origins of Molecular Biology* (Cold Spring Harbor Laboratory of Quantitative Biology, Cold Spring Harbor, N.Y., 1966).
9. C. Reid, *Hilbert* (Springer, New York, 1970).
10. Some people have questioned whether it is too early to claim substantial progress for the ethnomethodologists.
11. From interview data gathered by A. J. Miller.
12. M. Delbrück, reprinted in J. Cairns *et al.* (*8*, pp. 9–22).
13. B. F. Skinner, *The Behavior of Organisms* (Appleton, New York, 1938).
14. Greater devotion to text is revealed only in an apocryphal story of the Talmudic scholar who, when a copy of the *Talmud* was pierced by a needle, could name the word opposite the needle's point.
15. C. S. Fisher, *Arch. Eur. Sociol.* **8**, 216 (1967).
16. W. Goffman, *Nature* **212**, 449 (1966).
17. E. Schrödinger, *What Is Life? The Physical Aspects of the Living Cell* (Cambridge Univ. Press, Cambridge, England, 1944). Importance shown by N. C. Mullins (*7*, p. 58).
18. Paper cited and importance shown by C. Reid (*9*).
19. T. Kuhn, *The Structure of Scientific Revolutions* (Univ. of Chicago Press, Chicago, 1962).
20. D. J. De Solla Price, *Little Science, Big Science* (Columbia Univ. Press, New York, 1963); *Science* **149**, 510 (1965).
21. H. Butterfield, *The Origins of Modern Science* (Free Press, New York, 1957).
22. A. Koyré, *Etudes Galieennes, Histoire de la Pensée* (Herman, Paris, 1944).
23. Compare Kuhn (*19*) to H. Butterfield (*21*, pp. 13–28) to gain some impression of the relation of Kuhn's concepts to earlier work.
24. J. Ziman, *Public Knowledge* (Cambridge Univ. Press, Cambridge, England, 1968).
25. D. J. De Solla Price, *J. Amer. Soc. Inf. Sci.* **22**, 74 (1971).
26. Skinner and his followers doggedly rejected behavioral theory; their rationale was that it offered no explanatory advantage over operational formulations of psychological laws—a rationale that, in itself, is a major theoretical stand. In general, we speculate that these groups are either, as Butterfield would contend (*21*), picking up the other end of the stick (that is, viewing findings from an entirely new perspective), or creating a methodology through which a variety of new problems can be stated and examined. Quantum mechanics and molecular biology seemed to embody both aspects clearly. The audition researchers, alone among these groups, appear to have been mainly introducing a more sophisticated methodology, and it is curious to note that, around 1940, Delbrück was teaching biologists about mathematical tools similar to those the audition researchers had recently adopted.
27. A similar process occurred earlier in biochemistry. See R. Kohler, "The early history of biochemistry," a talk given to the history and sociology of science department of the University of Pennsylvania, Philadelphia (1971).
28. We thank Marilyn Jahn, A. James Miller, Carolyn Mullins, and Beth Krevitt for contributing in many ways to the preparation and writing of this article. Also, we thank M. Carl Drott, William Garvey, Dorwin Cartwright, and Georgess McHargue for reviewing this article. B.C.G.'s work was supported by Public Health Service research grant 1 RO1 LM 00911-01.

# SCIENTIFIC COMMUNICATION
## FIVE THEMES FROM SOCIOLOGY

(Originally published as: SCIENTIFIC COMMUNICATION: Five Themes From Social Science Research)

HERBERT MENZEL

*Department of Sociology, New York University*

THE recent upsurge of interest in the behavioral aspects of scientific and technical communication and information flow has two distinct sources, a theoretical one in the development of communication research, and a practical one in the concerns of policy makers in scientific organizations and information services.

For some time past, the attention of sociologists and social psychologists studying communication processes, once focused on so-called mass phenomena and mass publics, has turned to the interplay of communication processes with more and more definitely delineated and mapped aspects of social structure. One aspect of this shift in interest has been the increasing attention paid by behavioral scientists to the systems supplying information of a specialized sort, and to the publics which are consumers of this specialized information. The scientific and applied professions have been most prominent among the publics so studied.

At the same time those concerned with the planning of science information policy have become increasingly interested in so-called "user studies" as possible sources of guidance. For a decade or two, as the mushrooming of the scientific enterprise has led to a multifold increase in the supply of scientific information as well as in the demand for such information on the part of scientists and technologists, the adequacy of the science information system whose task it is to link this supply and this demand has become a matter of increasing concern. A multitude of astonishing new services has been introduced into the system, alleviating some of the concerns, but also generating new questions of optimal allocation of resources and even giving rise to some additional strains in the information system itself. Concerns have led to attempts at planning and these have, after some lag, more recently led to demands in some quarters that the information neeeds of science be ascertained as a basis for wise planning. While some have asked that the scientist users of scientific information be studied in order to ascertain these needs, others have countered that these needs can better be estimated by those who are experts in information handling. Both proponents and critics of the so-called "user study" approach have often confused it with opinion polling—that is, with quizzing scientists on what should be done (see Menzel, 1959a, 1964; Shaw, 1959).

Actually, studies of the information-gathering behavior and experiences of scientists have been going on, in one form or another, for at least 20 years (reviewed in Paisley, 1965). Behavioral scientists have taken some part in this work for about 10 years. Many of the studies have been quite primitive in the techniques of data gathering, simplistic in the conceptualization of variables and research goals, poor in comparability, and questionable in generalizability. But although many of the shortcomings remain, sounder and more sophisticated approaches have increasingly been used, with an especially gratifying concentration in the last 3 years or so (Menzel, 1966c). Outstanding among these most recent accomplishments is the Project on Scientific Information Exchange in Psychology of the American Psychological Association (1963, 1965), which has refined and innovated research techniques and has used them in a battery of studies giving comprehensive coverage to the communication situation in a discipline. It has drawn together the results in a process model which has suggested several policy changes and has aided in the choice between them. Recent highlights from this work are reported in other articles in this issue of the *American Psychologist.*

Enough of this work has now accumulated to make it possible to discern certain themes which emerge with increasing insistence as the sophistication of the studies advances. A discussion of five of these interrelated themes will constitute the bulk of this paper. The selection of these particular themes was, no doubt, influenced by the author's sociological bias, but it is believed that they warrant special attention in the interest of both practical and theoretical advances in the field of science communication research.

### Acts of Scientific Communicaton Constitute a System

The first of these themes is that of the desirability of taking a systemic view of the scientific communication in any discipline. It is necessary to look upon any one arrangement, institution, facility, or policy for scientific and professional communication as a component of the total system of scientific communication for a profession, a system which includes *all* the provisions, *all* the publications, *all* the facilities, *all* the occasions and arrangements, and *all* the customs in the discipline that determine how scientific messages are transmitted.[1]

The systemic view, however, means more than comprehensiveness with regard to the channels and mechanisms encompassed. Thus, for example, it also seems useful to conceive of the flow of scientific information as a set of interaction processes in a social system. The information-receiving actions of any one individual often involve several of his roles (as researcher, teacher, consultant, editorial referee, etc.) and approaches to several different channels, including individuals standing in diverse relationships to him and serving now as sources, now as relays, of information. The scientists who generate and use the information in a given discipline can therefore be usefully looked upon as interconnected publics.

Furthermore, it is necessary to be comprehensive with regard to the varied functions served by the science information system. And finally, it is necessary to be comprehensive in the delineation of transactions of scientific information, for these frequently involve much more than a single encounter between a scientist and some one communication channel.

The systemic view is urged upon us by a number of considerations. One cannot obtain a true picture of what the functions of the science communication system are, how often the need for each function arises, and how well each is performed, unless one considers all the channels through which scientific information travels. Conversely, one cannot obtain a true picture of the significance of any particular channel or arrangement unless one considers all the information functions that it may perform. Changes and innovations introduced in any one component of the system will have their consequences on the utilization and efficacy of other components. (This is made very clear in APA, 1965, pp. 127–140.) Numerous transactions of scientific information within a public of scientists may have to be considered before aggregate regularities and patterns are revealed behind what appears to be accidental and idiosyncratic in the individual case (Menzel, 1959b). And finally, even the effective transmission of a single message to an individual scientist may involve a multitude of contacts with diverse channels extending over a period of time—a topic to which we now turn.

### Several Channels May Act Synergistically to Bring About the Effective Transmisson of a Message

Any given transaction between a scientist as a receiver of information and the channel that brings him that information usually has a history behind it and a future ahead of it that may be very relevant to the evaluation of the success of that transaction and to the prognosis of whether this kind of transaction will happen again with similar results.

Often one channel of communication calls attention to a message to be found in another; sometimes a third channel is required to locate the precise document in which the message is contained; frequently one or more persons serve as relays between the source of a message and its ultimate consumer; and contacts at each intervening step may be initiated now by the receiver, now by the bringer of the message. The events which thus interplay are often distributed over a period of time. The possible relevance of a message to a man's work may not become apparent at the time it is first received, but only when that same message is repeated, sometimes more than once, or when it is put together with other information yet to be received, or when changes occur and needs come up in the course of the scientist's own future work.

In fact, not only an individual scientist, but an entire scientific community may for years turn its back on some already published and significant piece of work, until it is "brought home" by

[1] For an excellent and thorough laying out of the information system and its components in biomedical research, see Orr, Abdiam, Bourne, Coyl, Leeds, and Pings (1954).

repetition, appearance in new media, rediscovery in new contexts, or other supplementary messages. Information must often be publicized repeatedly or through diverse channels before it will enter the stream of communications which will lead it to its ultimate user; and from the point of view of the consumer of information, it is frequently necessary to be exposed to the information repeatedly before it will make an impact (Menzel, 1958, pp. 14–17, 32–49, 92–124). Much of this crucial multiple exposure is brought about in informal ways, largely through contacts between individual scientists. This phenomenon will be discussed in the next section.

## Informal and Unplanned Communication Plays a Crucial Role in the Science Information System

There is by now a fair amount of documentation (Ackoff, & Halbert, 1958; APA, 1965; Herner, 1954; Menzel, 1959b; Orr, Coyl, & Leeds, 1964; Pelz, 1956; Price, 1963; Rosenbloom, McLaughlin, & Wolek, 1965) for the great role played by informal, unplanned, person-to-person communication in the experiences of scientific investigators, often in ways that affect their work quite vitally. This comes as no surprise to communications researchers familiar with the "multistep flow of communications" that prevails in so-called mass communications. (For a recent summary, see Lazarsfeld & Menzel, 1963.) However, the situation in the sciences differs from "mass communication" in fundamental ways: The mass communication audience is typically apathetic, while the scientific audience is highly motivated; the familiar multistep flow serves to diffuse messages already contained in the mass media, while informal transmission of messages among scientists often antecedes their appearance in print; in mass communication, interpersonal links play their role primarily in persuasion, while in the sciences they seem to be crucial even in mere cognitive transmission. (For an example of persuasive communication in an applied profession, see Coleman, Katz, & Menzel, 1966.) For these reasons, the importance of interpersonal communication in the sciences cannot simply be explained by the same factors as in mass communication, but will have to be accounted for through the specific characteristics of the scientific public. (For one attempt to do this, see Menzel, 1966b.)

While informal communication in the sciences is largely unplanned, and sometimes appears accidental, there is actually a good bit of regularity to it. Certain individuals, for example, tend to be the most frequent carriers of information from one place to another, the recipients of correspondence, the hosts of visiting scientists, the visitors to other institutions—largely due to the positions or obligations that researchers assume in addition to their primary activity as researchers. It is the people who serve as editors of journals, who serve on grant-application review committees, who go to summer laboratories, and so on, that play the role of "the scientific troubadour," as it has been called.

There is also some regularity in the kinds of occasions, places, and times at which these information exchanges take place: at summer laboratories, in the corridors of scientific meetings, during and after colloquia and conferences. There is some regularity as to the patterns of initiative on the part of the conveyor and of the recipient of information through which unplanned communication comes about: seeking one kind of information and obtaining another; informing a colleague of current work and being rewarded with a relevant item of information; information brought up spontaneously by a colleague with whom one is together for another purpose; being sought out deliberately by a colleague who has information to convey; and so on (Menzel, 1959b).

And finally, there is some regularity as to the content of the information that seems preferentially to flow through these kinds of channels rather than through the more regular and systematized mechanisms of the printed word and the attendant bibliographic control devices. For example, there is a certain level of know-how information about the use and setting up of scientific apparatus that seems to go by preference through the word-of-mouth channels, perhaps because this kind of information is regarded as unworthy of being handled in detail in the printed word, and does not find a ready place under the subject terms of indexing procedures. Information that helps interpret results and information that helps a person become acquainted with a new field also seem to make their way differentially, often through the personal channels (APA, 1965, Report No. 11; Menzel, 1959b; Rosenbloom, McLaughlin, & Wolek, 1965).

The regularities inherent in the apparently accidental and unplanned ways of communicating hold out the hope of planned improvements in the system. On the one hand, as more is learned of the kinds of information that seem to go through these kinds of communication-switching devices, needs for better and more effective sources on the part of the formal devices become clear. On the other hand, as it is realized that some kinds of information will continue to be carried primarily through interpersonal interchanges, formal devices for making these informal interchanges more effective may be developed—planned mechanisms to make the so-called lucky accidents happen more often. These mechanisms may range from directories and newsletters that tell scientists who is doing what to the scheduling of working hours and the location of new institutes in such a way as to facilitate visits.

### Scientists Constitute Publics

The populations which are served by the science information systems—scientific researchers, practitioners in various disciplines and professions—can be usefully looked upon as publics, and described under the same categories that one uses when describing the more familiar publics of the mass media. These publics, can, for example, be described in terms of size, in terms of turnover, and in terms of the interaction that exists within them. They can also be described in terms of their interests in a range of topics, in terms of the fidelity with which they attend to given channels and in terms of the norms that they have created with regard to exposure to various channels.

Yet, while the scientific publics share certain characteristics with the mass publics, in certain other respects they are very different from the public of the newspaper, of the TV program, or the neighborhood public library. Number one, the scientists have a very high motivation to obtain the information that is channeled in their direction through the system that is designed to serve them. They go out of their way to reach out for this information. Second, they want this information to help in very specific activities—activities that form very essential parts of their professional roles and therefore of their lives. Third, because of both of these facts, they have very well-developed and very well-structured behavior patterns with regard to professional communication. In more concrete language, these professions have, in the course of their development, worked out a rich set of customs, habits, traditions, mechanisms, tricks, and devices as to how one goes about obtaining information, what one does by way of screening and listening for information, and what one need not listen or attend to. Planners of information policies must take into account this body of behavior patterns, of traditions, customs, and learned behavior. The members of these specialized publics have developed communication institutions and learned ways of interacting with them and with one another to a much higher degree than is true, for example, for the public of a newspaper. Furthermore, scientists themselves look upon the communications services and systems as instruments, and take an interest in their improvement as technologies.

Of course, the several scientific publics also differ from one another in many of these aspects (Menzel, 1966d). All of these aspects have implications for the wise planning of information services for these publics.

### Science Informaton Systems Serve Multiple Functions

The last theme to be taken up here is that it is rather important to draw qualitative distinctions between the several kinds of things that the science information systems are called upon to perform, especially in this current age of streamlining, of great technological strides, of great advances in logical systems. The reason is that these advances bring with them some risk that they may make some of these functions be served more efficiently and satisfactorily, while neglecting or even hampering others. Most of the great innovations have been instituted under the guiding themes of speed, efficiency, and comprehensiveness. The overriding aim has been to bring information to scientists promptly, to bring all the information that is relevant to the scientist's specific query, and to do so with a minimum of waste motion. The prototype of that activity is the exhaustive search. But this is only one of several types of services that are required of the science information system. To give but one example of another type, with characteristics almost the opposite of those of the exhaustive search, there is the requirement to call the scientist's attention to relevant developments in fields which he has not recognized as pertinent to his own work.

Can policies designed to satisfy some of these requirements really work to the detriment of others?

If search and retrieval services and selected distribution arrangements were working optimally, they would bring to each scientist exactly that which he has asked for and nothing else. But, by that very fact they would eliminate browsing, and would thereby put an end to the occasions when a scientist's attention is called to information which he had not appreciated as relevant to his own interests. This is just one example of perhaps the crudest kind of optimizing one science information function to the detriment of others.

But what actually are all the various kinds of functions that these information systems must perform; how many of them is it worth distinguishing? Distinctions along a number of axes have been suggested. The most basic criterion of classification is probably that of the scope and permanence with which the information needed by a particular scientist can be described in advance.[2] Along this dimension one can distinguish the exhaustive search; the reference function (to give the scientist the single best answer to a specific question); the current awareness function (to keep the person abreast of developments in his predetermined area of attention); a function which consists of stimulating researchers from time to time to seek information outside of their predesigned areas of attention; and a function which consists of enabling a scientist to follow through on this stimulation by "brushing up" or familiarizing himself with a well-defined field of inquiry which he had not previously included in his attention area. The two last-mentioned functions, it should be noted, transcend the informational requirements that each scientist can define for himself.

## Conclusion

The themes enumerated above have implications for science information policy, but the translation of these implications into concrete steps requires that the themes be specified through a considerable amount of empirical research. As indicated in the opening paragraphs, much research on the use of information and information sources by scientists has been carried out, but until very recently the great variety and subtlety of potentially useful research questions and approaches was not realized. Discussions of "methodology" in this field all too often are confined to a consideration of data-gathering techniques. Insufficient attention has been paid to the more fundamental questions of the conceptualization of units of observation, the choice of variables to be considered, the causal models to be employed, and the analytic designs to be used.[3]

## References

Ackoff, R. L., & Halbert, M. M. An operations research study of the scientific activity of chemists. Cleveland: Case Institute of Technology, Operations Research Group, 1958. (Mimeo)

American Psychological Association. *Reports of the American Psychological Association's Project on Scientific Information Exchange in Psychology.* Vol. 1. Washington, D. C.: APA, 1963.

American Psychological Association. *Reports of the American Psychological Association's Project on Scientific Information Exchange in Psychology.* Vol. 2. Washington, D. C.: APA, 1965.

Coleman, J., Katz, E., & Menzel, H. *Medical innovation—a diffusion study.* Indianapolis: Bobbs-Merrill, 1966.

Herner, S. Information-gathering habits of workers in pure and applied science. *Industrial and Engineering Chemistry,* 1954, 46, 228–236.

Lazarsfeld, P. F., & Menzel, H. Mass media and personal influence. In W. Schramm (Ed.), *The science of human communication,* New York: Basic Books, 1963. Pp. 94–115.

Menzel, H. The flow of information among scientists—problems, opportunities, and research questions. New York: Columbia University, Bureau of Applied Social Research, 1958. (Mimeo) (Available as Technical Report 144390 PB from the Clearinghouse, Department of Commerce, Springfield, Va.)

Menzel, H. Comment. *College and Research Libraries,* 1959, 20, 419–420. (a)

Menzel, H. Planned and unplanned scientific communication. In, *Proceedings of the International Conference on Scientific Information.* Washington, D. C.: National Academy of Sciences, 1959. Pp. 199–243. (b)

Menzel, H. Review of studies in the flow of information among scientists. New York: Columbia University, Bureau of Applied Social Research, 1960. 2 Vols. (Mimeo) (Available as Technical Report 156 941 PB from the Clearinghouse, Department of Commerce, Springfield, Va.)

Menzel, H. . The information needs of current scientific research. *Library Quarterly,* 1964, 34, 4–19.

[2] For a fuller treatment, see Menzel (1964).

[3] Some remarks on the conceptualization of units and on certain related methodological questions will be found in Menzel (1960) on the variety of analytic designs embodied in recent studies in Menzel (1966c) and on the feasibility of inferring science information needs from the past uses made of information services in Menzel (1966a).

Menzel, H. Can science information needs be ascertained empirically? In L. Thayer (Ed.), *Communication: Concepts and perspectives (Proceedings of the Second International Symposium on Communication Theory and Research)*. Washington, D. C.: Spartan Books, 1966. (a)

Menzel, H. Informal communication in science: Its advantages and its formal analogues. In Dan Bergen (Ed.), *The foundations of access to knowledge*. Syracuse: Syracuse University Press, 1966, in press. (b)

Menzel, H. Information needs and uses in science and technology. In C. Cuadra (Ed.), *Annual review of information science and technology*. Vol. 1. New York: Wiley, 1966. (c)

Menzel, H. Sociological perspectives on the information-gathering practices of the scientific investigator and the medical practioner. In D. McCord (Ed.), *Bibliotheca medica: Physician for tomorrow, dedication of the Countway Library of Medicine*. Boston: Harvard Medical School, 1966. (d)

Orr, R. H., Abdian, G., Bourne, C. P., Coyl, E. B., Leeds, A. A., & Pings, V. M. The biomedical information complex viewed as a system. *Federation Proceedings*, 1964, **23**, 1133–1145.

Orr, R. H., Coyl, E. B., & Leeds, A. A. Trends in oral communication among biomedical scientists. *Federation Proceedings*, 1964, 23, 1146–54.

Paisley, W. J. The flow of (behavioral) science information—a review of the research literature. Stanford: Stanford University, Institute for Communication Research, 1965. (Mimeo)

Pelz, R. C. Social factors related to performance in a research organization. *Administrative Science Quarterly*, 1956, **1**, 310–325.

Price, D. J. de S. *Little science, big science*. New York: Columbia University Press, 1963.

Rosenbloom, R. S., McLaughlin, C. P., & Wolek, F. W. Technology transfer and the flow of technical information in a large industrial corporation. Boston: Harvard University, Graduate School of Business Administration, 1965. 2 Vols. (Mimeo)

Shaw, R. Review of "flow of information among scientists." *College and Research Libraries*, 1959, **20**, 163–164.

## PART II: Innovation: Required Flows of Knowledge

This group of papers represents a field which has been largely neglected within information science, yet may become critical to its further advancement and societal support. The papers have been chosen to show, across a wide range of activities, the opportunities and difficulties inherent in applying knowledge. The first group of papers shows how information, as handled by scientific discipline, becomes knowledge. These papers show how information handled by organizations and society becomes services and products and meets societal goals.

Menzel considers information flows in a profession; Allen, in engineering; Glaser and Taylor, in behavioral science based on mental health services. Rothwell, an active researcher himself, reviews a range of studies, and Wolek and Griffith attempt an integration of policy with theory and findings.

# Communication networks in R & D Laboratories

Thomas J. Allen, *Associate Professor of Organisational Psychology and Management, Alfred P. Sloan School of Management, Massachusetts Institute of Technology*

Reprinted from R & D Management, Vol. 1, 1970.

*Abstract.* Communication networks in R & D laboratories are shown to have structural characteristics, which when properly understood can be employed to more effectively maintain the laboratories' personnel abreast of technological developments. Informal relations and physical location are shown to be important determinants of this structure. Informal relations can be developed through formation of project teams and intergroup transfers and loans. The effect of physical location on communications is especially strong and should be given serious consideration when designing research facilities.

This paper was first presented at a conference of the R & D Study Group of the Operational Research Society, February 1970.

## INTRODUCTION

To date, attempts to automate the transmission of scientific and technological information have been most notable for their failure. The reason for this does not lie in any lack of attention or inadequate effort allocated to the problem, since very large sums of money have been expended on storage and retrieval systems for scientific and technological information. Rather, it is due to the nature and complexity of the information itself, and to the uncertainty and very personal nature of each user's needs.

For this reason, the human being is still the most effective source of information, communication with a technically competent colleague being conducted on a two-way basis, with the output of the source tracking and responding to the expressed needs of the user. In this manner, the ability of the source to adapt flexibly and respond rapidly to communicated needs enables it to cope effectively with the uncertain nature of those needs.

A large number of recent studies show that increased use of organizational colleagues for information is strongly related to scientific and technological performance. The relation to performance is, perhaps, demonstrated most clearly in a recent study by a group at M.I.T. Some of the results of this study are presented in this paper as a basis for a discussion on strategies for properly structuring the flow of technical information in research and development organizations.

## THE INTERNAL CONSULTING STUDY

Eight pairs of individuals in different organizations, but working on identical problems, were compared on the extent to which each of them consulted with organizational colleagues. Since there were always two individuals attempting to solve the same problem, their solutions could be compared for relative quality and the sample split between 'high' performers and 'low' performers. Performance evaluations were made by competent technical evaluators in the government laboratories that had sponsored the projects. Dividing the sample into high and low performers allowed a further comparison to be made, now on an aggregate basis, of behaviour leading to high or low performance.

When such a comparison was made with respect to the number of times organizational colleagues were consulted during the project, it showed that high performers made far greater use of this source of technical information (Figure 1). As a matter of fact, high performers not only

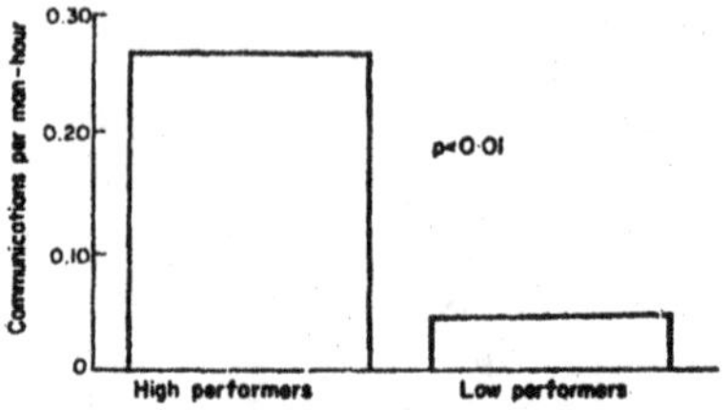


FIGURE 1. Extent of communication between R & D project members and organizational colleagues not assigned to the project.

reported a significantly greater frequency of consultation with organizational colleagues, they also spent significantly more time in their discussions with colleagues.

Furthermore, they relied on more people both within their own technical speciality and on other specialties (Figures 2a and 2b). The high performer was in closer

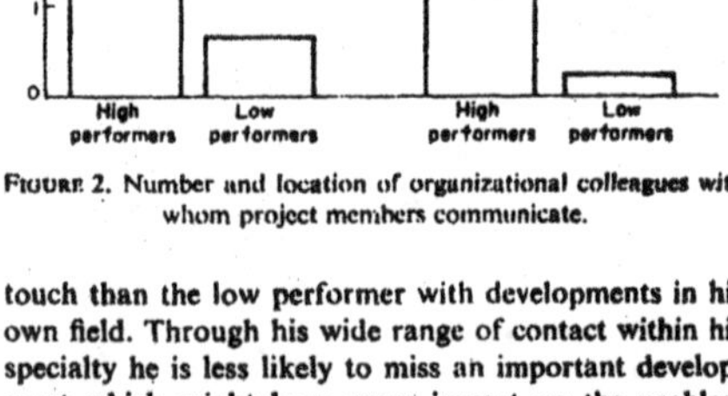


FIGURE 2. Number and location of organizational colleagues with whom project members communicate.

touch than the low performer with developments in his own field. Through his wide range of contact within his specialty he is less likely to miss an important development which might have some impact on the problem to which he is assigned. He also had wider contact with people in specialties other than his own. In fact, it was only the high performers who showed any real contact outside of their speciality (Figure 2b). The low performers seldom ventured outside of their field. These findings agree with those of Pelz & Andrews (1966) who noted that colleague contacts both within the immediate work group and with other groups in the organization were positively related to a man's performance and that the variety of contacts and their frequency each contributed independently to performance.

One cannot of course determine very easily whether communication causes high performance or whether high performers merely communicate more. Pelz & Andrews (1966), in their study, obtained data on which of the two parties initiated the contact. They then assumed that a man's high performance would be more likely to attract contact from others than to induce him to initiate contacts himself. They then looked only at contacts initiated by the information user and found that the relation with performance remained strong. They conclude:

> large amounts of colleague contact tended to go with high performance even when one looked only at scientists who themselves were the primary initiators of the contacts. Under these conditions it was difficult to believe that the contacts were primarily the *result* of previous high performance. Thus the hypothesis that contacts with colleagues stimulated performance seemed to be supported (p. 47).

### SUPPORT FROM OUTSIDE THE PROJECT: A PARADOX

Given the benefits to be derived from internal consultation, one would expect project members to rely heavily upon their technical staff for information. In fact, this is not the case. During the nineteen projects studied by Allen (1966), project members actually obtained more of their ideas from outside of their firms than from their own technical staff—although in general a poor performance was shown by sources outside of the firm. In fact, when individuals inside and outside of the firm were compared as sources of ideas, there was an inverse relation between frequency of use and performance.

Those information sources that reward the user by contributing more to his performance are used less than those that do not. Such a situation would seem to conflict with the principles of psychological learning theory. One might expect a person to return more frequently to those channels that reward him most consistently. The data show just the opposite to be true. The paradox can, however, be resolved with the introduction of an additional parameter. It can be safely predicted that an individual will repeat a behaviour that is rewarded more frequently than one that is unrewarded, only if the cost to him of the rewarded behaviour is less than or equal to the cost of the unrewarded behaviour. In other words, both cost and benefit may be taken into consideration when deciding upon a source of information.

Gerstberger and Allen (1968) actually studied this decision process in some detail. They found no relation at all between the engineers' perception of the benefits to be gained from an informal channel and the extent to which the channel was used. However, a very strong relation existed between extent of use and the engineers' perception of the amount of effort that it took to use the channel. Cost in that case was the overriding determinant of the decision. Working back from this finding, one might speculate that the failure to consult with organizational colleagues is attributable to a high cost associated with such consultation. In fact, there is evidence to indicate that the organizational colleague is a high cost source of information for research and development project teams (Allen *et al.*, 1968). It can, for example, be very costly for a project member to admit to a colleague that he needs his help.

### TECHNOLOGICAL 'GATEKEEPERS'

A number of recent studies have indicated that technologists do not read very much, and one might conclude that literature is not a very effective vehicle for bringing new information into the organization; and while it is found that outside personal contact is used very heavily by organizational technologists, further analysis suggests that this means of transfer is not much more instrumental than literature. The reason for this is that the average technologist cannot communicate effectively with outsiders. This is reflected in the results of several research studies which are consistent in their discovery of an inverse relation between outside personal contact and technical performance (Allen, 1964; Shilling & Bernard, 1964).

How then does information enter the organization? First of all, it is clear that entry does occur, because without it no R & D organization could long survive. No R & D organization, no matter how large, can be fully self-sustaining. In order for the organization to survive its members must maintain themselves abreast of current developments in those technologies which are central to the organization's mission. It must, in other words, constantly import technical information. Not only were the organizations under study surviving; they were, to all appearances, thriving. They were extremely successful, and highly regarded technically. They must, therefore have been successful, somehow, in acquiring information from outside, and disseminating it within their borders. The questions remains, how?

The first important clue lies in the observation that, of all possible information sources, only one appears to satisfactorily meet the needs of R & D project members. That one source is the organizational colleague. This has been shown in the case of R & D proposal competitions (Allen, 1964) for preliminary design studies (Allen, 1966; Allen *et al.*, 1968); for 'idea generating groups' (Baker, *et al.*, 1967); for engineers and scientists in a wide variety of industrial, governmental and university settings (Pelz & Andrews, 1966); and for the members of 64 laboratories in the biological sciences (Allen, 1964).

Following this clue, Allen & Cohen (1969) discovered that the process by which organizations most effectively import information is an indirect one (Figure 3). There existed, in the organizations that they studied, a small number of key people upon whom others relied very heavily for information. These key people, or 'technological gatekeepers', differ from their colleagues in their orientation toward outside information sources. They

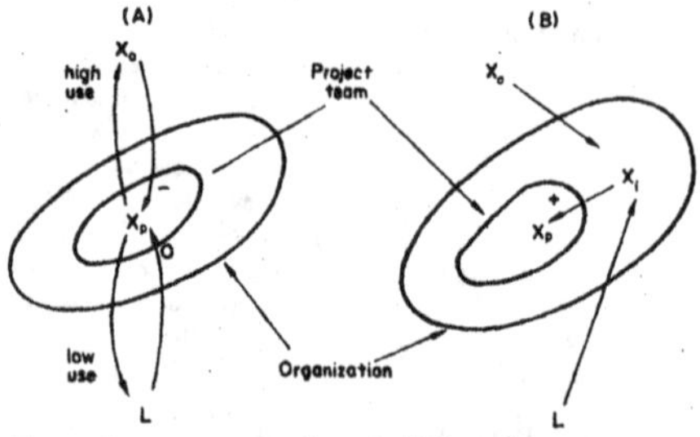


$X_p$ = project team member, in need of information;
$X_o$ = person outside of the organization;
$X_i$ = organizational colleague;
$L$ = literature.

FIGURE 3. The dilemma of importing information into the organization. Direct paths do not work (A), because literature is little used by the average technologist and because the direct contact with outside persons is ineffective. An indirect route, through the technological gatekeeper (B) has been shown to be more effective. Symbols next to incoming arrows indicate the polarity of the correlation with performance.

read far more, particularly the 'harder' literature. Their readership of professional engineering and scientific journals is significantly greater than that of the average technologist (Figure 4). They also maintain broader-ranging and longer-term relationships with technologists

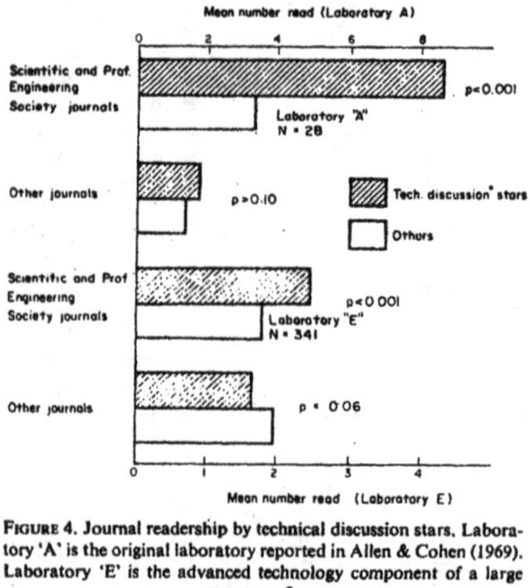


FIGURE 4. Journal readership by technical discussion stars. Laboratory 'A' is the original laboratory reported in Allen & Cohen (1969). Laboratory 'E' is the advanced technology component of a large aerospace firm.

outside of their organizations (Figure 5). The technological gatekeeper mediates between his organizational colleagues and the world outside, and he effectively couples the organization to scientific and technological activity in the world at large.

* Persons receiving one standard deviation or more above the mean number of technical discussion choices per person in their laboratory (Laboratory 'A') or in their department (Laboratory 'E').

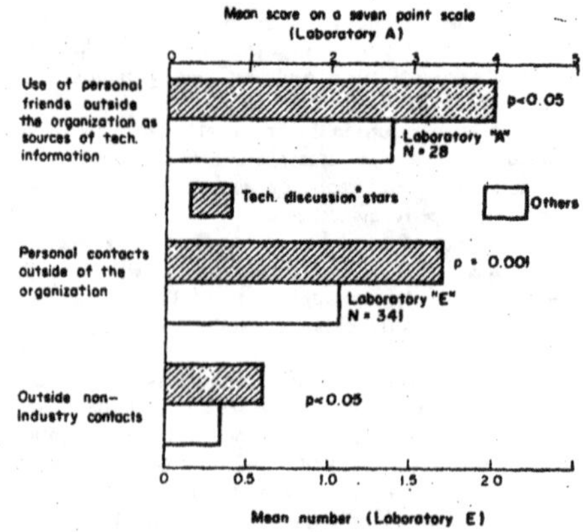


FIGURE 5. Personal contact outside of the organization by technical discussion stars. Laboratory 'A' is the original laboratory reported in Allen & Cohen (1969). Laboratory 'E' is the advanced technology component of a large aerospace firm.

NETWORKS OF GATEKEEPERS

Using the techniques of the earlier study (Allen & Cohen, 1969), the structure of the communication network in the research and advanced technology division of a large aerospace firm was measured. The laboratory under study was organized on a functional basis around five engineering specialties and three scientific disciplines.

The gatekeepers in each specialist department were identified, as well as the structure of the communication network in that department. Because of the complexity of the networks in such a large organization (Figure 6), an attempt was made to simplify them through graph-theoretic reduction.

A communication network (or portions thereof) can be characterized according to the degree of interconnectedness that exists among its nodes. There are several degrees of interconnectedness or 'connectivity' that can exist in a network (Flament, 1963). In the present analysis, only that degree of connectivity which Flament has called 'strong' will be considered. A strongly connected component, or strong component in a network, is one in which all nodes are mutually reachable. In a communication network, a potential exists for the transmission of information between any two members of a strong component (Flament, 1963; Harary *et al.*, 1965). For this reason, the laboratory's communication network was reduced into its strong components and their membership was examined.

When the departmental networks of the organization are reduced in this manner, two things become apparent. First of all, the formation of strong components is not aligned with formal organizational groupings, and second, while there were in each functional department anywhere from one to six non-trivial strong components, nearly all of the gatekeepers can be found together as members of the same strong component (see, for an example, Figure 7). On the average, 64% of all gatekeepers can be found

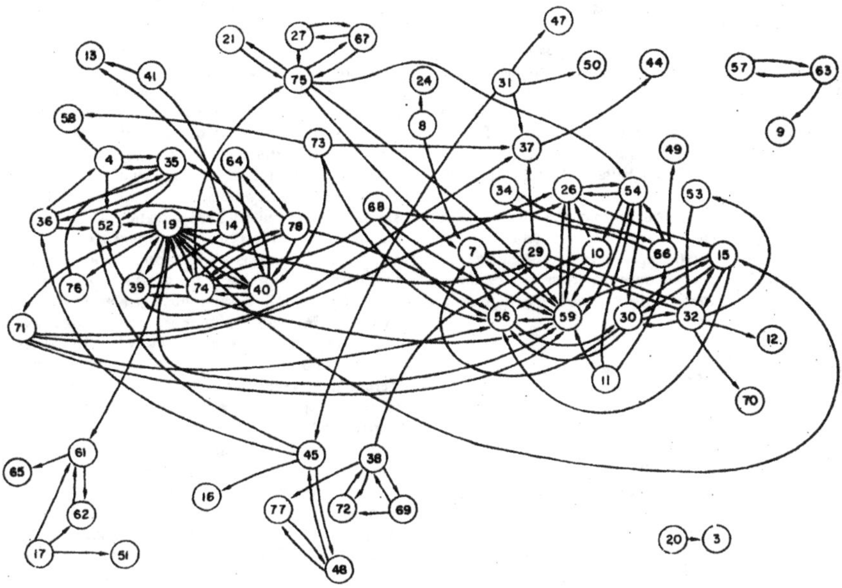

FIGURE 6. Typical communication network of a functional department in a large R & D laboratory.

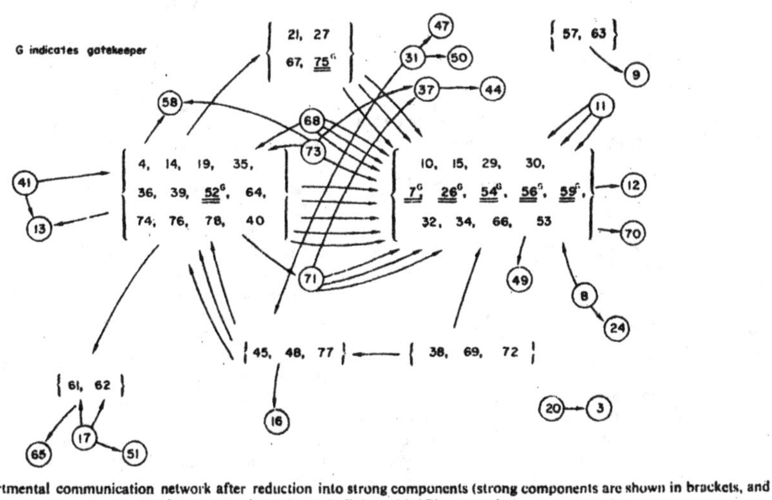


FIGURE 7. Departmental communication network after reduction into strong components (strong components are shown in brackets, and gatekeepers are shown by underlining with 'G' superscript).

in eight strong components, one for each of the five technological and three scientific specialties. In each technical specialty, there is one strongly connected network in which most of the gatekeepers are members. The gatekeepers, therefore, maintain close communication among themselves, thus increasing substantially their effectiveness in coupling the organization to the outside world.

In fact, if one were to sit down and attempt to design an optimal system for bringing in new technical information and disseminating it within the organization, it would be difficult to produce a better one than that which exists.

New information is brought into the organization through the gatekeeper. It can then be communicated quite readily to other gatekeepers through the gatekeeper network and disseminated outward from one or more points to other members of the organization (Figure 8).

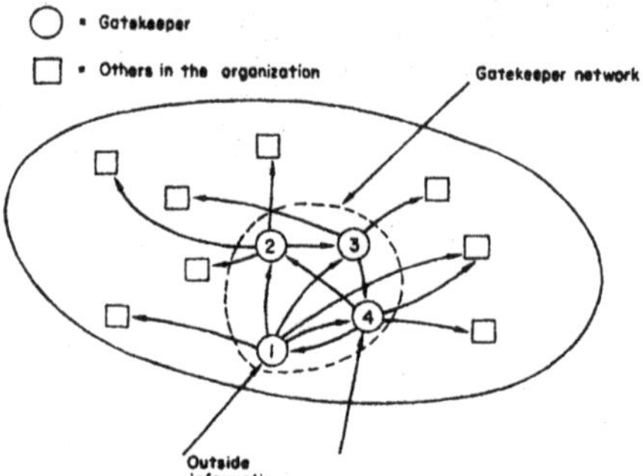


FIGURE 8. The functioning of the gatekeeper network. New information is brought into the organization by 1. It can be transmitted to 2, 3, and 4 via the gatekeeper network. It reaches its eventual users (squares) through their contacts with gatekeepers.

Perhaps the most interesting aspect of this functioning of the organizational communication network is that it has developed spontaneously, with no managerial intervention. In fact, there was scarcely a suspicion on the part of management that the network operated in this way.

### THE INFLUENCE OF NON-ORGANIZATIONAL FACTORS ON THE STRUCTURE OF COMMUNICATION NETWORKS

An organization's formal structure (that which generally appears on an organizational chart) is, as one would expect, a very important determinant of communication patterns. It is not the sole determinant, however. In addition to formal organizational structure, there are available to management at least two other factors that can be used to promote (or discourage) communication. The first of these operates through the extension of informal friendship-type relations within the organization. Allen & Cohen (1969) have shown how informal relations influence the structure of communication networks, and Allen *et al.* (1968) explore in detail how this influence comes about. Simply stated, people are more willing to ask questions of others whom they know, than of strangers. The key lies in the expected damage sustained by the ego if one's question is met with a critical response. To be told that you have asked a dumb or foolish question is the ultimate in rebuffs. Few people are willing to entertain such a risk. Now, out of all the people in the world, there are hopefully only a small percentage who would meet even a truly stupid question with such a retort. Even given that this percentage is very small, however, many people will follow the strategy of minimum regret and assume that everyone belongs to this set unless proven otherwise. This results in a situation in which, of all people who are known, only a small percentage are unapproachable, but all unknowns are unapproachable. To increase the proportion of people in the organization, who can be approached for information, management would be well advised to increase the number of acquaintanceships among its technical personnel. This it can do very easily. People will not become acquainted until they first meet. There are, however, a number of ways through which technical people can come to meet one another. Interdepartmental projects are one such device. People who come to know one another through service on projects or other inter-functional teams retain their effectiveness as channels between departments for some time even after the project or team had been disbanded. Interdepartmental teams can, and do, provide an indirect benefit, through the persistence of the relations that they establish, over and above their direct contributions to coordination. The same thing can be said for transfers within the organization. For a period of time following a transfer, the transferred individual will provide a communication path back to his old organization. His influence extends far beyond this direct link, though. Probably the most important contribution of the transferred person lies in his ability to make referrals. The number of communication paths that potentially become available when a man is transferred is the product of the number of acquaintanceships which he developed in the two parts of the organization. For some people this can be a very large number. So with only a very few transfers, a large number of communication paths can be created and coordination thereby improved.

Of course, the effect diminishes with time, since both people and activities will change in the old group, and the transferred person will gradually lose touch. Kanno (1968) has shown that following a transfer between divisions of a large chemical firm, the transferred persons provided an effective communication link back to their old divisions for 1–1½ years. The duration over which communications remain effective following a transfer is determined by many factors; principal among these are the rate of change of activities and turnover of personnel in the old organization. If projects are of short duration, with many new ones constantly being initiated and the turnover of personnel is high, one would expect that the effect of a transfer in promoting communication would be short-lived. Where the activity is more stable and turnover low, the transfer can be effective over a longer period of time. With estimates of these parameters and of the number of people (and their work) with whom the average transfer is acquainted, a systematic program of intra-organizational transfer can be developed. Such a program would contribute directly to communication, coordination and empathy among the sub-elements of the organization.

### THE EFFECTS OF GEOGRAPHICAL LOCATION

In addition to formal organizational and information relations there is a third very important factor that can be used to influence the structure of organizational communication networks, i.e. the physical configuration of the facilities in which that organization is placed.

The data on the effect of spatial separation to be presented now were obtained in three very different organizations. The first organization is a 48-man department in a medium-sized aerospace firm. The 48 people were all engineers and scientists, primarily in electrical and mechanical engineering and applied physics. The second organization that was studied is a 52-man section of a medical school laboratory. The third organization comprised 57 social psychologists, economists and applied mathematicians in a management school.

To determine the influence of physical separation on the probability of two people communicating, the distance between every possible pair of people was measured. Moving outward in 5-yard intervals from each person, a measurement was made of the proportion of people within each interval with whom the focal person communicated. The measurement of distance was the actual distance that the focal person would have to walk in order to reach another person's desk. All measurements were taken on a single floor.

The proportion of people with whom an individual communicates, or the 'probability of communication' as it is labelled in the figure, decays with the square of distance outward from the focal person (Figure 9). The

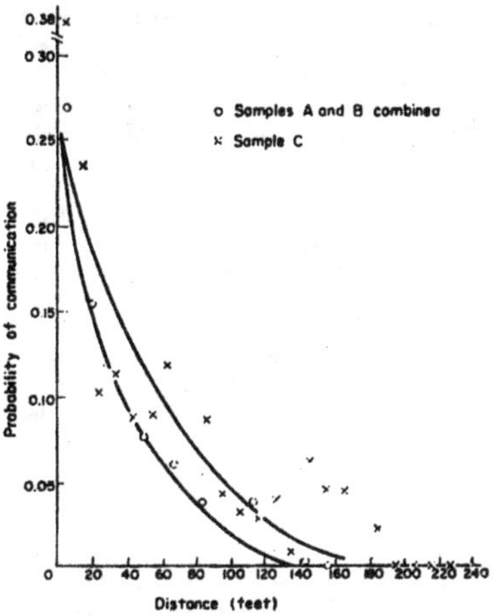


FIGURE 9. Probability of communication as a function of the distance separating pairs of people.

fact that the probability of communication decays with the distance separating people is not too surprising. Nor is the fact that it follows an inverse square law. What is surprising is the extreme sensitivity of probability to

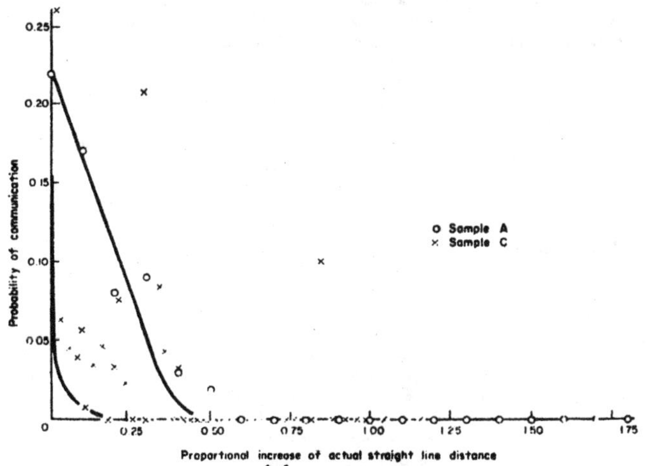


FIGURE 10. Probability of communication as a function of the magnitude of the nuisance factor.
O = Sample A
X = Sample C

distance. The function, naturally, must become asymptotic beyond the minimum point of the parabola. The striking thing is that it reaches this asymptote within 25 yards. This was true in all three organizations. In fact, for the first two organizations, the curves fall so close together that the data are combined in Figure 9. The result, therefore, appears to be general and independent of the nature of the technical work being performed.

As though, by itself, physical separation were not serious enough, there appear to be circumstances which can exacerbate its effect. The amount of difficulty, by way of corners to be turned, indirect paths to be followed, etc., encountered in traversing a path intensifies the effect of separation on communication probability. One index of this difficulty, something which might be called a 'nuisance factor' is the difference between the straight line and actual travel distances (Figure 10) separating two people. When communication probability is plotted as a function of the magnitude of the 'nuisance factor' (Figure 10) the effect is quite startling. This effect holds true whether the nuisance factor is computed on an absolute basis or as a proportion of straight line separation distance.

### ORGANIZATIONAL STRUCTURE

To encourage communication between project teams and the supporting technical staff, separation distances must be kept to a minimum. To locate a project in a separate facility is essentially to cut it off from support by the rest of the laboratory staff. There is a trade-off that must be made in locating project members. Effective coordination of all elements of project activity may require that all or most of the team members be located together in a specially assigned place. On the other hand, to maintain the specialists assigned to the project abreast of developments in their technical fields demands that they be kept in contact with the specialist colleagues. This, in turn, favours locating them with their specialist groups. Marquis (1969) has argued for the latter alternative on very large projects. All of the projects in Marquis's sample were of fairly long duration; several years. This may well hold the key to the trade-off. For long-term projects, technical personnel should remain in the same location with their specialist colleagues. Assignment to a project of long duration can force a man to lose touch with his field unless steps are taken to enable his free interaction with colleagues in the field. The result is technical obsolescence and difficulty for both the man and the organization in dealing with future assignments. In the case of a brief project, the length of separation will be too short to have these results, and the balance swings in favour of locating all project members together.

Long projects demand functional organization, while short-duration projects may be organized on a project basis with all team members located together.

Functional organization has the undesirable consequence of making intra-project coordination difficult. A possible solution to this problem lies in overlaying a coordinating team across the functional departments in what has come to be known as a matrix organization. This is not always as easy to accomplish as it first sounds, but when it functions properly it can achieve the desired goals of the functional organization without the loss in project coordination.

Project and matrix organization have the undesirable consequence of making communication between functional departments difficult. Transfers, where possible, and short-duration interdepartmental projects, assist in countering this problem. In addition, the overall configuration of the laboratory should be structured in such a way that inter-functional communication is eased. Where it is desirable to have communication between groups, they should be located near each other. Where this is impossible they can be made to share certain facilities that will force interaction. The nature of the facility is secondary. It may be as humble as a coffee pot or men's room or as grandiose as a computer or an expensive instrument. What matters is that it brings people into contact who would otherwise not meet. It is quite easy, in any organization, to think of a large number of such facilities for promoting interaction. Where possible they should be located where they will promote the desired patterns of group interaction. In those cases in which it is not feasible to manipulate the position of the interaction facility, then desired patterns of interaction should be given serious consideration in allocating the use of the facility among groups and in positioning groups around it. In the latter situation it must be borne in mind that the extent to which a facility will be used is also an inverse function of distance. Frohman (1968), for example, found the principal determinant of use of a technical library in an industrial firm to be the distance separating users from it. Interaction facilities must be positioned in such a way that they promote interaction among groups that would not otherwise interact, while at the same time they are not so far removed from any of the groups that they lose their effectiveness.

### SUMMARY AND CONCLUSIONS

The importance to research and development projects of technical staff support cannot be overstressed. Seldom, if ever, is management able satisfactorily to predict and obtain all of the talents that will be needed in a project and incorporate them in the project team. The project must, therefore, obtain much of its required information from sources beyond its own membership.

Research shows very clearly that the best source for this support lies in the technical staff of the laboratory itself. Attempts to bring information to the project directly from outside of the organization usually have been ineffective. The process by which an organization imports and disseminates outside information is more complex than people normally assume. The best way to maintain the project team abreast of outside developments lies in understanding and making proper use of existing information systems. This includes the use of technological gatekeepers for project support. Outside information can then be delivered to the project quite effectively, albeit by an indirect route. Research evidence indicates quite strongly that the indirect approach is far more effective than any direct approach to coupling project members to outside sources, whether personal or written.

There are available a wide variety of techniques for improving communication and coordination between projects and their supporting staff. A number of formal organizational mechanisms have been described in detail. In addition to these, use may also be made of the informal relationships that will develop when people come into contact with one another. A very effective means for increasing the level of acquaintanceships in an organization is the inter-group transfer. Physical location is also a very strong determinant of interaction patterns. People are more likely to communicate with those who are located nearest to them. Individuals and groups can therefore be positioned in ways that will either promote or inhibit communication. Architectural design thus becomes an important determinant of the structure that an organization's communication network will assume. Shared facilities or equipment can also be used to promote interaction between groups.

All of these factors must be taken into account and properly arranged in order effectively to couple the research and development project to its supporting information system.

This research was supported by a grant (GN597) from the Office of Science Information Service, National Science Foundation. Arun Firodia, Peter G. Gerstberger, Mario Y. Munoz and Paul W. O'Gara collaborated in the data analysis. The author gratefully acknowledges the cooperation of the management and employees of the laboratories that were studied.

## REFERENCES

Allen, T. J. (1964) 'The Use of Information Channels in R & D Proposal Preparation', Cambridge, Mass.: M.I.T. Sloan School of Management, Working Paper No. 97-64.

Allen, T. J. (1966) 'Managing the Flow of Scientific and Technological Information, Ph.D. Dissertation, Cambridge, Mass.: M.I.T. Sloan School of Management.

Allen, T. J., Gerstenfeld, A. & Gerstberger, P. G. (1968) 'The Problem of Internal Consulting in the R & D Laboratory', Cambridge, Mass.: M.I.T. Sloan School of Management, Working Paper No. 319-68.

Allen, T. J. & Cohen, S. I. (1969) 'Information flow in two R & D laboratories', Administrative Science Quarterly, Vol. 14.

Baker, N. R., Siegmann, J. & Rubenstein, A. H. (1967) 'The effects of perceived needs and means on the generation of ideas for industrial research and development projects', I.E.E.E. Transactions on Engineering Management, Vol. 14.

Flament, C. (1963) 'Applications of Graph Theory to Group Structure', New York: Prentice Hall.

Frohman, A. (1968) 'Communication problems in an industrial laboratory', Unpublished term paper, Cambridge, Mass.: M.I.T. Sloan School of Management.

Gerstberger, P. G. & Allen, T. J. (1968) 'Criteria used in the selection of information channels by R & D engineers', Journal of Applied Psychology, Vol. 52.

Harary, F., Norman, R. S. & Cartwright, D. (1965) 'Structural Models', New York: Wiley.

Kanno, M. (1968) 'Effect on Communication Between Labs and Plants of the Transfer of R & D Personnel', S.M. Thesis, Cambridge, Mass.: M.I.T. Sloan School of Management.

Marquis, D. G. (1969) 'Organizational factors in project performance', Program Management (ed. J. Galbraith), Cambridge, Mass.: M.I.T. Press (in press).

Pelz, D. C. & Andrews, F. M. (1966) 'Scientists in Organizations', New York: Wiley.

Shilling, C. W. & Bernard, C. W. (1964) 'Informal Communication Among Bio-Scientists', George Washington University Biological Sciences Communication Project, Report 16A-64.

Reprinted from ASLIB Proceedings, Vol. 20, 1968.

# ORGANIZATIONAL ASPECTS OF INFORMATION FLOW IN TECHNOLOGY

PROFESSOR T. J. ALLEN
*Massachusetts Institute of Technology*

*Paper presented at the 42nd Aslib Annual Conference, Canterbury, 22nd–25th September 1968*

FOR about five years now a small group of us at MIT have been conducting a series of investigations into the information needs of technologists, the manner in which these needs are presently met, the relation between various ways of fulfilling information needs and technological performance, and the nature of factors which determine the ways in which information needs will be fulfilled.

Since this series of research studies builds upon itself in a somewhat chronological pattern, perhaps the best way to present results is to go back to 1963 when we began and work forward to the present time.

We began in 1963 with the hope of studying the information consumption patterns of research and development projects. In pursuing this goal, we encountered two rather serious methodological difficulties, which we first had to overcome. Let me spend just a few minutes with these.

The first one is inevitable and omnipresent—that of obtaining a performance criterion for the project. We do, in all of our studies, want to determine some criterion of performance that we can relate to the behaviour we have observed.

The other is that each R and D project, by definition, is unique; if it was performed previously, it is no longer research. You can gather a lot of data on a particular case, and still be faced with the question of how much you can generalize to any other case.

There are two ways of getting around this latter difficulty. The first one is rather obvious. You gather data on a large number of projects, and control for the variation in the substance of the problems through statistical techniques.

The second, which I think is a bit more efficient, is to locate instances of matched pairs of research projects—in other words, two or more teams working on the same project. This is the strategy that we have employed. We have found a number of government-sponsored parallel projects in the early preliminary design phases at which time the government often funds two or more teams to perform the same project.

We have also found a number of similar instances in commercial projects. In other words, there are two or three teams, in some cases as many as twenty-five, working on essentially the same project. I will report today on some of our earliest findings on a number of government-sponsored projects.

The use of matched pairs also allows us to solve, to a large degree, the criterion problem. It is much simpler to obtain a relative performance measure on two identical projects, than it would be to obtain absolute performance measures. In other words, someone who is knowledgeable and competent in the required technical areas can determine which of the two teams produced the better solution to a particular problem. It is easier dealing, of course, on a sub-problem basis level rather than on the overall project evaluation. It is far easier, for example, to assess which of two competing teams has the better power supply design and which has the better guidance package design than it would be to get absolute evaluations for these subsystem designs.

Before I go into our results, I will describe very briefly how the data were collected.

Figure 1 shows our principal data-gathering tool. This is what we have come to call a solution development record. It is very simple. First of all, when we learn of a new project which is about to be initiated, we obtain the work statement for it and we factor the project down into a number of sub-problem areas, which are the units we study.

At the outset of the project we interview the individual who is primarily responsible for each subproblem. Figure 1 illustrates a typical subproblem. We ask the engineer at the very onset what approaches to the solution of this particular problem he is going to consider. We have him list them, if he is considering more than one, and we indicate them on a form that is mailed weekly to the principal investigator. Beside each alternative approach, we give him a series of numbers from zero to one. We tell the engineer that these represent the probability estimates. When the respondent receives the form on a particular day, he is to merely circle a number next to each alternative which represents his subjective probability that that approach will be the one upon which he will finally settle.

If he were, for example, considering only two approaches believing that they exhausted the field of possibilities, but was completely uncommitted between the two, he would circle 0.5 for each, as shown. Eventually, one of these goes to 1.0 and the rest go to zero, and we have a record of the engineer's decision process during the project.

Figure 2 illustrates plots over time of the actual probabilities that were submitted by two engineers who were working on the same design. Each considered five approaches and traded off among them during the course of the project. There is an overlap in the first three approaches. You can see that over a time we get a record of the trade-off process among alternatives. Armed with this, we can return after the project has been completed, place the plot before the engineer and ask him specific questions about it. If we were to ask him to simply recapitulate his solution process, I am afraid we would not be able to obtain very much information. Armed with the plots, however, we can ask specific questions about the reasons for changes. In the middle of August, for example, he may have come up with a new approach, and he can tell us what it was that first suggested this approach to him.

This method has enabled us to learn quite a bit about the types of information channels and information-gathering behaviour of the people we studied. Today, I am going to concentrate on one particular function that the information system provides to the engineer, and that is the actual generation of the solution

MASSACHUSETTS INSTITUTE OF TECHNOLOGY

Solution Development Record

Manned Uranus Landing in an Early Time Period Study

General United Aerospace Corporation

Name ____________________ Date ____________________

Estimate of Probability that Alternative will be Employed

Subproblem #1: Method of rendezvous at Uranus

Alternative approaches:

| | | | | | | | | | | | |
|---|---|---|---|---|---|---|---|---|---|---|---|
| orbital rendezvous mission with excursion vehicle | 0 | 0.1 | 0.2 | 0.3 | 0.4 | **0.5** | 0.6 | 0.7 | 0.8 | 0.9 | 1.0 |
| orbital rendezvous mission without excursion vehicle | 0 | 0.1 | 0.2 | 0.3 | 0.4 | 0.5 | 0.6 | 0.7 | 0.8 | 0.9 | 1.0 |
| direct mission | 0 | 0.1 | 0.2 | 0.3 | 0.4 | **0.5** | 0.6 | 0.7 | 0.8 | 0.9 | 1.0 |
| ____________ | 0 | 0.1 | 0.2 | 0.3 | 0.4 | 0.5 | 0.6 | 0.7 | 0.8 | 0.9 | 1.0 |

Subproblem #2: Design of the electrical power supply subsystem for the space vehicle

Alternative approaches:

| | | | | | | | | | | | |
|---|---|---|---|---|---|---|---|---|---|---|---|
| hydrogen-oxygen fuel cell | 0 | 0.1 | 0.2 | 0.3 | 0.4 | 0.5 | **0.6** | 0.7 | 0.8 | 0.9 | 1.0 |
| KOH fuel cell | 0 | 0.1 | 0.2 | **0.3** | 0.4 | 0.5 | 0.6 | 0.7 | 0.8 | 0.9 | 1.0 |
| Rankine cycle fast reactor | 0 | 0.1 | 0.2 | 0.3 | 0.4 | 0.5 | 0.6 | 0.7 | 0.8 | 0.9 | 1.0 |
| Rankine cycle thermal reactor | 0 | 0.1 | 0.2 | 0.3 | 0.4 | 0.5 | 0.6 | 0.7 | 0.8 | 0.9 | 1.0 |
| Brayton cycle reactor | 0 | **0.1** | 0.2 | 0.3 | 0.4 | 0.5 | 0.6 | 0.7 | 0.8 | 0.9 | 1.0 |
| ____________ | 0 | 0.1 | 0.2 | 0.3 | 0.4 | 0.5 | 0.6 | 0.7 | 0.8 | 0.9 | 1.0 |
| ____________ | 0 | 0.1 | 0.2 | 0.3 | 0.4 | 0.5 | 0.6 | 0.7 | 0.8 | 0.9 | 1.0 |
| ____________ | 0 | 0.1 | 0.2 | 0.3 | 0.4 | 0.5 | 0.6 | 0.7 | 0.8 | 0.9 | 1.0 |

FIG. 1.

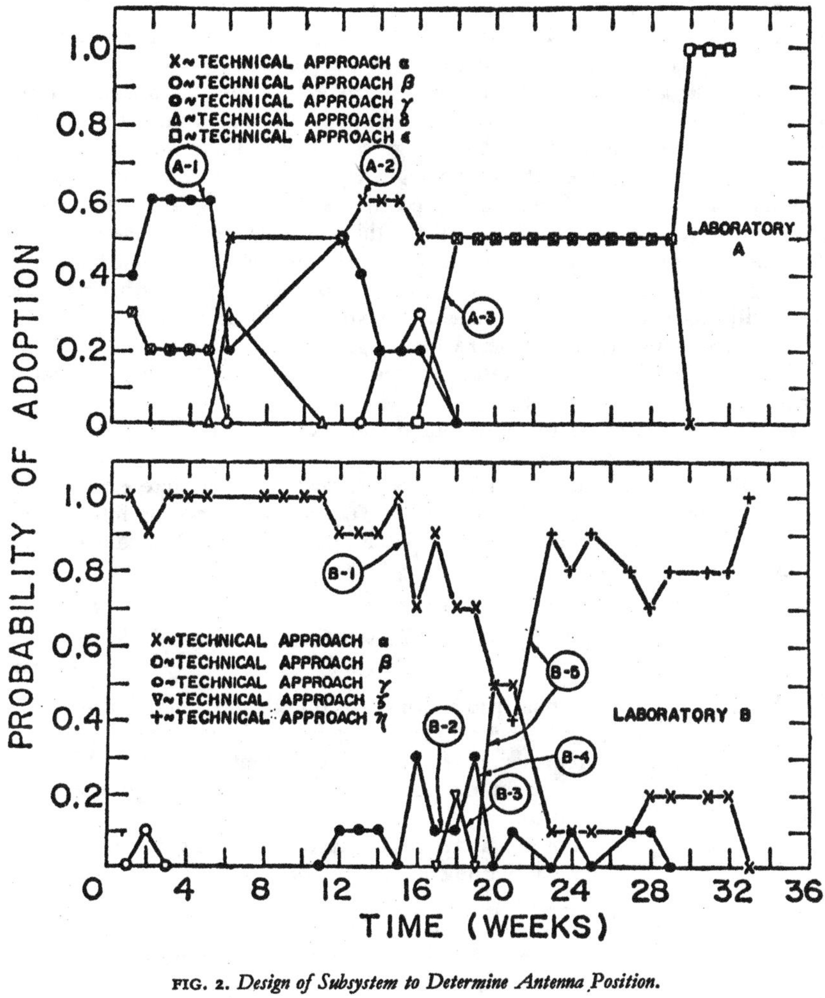


FIG. 2. *Design of Subsystem to Determine Antenna Position.*

alternatives—the generation of ideas. We are going to look back and see from which channels these ideas were originally derived. In this particular example (Figure 2), with regard to approach Epsilon, the story goes something like this. The researcher was going along, trading off among three alternatives, none of which really satisfied him. He was really searching around for other possibilities, and you can see other ideas coming up here and there in the plot.

About halfway through the project, a friend attended a meeting of the Society of Automotive Engineers and heard a paper that suggested an alternative of possible interest to our friend the engineer. He told him about the paper, gave him the name of the author; the engineer contacted the author, learned of a couple of literature references, looked up the references, and learned of a vendor who had the potential for making this particular device. He contacted the vendor, got some cost estimates and so forth—and as you can see, he carried it along during this period he was doing this information gathering—and eventually decided on this approach. So you see there were a number of messages that came to the engineer which suggested this alternative to him; the SAE paper, his friend, the literature contact that he made, the vendor, and so forth.

All of our interviews are tape-recorded and later coded for the sources from which these messages arrived.

In Table 1, we are shown a number of the channels that were examined as potential sources of ideas. We coded our tapes for these—for information coming from these particular channels. Each one of them is defined according to this table.

TABLE 1 *Typical Information Channels Considered in the Study*

| | |
|---|---|
| *literature* | books, professional, technical and trade journals and other publicly accessible written material. |
| *vendors* | representatives of, or documentation generated by suppliers or potential suppliers of design components. |
| *customer* | representatives of, or documentation generated by the government agency for which the project is performed. |
| *external sources* | sources outside the laboratory which do not fall into any of the above three categories. These include paid and unpaid consultants and representatives of government agencies other than the customer agency. |
| *technical staff* | engineers and scientists in the laboratory who are not assigned directly to the project being considered. |
| *company research* | any other project performed previously or simultaneously in the laboratory regardless of its source of funding. |

Table 2 shows the results of the message count on nineteen of these projects. In the first column we see the messages that were received. These are the messages which suggested any alternative that was considered.

TABLE 2 *Messages Received and Messages Accepted by R&D Scientists and Engineers as a Function of Information Channel (nine parallel sets comprising 19 R&D projects)*

| *Channel* | *Messages received* | *Messages accepted* | *Acceptance ratio* |
|---|---|---|---|
| literature | | | |
| scientists | 18 | 6 | 0.33 |
| engineers | 53 | 21 | 0.40 |
| external sources | | | |
| scientists | 5 | 5 | 1.00 |
| engineers | 67 | 32 | 0.48 |
| vendors | | | |
| scientists | 0 | 0 | — |
| engineers | 101 | 33 | 0.33 |
| customer | | | |
| scientists | 0 | 0 | — |
| engineers | 132 | 41 | 0.31 |
| technical staff | | | |
| scientists | 1 | 0 | 0 |
| engineers | 44 | 24 | 0.55 |
| company research | | | |
| scientists | 1 | 0 | 0 |
| engineers | 37 | 20 | 0.54 |
| unknown | 75 | 6 | — |

Differences in acceptance ratios between information channels are statistically significant at the 0.01 level: technical staff and vendors, external sources and vendors, technical staff and customer, company research and customer, external sources and customer. The difference between ratios for external sources and vendors is statistically significant at the 0.05 level.

Messages accepted are defined to be the messages which generated the solution — the one alternative which was finally accepted.

Taking the ratio between the two measures, as a first-order performance criterion, we see there is quite a variance in these acceptance ratios. They vary for engineers from about 0.30 all the way to 0.55.

Figure 3 shows that engineers differ quite a bit from scientists (at least from this limited sample) in their information-gathering behaviour. The literature is much less used by engineers. Vendors are used quite a bit. The acceptance ratio is rather low for vendors. The customer suggests a lot of possibilities, few of which are accepted. The technical staff suggests some. It has a very high acceptance ratio. Company research has a very high acceptance ratio. External sources have a relatively high acceptance ratio.

These are the three channels that were the highest: company research, technical staff, and external sources. They are what you might call expert sources. A man goes to them because he feels they have more knowledge than

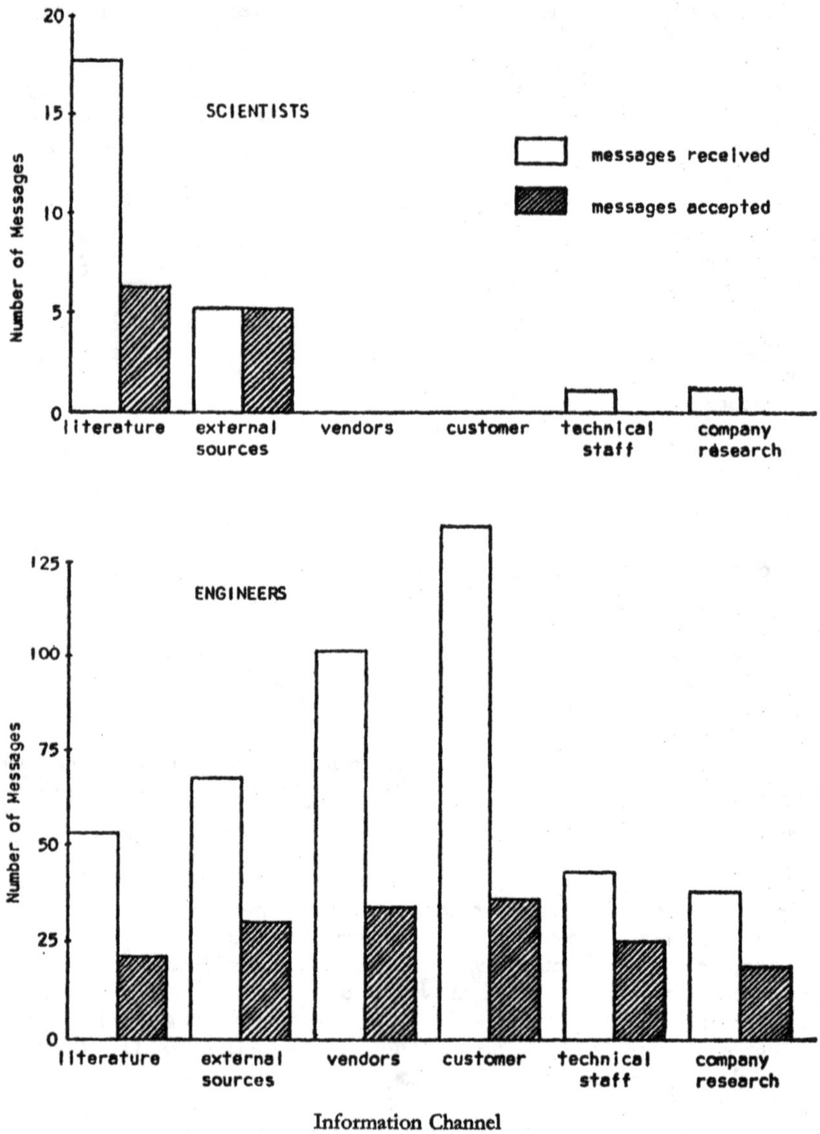


FIG. 3. *Messages Received and Messages Accepted by R. & D. Scientists and Engineers as a Function of Information Channel.*

he in a given area. He goes to them as experts, so there is something of a halo over any information which they give him.

In the sample of projects for the subproblem solutions, we were able to divide our sample into those that were rated higher, and those that were rated lower. You lose quite a lot of data in this way, because the evaluator in the government laboratory is often simply unable to discriminate between the technical quality of solution; one is as good as the other and the majority of our ratings are tied scores in this way. However, for 27 of the solutions we were able to get very definite distinctions in quality.

Dividing our sample into higher- and lower-rated solutions (Table 3), we find that using the literature contributes to twice as many lower-rated solutions as higher-rated solutions. Statistically the difference is not extremely great; the last column in Table 3 represents the probability that these results could have been generated by chance. We see that for the literature such a difference could occur by chance about 14 per cent of the time.

External sources generate more lower-rated solutions. In other words, they perform poorly. This could have occurred by chance only three times in a hundred.

Both vendors and the customer supply a nearly equivalent number of both high- and low-rated solutions.

Technical staff leans toward the high side, but again the results are not too significant.

Company research produces three times as many higher-rated as lower-rated solutions. The probability that this could have occurred randomly is about six one-hundredths.

Besides testing the performance of individual channels, we made a prediction concerning the performance of two classes or types of channel. Specifically, we hypothesized that channels whose origin lay outside of the laboratory organization would not perform as well as those inside. To test this hypothesis we had to first divide all of our solutions into three mutually exclusive sets (Table 4): (1) solutions that were derived from channels outside the laboratory; (2) solutions derived from channels inside the laboratory only; and (3) some solutions that were derived from a combination of both kinds of channel, or from neither.

TABLE 3 *Sources of Messages Resulting in Higher- and Lower-Rated Solutions. (27 Subproblem Pairs)*

| | PERCENTAGE OF SOLUTIONS SUGGESTED BY MESSAGES RECEIVED THROUGH EACH CHANNEL | | |
|---|---|---|---|
| *Information Channel* | 27 *higher-rated solutions* | 27 *lower-rated solutions* | *Level of statistical significance* |
| literature | 11% | 22% | 0.14% |
| external sources | 7.4 | 26 | 0.03 |
| vendors | 30 | 30 | 0.50 |

| | | | |
|---|---|---|---|
| customer | 56 | 44 | 0.21 |
| technical staff | 22 | 15 | 0.24 |
| company research | 22 | 7.4 | 0.06 |

The percentages in Tables 3 and 5 are distilled from 2 × 2 contingency tables in the following manner:

Taking the first row, literature, as an example, the original contingency table looked like this:

| | Solution rating: high | Solution rating: low | |
|---|---|---|---|
| Number of solutions based at least in part on messages from the literature | 3 | 6 | 3/27 = 11%<br>6/27 = 22% |
| Number of solutions not based on messages from the literature | 24 | 21 | |
| | 27 | 27 | |

TABLE 4 *Sources of Messages Resulting in Higher- and Lower-Rated Solutions (27 subproblem pairs)*

| *Information channel* | *Number of higher-rated solutions suggested* | *Number of lower-rated solutions suggested* |
|---|---|---|
| Channels outside the Laboratory external sources of vendors but not technical staff of company research (ESUV) ∩ (TSUCR) | 6 | 10 |
| Channels inside the Laboratory technical staff or company research but not external sources or vendors (TSUCR) ∩ (ESUV) | 7 | 1 |
| Other Channels both or neither (TSUCR) ∩ (ESUV) or (TSUCR) ∩ (ESUV) | 14 | 16 |

$x^2 = 5.63$, p 0.03

The external channels, we see, generated fewer high-rated solutions than low-rated solutions. The internal channels generated considerably more higher-rated than lower-rated solutions. This is statistically significant and quite strong.

So we see even more clearly that channels within a man's own organization tend to show a better performance than do channels outside. Now, if this were an isolated finding and resulted only from this particular study, I would not draw very strong conclusions from it, but it is something that keeps recurring.

Table 5 shows a summary of the evidence from several studies. First of all, we saw this phenomenon in a number of proposal competitions. We looked at the amount of time people spent with the literature, channels inside the laboratory organization, and channels outside the laboratory organization. We then correlated these with the technical quality of the proposals. We found no correlation between the use of the literature and technical quality. The literature appears consistently in the middle on our ratings; it is mediocre, at best, in its performance.

TABLE 5 *The Impact of the Organization in Technology*

| STUDY | PERFORMANCE RESULTS | |
|---|---|---|
| | *Internal channels* | *External channels* |
| Allen (1964). Twenty-two R and D proposal competitions | Weak positive correlation between use of channel and evaluation of technical quality of proposals. | Significant negative correlation between use of channel and evaluation of technical quality of proposals. |
| Allen (1966 (*a*), 1966 (*b*)). Nine sets of parallel R and D projects (nineteen projects) | Produce messages resulting in significantly more higher-rated solutions and fewer lower-rated solutions than would be expected by chance. | Produce messages resulting in significantly fewer higher-rated solutions and more lower-rated solutions than would be expected by chance. |
| Shilling and Bernard (1964). Scientists in sixty-four laboratories performing biological research | Significant direct correlations between degree to which internal discussion groups are used and seven of eight measures of laboratory performance. | Significant inverse correlations between degree to which paid consultants are used and all of eight measures of laboratory performance. |
| Hagstrom (1965). Seventy-nine scientists in the 'formal physical and biological sciences' | Correlation of channel use with performance positive but about half that found for sources outside the department (but within discipline). | Positive correlation between channel use and performance twice the magnitude of the correlation for channels within the academic department. |

Channels within the laboratory show a mild positive correlation, i.e. a weak positive correlation between their use and the technical evaluation.

Channels outside the laboratory, however, show a very strong inverse or negative correlation. On fourteen of the proposal competitions, in which we found more than one team using outside channels, we found negative correlations with the technical performance of the proposal.

Another study performed by Shilling and Bernard (1964) at George Washington University a couple of years ago in which they studied scientists in sixty-four laboratories performing biological research, showed inverse correlations between eight measures of laboratory performance and the extent to which paid consultants were used. Looking at the extent to which internal discussion groups were used, seven of the eight measures of laboratory performance showed a positive correlation for internal channels and a negative correlation for external channels.

We have one exception here. In a book published a year ago, in which the author studied seventy-nine scientists in the 'formal' physical and biological sciences, he found a very strong positive correlation between the extent to which, as information sources, they used other individuals outside of their own academic department and their rated performance in terms of papers published, and a much weaker, but still positive correlation between performance and the extent to which they communicated within their academic department. The people outside the academic department were within the same discipline as the scientists who were queried.

So this is one piece of evidence that appears conflicting at first. The distinction here, however, is that in the first three studies, the people were all in industrial or government organizations. None of them were university people. In the study by Shilling and Bernard, the university scientists did not use paid consultants, and for the particular part of the study which we have cited, university laboratories were taken out of the sample.

What is happening in the Hagstrom case may well be explained by the fact that the scientists are not in the types of organizations that we have in government and industry. The academic department is not a very important organization for their scientists. The real social system to which they owe their allegiance is the invisible college. We find that as long as they communicate within their invisible college, the communication is efficient.

With the industrial or government laboratory, we see that the organization imposes an impediment to communication. There is an impedance at this organizational boundary that introduces what might be called semantic noise (cf. Bar-Hillel and Carnap, 1953).

How does this come about? I think that over a time organizations develop a coding system, a common way of viewing the world which makes communication within the organization relatively efficient. This shared knowledge and shared coding scheme, a shared way of looking at events and describing them, improves and enhances communication. On the other hand, in the area of communicating across the organizational boundary, you will find that there may be a mis-match in the coding scheme, and this can introduce semantic noise, with a subsequent loss in efficiency.

Just to recapitulate what we have covered up to this point, we find that there is a problem centring around this differential in performance between internal and external channels. We also find that the literature is little used by engineers. The engineers just do not read. They have little contact with the literature.

How do we get at this a little better? One thing that occurred to us was to go back and look at the people who were the internal sources of information, the technical staff, to study them and see where they got their information. It must have come from somewhere. Perhaps these people are able to bridge the organizational boundary and communicate and transform between the two coding schemes. You never know, we might even find some engineers who read! When we look at the amount of contact between the average engineer and his technical literature, the situation is somewhat distressing. But actually in doing this we are looking only at the mean of a statistical distribution and ignoring its variance. It may well be that there are some engineers who do read, and in turn transmit the information that they gain to their colleagues in the organization.

To test this possibility we initiated a second series of studies within R and D laboratories looking at the information flow both within and into the laboratories. I am going to report on the first two of these today. We have since furnished a third and are still in the process of analysis, but it looks as though the results that I will present today are substantiated by the third study.

The first study was done in a small laboratory in the Boston area. We picked a small laboratory because we felt it would be easier to handle. There were thirty-four professionals in this laboratory.

The second study was performed in a forty-eight-man department of a medium size (5,000 employees) aerospace firm, and the third study is of a group of 400 engineers and scientists in a very large (approximately 100,000 employees) aerospace firm.

Our approach to studying communication network structure is very simple. We administered a questionnaire which measured a number of possible sociometric relations which might exist among the members of a laboratory (Table 6).

TABLE 6 *Sociometric Relations Studied*

| | |
|---|---|
| *Socialization* | Name the three or four persons from the laboratory with whom you meet most frequently on social occasions. |
| *Technical discussion* | Name the three or four people with whom you most frequently discuss technical matters. |
| *Special information* | (obtained during the interviews subsequent to the questionnaire)—the source, if any, from which the respondent reported having received special information that influenced him during the course of his last completed project. |
| *Research idea* | To whom in the laboratory would you first express an idea for a new research project. |

Figures 4 and 5 illustrate the pattern of two sets of relationships among the members of laboratory B (the first of the three laboratories described above). In Figure 4, the arrows indicate the direction of social contact choices; Figure 5 shows the pattern of technical discussion choices. The large circle labelled 'non-Ph.D.' in Figure 4 (*b*) represents the Ph.D. to non-Ph.D. choices, and shows very few social contacts in this direction. The circle labelled 'all Ph.D.s combined' in Figure 4 (*a*) gives an indication of which non-Ph.D.s choose into the Ph.D. group. Nine non-Ph.D.s do so, but in only two cases, subjects

24 and 28, is the choice reciprocated. Reciprocal choices are indicated in the diagram by double-headed arrows.

Sociograms are compared for two or more types of choice (e.g. technical discussion and socialization), by comparing the degree of overlap between two actual networks with the amount of overlap which would be expected under chance conditions. Since the number of overlapping choices expected by chance will vary as a function of the number of sociometric choices made by each individual, an expected number of overlaps is computed for each person who returned the questionnaire. This expected number is based on a binomial probability model in which the probabilities of overlap and non-overlap are a function of the number of actual choices made by each individual respondent.

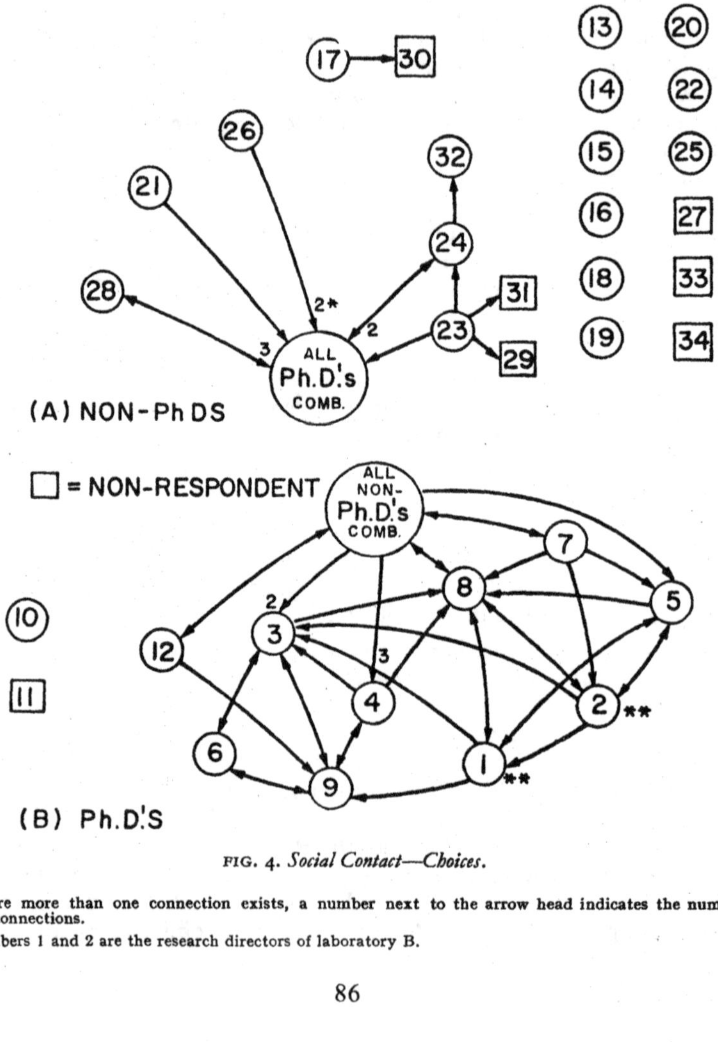


FIG. 4. *Social Contact—Choices.*

* Where more than one connection exists, a number next to the arrow head indicates the number of connections.

** Numbers 1 and 2 are the research directors of laboratory B.

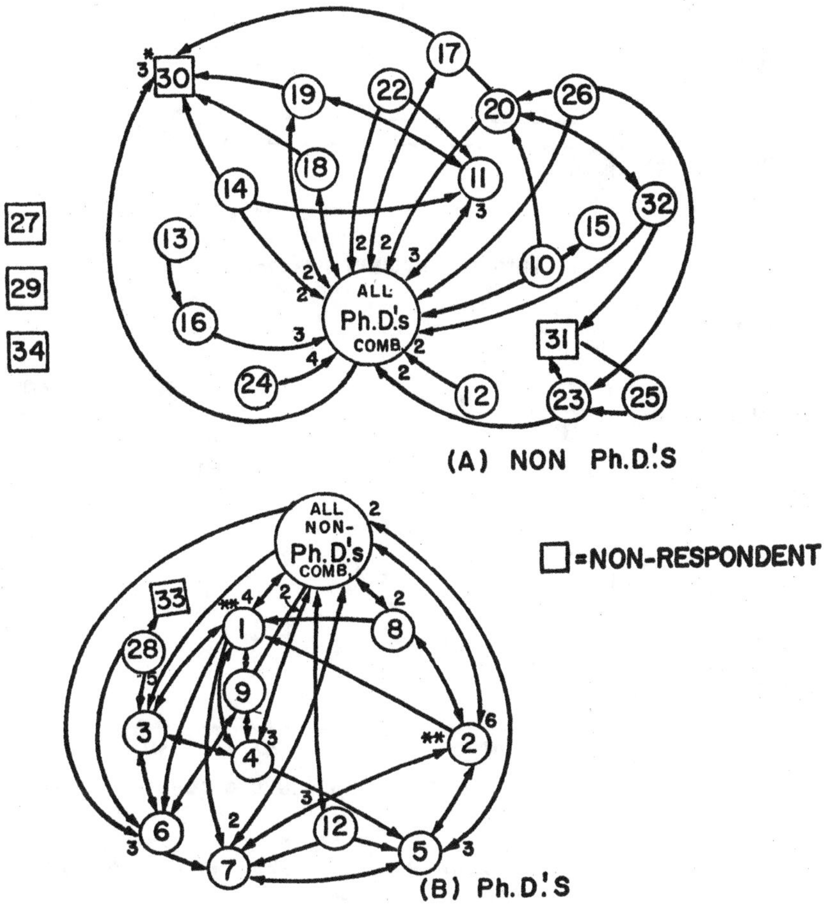


FIG. 5. *Technical Discussion—Choices.*

* Where more than one connection exists, a number next to the arrowhead indicates the number of connections.

** Numbers 1 and 2 are the research directors of laboratory B.

Expected values for the total sample are obtained by summing all of the individual values. The observed distribution of overlaps is then compared with this expected distribution by means of a one-sample Kolmogorov-Smirnov Test.

In Figures 6 through 9, the bar graphs compare the number of overlapping sociometric choices which were observed with the number predicted by the random model we have described.

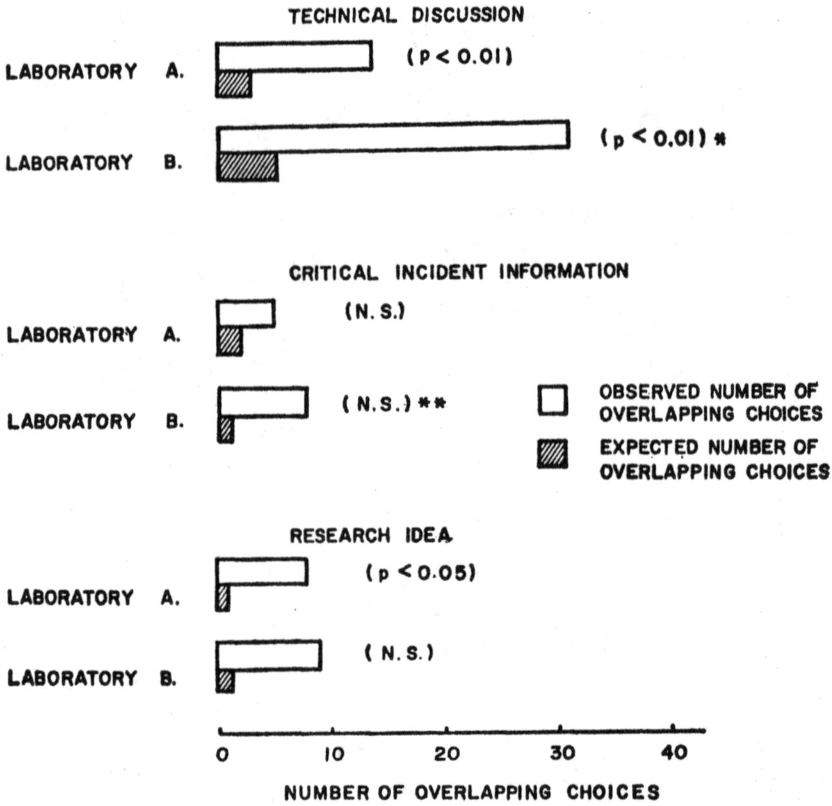


FIG. 6. *Overlap Between the Social Contact Network and Three Technical Information Flow Networks in an R. & D. Laboratory.*

* Determined by Kolmogorov on sample test.

** N.S. = Difference not statistically significant.

Figure 6 presents results of the comparison of three communication-oriented sociometric choices with the social contact choice. There is strong agreement between the selection of individuals for socialization and technical discussion in both laboratories. In laboratory B this is due in part, but not entirely, to the rather tight clique found among the Ph.D.s in the laboratory. As a matter of fact, among the Ph.D.s alone, the amount of overlap is not significantly above chance. The networks for critical incident information and for new research ideas show a decidedly weaker relation to the social contact network in the laboratory.

A question now remains concerning the impact of the formal organizational structure upon communication. In laboratory A, organizational relationships were taken directly from the departmental organization chart. People were considered to be members of common work groups when they reported to the same first line supervisor; the work group included each first line supervisor. In laboratory B, no organization chart was available. Since the organization of that laboratory is quite flexible and revolves around a number of long- and short-term projects, all under one or two research directors, consideration of formal structure is restricted to the *ad hoc* project groups. The respondents in laboratory B were asked to name 'the people whom you consider to be members of your present work group'. Figure 7 shows that while in both laboratories, much of the socialization occurs within work groups, the two networks are somewhat independent and should exert independent influences on information flow. If anything, the formal organization exerts an even stronger influence on communication (Figure 8) than does the informal socialization network. Work group structure influences not only technical discussion but new idea flow as well. This is not at all surprising, especially in laboratory A, where the most frequently named recipient for new research ideas is the naming individual's immediate superior.

Controlling for the effects of the formal organization, by comparing only those social and technical discussion links which are external to each individual's work group (Figure 9) produces a somewhat weaker relationship than that found when work group members were included. The formal organization is, then, the more important, but certainly not the sole determinant of information flow.

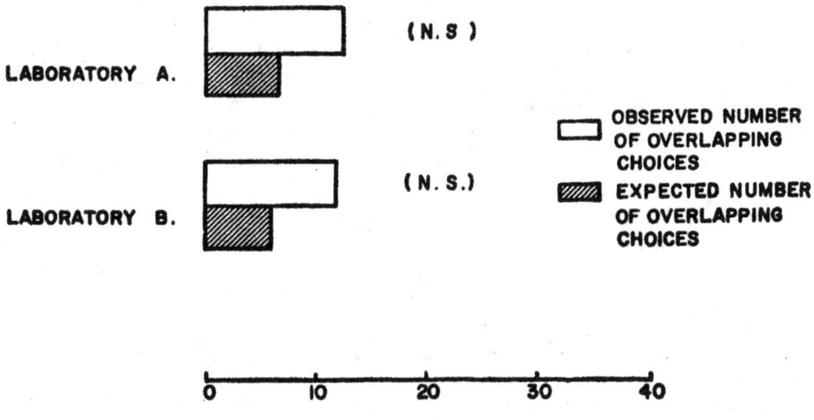


FIG. 7. *Overlap Between Work Group Structure and the Socialization Network in Two R. & D. Laboratories.*

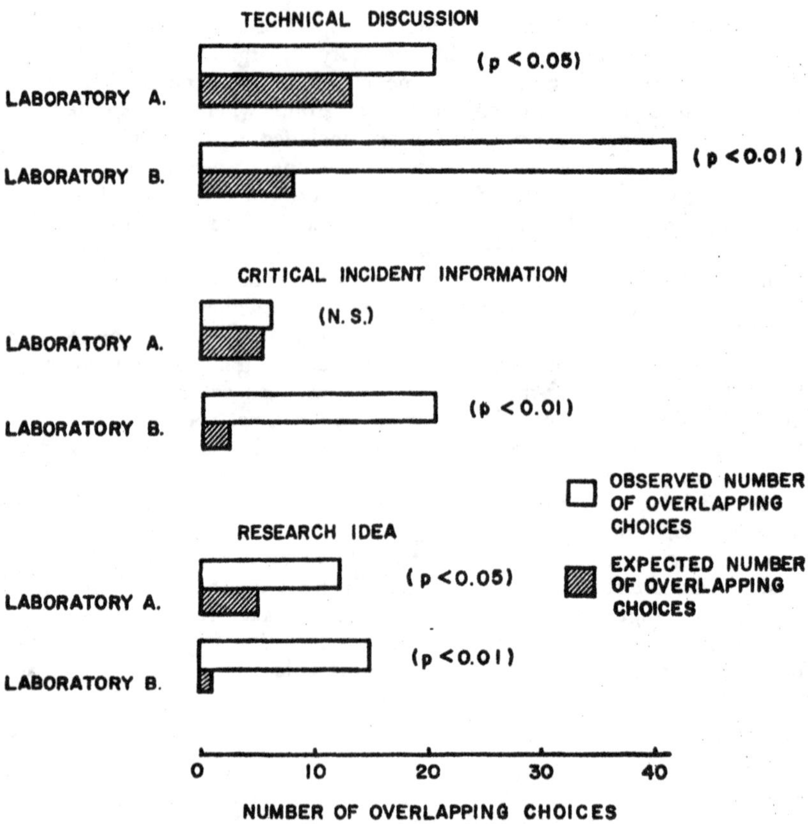


FIG. 8. *Overlap Between Work Group Structure and Three Technical Information Flow Networks in two R. & D. Laboratories.*

Figure 5 shows quite clearly that some individuals are much more highly chosen than others for technical discussion. These highly chosen individuals, or sociometric 'stars' may well be key links between the internal information network of the laboratory and the scientific and technological communities outside of the laboratory. To examine this possibility, the 'stars' in two sociometrically-determined information networks* will be compared with their colleagues to determine whether they display any systematic differences in their information gathering behaviour. Specifically, it is hypothesized that the stars will make greater use of such sources as literature and friends outside of the organization; in other words, that they will act as 'technological gate-keepers'.

* Stars being, in the first case, those people who are highly chosen for technical discussion, and in the second, those who were cited as sources of critical incident information. This analysis was performed in laboratory B only, because although stars existed in laboratory A, nothing is known of their information gathering behaviour. An attempt to go back to this laboratory and obtain data on the information gathering behaviour of stars and a matched sample of non-stars was abortive, as the result of poor co-operation.

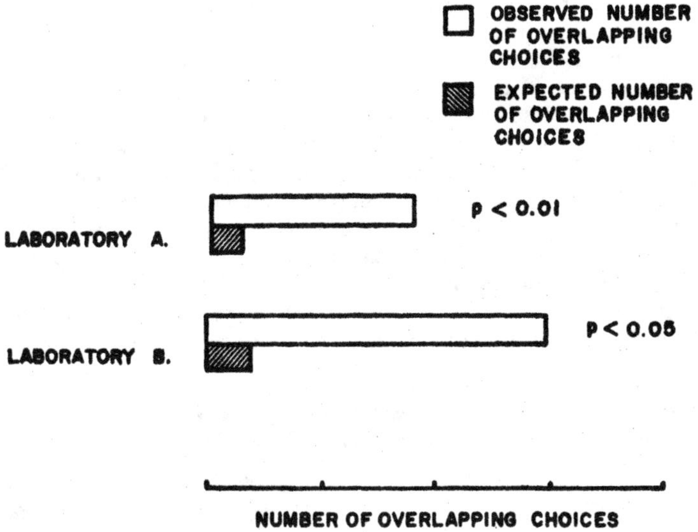


FIG. 9. *Overlap Between the Socialization and Technical Discussion Networks Exclusive of the Work Groups in a R. & D. Laboratory.*

TABLE 7 *Comparison of Communication Behaviour and Technical Discussion Choices*

| | NUMBER OF TIMES CHOSEN ON TECHNICAL DISCUSSION MATRIX | | |
|---|---|---|---|
| *Communication characteristics* | *Six or more* | *Four or fewer* | *Level of statistical significance* |
| Percentage who are above median in using personal friends outside the laboratory as an information source | 64% | 25% | 0.06 |
| Percentage who are above median in using technical specialists within the laboratory as an information source | 50% | 40% | 0.47 |
| Percentage who are above median in total number of technical periodicals read | 88% | 40% | 0.01 |
| Percentage who are above median in number of professional and scientific periodicals read | 75% | 35% | 0.001 |

* Based on Mann-Whitney U-test performed between the two groups.

In considering those members of the laboratory who are highly chosen for technical discussion* (Table 7), we find that the sociometric stars have more exposure to both the literature and to oral sources outside of the laboratory than does the average employee of the laboratory. This contrast is especially pronounced in the case of scientific and professional literature, that is journals published under sponsorship of scientific and engineering societies.

When requested to indicate the source of any information which influenced the course of their most recently completed research projects, twelve people cited seven other individuals within their own laboratory as the source of such information. In Table 8 these seven people are compared in terms of their own information gathering behaviour in the same manner as were the technical discussion stars. We again see the pattern of greater contact with experts outside of the organization and more exposure to the literature.

TABLE 8.—*Comparison of Communication Behaviour and Identification as the Source of Special Technical Information During One of the Laboratory's Projects*

| *Communication characteristics* | *Seven individuals cited* | *Others* | *Level of statistical significance* |
|---|---|---|---|
| Percentage who are above median in using personal friends outside the laboratory as an information source | 67% | 30% | 0.10 |
| Percentage who are above median in using technical specialists within the laboratory as an information source | 57% | 40% | 0.17 |
| Percentage who are above median in total number of technical periodicals read | 100% | 45% | 0.05 |
| Percentage who are above median in number of professional and scientific periodicals read | 86% | 35% | 0.03 |

* Based on a Mann–Whitney U-test performed between the two groups.

Individuals who are highly chosen as sources of potential sources of technical information are considerably different from their colleagues. They have greater contact with technical people outside of the organization and are more exposed to the technical literature. Furthermore, they all rely to very much the same degree upon internal consultation.

There appear then to be two distinct classes of individuals within this laboratory. The majority have few information contacts beyond the bound of the organization. A small minority in contrast have rather extensive outside contacts and furthermore serve as sources of information for their colleagues. There is then evidence of a two-step flow of information in the laboratory studied. Six or seven individuals act as technological gatekeepers for the rest

* Those who receive six or more technical discussion choices (eight respondents). This represents a split at one standard deviation above the mean number of technical discussion choices.

of the laboratory. As further support, it was found that two of these six or seven people were responsible for introducing all four of the 'most important technical ideas' that had been introduced into the organization during the preceding year.

The gatekeepers themselves show some variation in the type of information sources they use. Some rely more upon the literature than upon oral sources, while some operate in reverse. A comparison of relative exposure to technically oriented friends outside of the organization and to the scientific and professional literature shows a slight positive correlation (Kendall Tau = 0.27), but the relation does not approach statistical significance ($p = 0.21$). Quite fortunately, it would appear for the laboratory, the gatekeepers do not all tend the same gate.

In summary, I would like to recapitulate the principal conclusions of the studies. First of all, we find a serious misalignment between the quality of ideas generated through the channel study, and the frequency with which these channels are used by engineers. In other words, we found that people were using channels such as vendors and customers to a greater extent than seemed to be warranted by the evaluation that we were able to obtain. Secondly, the literature is not greatly used by engineers and is mediocre, at very best, in its performance.

The third conclusion is that the better performing groups rely more than the poorer performers upon sources within their laboratory—the technical staff and other company research programmes contrasted with sources outside the laboratory organization.

Our fourth and final conclusion is that a mismatch in information-coding schemes appears to be responsible for the ineffectiveness of communication across the organizational boundaries. The existence of key individuals, whom we call technological gatekeepers, provides a means of surmounting this organizational boundary impedance, and it is up to us, as research managers, to locate these individuals and to make use of them, to encourage them to develop a consultant function. I think very often we discourage this sort of behaviour on the part of potential consultants within our laboratories. We do not reward important consultants. We reward them for work on projects to which they are assigned, and the time they spend in actual consulting work tends to detract from their performance evaluations. I think that management should recognize the internal consultant as a very important contributor in R & D laboratories and align its reward systems accordingly.

## REFERENCES

ALLEN, T. J. *The use of information channels in R and D proposal preparation.* (Working Paper No. 97.) Cambridge, MIT Sloan School of Management, 1964.

ALLEN, T. J. The performance of communication channels in the transfer of technology. *Industrial Management Review*, **8**, 1966, p. 87–98.

ALLEN, T. J. Sources of ideas in parallel R and D projects. In: H. D. Lerner, *ed. Research program effectiveness.* New York: Gordon and Breach, 1966 (b).

HAGSTROM, W. O. *The scientific community.* New York: Basic Books, 1965.

SHILLING, C. W., *and* BERNARD, J. *Informal communication among bioscientists.* Washington, D.C.: George Washington University Biological Sciences Communication Project, 1964. (Report no. 16A.)

BAR-HILLEL, Y., *and* CARNAP, R. Semantic information. *British Journal of Philosophical Science,* **4**, 1953, p. 147–157.

## DISCUSSION

Professor Allen summarized his paper and went on to give a short account of work continued since it was written.

The average engineer, he said, derived only 10 per cent of his information from the literature, though the term average needed qualifying. The rest he obtained from internal and external consultants. It was found that though outside consultants were frequently used their use did not affect performance so much as the use of inside consultants. This was the result of 'semantic noise'; a communication barrier developed between an organization and the world outside, while insiders developed their own 'language'.

It was clear, however, that outside information was used and Professor Allen demonstrated that it came to particular personnel (which he called 'gatekeepers') within the organization, who digested it for their colleagues. Thus, incoming information was subjected to a two-step process.

An attempt had been made to identify gatekeepers, and it was shown that these people tended to be both PhDs who had acquired (through training and status) strong contact with the outside, and had substantial service with the organization, giving rise to strong internal contacts. Other features of gatekeepers and others were put forward including the observation that gatekeepers were also 'high contributors' as measured by patents produced and papers published.

The highly complicated communication network of an organization could, he said, be simplified, and subnetworks could be identified. These involved groups, one of which was a key group and contained a high proportion of gatekeepers. It was seen that there was a high degree of rationality in an informal communication system.

Professor Allen closed with an account of some work which showed that the law of least effort was applied by engineers in their choice of information sources. Of the three criteria, 'perceived accessibility' 'perceived ease of use' and 'perceived technical quality', the first was most important, the second minimal, and the third negligible.

Mr J. Farradane (City University) said it had long been known that engineers did not read and that there were gatekeepers. He was, however, disturbed to think that a pecking order existed where PhDs talked only to each other. He further commented that whereas Professor Allen talked of the individual going to the information service, the good information service went to the individual.

Professor Allen agreed that status was an important factor in communications: higher groups tended to be more cohesive. He thought that PhDs should be encouraged to communicate downwards.

Dr W. E. Batten (ICI) asked whether 'technical quality' was as perceived by the 'victim of the moment' or by the investigator. If the former, would it not automatically rank as the highest factor?

Professor Allen replied that, surprising as it seemed, the parameter in question was as perceived by the subject.

Mr J. M. Myers (SIRA) asked whether there was any observed correlation between use of external consultants and possession of in-house specialists.

Professor Allen replied that there was. An organization faced with a problem calling for specialist help that it did not itself possess went outside. However, it had been observed that large organizations also went outside even though they had the relevant specialists. This was because of ignorance of the existence of inside specialists and the difficulty of approaching the relevant person within the organization.

D. E. Bagley (HERTIS) asked whether gatekeepers were better informed about sources of information or whether they possessed particular personality traits. If the former, information use should be better taught at universities.

Professor Allen agreed that it should be possible to 'grow' gatekeepers. As he had shown, PhDs were more used to contact with both the literature and other specialists. One personality test had been tried, but without positive results.

Mr Dickson (Ealing Technical College) asked whether any gatekeepers in the study had been identified as librarians, and whether librarians should be trained in social science methodology.

Professor Allen replied that no gatekeepers were librarians, but thought there was certainly a gap that could be filled by librarians with specialist knowledge. For example, it would be advantageous if information technologists could advise on the design and architecture of R & D buildings.

# Factors Influencing the Success of Applied Research[1]

EDWARD M. GLASER *Human Interaction Research Institute, Los Angeles*[2]
SAMUEL H. TAYLOR *University of Southern California*[3]

Applied research projects under National Institute of Mental Health sponsorship are directed toward a search for new knowledge that can help solve problems encountered in meeting the mental health needs of society. The expectation is implicit that investigators, many of whom are more experienced in providing services than in carrying out research, will be capable of pursuing their project objectives in a scientific manner. It also is expected that the new knowledge, insights, and techniques that are produced will be applied in action for the benefit of people, or will be cross-validated through further demonstration and evaluation.

To date, there has been relatively little systematic study to determine the degree to which these expectations are, in fact, being realized. There is reason to believe that the scientific aims of projects sometimes have been outstripped by the need to provide services through the projects (Fairweather, 1967), with a consequent softening or vitiating of project conclusions. There also is reason to believe that even projects which report seemingly promising findings regarding the value of new methods or knowledge can adduce little evidence of the application of those findings elsewhere (Halpert, 1966).

Addressing itself to this problem, in 1967 the Applied Research Branch (ARB) of the National Institute of Mental Health (NIMH) conducted a program analysis study and rating of all projects funded by them that terminated within a specific 12-month period. Their purpose was to discover variables that may have been associated with *the degree of* project success. Success meant (*a*) that the project was directed to the original objectives or appropriate modifications thereof; (*b*) that the results were embodied in a clear and cogent report, complete and candid enough to enable replication by others; and (*c*) that the findings were disseminated adequately.

The study reported in this article, carried out by the Human Interaction Research Institute (HIRI), of which the authors are associates, presents the results of an intensive follow-up program conducted on 10 projects selected and rated by ARB; 5 were rated as very high and 5 were rated as relatively low in outcome, the ratings of high and low being determined by the above-enumerated criteria for success. The purpose of the HIRI study was to learn the more subtle and complex reasons underlying success or failure.

Seven of the 10 projects were either located within existing direct-service organizations or conducted their major data-collecting efforts in cooperation with such service organizations. The other three projects were more independent, either serving a nationwide constituency or being located within a university. However, even these projects were frequently in close contact with direct-service organizations in the conduct of their research. This is relevant because a crucial factor in the investigation was an effort to assess the various relationships and interactions between researchers and practitioners in applied mental health research.

[1] This study was carried out under National Institute of Mental Health Contract 43-67-1365. It was awarded first prize "for superior research related to psychological consultation" by the Division of Consulting Psychology at the 1972 APA Convention.

[2] Requests for reprints should be sent to Edward M. Glaser, Human Interaction Research Institute, 10889 Wilshire Boulevard, Los Angeles, California 90024.

[3] Taylor is associated with the School of Social Work at USC. He is also a Research Associate at the Human Interaction Research Institute, Los Angeles.

Although the authors necessarily examined the researcher–practitioner relationship factor retrospectively, particular attention was focused on tracing the quantity and quality of that interaction throughout the life cycle of each project studied.

The HIRI investigators had access to all NIMH documents related to each project, including the original grant application, comments of the Review Committee, and progress reports or other project publications. The principal research instrument for this study was a comprehensive interview schedule administered to key people associated with each project. These included the principal investigator, other staff members, administrators, and persons who would be most likely to be utilizers of the findings of the research project. This last-named category, referred to as practitioner-utilizers, was included because each of the 10 selected projects either alluded to or specifically identified in its grant application specific organizations or general categories of professionals who were proximate potential consumers of the project's findings.

To facilitate the identification and analysis of significant factors that influence applied research, the life cycle of a project was divided into six stages: (1) the *idea* that began the process; (2) the original *design* of the project, including revisions; (3) overall *funding* of the project; (4) the actual conduct of the *research;* (5) the *findings* of the research and their *dissemination;* and (6) actual or planned *use* of the findings by the agency or by others. For each stage, the primary focus of the inquiry was, What was done? What helped? What hindered or impeded progress?

To check on the accuracy of interviewer recording, a number of interviews were conducted by two interviewers instead of one, and their notations were checked against each other. Examination of the data revealed a high degree of concurrence. Further, two documents were prepared on each project. An objective question-by-question listing indicated the responses of principal investigators, administrators, and practitioners to facilitate a comparison and to determine what in all likelihood actually transpired at each stage within each project. A narrative was then prepared to provide a comprehensive and continuously linked story of the project's life cycle, with ample attention to central events and situations. All narratives and interviewers' records were then critically reviewed by both project staff and HIRI consultants with regard to the accuracy of the recorded responses and the interpretation of them (Williams, 1968).

This process facilitated the identification of similarities and differences (*a*) within each project, (*b*) among the projects, and (*c*) according to the category of respondent (principal investigators, administrators, practitioner-utilizers) among the projects. The key findings were organized with reference to the six stages in the life cycles of the applied research projects examined. These findings were as follows.

### *Idea*

Successful projects displayed a more receptive atmosphere and a more energetic solicitation of the reactions and contributions of other persons (administrators, practitioner-utilizers, experts, researchers, members of advisory groups) during the early idea stage than did the less successful projects. This early involvement appeared to enlist continuing support for the venture. The research idea was more likely to be directly relevant to pertinent practice issues of concern to the host agency in successful projects than in less successful ones.

Specifically, in the more successful projects the researchers had contacted an impressive number of experts as well as administrators and practitioners, and they could quickly document who had contributed particular ideas or refinements. Successful researchers appeared to have conducted more exhaustive explorations of both the theoretical and practical dimensions of their respective areas and transmitted a quality of genuine interest to other persons which served to elicit active involvement. In constrast, less successful researchers relied more on a handful of experts and exposed their early ideas to administrators, practitioners, and advisory groups more for the purpose of obtaining endorsement or access to potential sources of data rather than for the purpose of inviting critique.

By way of illustration, the principal investigator of a less successful project gained approval from the administrator of a community agency to use its clients in the study, but apart from the initial discussion there was no follow-up or involvement. When the project received funding, the principal investigator reestablished contact, but the community agency then reneged, citing costs and the fact that the staff was already overworked. Launching of the study was delayed, and damaging compromises were made in the rush to obtain another data resource. While the agency's reasons may have been legitimate, subsequent interviewing uncovered the fact that the community agency had been unclear regarding the purpose of the research (but were "impressed" by the researcher's status and reputation), and the agency's staff had little or no interest or investment in the topic.

In a more successful project, the principal investigator met with both the administration and the staff of a community agency that was to cooperate by providing data. In the meetings with the staff several revisions were suggested, and at subsequent meetings the principal investigator discussed which of the suggestions were to be adopted and which were not—and why. Further, it was agreed that one question that was of vital concern to the staff (but not to the principal investigator) would be included in the data-collection procedure. Regular two-way communication continued over the months, and although the agency experienced a funding cutback, the staff continued to collect data despite the fact that this entailed overtime without monetary compensation.

### *Design*

Successful projects usually were designed and substantially written by the principal investigator who was often a highly motivated person who developed a "network" for two-way communication in the earlier idea stages. All projects reported some degree of involvement with other people during the design-formulation phase; the successful projects evidenced a more dynamic, issue-laden interaction which frequently led to conflict and the need for revisions and compromise. Successful projects continued their early and active contacts with many other persons and groups and became aware of complexities and submerged obstacles when they received feedback from those with whom they had shared working drafts of the proposals. In this way they could make appropriate modifications at an early stage in the project life cycle, rather than being caught off-base by unanticipated problems when the research was under way. Further, the process of developing two-way communication and resolving conflict promoted the development of a coping capacity that was very valuable when problems were encountered in later stages.

One might conjecture that less successful projects would have reported more conflict and "disabling" revisions of the design prior to submission for funding, yet this was not the case. A respondent who was involved with an outstandingly successful project that had a major impact in its field reported:

> Because of [X's] policy of sending copies of letters and memos to everyone, including digests in the [newsletter], there was hell to pay when the first "rough" came out. . . .
>
> "They" were loaded for bear, tempers were lost and a lot of "blood" was spilled in those sessions . . . but they were able to compromise and find a middle ground because [X] had always leveled with them . . . kept them fully informed . . . and they trusted him and felt he understood and respected how *they* felt. Modifications were made and both sides adopted a wait-and-see policy.

In contrast, the less successful projects were comparatively calm and uneventful. One person associated with a less successful project seemed to focus the issue when he thought back over his various research experiences and commented:

> When a group of people or a team are truly involved and participating . . . they look ahead and conceive of their role in time and space in such a manner that includes what they see themselves doing in relation to the project. They usually attempt to interject their own pet theories and questions. . . . At the very least there's usually a rather heated discussion to work out the details, whether they be of an administrative nature or concern the ideas embodied in the design. . . . In our project *this did not happen!*

In other words, a clear and well-written study design in itself may be a virtue of limited value if this clarity is not linked to the interests and concerns of people in the research environment.[4] An untroubled and superficially harmonious beginning may be a poor augury rather than a good one. It may be that people do not know nor care enough to raise issues during the early stages.

---

[4] Each project examined in this investigation had survived the critical scrutiny of NIMH review committees; therefore, the authors' emphasis related to the extent to which each project's inquiry or demonstration was focused on issues that were of interest or concern to the agency and its personnel who were involved with the project in one way or another.

### *Funding*

All research projects reported concern about the availability and adequacy of funds, and all reported some modification in their grant applications, either in anticipation of a funding organization's particular interests or at the suggestion of an agent of the funding organization. Successful projects were more likely than less successful ones to have their NIMH grant augmented by direct financial or service contributions from host agencies.

There did not appear to be a direct association between the outcome of the project and the occurrence of an NIMH site visit, although projects that had site visits reported that the visitors' questions had been useful. However, successful projects more frequently availed themselves of the consultative services of their respective NIMH regional offices before or during the process of applying for funds.

Those projects that had the opportunity to start up with modest pilot studies reported that the pilot studies served to test out the workability of the design, to increase awareness of potential problems, to provide time for tooling up and recruiting personnel, and to aid in the future preparation of a realistic project budget.

### *Research*

Successful projects characteristically solicited consultation, involvement, and expertise from many different sources while their studies were under way. The project's own team members were encouraged to question and challenge all issues and procedures during the course of the research. These projects were not only receptive to such inputs, but also acknowledged their value and used them where appropriate. In contrast, less successful projects tended to discount, avoid, and discourage the suggestions and critical reactions of other persons; consequently, administrators and practitioners in the host or participating agencies often reacted negatively when called on for "cooperation" or special assistance when the project encountered problems.

Characteristic of the successful projects was the involvement of a principal investigator who had the requisite time and commitment to develop and maintain channels of two-way communication during the course of the research. Usually this required a full-time or at least substantial time investment rather than just a small part-time supervisory role. Further, problems or obstacles encountered by the project were identified at an early point and coped with before they got out of hand and seriously affected the outcome.

A recurrent challenge in both the successful and the less successful projects was maintaining the delicate equilibrium between a research orientation and the operational climate of the service agency. And at times all projects felt that they were the targets of overt or covert attempts at sabotage (Bergen, 1965). Practitioners in cooperating and host agencies often registered resentment about the special status (including salary differential) of the research staff; about being treated as lesser colleagues; about scanty communications concerning the progress and findings of the research (including failure to invite their questions and reactions); and about the abrupt departure of the principal investigator after his data were collected, without feedback or any other *quid pro quo* to the cooperating staff. Successful projects manifested more skill in dealing with many of the foregoing problems through small group discussions, through use of consultants, and, perhaps more important, through allocating enough time and energy to understand and cope with some of the less apparent aspects of the situation. It was true to some degree of all projects, however, that at times principal investigators were so preoccupied with the challenges posed by their own research that they were unable to use the wider perspectives that might have resolved certain problems.

A critical distinction between successful and less successful projects was the behavior of the principal investigators. Successful principal investigators negotiated differences and attempted to clear up misunderstandings with persons who were hostile or uncooperative. Members of the research team were strongly discouraged from adopting "we versus they" attitudes. In contrast, less successful projects became even more insular and developed a form of "tunnel vision" wherein the researcher could only see his own involvement in vital research and failed to see the other person's situation or consider possible alternative courses of action. Greater reliance was placed on pressuring top administration to mandate staff and middle management cooperation[5] (which often aggravated the situation) rather than utilizing face-to-face discussion and airing of differences at the points of conflict.

### *Development and Dissemination of Findings*

The key personnel from all projects reported observable findings that were of value to the field, and none felt that there had been any attempt by board or administration to suppress findings, even when they were controversial. However, in their judgment no project achieved optimum dissemination, chiefly because no formal arrangements had been made for this phase of the research. Even so, the range was substantial, since projects rated as more successful had achieved impressive levels of dissemination in contrast to those projects rated as less successful.[6] For example, all of the successful projects had published at least several journal articles, plus monographs, papers, and special reports, were active in workshops and institutes, and had ongoing contacts with interested agencies and researchers. Several of the successful projects each had published and recorded over 100 different publications and presentations. In response to the HIRI interviewer's questions about the findings and their dissemination, one respondent remarked somewhat reflectively:

> You know, just the questions you've asked make me painfully aware of what has *not* been done to report these findings to the groups who could use them. I'm behind schedule now, and I'll do the NIMH final report and then some journal articles, but I know I'll not get around to the rest of what should be done. I'm pressed for time as it is. . . . My intentions were good . . . why I can rattle off dozens of agencies who would want this information right now, but by the time I get around to it, it may not be as fresh and vital as it is now. Next time . . . .

The successful projects were more active and aggressive than the less successful ones in making use of conventional outlets for dissemination (journal publication, etc.) but, judging from the responses of administrators and practitioners, these channels of dissemination were only moderately effective. Institutes, workshops, and presentations that encouraged *two-way* discussion and clarification were identified as preferred methods of dissemination, and many of the respondents felt that such approaches would have been used more extensively if they had been facilitated by special financial and consultative support. This factor has been further substantiated by subsequent studies carried out by our organization in the field of research utilization (Glaser & Ross, 1971).

In those instances in which a project did not report or disseminate findings, this deficit could be attributed to one or more of the following possible reasons: (*a*) there were no findings; (*b*) there were potential findings, but the researchers resorted to what might have been unwarranted delays (such as interminable data collection) in formulating and presenting them; (*c*) there were innovative findings, but they were controversial, irrelevant, ambiguous, or of dubious (or at least undemonstrated) potential benefit.

The successful projects reported that they were both prodded and solicited by involved persons in their ongoing network of communications to publish and make presentations regarding their findings. It was clear that the less successful projects, more insular throughout their life cycle, did not have such an informed and encouraging constituency.

### *Utilization*

Projects rated as successful were able to enumerate and identify more instances in which their research findings were utilized by practitioners and researchers than were the less successful projects, but dissemination was one of the criteria for designating the successful projects. There was some reluctance on the part of many principal investigators to take the initiative in promoting the utilization of their findings; some felt that such activity was unprofessional.

Administrators generally reported that they tended to endorse or reject implementation, but ultimately it was the practitioners who determined whether the findings would be incorporated into agency practice, or abandoned. If the practitioners in the host agency were actively involved in the development of the project, if they had good

[5] While top administration often tried to help, less successful projects which had not at earlier stages developed open interactive relationships nor encouraged involvement found that administrators keenly resented the inference that agency staff were the "cause" of project problems.

[6] Obviously, an inescapable element of circularity is built into this achievement as reported here, due to the fact that dissemination of findings was one of the NIMH study's classification criteria for success.

rapport with the research team and did not feel exploited, if their responses to the developing findings were sought and heeded, then there was greater likelihood that they would use the findings in their practice and that this endorsement also would be instrumental in promoting use of the findings in comparable agencies elsewhere.

The concept of effective utilization need not mean acceptance or adoption of a total package. Typically, particular components or aspects of the findings were used by consumer agencies according to agency needs. The same open two-way approach which characterized effective dissemination also contributed to more widespread utilization, through special institutes, workshops, and other devices that permit clarifying of questions and dispelling of misgivings. Researchers, administrators, and practitioners all agreed that insufficient time, money, and skill had been allocated to utilization efforts. In the author's opinion, promising research projects would benefit by having a dissemination-utilization expert on the research team (or available for consultation) from the very beginning to guide planning for dissemination of results and to promote linkage with potential consumer groups. Further facilitation would be provided if the funding agency included in the contract the financial support required for adequate dissemination (Glaser, 1972).

• • •

Generalizing from the foregoing findings, the authors formulated the following profiles of the successful project and the less successful project.

### *The Successful Project*

The successful project was characterized by high communication, awareness, and involvement with persons and groups within and outside the immediate environment from its earliest moments. The project staff made efforts to induce interest and cooperation from a wide group of supporters and potential users. Interaction and communication proceeded at a high rate through both formal and informal channels. Potential obstacles were shared concerns. The resolution processes often provided unanticipated benefit and strengthened the project. The development and maintenance of a network of communication took time and effort, but observable rewards justified the expenditure.

The research was designed by the principal investigator, who devoted full time to the project. The host agency indicated its commitment by contributions of services and supplementary funds. The focus of the research was aimed at a felt need which enjoyed a shared interest from other people. *Ipso facto,* therefore, the product was readily marketable. Potential consumers were involved and informed. They encouraged early efforts at dissemination of findings and were ready to consider implications for utilization.

Throughout the life of the project there was ample evidence of adequate project structure (i.e., committees, liaison, linkage). There was leadership capability, with a consensus among those involved regarding priority of goals. Dissemination was planned for, and a higher level of utilization was achieved. The communication component paid off again and again: when severe problems were encountered by successful projects, their base of involved supporters was sufficient to cope with the problems.

### *The Less Successful Project*

While there was some interaction and internal communication, there was little sustained effort to open up the process to others. Communication was sporadic, and involvement was limited to a small nucleus. The problem to be investigated may well have appealed to a constituency of interactors, but involvement was not welcomed. In fact, there was a pervasive and discernible quality of insularity. Administrators and practitioners resented being excluded.

Characterized by calm during the idea, design, and funding stages (in contrast to the successful projects which were dynamic and laden with conflict), these projects erupted soon after the research stage began. Problems developed suddenly and often were unanticipated. Coping efforts were hindered by the fact that part-time principal investigators did not have the time to devote to resolution efforts. Nor did they have an invested group of supporters to help and share responsibility. Each problem reverberated throughout the project, causing extensive shock. Plans were delayed or abandoned enroute. Despite the problems, there were successful findings worth reporting, but there was insufficient time for reports and little "push" comparable to the encouragement received by successful projects.

## *Conclusion*

It is acknowledged that practitioners and researchers may have different value systems, orientations, and styles of thinking. The training, professional goals, and organizationally assigned roles of the participants may be so vastly different or even antagonistic that it is difficult to define a common ground for meaningful dialogue. It is suggested that the absence of or inability to obtain involvement of others will impede or prevent the achievement of a successful research outcome regardless of the expertise of the researcher. The likelihood of such a result is increased by the degree that the researcher must depend on the cooperation of others in the organization who do not share the research mission (Wolkon, 1971). Since the very reason for conducting research in a practice setting usually implies the need for such cooperation and such a unique vantage point for the inquiry, this is a serious problem which goes to the heart of applied research.

Anyone engaged in applied research within or in cooperation with an agency for the purpose of obtaining a type or quality of data not readily obtainable elsewhere is of necessity thrown into a position of administrative responsibility related to the structure of that agency. Therefore, it is incumbent upon the researcher to understand and use appropriate organization and management theory and practice in relations with the agency if he wishes to be able to carry out the research and obtain an optimal level of utilization of findings. He should be prepared to communicate with various groups beyond those most proximate to the project itself. He should understand how bureaucracies function. He should be ready to utilize communication theory and practice to overcome obstacles and facilitate the development of an open, interactive climate (Shyne, 1969).

If the researcher is not prepared, either by personal disposition or knowledge, he would do well to engage someone as a part of the research team who can undertake these tasks. These tasks appear to be essential in conducting applied research in a service setting, as opposed to carrying out solo research in a library or working in a comparatively controlled laboratory situation.

It is recognized that the preceding comments may discourage some researchers who prefer to devote their energies to the research process exclusively rather than be distracted by other responsibilities. However, concern for the organizational environment and its functioning is relevant. This study indicates that ignoring it serves to reduce substantially a project's chances for success. This does not suggest that the researcher must function as a public relations expert; it does imply that he ought to understand and be ready to relate competently to the organizational systems with which he works. Very possibly, researchers who are unsure about their competence in relating effectively to a service organization should consider obtaining consultation. Further, funding organizations such as NIMH and others might consider trial programs wherein information dissemination consultants are made available to projects from their inception in an effort to determine if this brings about improved outcomes as well as better diffusion and utilization results.

### REFERENCES


Bergen, B. Professional communities and the evaluation of demonstration projects in community mental health. *American Journal of Public Health*, 1965, **55**, 1057–1066.

Fairweather, G. *Methods for experimental social innovation*. New York: Wiley, 1967.

Glaser, E. M. The diffusion and utilization of existing knowledge. Paper presented at the meeting of the Western Psychological Association, Portland, Oregon, April 1972.

Glaser, E. M., & Ross, H. L. *Increasing the utilization of applied research results*. (Final report, Grant 5R12 MH09250-2) Washington, D.C.: National Institute of Mental Health, United States Department of Health, Education, and Welfare, 1971.

Halpert, H. Communications as a basic tool in promoting utilization of research findings. *Community Mental Health Journal*, 1966, **2**, 231–232.

Shyne, A. Warm bodies and lively minds: Recruiting and retaining research staff. *Social Work*, 1969, **14**, 107–113.

Williams, J., Jr. Interviewer role performance: A further note on bias in the information interview. *Public Opinion Quarterly*, 1968, **32**, 287–294.

Wolkon, G. Consent, cooperation and control in rehabilitation research. In R. O'Toole (Ed.), *The organization, management and tactics of social research*. Cambridge, Mass.: Schenkman, 1971.

*Reprinted from* ASLIB Proceedings, *Vol. 27, No. 5, 1975*

# Patterns of information flow during the innovation process*

*Roy Rothwell*

**Science Policy Research Unit, University of Sussex**

## 1 Introduction

THERE IS A COMPREHENSIVE and growing body of empirical evidence, gathered through retrospective studies of innovation attempts, which demonstrates clearly that good communications, with the consequent efficient flow of information both within the innovating organization and between the organization and its environment, is a prime requisite for innovative success. [1,2] The relative importance of literature and other formal sources of information utilized during innovation, in relation to informal interpersonal sources will be mentioned only briefly since this topic has been discussed at some length elsewhere.[3]† This paper represents an attempt to analyse some of the available empirical data which relate to the information seeking habits of innovators in their search for scientific and technological information. It traces the patterns of search through the various phases of the innovation process, discusses the different information seeking habits of scientists and technologists, describe the effect of firm size on the pattern of information search and highlights the necessity of matching the degree of complexity of a message to the level of sophistication of its recipient. Finally it discusses the significance of these findings to those whose task is the management of innovation.

## 2 Patterns of information flow during innovation

It can be seen from Figure 1 that there are three main sub-processes contained within the overall innovation process: idea generation, problem solving and implementation and diffusion. Most of the scientific and technological information requirements for the innovation will be met during the first two of these sub-processes and this section considers the sources of ideas utilized during idea generation and those used in problem solving, and establishes differences between the two.

### 2.1 *Sources of ideas leading to innovation*

In this section data relating to the sources of ideas which actually led to the initiation of new developments is presented.

* The definition of innovation employed here is: 'the technical production and commercial steps which lead to the marketing of a new product, or the first commercial use of a new process or equipment'. A simple model of the innovation process is given in Figure 1.

† The great majority of studies suggest, in fact, that the bulk of information utilized during innovation is 'person embodied' rather than transmitted via the printed word.

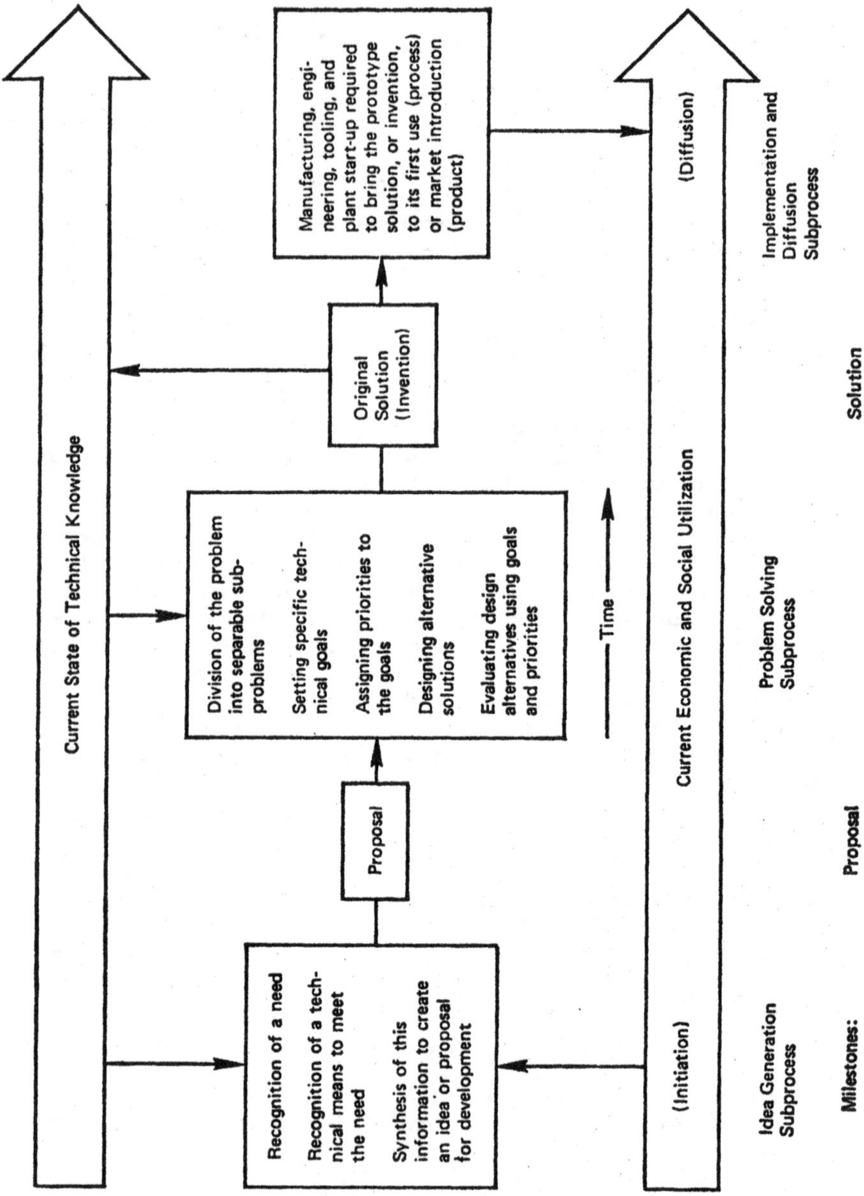


FIG. 1: *The process of technical innovation*

Reproduced from J. M. Utterback, 'The process of innovation, a study of the origination and development of ideas from new scientific instruments', *IEEE Transactions on Engineering Management*, EM–18, 1971, p. 124.

### 2.1.1 *Myers and Marquis*[4]

Myers and Marquis studied 567 successful innovations in the U.S.A. which were spread over a number of industries (railroads, railroad suppliers, computer manufacturers, computer suppliers and housing suppliers). They identified 153 major inputs from sources which unambiguously evoked the basic idea for the innovation. The institutional sources of these ideas were as follows:

| | |
|---|---|
| 59.5% | private industrial organizations, including the innovator |
| 15.3% | vendor or potential supplier |
| 3.3% | government agencies |
| 20.9% | unknown |

### 2.1.2 *Project SAPPHO*[5]

Project SAPPHO studied a total of 86 innovations, 43 successful, 43 unsuccessful, in two industries: chemical processes and scientific instruments. (There was no correlation between the source of an idea and either success or failure.) The sample was international.

The 86 ideas that stimulated innovation derived from the following sources:

| | | *Externally originated ideas as a percentage of all externally originated ideas* |
|---|---|---|
| 53% | in-house | — |
| 18.5% | private industry | 39% |
| 10% | universities | 22% |
| 5% | individuals | 11% |
| 13.5% | government agencies | 28% |

### 2.1.3 *Bolton Committee of Inquiry on Small Firms*[6]

This was a study which sought the contribution to post-war innovations in the U.K. from firms of different sizes. The study listed the sources of ideas which led to initiation of 1,667 important successful innovations in manufacturing industry.

The distribution of ideas, by source, was found to be as follows, aggregated for firms of all sizes:

| | |
|---|---|
| 53.7% | in-house |
| 2.53% | university |
| 6.88% | government agencies |
| 4.2% | research associations |
| 17.6% | private industry |
| 13.74% | abroad |
| 1.25% | private individuals |

### 2.2 *Sources of ideas utilized during problem solving*

In their section the sources of ideas which were used in the solution to problems encountered during the course of the innovation will be listed.

2.2.1 *Myers and Marquis*

Myers and Marquis identified 414 major information inputs in their investigation which expedited the solution to an important problem encountered during innovation. The sources were as follows:

| | |
|---|---|
| 46% | private industry, including the innovator |
| 14.3% | vendor or potential supplier |
| 3.0% | government agencies |
| 36.7% | unknown |

2.2.2 *Project SAPPHO*

Firms utilized 53 external agencies as sources of scientific and technical information which was used during the innovation:

| | |
|---|---|
| 41% | private industry |
| 19% | universities |
| 4% | individuals |
| 22% | government agencies |
| 4% | research associations |

2.2.3 *Langrish*

Langrish studied 82 innovations in the U.K., which gained the Queen's Award to Industry for Innovation. The sources of 102 external ideas made use of in 51 of the innovations were identified:

| | | |
|---|---|---|
| 64% | private industry | (23% U.K., 26% U.S.A., 15% other) |
| 21% | government | (17% U.K., 2% U.S.A., 2% other) |
| 10% | university | (7% U.K., 0% U.S.A., 3% other) |
| 7% | Second World War effort | |

A number of conclusions regarding industrial innovation can be drawn from the above data:

(a) private industry plays the major information providing role during project initiation and problem solving in both the U.K. and the U.S.A.

(b) government agencies appear to play a more significant role in the U.K. than in the U.S.A. in providing both idea generation and problem solving information. It is possible that this reflects the higher level of Government funding of private industry R & D in the U.S.A. compared with the U.K. resulting in greater in-house R & D capability on the part of American firms.*

(c) according to Myers and Marquis and project SAPPHO there exist remarkable similarities between the institutional sources of ideas used in idea generation and those used during problem solving.

**3 In-house vs external sources**

It was seen in the preceding section that similarities exist between the ***institutional*** sources of ideas which result in new development projects and those which are utilized during problem solving. However, if one classifies the source

* In 1969/70 Government in the U.K. funded about 30% of the total expenditure on R & D in private industry. An estimate in the U.S.A. put the Federal Government share in 1973 at 40%. Sources: Studies in Official Stats. No. 21 'R & D Expenditures', HMSO, 1973. 'National Patterns of R & D Resources' NSF. 74-304 Washington, U.S.A.

of an idea as simply 'in-house' or 'external', then a very definite pattern emerges.

3.1 *Myers and Marquis*

| *153 Project initiation ideas* | *414 Problem solving ideas* |
|---|---|
| 39% Internal | 60% Internal |
| 50% External | 29% External |
| 11% Multi-channels | 11% Multi-channels |

3.2 *Utterback*[8]

Utterback studied the different communication events associated with the initiation and subsequent development of 32 award winning scientific instrument innovations in the U.S.A. The following pattern was observed:

| *Project stimulating inputs (Idea generation)* | *Other inputs prior to funding (Project definition)* | *Inputs following funding (Problem solving)* |
|---|---|---|
| Internal 34% | 47.8% | 64.4% |
| External 66% | 52.2% | 35.6% |

Unfortunately no comparable data exists from the SAPPHO and Bolton Committee studies concerning the relative percentages of problem solving ideas which arise in-house and those which arise external to the innovating organization. However, both studies show that approximately half of the inputs which lead to the initiation of new projects arise internally and half externally (although the Bolton Committee data suggests that this fraction is a function of firm size). Nevertheless, there is a clear indication from the above two studies (Myers and Marquis and Utterback) that the information seeking behaviour of scientists and technologists depends on the stage of the innovation process at which information is being sought. Since many innovations are stimulated by the recognition of a definite need (evidence suggests that for *successful* innovations the fraction is about three-quarters of the total), and since much of the 'new science' or 'new technology' which stimulates the other innovations will be developed outside any one innovating organization, often within universities and government laboratories, and will therefore generally be well known it is not, perhaps, altogether surprising that the majority of ideas leading to the initiation of new projects originate externally to the innovating organization. Furthermore, since one might expect the search for problem solving information to proceed from easily accessible sources to more difficult ones—through literature and memory, through interaction with colleagues, through experimentation and finally through external search—it is not altogether unexpected that most problem solving information is found in-house.

Myers and Marquis further studied the information *channels* used during idea generation and those employed in problem solving. In idea generation personal contact accounted for 34% of the ideas, 4% inside the firm and 30% external to the firm. During problem solving personal contact accounted for 22% of the ideas, 5% inside the firm and 17% outside the firm. During both the functions R & D and experience accounted for a large proportion of the total (25% and

29% respectively). Literature accounted for only 10% of ideas during idea initiation, all of which were external, and 9% during problem solving, of which 2% were internal and 7% external. It can be seen that channel usage is quite similar in both phases. According to Utterback 15.3% of the project initiating inputs were literature, 44% external discussion and 13.6% analysis and experimentation. In problem solving the percentages for the same channels were 8.4%, 21.7% and 51.8% respectively: clearly some differences in channel usage during the different phases of innovation are indicated in the latter study.

There exists also evidence to suggest that information seeking behaviour (in-house or external) varies according to the seeker's professional discipline, *i.e.* scientist or technologist. For example, Allen[9] studied 17 *development programmes* and discovered that out of 706 messages which resulted in technical ideas considered during the course of the projects, exactly half originated internally and half externally. In a similar study of 2 *research projects* Allen found that 65% of messages originated outside the laboratory and 35% inside. In another study, Gibbons and Johnston[10] investigated the types and sources of information which contributed to the resolution of technical problems encountered during 30 innovations in a variety of industries: one of their major findings was that 'the problem-solver with a university education relied more on information obtained outside the company, from scientific literature and from scientists in universities, whereas problem-solvers with industrial education relied on their own expertise based on education, experience, and industrial contacts to resolve technical problems'. A consequence of this is that '. . problem solvers with industrial education appear to be better at relatively small scale innovation while those with a university education can solve the technical problems arising during a large scale, less standardized innovation more efficiently'.*

Gibbons and Johnston also found differences in the mode of coupling between scientific sources and technological sources: 'the former (scientific sources) were used not at all, or to a considerable extent (limited multiple use) whereas the pattern of use for the latter (technological sources) was distributed much more evenly throughout all the innovations . . .'.†

## 4 Communication and firm size

It was stated earlier that the percentage of project initiating ideas originating in-house was a function of firm size. The pattern, according to the Bolton Committee data, is shown below:

| Firm size (no. of employees) | 1–199 | 200–999 | 1000+ |
|---|---|---|---|
| Percentage of ideas originating in-house | 70.55 | 65.65 | 48.87 |

* This might go some way towards explaining the figures quoted by Holt[11] who says '. . ideas for the technical solution of minor innovations originate mostly inside, whereas about two-thirds (65%) of basic (major) innovations come from outside'.

† It is interesting to note that Gibbons and Johnston found a somewhat higher contribution from the literature than most other workers: 42% of 'external' information was derived from literature, as was 24% of 'personal' information (*i.e.* information obtained by the innovator prior to the commencement of the project). The aggregate contribution based on all categories of internal and external information was 29%.

On the face of it this appears surprising since larger firms will generally have a greater in-house R & D capacity and might thus be expected to generate relatively more of their own ideas.* However, evidence does suggest that larger firms are more outward looking and have more contacts with external agencies than smaller firms, and Table 1 shows the percentages of firms in the different size categories which contacted Research Associations and/or Technical Associations and/or Management Consultants, etc.

| NO. OF EMPLOYEES | 0–49 | 50–999 | 100+ |
|---|---|---|---|
| NO. OF FIRMS | 17 | 29 | 7 |
| *Source of external aid* | *% of firms making contact* | | |
| Research Association | 30 | 41 | 86 |
| Technical Association | 48 | 88 | 100 |
| Management Consultant | 0 | 17 | 43 |
| Technical Consultant | 6 | 20 | 43 |
| Government | 60 | 58 | 86 |
| Supplier | 66 | 61 | 71 |

SOURCE: S. Hyman.[12]

TABLE 1

Further evidence of this firm size effect is provided in a report by the U.K. Universities and Industry Joint Committee[13] (UIJC) who investigated the degree of coupling between university and industry as a function of firm size. On all of the measures of contact considered (sponsor university work, use university consultants, regular contact with universities and use of published information on university work) large firms had by far the greatest number of contacts (average score for firms having between 1–199 employees was 12%; average score for firms having over 5000 employees was 72%). Of 403 firms having less than 200 employees, 75% had no contact with universities whatsoever whereas out of 96 firms with greater than 5000 employees, only 9% had no contact with universities.

A significant result of the UIJC enquiry lies in the fact that a positive correlation was demonstrated between the number of scientists in the senior management of small companies and the number of contacts with universities. However, of the sample of small firms studied, 71% did not recruit graduates: the corresponding proportion for the large firms was only 10%! Furthermore in 1968, small firms employed slightly more than 15% of all qualified scientists and engineers in manufacturing, which is a concentration of 0.7%, only half that of large firms.[14]

Larger firms will generally have sufficient resources to enable them to subscribe to many journals, to send employees to conferences and seminars and to

* An F.B.I. survey in 1960 suggested that in the U.K. small firms' share of industrial R & D expenditure was less than 3%: at the same time the share of small firms in employment was about 20%. More recent data from OECD has shown that in most member countries the hundred largest R & D performers accounted for more than three quarters of total industrial R & D expenditure. Sources: FBI, 'Industrial Research in Manufacturing Industry', 1961. OECD: 'The Overall Level and Structures of R & D Effort, in Member Countries, Paris, 1969.

establish comprehensive library and SDI services etc., whereas small firms cannot finance these operations nor do they have time or personnel to spare for them.* Large firms, will, therefore, have many more contacts with external information sources than will small firms which would go some way towards explaining their apparently greater awareness of external developments. However, this is not the whole story, and the answer might also lie to some extent in the different types of person employed by large and small firms. It has been demonstrated that scientists are more outward looking in their information seeking behaviour than technologists and they look more towards primary sources of information, (*e.g.* scientific journals, university laboratories) than do the latter.† This is because scientists, whether they be in university or industry, speak the same language: they understand one another. Technologists, in contrast, tend to be inward looking and to make use of secondary literature such as trade journals and textbooks. Most of them certainly do not understand university science or the arguments of scientists and, indeed, many have little interest in doing so: these are neither within their scope of learning nor their terms of reference in industry. It is not surprising then, when one considers not only the relative levels of resources available to large and small firms, but in addition the type of person employed by them (remember, large firms have double the concentration of QSEs than their smaller counterparts), that large firms interact more with external agencies than do their smaller counterparts.

## 5 'Levels' of information

The question raised above concerning the differences in level of understanding between scientists and technologists is of extreme importance to those whose job it is to satisfy industry's STI requirements. Not only must information be made readily available to those seeking it but it must also be couched in terms which they understand and presented at levels of sophistication which match, but most certainly do not exceed, their own levels of comprehension.

As an example of this consider a firm which requires information concerning the possible use of metalliding‡ in changing the surface properties of a metallic component. The relevant information can be presented at two levels. First, information describing the thermo-dynamics of the system: effect of surface impurities, dislocation densities, temperature of salt bath, etc. on the metal ion transfer and diffusion rates. Second, a simple tabulation or graphical representation of data showing changes in surface hardness and in dimensions of the component as a function of time at different temperatures. The scientist might deduce the second from the first whereas the technologist almost certainly will not. Clearly the technologist's need will only be met when he is presented with the second set of data, which contains relevant information at a level at which he can understand it.

* See R. Rothwell and J. Townsend, 'The communication problems of small firms', *R & D Management*, 3, (3), (Notes and Comments), June 1973.

† See Allen, ref. 9; Gibbons and Johnston, ref. 10.

‡ A process whereby the surface properties of a metal are altered by immersion in a bath of molten salts.

## 6 Conclusions and implications for Management

From the above discussion the following four general conclusions can be drawn:

(a) the information seeking behaviour of innovators tends to very depending on the phase in the innovation process during which information is being sought, from an outward looking attitude at 'idea generation' to introspection during 'problem solving'. (Myers and Marquis,[4] Utterback[8])

(b) The information habits of scientists differ significantly from those of technologists, the former coupling strongly with extra-organizational sources and relying heavily on primary literature, the latter using mainly in-house sources and secondary literature. (Allen,[9] Gibbons and Johnson[10])*

(c) the STI retrieval behaviour of organizations is a function of size, the larger organizations having a greater tendency (and ability) to interact with external agencies than their smaller counterparts.

(d) information must not only be made more easily accessible to the seeker, but it must also be presented to him at a level commensurate with his ability to understand it.

Clearly, these conclusions have profound implications for both information scientists and for those whose task is the management of innovation. Since the majority of information inputs to the idea generation phase of innovation arise externally to the innovating organization, it is essential that the information officer be made aware of the firm's strategies and long term plans for new development. It is only in this way that information officers can present information to R & D management, which is relevant to their future interests and which may, indeed, anticipate their needs. The objectives, the needs and the problems of the organization must be spelt out clearly to the information officer, thus enabling him to construct current and future profiles of its information requirements. The causal role of speedy and efficient information retrieval and dissemination in successful innovation must be recognized and accepted by top management and the information department must be set on a level with R & D, production and marketing. It is only when management appreciates the full importance of the information function that the information department can play its full role in stimulating and assisting innovation and growth.

### REFERENCES


1 ROBERTSON, A. B. 'Information flow and industrial innovation', *ASLIB Proceedings*, **25**, (4), April 1973, pp. 130–39.

2 ROTHWELL, R. *and* ROBERTSON, A. B. 'The role of communications in technological innovation', *Research Policy*, **2** (1973), pp. 204–25.

3 HOLMES, P. 'The role of information in Science and Technology', OSTI Report No. 5180.

4 MYERS, S. *and* MARVUIS, D. G. 'Successful industrial innovation', N.S.F. 69–17, 1969.

5 ROTHWELL, R. *et al.* 'Sappho updated; Project SAPPHO Phase II', *Research Policy*, **3**, (3), 1974, pp. 258–91.


* In the case of Allen the differences were observed between scientists performing research and engineers doing development work. The differences observed by Gibbons and Johnson were between graduates and non-graduates. Perhaps a suitable general distinction could best be made between 'qualified research staff' and 'development staff'.

6 FREEMAN, C. *et al.* (1971), 'The role of small firms in innovation in the U.K. since 1945', Committee of Enquiry on Small Firms, Research Report No. 6, H.M.S.O.
7 LANGRISH, J. *et al. Wealth from knowledge*, London, Macmillan, 1971.
8 UTTERBACK, J. M. 'The process of innovation, a study of the origination and development of ideas from new scientific instruments', *IEEE Transactions on Engineering Management*, EM-18, 1971, p. 124.
9 ALLEN, T. J. 'Performance of information channels in the transfer of technology', *Industrial Management Review*, 1966, p. 87.
10 GIBBONS, M. *and* JOHNSTON, R. D. 'The interaction of Science and Technology, Manchester University, Department of Liberal Studies in Science, 1972.
11 HOLT, K. 'Stimulation of creativity—generation of ideas', Proceedings of the 6th International TNO Conference, Netherlands, March 1973.
12 HYMAN, S. *Associations and consultants*, London, Allen and Unwin, 1970.
13 'Industry, Science and the Universities', University and Industry Committee, CBI, July 1970.
14 COX, J. 'Committee of Enquiry on Small Firms', Research Report No. 2, H.M.S.O., 1971.

Reprinted from Science Studies, Vol. 4, 1974.

# Discussion Paper

## POLICY AND INFORMAL COMMUNICATIONS IN APPLIED SCIENCE AND TECHNOLOGY

Francis W. Wolek
*Wharton School,*
*University of Pennsylvania**

and

Belver C. Griffith
*Graduate School of Library Science,*
*Drexel University*

Over the past ten to fifteen years there has been a marked growth of interest in, and applied work on, the dissemination of scientific and technical information. In search of ways to stimulate progress in science and technology, policymakers have supported an extensive body of research on the information needs and practices of users of professional information. This research has consistently demonstrated a strong reliance on informal channels of communication, especially in applied fields.[1] This reliance is somewhat troublesome, for it is the *formal* channels which seem to be much more amenable to control and institutional support.

This paper is a review of existing thought on informal communication in terms of its significance for progress in applied science and technology. It is directed at the policy problems intrinsic to encouraging productive informal communication.

### *A SYSTEMS CONTEXT FOR POLICY ON INFORMAL COMMUNICATION*[2]

The predominant orientation of policy on scientific and technical communication is spelled out in the introduction of the SATCOM report as follows:

* Philadelphia, Pennsylvania 19174, U.S.A.

[1] Many surveys of information flow have documented this strong reliance on informal channels. Among those for the applied fields are surveys by: S. Herner, 'Information Gathering Habits of Workers in Pure and Applied Science,' *Industrial and Engineering Chemistry*, **46** (1954), 228–36; T. J. Allen, 'Performance of Information Channels in the Transfer of Technology,' *Industrial Management Review*, **8** (1966), 87–98; and R. S. Rosenbloom and F. W. Wolek, *Technology and Information Transfer* (Boston: Harvard Business School, 1970). Several papers have also attempted to explicate the functions of informal channels, thus showing that such communication is not merely a preferred practice of scientists and engineers, but an integral factor in the advancement of scientific and technical knowledge. Among this latter group of papers are two in D. Bergen (ed.), *The Foundations of Access to Knowledge* (Syracuse: Syracuse University Press, 1968)—one by H. Menzel, 'Informal Communication in Science: Its Advantages and its Formal Analogies' (153–67), and the other by W. D. Garvey and B. C. Griffith, 'Informal Channels of Communication in the Behavioural Sciences, (129–46). Another relevant paper is by F. W. Wolek: 'The Engineer: His Work and Needs for Information,' *Proceedings of the American Society of Information Science*, **6** (1969), 471–6.

[2] For note 2 see next page

New science and technology rest firmly on the base of information generated in the past; thus the effectiveness of future work in universities, government laboratories, and industry depends on the efficiency of present information transfer. Information costs are usually no more than a few per cent, at most, of the cost of doing scientific and technical work. The improvement in the efficiency of such work that could result from increasing the effectiveness of information-handling procedures would offset—easily and several-fold—information costs substantially greater than the present level of expenditures for this purpose.[3]

In short, to promote progress in science and technology, improve the efficiency of information transfer; in particular, reduce the costs of information and improve the timeliness of information available to the scientist and technologist. How relevant is this injunction for policy on informal communication? The answer to this question involves us in one of the primary themes of recent thought on professional communication; namely, that formal and informal communications are interdependent elements of the same system.[4]

The emergence of this 'systems' view is a recent phenomenon. In the early stages of work on computerized document systems, informal channels were often seen as *competitors* of formal channels. Reliance on the informal was sometimes interpreted as a sign of both weakness and need for better formal systems.[5] Others attempting to separate policy on informal from policy on the formal communication prompted Herbert Menzel to note that:

Formal and informal scientific communication are complementary; they must not be thought of as alternatives in the sense that certain messages are obtained exclusively through the printed work, the library, and the mechanized search-and-retrieval

[2] In several of his papers, Herbert Menzel has pointed out six major advantages of informal over formal communication. In one of these papers, 'Planning the Consequences of Unplanned Action in Scientific Communication,' in A. de Reuck and S. Knight, eds., *In Communication in Science* (London: J. A. Churchill, Ltd., 1967), 57–77, he noted (p. 60): 'The six advantages of informal communication . . . all reside in the interpersonal nature of this communication—in the fact that it is a direct communication between individuals and as such can be highly reactive as well as specifically tailored to each individual's needs.' We follow Menzel in our definition of informal communication. Accordingy, some written communications, such as person-to-person letters, are seen to be informal, whereas some oral communications, such as presentation of a paper at a professional meeting, are seen to be formal. The criterion is whether the communication allows for direct interaction between source(s) and receiver(s).

[3] National Academy of Sciences, *Scientific and Technical Communication: a report of the Committee on Scientific and Technical Communication* (Washington, D.C.: National Academy of Sciences, 1969), 1.

[4] Some work has been directed at the efficiency of informal channels. For example, several organizations have developed listings of their personnel which can be searched by the indexing methods found in document retrieval systems. Several studies also comment on the need to promote visits and travel as a way of stimulating informal contacts. Finally, Thomas Allen and Peter Gertsberger (*Human Factors*, in press) have recently found a positive effect on informal communication when offices are arranged without permanent desks for individual workers (a 'non-territorial' office).

[5] This view is expressed by Christopher Scott in 'The Use of Technical Literature by Industrial Technologists', *IEEE Transactions on Engineering Management*, **EM-9** (1962), 76–86.

system, whereas others are obtained by the exclusive use of word-of-mouth and the telephone. The much more typical event is one in which the receipt of single messages is secured by the successive interplay of these two kinds of communication.[6]

According to this systems viewpoint, the information which a professional receives in any given incident or through any given channel might be valueless without other information received through other channels.

What is important for policy in this new view of communications ? One key idea is that of *balance* between formal and informal activities to avoid bottlenecks to professional progress. For example, a scientific society which was ignorant of the systems' structure (as pointed out by Garvey and Griffith[7]) might encourage only such primary publications as journals. By inadequately supporting the informal channels so crucial to verifying the importance of specific contributions, the society might establish a bottleneck rather than increased flow of new science. Similarly, efforts to develop informal channels may be wasted unless secondary publications, important in the dissemination and cataloguing of knowledge, are adequately supported.

A second key point for policy is that of *precedence*; that is, people may need to be prepared for some communications. Speaking on this point, Wolek noted:

If the manager does decide to support some services for interpersonal communication, he must be careful to see these as elements in a larger system. He may, for example, decide to institute a series of meetings on selected subjects with the idea of bringing people together for an 'informal exchange of ideas'. If management has not provided literature sources which will allow the participants to share the same background and has not provided opportunities for participants to test their knowledge with friends beforehand, the expected change may not transpire. All that may happen is that the participants will learn of a new set of names of persons interested in and competent in a subject. This result may be very worthwhile and may justify the meeting, but it will not satisfy managers and participants who expected a real exchange.[8]

A third key point for policy is that of *suboptimization*. In the present context this idea has been emphasized by Menzel as follows:

Can policies designed to satisfy . . . requirements of speed, efficiency and comprehensiveness really work to the detriment of others ? If search and retrieval services and selected distribution arrangements were working optimally, they would bring to each scientist exactly that which he has asked for and nothing else. But, by that very fact, they would eliminate browsing, and would thereby put an end to the occasions when a scientists' attention is called to information which he had not appreciated as relevant to his own interests.[9]

[6] Menzel, *op. cit.* note 2, 153.

[7] W. D. Garvey and B. C. Griffith, 'Scientific Information Exchange in Psychology', *Science*, **146** (25 December 1964), 1655–9, and 'Scientific Communication: Its Role in the Conduct of Research and Creation of Knowledge', *American Psychologist*, **26** (1971), 349–62.

[8] F. W. Wolek, 'Preparation for Interpersonal Communication', *Journal of the American Society of Information Science*, **23** (1972), 3–10.

[9] H. Menzel, 'Scientific Communication: Five Themes from Social Science Research', *American Psychologist*, **21** (1966), 999–1004.

Thus, while it may be relevant to think about the efficiency of informal channels, it is clear that the policymaker must understand more than ways to improve the efficiency of specific channels of information transfer. He must also understand the relations between different channels (i.e., the structure of the communications system) so that he can plan for such structural attributes as balance among channels, preparedness of communicators, and overall (vs. sub-) optimization of the system. The basic knowledge needed for understanding this system in the basic sciences has begun to accumulate (e.g., the work of Garvey and Griffith[10] in psychology and Orr[11] in the biomedical sciences). However, much additional research is needed to establish the optimal structure of a system where new pieces of hardware are the primary goal.

## *THE SOCIAL CONTEXT OF INFORMAL COMMUNICATION*

The previous section argued that informal communication must be examined within the context of a system. The present section expands this argument; it is not just any system, it is a system within a special social context which must provide the context for sound policy.

Many policy makers have developed doubts about fostering informal communication, for reasons which illuminate the requirements of a sound informal communication policy. For example, the report of the Committee on Information in the Behavioural Sciences describes several 'limitations' of informal communication. The first of these limitations is that informal communication is 'fortuitous'; that:

> While scientists working in related research areas are likely to come into contact, there is no certainty that this will occur.[12]

This point is an especially telling one. For, to the degree that informal communication is fortuitous, there is no assurance that subsequent action is based upon the correct, complete, and best available information. From this standpoint, a profession or organization which encouraged informal communication might well wonder whether it hadn't also encouraged second rate or redundant work, and thereby provided an invitation to be innundated by unorganized communication which had not been subject to qualified evaluation. Indeed, the latter points were among the primary arguments leading to the withdrawal of governmental funding from the Information Exchange Group (IEG) experiment, which supported informal channels (largely by preprint distribution) in the biological sciences.[13]

[10] Garvey and Griffith, *op. cit.* note 7.

[11] R. H. Orr, G. Abdian, C. P. Bourne, E. B. Coyle, A. A. Leeds, and V. M. Pings, 'The Biomedical Information Complex Viewed as a System', *Federation Proceedings*, **23** (1964), 1133–45.

[12] Committee on Information in the Behavioral Sciences, *Communication Systems and Resources in the Behavioral Sciences* (Washington, DC: National Academy of Sciences, 1967), 45.

[13] For the views of the chairman of one of the groups see: D. Green, 'Death of an Experiment', *International Science and Technology* (May 1967), 82–4, 86, 88. An historical review of the experiment may be found in W. F. Heany and D. C. Weeks, *Informal Communication among Scientists* (George Washington University Medical Center, 1971) **AD-726, 650.**

Available research, on the other hand, strongly suggests that what may appear on the surface to be without rhyme or reason often has an underlying structure. For example, Herbert Menzel[14] has noted a large 'planned' component in 'unplanned communication', in that seemingly voluntary contributions of information are based on prior knowledge of the receiver's interest. Allen[15] has found that informal communications in an organization conform to well-defined networks based on the abilities of various people to monitor developments in different fields and to interpret these for internal tasks (what Allen calls 'gatekeeping'). Allen notes also that:

> The most intriguing aspect of this [network] is that it is developed spontaneously, with no management intervention. There was scarcely a suspicion on the part of management that the network operated in this way.[16]

Informal contacts may also reflect certain aspects of the organization of work in a speciality area, as has been shown by research on the structure of 'invisible colleges'. For example, a recent paper by Griffith and Mullins[17] emphasizes the key role that certain highly coherent, 'activist' groups played in scientific change. In a variety of fields, small groups of highly productive researchers have organized to pursue the goal of making very substantial changes in the direction of scientific work. The operation of these groups is nearly completely sustained by informal communication.

The basic point has been stressed by Rosenbloom and Wolek as follows:

> The predominant use of local information sources in operational circumstances is often . . . explained as a manifestation of the simple economics of turning around (or picking up the phone) and 'asking the next guy'. The most important point about operating organizations, however, is that they ensure that usually there is a 'next guy' to talk to . . . . That is, the unifying element in such work is provided by the mission of the organization, which not only relates task to task and person to person, but which when fulfilled, also justifies the development and support of a team of experts. Organization, in the sociological sense, is the key element.[18]

The mere fact of informality in communication is not a reliable indicator of appropriate organization. Rather, it is essential to define the precise nature and extent of social relationships between communicators. To judge whether a contact is fortuitous, policy makers must understand the extent of, and basis for, previous contacts, the criteria used to judge the relevance and validity of information, and factors such as common acquaintances and common memberships which affect the probability of contact.

[14] H. Menzel, 'Planned and Unplanned Scientific Communication', *Proceedings of the International Conference on Scientific Information, I* (Washington DC: National Academy of Sciences, 1959), 189–233.

[15] T. J. Allen, 'Roles in Technical Communication Networks', in C. E. Nelson and D. K. Pollock, eds., *Communications among Scientists and Engineers* (Lexington, Mass.: D.C. Heath and Co., 1970), 191–208.

[16] *Ibid.*, 200.

[17] B. C. Griffith and N. C. Mullins, 'Coherent Social Groups in Scientific Change', *Science*, **177** (15 September 1972), 959–64.

[18] Rosenbloom and Wolek, *op. cit.* note 1, 104–5.

What is important for policy about this emphasis on social systems? It strongly suggests that communication and organization are inseparable; that communication without organization makes nonsense and organization without communication is impossible. If policymakers wish to stimulate progress in a particular field, they may need to do more than increase the flow of information; they may also need to ensure the presence of a community of professionals to make sense of the information. Professional societies and governments may need to foster conditions where professionals are sufficiently known and accessible to each other that they may mutually evaluate and integrate the new information.[19]

The interdependence of organization and communication is also relevant for policymakers of companies and agencies. For example, Allen[20] argues that the formal organization of a firm can hamper the existence of an effective informal network. Formally recognized purposes, and formally sanctioned relationships, are not necessarily the ones which professionals feel to be important to their work. Informal networks may be established which must then compete with formal channels. The potential here for wasted effort and misguided direction are clearly relevant to the policymaker.

The basic point is also applicable for policymakers who command a consensus for greater productivity or different directions in a particular organization. Significant flows of information rely fundamentally on relationships between people; the mere adoption of something like a computerized retrieval system will not necessarily bring about desired changes.[21] An increased flow of information from some particular direction requires the presence of people who share background and goals with the desired sources on the one hand, and, on the other hand, share other goals and backgrounds with internal colleagues. Persons filling such 'gatekeeper' roles must have the skills and organizational pre-requisites to fulfil their functions.[22]

[19] Eric Trist, 'Social Research Institutions: Types, Structures, Scale', *International Social Science Journal*, **22** (1970), 301–24, has described a need for a new form of organization in applied science, which he calls 'domain-centered' research. Such research would be interdisciplinary in the domain of problems relevant to such broad social concerns as pollution control. The Institute of Life Insurance has formally organized an information-exchange network on events which have implications to the industry and firms in it. This interesting organization is described in a case history (No. 9-371-380) published by the Harvard Business School (1971).

[20] T. J. Allen, unpublished dissertation, Sloan School of Management, MIT, 1966.

[21] For example, a system installed by the DuPont Company (Federal Council for Science and Technology, *Proceedings: Second Symposium on Technical Information and the Federal Laboratory*, 1964, 41–5) failed to provide more than a slight increase in document use, and then only by established document users.

[22] The work of Allen (*op. cit.* note 15) and Winford Holland ('Characteristics of Individuals with High Information Potential in Government Research and Development Organizations', *IEEE Transactions in Engineering Management*, **19** [1972], 38–44) have shown that gatekeepers have distinguishing characteristics which allow management to identify them. Paul Lawrence and Jay Lorsch, in *Organization and Environment* (Homewood, Ill.: R. D. Irwin, Inc., 1969), have also described characteristics of persons who have the role of integrating different groups concerned with product innovation. For a discussion of the important interdependencies between marketing, production, and technical personnel in innovation, see the paper by R. S. Rosenbloom in *New Ideas for Successful Marketing* (Chicago: American Marketing Association, 1966).

## *PROFESSIONAL COMMUNITIES*

A theme which has increasingly characterized research on scientific communication is that science is a social process involving communities of similarly-interested people.[23] This concept of a community of freely interacting professionals seeking consensus on established knowledge is quite consistent with the traditional views of science. However, existing studies of innovation suggest that such a view is also relevant for applied science and technology.[24] An especially significant study is that of Ronald Havelock,[25] who investigated the structure of what he calls a 'national problem solving system'.

Given common interests, it might be reasonable to expect that there is much to be gained, from the viewpoint of both society and the individual organization, by stimulating inter-organizational flows of information. Three surveys of industrial practice have confirmed the value of having organizations maintain close contact with technical progress external to their own organizations. One of these, a study of 152 English companies, found that:

> The greater a firm's technical achievements, the readier it is to share its knowledge with other firms and to contribute to journals, conferences, and so forth. . . . The most backward and parochial firms are secretive on technical matters.[26]

More recent confirmation is from the Project SAPPHO group in England which found that a measure of the 'effectiveness of the innovating organization's communications with the outside scientific and technical community' strongly differentiated successful from unsuccessful cases of innovation.[27] The third survey, Miller's

[23] Among other references cited below, two studies which have espcially focused on this concept are those of W. O. Hagstrom, *The Scientific Community* (New York: Basic Books, Inc., 1965), and R. Stankiewicz, 'The Role of Informal Communication in Integration and Coordination of Research', unpublished report of the Department of Sociology and Research Policy Programme, University of Lund (Sweden), 1968.

[24] One of these (Illinois Institute of Technology Research Institute, *Technology in Retrospect and Critical Events in Science—TRACES*, a report prepared for the National Science Foundation, 1968) involved the detailed analysis of events leading to five innovations. After reviewing these events, the authors emphasized the 'highly effective personal communication' which characterized interaction between disciplines and between applied and non-mission-directed workers. Two other recent studies of technological innovation in England have also emphasized the basic point that interaction between many different organizations is essential to technological innovation. These two studies are: (1) J. Langrish, *et al.*, *Wealth From Knowledge* (London: Macmillan, 1972) and (2) C. Layton, *Ten Innovations* (London: George Allen and Unwin, 1972).

[25] Ronald G. Havelock, 'A National Problem Solving System; Highway Safety Researchers and Decision Makers', Final Report prepared for the National Highway Traffic Safety Administration, U.S. Department of Transportation, May 1971, available from the Institute for Social Research of the University of Michigan.

[26] C. F. Carter and B. R. Williams, *Industry and Technical Progress* (London: Oxford University Press, 1957), 179.

[27] Science Policy Research Unit, University of Sussex, *Success and Failure in Industrial Innovation* (London: Centre for the Study of Industrial Innovation, 1972). This study analyzed successful *vs.* unsuccessful examples of essentially the same attempts at innovation. The measure of external communications strongly differentiated successful from unsuccessful cases (i.e., it was the second most powerful predictor, being accurate in 75% of the data points) for 12 innovations in the field of scientific instrumentation. The measure was less powerful in predicting the success of chemical process innovations.

study of technological innovation in the steel industry,[28] found a clear association between (1) the financial success of a firm and its propensity to innovate, and (2) the propensity to innovate and openness to communication from the external environment.

Despite the findings of the three studies cited above, it seems clear that the benefits of tapping the professional community are not obtained by some simple mechanism of 'keeping contact'. Indeed, initial drafts of this paper excited much scepticism about the above findings on the part of industrial executives. Some research has also encouraged caution about the idea of openness to professional communities. For example, Allen[29] found a negative correlation between external consultation and the quality of technical work. Speaking on this finding, Allen noted:

> Laboratories which do not have the necessary technical manpower resources attempted unsuccessfully to substitute through reliance upon outside technical personnel.[30]

Roger Miller has summed up the basic point behind these notes of caution as follows:

> The innovative organization inserts itself in its environment, accepts the dependency which it implies but attempts to manage it. Moreover, it establishes units that become boundaries between the organization and the environment.[31]

What does it mean to 'manage' the relationship between an organization and the relevant professional communities ? Current research is vague on this matter, yet the general directions seem clear. For example, the organization and its professionals must have an established position in the profession if professional sources are to be accessible. The organization's professionals must also have sufficient experience, obtained by actually working in the professional field, so that they have the background to interpret events correctly and to build on discoveries. Finally, those in touch with professional developments must have the internal contacts and experience to interpret these developments with internal staff. Much additional research is needed to make these suggestions operationally useful.

## *POLICY ON INTER-ORGANIZATIONAL COMMUNICATION*

The concerns which policymakers have expressed about informal communication may also be used to illuminate the requirements of sound policy on inter-organizational communication. For example, some executives have expressed concern that, in order to maintain status with, and accessibility to, experts outside one's organization, professionals excessively bias their work towards professional ends at the expense of organizational ends. On the other hand, others are concerned that without the training that comes from preparing and analyzing formal publications, professionals will lack the orientation and skills to generalize from their

[28] R. E. Miller, *Innovation, Organization and Environment* (Sherbrooke, Canada: University of Sherbrooke, 1971).

[29] Allen, *op. cit.* note 20.

[30] *Ibid.*, 95.

[31] Miller, *op. cit.* note 28, 132–3.

experience and thus to formulate creative ideas. David Barton, a senior engineer at an industrial laboratory, has expressed this concern as follows:

Mission-oriented work attracts a greater percentage of engineers whose mental processes are confused and who cannot perceive and express the simple relationships underlying their jobs. These men are more likely to engage in oral snow jobs known to sociologists as 'interpersonal communications' than in writing the structured memos, reports and papers expected of discipline-oriented engineers and scientists. Many mission-oriented men eventually wind up in sales or program management jobs where interpersonal communications are highly rewarded and rigorous thinking and expression are discouraged and prohibited.[32]

Two other concerns bear respectively on the structure and operation of informal systems. First, the Committee on Information in the Behavioral Sciences has charged that informal communication is 'undemocratic'; that:

The informal communication system as it operates at present, it has been observed, exhibits a bias against scientists who are younger or affiliated with small, poorly financed, or less prestigous institutions.[33]

Later findings[34] clearly substantiated these impressions, extending the class of 'disadvantaged scientists' to include youthful researchers, and in some fields, those working in foreign countries. Policymakers who have recognized these findings have legitimately been concerned that support for informal communication could act so as to 'freeze' the membership of accepted contributors to professional knowledge, and thus to freeze the growth of such knowledge itself.

The security of proprietary information is another relevant issue in the operation of informal systems. Just as the scientist who establishes priority earns status, so the organization which establishes a lead over its competition will receive advantages in the marketplace. Information which is 'leaked' to competitors can destroy the chances for these rewards, and a system which permitted such leaks could destroy a primary motivator of scientific and technical progress.[35]

There is certainly great appeal to the prospect of active dialogue with the best minds in the world; however, the findings cited above suggest that there are also costs to be incurred from fostering active contact between organizations. Proprietary information may be leaked; expertise which has value to outsiders may require work with little organizational value; and networks which monitor and organize progress may also exclude persons who are valuable to the organization. Policy on communication, therefore, means more than supporting ideas for improving the efficiency of

[32] Personal letter, 19 March 1970.

[33] Committee on Information in the Behavioral Sciences, *op. cit.* note 12, 45.

[34] B. C. Griffith and J. Miller, 'Networks of Informal Communication among Scientifically Productive Scientists', in C. E. Nelson and D. K. Pollock, *op. cit.* note 15, 125–40.

[35] The extent to which some organizations feel and act on this concern is spelled out in a fascinating case study by J. Brooks, *New Yorker* (11 January, 1964), 37. The case involved the extensive legal actions of a manufacturer of space suits to block the move of one of its engineers to a competing firm. The case shows that the issue of proprietary information is broad, bearing on the nature of the fiducial relationship of employers with employees and consultants. As yet, we have little understanding of the applied scientist's personal conflicts regarding rights of ownership to creative work done in the employ of others.

information channels. Policy must include the making of reasoned tradeoffs between security and up-to-dateness, between orderly growth and radical innovation, and between elite networks and open communities.

Before making these tradeoffs, policymakers need to understand the actual extent of the threats they may dimly perceive. To do this, they must understand the social organization and operation of informal networks. On what basis do people enter into repeated informal contact? What norms of behaviour govern such relationships? What procedures and activities constitute their operation? What impacts are sought for and obtained on members and others? Without answers to such questions, reasoned tradeoffs, and thus, reasoned policy, cannot be made. Studies on the social organization of communication networks[36] have provided insight into these issues for the scientific disciplines. However, similar research in the more complex, multi-institutional world of applied science and technology needs to be done.

## *SUMMARY*

This paper began with a statement of the primary rationale behind research and policy on professional communication: to promote progress in science and technology and to improve the efficiency of information transfer. Work based on this ethic of efficiency has undoubtedly contributed to progress. Abstracting services, computerized retrieval systems, review publications, and decreased lead times have been, and are, productive. However, the ethic of efficiency is not adequate as the sole guideline for policy on communication and is especially limited for policy on the informal communications which are so central to work in applied fields.

A simple improvement in the efficiency of one channel of communication will not be translated into great gains in scientific and technical output. Changes in one channel require commensurate changes in others and, even more importantly, changes in the formal and informal relationships between users of the information. Thus, for policymakers to effect improvements and changes in the flow of information, they must have a firm understanding of the existing and desired relationships which bind groups of professionals into productive communities.

[36] This literature includes studies by (1) Derek Price: *Little Science, Big Science* (New York: Columbia University Press, 1965); 'Collaboration in an Invisible College' (with D. Beaver), *American Psychologist*, **21** (1966), 1011–8; (2) Diana Crane: 'The Nature of Scientific Communication and Influence', *International Social Science Journal*, **22** (1970), 28–41; 'Social Structure in a Group of Scientists: A Test of the Invisible College Hypothesis', *American Sociological Review*, **34** (1969), 335–52; and *Invisible Colleges* (Chicago: University of Chicago Press, 1972); (3) Nicholas Mullins: 'The Development of a Scientific Speciality', *Minerva*, **10** (1972), 51–82; and 'The Distribution of Social and Cultural Properties in Informal Communication Networks among Biological Scientists', *American Sociological Review*, **33** (1968), 786–97; (4) David Krantz: 'The Separate Worlds of Operant and Non-Operant Psychology', *Journal of Applied Behavioral Analysis*, **4** (1971), 61–70; and 'Schools and Systems: The Mutual Isolation of Operant and Non-Operant Psychology as a Case Study', *Journal of the History of the Behavioral Sciences*, **8** (1973), 86–102.

## PART III: The Structure of Literature and Documents

The past five years have seen a remarkable growth of new techniques and ideas in the study of the structure of literature. Advances include the co-citation techniques developed by Marshakova, Small and Griffith[1]; the development of more sophisticated statistical techniques for evaluating literature by Narin and coworkers; and a most remarkable burst of creativity by two pioneering research workers (Brookes and Price). Accordingly, the selection of individuals papers was difficult. I have avoided the detailed papers of Small and Griffith on the development techniques using co-citation and chose, instead, Small's study of the strong relationship between literature and scientific achievement in a small, but highly significant, biomedical specialty, collagen. This paper clearly shows the close relationship between the clustered documents and scientific advances in the specialty. The choice of a paper from among the works of Narin was difficult, so again I chose one which suggested the high power of citation measures, in this case relative to traditional evaluations of graduate programs through panels of experts. The remaining papers flow naturally to anyone currently following this literature as Brookes and Price, seemingly ignorant of one another's work, recently advanced powerful theories. The Drott and Griffith paper is added as a bit of reality, and the final Price paper as a vision of the future.

---

[1]These papers, not included in this volume, are: Henry Small, "Co-citation in the scientific literature," *Journal of the American Society for Information Science,* 24:265-69, 1973; I.V. Marshakova, "Bibliographic coupling system based on cited references," *Nauchno-Tekhnicheskaya Informatisiya Seriya* 2(6): 3-8, 1973; Griffith, Small, Stonehill, & Dey, "The Structure of Scientific Literature II," *Science Studies, 4: 336-65, 1974.*

Text processing for retrieval has proven a very difficult type of research to undertake. In the first place, building and manipulating data bases containing considerable amounts of text is expensive and has the potential of consuming large amounts of computer time. The second difficulty with this type of study has been the problem of replicability of results. There appear to be a number of factors which are highly dependent on the specific nature of the data base and query, thus making it difficult to establish the value of any particular manipulative strategy. The future of this research will depend both upon the ability to resolve these inconsistencies and on the applicability of the proposed techniques to data bases which are of a real world size.

The literature which seeks to provide evaluation measures is also filled with difficulties. One of the central issues is the question of relevance. In a variety of papers, Saracevic has thoroughly illuminated the many problems associated with assigning a relevance value to documents. His work is definitive; he closes off that problem as a fruitful area of research, given today's tools. Judged relevance thus emerges as a far too labile concept to be used in fine tuning information systems.

In considering the retrieval measures which are proposed, it is important to distinguish the intended use of the measure. Measures whose aim is to set the actual value of a retrieval set to an end user face a much more difficult problem than those measures which primarily order the results of different retrieval strategies applied to the same queries on a single data base. The first encounters, again, all the perils associated with relevance.

This elaboration of techniques, I should note, has occurred in a retrieval world that is now dominated by online machine retrieval and is independent of that activity; at this point, the theory and technology are running in nearly opposite directions. The success of the latter using bits of natural language and indexing and elaborations of post-coordination of terms, truncation and Boolean searches may eventually spell the end of this quest for improved retrieval through research. The literature of online systems cannot be presently included because it is tied closely to specific systems and products and would have little ability to age gracefully.

Reprinted from the Journal of the American Society for Information Science, Vol. 29, No. 2, 1978. Copyright © 1978 by the American Society for Information Science. Reprinted by permission of John Wiley & Sons, Inc.

# Publication Ratings versus Peer Ratings of Universities

**Richard C. Anderson, Francis Narin, and Paul McAllister**
*Computer Horizons, Inc., 1050 Kings Highway North, Cherry Hill, NJ 08034*

**This paper presents a quantitative comparison of peer versus bibliometric procedures for rating the quality of U.S. universities. The peer ratings used are the Roose-Andersen rating of the quality of graduate faculty in 10 scientific fields. The bibliometric ratings used are (1) the number of university papers in each field; (2) the average "quality" of the papers based on their citation rates, expressed as influence per paper in each field; and (3) total influence, the product of number of papers and influence per paper. The bibliometric ratings are based on 127,000 university papers, from 450 journals in 10 fields for 1965 to 1973. Roose-Andersen ranks and scores are found to correlate most highly with the total influence of the university's papers, followed closely by correlations with the total number of papers, and much less closely with the average influence per paper. A partial correlation and regression analysis indicate that the Roose-Andersen scores have two additive components: bibliometric size and bibliometric quality. Further analysis explores the extent to which a university's prestige in one department correlates with the assessment of other departments within that university, and the extent to which the university's overall bibliometric size correlates with the assessment of departments within that university. It is shown that the ratings of departments within a university are not independent, and that these dependencies are associated with the bibliometric size of the university. University ranks and scores in different fields are shown to be much more highly correlated when based on peer assessment than when based on bibliometric measures.**

## Background

Considerable effort has been expended by various investigators to find a suitable measure for the quality of graduate education in the United States. Some of these measures have been almost completely subjective, essentially peer evaluations based on surveyed opinions. Other measures incorporate more objective methods such as publication output and citation analysis.

The primary subjective measures of quality have been the reports from the American Council on Education. The 1966 report by Allan M. Cartter was essentially a survey analysis of informed opinions from 900 department chairmen, 1,700 outstanding senior scholars and scientists, and 1,400 younger professions [1]. Thirty academic fields in over 100 universities were selected for study. Ratings were constructed for both the quality of the graduate faculty and the effectiveness of the doctoral program. The 1969 follow-up study by Roose and Andersen [2] was similar in concept and conduct to the Cartter report. The Roose-Andersen study, based on the completing of a questionnaire by some 6,000 scholars, included seven more disciplines and 25 more institutions than the Cartter report. The impact of these studies was wide: over 26,000 copies of Cartter's report were distributed between 1966 and 1970 [3].

Because of this wide interest in the Cartter and Roose-Andersen articles, a number of other studies have sought to develop more objective measures which would correlate with their subjective quality rankings. Beyer and Snipper [4] performed a discriminant analysis, based on the responses to questionnaires describing departmental characteristics in four disciplines. Two of the most important variables were found to be the quality of the department where the faculty PhDs were obtained, and the number of PhDs granted by the department.

An extensive 1970 study by Hagstrom compared inputs, outputs, and the prestige of American university science departments [5]. Using multiple linear regression Hagstrom was able to explain approximately 75% of the variability of the rated quality by using a set of nine independent variables. He found the most significant variable to be the number of research articles produced by a department, followed closely by citations to works by the department.

For the field of sociology, Solomon [6], in 1972, compared the Cartter and Roose-Andersen rankings for graduate programs with a set of productivity indices compiled from published books and major articles. The Spearman rank correlation obtained was 0.81 on a departmental basis.

In 1975, Drew and Karpf collected data on faculty publication rates for the fields of mathematics, physics, and chemistry [7]. They counted department publications in 20 prestigious journals in each field for 1960 to 1963 and 1965 to 1968 by noting the institutional affiliation of the author. The publication counts gave correlations of 0.87, 0.84, and 0.86 for mathematics, physics, and chemistry, respectively, when compared with the Cartter study. When correlated with the Roose-Andersen study, correlations of 0.76, 0.83, and 0.87 were obtained for mathematics, physics, and chemistry, respectively. Drew and Karpf examined several other objective factors for ranking departments but found that none of these gave correlations as high as the rate of publication.

## Introduction

The impact and widespread utilization of the Roose-Andersen findings render them natural standards for comparison. The intent of this paper is to explore the nature of the Roose-Andersen evaluations with the aid of recently developed bibliometric techniques.

The methodology described in this paper offers several advantages in assessing university departmental quality over the previously mentioned studies. The principal advantage of the methodology lies in its ability to separate the total influence of a university's papers into two factors: one expressing the influence per paper, or quality of the published work, and another expressing size, as measured by the number of papers.

In addition, the size of the data base is considerably larger than any of the samples used in previous studies. Approximately 127,000 university papers from 450 journals are utilized in this analysis.

Finally, both the Roose-Andersen ranks and actual Roose-Andersen quality scores are considered. Use of ranks only has a serious statistical disadvantage since the distance between ranks is meaningless. This problem is not as serious when the actual scores are employed.

The specific objective of this study is to investigate the relationships between three bibliometric measures and the Roose-Andersen ranks and scores. The bibliometric measures to be studied are *Total number of papers*, a bibliometric size measure; *Influence per paper*, a size-independent measure of citation influence; and *Total influence*, defined as total papers X influence per paper. The relationships among these variables are examined within each of 10 scientific fields and across all 10 fields. Within a field, each university is given four separate ranks based on Roose-Andersen quality of graduate faculty score, total number of papers, average influence per paper, and total influence. Correlations are then calculated to measure the degree of association between the Roose-Andersen ranks and scores and ranks and scores based on the three bibliometric measures.

Because of the strong relationships which exist among total papers, average influence per paper, and total influence, the use of partial correlations becomes necessary. Three sets of first-order partials yield useful information. The size component of the Roose-Andersen evaluations is assessed by analyzing the correlation between Roose-Andersen score and number of papers, with average influence per paper held constant. Similarly, the quality component can be extracted by considering the correlation between Roose-Andersen score and average influence per paper, with total number of papers held constant. The third set of partial correlations studies the bibliometric relationship between total number of papers and average influence per paper, with Roose-Andersen score held constant. The Roose-Andersen scores are shown to have both a size and a quality component.

To further explore the nature of the Roose-Andersen evaluations, an attempt is made to determine to what extent a university's prestige in one department influences the assessment of other departments within that university. Rank correlations are calculated for each possible pair of fields using the ranks of all universitites which have departments in both fields. It will be shown that the ratings of departments within the same university are not independent and that these dependencies are associated with the size of the university.

## Collection of the Data

Selection of the institutions for this study was determined by the amount of research support the institution had received from the National Institutes of Health (NIH). This particular criterion was chosen because we had previously assembled university publication data for an NIH supported study [8]. The institutions selected were those which had received at least $500,000 in NIH grant funding at least one fiscal year between 1965 and 1972. Of those institutions, 115 were universities covered in the Roose-Andersen ratings. Table 1 lists those 115 universities used in this study.

The specific papers analyzed included all articles, notes, and reviews listed under all variants of the 115 institutional names in the Corporate Index of the *Science Citation Index* (*SCI*) from 1965 to 1973 inclusive [9]. If the authors of a paper were affiliated with more than one institution, the paper was apportioned equally among the different institutions. Only journals covered continuously by the *Science Citation Index* since 1965 were included in the analyses. Note that, since the Roose-Andersen study was done in 1969, the 1965 to 1973 publication set neatly spans the time period from four years before to four years after the Roose-Andersen study.

Because the publication data were extracted from an already existing set, the number of schools used in the comparison varied from field to field: a low of 55 schools was used in the pharmacology comparisons to a high of 88 schools in the chemistry comparisons. The University of California and the State University of New York were omitted from the comparisons in every field, because the individual campuses of these universities are not easily separable in the *SCI* data prior to 1973.

For schools with distinct campuses, the campus with the highest publication count was chosen in each field. This campus would probably be the one the Roose-Andersen participants had in mind when answering their questionnaires. A brief analysis showed that combining the campuses would have a minimal effect on the publication ranks of the individual schools and, therefore, on the comparisons with the Roose-Andersen data. Omitting all the schools with multiple campuses would have eliminated a number of major schools and seemed a needless loss of information.

Table 2 summarizes the data base. The first column of the table shows the Roose-Andersen field. The next column shows the number of universities in each field which are both in the Roose-Andersen ranking and in our data base. The third and fourth columns show, respectively, the number of journals in each field in the data base, and the number of papers from the universities in these journals. The procedure for assignment of journals to subfields is dis-

TABLE 1. 115 universities in the data set.

| | | |
|---|---|---|
| University of Alabama, Birmingham | Kansas State University, Manhattan | University of Rochester* |
| University of Alaska, College | University of Kentucky, Lexington | Syracuse University |
| Arizona State University, Tempe | University of Louisville | University of North Carolina, Chapel Hill |
| University of Arizona, Tucson | Louisiana State University, New Orleans | Duke University, Durham* |
| University of Arkansas, Little Rock | Tulane University, New Orleans* | North Carolina State University, Raleigh |
| Loma Linda University | Johns Hopkins University | Wake Forest University |
| University of Southern California, Los Angeles | University of Maryland, Baltimore | University of Cincinnati, Cincinnati |
| California Institute of Technology, Pasadena | University of Maryland, College Park* | Case Western University, Cleveland* |
| Stanford University* | University of Massachusetts, Amherst | Ohio State University, Columbus* |
| University of Colorado, Boulder* | Boston University* | University of Oklahoma, Oklahoma City |
| Colorado State University, Fort Collins | Harvard University, Boston* | Oklahoma State University, Stillwater |
| University of Connecticut, Farmington | Tufts University, Boston | Oregon State University, Corvallis |
| University of Connecticut, Storrs | Harvard University, Cambridge | University of Oregon, Eugene |
| Yale University, New Haven* | Massachusetts Institute of Technology | Thomas Jefferson University, Philadelphia |
| George Washington University, D.C. | Brandeis University, Waltham | University of Pennsylvania, Philadelphia* |
| Georgetown University, D.C. | University of Michigan, Ann Arbor* | Temple University, Philadelphia |
| Howard University, D.C. | Wayne State University, Detroit | University of Pittsburgh* |
| University of Miami, Coral Gables* | Michigan State University, East Lansing | Pennsylvania University, University Park |
| University of Florida, Gainesville* | University of Minnesota, Austin | Brown University, Providence |
| Florida State University, Tallahassee | University of Minnesota, Minneapolis* | University of Puerto Rico |
| University of Georgia, Athens | University of Mississippi, Jackson | University of Tennessee, Knoxville |
| Emory University, Atlanta | University of Missouri, Columbia* | Vanderbilt University, Nashville* |
| Georgia Institute of Technology, Atlanta | St. Louis University* | University of Texas, Austin |
| University of Hawaii, Honolulu | Washington University, St. Louis* | Texas A&M University, College Station |
| University of Chicago, Chicago* | University of Nebraska, Lincoln | University of Texas, Dallas |
| Illinois Institute of Technology, Chicago | Creighton University, Omaha | University of Texas, Galveston |
| University of Illinois Medical Center, Chicago | University of Nebraska, Omaha* | Baylor University, Houston |
| Loyola University, Chicago | Dartmouth College, Hanover | Rice University, Houston |
| Northwestern University, Chicago* | Rutgers University, New Brunswick | University of Texas, Houston |
| Northwestern University, Evanston | Princeton University, New Jersey | University of Utah, Salt Lake City* |
| University of Illinois, Urbana* | University of New Mexico, Albuquerque | Vermont University & State Agriculture College |
| Indiana University, Bloomington* | Union University, Albany | Virginia Polytechnic Institute |
| Indiana University, Indianapolis | Cornell Univeristy, Ithaca | University of Virginia, Charlottesville |
| Purdue University, Lafayette* | City University of New York | Virginia Commonwealth University, Richmond |
| University of Notre Dame | Columbia University, New York* | Washington State University, Pullman |
| Iowa State University, Ames* | Cornell University, New York | University of Washington, Seattle* |
| University of Iowa, Iowa City* | Rockefeller University, New York | University of Wisconsin, Madison* |
| University of Kansas, Kansas City | Yeshiva University, New York | West Virginia University, Morgantown |
| University of Kansas, Lawrence* | | |

*Asterisk indicates university campus included in all ten fields of analysis.

TABLE 2. Publication data base.

| Roose-Andersen Field | No. of Schools Common to Roose-Andersen and Publication Set | Number of Journals in Publication Set | No. of Papers (Articles, Notes, Reviews) in Publication Set |
|---|---|---|---|
| Biochemistry | 85 | 27 | 19,794 |
| Chemistry | 88 | 130 | 30,465 |
| Developmental Biology | 74 | 21 | 2,673 |
| Mathematics | 81 | 57 | 13,198 |
| Microbiology | 86 | 20 | 5,844 |
| Pharmacology | 55 | 19 | 3,475 |
| Physics | 83 | 125 | 36,903 |
| Physiology | 85 | 15 | 3,497 |
| Psychology | 83 | 31 | 9,627 |
| Zoology | 78 | 14 | 2,270 |
| Total | – | 459 | 127,746 |
| (Average) | (80) | (46) | (12,775) |

cussed in our biomedical paper [10] and detailed for all 2,300 *SCI* covered journals in our recent monograph [11].

#### Influence Methodology

A very brief explanation of the influence methodology will be given here. The primary purpose of this methodology is to extract a measure of the influence of an individual journal from its citation relationship with other journals. In essence, the influence per paper for a journal is the weighted number of times an average paper in the journal is cited, where the weighting is based on the influence of the citing journal. Thus a citation from a highly prestigious journal such as the *Journal of Biological Chemistry* counts more heavily than a citation from a less prestigious journal. For a substantial collection of papers, such as the 127,000 papers studied here, influence per paper provides a convenient alternative to the time and expense of counting citations to each paper. The influence computations are performed on a field-by-field basis, so that field-to-field differences in referencing are compensated for. The detailed formulation of journal influence as an eigenvalue problem is given elsewhere [12].

For comparison with Roose-Andersen evaluations, three bibliometric measures are considered as possible indicators of a university's research output in a given field. The first is the total number of university papers in a field. This figure measures nothing about the quality of the published research.

The second indicator is the average influence per paper for a university in a field. Let $U_j$ be the number of university papers in journal $j$, and $I_j$ the influence per paper of journal $j$, then

$$\text{University influence per paper in a field} = \frac{\sum_{\text{all } j \text{ in field}} U_j \times I_j}{\sum_{\text{all } j \text{ in field}} U_j}$$

The average influence per paper is a size-independent measure of the quality of an institution's publications.

The third indicator is the total influence of a university's papers in a field. It is simply the number of papers times the university's average influence per paper in the field.

#### Correlation of Bibliometric Measures with Roose-Andersen Evaluations

Universities were ranked, within each field, on the basis of the three bibliometric measures and their Roose-Andersen scores. Three different sets of Spearman rank correlations were calculated (1) between the Roose-Andersen score and the number of university papers, (2) between the Roose-Andersen score and the average influence per paper of the university publications, and (3) between the Roose-Andersen score and the total influence of the university papers. Table 3 summarizes these results.

Almost all of the correlations are quite high. The range of Spearman rank correlations between Roose-Andersen and total number of papers is 0.64 to 0.90. Clearly, a substantial correlation exists between this publication size measure and a university's Roose-Andersen ranking.

The next column, correlations between Roose-Andersen rank and average influence per paper, also reveals high correlations, most of which are between 0.50 and 0.85. Since influence per paper is the closest publication measure to "quality," or size-independent influence, the Roose-Andersen rankings also seem to reflect the quality or influence of the journals in which the universities are publishing. Except for mathematics and psychology, the rankings correlate with average influence per paper to a notably lesser degree than they correlate with the bibliometric size of a university.

The last column in the table, correlations with total influence, shows that in every field the correlations between the Roose-Andersen ranking and the publication ranking increase when size (total papers) and quality (influence per paper) are combined into total influence.

Figure 1 graphically shows this effect of influence weighting on the rank correlations. The foot of each arrow lies along the diagonal at the value of the Spearman rank correlation between total papers count and the Roose-Andersen rankings. The head of the arrow shows the correlation between total influence, or influence-weighted papers, and the Roose-Andersen ranking. In every case there is an increase in the correlation when the papers are influence weighted. The field which has the smallest increase in correlation, developmental biology, had a relatively small correlation between Roose-Andersen and average influence per publication. Physics, the only other field that does not show a notable increase, had such an extremely high correlation of 0.898 on paper count alone, that the influence weighting only minimally increased this correlation.

Overall, the addition of the influence per paper "quality" factor yields a definite increase in the correlations between publication ranking and the Roose-Andersen ranking.

The use of rank data, however, has one important drawback; the distance between ranks is meaningless. This important concept of distance is lost when only the ranks are used. To make full use of all the information contained within our data, further analysis was carried out using the actual values of the three bibliometric variables and the actual Roose-Andersen scores for universities. Only university ranks were reported in the 1969 Roose-Andersen study, but the actual scores assigned to universities have been obtained from the authors. The availability of this interval scale data permits the calculation of product moment correlations.

The patterns which emerged with the Spearman rank correlations are not altered by the switch to product moment correlations. The correlations between the Roose-Andersen score and each of the three bibliometric variables are all positive and quite high. Furthermore, the correlations of Roose-Andersen with total influence have the highest values, followed by Roose-Andersen score versus

TABLE 3. Spearman rank correlations between publication rankings and Roose-Andersen rankings.

| Field | No. of Universities | No. of Papers | Correlation With Total No. of Papers[a] | Correlation With Influence/ Paper | Correlation With Total Influence |
|---|---|---|---|---|---|
| Biochemistry | 85 | 19,794 | 0.827 (13.50) | 0.723 (9.60) | 0.856 (15.21) |
| Chemistry | 88 | 30,465 | 0.804 (12.62) | 0.694 (8.98) | 0.855 (15.36) |
| Developmental Biology | 74 | 2,673 | 0.635 (7.02) | 0.287 (2.56) | 0.647 (7.25) |
| Mathematics | 81 | 13,198 | 0.699 (8.75) | 0.834 (13.53) | 0.852 (14.57) |
| Microbiology | 86 | 5,844 | 0.703 (9.11) | 0.507 (5.42) | 0.812 (12.81) |
| Pharmacology | 55 | 3,475 | 0.675 (6.73) | 0.551 (4.85) | 0.731 (7.86) |
| Physics | 83 | 36,903 | 0.898 (18.49) | 0.545 (5.89) | 0.910 (19.82) |
| Physiology | 85 | 3,497 | 0.694 (8.84) | 0.549 (6.01) | 0.746 (10.27) |
| Psychology | 83 | 9,627 | 0.721 (9.43) | 0.720 (9.39) | 0.859 (15.21) |
| Zoology | 78 | 2,270 | 0.654 (7.60) | 0.275 (2.51) | 0.777 (10.82) |

[a]Values in parentheses are the standard normal deviates ($z$ value).

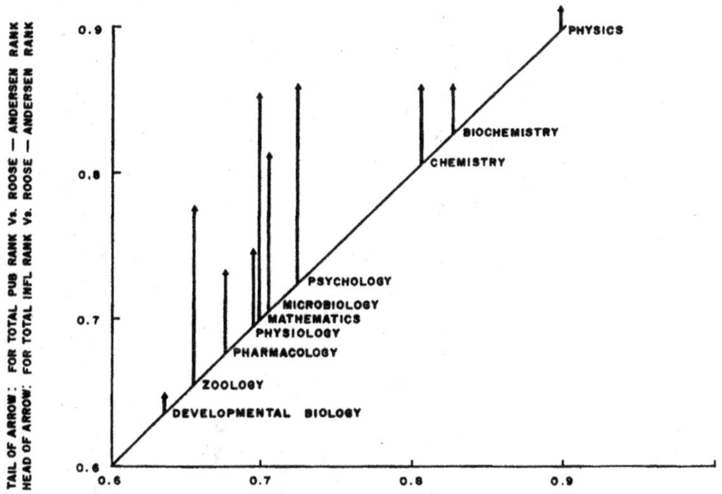


FIGURE 1. Effect of influence weights on correlations between publication rank and Roose-Andersen rank.

total publications, and Roose-Andersen score versus influence per paper. Figure 2 summarizes this. Figure 3 presents the relationships among the three bibliometric measures themselves. There is a strong positive correlation between total influence and both total papers and influence per paper. This is not surprising since the latter two variables are simply multiplied together to find total influence. The relationship between total papers and influence per paper is notably weaker. The reader will remember that influence per paper was derived so as to measure quality independently of the number of papers. Thus influence per paper permits size-independent quality comparisons of universities. The size-independent derivation of influence per paper in no way excludes the possibility of either a university publishing mainly in high or low influence journals. Although the correlations between total publications and influence per paper are not all strong, there is a definite pattern for positive correlations. Thus, there may be a tendency for larger universities to also publish papers in more influential journals.

### Partial Correlation

The preceding section has shown that quantity and quality of university publications appear, in general, to be positively correlated. Participants in the Roose-Andersen survey were supposedly judging the quality of graduate departments in American universities. It is doubtful that these participants were consciously aware of the positive correlation between quantity and quality. Therefore, they probably did not try to separate these two factors when making their judgments. This leads one to wonder if their quality assessments were influenced by the sizes of the universities as measured by their total publication outputs.

The possibility of Roose-Andersen scores being a combination of both quantity and quality of papers suggests the use of partial correlations to explore this structure.

Confirmation of the quality component in the Roose-Andersen ratings is the initial step. Both the Spearman rank and simple product moment correlations portray a strong positive association between Roose-Andersen scores and the influence per paper quality measure. Since both of these variables are positively correlated with total publications, the value of interest would be the correlation between Roose-Andersen score and influence per paper with the total number of papers held constant. Table 4 presents both the simple correlations between Roose-Andersen score and influence per paper, and the first-order partial correlations between these two variables with total papers held constant. The striking feature is that the partial correlations are very similar to the simple correlations. Half of the partials are larger than the simple correlations and half are smaller, but all of the changes are slight. These results imply that when the effect of total number of papers is removed

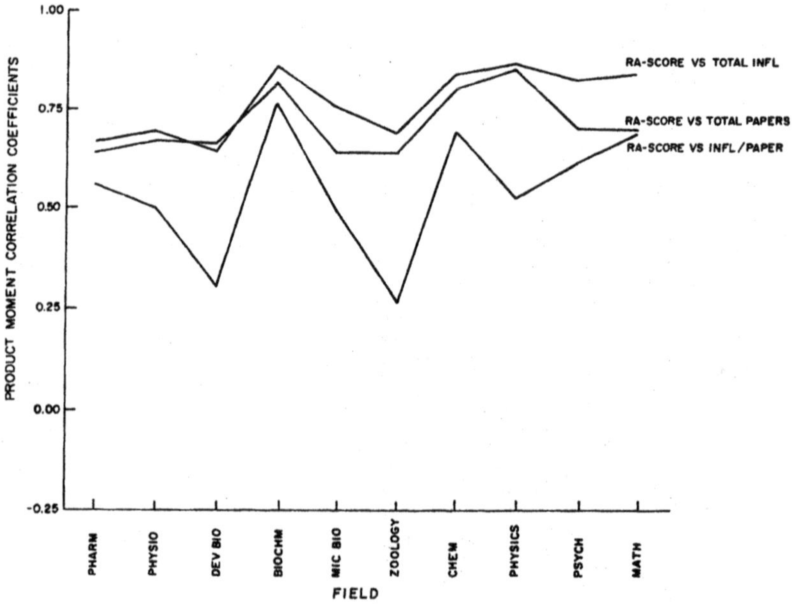


FIGURE 2. Correlations between Roose-Andersen and bibliometric scores for universities.

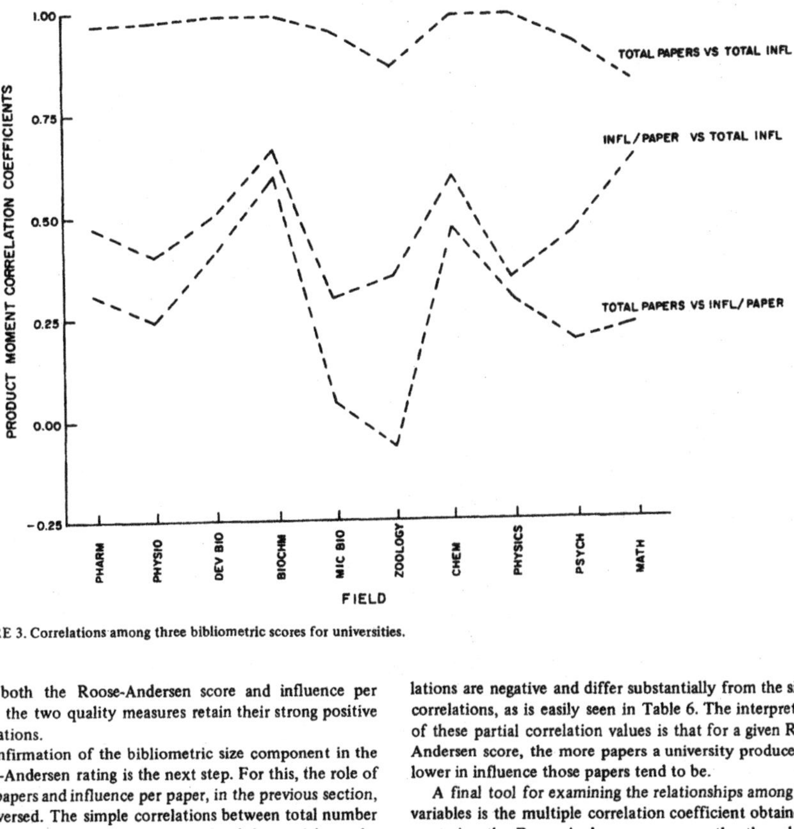


FIGURE 3. Correlations among three bibliometric scores for universities.

from both the Roose-Andersen score and influence per paper, the two quality measures retain their strong positive correlations.

Confirmation of the bibliometric size component in the Roose-Andersen rating is the next step. For this, the role of total papers and influence per paper, in the previous section, are reversed. The simple correlations between total number of papers and Roose-Andersen score and the partial correlations with influence per paper held constant are listed in Table 5. Again the differences between the simple and partial correlations are negligible. Furthermore, the differences from field to field are slight, indicating the strength of the relationship over all fields. These patterns provide strong evidence for the conclusion that Roose-Andersen ratings have a large component due to the bibliometric size of the university being evaluated. That is, when quality is held constant, as measured by influence per paper, the Roose-Andersen scores remain highly correlated with the quantity measure, total number of papers.

The completion of this current line of reasoning is to further examine the relationship between influence per paper and total number of papers. For each field, the simple correlation between average influence per paper and total number of papers and the first-order partial correlation between these variables with Roose-Andersen score held constant were computed. Nine of the ten partial correlations are negative and differ substantially from the simple correlations, as is easily seen in Table 6. The interpretation of these partial correlation values is that for a given Roose-Andersen score, the more papers a university produces, the lower in influence those papers tend to be.

A final tool for examining the relationships among these variables is the multiple correlation coefficient obtained by regressing the Roose-Andersen scores on the three bibliometric variables—total papers, influence per paper, and total influence. In general, the combination of total papers and influence per paper is more useful in explaining the Roose-Andersen scores than any of the bibliometric variables individually.

Since total influence is simply the product of total papers times the average influence per paper, its addition to the model gives a means for assessing the extent to which these two variables interact multiplicitively. Table 7 shows that the three-variable model has no apparent advantage over the model with only total papers and influence per paper. There is almost no increase in the multiple correlation nor is there a meaningful decrease in the standard error of estimation for the three-variable model. The conclusion is that there is no multiplicitive interaction between total number of papers and average influence per paper and that these two bibliometric variables have an additive relationship in explaining Roose-Andersen scores.

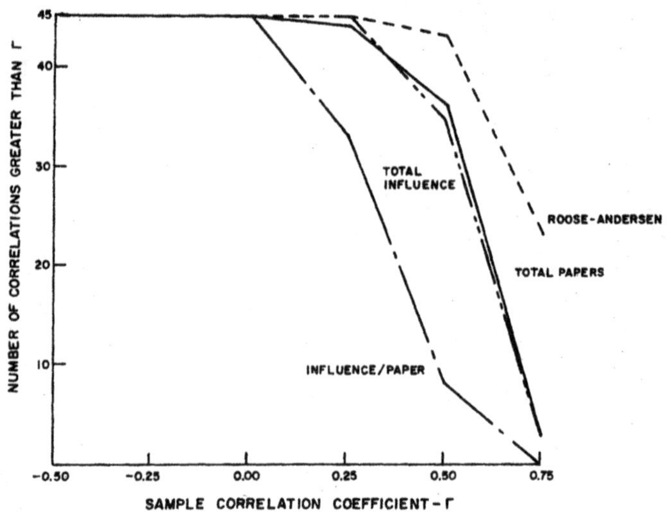


FIGURE 4. Frequency of occurrence of cross-field Spearman rank correlations between university scores in pairs of fields.

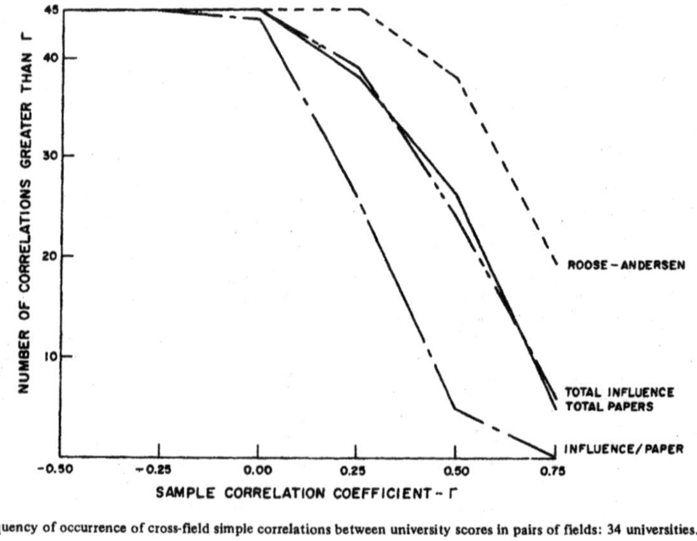


FIGURE 5. Frequency of occurrence of cross-field simple correlations between university scores in pairs of fields: 34 universities.

TABLE 4. Simple and first-order partial correlations between Roose-Andersen score and influence per paper for universities.

| | Pharmacol. | Physiol. | Dev. Biol. | Biochem. | Microbiol. | Zoology | Chem. | Phys. | Psychol. | Math. |
|---|---|---|---|---|---|---|---|---|---|---|
| Simple Correlations | 0.557 | 0.500 | 0.305 | 0.765 | 0.488 | 0.261 | 0.690 | 0.523 | 0.617 | 0.695 |
| First-Order Partial Correlations Controlled for Total Papers | 0.496 | 0.465 | 0.052 | 0.604 | 0.600 | 0.396 | 0.592 | 0.552 | 0.694 | 0.762 |

**Cross-Field Correlations**

In the previous section it was shown that the separation of paper count and influence per paper can be used to differentiate some of the effects of bibliometric size and quality in Roose-Andersen rankings and scores. In this section, it will be shown that these techniques can also be used to isolate the cross-field "halo" effect of neighboring departments upon the responses of Roose-Andersen participants.

A reasonable assumption can be made that a scientist evaluating the quality of a university's graduate faculty in biochemistry would be affected by his perception of the overall prestige of the university. Generally, the larger, more prestigious schools are strong in all fields. As a result, the scores given individual departments by Roose-Andersen participants might tend to be higher when the department being evaluated is in a large, eminent university.

The analysis of this phenomenon begins with the computation of Spearman rank correlations between Roose-Andersen rankings across fields. That is, for all pairs of fields, the Spearman rank correlation was found using the ranks of all universities which were included in both fields. A graphic technique has been employed to summarize these findings. Figure 4 presents the Spearman rank cross-field correlations based on Roose-Andersen score, total number of papers, total influence, and influence per paper. The graph for each variable was constructed by simply counting the number of correlations greather than the value specified on the horizontal scale.

Seventeen of the Roose-Andersen cross-field correlations are greater than 0.80 and 23 are greater than 0.75. The rank correlations based on number of papers from the universities in the different fields are lower than those based on Roose-Andersen rankings; only two correlations exceed 0.80 and only three are greater than 0.75. For total influence the correlation patterns and overall relationships are much the same as for total number of papers.

It is interesting to note that the highest correlation based on total number of papers is 0.86 between the fields of chemistry and physics, while the next highest correlation, 0.80, is between mathematics and physics. The correlation between mathematics and chemistry is also high at 0.78. Rankings of schools in chemistry, physics, and mathematics seem particularly closely related. This result is intuitively appealing because of the close interrelationships of the three fields.

This analysis is concluded by examining the cross-field Spearman rank correlations based on influence per paper departmental rankings. These correlations are considerably lower than the cross-field correlations based on total publications or total influence, and much lower than the correlations based on Roose-Andersen ranking.

The preceding evidence provides support for the hypothesis that the Roose-Andersen evalutions are affected by the overall prestige of the university. It also shows that the ranks of departments within a university are strongly correlated with respect to their total number of papers. In contrast, when cross-field correlations based on influence per paper ranks are used the quality of one department comes much closer to having no correlation with the quality of other departments.

These simple cross-field rank correlations, however, do not completely expose the structure of the nonindependent departmental ratings. The techniques necessary for further analysis require that only those schools which appear in all 10 fields be included. In Table 1 asterisks identify the 34 universities which meet this requirement. As a comparison to the results obtained for the larger set of universities the simple cross-field product moment correlations were calculated using the data from the 34 schools. Figure 5 shows that 38 of the Roose-Andersen cross-field correlations are

TABLE 5. Simple and first-order partial correlations between Roose-Andersen score and total publications for universities.

| | Pharmacol. | Physiol. | Dev. Biol. | Biochem. | Microbiol. | Zoology | Chem. | Phys. | Psychol. | Math. |
|---|---|---|---|---|---|---|---|---|---|---|
| Simple Correlations | 0.643 | 0.670 | 0.659 | 0.824 | 0.636 | 0.636 | 0.801 | 0.852 | 0.702 | 0.698 |
| First-Order Partial Correlations Controlled for Influence per Paper | 0.600 | 0.651 | 0.615 | 0.713 | 0.707 | 0.679 | 0.745 | 0.859 | 0.758 | 0.763 |

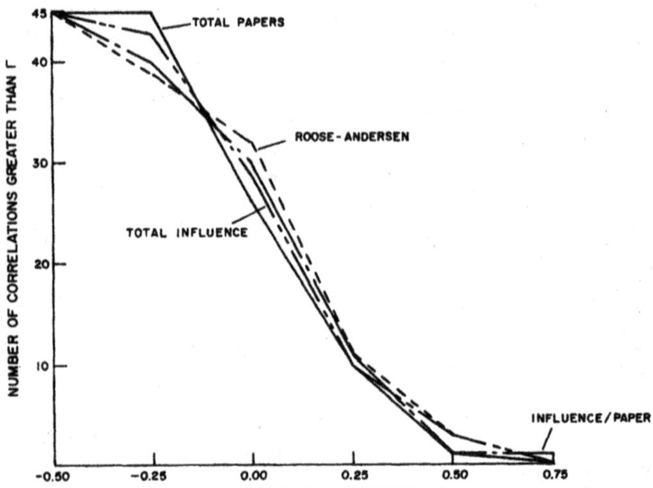


**FIGURE 6.** Frequency of occurrence of cross-field partial correlations between university scores in pairs of fields with scores in all other fields held constant: 34 universities.

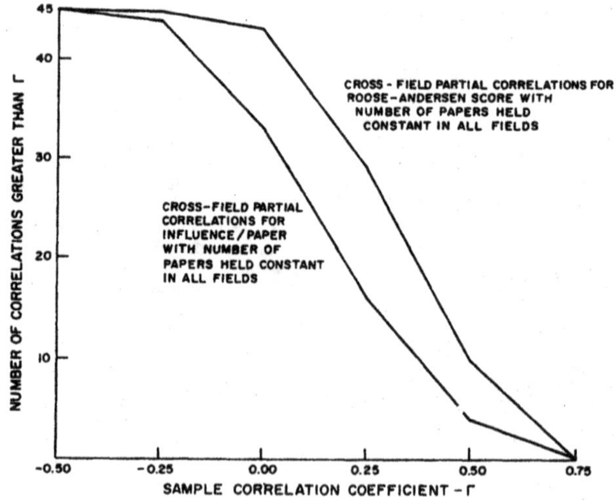


**FIGURE 7.** Frequency of occurrence of cross-field partial correlations between university scores in pairs of fields with number of papers held constant in all fields: 34 universities.

TABLE 6. Simple and first-order partial correlations between total publications and influence per paper for universities.

| | Pharmacol. | Physiol. | Dev. Biol. | Biochem. | Microbiol. | Zoology | Chem. | Phys. | Psychol. | Math. |
|---|---|---|---|---|---|---|---|---|---|---|
| Simple Correlation | 0.303 | 0.247 | 0.409 | 0.595 | 0.040 | −0.069 | 0.472 | 0.289 | 0.188 | 0.237 |
| First-Order Partial Correlations Controlled for Roose-Andersen Score | −0.087 | −0.136 | 0.290 | −0.098 | −0.401 | −0.316 | −0.187 | −0.351 | −0.438 | −0.482 |

greater than 0.50, but only five of the influence per paper correlations exceed 0.50. The cross-field correlations based on total papers and total influence are seen to fall between these extremes. Thus, the cross-field product moment correlations for the 34 schools exhibit the same patterns as observed when all universities were considered.

Our hypothesis is that the overall prestige of a university affects the ratings of all departments within the university. A logical course of action is to look at the correlation between two fields' Roose-Andersen scores with the Roose-Andersen scores of the remaining eight fields held constant. The Roose-Andersen line on Fig. 6 shows this analysis. Two-thirds of these cross-field partial correlations fall in the range −0.25 to 0.25, indicating virtually no correlation between fields' Roose-Andersen scores, when the effects of the other eight fields are removed. This is further evidence that the evaluation of one field within a university is not independent of the evaluation of other fields. Interestingly, the behavior of the cross-field partial correlations for the three bibliometric variables is nearly identical to that seen in the Roose-Andersen scores. Pairs of departments do not seem to be correlated with respect to quantity of papers, quality of papers, or the combination of both when the levels of these variables are held constant in all other fields.

The next step is to investigate which factors contribute to the strong cross-field correlations observed for the Roose-Andersen scores. It was previously shown that Roose-Andersen scores for pairs of departments within a university are highly correlated. Those pairwise relationships are nearly as strong for total number of papers, but weaker when influence per paper is considered.

Furthermore, it was demonstrated that Roose-Andersen scores are strongly related to the quantity (number of papers) and quality (influence per paper) of university publications. Also, quantity and quality were shown to be somewhat correlated.

To effectively isolate the relationships which are causing the Roose-Andersen scores to be highly correlated across fields, the simple cross-field correlations were examined for total number of papers versus Roose-Andersen score, for influence per paper versus Roose-Andersen score and for total number of papers versus influence per paper. The Roose-Andersen scores are highly correlated with both the quantity and quality of university publications, not just within fields, but across all fields. The relationship between quantity and quality, however, is not nearly as strong across fields. Because of these interrelations, partial correlations are again necessary. The first step is to remove the effect of the total number of papers from both the Roose-Andersen and influence per paper cross-field correlations. The result is essentially the cross-field correlations for Roose-Andersen score and influence per publication with the quantity of publications held constant in all fields. Figure 7 summarizes the results of these calculations. Both curves show that about two-thirds of the correlations are between 0.00 and 0.50, indicating that when the quantity effect is removed, the departments come much closer to having no correlation with respect to their Roose-Andersen score and influence per paper ratings.

If the influence per paper curve in Fig. 7 is compared with the corresponding curve in Fig. 5 (simple cross-field correlation), it will be seen that they are rather similar,

TABLE 7. Multiple correlation coefficients between Roose-Andersen scores and bibliometric scores for universities.

| Bibliometric Correlation | Pharmacol. | Physiol. | Dev. Biol. | Biochem. | Microbiol. | Zoology | Chem. | Phys. | Psychol. | Math. |
|---|---|---|---|---|---|---|---|---|---|---|
| Total Papers | 0.64 | 0.67 | 0.66 | 0.82 | 0.64 | 0.64 | 0.80 | 0.85 | 0.70 | 0.70 |
| Influence/Paper | 0.56 | 0.50 | 0.30 | 0.76 | 0.49 | 0.26 | 0.69 | 0.52 | 0.62 | 0.70 |
| Total Influence | 0.66 | 0.70 | 0.64 | 0.85 | 0.75 | 0.69 | 0.84 | 0.87 | 0.82 | 0.84 |
| Total Papers and Influence/Paper | 0.75 | 0.75 | 0.66 | 0.89 | 0.79 | 0.70 | 0.88 | 0.90 | 0.86 | 0.88 |
| Total Papers and Influence/Paper and Total Influence | 0.78 | 0.76 | 0.66 | 0.89 | 0.80 | 0.71 | 0.88 | 0.90 | 0.87 | 0.89 |

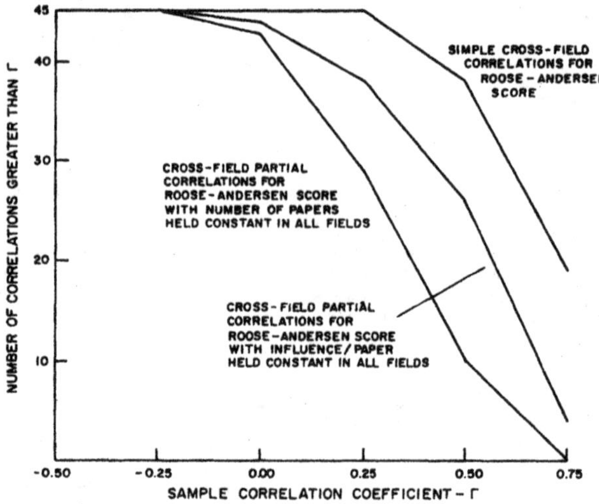


FIGURE 8. Frequency of occurrence of cross-field correlations between Roose-Andersen scores in pairs of fields: 34 universities.

with very few correlations greater than 0.50. This implies that influence per paper values for departments within the same university are not affected by the quantity of university publications. However, if a similar comparison is made for the Roose-Andersen curves, there are 19 simple cross-field correlations greater than 0.75, but none of the partial correlations exceed this value. The conclusion is that the Roose-Andersen scores for departments within a university are strongly related to the quantity of university publications.

The final stage of this analysis is to examine the cross-field correlations based on Roose-Andersen scores with influence per publication held constant in all fields. Figure 8 shows that 26 of these correlations are greater than 0.50. This compares with 38 of the simple cross-field correlations and only 10 of the partial correlations with the effect of total publications removed. Removal of the quantity (number of publications) effect reduces the amount of Roose-Andersen cross-field correlation substantially more than removal of the quality (influence per paper) effect. The most important factor contributing to the strong Roose-Andersen cross-field correlations is the number of university publications. We conclude, therefore, that in rating a given department within a university, the Roose-Andersen evaluations are strongly related to the total number of papers which were produced by all of the departments in that university.

## Conclusions

Two main conclusions may be drawn from the analyses presented in this paper. First, both the Roose-Andersen ranks and scores are highly positively correlated with a measure of university size (number of papers) and the citation quality of the university's publications (influence per paper). Within each field, when the quality is held at a constant level, Roose-Andersen score and university size retain their strong positive association. Similarly, for universities of the same size, Roose-Andersen score and citation quality are positively correlated. Thus, the Roose-Andersen evaluations have both a size and quality component.

The second conclusion is that the size component in the Roose-Andersen evaluations tends to inflate the scores of all departments within a large university. It was shown that the rating given by Roose-Andersen participants for one department within a university was not independent of the rating given other departments in the same university. When the number of papers was held constant in all fields, the quality component of the Roose-Andersen ratings came much closer to being uncorrelated for departments within the same university. However, when the quality of all departments was held constant, the Roose-Andersen cross-field correlations were quite high and positive, indicating that Roose-Andersen evaluations are strongly related to overall university size.

## Acknowledgments

This work was supported by the National Science Foundation under Contracts NSF-C627 and NSF-PRM7681724. The contributions of E. Haynes, Office of Planning and Resources Management Staff, NSF, as Project Officer, is gratefully acknowledged. The authors also wish to acknowledge the assistance of Stephen B. Keith of Computer Horizons,

Inc. in the preparation of the data base. Much of the publication data base was developed under NIH Contract N01-OD-3-2109. The authors also wish to acknowledge the assistance of Dr. Charles J. Andersen of the American Council on Education for providing the Roose-Andersen scores to us, and for his helpful advice and discussion.

## References


1. Cartter, A.M. *An Assessment of Quality in Graduate Education.* Washington, DC: American Council on Education; 1966.
2. Roose, K.D.; Andersen, C.J. *A Rating of Graduate Program.* Washington, DC: American Council on Education, 1970.
3. Roose, K.D.; Andersen, C.J. Ref. 2; p. ix.
4. Beyer, J.M.; Snipper, R. "Objective Versus Subjective Indicators of Quality in Graduate Education." *Sociology of Education.* 47:541-557; 1974.
5. Hagstrom, Warren O. "Inputs, Outputs, and the Prestige of University Science Departments." *Sociology of Education.* 44:375-396; 1971.
6. Solomon, W.E. "Correlates of Prestige Ranking of Graduate Programs in Sociology." *American Sociologist.* 7:13-14; 1972.
7. Drew, D.E.; Karpf, R.S. *Evaluating Science Departments: A New Index.* Rand Corporation Paper Series, October 1975.
8. Frame, J.D; Narin, F. "NIH Funding and Biomedical Publication Output." *Federation Proceedings.* 35:2529-2532; 1976.
9. *Science Citation Index.* Philadelphia, PA: Institute for Scientific Information.
10. Narin, F.; Pinski, G.; Gee, H.H. "Structure of the Biomedical Literature." *Journal of the American Society for Information Science.* 27:25-45; 1976.
11. Narin, F. *Evaluative Bibliometrics: The Use of Publication and Citation Analysis in the Evaluation of Scientific Activity.* Contract NSF C-627. National Science Foundation. March, 1976. NTIS: RPB252339/AS.
12. Pinski, G. "Citation Influence for Journal Aggregates of Scientific Publications: Theory, with Application to the Literature of Physics." *Information Processing and Management.* 12:297-312; 1976.

Reprinted from the Journal of Documentation, Vol. 33, No. 3, 1977.

# THEORY OF THE BRADFORD LAW

B. C. BROOKES

*School of Library, Archive, and Information Studies, University College London*

The Bradford law is explored theoretically by means of a very mixed Poisson model which, it is claimed, elucidates the uncertainties surrounding the law and its applications. It is argued that Bradford succeeded in formulating an empirical regularity which has pure and hybrid forms but that all the variants can be subsumed under a simple logarithmic law which, for reasons explained, escapes exact expression in conventional frequency terms. The theoretical aspects discussed include the hybridity of form, estimations, sampling problems, the stability of ranks, homogeneity of data, and tests of significance. Some numerical examples, some simulated and some drawn from social contexts outside bibliography, are used both to illustrate theoretical issues and also to indicate the wide generality of the Bradford law. Possible applications and developments of the theory are indicated.

## 1. INTRODUCTION

IT IS NOW 40 years since Bradford[1] first enunciated his empirical law of documentation. Its mysteries have evoked many papers, some published in this Journal. The ambiguities of Bradford's own formulation of the law posed only some of the problems it has raised. The major problem has been that in some indefinable way the Bradford law seemed to stand apart from other mathematical regularities and, in spite of many ingenious efforts, to be unrelatable to conventional mathematical or statistical ideas. At the same time, the Bradford law has been applied, sometimes successfully but sometimes not, to bibliometric problems though rarely with confidence.

In this paper I describe how Bradford's law can be regarded as a particular example of an empirical law of social behaviour which pervades all social activities. Bradford, without knowing what he was doing in this respect, may have initiated a new branch of statistics—the statistics of individuality—which may also lead to an extension of fundamental mathematical ideas which would make mathematics more useful in the social sciences.

However, this paper will focus on the task of explaining Bradford's law in this wider context and on its applications to documentation.

## 2. ACTIVE SOURCES AND GENERATED ITEMS

To take discussion of the Bradford law out of the narrow context of scientific journals and papers relevant to some topic—the context in which Bradford noted the regularities—I use the term *sources* instead of *journals* and of generated *items* instead of 'published papers relevant to some specified topic'. We then consider a finite number of sources—an *ensemble*—each of which is capable of generating (or utilizing or consuming) countable discrete items of some *homogeneous* kind.

The number of sources has to be finite because the Bradford law is divergent.

But in all social contexts the number of sources and the total output must always be finite. The only loss that follows from emphasis on these finitudes is that some mathematical and statistical concepts we have learned to rely on in solving physical problems must be abandoned. The correct use of the Bradford law demands a social realism and a recognition of individuality which escapes the mesh of conventional mathematical techniques and the concepts of random sampling theory.

### 3. THE SAMPLING OBSERVATION PERIOD

The analysis of the Bradford law has hitherto been applied to theoretical models which are too static, too deterministic and too physical. All Bradford data are derived by observing the *activities* of a set of sources over some appropriate period and by noting these activities, as measured in terms of the numbers of items each source accounts for in that time.

Thus the Bradford law is concerned with:

(*a*) a finite set of active sources (an *ensemble*) whose activities are made manifest by the generation or consumption of a specified type of item.
(*b*) observation of those activities over a specified *sampling* period.
(*c*) items of some *homogeneous* kind which are discrete and countable.

One of the points that has so far escaped analysis is the fact that the statistical distributions of such an ensemble of activity must depend on relationships between the number of active sources, the range and intensity of their activities, and the period of observation which provides the sample data. All Bradford distributions are *samples* of some on-going activity but, all too often, the sample data have been regarded as constituting a total population.

### 4. RANDOMIZATION AS A MIXED POISSON PROCESS

Another factor that has been disregarded is that social activities of the kind we are considering are not constant or determined as are those of physical processes. For example, the editorial board of a journal which publishes papers on Bradford's law (or any other topic) does not know when papers on this topic will be submitted for consideration. To any author, the writing of a paper requires deliberation and sustained activity and so he is unlikely to regard the writing of a paper as a random process. But to the editorial board of the journal he submits it to, to printers and readers and indexers—in fact, to almost everyone else—the publication of the paper is an unforeseen random event. So the *randomness* of Bradford-type data has to be allowed for.

The simplest and most realistic way of randomizing a Bradford process is to regard any source as an independent Poisson generator. If the mean activity of the source is $\mu$ items per unit time, then over an interval of duration $t$ the expected productivity is $\mu t$, but any realization of the process will be a random number from the Poisson distribution of mean $\mu t$.

Adoption of Poisson randomization adds no new parameters because in any theoretical model, some mean activity $\mu$ would have to be assumed. The variance of a Poisson distribution is also $\mu$, so we can also estimate the range of possible values of $\mu t$. The Poisson distribution is also discrete; whether $\mu$ is fractional or not, only integral values (or zero) can occur. Moreover, the Poisson distribution, it is sometimes said, 'has no memory'; it is a pure random process of which observation can begin at any moment convenient to the observer without affecting the distribution of events observed.

So each member of the ensemble of $n$ sources will be assumed to have a different value of $\mu$—say $\mu_r$ (with $r = 1, 2, 3 \ldots n$)—and to act independently of all others. If the activity of the ensemble is observed for a period $t$, the expected total activity of the ensemble will be $\sum_{r=1}^{n} \mu_r t = t \sum_{r=1}^{n} \mu_r = tR$, say. This mean total activity will also be a Poisson variate since the sum of any number of Poisson variates is also a Poisson variate.

As a Bradford-type ensemble may consist of $10^5$ or more sources, each of which may have its own unique Poisson mean, the ensemble constitutes a very mixed Poisson process indeed. Yet some of the sources expected to show activity may in fact remain observationally inert during the observation period. The probability that a Poisson source of mean $\mu_r$ shows no activity during a period $t$ is $\exp(-\mu_r t)$, a function which decreases monotonically towards zero as $t$ increases. As in other sampling techniques, the larger the sample taken, i.e. the longer the period of observation, the more confident we are about the data we collect and the inferences we draw.

On the other hand, we have to remember that in the social scene 'nothing is permanent but change', that human life is finite, and that observation periods of social activities have to be related to the rates of change of the social phenomena we are observing. What we need in such circumstances are simple monitoring techniques applicable to living processes rather than elaborate once-for-all detailed investigations whose conclusions are out of date before the calculations are completed. When properly understood, it will be argued, the ranking technique adopted by Bradford has great advantages over conventional statistical analysis of frequency distribution in providing simple monitoring of any social affairs—literary, economic, political—in which we may be interested.

The use of the Bradford law imposes a social realism. In conventional statistics Bradford-type data are correctly regarded as random selections from a distribution but in a way which ignores the socially recognized fact that some humans consistently demonstrate greater particular skills or stronger drives, appetites, or propensities than others. The Poisson model of the Bradford law accommodates both the randomization and this individualization of human performance.

### 5. THE BRADFORD HYBRIDITY

Another confusion that has hindered understanding of the Bradford law arises from the fact that the law as Bradford formulated it is a *hybrid*. Bradford's own diagram shows a curve rising from $r = 1$ to some intermediate point $r = c$ at which the rising curve runs smoothly into a linearity which then extends to $r = n$, as in graph I of Fig. 1. The rising curve and the log-linearity describe *two* effects, not one, and the two parts of the graph require two different mathematical formulations.

In his verbal formulation, Bradford avoided this issue by embracing the courses of ranks 1 to $c$ in the 'nuclear' zone, with the remaining sources grouped into zones whose productivities conform with the log law.

Experience of Bradford-type data from many contexts suggests that the position of the point $c$ can vary widely. There are two extremes. When $c = 1$, the nucleus disappears and the graph reduces wholly to a linearity such as graph II

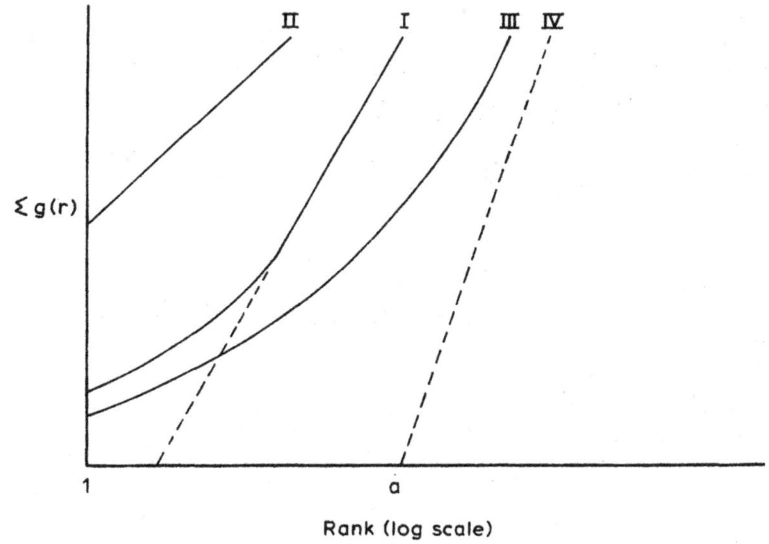


FIG. 1. *The Bradford forms*

in Fig. 1. When $c > n$, the graph reduces wholly to a continuously rising curve with no linearity whatever, such as graph III in Fig. 1. In this second case, however, if the rising curve conforms with the Bradford law, then it is possible to transform the origin of ranks to some point $a$ such that when the corresponding source frequencies are cumulatively summed as usual, a log-linearity, such as graph IV, results.

It seems reasonable to assume therefore that the dominant component of the Bradford law is that which corresponds to the linearity. However, the most frequently occurring form is the hybrid, Bradford's graph I of Fig. 1. So, after analysis of the simple logarithmic form, we have to return to the problems posed by hybridity and explain how they arise as modifications of the simpler linear forms.

## 6. THE EMPIRICAL LOG LAW

The formulation of the Bradford law now has to be generalized to express both the results of the above analysis of its hybridity and also the social contexts outside bibliography in which data conforming with the law are found.

If, in social contexts, we observe the activities of the individual sources of an ensemble, each of which is generating or consuming or utilizing discrete items of some homogeneous kind then, when the sources are ranked in order of decreasing activity, the cumulative totals are found to conform with the law:

$$\sum_{r=c}^{s} g(r,t) = t \log_b \{(a+s)/a\} \tag{6.1}$$

over some range $r = c$ to $r = n$ of the sources, where $t$ is the period of observation.

This formulation includes both the pure logarithmic and the hybrid forms. One element, however, is still missing—the form of the rising curve over $r = 1$ to $r = c$ in the hybrids. We return to this point in a later section.

## 7. THE MIXED POISSON MODEL

Consider a population, which may be mathematically infinite, some members of which engage in an activity whose public results emerge as an intermittent production of items. Most members of the population may be uninterested in the particular activity but those who are engaged display a wide range of activity. Some are very active (or successful) indeed, more are only moderately so while most are relatively inactive. It will be assumed that, if the population were distributed according to their activities, they would conform with the inverse law.

$$df(\mu) = \frac{k}{\mu}\,d\mu \qquad 0 \leqslant \mu < m. \tag{7.1}$$

Some upper limit $m$ has to be imposed because the inverse law is otherwise divergent. But, in any case, all human activities remain finite. Since $f(\mu) \to \infty$ as $\mu \to 0$, the lower limit of zero implies that the population is mathematically infinite. This infinity creates no serious difficulties however; it implies only that the total population can be as large and the active population as small as we wish.

In the Poisson model of such a population, consider a member who produces an average of $\mu$ items per unit time. The chance that his activity will be observed during the unit sampling period is $p = (1 - e^{-\mu})$, and the chance that it will not is $q = 1 - p = e^{-\mu}$.

As there are $\frac{k}{\mu}\,d\mu$ members of the population with mean activity $\mu$, the expected number of those observed to be active is

$$(1 - e^{-\mu})\frac{k}{\mu}\,d\mu. \tag{7.2}$$

Integrating over all possible values of $\mu$, the total observed active population will be

$$\int_0^m (1 - e^{-\mu})\frac{k}{\mu}\,d\mu. \tag{7.3}$$

As it stands, this integral gives rise to difficulties of integration when $\mu = 0$. There are various ways around this difficulty but the simplest for the immediate purpose is to rewrite it as

$$\int_0^m e^{-\mu}(e^{\mu} - 1)\frac{k}{\mu}\,d\mu = k\int_0^m \frac{e^{-\mu}}{\mu}\left(\mu + \frac{\mu^2}{2!} + \frac{\mu^3}{3!} + \ldots \frac{\mu_r}{r!} + \ldots\right)d\mu$$

which includes the expanded form of the Poisson distribution truncated because of the absent zero term. We now integrate term by term to get the required frequency distribution of successes:

$$f(1) = k\int_0^m e^{-\mu}\,d\mu = k\,(1 - e^{-m})$$

$$f(2) = \frac{k}{2!}\int_0^m e^{-\mu}\,\mu\,d\mu = \frac{k}{2!}\{1 - e^{-m}\,(1 + m)\}$$

$$f(3) = \frac{k}{3!}\int_0^m e^{-\mu}\mu^2\,d\mu = \frac{k}{3!}\left\{1 - e^{-m}\left(1 + m + \frac{m^2}{2!}\right)\right\}$$

with
$$f(r) = \frac{k}{r!}\left\{1 - e^{-m}\left(1 + m + \frac{m^2}{2!} + \ldots \frac{m^{r-1}}{(r-1)!}\right)\right\}$$

$$= \frac{k}{r!}\left\{1 - e^{-m}\left(e^m - \frac{m^r}{r!} - \frac{m^{r+1}}{(r+1)!} - \ldots\right)\right\}$$

$$= \frac{k}{r!}\sum_{s=r}^{\infty}\frac{m^s}{s!}. \tag{7.4}$$

The recurrence relation

$$f(r) = \frac{1}{r}f(r-1) - \frac{1}{r!}e^{-m}\frac{m^{r-1}}{(r-1)!}$$

can be helpful.

This is the *frequency* distribution of the frequency-rank log law. Like the Poisson distribution from which it is derived, it is expressed as an infinite but converging series: the value of $f(r) \to 0$ as $r \to \infty$ and in empirical contexts the series stops when $f(r)$ reduces to about 1.

For large values of $m$ the distribution conforms closely with

$$\int_1^m \frac{k}{\mu}\,d\mu = k \log m$$

which implies that the observably active sources are then uniformly distributed along the axis of $\log \mu$ in conformity with the Poisson model of the log law. This frequency distribution reverses the order of the frequency-rank distribution and so gives priority and emphasis to the sources of least activity.

The main advantage of the model is that it shows how the log law, and therefore how the hybrid forms of the Bradford law, can be derived in a realistic and natural way from orthodox frequency statistics. It shows that the Bradford hybrid distributions can be regarded as a mix of two mixed Poisson distributions in which two sets of Poisson means each constitute a sequence of uniform density over adjacent intervals of a logarithmic axis, deviating from this regularity, however, as the value of $\mu$ declines through 3, 2, and 1 towards 0.

## 8. THE LOG LAW OF NUMBERS

Is the non-hybrid Bradford i.e. the pure logarithmic law of the Poisson model of the previous section, to be found in social data? Yes: one particularly interesting example arises from the social use of numbers.

If the *first* digits 1, 2, . . . $r$ . . . 9, excluding the zero which plays a special place role in our numeral system, of the numbers which occur in social use, as, for example, in the sports and business columns of our newspapers, are selected at random, then it has been observed that in *a large enough sample*, these digits conform with the law

$$p(r) = \log_{10}(r + 1) - \log_{10} r$$
$$P(r) = \log_{10}(r + 1)$$

which is the logarithmic law with $a = 1$ and $b = 9 + 1 = 10$.

To statisticians[2] this is known as 'the law of anomalous numbers'. It was the first (1906) of the empirical Bradford-type laws, though statisticians mistakenly regard it as a *frequency* rather than as the *frequency-rank* distribution it patently is. As the name makes explicit, statisticians regard it as a peculiar anomaly. Henceforward, this natural social law will be referred to in this paper as the *log law of numbers*.

The main interest of this law is that it provides a means of exploring the sampling problems of Bradford law applications because the 'true' rank of any number is known *a priori*. We know, for example, that the digit 8 will be ranked 8th in any large enough random sample of the digits 1–9 because the cardinal value of any number signifies its expected ordinality or rank. Moreover, the computer generation of random numbers conforming with the Poisson model of the log law can be used to test sampling hypotheses. So the log law of numbers plays a key theoretical role in analysis of Bradford-type frequency-rank distributions.

In Table 1 are shown some results of a computer simulation of the log law of numbers for the digits 1–9, where $N$ is the sample size.

TABLE 1. *Simulation of the log law of numbers*

| | $N =$ | 100 | | 1000 | | 10000 | |
|---|---|---|---|---|---|---|---|
| $n$ | $q(n)$ | $f$ | $r$ | $f$ | $r$ | $f$ | $r$ |
| 1 | 0·3010 | 31 | 1 | 280 | 1 | 3019 | 1 |
| 2 | 0·1761 | 15 | 2 | 190 | 2 | 1697 | 2 |
| 3 | 0·1249 | 9 | 4 | 141 | 3 | 1260 | 3 |
| 4 | 0·0969 | 10 | 3 | 76 | 4 | 1018 | 4 |
| 5 | 0·0792 | 7 | 6 | 67 | 6 | 775 | 5 |
| 6 | 0·0669 | 4 | 9 | 70 | 5 | 719 | 6 |
| 7 | 0·0580 | 9 | 5 | 65 | 7 | 554 | 7 |
| 8 | 0·0512 | 7 | 7 | 57 | 8 | 479 | 8/9 |
| 9 | 0·0458 | 7 | 8 | 54 | 9 | 479 | 9/8 |

There is no *a priori* reason why the log law of numbers should not be extended beyond the digit 9 to any finite number so that (as I have explained elsewhere)[3] I assume that the law is valid for any finite range of integral numbers $n_1$ to $n_2$, with appropriate changes of the parameters to reduce the total probability to 1.

(Implicit in this result are intriguing problems relating to applications of conventional probability theory to social phenomena, but these problems will be discussed in a subsequent paper.)

## 9. THE STABILITY OF BRADFORD RANKS

It has often been noted that, in different Bradford samples of the same ensemble at different times, the sources are differently ranked or that the ranks of sources change as the sample size grows. Sometimes such changes are cited as evidence that the Bradford law itself is at fault, but sometimes the ranks of a relatively small sample are seemingly held to be immutable as though the ranking process eliminates the sampling errors that always attend more conventional forms of sampling.

So the question to be discussed here, assuming that the sample data conform with the logarithmic laws, is: How large must the total sample be to ensure that the 'true' ranks have emerged and that no more changes of rank will occur?

In considering this problem we switch from observation over time to the collection of a total sample of $N$ items. Consider an ensemble of $n$ sources over the interval $(1, n + 1)$ for which the rank probability density function is

$$p(r) = \log_b (r + 1) - \log_b r.$$

The expected productivity of the source of rank $r$ will then be $N p(r)$ items. We assume that $N p(r)$ is a Poisson variate.

It is well known that, as the mean of a Poisson variate increases, the Poisson distribution tends to a gaussian with the same mean and variance. It will be assumed (and confirmed) that the frequencies involved justify the substitution of gaussian for the Poisson variates.

If the two sources of rank $r$ and $(r + 1)$ are to be correctly ranked then we require that 'low' values of the variate $N p(r)$ are likely to exceed 'high' values of the variate $N p(r + 1)$, i.e. that

$$Np(r) - d\sqrt{Np(r)} > Np(r + 1) + d\sqrt{Np(r + 1)} \tag{9.1}$$

where $d$ is a parameter (obtainable from normal probability tables) which establishes the degree of confidence required.

On solving (9.1) for $N$ we have

$$\sqrt{N} = d\{\sqrt{p(r)} - \sqrt{p(r + 1)}\} \tag{9.2}$$

and the value of $N$ can be calculated for different values of $d$ and $r$. A short table of such calculation for various values of $r$ and for $d = 1{\cdot}645$ which corresponds to a confidence level of 95% is given in Table 2.

TABLE 2. *Minimum sample sizes: 95% confidence; Poisson model; log law of numbers*

| $n$ | 2 | 5 | 10 | 100 |
|---|---|---|---|---|
| $N$ | 78 | 2350 | 25800 | $96{\cdot}5 \times 10^6$ |

The frequencies required increase rapidly with $n$ and in social affairs would often exhaust the data available. Exhaustion of the data, when it does occur, cannot be helped. We have to learn that in social affairs the data cannot always be as plentiful as we would wish. But then, of course, the ranks *are* immutable.

## 10. CORRELATION OF RANKS

Because more appropriate measures have not been available, the rank correlation coefficients of Spearman and of Kendall are often applied to correlate the ranks of two Bradford-type distributions. But these coefficients wholly ignore the sizes of the samples, as measured in terms of total frequencies, and on which the

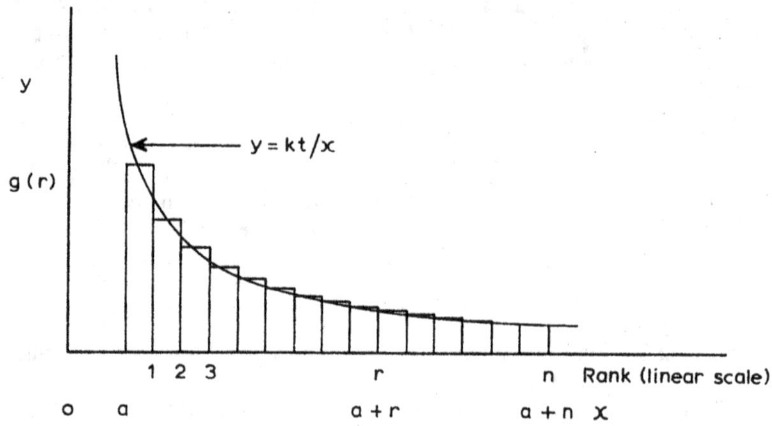


FIG. 2. *Ranks and the x-axis*

stabilities of the ranks depend. Moreover, they are based on assumptions which are certainly not satisfied by logarithmic frequency-rank distributions.

Some less inappropriate measures have become available as the result of work on 'order' statistics, notably by Kolmogorov and Smirnov. These new measures are derived from analysis of the ranked random samples drawn from conventional probability distributions and so come closer to our present needs. The calculation itself is very simple: one has to look only for the biggest difference between the two cumulative ranked distributions and then one relates the ratio of the difference to the total frequencies to (as usual) special statistical tables. Thus the new measure takes account of frequencies (and of sample size) as well as of ranks. Readable accounts of these new techniques and the required special tables are given in the textbook by Lindgren.[4]

But even these new measures, though better than the simple rank coefficients, are still not quite appropriate to Bradford-type distributions because the concepts on which they are based still give primacy to frequency statistics and to notions of random sampling which ignore social realities.

So new measures specially contrived for such distributions are needed. Though some difficult technical problems have first to be resolved, it looks to me as though the concept of correlation, inherited from conventional statistics, may have to be abandoned in social contexts. But these issues require a separate paper.

## II. TESTS OF SIGNIFICANCE

The concepts of social and of statistical significance are not always congruent. For example, in an election determined by independent votes the primary issue is usually: Who is the winner? i.e. Who is ranked *first*? The capture of a parliamentary seat from one political party by another may depend on a very small change in the pattern of voting—as in a 'marginal' seat. The small change of votes may not be *statistically* significant at any conventional level yet a change of winner is regarded as *politically* or *socially significant.*

So when the differences between two ranked distributions are being considered we need to be clear about the issue we are concerned with. If the issue is *statistical* then the well-known $\chi^2$ techniques are available. But if the issue is essentially *social*, the $\chi^2$ technique may not be appropriate.

At parliamentary election times the possible changes are usually discussed in terms of percentage 'swings' in the party allegiances of the electorate. A generalization of this concept to make it applicable to Bradford ensembles of many sources is the *transfer coefficient* $T$. The frequencies of the two distributions are first converted to percentages of their respective distribution totals. If $f_j$ and $g_j$ are the percentages corresponding to source $j$ (not *rank* $j$) in the two distributions, then

$$T = \tfrac{1}{2} \Sigma \, | f_j - g_j |. \qquad (11.1)$$

Within a single distribution, possible levels of *social* significance can be related to the *minimum* ranks of $T$ required to exchange ranks 1 and $r$ ($r = 2, 3, 4 \ldots . n$) for which

$$T = \tfrac{1}{2} \sum_{j=1}^{r-1} \{f_j - (r - 1) f_r\}. \qquad (11.2)$$

Some numerical examples of this measure are given in Appendix III, but more experience of its application is needed.

## 12. THEORETICAL MODEL AND PRACTICAL PERFORMANCE

Though the expected means $\mu_r$ can take any value required, the Poisson model does not fit the graph of $y = k/x$ exactly because the realization of a Poisson activity results in a discrete whole number. But any practical realization of the Poisson model, with the sources in their 'correct' positions, fits the graph even less well. The output $f(r)$ corresponding to the source of rank $r$ is a random sample from the Poisson distribution of mean $\mu_r$ and therefore has a standard deviation of $\mu_r^{\frac{1}{2}}$. So when the Poisson model is realized, as in computer simulation, some sources exceed their Poisson mean while others fall short of it. But when, as in practice, the actual outputs are reranked, a step-distribution results which is again a reasonably good fit to the graph of $y = k/x$ (Fig. 3).

Ranking is a smoothing process which imposes on the middle values the double rule: $f(r - 1) \geqslant f(r) \geqslant f(r + 1)$ so that each value of $f(r)$ is related to the values of its two neighbours. If $f(r)$ does not conform with this double rule then some reranking has to be done until it does. But at the ends of the ranked distribution this rule is relaxed. At the upper end, the output of the source of rank 1 has to satisfy only the single condition $f(1) \geqslant f(2)$ and so it has greater freedom to diverge from the regularity imposed on the others. At the lower end, also, the output of the last source of rank $n$ has only to satisfy the single condition $f(n) \leqslant f(n - 1)$, but if $f(n - 1)$ is already reduced to the value 1, $f(n)$ can take only the values 1 or 0, in spite of the relaxation afforded by the absence of the double conditions.

## 13. ESTIMATING THE NUMBER OF SOURCES

It is first necessary to clarify what is meant by 'the number of sources'. The frequency-rank technique associated with the Bradford law,[5] which depends on the use of semi-logarithmic graph paper, estimates the $N$ sources for which $\mu \geqslant 1$. The mixed Poisson model, however, can be used to estimate the total population, $P$, of sources engaged in the activity. The difference, $P$–$N$, is the

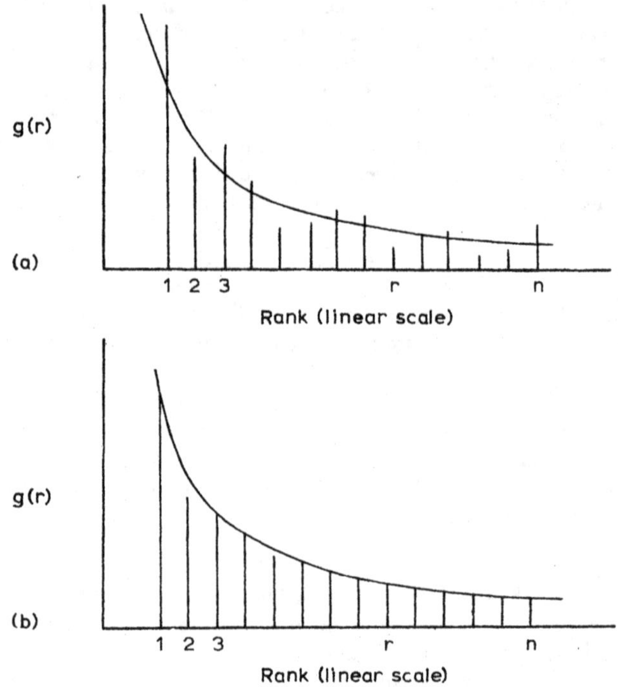


FIG. 3. *Effects of ranking: a, before*$_2$ *b, after*

number of sources which are *not* likely to be observed in action during the sampling period. Most of these sources are, of course, of low mean activities. They constitute the zero terms $\Sigma f(0)$, of the truncated mixed Poisson series which is the frequency distribution of the successful sources. The numerical value of $\Sigma f(0)$, and therefore of $P$, can be estimated from empirical data.

The sum of the terms of a truncated *simple* Poisson distribution of mean $\mu$ is

$$S = P\,e^{-\mu}\,(\mu + \mu^2/2! + \mu^3/3! + \ldots + \mu^r/r! + \ldots)$$

$$= P\,e^{-\mu}\,(e^{\mu} - 1) = P(1 - e^{-\mu}) = \sum_{r=1}^{\infty} f(r).$$

The algebraic sum of the same terms when the signs are alternated is

$$A = P\,e^{-\mu}\,(\mu - \mu^2/2! + \mu^3/3! - \ldots + (-1)^{r+1}\,\mu^r/r! + \ldots)$$

$$= P\,e^{-\mu}\,(1 - e^{-\mu}) = P\,e^{-\mu} - P\,e^{-2\mu} = f_1(0) - f_2(0)$$

where $f_1(0)$ is the zero term for unit period and $f_2(0)$ the zero term for a two-unit period. So $A$ is the expected number of *new* sources that would show activity if the observation period were doubled.[6]

We now regard the Poisson population as a *binomial* distribution of successes and failures. The probability $p$ of success is $1 - e^{-\mu}$, the probability that at least one item will be generated, and the probability $q = 1 - p$ of failure is $e^{-\mu}$. We can then write

$$p = \frac{S}{P} = \frac{S - A}{S} \text{ giving } P = \frac{S^2}{S - A}\,. \qquad (13.1)$$

This result can be verified by putting $S = P(1 - e^{-\mu})$, $A = P(e^{-\mu} - e^{-2\mu})$. We then have $S^2 = \{P(1 - e^{-\mu})\}^2$ and $S - A = P(1 - e^{-\mu})^2$. Similarly, $AS/(S - A) = f(0)$.

If the truncated Poisson distribution is simple, this technique yields the value of $P$, and therefore of $f(0)$, 'exactly', i.e. within the limits of sampling variance. But if the distribution is a mix of two or more Poisson distributions, the result of performing the above calculation yields

$$\frac{S^2}{S - A} = \frac{(\sum S_r)^2}{\sum S_r - \sum A_r} \qquad (13.2)$$

which is not equal to

$$\sum \left\{ \frac{S_r^2}{S_r - A_r} \right\},$$

the sum we seek. In fact, (13.1) underestimates $S^2$ by $S^2\sigma^2/\mu^2$ where $\mu$ and $\sigma^2$ are the mean and variance of the distribution of $p$. So (13.1) should be corrected to

$$P = \frac{S^2}{S - A}\left(1 + \frac{\sigma^2}{\mu^2}\right). \qquad (13.3)$$

The values of $\mu$ and $\sigma^2$ have to be estimated from the truncated data, a problem requiring analysis to be reported in a subsequent paper.

Hitherto, Bradford distributions have not been regarded as truncated; the zero term has been thought to be inaccessible. But as the zero term can now be found the problems of dealing with the Bradford and related distributions are much simplified if the zero terms are admitted. The Bradford plus zero term then becomes a mixed Poisson distribution of a regular kind which is much more amenable to statistical analysis by conventional methods.

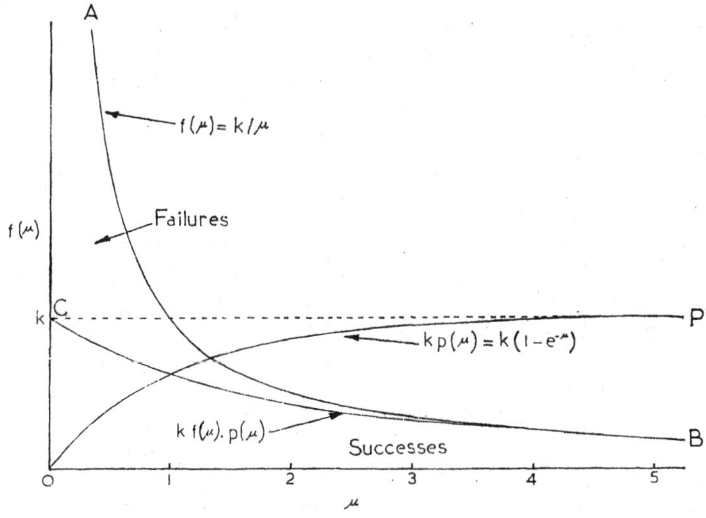


FIG. 4. *Estimating the number of sources*

Thus, the frequency distribution of means then becomes

$$\mathrm{d}f(\mu) = e^{-\mu} \,.\, e^{\mu} \frac{k}{\mu} \,\mathrm{d}\mu$$

$$= \frac{k}{\mu} \,\mathrm{d}\mu \qquad (a < \mu < \lambda\, a)$$

where $a > 0$ and $\lambda > 1$, so that

$$f(\mu) = k \ln \lambda \quad \text{or} \quad k = (\ln \lambda)^{-1}.$$

We then have

$$\mu = \int k \,\mathrm{d}\mu = a\,(\lambda - 1)/\ln \lambda$$

$$\sigma^2 = \int \mathrm{kv}\,\mathrm{d}\mu = a^2 (\lambda - 1)\,(\lambda^2 - \lambda + 2)/2\,(\ln\lambda)^2 \qquad (13.4)$$

for the mean and variance respectively.

This frequency distribution is transformed into the frequency-rank distribution, familiar to those who have used the Bradford techniques, by putting $\log \mu = -z$, so that $\mathrm{d}\mu/\mu = -\mathrm{d}z$. We then have $\mathrm{d}f(\mu) = -k\mathrm{d}z = \mathrm{d}f(z)$ which implies that the density of sources along the logarithmic axis is uniform—a distribution equivalent, of course, to the inverse of the distribution of means from which the mixed Poisson model is derived. We also have

$$f(z) = k[z] = k \log \{(a + n)/a\} \qquad (13.5)$$

since $z = -\log (a + n)$ and $-\log a$ when $\mu = a + \mathrm{n}$ and $a$ respectively. In this case $k$ is the number of sources, $N$, for which $\mu \geqslant 1$ and so the graphical technique which depends on (13.4) is validated.

The graphical method is simple to use but it does require the data to be related to some homogeneous activity. The alternating sign technique is more robust and can be applied to heterogeneous mixes of activities. On the other hand, the graphical method provides an estimate of $N$ even if only a few of the most active sources and their activities have been observed, whereas the frequency method requires the sample to be as comprehensive as possible.

## 14. DETERMINING THE RANK ORIGIN

When cumulated Bradford data are graphed with $r = 1, 2, 3 \ldots.$ on semi-logarithmic paper, a curve which continues to rise often emerges. To test whether such a graph conforms with Bradford's law, first find the ranks $v$ and $w$ which correspond to cumulated sums of items $S$ and $2S$ respectively. We then have

$$S = k \log \{(a + v)/a\}$$

$$\text{and } 2S = k \log \{(a + w)/a\}$$

$$\text{so that} \quad \log \{a + w)/a\} = 2 \log \{(a + v)/a\}$$

$$\text{or} \quad (a + w)/a = \{(a + v)/a\}^2$$

$$\text{from which} \quad a = v^2/(w - 2v).$$

This value of $a$ is an estimate which should be checked over further values covering the whole range of the distribution. If the estimates are reasonably equal, the data conform with the Bradford law. If the data are now reranked $a + 1$, $a + 2$, $a + 3$ . . . and are replotted, a linearity is obtained. (This technique was introduced by Elizabeth Wilkinson,[7] but is repeated here for the sake of completeness.) When applied to the data of Appendix I, it gives $a = 66 \cdot 27$.

The technique enables the distribution to be fitted to the appropriate interval under the graph of $y = k/x$. The greater the value of $a$ the more nearly uniform the distribution becomes. It is a parameter whose usefulness as a measure of the overall restraint imposed on the source activities has not yet been exploited.

## 15. HYBRID BRADFORD FORMS

With only minor and obvious modifications, all that has been said about the pure logarithmic form discussed so far can be applied to the hybrid forms of the Bradford law of which two types have now been observed.

In the Type I described by Bradford the initial curve rises more and more steeply over the nuclear sources of ranks 1 to $c$ until it runs into a linearity. The first example of Type II was noted by Mr Valentine Reilly who observed it in a Bradford graph in which the sources were the natural languages—English, French, German, Russian, Spanish . . .—and the items were papers on a topic of agricultural science published in the world's literature. In this type, the initial curve rises steeply at first but then less and less steeply until it runs into the linearity (Fig. 5).

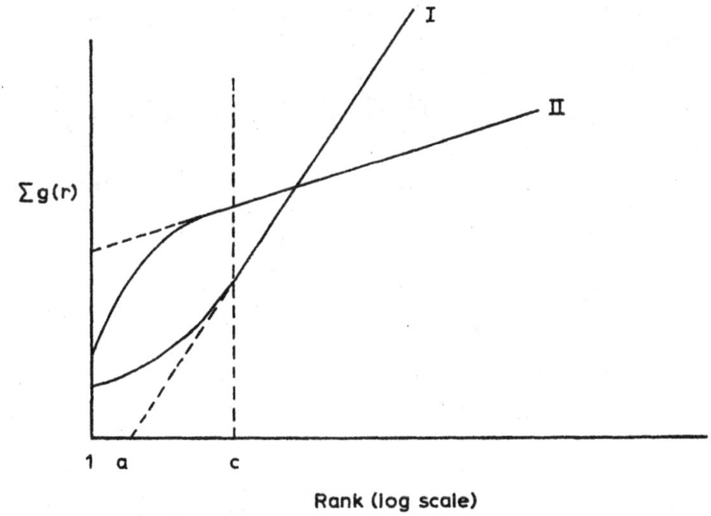


FIG. 5. *The two hybrid forms: I, nuclear restraint; II, nuclear enhancement*

In an earlier paper[5] I suggested that the rising curve corresponding to the nucleus could be expressed in the form

$$G(r) = a\, r^{\beta}, \qquad r = 1, 2 \ldots c,$$

but I now believe that these initial curves are more accurately described as second logarithmic distributions in which the intervals on the $x$-axis of the successive ranked sources have been either contracted (Type I) or expanded (Type II) as compared with the unit intervals of the linear part of the graph.

In both situations a hybrid Bradford distribution results which can be expressed as a hybrid logarithmic distribution with rank distribution function

$$Q(r) = \log_b \{(a + \sum_r \alpha^{c-r})/a\} \qquad r = 1, 2 \ldots c, \qquad (15.1)$$

$$= \log_b \{(a + r)/a\} \qquad r = c + 1, \ldots n,$$

where $b = (a + n)/a$ and where $\alpha < 1$ for Type I and $\alpha > 1$ for Type II.

Graphs of the pure logarithmic form arise when *all* the source activities are subject to precisely the same set of conditions. Graphs of the hybrid forms arise when *some* of the sources—those ranked 1 to $c$—are subjected to some additional *restraint* (Type I) or enjoy some *enhancement* (Type II). The additional restraint packs the sources 1 to $c$ more closely on the $x$-axis; the enhancement pulls them more widely apart. But within the ranks 1 to $c$ the intervals form the geometric series $\alpha^c, \alpha^{c-1}, \ldots \alpha$, so that the most active sources are those whose activities are most modified by the hybridizing conditions. If these sources are reranked on the log-scale according to these intervals then the whole hybrid distribution is represented by one linear graph (Fig. 6).

In Type I, items that, under equal conditions, would have been produced by the nuclear sources are distributed over the remaining sources; and in Type II items that, under equal conditions, would have been produced by the extra-nuclear sources are attracted to the nuclear sources. Type I is exemplified by the data on conference participation (Appendix III). Every member of the conference has an equal chance of contributing, subject only to the rule that when two or more members indicate to the chairman their readiness to speak, the chairman chooses. In such cases, the chairman often gives preference to the member who, up to that point, has contributed least. The most active members are those who most frequently risk losing that preference and constitute the nuclear graph of the conference. And Type II is exemplified by data on the languages of scientific publications. A Dutchman, a Dane, a Finn may prefer to publish his papers in one of the major languages of his science and so reach a readership much wider than that offered by his own natural language. In both cases the transfer of items is proportional to log $\alpha$.

In the two hybrid forms there are analytical conditions which the parameters $a$, $c$, and $\alpha$ must satisfy but which are not of immediate relevance to the present paper.

## 16. HOMOGENEITY OF DATA

Most of the Bradford anomalies referred to me for elucidation have arisen because the items considered have not been *homogeneous*.

Consider the student members of a large school (formal membership of which identifies the potential sources) and assume that we could discover how many apples and bananas they individually consumed over some specified period. We then regard each child as a source (or sink). These sources could then be ranked in three ways: in order of their decreasing totals of *apples only* or of *bananas only* or of *apples and bananas*, i.e. 'fruit'! Though I have no data to corroborate my

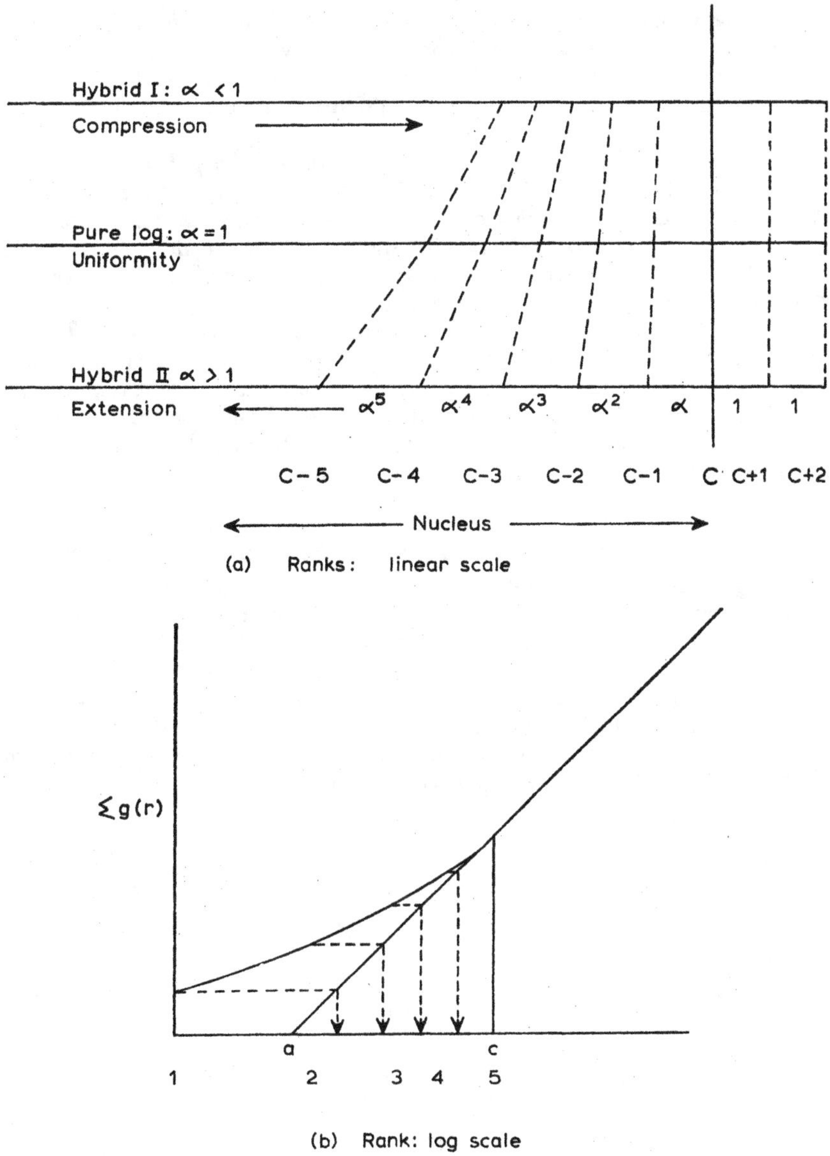


FIG. 6. *Linearizing the hybrid nuclear zones: Type I*

hypothesis, I guess that the distribution of apples and of bananas would both be Bradfordian but that the distribution of 'fruit', i.e. of apples *and* bananas, a conflation of the two Bradfords, would *not* be Bradfordian. The graph for fruit may be linear, for example, but yield a hopelessly wrong end-point.

Problems of homogeneity arise in bibliographic contexts. For example, citations *from* a literature *S* are not homogeneous unless they are limited to citations *to*

*S* also. Many citations found, say, in papers on fluid mechanics may relate to documents which are mathematical or medical or which relate to applications over diverse fields. Only citations *from S to S* would be homogeneous in the sense required. The lists of citations published by ISI do not conform with the Bradford law.

Again, a search for papers on a topic such as *Technique A applied to the study of B* as, for example, *Application of statistical techniques to genetics*, may cause difficulties. Papers in *genetics* are well indexed but *statistical applications* can range from the trivial and unindexed to the very sophisticated which are more likely to be indexed: such applications range so widely that the purpose of the search needs to be defined more precisely for homogeneity.

So when asked to elucidate some Bradford anomaly I first look at the homogeneity of the sources—are they adequately defined?—and then at the homogeneity of the items. In both cases it should be possible to say at once of any potential source or any potential item whether it is to be included or not. In fact, I have gradually come to use conformity with the Bradford law as a test of the homogeneity of the data of both sources and items.

## 17. THE ACTIVITY PROFILES OF SYSTEMS: FREEDOM AND CONTROL

If we regard the operating units of a system as an ensemble of sources and their activities, recorded in some common measure, as the related Bradford items, then the operating units of the system can be ranked and the usual Bradford-graph can be drawn. Such graphs reveal much about the system at a glance.

The whole range of Bradford forms appears in such profiles. In Fig. 7 the linear logarithmic graph A typifies a system of units which work wholly independently and with no overall control whatever; the public library system of South Korea is of this type. The items are 'transactions'.

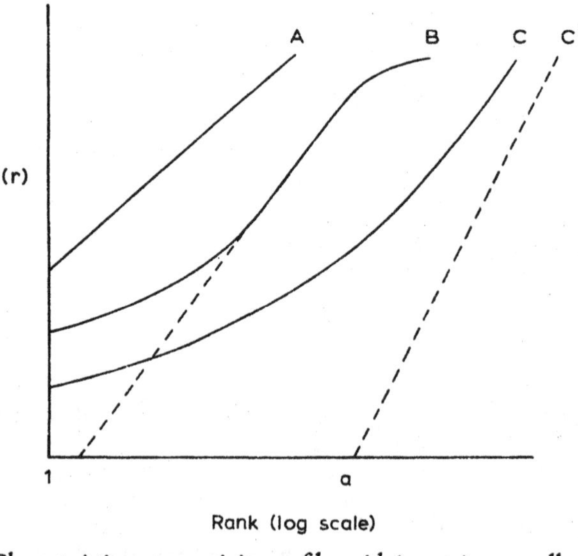


FIG. 7. *Characteristic system activity profiles with increasing overall control*

The hybrid form B, together with the droop at the upper end which signifies incompleteness, typifies a library system which is partly controlled and which is also growing: the library system of the State of Illinois is of this type. One of its present policies is to extend its range of library services into the more rural regions of the State, aiding the founding of new libraries with central funds and professional advice.

The rising curve C, which transposes into the pure linear form $C^1$, represents a library system with overall control; the libraries of British universities conform with this type of system.

So the 'bibliograph' applied to systems betrays the degree of control imposed overall. The measure of that control is given by the value of $a$ (or of $\log a$). In view of the recent proposed limitations on capital expenditure I expect the value of $a$ for the British university library system to increase steadily over the next few years.

In the quantitative analysis of such profiles, the usual end-point estimation is of no interest unless a specified minimum level of activity is demanded of all units admitted to the system. The interest in system profiles lies elsewhere.

My collected data on library systems suggests that the evolutionary trend of library systems (and probably of other systems too) is from the 'free-for-all', 'private enterprise' state of system A, through the partly controlled 'mixed economy' state of system B, to the completely controlled 'socialist' state of system C, the profile moving steadily from left to right over the graph. The movement to the right can theoretically continue, with firmer and firmer overall control, until all the units operate on equal terms, as $a \to \infty$.

The main value of such profiles is that, given valid data, they reveal in a simple graphical way the objective state of any system of operating units and so can be used as aids in the formulation of managerial policies and in monitoring their effects.

## 18. SAMPLING THE BRADFORD DISTRIBUTION

### (a) *The observation period*

It has already been emphasized that every set of Bradford data is a random sample whose magnitude is determined by the observation period. The effects of varying this observation period have already been discussed in Section 7.

### (b) *By sampling the items*

Sampling of the *items* may be regarded as a random binomial process in which the proportion $p$ is selected and $q = 1 - p$ is rejected. Such sampling is equivalent overall to a reduction of the source mean activities from $\mu_r$ to $p\mu_r$. It is therefore equivalent to a reduction of the observation period from, say, $t$ to $pt$.

### (c) *By sampling the sources*

Sampling of the *sources* involves a change of scale of the rank intervals. If the proportion of sources selected at random is $p$, then the expected total number of sources in the sample will be $pn$, and the interval units will be contracted also in the same proportion. So the constant $a$ of the original distribution now becomes $pa$.

If the original distribution had the cumulative frequency function

$$G(r) = (a + n) \log \{(a + r)/a\} \quad r = 1, 2, \dots n,$$

the sample distribution function will be

$$\begin{aligned} G_1(s) &= (pa + pn) \log \{(pa + s)/pa\} \qquad s = 1, 2, \ \ldots pr \ldots pn \\ &= p(a + n) \log \{(pa + pr)/pa\} \\ &= p\ G(r). \end{aligned}$$

But, of course, the new source ranks $s$ can increase only by intervals of 1, so we must write

$$G_1(s) = (a_1 + m) \log \{(a_1 + s)/a_1\} \qquad s = 1, 2, \ \ldots pn,$$

where $m = pn$ and $a_1 = pa$.

The three kinds of sample are illustrated in Fig. 8.

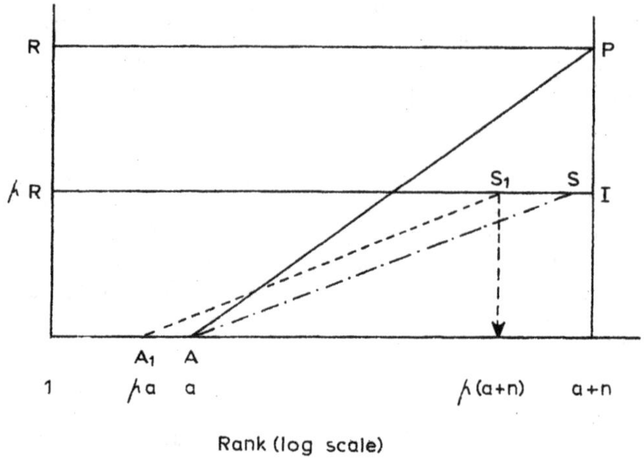


FIG. 8. *Sampling of the Bradford distribution* AP *by time or by items* (AS) *and by sources* (AS)

(d) *Sampling the Bradford totality of items*

On the Poisson model the Bradford totality of items is also a Poisson variate and Poisson variates have a relatively large variance. If the expected totality is $R$ then the standard deviation of $R$ is $R^{\frac{1}{2}}$.

However, in most cases we cannot assume that the parameters of any given Bradford ensemble—the values of $a$, $n$, $\mu_r$—will remain constant indefinitely. All are likely to be changing in unknown ways. So though we may be seeking to estimate the value of $R$ we are much more likely to be seeking (as in bibliography) one particular estimate of $R$ than in seeking the distribution of all possible values of $R$. And this particular value of $R$ will have to be realized at least in part, i.e. will have to be sampled. So we have to collect *some* data and the easiest data to collect are those from the more prolific sources which enable the bibliograph to be drawn in part. We then have to estimate the remainder, which is also a Poisson variate, and this remainder decreases rapidly as the Bradford data are collected.

If, for example, $a = 10$, $n = 990$ so that $R = k \log \{(a + n)/a\} = k \log 1000/10 = k \log 100$, we have to collect data on only the 90 most prolific sources to reduce the remainder derived from the unknown 900 less prolific sources by half. If $R'$ is this remainder, we have

$$R' = k \log 100 - k \log \{(10 + 90)/10\}$$
$$= k \log 100 - k \log 10 = k \log 10 = \tfrac{1}{2} R.$$

More generally, if the outputs of the most active $m$ sources are known, the remainder is reduced to

$$R_m = k \log \{(a + n)/(a + m)\}$$

with the corresponding variance also of $R_m$.

## 19. BRADFORD AND ZIPF DISTRIBUTIONS

The Zipf distribution has now been defined in so many ways in the literature of statistics, in frequency rather than in rank terms, that it is not now clear exactly how it should be defined. In earlier papers on Bradford's law I have taken the Zipf law to be what I would now express as

$$Q(r) = \log_b \{(a + r)/a\} \quad 0 < a \leqslant 1 \tag{19.1}$$

which is the logarithmic law with a restricted value of the parameter $a$. This restriction ensures that the cumulative graph meets the rank-axis to the left of the rank origin at 1.

Bradford's law as generalized in the present paper embraces both this version of the Zipf law and all logarithmic laws for which $a > 1$, so that the Zipf law, at least as I have understood it, is now subsumed under the more general Bradford or logarithmic law.

The Zipf law arose from the statistical study of vocabulary. Zipf noted that if the frequencies of occurrence of the words in a given text are counted, and the words are then ranked in order of decreasing frequency of occurrence, then the words conform closely with the law

$$g(r) = k/r \quad r = 1, 2, 3 \ldots .$$

which is an approximation to the log law. But Zipf himself preferred to work on the frequency formulation of his law and considered the Riemann series $f(r) = k/(a + r)^{\alpha}$ with $\alpha \approx 2$, as the most promising candidate (and the Zeta-function integrals to which the frequency function, equation (7.5), of the Bradford law approximates supports this idea). This problem of finding a frequency formulation of vocabulary data has occasionally attracted the attention of statisticians but, though their functions become steadily more elaborate,[8] none has yet won general consent. Most of them, however, fit some data part of the way. And it seems that none of the contributors to this problem have yet appreciated that the empirical data are samples whose frequency formulation will vary with the size of the sample relative to the total population—in this case, of an author's vocabulary.

So, as Zipf abandoned the use of ranks in favour of frequencies, whereas Bradford's law can be expressed simply only in terms of ranks, I see no further reason to continue to use Zipf's name descriptively in the context of Bradford's law. When as many ambiguities surrounded the Zipf law as once surrounded the Bradford law, the use of Zipf's name in the present context serves no useful purpose.

However, there is one relation between the law of vocabulary (Zipf's law) and Bradford's law which is of documentary interest. Imagine that we have 'done a Zipf count' on all the words that occur in the documents which constitute the English-language literature of some scientific subject $S$. The most frequently occurring words, and therefore those of ranks, 1, 2, 3 . . . $i$, in the total vocabulary will be those of the matrix of the English language, the everyday words—*a*, *the*, *it*, . . . in which the technical terms of $S$ are embedded. We now assume that the first technical term which is specific enough to be acceptable as an information-bearing index term has the rank $i + 1$ and that further indexing terms appear thereafter at random but at an average of $k$ words, where $k < i$. What is the rank distribution of index terms?

The distribution functions will be:

Of *all* words from $r = 1$,

$$Q(r) = \log_b \{(a + r)/a\}, \quad a \approx 1, \text{(Zipf)}$$

$$\approx \log_b (1 + r) \text{ when } b = n + 1.$$

Of *all* words from $r = i + 1$ onwards,

$$Q'(r) = \log_c \{(i + r)/i\} \quad r = 1, 2, 3 \ldots (n - i)$$

where $c = (n - i)/i$.

Of every $k$th word thereafter

$$Q_1(s) = \log_d \{(\alpha + s)/d\} \quad s = 1, 2, , , (n - i)/k \tag{19.2}$$

where $\alpha = i/k$, $d = ic/k$, since here the scale of the rank axis is reduced in the ratio $1/k$.

But (19.2) is the distribution function of a Bradford distribution of parameter $\alpha$. And so posted index terms conform with the Bradford law, as Griffiths[9] has reported.

## 20. BRADFORD'S LAW AND INFORMATION THEORY

Goffman and Morris[10] noted that a homogeneous library service conforms with the pure Bradford law. Its activity can therefore be represented in the form

$$R = (a + n) \log \{(a + m)/a\} \tag{20.1}$$

where $m$ is the number of books loaned at least once in the observation period, $n$ is the number of books available for loan, and $a$ is the measure of restraint on the users.

From information theory, the Shannon–Hartley formula for the capacity of a telecommunications channel is

$$C = B \log \{(N + S)/N\} \tag{20.2}$$

where $B$ = bandwidth: cf. number of books available, plus $a$.

$N$ = noise power: cf. restraint on users.

$S$ = signal power: cf. number of books loaned.

So the Bradford law expresses the 'channel capacity' of the library as a channel of communication between the users and the authors of its books, and does so in terms of its stock and its activity. It offers a means of calculating the distribution of books in a library system which optimizes *R* the total channel capacity of the system.

The analogy is not fortuitous. The same formula (20.1) expresses Zipf's formula for an author's use of his vocabulary. And Zipf also noted that it described the activities of telephone exchanges also. So Bradford's law expresses a very general characteristic of the *physical* aspects of human communication, of its use of the instruments—words, numbers, books, papers, telephone, traffic—which has not yet been generally recognized or exploited in the design of information systems.

## 21. THE BRADFORD LAW IN OPERATIONAL RESEARCH

The analytical techniques of OR are implicitly physical. They usually demand identification and measurement of all the variables that bear on the central objective and study of their interrelations so that the total pattern is made plain. In many cases, however, the Bradford law offers a much simpler and more easily grasped solution because the effects of the variables which bear on the central objective directly affect only the single key parameter of the law in an additive way and so they do not need to be analysed in detail, nor even identified. This is a big subject and only one possible application can be outlined here.

A question which must now concern many librarians is to consider how present economic restraints may affect the usage of their libraries. Consider a simple example.

Most libraries offer a variety of services to a mixed user population, mixed in the sense that some user groups may command greater privileges than others. The first need is to reduce any problem concerning the library service as a whole to a set of homogeneous services in each of which only one service relates to only one category of users—to ensure that the Bradford law applies.

Conformity with the Bradford law in such situations implies that the group of users of any service range from the most active, enthusiastic and knowledgeable users to casual intermittent users who are near the threshold beyond which use of the service ceases, and that the range of users constitutes a Bradford ranking.

All the data that are then strictly needed are (i) the total number of such users—say $n$, and (ii) the actual activity of the few most active and therefore most prominent users over some reasonable typical period. With these data the parameter $a$ can be found.

The important point about this parameter $a$ is that it measures, in precisely the operational terms required, the effect on the users of any level of restraint already imposed on them by the library (and there are always some). If further restraints have to be imposed as, for example, a shortening of the hours of access to the library, the numerical value of $a$ will increase. By how much? The answer (as will any other kind of analysis) has to be found empirically, but the results of any additional restriction can be assessed quickly and simply by studying its effects on the small group (10?) of the most prominent group users of the particular service. The new value of $a$, say $a_1$, can thus be found.

With this new value, the overall effect can be estimated. The Bradford law asserts that (Fig. 9) the whole group of users will be pushed a distance $(a_1 - a)$ to the right along the rank axis. A total of $(a_1 - a)$ users will therefore be pushed past the threshold at $T$ and will be lost. And the proportion of the total service that will be lost is proportional to the area hatched in the diagram. It is

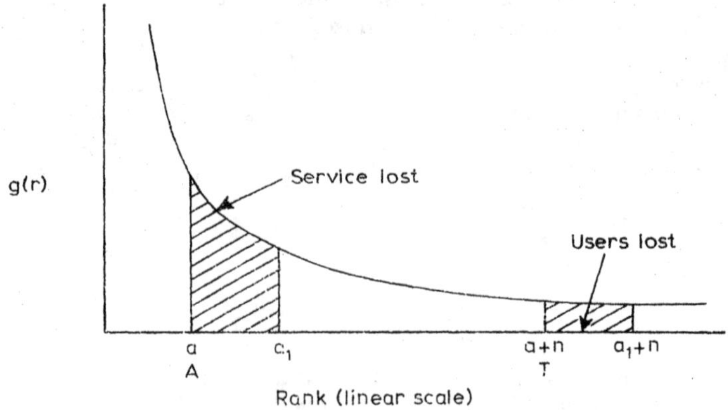


FIG. 9. *Effects of cuts on a homogeneous library service*

$$\int_a^{a_1} k/r \, \mathrm{d}r \Big/ \int_a^t k/r \, \mathrm{d}r = \log (a_1/a)/\log (t/a).$$

This example is necessarily crude. In practice, the Bradford technique offers a monitoring service of little cost which, with experience, enables the effects of such changes to be predicted.

## 22. DEVELOPMENT OF THE MIXED POISSON MODEL

The mixed Poisson model presented here is only a beginning. It opens up further exploration of the Bradford law by application of the well-developed theory of stochastic processes which deals in a general way with the seeming chaos of random phenomena. In its present form it is the simplest possible stochastic model of the Bradford law, but it can easily be modified, for example, to embrace problems of growth and obsolescence—the classical 'birth and death' process of stochastic theory. But such development requires the application of more advanced statistical techniques. Yet, at the same time, Bradford's remarkable empirical law has an important contribution to make to the theory of stochastic processes as applied to social phenomena.

## 23. THE STATISTICS OF INDIVIDUALITY

I have argued elsewhere that the mathematics and statistics we now see were derived from the physical sciences where they have been applied with immense success. Applied to social affairs, however, mathematics and statistics have been much less successful, because inherent in them are physical concepts which do not apply to humans; I need only point to the confusions of economic theory to make this point. One of the reasons why it has taken 40 years to elucidate the Bradford law is that all of us (including myself) who have worked on it believed that its mysteries would yield to analysis by the techniques we have inherited from the physical sciences.

Bradford *ranked* the sources in order of their performance as indicated by the relevant frequencies and was able to express the law he noted very simply. But *ranked* frequency data are alien to physical mathematics, though in social affairs ranking is very commonly used—from such serious matters as parliamentary elections and academic achievements to sporting activities such as cricket, football and all other competitive games, and to other fields of entertainment such as the weekly 'top-of-the-pops' charts indicate. So *ranking by frequency* is a technique widely used and understood.

The main difference between conventional and rank statistics is that in conventional physical statistics the entities of interest are grouped into anonymous classes defined only by the fact that they share some common numerical characteristic. In conventional statistics the end-of-season table of a football league would look like:

| Points | 21–30 | 31–40 | 41–50 | 51–60 | 60+ | Total |
|---|---|---|---|---|---|---|
| Frequency | 2 | 6 | 7 | 5 | 2 | 22 |

a table which would not satisfy the ardent adherents of Manchester United or Aston Villa. So football league tables name each team and rank them individually according to the number of points they have earned. Every team is named and ranked. We like to see the results of parliamentary elections and other social competitions similarly displayed. The naming and the ranking are of social interest.

Bradford was therefore a pioneer in social mathematics. Unfortunately the techniques to deal with social statistics as competently as with physical statistics are not yet established. But they are desperately needed. Ranking is more primitive than measuring. We learn to rank before we learn to speak or count. It is *because* ranking is a primitive action which permeates all social activities that it is time it were taken more seriously, by statisticians and mathematicians.

It may be that Bradford, working in the quiet field of bibliography, through his ranking technique and his discovery of an empirical social law (which describes how we rank ourselves in every ensemble we join), has founded a new discipline now needed—the statistics of individuality.

## 24. BRADFORD'S LAW IN RESEARCH

My last point about the Bradford law is that those who begin to work with it are at first delighted to discover new contexts in which it 'works'. However, after a few experiences of this kind, as with other natural laws, it is the contexts in which the law does *not* work as expected which create the interesting problems and reveal new discoveries.

First, the data on both sources and items have to be checked. Are they complete? Are they homogeneous? Then all the basic assumptions have to be considered, one by one. It is only in this way, by analysis of anomalies and misfits, that the Bradford law can become a fruitful analytical research tool.

The log law is the basic empirical law of the social activities of a population and represents the free play of individualistic activities. The hybrid forms of the Bradford law, however, are of the greater social interest, because they provide a simple *measure* of the extent to which anarchic individualism can be modified by social interaction.

The data in Table A1 were published in *The Times* (15 September 1976), just after the end of the 1976 cricket season. The short table shows the 20 batsmen who scored more than 1,450 runs in the first-class game. The cut-off at 1,450 runs is made only to reduce the size of the table to a reasonable length for illustration purposes.

TABLE A1. *Cricket data*

| $r$ | $f(r)$ | $F(r)$ | $G(r)$ | $g(r)$ |
|---|---|---|---|---|
| Z.A. | 2554 | | | |
| D.A. | 2110 | | | |
| 1 | 1821 | 1821 | 1825 | 1825 |
| 2 | 1818 | 3639 | 3622 | 1797 |
| 3 | 1759 | 5398 | 5394 | 1722 |
| 4 | 1752 | 7150 | 7140 | 1746 |
| 5 | 1727 | 8877 | 8862 | 1722 |
| 6 | 1695 | 10572 | 10559 | 1697 |
| 7 | 1692 | 12264 | 12233 | 1674 |
| 8 | 1624 | 13888 | 13885 | 1652 |
| 9 | 1620 | 15508 | 15514 | 1629 |
| 10 | 1588 | 17096 | 17122 | 1608 |
| 11 | 1572 | 18668 | 18709 | 1587 |
| 12 | 1569 | 20237 | 20276 | 1567 |
| 13 | 1554 | 21791 | 21822 | 1546 |
| 14 | 1546 | 23337 | 23349 | 1527 |
| 15 | 1526 | 24863 | 24858 | 1509 |
| 16 | 1488 | 26351 | 26348 | 1490 |
| 17 | 1470 | 27821 | 27820 | 1472 |
| 18 | 1453 | 29274 | 29274 | 1454 |

Inspection of the data suggests that it may be a hybrid Bradford of Type II because the first two batsmen (Zahir Abbas and Dennis Amiss) stand clear of the rest and are temporarily omitted from the calculation that follows. The graph of Fig. 10 of the cumulated data, $F(r)$, shows a curve which continues to rise but that it is worth considering whether a transposition of the origin of ranks could yield a linear logarithmic graph.

If the data conform with the logarithmic law they have to fit the equation

$$G(r) = (a + n) \log_b \{(a + r)/a\}, \; n = 18,$$

where $b = (a + n)/a$. For ease of calculation we now write

$$G(r) = (a + n) \frac{\ln\{(a + r)/a\}}{\ln\{(a + n)/a\}}$$

and so substitute logarithms to the base $e$ (or to the base 10) for logarithms to the base $b$.

The first task is to find the value of $a$ from the data. Here we have $G(n) = 29274$ so the median lies at the value of $r$ corresponding to $29274/2 = 14637$. On examining the data of Table A1, this value of $r$ is approximately $8 + (14637$

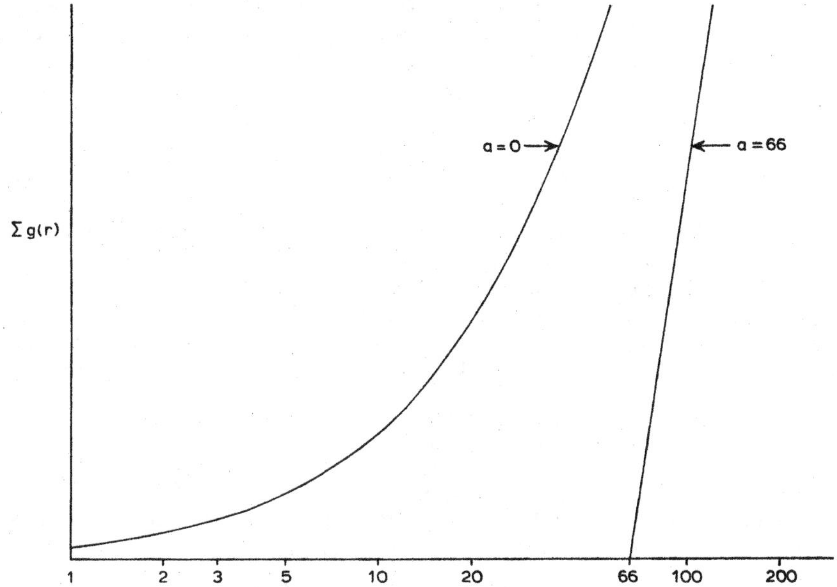


FIG. 10. *Bradford distribution of batting totals*

$- 13888)/1620 = 8 \cdot 46$. The value of $a$ is then given by Wilkinson's technique:

$$a = 8 \cdot 46^2/(18 - 2 \,.\, 8 \cdot 46) = 66 \cdot 27.$$

We can now write

$$G(r) = k \ln\{(a + r)/a\}$$

where $a = 66 \cdot 27$, $k = 29274/\ln\{(66 \cdot 27 + 18)/66 \cdot 27\} = 121828$, so that

$$G(r) = 121828 \ln\{(66 \cdot 27 + r)/66 \cdot 27\}.$$

The values of $G(r)$ for $r = 1$ to $r = 18$ are given in Table A1. The values of $g(r)$ are found by successive subtraction of the corresponding values of $G(r)$.

It is evident that, by conventional statistical standards, the fit is very close indeed. For the $\chi^2$-test we find that $\chi^2 = 1 \cdot 977$ which indicates a good fit even for *one* degree of freedom (for which $\chi^2 = 1 \cdot 64$ at 20% and $2 \cdot 71$ at 10%). For the Kolmogorov–Smirnov test, we seek the largest difference between $F(r)$ and $G(r)$ and find it to be 41 when $r = 11$. So $D_n = 41/29274 = 0 \cdot 0014$ which is considerably less than the critical limits for this test which are $0 \cdot 244$ at the 20% and $0 \cdot 309$ at the 5% levels.

These frequency statistics techniques are derived from different concepts of random sampling and are therefore not strictly applicable. But they are also much too crude for rank statistics which, because of the smoothing of the data which ranking implies, need new measures of goodness to fit.

However, the point remains that these cricket data fit the logarithmic law extraordinarily well. In fact, the close fit continues for the 82 batsmen who scored more than 800 runs. The law applies equally well to bowling performances when the items considered are the *totals* of wickets taken. The value of $a$ is approximately the same also.

In this context, little meaning can be attached to the end-point as it arises in bibliographic Bradford problems, but as we know the values of $k$ and $a$ we can easily estimate how many batsmen scored at least $M$ runs. The equation of the related hyperbolic curve $y = k/r$ here becomes

$$y = 121828/(66{\cdot}27 + r)$$

and if we put $y = M$ we can solve this equation for $r$. Thus if $M = 1000$, $r = 121{\cdot}83 - 66{\cdot}27 = 55{\cdot}56$ or 56 to the nearest integer; if $M = 900$, $r = 69$, and if $M = 800$ we similarly get $r = 86$. As the actual numbers are known to be 56, 69, and 82 respectively, it looks as though the log law is beginning to get short of batsmen in the 800's.

Returning to the two batsmen omitted from the above considerations, we can now accommodate them, if desired, under the linear graph already established by assigning them intervals larger than the unit intervals of the remainder. For Amiss we solve the equation

$$\ln\{66{\cdot}27/(66{\cdot}27 - a_1) = 2110/121828$$

which yields $a_1 = 1{\cdot}14$ and for Abbas we find $a_2 = 1{\cdot}35$. So the original value of $a$ has to be modified (in the Hybrid II) to $(29274 + 4554)\ln\{63{\cdot}58 + 18 + 2{\cdot}49)/63{\cdot}58\} = 121095$. This gives the single graph

$$G(r) = 121095 \ln\{(63{\cdot}58 + r)/63{\cdot}58\}$$

with $r = 1{\cdot}35, 2{\cdot}49, 3{\cdot}49, 4{\cdot}49 \ldots 20{\cdot}49$ or, preferably,

$$G(r) = 121095 \ln\{(64{\cdot}07 + r)/63{\cdot}58\}$$

with $r = 0{\cdot}86, 2, 3, 4 \ldots 20$.

which yields the first two enlarged intervals without undue disturbance of the remaining ranks.

To explain how two batsmen escaped from the logarithmic regularity of all their fellows, and so made a hybrid Bradford distribution of the enhanced type, requires a greater knowledge of the cricket scene than I command. I can only applaud their exceptional skills.

It has to be emphasized that the extraordinarily exact regularity in the performance of cricketers which is illustrated here escapes capture by frequency statistics and can be observed only by means of the ranking technique that Bradford adopted in his bibliographical studies.

## APPENDIX II. SIMULATION OF THE MIXED POISSON MODEL

A simulation of the mixed Poisson model was undertaken to see how the output changed with time. A *closed* set of 100 Poisson sources was aligned as a regular logarithmic array and so that $\mu_r = 100 \ln\{(1 + r)/r\}$ which makes $\mu_{100} = 0{\cdot}995$ for $t = 1$. The simulated output was then observed at intervals of time equivalent to $t = 0{\cdot}2, 0{\cdot}4, 0{\cdot}6, 0{\cdot}8, 1, 2, 3, 4, 5$ units.

The graph of Fig. 11 shows how the frequencies of the logarithmic distribution build up from $t = 0$. It will be seen that $f(0, t)$ falls steeply at first and then less and less steeply as $f(0, t)$ decreases but that it reaches zero (in the practical sense) only when $T \approx 4$. Meanwhile $f(1, t)$ increases steeply initially but reaches a maximum at about $T = 0{\cdot}4$ and thereafter declines slowly to zero before $T = 5$. There-

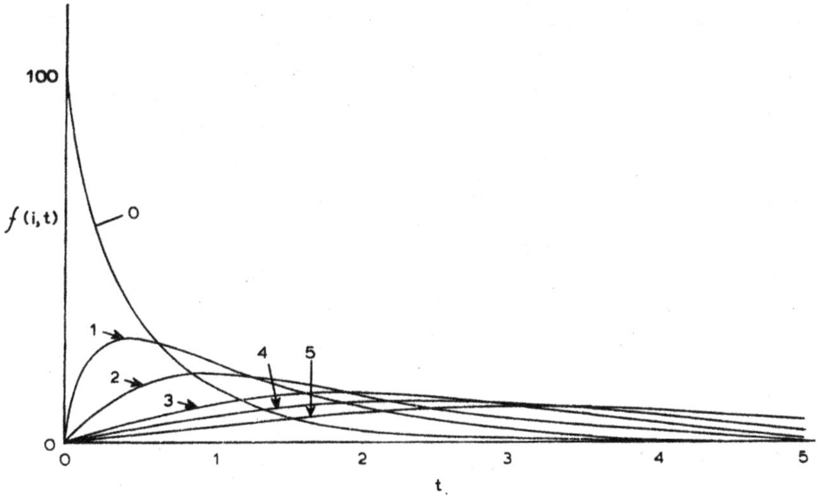


FIG. 11. *Simulation of the Bradford frequency distribution*

after, as $i$ increases, the graphs rise ever more slowly to a maximum and then decline.

The simulation data make it possible to check the alternating sign test for 'completion' (Section 13):

| $t$ | 1 | 2 | 4 |
|---|---|---|---|
| $f(0, t)$ | 15 | 3 | 0 |
| $-\Sigma(-1)^i f(i, t)$ | 12 | 3 | 0 |

The table indicates that 12 sources become active for the first time between $t = 1$ and $t = 2$; that 3 more were found between $t = 2$ and $t = 4$, and that, by $T=4$ all sources had been found.

I am indebted to Miss Jose-Marie Griffiths for the computer simulation.

## APPENDIX III. DATA ON CONFERENCE BEHAVIOUR

The set of data discussed here was kindly provided by Mr Bernard Williams. The data relate to a three-day conference held at NRC. It was attended by 50 members all of whom, together with the chairman and the recorder, remained unchanged for the duration of the conference. So here we have an ensemble of 52 potential sources which remained 'closed'. How did they behave as contributors to the formal discussions which followed each paper?

Expressed as a frequency distribution the scores were:

| $i$ | 1, | 2, | 3, | 4, | 5, | 6, | 7, | 8, | 9, | 10, | 11, | 12, | 13, | 14, | 15 |
|---|---|---|---|---|---|---|---|---|---|---|---|---|---|---|---|
| $f(i)$ | 9, | 6, | 3, | 4, | 1, | 2, | 1, | – | 2, | 1, | 1, | – | 1, | 1, | 1. |

And as a ranked order:

15, 14, 13, 11, 10, 9, 9, 7, 6, 6, 5, 4, 4, 4, 4,
3, 3, 3, 2, 2, 2, 2, 2, 2, 1, 1, 1, 1, 1, 1,
1, 1, 1,

The cumulative sums 15, 29, 42, 53, 63, . . . are graphed as in Fig. 12. The result is a typical Bradford hybrid which, when the steepest line of best fit is drawn, indicates that the members ranked 1, 2, 3, and 4 were all restricted to some extent.

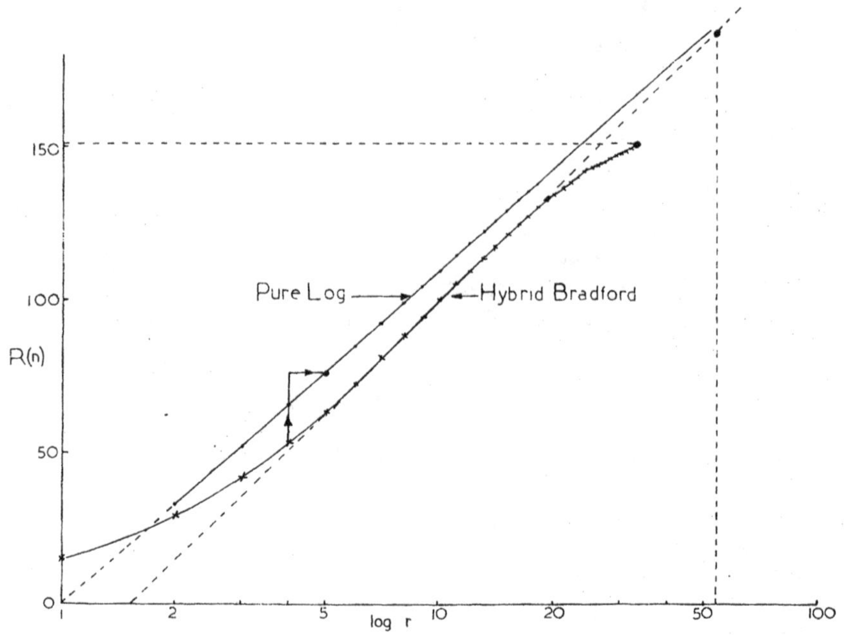


FIG. 12. *Bradford distribution of conference performance*

To find the parameters of the linearity we take two points from the data which lie on the line. When $r = 10$, $\sum g(r) = 100$ and when $r = 5$, $\sum g(r) = 63$. Hence we can write

$$100 = k \log 10 - k \log a$$
$$63 = k \log 5 - k \log a.$$

From these two equations we find $k = 53 \cdot 32$ and $a = 1 \cdot 53$. As $k = a + n$, $n = 52$ to the nearest integer, which is the estimated number of potentially active sources within the time-span of the conference.

The effect of the chairman's preference for speakers from 'the back row' is indicated by the loss of contributions by the nuclear group. This loss totals $k \ln a = 53 \cdot 32 \ln 1 \cdot 53 \approx 23$. To consider the chairman's role in redistributing these 23 contributions from the nuclear group of 4 to the peripheral group, the corresponding 'free-for-all' log linearity can be constructed. First, the 23 items are added to the observed contribution of the nuclear group so that the cumulative total for the sources ranked 1 to 4 is raised from 53 to $53 + 23 = 76$.

The simple log law then gives

$$76 = k' \ln (1 + 4), \text{ since } a' = 1,$$

or $k' = 76/\ln 5 = 47 \cdot 2$. Thus the number of members willing to contribute under the harsher conditions of the free-for-all is reduced from 52 to 47. Assuming that the same number of contributions, 151, would be made in the free-for-all, the number of contributors $n$ is given by

$$151 = 47{\cdot}2 \ln (1 + n)$$

which yields $n = 24$. Thus the chairman's selection of speakers, when selection was possible, diverted 23 contributions from the nuclear group to the peripheral group of 48 numbers and also increased the number of contributors from the 24 of the free-for-all to the 33 observed.

Thus the Bradford hybrid shows how social forces can modify individualistic behaviour and also provides a measure, in this case of the effect of the social acceptance of the chairman's role, of these social forces on individualistic behaviour. The members of this homogeneous conference group unwittingly but naturally adapted their contribution behaviour to conform with the hybrid Bradford law.

When the transfer coefficient $T$ (Section 11) is applied to the conference data, we have:

$$T(1, 2) = \tfrac{1}{2}(15 - 14)/151 = 0{\cdot}33\%$$
$$T(1, 3) = \tfrac{1}{2}(15 + 14 - 2{\cdot}13)/151 = 0{\cdot}99\%$$
$$T(1, 4) = \tfrac{1}{2}(15 + 14 + 13 - 3{\cdot}11)/151 = 2{\cdot}98\%$$

with $T(1, 5) = 4{\cdot}30\%$ and $T(1, 6) = 5{\cdot}96\%$.

## REFERENCES


1. BRADFORD, S. C. *Documentation*. Crosby Lockwood, London, 1948.
2. FELLER, W. *An introduction to probability theory and its applications*. Vol. II. Wiley, New York, 1968.
3. BROOKES, B. C. *The statistics of individuality*. (To be published.)
4. LINDGREN, B. W. *Statistical theory*. 2nd ed. The Macmillan Co., New York, 1968.
5. BROOKES, B. C. Bradford's law and the bibliography of science. *Nature*, *224*, 1969, 953–5.
6. BROOKES, B. C. A sampling theorem for finite discrete distributions. *J. Doc.*, *31*, 1975, 26–35.
7. WILKINSON, E. M. The ambiguity of Bradford's law. *J. Doc.*, *28*, 1972, 122–30.
8. SICHEL, H. S. On a distribution law for word frequencies. *J. Am. Statist. Assoc.*, *70*, 1975, 542–7.
9. GRIFFITHS, J. M. Index term input to IR system. *J. Doc.*, *31*, 1975, 185–91.
10. GOFFMAN, W. *and* MORRIS, T. Bradford's law and library acquisitions. *Nature*, *226*, 1970, 922–3.



(*Revised version received 12 July 1977*)

Reprinted from the Journal of the American Society for Information Science, Vol. 29, No. 5, 1978. 

# An Empirical Examination of Bradford's Law and the Scattering of Scientific Literature

**M. Carl Drott and Belver C. Griffith**
*The Graduate School of Library Science, Drexel University, Philadelphia, PA 19104*

**Twenty-three data sets representing the documents retrieved by a wide variety of searches were examined for correspondence to Bradford's Law. Regression lines fit to the data sets showed all correlations in excess of 0.96. Thus, the fitted line, as customarily specified by slope and intercept, can serve as a good representation of an entire data set. Slope can be shown to be almost entirely determined by the total number of articles retrieved. Over two-thirds of the variance in the intercept is accounted for by the total number of journal titles retrieved. These findings weigh against earlier speculation that slope and intercept depended on such characteristics as breadth of subject area, topic, time period, or search technique. The findings show that Bradford's Law is the reflection of some underlying process not related to the characteristics of the search mechanism or the nature of the literature. The authors conclude that there is instead a basic probabilistic mechanism underlying the law.**

In a field as complex as information science it is both surprising and comforting to find a quantitative relationship which holds over a large number of situations and subject fields. One such relationship appears to be Bradford's Law which describes the dispersion of articles on a particular subject among journal titles. This relationship was first recognized by Bradford [1] and its mathematical form has been explored by Vickery [2], Leimkuhler [3], and Brookes [4-6]. Numerous investigators have reported empirical confirmation using data from a wide variety of sources.

It is the purpose of this paper to examine some questions which arise in connection with the application and usefulness of Bradford's Law. It has been suggested that a variety of situational factors, such as the sources of data, the methods of data collection, and the subject field of the data, may be related to the mathematical parameters associated with Bradford's Law. The data conforming to Bradford's Law may be for literature covering a broad subject area or a narrow scientific subspecialty, the field may be in the realm of "hard" science, social science, or technology. Articles may be located by searching a single abstracting and indexing service or by a comprehensive examination of all available sources.

The mathematical parameters which characterize a line fit to data, and therefore, the conformity of data to Bradford's Law, include slope, intercept, and, often, some measure of goodness-of-fit (e.g., variance accounted for). For example, it has been suggested that the slope can be used to estimate the completeness of a particular search and that the intercept is an indicator of subject breadth.* Bradford's Law has been applied to decisions involving tests of collection adequacy, journal acquisition and retention policies, and the evaluation of indexing services.

The most widely used mathematical formulation of Bradford's Law is that proposed by Brookes:

$$R(n) = k \log n,$$

where $n$ is the rank of a journal in terms of relevant papers published and retrieved, and $R(n)$ is the cumulative number of papers published by the first $n$ journals and retrieved in the search. Data is commonly displayed in the form of a semilogarithmic plot of log rank versus cumulative number of papers. In such a figure the slope of the line corresponds to the constant $k$.

In dealing with actual data, certain divergences from the mathematical form have been observed. In particular, journals with numerically low rank (those journals contributing the most papers) tend to produce fewer papers than the formula would predict. On the other hand, journals with numerically high rank (those contributing few papers) have also been reported to contribute fewer papers than would be predicted. The general practice, and the one which we shall follow, is to deal with each of these segments of the data separately.

The effect of the failure of the initial points to fit on the straight line requires a revision of the formula for the line to

$$R(n) = k \log (n/s)$$

(a variation originally proposed by Brookes) where $s$ is the intercept on the $x$ (log rank) axis.

*The origins of these claims are difficult to determine. They appear in a number of empirical studies and review articles and are alluded to in some texts. If attributed, these ideas are most often credited to Brookes. A careful reading of Brookes, however, shows that he did not make such claims. Brookes does include some speculation on these possibilities but carefully identifies them as extrapolations from a mathematical approximation. In view of the confused record, and our own negative opinion of the validity of these claims, we believe it would be unfair for us to attribute them to specific individuals.

### Collection of Data

In order to examine the various aspects of Bradford's Law we have drawn data from a variety of sources. First we have taken data from published articles which report that their data fit Bradford's Law. The selection of these articles has been somewhat arbitrary in that we have selected for diversity of subject areas and data sources. We were also limited to articles presenting complete tabular data (as opposed to graphical data only).

We have used searches based upon the technique of cocitation clustering developed by Small and Griffith [7-9]. Briefly, document pairs are identified by being frequently cited together by other articles (in this case, we required that pairs be cocited at least 11 times per year). The resulting group of documents cocited pairwise with each other is called a cluster. All documents citing at least a pair of documents from a cluster are retrieved as being relevant to that cluster. In practice this results in sets of documents which are intuitively reasonable and whose relevance is confirmable by experts in the subject field. We have used this technique to perform searches on an area of hepatitis research, on a biochemical specialty area in viral genetics and on a specialty which combines aspects of chemistry and physics in the study of molecular orbital theory. We supplemented these searches with several searches performed on the Medline system.

### Sources of Data

In order to predict what patterns of regularities the parameters of the Bradford Distribution should portray, it is necessary to examine the sources and nature of our data. This section presents brief descriptions of the data drawn from the literature and of the sources of our own data. We acknowledge in advance the inadvertent injustices which we may do in summarizing the work of others and urge readers to examine the original papers listed in the bibliography.

We performed both Medline and cocitation searches for a biomedical speciality dealing with hepatitis research. Central to this area of study is a recently discovered substance called Australia antigen (HBAu), of which the presence in blood is associated with hepatitis. This field has important clinical applications in screening for blood banks and may have theoretical importance in the more general study of disease processes. The most important papers in our cocitation cluster are by Blumberg [10] and Prince [11]. Important descriptors for Medline are "Hepatitis Virus" and "Australia Antigen."

The general area of viral genetics is the fastest growing research field in all of science. We have selected a subspeciality which deals with cytoplasmic RNA and polyadenylic acid sequences in RNA. These studies are important in the development of basic theories of molecular biology and may have long-range application to cancer and related diseases. Important papers on this subject include those by Loening [12] and Bishop [13].

The study of molecular orbital theory deals with both chemistry and physics. The field involves special approximations to the equations of quantum mechanics. The methods involved, while oriented towards problem solution, have high theoretical content. The central works in the field are those by Pople [14].

The two data sets from Bradford were drawn from comprehensive bibliographies compiled by the staff of the Science Museum Library. Sources included numerous abstracting journals and scanning of incoming periodicals by the library staff. The two specific subject areas were chosen because it was felt that their bibliographies were unusually complete. The subject areas were identified as applied geophysics and lubrication but were not defined further. The time periods covered were 1928 through 1931 and 1931 through June 1933, respectively.

Freeman [15] presents data on a bibliography on the topic of marine biology. The topic is defined by noting that it is a portion of marine science which is not physical oceanography. Articles on the topic published in 1967 or 1968 were selected from the *Current Bibliography for Aquatic Sciences and Fisheries.*

The data presented by East and Weyman [16] was collected by taking every abstract under the heading "plasma physics" from the 1965 *Physics Abstracts.* The abstracts representing journal articles were selected from this list (approximately two-thirds of the total items). The data presented include only those journals appearing 12 times or more.

Lancaster's [17] data are a part of a much larger study of the Medlars demand search system. The sample is the articles retrieved by 302 searches covering a variety of medical topics. The searches were selected to be somewhat representative of searches performed on the system in 1966 and 1967. The data are divided into two groups, representing two levels of indexing used by the National Library of Medicine. Approximately one-third of the journals covered are designated as "depth" journals. Articles from these sources are indexed with about 10 terms per article. Articles from the remaining "nondepth" journals receive about 4 terms per article.

The two data sets from Lawani [18, 19] bear the relationship of set and subset. The larger data set represents a search on the topic of tropical and subtropical agriculture. The sample consists of all journal articles abstracted by *Tropical Abstracts* for the period 1967 through 1970. The data subset covers 1970 only.

The data by Wood [20] are based on a survey of users of social science periodicals at the National Lending Library. The data covers all social sciences material which was requested (even if it was unavailable). The use being surveyed is essentially interlibrary loan. Data were collected for one month in 1968.

The Cole [21] data are based upon answers to reference questions at the British Petroleum Company, Technical Information and Library Service. It is a 20% sample of questions answered in a nine-year period prior to 1958. It should be noted that 13 people accounted for 30% of all of the questions asked. Questions dealt with all aspects of the petroleum business.

The Goffman [22] study covered all journal articles appearing in *Index Medicus* under the heading "Transplantation Immunology." The period covered was 1965 through 1968.

Seethrama [23] draws his data from a comprehensive annotated bibliography, *Comparative Survey Analysis*, compiled in 1969 by S. Rokkan and an international committee. Both the topic and the bibliography are international in scope.

This collection of data sets provides us with rather wide-ranging possibilities for contrast and comparison. For example, we have two data sets based on reference questions (Wood and Cole), several on medicine including Goffman, our own Australia antigen searches, and the much broader Lancaster data sets. We have two topics in physics (East and our molecular orbital theory searches), and two which bear on social science topics (Seethrama and Wood). We have the same industry from different points of view (Bradford lubrication and Cole). Our own searches give us several specialities over time and the same speciality searched by different methods.

Some of our data sets were compiled by complete bibliographical search (e.g., Seethrama and Bradford), while others depended upon a single abstracting and indexing service (e.g., Goffman and East). A variety of time spans are represented. The size of the retrieved sets varies from about 300 articles in 100 journals to more than 8000 articles in 700 journals.

Thus we have provided a rather rich environment for examining differences and similarities reflected by the fit of data to Bradford's Law.

#### Preparing Data for Analysis

Before we begin our analysis, it is necessary to consider several problems inherent in fitting this type of data.

The first problem is that, as mentioned above, the first and last data points may not fit the expected straight line. One of our analytical options deletes the data on the top four journals and all journals contributing only one article each. These criteria, while somewhat arbitrary, are at least replicable. The slope and goodness-of-fit seem relatively insensitive to the exact rule selected for deleting points.

The second problem in fitting data is an apparent relationship between the total number of articles in a data set and the slope of the curve. This makes comparison of different Bradford plots very difficult. As a solution to this problem we used an analysis in which both frequency and rank are expressed as percentages.

The third problem with the usual form of data presentation is the smoothing effect introduced by the use of the cumulative number of articles. In order to deal with this problem we use a noncumulative distribution such as that used by Hockings [24]. In this analysis the variables are log rank and log frequency (the number of articles contributed by the journal of that rank). One possible value of this form of analysis was illustrated during our own work when several data points were keypunched incorrectly. The effect of this error on the fit of a standard Bradford curve was small and escaped detection. On the log-log data, however, the correlation dropped dramatically.

Each of the variations in data analysis suggested above has merit but none stands out with particular appeal. Thus we have done our analysis using each of the possible variations.

#### Fitting Data to Bradford's Law

There seems to be no generally accepted approach to fitting data to Bradford's Law. In much of the literature the data is simply plotted and the fit is determined by inspection. We have not found any approach to fitting this type of data which seems to have particular theoretical appeal. Therefore as a first test of the value of more precise measures we have simply fit a regression line to the data sets and observed the corresponding values of slope and correlation. There are, of course, several reasons why such an approach is mathematically suspect. However, we believe that the results give a good indication of what a more refined technique might produce. The benefits of our approach are that the computational techniques are simple and well known, that computer implementations of these calculations are widely available, and that this analysis can be readily replicated.

We performed our analysis by modifying each data set according to the possible combinations of the options discussed above. The resulting slopes and correlations constitute a 16 × 23 table which appears in Appendix A. These results, while of possible interest, are too massive for full discussion here. It is sufficient for our purposes to note that none of the data modifications seems to produce outstandingly different results. Thus we will limit our discussion to the results presented in Table 1. These results are the slope and the correlation for a regression line fit to the cumulative number of articles versus log journal rank for each data set. We also present the $x$ (log rank) intercept. For consistency with previous analyses, the intercept was calculated on the truncated data (first four journals and all journals occurring only once removed).

It is important to call attention to the fact that we have used logarithims to the base 10 throughout our analysis. There seems to be some tendency in the literature to use common logarithms when employing graphical methods but to switch to natural (base $e$) logarithms when solving algebraically.

#### Data Analysis

The most striking aspect of the analysis presented in Table 1 is the lack of apparent pattern. Consider, for example, the searches on Australia antigen done for the same year but by different techniques. The slopes are similar but with unexplained divergencies. In 1972, the slope of the data for Australia antigen by cocitation is closer to the two data sets on cytoplasmic RNA than it is to the slope for Australia antigen by Medline. In 1973 the pattern is even less clear with the slope of the Medline search data having more in common with Bradford's data on lubrication and

TABLE 1. Values of Bradford's Law parameters obtained from least-squares fits.

| Data Set | Journals | Articles | Slope[a] | Intercept[b] | Correlation[a] |
|---|---|---|---|---|---|
| 1. Australia antigen–Cocite–71 | 97 | 277 | 131.5 | 1.01 | 0.996 |
| 2. Australia antigen–Cocite–72 | 100 | 320 | 167.3 | 1.83 | 0.994 |
| 3. Australia antigen–Cocite–73 | 115 | 291 | 151.7 | 2.02 | 0.985 |
| 4. Australia antigen–Medline–69/70 | 95 | 257 | 103.8 | 0.32 | 0.993 |
| 5. Australia antigen–Medline–71 | 84 | 196 | 85.5 | 0.53 | 0.984 |
| 6. Australia antigen–Medline–72 | 133 | 282 | 149.2 | 2.40 | 0.982 |
| 7. Australia antigen–Medline–73 | 197 | 497 | 233.4 | 1.77 | 0.987 |
| 8. Cytoplasmic RNA–71 | 72 | 301 | 157.6 | 1.44 | 0.992 |
| 9. Cytoplasmic RNA–72 | 83 | 354 | 168.9 | 0.88 | 0.993 |
| 10. Molecular orbital theory–72 | 119 | 648 | 288.3 | 0.75 | 0.998 |
| 11. Molecular orbital theory–73 | 100 | 445 | 184.5 | 0.40 | 0.999 |
| 12. Bradford–applied geophysics | 326 | 1332 | 575.2 | 2.05 | 0.996 |
| 13. Bradford–lubrication | 164 | 395 | 198.8 | 2.31 | 0.992 |
| 14. Freeman–marine biology | 525 | 4006 | 1602 | 2.12 | 0.992 |
| 15. East–plasma physics | 70 | 7383 | 3636 | 0.59 | 0.997 |
| 16. Lancaster–Medlars depth | 667 | 4879 | 2561 | 9.55 | 0.985 |
| 17. Lancaster–Medlars nondepth | 735 | 1607 | 881.7 | 13.12 | 0.968 |
| 18. Lawani–tropical agriculture–70 | 374 | 2294 | 1206 | 5.86 | 0.987 |
| 19. Lawani–tropical agriculture–67-70 | 681 | 8808 | 3960 | 5.50 | 0.975 |
| 20. Wood–social science | 62 | 663 | 411.1 | 3.48 | 0.967 |
| 21. Cole–petroleum reference questions | 197 | 897 | 382.7 | 1.26 | 0.998 |
| 22. Goffman–transplant immunology | 272 | 1120 | 438.5 | 0.97 | 0.999 |
| 23. Seethrama–survey bibliography | 173 | 651 | 270.0 | 0.86 | 0.999 |

[a]Values of slope and correlation are based on a linear regression fit to cumulative articles versus log rank for each complete data set.

[b]Intercept is for a regression line fit to the data sets after removal of the first four journals and all journals contributing only one article.

Seethrama's bibliography of survey research than with any of the other six searches on Australia antigen. Turning to other data sets, viral genetics is one of the fastest moving areas in science while, by comparison, molecular orbital theory is changing and developing much more slowly. Contrary to this the slopes for consecutive years suggest greater stability for cytoplasmic RNA than for molecular orbital theory.

Looking at the data sets with the greatest slope we have Lawani's four-year study of tropical agriculture, followed by East's coverage of plasma physics and Lancaster's most important medical journals. If these topics share some unique common bond it is hard to see just what it is that sets them apart from the other data sets. Thus, generally, there seems to be no pattern of slope changes between fields. Rank-ordering the slopes shows an intermixing of theoretical and applied areas, of rapidly developing fields and those which change more slowly, and of general and highly specific subject areas.

There seems to be no particular pattern in the correlation. It is immediately striking that all of the correlations are extremely high. Our investigations with various data modifications mentioned above show that the correlations remain high for all transformations. Thus high correlation does not appear to be an artifact of the specific analytical method. The one general pattern of correlation which may be identified is a slight tendency for the subject areas which have the most articles to have poorer correlations. We see no particular importance in this.

Table 1 also gives the $x$ intercept for straight lines fit to the truncated Bradford curve (cumulative articles, first and last points removed). It has been suggested that the $x$ intercept (on the log rank axis) is related to the breadth of the field. Some of the data is promising with respect to this statistic. For example, the two Lawani data sets are searches on the same topic (tropical agriculture) which differ only in time span. The intercepts are very similar. The Lancaster data on Medlars nondepth journals shows a very high value for the intercept. The wide dispersion of articles over titles seems appropriate in such a case. On the other hand, it is not clear why Freeman's data on marine biology and our Medline search of Australia antigen in 1972 should have intercepts which indicate similar breadth. Nor is it clear why Bradford's data on lubrication should represent a topic of greater breadth than Cole's petroleum reference questions.

One of the major problems seems to be the sensitivity of the intercept to the exact line which is used to determine it. For example, in our Medline searches the use of truncated data rather than full data produced differences in the computed slope which ranged from 3% to 7%. The differences in $x$ intercept for the same data ranged from 5% to 21%. This sensitivity seems even more acute when lines are fit to the data by unspecified means (presumably inspection). For example, Freeman reports an intercept of 3.2 compared with our calculated value of 2.1, while Lawani, reporting on his larger data set, gives an intercept of 8.4 compared with a calculated 5.5. It is clear that anyone who wishes to claim some metric or predictive value for the intercept must first specify a replicable method by which the intercept can be determined.

It can be seen from the above discussion that claims

TABLE 2. Pearson correlations of selected data set parameters ($n = 23$).

| | Total Articles | Slope | Intercept ($x$) |
|---|---|---|---|
| Total journals | 0.59 | 0.58 | 0.82 |
| Total articles | | 0.99 | 0.34 |
| Slope | | | 0.38 |

TABLE 3. Prediction of data set parameters in terms of variance accounted for by variables.

| | Variables | |
|---|---|---|
| Parameters | Total Journals[a] | Total Article[b] |
| $x$ intercept | 0.67 | 0.02 |
| Slope | 0.00 | 0.99 |

[a]Predictor entered first for $x$ intercept.
[b]Predictor entered first for slope.

which relate to the interpretation of parameters of Bradford's Law bear a heavy burden of proof. On the surface, at least, these claims cannot be supported by the diverse data sources presented here. Yet, as we have noted above, while no overall pattern emerges, there may be regularities which would present some subtle pattern upon more detailed study of the data and its sources. We cannot refute such an argument; however, in the following section we shall argue for a simpler explanation, namely, that these regularities are most easily explained by the sizes (in terms of articles and journals) of the respective data sets.

#### Data Set Parameters

The literature on Bradford's Law has generally taken the view that the relationship between the cumulative total articles and the log of the journal rank was most appropriately explained in terms of the extrinsic characteristics of the data sets. By extrinsic characteristics we mean those descriptive variables which characterize a data set as the result of a unique bibliographic process of information retrieval. In this section we shall argue for an alternative point of view, namely, that the observed relationship is best explained as an intrinsic probabilistic relationship whose density function can be characterized by the total number of articles in the data set and the total number of journals.

As we have observed above, the correlations of regression lines fit to the data sets are extremely high. In other words, nearly all (between 94% and 99%) of the variance is accounted for by a relationship that can be fully described by the slope and the $x$ intercept. We exploited this finding in the section above by searching, without success, for a relationship between slope or intercept and the extrinsic characteristics of the data sets. Our conclusion was that there were no special patterns associated with the subject matter, source, or breadth of the data sets.

In order to explore the possibility that the data sets are a reflection of the operation of a single probabilistic law we

TABLE 4. Comparison of $x$ intercepts.

| Data Set | Observed Intercept[a] | Calculated Intercept[b] | % Error |
|---|---|---|---|
| 1. Australia antigen–Cocite–71 | 1.005 | 1.098 | +9 |
| 2. Australia antigen–Cocite–72 | 1.831 | 1.128 | -38 |
| 3. Australia antigen–Cocite–73 | 2.022 | 1.347 | -33 |
| 4. Australia antigen–Medline–69/70 | 0.323 | 1.076 | +233 |
| 5. Australia antigen–Medline–71 | 0.534 | 0.940 | +76 |
| 6. Australia antigen–Medline–72 | 2.399 | 1.601 | -33 |
| 7. Australia antigen–Medline–73 | 1.774 | 2.436 | +37 |
| 8. Cytoplasmic RNA–71 | 1.444 | 0.741 | -49 |
| 9. Cytoplasmic RNA–72 | 0.878 | 0.880 | 0 |
| 10. Molecular orbital theory–72 | 0.748 | 1.300 | +74 |
| 11. Molecular orbital theory–73 | 0.400 | 1.092 | +173 |
| 12. Bradford–applied geophysics | 2.054 | 4.001 | +95 |
| 13. Bradford–lubrication | 2.308 | 2.003 | -13 |
| 14. Freeman–marine biology | 2.115 | 6.013 | +184 |
| 15. East–plasma physics | 0.593 | 0.614 | +3 |
| 16. Lancaster–Medlars depth | 9.545 | 7.750 | -19 |
| 17. Lancaster–Medlars nondepth | 13.12 | 9.651 | -26 |
| 18. Lawani–tropical agriculture–70 | 5.856 | 6.806 | +16 |
| 19. Lawani–tropical agriculture–67-70 | 5.502 | 3.694 | -33 |
| 20. Wood–social science | 3.479 | 0.496 | -86 |
| 21. Cole–petroleum reference questions | 1.255 | 2.320 | +85 |
| 22. Goffman–transplant immunology | 0.965 | 3.306 | +243 |
| 23. Seethrama–survey bibliography | 0.860 | 2.055 | +139 |

[a]Based on a least-squares fit to each data set.
[b]Based on the formula: intercept = (articles × −0.00029) + (journals × 0.01401) − 0.18022.

TABLE 5. Variance reduction from a multiple-regression fit.

| Dependent Variables | Independent Variables | | | |
|---|---|---|---|---|
| | Scale Effect[a] | Intercept[b] | Slope[b] | Total Variance Reduction |
| Total articles | 0.34 | 0.06 | 0.60 | 1.00 |
| Total journals | | 0.60 | 0.00 | 0.93 |

[a]The relationship of total articles to total journals.
[b]Variables were entered with the smaller prediction effect first.

have calculated correlations based on our 23 data sets. These results appear in their entirety as Appendix B and are summarized for purposes of this paper as Table 2. The most striking correlations are 0.99 between the total number of articles and the slope and 0.82 between the total number of journals and the intercept. Both of these correlations are higher than would be explained by the correlation of 0.59 between the number of articles and the number of journals. Our findings in this area have been verified by both factor analysis and multiple regression; to avoid redundancy, we do not present the full analyses.

The correlation between the total number of articles and the slope explains over 98% of the variance in the slope. This strongly suggests that the slope is simply another way of expressing the number of articles found. Indeed, so much of the variance is explained that it is nearly impossible that any extrinsic variable could have any effect. Thus, to the extent that the slopes characterize the data sets, our case for an intrinsic probability distribution is supported.

We shall now turn our attention to the intercept as a data set characteristic. Table 2 shows that the relationship between the total number of articles and the intercept explains 67% of the variability in the intercept. We used multiple regression to determine whether we could better predict the data set parameters by using both of our variables. Tables 3 presents the results, reflecting a procedure of placing the stronger predictive variable into the relationship first. These results make clear that there is exceedingly little variance left to be accounted for by any variable. In order to check that the remaining 31% of the variance in the intercept was not explainable simply in terms of other data set characteristics, we used our regression equation to estimate intercepts for each of our data sets. A comparison of these estimated intercepts with the intercepts calculated from the full data sets is presented in Table 4. While the errors are highly variable and sometimes quite large we are unable to discern any pattern to which the remaining variance might be attributed.

In summary, we have shown that a data set can be appropriately characterized by the slope and intercept of a regression line fit to it. We have further shown that most of the variance in these parameters is explained by considering the total number of articles and the total number of journals to be the arguments of a probability function which generates the data sets. We have argued that the remaining variance is not readily explainable in terms of the extrinsic characteristics of the data sets. As a final analysis which may be of assistance in creating further theoretical models, we have shown the effect of predicting each of our variables using the other variable and the two data set parameters. This result is presented as Table 5. The basis of this analysis is a recognition that the variables, total articles and total journals, must be related logically and, in fact, are related empirically. We have labeled this relationship as a scale effect. The remaining variables were entered with the smaller prediction effect first.

## Conclusion

We began this research with the expectation that the various contrasts among our data sets would allow us to explicate the relationship between Bradford's Law and extrinsic characteristics of the data sets such as subject matter, rate of growth, and manner of search. The application of such relationships to management decisions in libraries and information centers has been widely speculated upon in the literature. Our analysis however, suggests that this entire point of view must be reconsidered. We have shown instead that data sets conforming to Bradford's Law can be well characterized by two numbers; the slope and the $x$ intercept of a regression line. These two numbers can be predicted almost completely by the two variables, total number of articles and total number of journals. We argue that this finding, and the failure to find any relationship to the extrinsic variables, supports the viewpoint that we are observing an intrinsic probabilistic process.

We began this paper by discussing the mathematical descriptions of Bradford's Law. Our findings strongly support these descriptions and add the relationship of the $x$ intercept to the total number of journals. We need further research to explicate the underlying probabilistic process which accounts for these mathematical regularities.*

## Acknowledgments

Much of the initial data selection and preparation was performed by A. Ben Wagner, who also provided important intellectual input. Janet V. Edelmann assisted with the programming and data analysis. We also thank Henry Small of The Institute for Scientific Information for assistance in selecting the cocitation data sets. Finally we acknowledge an important debt to all of the authors whose data we have used. Without their careful data collection and clear presentation, this work could not have been done.

This work was supported in part under Public Health Service Grant Number 5 R01 LM00911-0251 from the National Library of Medicine. Computing was also supported by Drexel University.

*As these analyses were being completed, two remarkable attempts to derive Bradford's Law formally were received from B.C. Brookes and Derek Price. Later work is planned to determine the compatibility of our empirical results with either theory.

## Appendix A

This section presents the slopes and correlations resulting from regression lines fit to each of our 23 data sets under various analytic options. These options are described above and summarized briefly below. Calculations were performed by a specially written program using the PL/1 language on an IBM 370/168 computer. The calculations were checked using an independently written program in the BASIC language on a DEC-10 computer. Details of the calculations are available from the first author.

The calculations in Table A1 are in the standard form found in the literature—namely cumulative number of articles versus log rank. Alternatively, Table A2 uses the form: number of articles in *i*th journal versus rank of *i*th journal.

Calculations indicated "Complete Distribution" use the full data provided in the original paper. "Truncated Distribution" indicates that the data for the first four journals (i.e., rank 1-4) were removed along with all journals contributing only one article each (if any). The columns "Articles After Truncation" and "Journals After Truncation" indicate the sizes of the respective data sets after truncation.

The percent option expresses the data for both articles and journals as percentages. The variables are (cumulative articles/total articles) versus log (rank/total journals) with appropriate variations for noncumulative and truncated data sets.

## Appendix B

The Table B1 presents the Pearson correlations between the various data set parameters which were presented in Appendix A. Correlations were calculated using the computer program from the Statistical Package for the Social Sciences (SPSS). As a check on the calculation, rank correlations (Spearman's and Kendall's) were also calculated and compared with the Pearson correlations. Correlations were also calculated after deleting the two most abberant data sets. None of these variations had any significant effect on the outcome and hence they are not reprinted here.

In addition to the variables presented in Appendix A we have added correlations for the ratio of the total number of articles divided by the total number of journal titles for each data set. We have also included cocitation—a binary variable which has a value of one for data sets obtained by cocitation and a value of zero for all other sets. Neither of these new variables enters significantly into our analysis.

TABLE A1. Slopes and correlations for regression fit using cumulative number of articles.

| Data Set | Journals after Truncation | Articles after Truncation | Complete Distribution | | | Truncated Distribution | | |
|---|---|---|---|---|---|---|---|---|
| | | | Raw Scores | | Percentages | Raw Scores | | Percentages |
| | | | Slope | *r* | Slope[a] | Slope | *r* | Slope[a] |
| 1. Australia antigen–Cocite–71 | 37 | 132 | 131.5 | 0.996 | −1.85 | 134.9 | 0.998 | −0.923 |
| 2. Australia antigen–Cocite–72 | 46 | 185 | 167.3 | 0.994 | −1.84 | 186.0 | 0.998 | −1.03 |
| 3. Australia antigen–Cocite–73 | 51 | 160 | 151.7 | 0.985 | −1.73 | 155.0 | 0.993 | −0.758 |
| 4. Australia antigen–Medline–69/60 | 26 | 85 | 103.8 | 0.993 | −1.88 | 96.6 | 0.999 | −0.661 |
| 5. Australia antigen–Medline–71 | 23 | 64 | 85.5 | 0.984 | −1.83 | 80.0 | 0.997 | −0.617 |
| 6. Australia antigen–Medline–72 | 48 | 147 | 149.2 | 0.982 | −1.69 | 144.3 | 0.992 | −0.593 |
| 7. Australia antigen–Medline–73 | 78 | 271 | 233.4 | 0.987 | −1.74 | 220.9 | 0.993 | −0.695 |
| 8. Cytoplasmic RNA–71 | 31 | 171 | 157.6 | 0.992 | −1.94 | 195.2 | 0.996 | −0.911 |
| 9. Cytoplasmic RNA–72 | 33 | 189 | 168.9 | 0.993 | −1.97 | 193.2 | 0.995 | −1.10 |
| 10. Molecular orbital theory–72 | 66 | 382 | 288.3 | 0.998 | −1.97 | 304.9 | 0.999 | −1.14 |
| 11. Molecular orbital theory–73 | 46 | 211 | 184.5 | 0.999 | −1.99 | 188.4 | 0.999 | −1.01 |
| 12. Bradford–applied geophysics | 153 | 880 | 575.2 | 0.996 | −1.84 | 612.4 | 0.997 | −0.895 |
| 13. Bradford–lubrication | 58 | 225 | 198.8 | 0.992 | −1.72 | 201.2 | 0.998 | −0.623 |
| 14. Freeman–marine biology | 309 | 3211 | 1602 | 0.992 | −1.94 | 1783 | 0.997 | −1.17 |
| 15. East–plasma physics | 66 | 4404 | 3636 | 0.997 | −1.99 | 3662 | 0.995 | −2.45 |
| 16. Lancaster–Medlars depth | 532 | 4438 | 2561 | 0.985 | −1.73 | 2717 | 0.991 | −1.38 |
| 17. Lancaster–Medlars nondepth | 351 | 1166 | 881.7 | 0.968 | −1.50 | 782.9 | 0.971 | −0.633 |
| 18. Lawani–tropical agriculture–70 | 257 | 1939 | 1206 | 0.987 | −1.77 | 1318 | 0.993 | −1.17 |
| 19. Lawani–tropical agriculture–67/70 | 396 | 7768 | 3960 | 0.975 | −1.88 | 4775 | 0.992 | −1.13 |
| 20. Wood–social science | 58 | 531 | 411.1 | 0.967 | −1.60 | 501.2 | 0.988 | −1.60 |
| 21. Cole–petroleum reference questions | 93 | 552 | 382.7 | 0.997 | −1.90 | 423.2 | 0.999 | −0.948 |
| 22. Goffman–transplant immunology | 113 | 650 | 438.5 | 0.999 | −1.87 | 460.9 | 0.999 | −0.931 |
| 23. Seethrama–survey bibliography | 67 | 360 | 270.0 | 0.999 | −1.89 | 287.4 | 0.999 | −0.821 |

[a]Correlations for percentage distributions exceeded 0.99 and were therefore omitted.

TABLE A2. Slopes and correlations for regression fit using noncumulative number of articles.

| Data Set | Complete Distribution | | | Truncated Distribution | | | Intercept[a] | |
|---|---|---|---|---|---|---|---|---|
| | Raw Scores | | Percentages | Raw Scores | | Percentages | $y$ | $x$ |
| | Slope | $r$ | Slope | Slope | $r$ | Slope | | |
| 1. Australia antigen–Cocite–71 | −0.854 | −0.975 | 5.29 | −0.812 | −0.978 | 2.84 | −0.288 | 1.005 |
| 2. Australia antigen–Cocite–72 | −0.896 | −0.972 | 5.30 | −0.814 | −0.972 | 3.13 | −48.85 | 1.831 |
| 3. Australia antigen–Cocite–73 | −0.752 | −0.972 | 5.25 | −0.606 | −0.968 | 2.66 | −47.40 | 2.022 |
| 4. Australia antigen–Medline–69/70 | −0.796 | −0.944 | 5.36 | −0.896 | −0.951 | 2.05 | 47.41 | 0.3231 |
| 5. Australia antigen–Medline–71 | −0.719 | −0.946 | 5.14 | −0.665 | −0.945 | 2.00 | 21.81 | 0.5338 |
| 6. Australia antigen–Medline–72 | −0.680 | −0.966 | 5.35 | −0.596 | −0.969 | 2.38 | −54.85 | 2.399 |
| 7. Australia antigen–Medline–73 | −0.748 | −0.973 | 5.76 | −0.692 | −0.975 | 2.71 | −55.02 | 1.774 |
| 8. Cytoplasmic RNA–71 | −1.07 | −0.960 | 5.16 | −1.22 | −0.952 | 2.47 | −31.12 | 1.444 |
| 9. Cytoplasmic RNA–72 | −1.09 | −0.968 | 5.37 | −1.30 | −0.983 | 2.93 | 10.89 | 0.8783 |
| 10. Molecular orbital theory–72 | −1.11 | −0.983 | 5.75 | −1.07 | −0.999 | 3.30 | 38.40 | 0.7483 |
| 11. Molecular orbital theory–73 | −1.05 | −0.984 | 5.60 | −1.06 | −0.982 | 2.84 | 74.91 | 0.4003 |
| 12. Bradford–applied geophysics | −0.963 | −0.977 | 6.42 | −0.899 | −0.982 | 3.28 | −191.4 | 2.054 |
| 13. Bradford–lubrication | −0.764 | −0.964 | 5.55 | −0.826 | −0.978 | 2.42 | −73.09 | 2.308 |
| 14. Freeman–marine biology | −1.19 | −0.978 | 7.29 | −1.14 | −0.990 | 4.33 | −580.0 | 2.115 |
| 15. East–plasma physics | −1.20 | −0.976 | 5.26 | −1.35 | −0.979 | 6.42 | 831.41 | 0.5929 |
| 16. Lancaster–Medlars depth | −0.983 | −0.935 | 6.89 | −0.902 | −0.963 | 5.58 | −2662 | 9.545 |
| 17. Lancaster–Medlars nondepth | −0.626 | −0.953 | 6.60 | −0.505 | −0.969 | 3.56 | −875.3 | 13.12 |
| 18. Lawani–tropical agriculture–70 | −1.02 | −0.941 | 6.43 | −0.891 | −0.965 | 4.38 | −1011.7 | 5.856 |
| 19. Lawani–tropical agriculture–67/70 | −1.41 | −0.939 | 7.43 | −1.27 | −0.933 | 4.31 | −3536 | 5.502 |
| 20. Wood–social science | −0.518 | −0.993 | 4.54 | −0.523 | −0.990 | 4.54 | −271.4 | 3.479 |
| 21. Cole–petroleum reference questions | −1.03 | −0.979 | 6.07 | −1.00 | −0.985 | 3.10 | −41.68 | 1.255 |
| 22. Goffman–transplant immunology | −0.970 | −0.978 | 6.34 | −0.957 | −0.990 | 3.23 | 7.14 | 0.965 |
| 23. Seethrama–survey bibliography | −0.967 | −0.974 | 5.93 | −1.06 | −0.988 | 2.67 | 18.82 | 0.8600 |

[a]Intercepts are calculated on the truncated distributions using raw scores.

TABLE B1. Pearson correlations: slopes and other parameters.

| | Articles | Bradford | Bradford Percent | Bradford–% Deleted | Bradford Deleted | Noncumulative | Noncumulative Percent | Noncumulative Deleted | Noncumulative–% Deleted | Ratio | Intercept $y$ | Intercept $x$ | Cocite |
|---|---|---|---|---|---|---|---|---|---|---|---|---|---|
| Total journals | 0.59 | 0.58 | 0.40 | 0.59 | 0.12 | −0.25 | 0.86 | 0.00 | 0.41 | −0.16 | −0.81 | 0.84 | −0.39 |
| Total articles | | 0.995 | −0.09 | 0.99+ | −0.49 | −0.64 | 0.57 | −0.49 | 0.78 | 0.55 | −0.62 | 0.34 | −0.35 |
| Bradford (cumulative)[a] | | | −0.07 | 0.99+ | −0.52 | −0.60 | 0.53 | −0.46 | 0.81 | 0.59 | −0.62 | 0.38 | −0.36 |
| Bradford–percent | | | | −0.08 | 0.47 | 0.64 | 0.25 | 0.75 | 0.03 | −0.38 | −0.24 | 0.65 | −0.26 |
| Bradford–deleted | | | | | −0.49 | −0.63 | 0.55 | −0.47 | 0.78 | 0.53 | −0.67 | 0.37 | −0.35 |
| Bradford–percent deleted | | | | | | 0.33 | 0.27 | 0.41 | −0.78 | −0.83 | −0.03 | 0.08 | 0.12 |
| Noncumulative | | | | | | | −0.48 | 0.92 | −0.39 | −0.31 | 0.33 | 0.14 | −0.16 |
| Noncumulative–percent | | | | | | | | −0.22 | 0.29 | −0.23 | −0.67 | 0.53 | −0.26 |
| Noncumulative–deleted | | | | | | | | | −0.30 | −0.41 | 0.08 | 0.33 | −0.19 |
| Noncumulative–percent deleted | | | | | | | | | | 0.67 | −0.37 | 0.39 | −0.30 |
| Ratio of articles/journals | | | | | | | | | | | 0.19 | −0.15 | −0.21 |
| Intercept $y$ | | | | | | | | | | | | −0.65 | 0.26 |
| Intercept $x$ | | | | | | | | | | | | | −0.31 |

[a]The nine variables Bradford (cumulative) through noncumulative–percent deleted are slopes.

## References


1. Bradford, S.C. *Documentation.* Washington, DC: Public Affairs; 1950.
2. Vickery, B.C. "Bradford's Law of Scattering." *Journal of Documentation.* 4(3):198-203; 1948.
3. Leimkuhler, F. "The Bradford Distribution." *Journal of Documentation.* 23(3):197-207; 1967.
4. Brookes, B.C. "The Derivation and Application of The Bradford-Zipf Distribution." *Journal of Documentation.* 24(4): 247-265; 1968.
5. Brookes, B.C. "The Complete Bradford-Zipf 'Bibliograph'." *Journal of Documentation.* 25(1):58-60; 1969.
6. Brookes, B.C. "Bradford's Law and The Bibliography of Science." *Nature.* 224(5223): 953-956; 1969.
7. Small, H. "Co-citation in The Scientific Literature: A New Measure of the Relationship Between Two Documents." *Journal of the American Society for Information Science.* 24(4): 265-269; 1973.
8. Small, H.; Griffith, B.C. "The Structure of Scientific Literatures. I. Identifying and Graphing Specialties." *Science Studies.* 4(1): 17-40; 1974.
9. Griffith, B.C.; Small, H.; Stonehill, J.A.; Dey, S. "The Structure of Scientific Literatures, II. Toward a Macro- and Microstructure for Science." *Science Studies.* 4(4): 339-365; 1974.
10. Blumberg, B.S.; Alter, H.J.; Visnich, S. "A New Antigen in Leukemia Sera." *Journal of The American Medical Association.* 191(7):541; 1965.
11. Prince, A.M. "An Antigen Detected in Blood During Incubation Period of Serum Hepatitis." *Proceedings of The National Academy of Sciences of the U.S.A.* 60(3):814; 1968.
12. Loening, V.E. "Fractionation of High-Molecular Weight Ribonucleic Acid by Poly-Acrylamide-Gel Electrophoresis." *Biochemical Journal.* 102(1):251; 1967.
13. Bishop, D.H.; Claybrook, J.R.; Spiegelman, S. "Electrophoretic Separation of Viral Nucleic Acids on Polyacrylamide Gels." *Journal of Molecular Biology.* 26(3):373; 1967.
14. Pople, J.A.; Segal, G.A. "Approximate Self-consistent Molecular Orbital Theory. 3. cndo Results for AB2 and AB3 Systems." *Journal of Chemical Physics.* 44(9):3289; 1966.
15. Freeman, C. "Bradford Bibliography and The Literature of Marine Science." *Australian Academic and Research Libraries.* 5(2):65-71; 1974.
16. East, H.; Weyman, A. "A Study in The Source Literature of Plasma Physics." *ASLIB Proceedings.* 21(4):160-171; 1969.
17. Lancaster, F.W. *Evaluation of The MEDLARS Demand Search Service.* Washington, DC: U.S. Department of Health, Education, and Welfare; 1968.
18. Lawani, S.M. "Periodical Literature of Tropical and Subtropical Agriculture." *UNESCO Bulletin of Libraries.* 26(2):88-93; 1972.
19. Lawani, S.M. "Bradford's Law and The Literature of Agriculture." *International Library Review.* 5(3):341-350; 1973.
20. Wood, D.N.; Bower, C.A. "The Use of Social Science Periodical Literature." *Journal of Documentation.* 25(2): 108-122; 1969.
21. Cole, P.F. "A New Look at Reference Scattering." *Journal of Documentation.* 18(2):58-64; 1962.
22. Goffman, W.; Morris, T.G. "Bradford's Law and Library Acquisitions." *Nature.* 226(5249):922-923; 1970.
23. Seetharama, S. "Documents on Survey Analysis." *Library Science with a Slant to Documentation.* 9(3):384-395; 1972.
24. Hockings, E.F. "Selection of Scientific Periodicals in an Industrial Research Library." *Journal of The American Society for Information Science.* 25(2):131-132; 1974.

*Reprinted from the* <u>*Journal of the American Society for Information Science*</u>*, Vol. 27, No. 5, September-October 1976.* 

# A General Theory of Bibliometric and Other Cumulative Advantage Processes*

**A Cumulative Advantage Distribution is proposed which models statistically the situation in which success breeds success. It differs from the Negative Binomial Distribution in that lack of success, being a non-event, is not punished by increased chance of failure. It is shown that such a stochastic law is governed by the Beta Function, containing only one free parameter, and this is approximated by a skew or hyperbolic distribution of the type that is widespread in bibliometrics and diverse social science phenomena. In particular, this is shown to be an appropriate underlying probabilistic theory for the Bradford Law, the Lotka Law, the Pareto and Zipf Distributions, and for all the empirical results of citation frequency analysis. As side results one may derive also the obsolescence factor for literature use. The Beta Function is peculiarly elegant for these manifold purposes because it yields both the actual and the cumulative distributions in simple form, and contains a limiting case of an inverse square law to which many empirical distributions conform.**

**Derek de Solla Price**
*Department of History of Science and Medicine*
*Yale University*
*New Haven, CT 06520*

## • Introduction

It is common in bibliometric matters and in many diverse social phenomena, that success seems to breed success. A paper which has been cited many times is more likely to be cited again than one which has been little cited. An author of many papers is more likely to publish again than one who has been less prolific. A journal which has been frequently consulted for some purpose is more likely to be turned to again than one of previously infrequent use. Words become common or remain rare. A millionaire gets extra income faster and easier than a beggar.

In statistics, such a process is commonly described by a skew or hyperbolic distribution function of the type that has been characterized by Simon (*1*) and correctly shown by him to be given by the Beta Function (this is not the "Beta Density" which is discussed by Feller (*2*) II:49 and includes a dependent variable) rather than the more commonly used "contagious" distributions, for example the negative binomial (*3,4,5*) or its limiting form, Fisher's logarithmic series distribution.

Although the relation between such distributions, the stochastic processes which lead to them and the Urn models from which they may be derived, seem well known and go back more than 50 years to Yule's (*6*) first use of such probability models to explain the distribution of biological genera and species, it does not seem that the full elegance of the Beta Function is widely appreciated; certainly not in the context of bibliometrics though good theoretical treatments have been given by Hill (*7,8*), Crowley (*9*), Hill and Woodroofe (*10,11*) and Sichel (*12*), all discussing the general varieties of contagious process that yields hyperbolic distributions. As we shall show, this distribution which we propose to call the *Cumulative Advantage Distribution* (*CAD*), [after the pioneering sociological work in which Cole and Cole (*13*) following Merton discuss accumulative advantage in social stratification of the scientific community] can be derived either from a modification of the Polya Urn model, or as a stochastic birth process. It provides a

*This research was funded by NSF grant SOC73-05428.

sound conceptual basis for such empirical laws as the Lotka Distribution for Scientific Productivity, the Bradford Law for Journal Use, the Pareto Law of Income Distribution, and the Zipf Law for Literary Word Frequencies. It is therefore an underlying probability mechanism of widespread application and versatility throughout the social sciences. Though I cannot hope to deal adequately with all its mathematical aspects, this account should make the general theory more available and thereby remove much of the present restriction to empirical laws whose functions is useful but not fundamental.

## • The Urn Model

The idea to use urn models to describe statistical after-effects or "contagion" seems to be due to Polya (see Feller (*2*) I:119, n.1). In general, the model supposes that fate has in storage an urn containing red and black balls; at regular intervals a ball is drawn at random, a red ball signifying a "success" and a black ball a "failure." If the composition of the urn remained fixed, the chances of success and failure would not vary, but if at each drawing the composition is *changed* by some rule, the *chances* will change as an after-effect of the previous history. A more general rule would be that after each drawing the ball is replaced and $c$ balls of the color drawn and $d$ balls of the opposite color are added before the next drawing takes place. For the Polya Urn Scheme, which can be shown to lead to a negative binomial distribution, $c > 0$, $d = 0$, so that at each drawing the number of balls of the color drawn *increases* while that of the other color remains unchanged. Thus, each occurrence of a red or of a black increases the probability of a *further* such occurrence. It is easy to see that only the numbers of reds and of blacks previously drawn, and not their sequence, determine the probabilities for the next drawing.

In the Polya Urn Scheme, success is rewarded by an increased chance of further success, but failure (*i.e.*, a black ball) is "punished" by an increased chance of further failure. Contagion, so to speak, is double-edged. In sociology, Merton calls this the Matthew Effect since "unto him that hath is given and unto him that hath not is taken away, even that which he hath." In fact, as we shall show, many of the known empirical data can be made to agree with a law which proceeds from the first part of the verse, but without the negative feedback of the second part. A trivial modification can make the effect of contagion single-edged so that success *increases* the chance of further success, but failure has no subsequent effect in changing probabilities. In effect, for many of the applications discussed, failure does not constitute an event as does success. Rather it must be accorded the status of a "non-event"; thus lack of publication is a non-event and only publication becomes a markable event. It seems to me that this difference between single- and double-edged contagious after-effects is the criterion on which one may decide whether the negative binomial or Cumulative Advantage distributions should apply.

For this urn model we shall suppose that after each drawing the ball is replaced; if a red is drawn then $c$ red balls are added, but if a black is drawn no extra balls are put in the urn. If we start with $b$ black balls and $r$ red, the conditional probability of success after $n$ previous successes will be $(r+nc)/(b+r+nc)$ and the corresponding conditional probability of failure will be $b/(b+r+nc)$.

The simplest case of this Cumulative Advantage Urn Scheme is to take $b = r = c = 1$ for, apart from the multiplicative constant $c$, any other starting configuration can be regarded as the state after some number of successes have occurred either under this rule, or in the complementary game with red and black reversed. The conditional chance of success after $n$ successes is $(1+n)/(2+n)$ and the conditional chance of failure is $1/(2+n)$. Consider now, again as the most simple case, a population of $N$ such urns, each originally in its ground state of $n = 0$. Going through the urns one by one we make drawings, continuing with the *same* urn as long as it produces successes and terminating and going on to *another* urn at the first failure. By the time all the $N$ urns have been played, there will result a simple distribution which may be taken as a limiting case of the cumulative advantage process.

Half the urns will have produced a failure on their first drawing and therefore remain in that state. Of the half population that produce a first success, two-thirds will be successful again and one-third will fail and terminate; of the $N/3$ with two successes, three-quarters will succeed yet again, and so on. The expected number of urns with at *least* $n$ successes by the end of the game will be $N/(n+1)$ and the expected number with *exactly* $n$ successes is

$$\frac{N}{n+1} - \frac{N}{n+2} = \frac{N}{(n+1)(n+2)} .$$

Introducing a standard notation for the number of members of the population with exactly $n$ successes, $N(n)$, and for the cumulative number of those with $n$ or more successes, $S(n)$, we have:

$$N(n) = \frac{N}{(n+1)(n+2)} \tag{1}$$

$$S(n) = \frac{N}{n+1} \tag{2}$$

Setting $S(n) = 1$, it is seen that there is just one urn, that with the highest score of successes, in the range $N < n+1 < \infty$, thus the highest possible score is at least $N - 1$. Proceeding similiarly by setting $S(n) = m$, we may show that the $m$th highest score is in the range

$$N/m < n+1 < N/(m-1).$$

The total number of successes over the whole population may be found by summing $S(n)$ from the highest scorer downwards, though we must be careful to exclude the infinity that would be introduced by the upper limit of the highest scoring member of the population. With this exclusion, the sum of the lower limits is a harmonic series

$$\sum_{n=1}^{n=N-1} S(n) = N \sum_{n=2}^{n=N} \frac{1}{n} = N(C - 1 + \log_e N + o\left[\frac{1}{n}\right]),$$

where C is Euler's Constant, 0.577215665. . . The mean minimum score of successes per urn increases logarithmically as the size of the population. The mean value for the maxima, excluding only the highest scorer, is a similar expression, substituting $N+1$ for $N$. It is, therefore, convenient for most purposes to take this value, which has been derived as representing a mean value, the indeterminate upper bound of the highest score being excluded.

## • The Cumulative Advantage Distribution

The Urn Scheme which has been discussed is, as has been stated, the simplest case of a Cumulative Advantage principle. A more general case, corresponding to a situation in which the population does not commence in a uniform ground state, may be studied better by considering a stochastic pure birth process, the general case which has been given by Feller [*(2)* 1:448]. For this we shall suppose the population to consist of a number of individuals, each of whom is in a state that can be characterized by a single number, $n$, the total of "successes" thus far achieved. We further suppose that transitions or jumps can occur only by the incidence of a further success which transforms the individual from a state $n$ to a state $n+1$, but never in the reverse direction.

A picturesque illustration of such a stochastic process would be a sort of "negative" radioactivity in which atoms of atomic (success) weight $n$ could decay (negatively!) into atoms of the next higher weight. At any time the population consists of atoms distributed over the entire spectrum of atomic weights, all decaying upwards in the series at appropriate rates. If no new atoms at ground state were added, the entire population would decay towards infinite atomic weight; but if new ground state atoms are *continually* added, it can be shown that a stable population distribution can be produced, provided that a principle of cumulative advantage governs the transitions. The simplest expression of such a principle is to suppose that successes fall equally on the heads of all *previous* successes, so the frequency of transitions from state $n$ to $n+1$ will be proportional to $n$.

This is fine if one begins from a ground state of unity rather than zero, as one does for example in considering a population of authors of $n$ papers, an "author" of zero papers being undefined. In such a case, however, of the citedness of papers, it is useful to attach some meaning to the transition from zero citations to the first. If we wish to retain the proportionality between transition frequency and the state number, the number of successes must be counted as one *more* than the number of citations. In a way, this is tantamount of considering the *original* publication as the first citation, which seems reasonable, though one may wish the option of counting publication as some other number of successes, more or less than unity. Such a modification is relatively easy to make after the theory is developed for one may suppose the actual number of citations to be $n+k$, where $n$ is the number of successes, and $k$ is an arbitrary constant, presumably in the region of unity. Even more generally, we may set $n = ax+b$ where $x$ is some other arbitrary state descriptor such as income in dollars.

Consider then a population of $P$ individuals, of which a fraction $f(n)$ are in state $n$, where

$$\sum_{1}^{\infty} f(n) = 1,$$

and the mean number of previous successes

$$\sum_{1}^{\infty} nf(n) = R.$$

Now suppose that a small number $dP$ of new individuals are added to the population, and with them $RdP$ new successes are sprinkled at random over all members. Since these new successes are to be sprinkled evenly over the $RP$ previous successes, there are $dP/P$ new successes per previous one, and for the class of $Pf(n)$ individuals with $n$ previous successes each, there will, therefore, be $nPf(n).dP/P$ new successes, and therefore transitions from this $n$th state to the $(n+1)$th. There must be therefore $nf(n)dP$ transitions out of the $n$th state, and there will be also $(n-1)f(n-1)dP$ transitions into it, from the class below receiving its quota of new successes. The change in the number of individuals in the $n$th state is therefore

$$\frac{d}{dP}Pf(n) = -nf(n) + (n-1)f(n-1) \qquad n > 1$$

$$= -f(1) + 1 \qquad n = 1 \quad (3)$$

so that $P\frac{d}{dP}f(n) = -(n+1)f(n) + (n-1)f(n-1) \quad n > 1$

$$= -2f(1) + 1 \qquad n = 1 \quad (4)$$

and the distribution over the states is defined by this series of difference-differential equations. It can readily be seen that for a stable distribution, for which $f(n)$ is independent of $P$, the left hand side of Equation (4) becomes zero, and one may solve recursively

$$f(n) = \frac{n-1}{n+1}f(n-1) = \frac{n-1}{n+1}\cdot\frac{n-2}{n}\cdot\frac{n-3}{n-1}\cdots\frac{1}{3}\cdot\frac{1}{2} = \frac{1}{n(n+1)} \quad (5)$$

which is the form found for the Urn Model.

Suppose now that the distribution is slowly changing with $P$, and take it to be separable as the product of a function of $P$ independent of $n$, and a function of $n$ independent of $P$, thus

$$f(n) = F(P)g(n). \quad (6)$$

Substituting this in Equation (4) we get

$$\frac{P}{F(P)}\frac{dF(P)}{dP} = \frac{(n+1)g(n) + (n-1)g(n-1)}{g(n)} \qquad n > 1$$

$$= \frac{-2g(1) + 1}{g(1)} \qquad n = 1 \quad (7)$$

Since the variables have been separated, both sides of Equation (7) must be constant of all $P$ and for all $n$; let us call this constant $m$. It then follows that

$$\frac{P}{F(P)}\frac{dF(P)}{dP} = m \quad (8)$$

therefore $F(P) = CP^m$

and $$\frac{-(n+1)g(n) + (n-1)g(n-1)}{g(n)} = m \qquad n > 1$$

$$\frac{-2g(1) + 1}{g(1)} = m \qquad n = 1 \quad (9)$$

Therefore

$$g(n) = \frac{n-1}{n+1+m}g(n-1)$$

$$= \frac{n-1}{n+1+m}\cdot\frac{n-2}{n+m}\cdots\frac{1}{3+m}\cdot\frac{1}{2+m}$$

$$= \frac{(n-1)!(m+1)!}{(n+1+m)!} \quad (10)$$

This last result may be expressed most elegantly by using the notation of the Beta Function, otherwise known as Euler's First Integral,

$$B(a,b) = B(b,a) = \int_0^1 x^{a-1}(1-x)^{b-1}\,dx = \frac{\Gamma(a)\Gamma(b)}{\Gamma(a+b)} = \frac{(a-1)!(b-1)!}{(a+b-1)!}$$

So that from Equations (6), (8) and (10) we have a solution of Equation (3) as

$$f(n) = CP^m B(n,m+2) \quad (11)^*$$

and hence for any particular value of $P$, the distribution we have considered is proportional to the values of the Beta Function $B(n,m+2)$. This may be expressed in the usual way as a discrete probability density by chosing the constant of proportionality so that

$$\sum_1^\infty f(n) = 1,$$

and on this basis we propose as the Cumulative Advantage Distribution, the density

$$f^*(n) = (m+1)\,B(n, m+2)$$

though in most cases it will prove more convenient to use the unnormalized form and work directly with tables of the Beta Function.

The Beta Function, of course, assumes simple forms for integral values of $a$ and $b$. It should be noted for example that

$$B(n,1) = 1/n$$
$$B(n,2) = 1/n(n+1)$$
$$B(n,3) = 2/n(n+1)(n+2)$$
$$B(n,4) = 6/n(n+1)(n+2)(n+3), \text{ etc.}$$

*A linear combination of such solutions for any values of $m$ constitutes a more general solution, but I see at present no physical significance in such a compound expression.

We tabulate the function for integral values of the arguments by taking $B(1,b) = 1/b$ and then calculating successively

$$B(2,b) = B(1,b)/(b+1), B(3,b) = B(2,b) \cdot 2/(b+2), B(4,b) = B(3,b) \cdot 3/(b+3), \text{etc.}$$

## • Properties of the Beta Function

It should be noted that $f(n)$ contains only the single parameter $m$, the simple limiting case discussed above in the Cumulative Advantage Urn Model corresponding to $m = 0$. The distribution is therefore remarkably simple in form, having one free parameter like the Poisson distribution, rather than two or more as in other contagious probability forms like the negative binomial. The properties of the Beta Function are, of course, well known, though their use in this context seems not to be widespread since it appears that no previous extensive tabulation of the function has been published.

Perhaps the most important property for our purposes is that

$$B(a,b) - B(a+1,b) = B(a,b+1) \tag{12}$$

so that the values of $B(a,b+1)$ are the first differences of $B(a,b)$ and, in general, $B(a,b+c)$ for the run of values of $a$ are the $c$th differences of $B(a,b)$. A table of the Beta Function for integral values of $a$ and $b$ has therefore for $b = 1$, a table of the reciprocals of the nature numbers, and for higher values of $b$, the $b$th differences of this harmonic series. Conversely, since differences are taken by increasing the value of $b$, we get a sum by decreasing it. Each run of $B(a,b)$ gives the sum from infinity to $a$ of $B(a,b+1)$. Since the Cumulative Advantage Distribution is given in Equation (11) by the Beta Function with $b = m+2$ for the relative number of the population with *exactly* $a = n$ successes, the cumulative sum for all $a = n$ must be given by the adjacent tabulation for $b = m+1$. In a tabulation for integral $m$ (see Table 1) we shall have therefore, in adjacent columns, the frequency distribution on the right and the cumulative frequency distribution on the left.

As a special case it may be noted that the top number in any column, *i.e.*, the value $B(1,b)$, is the sum of the entire column to the right of it, *i.e.*,

$$\sum_a B(a,b+1).$$

Because, as was noted above in the Urn Model, the total number of successes is the sum of the *cumulative* frequencies, the top entry to the left of the pair of columns just mentioned gives this sum of successes, all numbers being, of course, scaled to the total population. In all then, for any particular value of $m > 1$, we shall be concerned with three adjacent columns of the Beta Function table:

$B(1,m)$ gives the total number of successes,

$B(1,m+1)$ gives the size of the population (except for a factor if we wish to make this equal to $P$), and subsequent entries in this column $B(n,m+1)$ given the cumulative frequency, *i.e.*, the number of members with success scores of at least $n$.

$B(n,m+2)$ gives the actual frequencies, *i.e.*, the number of members with success scores exactly $m$.

Since the size of the population is $B(1,m+1) = 1/(m+1)$, we may norm to a population $P$ by multiplying all entries by $P(m+1)$. As leading results from such a normalization, we note that the total number of successes becomes $P(m+1)B(1,m = P(m+1)/m$, and the mean is therefore $1+1/m$; and that the proportion of individuals with exactly one success is $(m+1)B(1,m+2) = (m+1)/(m+2)$. These results may be used as estimators for the parameter $m$, but for this another very useful indication is that for large values of $a$,

$$B(a,b) = \frac{(b-1)!}{(a+b-1)(a+b-2)\ldots(a+1)a} \simeq \frac{(b-1)!}{(a+\frac{b-1}{2})^b} \tag{13}$$

So, rather more approximately,

$$B(a,b) = (b-1)!a^{-b} \tag{14}$$

and as a result, for reasonably large values of $n$, the Cumulative Advantage Distribution follows an inverse power law with exponent $m+2$; and the cumulative distribution is also an inverse power law, but with exponent $m+1$. This is indeed the characteristic of several very well known empirical laws of social science, including bibliometrics (for which see the splendid critical summary by Fairthorne (*14*) and the recent literature review by Narin (*15*). In most cases such as the Pareto and Lotka distributions, it appears that $m$ is small so that one is not far distant from the limiting case $m = 0$ which was discussed in the Urn Model.

## • The Limiting Case—Lotka and Bradford

It must be observed that in this limiting case we can no longer use an estimation from the mean, since the cumulative distribution $B(n,1)$ is the harmonic series $1/n$ and its sum is divergent. In this case, we must argue that

Table 1

| a= | b= 1 | b= 2 | b= 3 | b= 4 | b= 5 | b= 6 | b= 7 | b= 8 | b= 9 | b= 10 | b= 11 |
|---|---|---|---|---|---|---|---|---|---|---|---|
| 1 | 10000000 | 5000000 | 3333333 | 2500000 | 2000000 | 1666667 | 1428571 | 1250000 | 1111111 | 1000000 | 909091 |
| 2 | 5000000 | 1666667 | 833333 | 500000 | 333333 | 238095 | 178571 | 138889 | 111111 | 90909 | 75758 |
| 3 | 3333333 | 833333 | 333333 | 166667 | 95238 | 59524 | 39683 | 27778 | 20202 | 15152 | 11655 |
| 4 | 2500000 | 500000 | 166667 | 71429 | 35714 | 19841 | 11905 | 7576 | 5051 | 3497 | 2498 |
| 5 | 2000000 | 333333 | 95238 | 35714 | 15873 | 7937 | 4329 | 2525 | 1554 | 999 | 666 |
| 6 | 1666667 | 238095 | 58524 | 19841 | 7937 | 3608 | 1804 | 971 | 555 | 333 | 208 |
| 7 | 1428571 | 178571 | 39683 | 11905 | 4329 | 1804 | 833 | 416 | 222 | 125 | 73 |
| 8 | 1250000 | 138889 | 27778 | 7576 | 2525 | 971 | 416 | 194 | 97 | 51 | 29 |
| 9 | 1111111 | 111111 | 20202 | 5051 | 1554 | 555 | 222 | 97 | 46 | 23 | 12 |
| 10 | 1000000 | 90909 | 15152 | 3497 | 999 | 333 | 125 | 51 | 23 | 11 | 5 |
| 11 | 909091 | 75758 | 11655 | 2498 | 666 | 208 | 73 | 29 | 12 | 5 | 3 |
| 12 | 833333 | 64103 | 9158 | 1832 | 458 | 135 | 45 | 17 | 7 | 3 | 1 |
| 13 | 769231 | 54945 | 7326 | 1374 | 323 | 90 | 28 | 10 | 4 | 2 | 1 |
| 14 | 714286 | 47619 | 5952 | 1050 | 233 | 61 | 18 | 6 | 2 | 1 | |
| 15 | 666667 | 41667 | 4902 | 817 | 172 | 43 | 12 | 4 | 1 | 1 | |
| 16 | 625000 | 36765 | 4085 | 645 | 129 | 31 | 8 | 3 | 1 | | |
| 17 | 588235 | 32680 | 3440 | 516 | 98 | 22 | 6 | 2 | 1 | | |
| 18 | 555556 | 29240 | 2924 | 418 | 76 | 17 | 4 | 1 | | | |
| 19 | 526316 | 26316 | 2506 | 342 | 59 | 12 | 3 | 1 | | | |
| 20 | 500000 | 23810 | 2165 | 282 | 47 | 9 | 2 | 1 | | | |
| 21 | 476190 | 21645 | 1882 | 235 | 38 | 7 | 2 | | | | |
| 22 | 454545 | 19763 | 1647 | 198 | 30 | 6 | 1 | | | | |
| 23 | 434783 | 18116 | 1449 | 167 | 25 | 4 | 1 | | | | |
| 24 | 416667 | 16667 | 1282 | 142 | 20 | 4 | 1 | | | | |
| 25 | 400000 | 15385 | 1140 | 122 | 17 | 3 | 1 | | | | |
| 26 | 384615 | 14245 | 1018 | 105 | 14 | 2 | | | | | |
| 27 | 370370 | 13228 | 912 | 91 | 12 | 2 | | | | | |
| 28 | 357143 | 12315 | 821 | 79 | 10 | 2 | | | | | |
| 29 | 344828 | 11494 | 742 | 70 | 8 | 1 | | | | | |
| 30 | 333333 | 10753 | 672 | 61 | 7 | 1 | | | | | |
| 31 | 322581 | 10081 | 611 | 54 | 6 | 1 | | | | | |
| 32 | 312500 | 9470 | 557 | 48 | 5 | 1 | | | | | |
| 33 | 303030 | 8913 | 509 | 42 | 5 | 1 | | | | | |
| 34 | 294118 | 8403 | 467 | 38 | 4 | 1 | | | | | |
| 35 | 285714 | 7937 | 429 | 34 | 3 | | | | | | |
| 36 | 277778 | 7508 | 395 | 30 | 3 | | | | | | |
| 37 | 270270 | 7112 | 365 | 27 | 3 | | | | | | |
| 38 | 263158 | 6748 | 337 | 25 | 2 | | | | | | |
| 39 | 256410 | 6410 | 313 | 22 | 2 | | | | | | |
| 40 | 250000 | 6098 | 290 | 20 | 2 | | | | | | |
| 41 | 243902 | 5807 | 270 | 18 | 2 | | | | | | |
| 42 | 238095 | 5537 | 252 | 17 | 1 | | | | | | |
| 43 | 232558 | 5285 | 235 | 15 | 1 | | | | | | |
| 44 | 227273 | 5051 | 220 | 14 | 1 | | | | | | |
| 45 | 222222 | 4831 | 206 | 13 | 1 | | | | | | |
| 46 | 217391 | 4625 | 193 | 12 | 1 | | | | | | |
| 47 | 212766 | 4433 | 181 | 11 | 1 | | | | | | |
| 48 | 208333 | 4252 | 170 | 10 | 1 | | | | | | |
| 49 | 204082 | 4082 | 160 | 9 | 1 | | | | | | |
| 50 | 200000 | 3922 | 151 | 9 | 1 | | | | | | |
| 51 | 196078 | 3771 | 142 | 8 | 1 | | | | | | |
| 52 | 192308 | 3628 | 134 | 7 | 1 | | | | | | |
| 53 | 188679 | 3494 | 127 | 7 | | | | | | | |
| 54 | 185185 | 3367 | 120 | 6 | | | | | | | |
| 55 | 181818 | 3247 | 114 | 6 | | | | | | | |
| 56 | 178571 | 3133 | 108 | 5 | | | | | | | |
| 57 | 175439 | 3025 | 103 | 5 | | | | | | | |
| 58 | 172414 | 2922 | 97 | 5 | | | | | | | |
| 59 | 169492 | 2825 | 93 | 4 | | | | | | | |
| 60 | 166667 | 2732 | 88 | 4 | | | | | | | |
| 61 | 163934 | 2644 | 84 | 4 | | | | | | | |
| 62 | 161290 | 2560 | 80 | 4 | | | | | | | |
| 63 | 158730 | 2480 | 76 | 3 | | | | | | | |
| 64 | 156250 | 2404 | 73 | 3 | | | | | | | |
| 65 | 153846 | 2331 | 70 | 3 | | | | | | | |
| 66 | 151515 | 2261 | 67 | 3 | | | | | | | |
| 67 | 149254 | 2195 | 64 | 3 | | | | | | | |
| 68 | 147059 | 2131 | | | | | | | | | |

**Table 2**

| a= | b= 1.0 | b= 1.1 | b= 1.2 | b= 1.3 | b= 1.4 | b= 1.5 | b= 1.6 | b= 1.7 | b= 1.8 | b= 1.9 | b= 2.0 | b= 2.1 | b= 2.2 | b= 2.3 |
|---|---|---|---|---|---|---|---|---|---|---|---|---|---|---|
| 1 | 10000000 | 9090909 | 8333333 | 7692307 | 7142857 | 6666666 | 6249999 | 5882352 | 5555555 | 5263157 | 5000000 | 4761904 | 4545454 | 4347826 |
| 2 | 5000000 | 4329004 | 3787879 | 3344481 | 2976190 | 2666666 | 2403846 | 2178649 | 1984127 | 1814882 | 1666667 | 1536098 | 1420454 | 1317523 |
| 3 | 3333333 | 2792906 | 2367424 | 2026958 | 1750700 | 1523809 | 1335470 | 1177648 | 1044277 | 930709 | 833333 | 749316 | 676407 | 612801 |
| 4 | 2500000 | 2043590 | 1691017 | 1414157 | 1193659 | 1015873 | 870959 | 751690 | 652673 | 569822 | 500000 | 440774 | 390235 | 346869 |
| 5 | 2000000 | 1602815 | 1300782 | 1067288 | 884192 | 738817 | 622113 | 527502 | 450120 | 386320 | 333333 | 289032 | 251764 | 220234 |
| 6 | 1666667 | 1313783 | 1049018 | 847054 | 690775 | 568321 | 471298 | 393658 | 330970 | 279942 | 238095 | 203544 | 174836 | 150845 |
| 7 | 1428571 | 1110239 | 874182 | 696209 | 560088 | 454656 | 372077 | 306747 | 254592 | 212614 | 178571 | 150773 | 127929 | 109045 |
| 8 | 1250000 | 959466 | 746253 | 587164 | 466740 | 374423 | 302854 | 246808 | 202517 | 167225 | 138889 | 115979 | 97337 | 82077 |
| 9 | 1111111 | 843487 | 648915 | 505087 | 397225 | 315304 | 252378 | 203553 | 165320 | 135131 | 111111 | 91864 | 76343 | 63749 |
| 10 | 1000000 | 751622 | 572572 | 441339 | 343753 | 270260 | 214283 | 171213 | 137766 | 111576 | 90909 | 74485 | 61347 | 50773 |
| 11 | 909091 | 677137 | 511225 | 390565 | 301538 | 235009 | 184727 | 146335 | 116751 | 93761 | 75758 | 61558 | 50284 | 41279 |
| 12 | 833333 | 615579 | 460941 | 349286 | 267493 | 206808 | 161270 | 126747 | 100333 | 79952 | 64103 | 51690 | 41904 | 34141 |
| 13 | 769231 | 563889 | 419037 | 315145 | 239546 | 183829 | 142297 | 111020 | 87246 | 69023 | 54945 | 43991 | 35412 | 28650 |
| 14 | 714286 | 519898 | 383626 | 286496 | 216257 | 164812 | 126702 | 98181 | 76635 | 60221 | 47619 | 37873 | 30286 | 24343 |
| 15 | 666667 | 482024 | 353339 | 262153 | 196597 | 148863 | 113707 | 87550 | 67905 | 53025 | 41667 | 32933 | 26173 | 20908 |
| 16 | 625000 | 449091 | 327166 | 241245 | 179814 | 135330 | 102748 | 78637 | 60629 | 47064 | 36765 | 28889 | 22826 | 18128 |
| 17 | 588235 | 420202 | 304341 | 223117 | 165347 | 123730 | 93407 | 71085 | 54498 | 42068 | 32680 | 25537 | 20066 | 15850 |
| 18 | 555556 | 394665 | 284274 | 207267 | 152766 | 113698 | 85372 | 64622 | 49280 | 37839 | 29240 | 22729 | 17767 | 13961 |
| 19 | 526316 | 371936 | 266507 | 193306 | 141741 | 104952 | 78403 | 59046 | 44800 | 34226 | 26316 | 20355 | 15832 | 12379 |
| 20 | 500000 | 351581 | 250675 | 180927 | 132014 | 97273 | 72313 | 54197 | 40923 | 31115 | 23810 | 18329 | 14189 | 11042 |
| 21 | 476190 | 333252 | 236486 | 169884 | 123378 | 90486 | 66957 | 49951 | 37544 | 28415 | 21615 | 16587 | 12783 | 9904 |
| 22 | 454545 | 316665 | 223703 | 159981 | 115667 | 84454 | 62216 | 46210 | 34580 | 26058 | 19763 | 15079 | 11571 | 8926 |
| 23 | 434783 | 301586 | 212132 | 151055 | 108746 | 79063 | 57998 | 42895 | 31965 | 23986 | 18116 | 13765 | 10519 | 8081 |
| 24 | 416667 | 287820 | 201613 | 142974 | 102507 | 74222 | 54226 | 39943 | 29645 | 22156 | 16667 | 12614 | 9601 | 7346 |
| 25 | 400000 | 275207 | 192012 | 135627 | 96857 | 69856 | 50837 | 37301 | 27577 | 20531 | 15385 | 11599 | 8794 | 6704 |
| 26 | 384615 | 263608 | 182218 | 128923 | 91720 | 65902 | 47779 | 34926 | 25724 | 19080 | 14245 | 10700 | 8083 | 6139 |
| 27 | 340370 | 252908 | 175135 | 122784 | 87034 | 62308 | 45009 | 32782 | 24059 | 17781 | 13228 | 9900 | 7453 | 5640 |
| 28 | 357143 | 243008 | 167682 | 117144 | 82744 | 59028 | 42491 | 30841 | 22555 | 16612 | 12315 | 9186 | 6891 | 5198 |
| 29 | 344828 | 233822 | 160791 | 111946 | 78803 | 56027 | 40194 | 29075 | 21193 | 15556 | 11494 | 8545 | 6389 | 4803 |
| 30 | 333333 | 225277 | 154402 | 107143 | 75174 | 53271 | 38093 | 27465 | 19954 | 14600 | 10753 | 7968 | 5939 | 4450 |
| 31 | 322581 | 217309 | 148464 | 102693 | 71823 | 50735 | 36164 | 15992 | 18825 | 13730 | 10081 | 7447 | 5533 | 4133 |
| 32 | 312500 | 209862 | 142931 | 96857 | 68719 | 48393 | 34389 | 24641 | 17792 | 12937 | 9470 | 6974 | 5166 | 3848 |
| 33 | 303030 | 202888 | 137765 | 84712 | 65839 | 46226 | 32752 | 23398 | 16844 | 12212 | 8913 | 6545 | 4834 | 3590 |
| 34 | 294118 | 196343 | 132931 | 91123 | 63159 | 44216 | 31237 | 22252 | 15973 | 11547 | 8403 | 6153 | 4532 | 3356 |
| 35 | 285714 | 190190 | 128399 | 87767 | 60661 | 42348 | 29833 | 21192 | 15170 | 10936 | 7937 | 5795 | 4256 | 3143 |
| 36 | 277778 | 184395 | 124143 | 84624 | 58328 | 40608 | 28529 | 20211 | 14428 | 10373 | 7508 | 5467 | 4005 | 2949 |
| 37 | 270270 | 178927 | 120138 | 81674 | 56145 | 38983 | 27315 | 19299 | 13741 | 9853 | 7112 | 5166 | 3774 | 2772 |
| 38 | 263158 | 173761 | 116364 | 78902 | 54098 | 37465 | 26183 | 18451 | 13103 | 9372 | 6748 | 4888 | 3562 | 2610 |
| 39 | 256410 | 168873 | 112802 | 76292 | 52176 | 36042 | 25125 | 17661 | 12511 | 8926 | 6410 | 4632 | 3367 | 2461 |
| 40 | 250000 | 164241 | 109435 | 73831 | 50368 | 34707 | 24135 | 16924 | 11959 | 8511 | 6098 | 4396 | 3187 | 2324 |
| 41 | 243902 | 159845 | 106247 | 71507 | 48664 | 33453 | 23206 | 16234 | 11444 | 8125 | 5807 | 4176 | 3021 | 2198 |
| 42 | 238095 | 155668 | 103226 | 69309 | 47058 | 32272 | 22335 | 15587 | 10963 | 7765 | 5537 | 3973 | 2867 | 2081 |
| 43 | 232558 | 151695 | 100359 | 67229 | 45540 | 31159 | 21515 | 14981 | 10512 | 7429 | 5285 | 3784 | 2725 | 1973 |
| 44 | 227273 | 147912 | 97634 | 65256 | 44104 | 30109 | 20743 | 14411 | 10090 | 7115 | 5051 | 3608 | 2592 | 1873 |
| 45 | 222222 | 144304 | 95042 | 63383 | 42744 | 29116 | 20016 | 13875 | 9693 | 6820 | 4831 | 3443 | 2469 | 1780 |
| 46 | 217391 | 140861 | 92573 | 61603 | 41454 | 28177 | 19328 | 13370 | 9320 | 6544 | 4625 | 3290 | 2354 | 1693 |
| 47 | 212766 | 137571 | 90220 | 59910 | 40230 | 27287 | 18679 | 12894 | 8969 | 6284 | 4433 | 3146 | 2246 | 1612 |

some maximum value of $n$ must exist, as before that for which the cumulative number of cases becomes unity; this leads again to a mean given by $C + \log_e P$. If in this case we take a running cumulative sum of the score of successes, starting at the maximum, and consider it as a function of rank, one gets the same sort of logarithmic relationship. From Equation (2), again with a proviso to exclude the infinity due to the upper range of the highest score, we count the highest score as $P$-1 and the $r$th highest as $P/r - 1$. The sum of the scores from the top to the $r$th individual is therefore:

$$Q(r) = (P-1)+(P/2-1)+(P/3-1)\ldots(P/r-1)$$
$$= P(1+1/2+1/3\ldots 1/r)-r \qquad (15)$$
$$= P(C+\log_e r)-r. \qquad (16)$$

If $r$ is large compared with $e^C$=1.781 and small compared with $P$, this last equation becomes

$$Q(r) \simeq P\log_e r \qquad (17)$$

so that the total success score is proportional to the logarithm of the rank from the top. This is well known as the basis from which one may derive the Bradford Distribution (*15, 16, 17*) in which geometric "zone" increases in rank to correspond to arithemetic increments in the total score. In the simplest two-zone form, it states that half the successes are due to the highest scoring elite comprising $\sqrt{P}$ of the individuals. Though we did not realize it at the time of publication (*18*), this turns out to be precisely the same mathematical basis for the so-called Price Law that asserts, on the basis of the Lotka distribution, that the top $\sqrt{P}$ authors will produce at least half the total papers published by the population $P$.

We see, therefore, that two of the most popular empirical laws of bibliometrics and some other findings can be derived immediately from the underlying theory of Cumulative Advantage in its limiting case $m = 0$, and their forms have much more general application than had been supposed. Insofar as the empirical laws do not quite fit all of the data, a very probable cause is that, in such cases, the limit is approached but not reached, so that $m$ is small but non-zero. Two additional small modifications for practical use may be noted: for the usual step form of the Bradford graph, it is better to use the actual harmonic series terms of Equation (16) rather than the logarithmic approximation of Equation (16); and the Groos (*19*) "Droop", having no underlying theoretical basis, is simply due to the poor ability of gathering individuals with very low scores. It may, in fact, be explained as a Poisson probability for rare events (successes) that would lead one to gather only a fraction $1-e^{-p}$ of individuals when there is only a small expectation $p$, that is, only a few successes each. For small values of $n$ one should therefore apply this correction.

All such modifications notwithstanding, it follows from Equation (17) that if we have a population in which there operates—for whatever cause—a Cumulative Advantage Process in its limiting case;

$$Q(r)/Q(P) = \log r/\log P. \qquad (18)$$

Thus for example, if we suppose, as turns out from the other data to be reasonable, that citation of a journal is governed by such a process, we may calculate the fraction of all citations to journals or papers that will be collected by starting from the $r$ most cited journals instead of the total population of $P$ journals. Barr (*20*) estimated that there were about 26,000 journals of interest to scientists and technologists in 1966; for that same year the *Science Citation Index®* used 1573 source journals. If we suppose that these were all the most highly ranked journals, they would yield log 1573/log 26000 = 0.72 of all citable papers of that year, which may be regarded as the built-in efficiency of an operation based on a selection rather than the entire population.

In the same way, it is trivial mathematically, but by no means so economically, to observe that if we have, say one million individuals of the highest rank in a Cumulative Advantage population in its limiting case, the doubling of the population by the addition of the next highest ranked million will increase the total bulk of successes by only $\log 2/\log 10^6 \simeq 5\%$. Thus, if "successes" be book use in a library, citations to a body of literature, frequencies of word use or incomes of the rich, once one has a large body of individuals selected by their being of the highest ranks in success rate, the pay-off for *adding* to the population becomes rather small. Since it happens that the cost of managing or holding a collection is proportional to more than the first power of the size of the collection, the acquisition of an additional 5 percent of value in the return is paid for by more than a doubling in cost. We, therefore, see the operation of a very powerful principle of marginal utilities in such cumulative advantage situations. It is the marginal economy, of course, that produces the force leading one to the elitism (*21*) of small libraries, vocabularies and document collections and small social groups of those with many successes behind them. For the *Science Citation Index®*, the operation would not be possible if it were not for the Cumulative Advantage situation. Taking as sources the most obvious and best 6 percent or so of all citable journals one can, as has been shown, acquire citations to about 72 percent of all citable papers.

## • Application of Cumulative Advantage Theory to Lotka's Law

Although much comment has been made about Lotka's Law of Scientific Productivity, including interesting theoretical pseudo-derivations by Shockley (*22*) and by Zener (*23*), its very simplicity seems to have militated against the collection of empirical data that would give a parameter $m$ in terms of the mean value or by some other way. Lotka's (*24*) original data, tested only for relatively small $n$, was based partly on lifetime productivities and partly on the ten year indexes. In a way, it is rather misleading, for one is led to suppose that the $1/n^2$ law can be identified with the limiting case of the Cumulative Advantage Distribution for $m = 0$, for which $N(n) = 1/n(n+1)$. It is possible if scientists did not have a finite research lifetime, and if we had a total bibliography over all time, such a law might hold. For Lotka's test, however, it is only necessary that the first few values for small $n$ fit the inverse square law so that

$$N(1)/N(2) = 2^2, \; N(1)/N(3) = 3^2, \text{etc.}$$

More crucially, as was shown by Price (*25*) p. 46-48, the ranking of the most productive authors, in Lotka's data and in many other examples, follows the law $S(n) = c/n^2$ which leads one to suppose that $m$ is in the region of unity rather than zero.

If the value of $m$ were exactly unity (which it doubtless is not), we would have

$$N(n) = B(n,3) = 2/n(n+1)(n+2), \; S(n) = B(n,2) = 1/n(n+1),$$

$S(1) = 1/2$ and $Q(1) = B(1,1) = 1$, so that the mean

$Q(1)/S(1) = 2$. It follows therefore that $N(1)/N(2) = 4$ exactly as required, and $N(1)/N(3) = 10$ which is close to $3^2$. A still more crucial test for the distribution in the tail is given by the computation of the highest scoring member by setting $PS(n) = 1$. For $m = 1$, taking a population of the order of a million authors we must have $n(n-1) \simeq n^2 = 10^6$ which gives a maximum score of $n = 1000$, in reasonable accordance with the order of magnitude of existing world records. Another reasonable estimate is to be had from the proportion of single paper authors, $N(1)/S(1) = 2/3$ for $m = 1$, which is somewhat higher than the approximately 60 found empirically and theoretically by Lotka.

The small discrepancy could be reduced by using a slightly smaller value for $m$, say 0.7, rather than unity. This value makes the maximum score for a million authors $(10^6)^{1/1.7} = 3400$ in close agreement with the remarkable actual world record of 3904 papers attributed to T.D.A. Cockerell (1866-1948), an entomologist of the University of Colorado. Also for this value we have $N(1)/N(2) = 3.7$ and $N(1)/N(3)8.7$, both rather

| | $m = 1.0$ | | $m = 0.7$ | |
|---|---|---|---|---|
| $n$ | $N(n)$ | $S(n)$ | $N(n)$ | $S(n)$ |
| 1 | .333 | .500 | .370 | .588 |
| 2 | .083 | .166 | .100 | .218 |
| 3 | .033 | .083 | .043 | .118 |

near to the values of 4 and 9 required by the inverse square law, and the mean value of productivity becomes

$$1+1/0.7 = 2.43.$$

The actual value of $m$ is likely to vary with the sampling used in any particular case. For modern data there must be much uncertainty because we have as yet no adequate model or theory for the attribution of credit in the case of multi-author collaborative papers; there remains also some doubt as to the effect of finite lifetime on author productivity. Such difficulties notwithstanding, it is clear from the only extensive demographic study of authorship thus far, that by Price and Gürsey (*26*), that authors differ not so much in their *rate* of publication of papers, but in the span of *time* they spend at the publication front. The greater number of those arriving at the research front emit only their initial publications and are therefore to be considered as "transients"; they number perhaps two-thirds of all authors. This is just what would be expected in a Cumulative Advantage process with $m$ near unity; it corresponds in fact to an Urn Model where one begins with one red ball of success and two blacks for failure. Two-thirds of all first choices will result in failure and the end of that particular "game" of publication, but for the one-third that *succeed* there will be an even chance of a *second* success, and thereafter the chance will approach unity asymptotically. It seems therefore that in all qualitative aspects and also quantitatively the Cumulative Advantage Distribution and process account for journal distributions and author productivities.

## • Application to Citation Data

By far the most stringent test of the Cumulative Advantage principle is the application to citation data where we have a wealth of computer-generated counts instead of the short series of hand counts for productivity. Though the data are rich, the empirical generalizations and underlying theoretical constructs have been sparse. Price (*27*) reported that the number of papers cited $n$ times in a year followed an inverse power law (a

Zipf Law) with exponent in the range 2.5-3.0, and I. Yermish (*28*) has since shown that an exponent of 3.036 gives a correlation of 0.9937 with the data for 1972. The only far-reaching theoretical analysis known to me is by Charles J. Crowley (*29*) where it is supposed that a negative binomial distribution would have the required properties, and this is unfortunately tested on very limited data. One other previous contribution deserves special mention even though its ingenious and elegant mathematics were introduced in connection with the Bradford Law rather than citation data. Brookes (*30*) showed that the sampling of a truncated hyperbolic distribution could be accounted for by an analogue of the Taylor's Theorem, a result which I conjecture may be equivalent to convoluting or changing the value of $m$ to $m+h$ in the Beta Function, $B(n,2+m)$ of the Cumulative Advantage Distribution.

In all that follows, it must be remembered that for citations there is a problem associated with the zero ground state. We have supposed above that the *publication* of a paper might be counted as its first citation "success." If it is *not*, then the value of $n$ in the Beta Function must be taken as the number of citation successes plus $k$, where $k$ is some parameter different from unity. This will affect the values of $N(n)$ and $S(n)$ for small values of $n$ only, and it may be used as an additional parameter to adjust such values to agree with the empirical data. Because of the possibility of such a 'fudge' factor being used, we shall not rest any vital tests upon such values for small $n$, and provisionally $k$ is set at unity.

For the total citation network for all time, it is clear that the maximum number of successes per paper is equal to the total population of papers, for it has its own publication and can be cited by all other papers. It follows then that the average number of successes, which must be one more than the average number of references from each paper to the same journal literature, must be $C-\log_e P$ which is here tabulated for typical values of population:

| *P* | *Mean Successes* | *Refs/Paper* |
|---|---|---|
| 1,000 | 7.48 | 6.48 |
| 10,000 | 9.79 | 8.79 |
| 100,000 | 12.09 | 11.09 |
| 1,000,000 | 14.39 | 13.39 |
| 10,000,000 | 16.70 | 15.70 |
| 100,000,000 | 19.00 | 18.00 |

Since there are, in fact, about 13 references per article today across the whole field of literature, this provides an over-estimate, especially since many of these are to non-journal items outside the source network. What has probably happened also is an overestimation of the maximum possible success rate; even the most cited paper, that of Lowry 1951, is cited only by about 1 percent of all papers. With this correction, a rate near the actual ten journal references per article gives a total archive of 3,400,000 papers which is perhaps a slight *under*estimate. It may well be that this tells us that the scientific literature consists not of a unity, but of some hundreds of nearly autonomous subfields. Alternatively it might be due to some process whereby only a fraction, *ca.* 10/13 of all successes, are actually manifested as citations.

A remarkable consequence of this derivation is that each doubling of the archive should add $\log_e 2 = 0.7$ refs/ paper. Since the total population of papers grows exponentially with a doubling time of *ca.* ten years, we should expect that the number of refs/paper must have been increasing by unity about every 15 years, a fact that agrees well with the much smaller incidence of citation in the early years of this century. I do not believe this postdiction of the bibliometric record has ever before been stated or observed.

For an actual citation index, such as those published on a quarterly, annual and quinquennial basis by the Institute for Scientific Information, we must take into account that this is a sampling in two distinct ways. First, we have the fact that it is based upon a selection of the largest and most cited journals, and, as we have seen, if this in itself is governed by a Cumulative Advantage Distribution, it is probable that this collects a fraction of about 72 percent of the entire cited literature. Secondly, the index is based upon only a restricted range over time of the previous literature, which we shall suppose to be in exponential growth at a rate $K$, which is approximately 0.07 per year. Letting the number of journal references per source article be $R$, it follows that in a one-year citation index there will be $KR$ references back per article existing in the corpus. As has long been known [see Price (*27*)], this works out to about one citation per article per year. Since in the Cumulative Advantage Distribution we have a mean of $1+1/m$ successes/item, it follows that the mean number of citations $M$ is one less than this, $1/m$. We are led therefore to suppose that a one year citation index must have $m$ near unity, and it will therefore follow from Equation (14), for large $n$, an inverse cube law, $1/n^3$. For a many-year index the mean number of citations per corpus paper will be larger, so that $m$ is small, and one gets closer to the inverse square law which is the limiting case. For a correspondingly shorter period, the value of $m$ must be larger than unity; for example, it must be that $m \simeq 4$ for a quarterly index, so that the distribution for large $n$ will fall off as $1/n^6$. It follows also that the cumulative distributions will fall off as $1/n^2$ for the annual, nearly $1/n$ (perhaps $1/n^{1.2}$) for the quinquennial, and $1/n^5$ for the quarterly citation indexes.

Table 3. Empirical data for number of papers cited $n$ times in *Science Citation Index®*

| $n$ | Quarterly | Σ | Annual | Σ | 6-year Cum | Σ |
|---|---|---|---|---|---|---|
| | | 10,000 | | 10,000 | | 10,000 |
| 1 | 7,968.2 | | 7,280.9 | | 6,689.7 | |
| | | 2,031.8 | | 2,719.1 | | 3.310.3 |
| 2 | 1,223.0 | | 1,328.9 | | 1,260.0 | |
| | | 808.8 | | 1,390.2 | | 2,050.3 |
| 3 | 532.7 | | 550.5 | | 555.2 | |
| | | 276.1 | | 839.7 | | 1,495.1 |
| 4 | 154.3 | | 312.3 | | 329.9 | |
| | | 121.8 | | 527.4 | | 1,165.2 |
| 5 | 66.6 | | 154.9 | | 225.3 | |
| | | 55.2 | | 372.5 | | 939.2 |
| 6 | 24.4 | | 97.5 | | 181.8 | |
| | | 30.8 | | 275.0 | | 758.1 |
| 7 | 6.5 | | 64.3 | | 114.3 | |
| | | 24.3 | | 210.7 | | 643.8 |
| 8 | 8.1 | | 45.2 | | 90.1 | |
| | | 16.2 | | 165.5 | | 553.7 |
| 9 | 3.2 | | 31.4 | | 88.5 | |
| | | 13.0 | | 134.1 | | 465.2 |
| 10 | 1.6 | | 24.4 | | 69.2 | |
| | | 11.4 | | 109.7 | | 396.0 |
| 11 | 0 | | 18.3 | | 56.3 | |
| | | 11.4 | | 91.4 | | 339.7 |
| 12 | 1.6 | | 14.2 | | 35.4 | |
| | | 9.8 | | 77.2 | | 304.3 |
| 13 | 1.6 | | 11.0 | | 24.1 | |
| | | 8.2 | | 66.2 | | 280.2 |
| 14 | 3.2 | | 8.9 | | 40.2 | |
| | | 5.0 | | 57.3 | | 240.0 |
| 15 | 0 | | 7.3 | | 24.1 | |
| | | 5.0 | | 50.0 | | 215.9 |
| 16 | 0 | | 6.1 | | 20.9 | |
| | | 5.0 | | 43.9 | | 195.0 |
| 17 | 1.6 | | 5.2 | | 9.7 | |
| | | 3.4 | | 38.7 | | 185.3 |
| 18 | 0 | | 4.2 | | 22.5 | |
| | | 3.4 | | 34.5 | | 162.8 |
| 19 | 0 | | 3.8 | | 9.7 | |
| | | 3.4 | | 30.7 | | 153.1 |
| 20 | 0 | | 3.0 | | 24.1 | |
| | | 3.4 | | 27.7 | | 129.0 |
| >20 | 3.4 | | 27.7 | | 129.0 | |
| Average cites/paper cited | 1.345 | | 1.66 | | 2.641 | |

Sources:
Quarterly, hand count of 6157 papers from 1975 index.
Annual, computer count of 1,882,864 papers from 1967 index.
5-Year Cum, hand count of 6214 papers from 1965-1969 index.

In an empirical test from machine-generated data for the annual and from hand-counts for the quarterly and quinquennial indexes (see Table 3 and Fig. 1), I find for the actual distributions exponents of 2.1 for five years, 3.2 for one year, and 5.3 for a quarter year, and independently for the cumulative distributions, values of 1.4, 2.3 and 4.0 respectively. It would appear therefore that for an annual index we have $m \simeq 1.25$, and for the quinquennial it has an appropriate value about one-fifth of this, $m \simeq 0.25$, but for the quarterly where we should have $m \simeq 5.0$, we have in fact $m \simeq 3.15$ which may be due to the smallness of the sample counted, or it may have some deeper basis such as the constant $k$ associated with the ground state transition not being unity.

Another interesting test of the citation data is afforded by the rank list of highly cited items. According to the tabulation by Garfield (*31*), the most cited paper, that of Lowry *et al* had 29,655 citations in the interval 1961-1972, followed by items with 6281, 5825, 5273 and 5054 citations in the same ten year period. The tenth most cited paper had 3621; the 20th, 2054; the 30th, 1695; the 40th, 1317 and the 50th, 1207. The trend follows approximately (except for the anomalous top item) a typical power law that the number of citations is $10{,}000/\text{rank}^{2/3}$, which is equivalent to a cumulative distribution proportional to $1/n^{1.5}$ suggesting that for a ten year index we should have $m \simeq 0.5$.

In this period the citation index contained a total of *ca.* 3,500,000 source items, and although the annual rate grew by about a factor of three, some of that was due to an expansion in the extent of the Institute for Scientific Information operation relative to the total available literature, so one may suppose that the actual corpus, growing at *ca.* 7 percent per annum, must have doubled in the period. The corpus at the end of the period therefore must have been about 7 million papers, so that Lowry's paper had been cited by more than four papers in every 1000, a surprisingly large fraction when one remembers that most scientific literature has nothing to do with organic chemistry. Quite apart from the trend of most cited items, we may use this highest score as an estimator, since from Equation (14) it follows that, setting the cumulative total of unity, the score of the highest cited item must be given by $7{,}000{,}000/n^{1+m} = 1$ and for $n = 29{,}655$ we have $m = 0.53$.

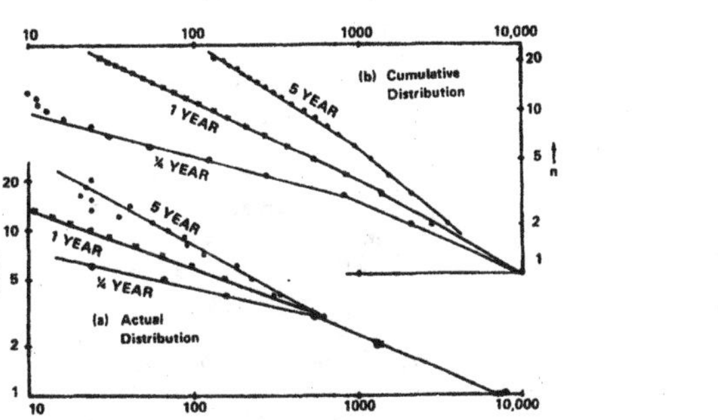


Fig. 1. Number of papers with (a) exactly and (b) at least n citations in ¼, 1, and 5-year indexes.

It should also be possible to estimate the value of $m$ from the Garfield Constant (*32*), the number of citations per cited item. This parameter, $G$, has been slowly rising for the annual index from about 1.60 in the early 1960s to about 1.80 in the mid-1970s; for the 1965-1969 quinquennial index it was 2.55 and for quarterly indexes it is *ca.* 1.3. For the Cumulative Advantage Distribution the number of papers cited (*i.e.*, having at least two successes) is given by $S(2) = B(2,m+1) = 1/(m+1)(m+2)$ and the number of citations by

$$Q(2) = B(2,M) = 1/m(m+1),$$

hence $G = 1+2/m$ and the Garfield Constant is therefore one more than twice the mean number of citations per paper.

The fraction of all cited papers that occur in a citation index based upon a limited time interval $T$, compared with those in one based upon all time may be calculated by supposing that we have a Poisson process with an expectation $RKT$ where $R$ is the number of references/paper, and $K$ is the growth rate. The fraction of papers not "hit" is $e^{-RKT}$ so those "hit" by citation are $1-e^{-RKT}$ and combining this with the efficiency $F$ (due to the journal selection) we have $M = F(1-e^{-RKT})$. For $F = 0.72, R = 9, K = 0.07$/year we get:

| Span of Index in Years | Calculated Mean Citations = $M$ | Calculated $G = 1+2M$ |
|---|---|---|
| 1/4 | 0.105 | 1.21 |
| 1 | 0.336 | 1.67 |
| 5 | 0.689 | 2.38 |

Alternatively, if we take $G$ to be 2.55 for the quinquennial and 1.80 for the annual index, it follows from a simple numerical solution of the simultaneous equations that we must have $F = 0.79$ and $RK = 0.73$. It seems reasonable that the efficiency of the citation index should have improved by enlarging the journal list from 0.72 in 1966 to 0.79 in 1974 (indeed, computing from the current size of the roster of source journals log 2500/log 26,000 = 0.77), and for the value of $RK$ we might have a growth rate 0.08 per year and 9.1 references to the journal literature per article. The agreement is surprisingly good though the values of $M$ seem to correspond to $m+2$ rather than to $m$ which I should expect.

## • Citations as a Function of Time and Field

It should be noted that the Cumulative Advantage Distribution has been derived without explicit reference to time as a variable, and unlike such many-parameter functions as the negative binomial, it contains little scope for adjusting the constants to fit different fields or other sorts of population. The distribution depends only on the size of the population and the mean number of successes per item. We have supposed that successes generate future successes without any particular time scale. For an exponentially growing population, however, it is clear that if we start with $RP$ successes there will be added $KRP$ where $K$ has a value of the order of 0.07 per year, and hence the exponential growth may be regarded as due to each success producing 0.07 new successes per year, or one further success every *ca.* 14 years. Such a concept is, of course, equivalent to a model explaining exponential growth as a tendency for successes to breed new successes at a constant birth rate.

The birth rate is however quite small. A paper needs to have some 14 previous successes before it reaches a rate of one new success per year. In view of this smallness of the constant, it is clear that the first few citations could not cumulate in such a slow fashion—it would take far too long for Lowry to become Lowry! What clearly happens is that immediately after publication, in as long as it takes for the work to become known (which may indeed precede publication through the use of informal communication) the paper is weighed by peers and in its incunable period produces a first pulse of citations which in most cases probably determines all future citation history; only rarely is there a much retarded discovery or subsequent rounds of rediscovery and new application.

In the absence of such anomalies the future citation history of a paper will depend only on the size of the initial pulse and since $dn = Kndt$, we have $n = n_0e^{Kt}$ so that the number of citations is expected to grow at the same exponential rate as the literature, where $t$ is the time elapsed from the initial pulse of $n_0$ citations. The pulse size is clearly a determinant of the effectiveness of the paper at the research front. It must thus be a measure of "quality," perhaps also containing a factor proportional to the size of the paper (in pages?).

An interesting point that must have further investigation is that there must be a feedback from the citations as a cumulative advantage process to the author's productivity which follows just the same pattern. We must suppose that the size of the initial pulses modulates the author's behavior and causes either a continuance of publication or a cessation. If the initial paper(s) are well received, the author's self-estimate, and also those who may determine things such as promotion and tenure, will enable the circumstances and motivation to be high enough to make another attempt. At subsequent determinations the cumulation of past success makes the threshold needed smaller so there arise larger and larger cumulating advantages leading to continuance in publication. Price and Gürsey (*33*) showed that transient authors have only a chance of about one in four of having their sole paper cited, non-core continuants have about 0.7 chance of being cited, and core continuants are almost all cited every year. The correlation between citation and productivity is therefore very high and most effective in the crucial decision to remain at the research front or retire from it.

The citation of papers, as has been shown, depends only on their nature and not on the number of papers available to cite them, though this too grows at the same exponential rate. This point was confirmed by Gomperts (*34*) who showed that in the field of vibrating plates the citations per paper were independent of the size of the citing literature, though of course the rate must vary from paper to paper. Looking back on the literature from any date however, by observing the references in source papers of that date, one must get a distribution that depends on the number of papers available for citation at any previous date. In 1965 I suggested that the time distribution of citations per cited paper should enable one to disentangle the literature growth from any obsolescence factor that might apply. Now, the cumulative advantage theory enables this to be done, for as has been seen the citations per cited paper (the Garfield Constant) is related to the mean $M$ and therefore to the parameter $m$. We have $G = 1+2M = 1+2/m$. Taking the data from Price (*27*) we get the mean citations, and therefore for the amount the literature of that age is used relative to the use per paper of most recent literature, the following table:

| Age in years | $G$ | $1\text{-}G/1\text{-}G_0$ |
|---|---|---|
| 0 | 1.75 | 1.00 |
| 4 | 1.7 | 0.93 |
| 9 | 1.6 | 0.80 |
| 15 | 1.5 | 0.67 |
| 20 | 1.4 | 0.53 |
| 28 | 1.3 | 0.40 |
| 42 | 1.2 | 0.27 |
| 55 | 1.15 | 0.20 |
| 80 | 1.1 | 0.13 |

| Age in years | Relative use in percent |
|---|---|
| 2 | 98 |
| 3 | 96 |
| 5 | 90 |
| 8.5 | 80 |
| 10 | 75 |
| 12 | 70 |
| 17 | 60 |
| 23 | 50 |
| 30 | 40 |
| 49 | 25 |
| 58 | 20 |
| 100 | 10 |
| 150 | 5 |
| 230 | 2 |
| 300 | 1 |

Since the data on which this is based shows no effect whatsoever due to the enormous curtailments of publication volume in both World War I and World War II we can be sure that what we have here is pure obsolescence, unaffected by the size of the available literatures. The time variation is rather different from anything that had been previously proposed and follows a typically *S*-shaped logistic decline with the logarithm of time as the independent variable. I conjecture that the form might be $y = e^{-x}(1+x)$ where $x = \log_e (t/10 \text{ years})$ and that it probably arises from the usual differential equation defining the exponential growth of the literature, $dy/dt = Ky$ being modified to include a term on the right of the second degree, $dy/dt=Ky-Ly^2$.

At any event, what seems to happen in the process of obsolescence as we now can see it, is that during the first several years after publication the utility of relative citability of a paper declines only very slowly and parabolically in the logarithm of years elapsed. Even after *a century* the chance of citation has decreased by only a factor of ten. Most citations are to recent papers because most papers *are* recent, and it is dubious if there is anything of an immediacy effect due to rapid short-range obsolescence as I once conjectured. Obsolescence would seem to be an essentially long-range phenomena, akin to the effect of finite lifetime of authors in curtailing publication productivity. Since we now have the empirical values of $G$ for papers of various ages, one may use the obsolescence data to derive from the time spectrum of citation the volume of publication that must exist at the various dates in the past century. One may also derive the citation frequency distributions for papers of varying age. It is evident immediately that highly cited papers will fall off more slowly with elapsed time than less cited papers.

## • Philosophical Epilogue

I cannot conclude this first paper on the Cumulative Advantage Distribution without some remarks on its conceptual significance. The surface has only been scratched and doubtless the application of this theory will raise as many problems as are solved and demand much more empirical testing and rigorous statistical mathematics in expression. What intrigues me most is that this new underlying theory which seems to pull together so many diverse phenomena and qualitative laws into good quantitative predictability does so in a way that has an element of causal asymmetry. One would have supposed, for example, that the process of citation depended equally on the cited paper and the citing paper. It is with this in mind that some recent investigators (*35*) have been taking long hard looks at the apparent caprice with which a paper may or may not decide to cite previous work and may even make token or ritualistic citations.

In this theory, it would appear that the course of future citation successes is determined statistically by the past history of the cited paper; and so one is driven to suppose that citations are generated by a pull mechanism from previous citation rather than from a push mechanism of the papers that do the citing. We even derive a relationship which goes some of the way to explaining the average number of references per paper as a consequence of the success distribution of the already existing corpus of literature, without there being much possible allowance for what such a reference actually implies.

It seems to me that the injection of some version of an underlying theory of this nature goes a long way towards solving the problem of what it is that we have been measuring and counting in bibliometric research and the other social science fields where cumulative advantage appears to operate.

## Acknowledgments

I wish to record my personal gratitude to the Office of Science Information Service of the National Science Foundation for their friendly counseling over many years, and to Eugene Garfield and his staff at the Institute for Scientific Information for extensive and freely given cooperation in all matters pertaining to citation indexing which has made possible these interesting investigations. I thank also Mark d. Price for computing the table of the Beta Function, I. Richard Savage for some discussions of statistical matters, Gabriel Pinski and Christopher Anagnostakis for detecting and correcting an error in my initial proof of the distribution law, and Belver C. Griffith for a seemingly innocent remark which led me from an erroneous draft reply to a Garfield editorial towards the present work, which brings to a head this long series of researches.

### References

1. **Simon, H.A.** 1957. *Models of Man: Social and Rational.* Chapter 9: On a Class of Skew Distribution Functions. New York: John Wiley & Sons, 1957.
2. **Feller, W.** *An Introduction to Probability Theory and Its Applications.* (3rd ed.) New York: John Wiley & Sons, I (1968), II (1966).
3. **Bliss, C.I.; Fisher, R.A.** 1953. "Fitting the Negative Binomial Distribution to Biological Data and Note on the Efficient Fitting of the Negative Binomial." *Biometrics.* The Biometric Society. 1953; 9(2): 176-200.
4. **Bliss, C.I.** "The Analysis of Insect Counts as Negative Binomial Distributions." *Proceedings of the Tenth International Congress of Entomology.* 2: 1015-1032 (1956 [1958]).
5. **Williamson, E.; Bretherton, M.H.** 1963. *Tables of the Negative Binomial Probability Distribution.* New York: John Wiley & Sons, 1963.
6. **Yule, G.U.** 1924. "A Mathematical Theory of Evolution, based on the Conclusions of Dr. J.C. Willis, F.R.S." *Philosophical Transactions of the Royal Society* 1924 B. 213: 21-87.
7. **Hill, B.** 1970. "Zipf's Law and Prior Distributions for the Composition of a Population." *Journal of the American Statistical Association.* 1970; 65 (331): 1220-1232.
8. **Hill, B.** 1974. "Rank Frequency Forms of Zipf's Law." *Journal of the American Statistical Association.* 1974; 69 (348): 1017-1026.
9. **Crowley, C.J.** 1975. "The Distribution of Citations to Scientific Papers: A Model." Presented at Midwest Sociological Society meeting, Chicago, April 1975 (unpublished).
10. **Hill, B.; Woodroofe, M.** 1975. "Stronger Forms of Zipf's Law." *Journal of the American Statistical Association.* 1975; 70 (349): 212-219.
11. **Woodroofe, M.; Hill, B.** 1975. "On Zipf's Law." *Journal of Applied Probability.* 1975; 12: 425-434.
12. **Sichel, H.S.** 1975. "On a Distribution Law for Word Frequencies." *Journal of the American Statistical Association.* 1975; 70 (352, part 1): 542-547.
13. **Cole, J.R.; Cole, S.** 1973. *Social Stratification in Science.* Chicago, IL: University of Chicago Press, 1973.
14. **Fairthorne, R.A.** 1969. "Progress in Documentation: Empirical Hyperbolic Distributions (Bradford-Zipf-Mandelbrot) for Bibliometric Description and Prediction." *Journal of Documentation.* 1969; 25 (4): 319-343.
15. **Narin, F.** 1976. *Evaluation Bibliometrics: The Use of Publication and Citation Analysis in the Evaluation of Scientific Activity.* Cherry Hill, NJ: Computer Horizons, 1976.
16. **Brookes, B.C.** 1969. "Bradford's Law and the Bibliography of Science." *Nature.* 1969; 224 (5223): 953-956.
17. **Naranan, S.** 1970. "Bradford's Law of Bibliography of Science: an Interpretation." *Nature.* 1970; 227: 631-632.
18. **Allison, P.D.; Price, D.de S.; Griffith, B.C.; Moravcsik, M.J.; Stewart, J.A.** 1976. "Lotka's Law: A Problem in its Interpretation and Application." *Social Studies of Science.* 1976; 6: 269-276.
19. **Groos, O.V.** 1967. Bradford's Law and the Keenan-Atherton Data." *American Documentation.* 1967; 18: 46.
20. **Barr, K.P.** 1967. "Estimates of the Number of Currently Available Scientific and Technical Periodicals." *Journal of Documentation.* 1967; 23 (No. 2): 110-116.
21. **Price, D. de S.** 1971. "Some Remarks on Elitism in Information and the Invisible College Phenomenon in Science." *Journal of the American Society for Information Science.* 1971; 22 (2): 74-75.
22. **Shockley, W.** 1957. "On the Statistics of Individual Variations of Productivity in Research Laboratories." *Proceedings of the Institute of Radio Engineers.* 1957; 45: 279-290, 1409-1410.
23. **Zener, C.** 1968. "An Analysis of Scientific Productivity." *Proceedings of the National Academy of Sciences.* 1968; 59 (4): 1078-1081.
24. **Lotka, A.J.** 1926. "The Frequency Distribution of Scientific Productivity." *Journal of the Washington Academy of Sciences.* 1926; 16 (12): 317-323.
25. **Price, D.de S.** 1963. *Little Science, Big Science.* New York: Columbia University Press. 1963.
26. **Price, D.de S.; Gürsey, S.** 1976. "Studies in Scientometrics. Part I: Transience and Continuance in Scientific Author-

ship." *International Forum on Information and Documentation.* International Federation for Documentation Proceedings. 1976; 1 (2): 17-24.

27. **Price, D.de S.** 1965. "Networks of Scientific Papers." *Science.* 1965; 149 (3683); 510-515.
28. **Yermish, I.** Private communication. 1976, March 17.
29. **Crowley, C.J.** 1975. "The Distribution of Citations to Scientific Papers: A Model." paper presented at Midwest Sociological Society meeting, Chicago. April 1975 (unpublished).
30. **Brookes, B.C.** 1975. "A Sampling Theorem for Finite Discrete Distributions." *Journal of Documentation.* 1975; 31 (1): 26-35.
31. **Garfield, E.** 1974. "Selecting the All-Time Citation Classics. Here Are the Fifty Most Cited Papers for 1961-1972." *Current Contents.* Editorial, (2): 1974 January 9.
32. **Garfield, E.** 1976. "Is the Ratio Between Number of Citations & Publications Cited a True Constant." *Current Contents,* Editorial, Current Comments, (6) 1976 February 9.
33. **Price, D.de S.; Gürsey, S.** 1976. "The Relation between Source Author and Cited Author Populations." *International Forum on Information and Documentation.* International Federation for Documentation. 1976; 1 (3): 19-22.
34. **Gomperts, M.C.** 1968. "The Law of Constant Citation for Scientific Literature." *Journal of Documentation.* 1968; 24 (2): 113-117.
35. **Moravcsik, M.J.; Murugesan, P.** 1975. "Some Results on the Function and Quality of Citations." *Social Studies of Science.* 1975; 5: 86-92.

*Reprinted from the Journal of the American Society for Information Science, Vol. 29, No. 4, 1978. Copyright © 1978 by the American Society for Information Science. Reprinted by permission of John Wiley & Sons, Inc.*

# Cumulative Advantage Urn Games Explained: A Reply to Kantor

**Derek de Solla Price**
*Yale University, New Haven, CT*

I am delighted with the challenge afforded by Kantor's paper. It provided an opportunity to examine the properties of the entire class of distributions arising from the models that he postulates. It made me analyze the difference between his models and mine and thereby rethink and clarify the nature of the Cumulative Advantage Distribution from a formulation that may have made it previously obscure to many, including myself.

The basic difference between our models is that Kantor's model is time dependent and relates to a more or less regularly occurring series of games in which the entire population of players participates. My model is for lifetime scores of a series of games played tournament style, gradually reducing the large field of players to a small elite of highly successful champions. In both types of model one can set up schemes with or without cumulating advantage, cumulating disadvantage, or even both. They probably all approximate real-life situations, however, the trouble is that Kantor's model, and all others in this time-dependent category, are, as he points out, nowhere near the right form to correspond to distributions of author productivity, frequency, or journal distribution. My time-independent distributions do.

To fully understand Kantor's proposal let us first consider its analog where the games of drawing from an urn are without any sort of changing chances. The entire population of players is each provided with an urn containing one red ball of success and one black ball of failure. At each tick of some great celestial metronome (be it annual or, more exaggeratedly, daily, or each second) the players pick a ball and thereby fail or succeed. It is easy enough [Fig. 1(a)] to see that after $n$ such games the probabilities of all such scores are arranged as the binomial coefficients in the expansion of $(1 + 1)^n$. Indeed the probability of a score $m$ is ${}_nC_m/2^n$. With an even chance of winning any particular game the average (and modal) score will be about $n/2$ and as the number of games becomes infinite the mean scores will also become infinite. The distribution of all possible scores at any time is, of course, a plain binomial.

As Kantor shows [Fig. 1(b)], if one adds cumulative advantage to this model by adding a red ball at each success but otherwise leaving the blacks unchanged it skews the distribution towards to top end. I find it fascinating that it would seem from his calculations as if increasing "skill" with success in such daily sets of tennis results in a situation where you settle down to winning all but a couple or so of the sets played. With more than an even chance of winning all sets beyond the first win only the very rare individual with lengthy runs of rotten luck will escape scores only slightly less than the number of sets played.

If one sets up a model of cumulating *dis*advantage by adding black balls rather than red, obviously one produces the same effect in mirror image with a skew to low scores and there will be a mode of two or so wins when the number of games is in the range that Kantor calculates, but it will still be a skewed binomial distribution.

There is an interesting special case if one both rewards success by an extra red ball *and* punishes failure with an extra black. Starting from the simplest pair as before, it appears [Fig. 1(c)] that the two processes balance and after any number of games there will be an equal probability of the entire range of possible scores. Thus the cumulation of both advantage and disadvantage produces such a skewing in both directions so that the resultant distribution is perfectly flat.

I do not feel that any model of this type can be used for such a phenomenon as publication or citation. In such processes there are no discrete failure events, only intervals separating events of success. At the extreme, consider the case actually most common in which an author produces no more than a single paper in a lifetime, or a paper which is cited once and newer again. How can it be possible to regard the entire history as made of a series of games, annual or daily or at any other rate, of which only one is a success?

I suppose instead that we deal with probabilistic changes of state so that some fixed proportion of the population will *in their entire lifetime* move up from the lowest state to the next. Correspondingly, to each higher state there are fixed probabilities of upward transition. What matters in publication or citation is not the rate of winning so much as the coming into being or passing away from such activity.

The simplest model of this sort assumes a constant transition probability. Let us postulate a series of sequential steps of such difficulty that only half of those that attempt such a step succeed [Fig. 2(a)]. The resultant distribution shows a simple exponential falloff with the number making each score just half of the score one unit below. A similar exponential falloff would occur for any value of the constant factor. It should be noted that the distribution says

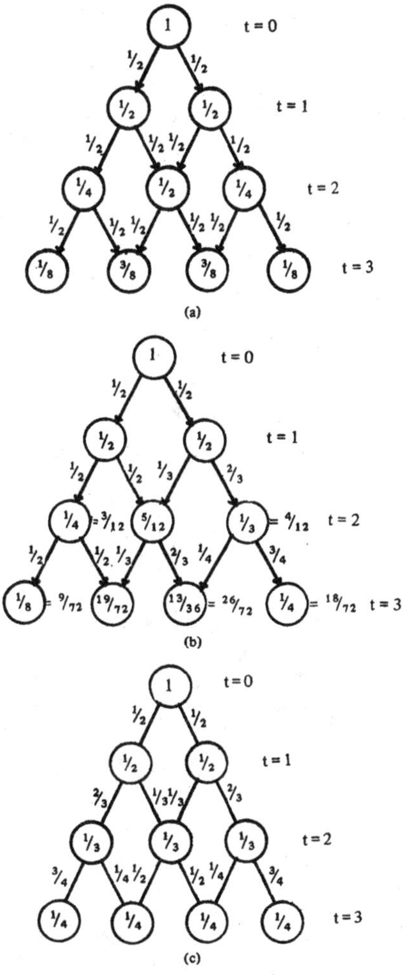


FIGURE 1. Proportions of players and their contingent probabilities of further success or failure after the first few urn games. (a) shows the case in which there remains an even chance of either outcome at each game in the series. (b) is Kantor's model showing a case in which the contingent probability of success is unchanged by failure but increased by success. (c) shows a game in which the result of success is an increased contingent probability of success and the result of failure is an increased contingent probability of failure. The first model corresponds to sets of some compulsory game of pure chance like coin tossing. The second adds a factor of skill on the part of the player as in compulsory attempts on a daily crossword puzzle. The third supposes that the players tire with failure or their opponents gain skill as in compulsory tennis singles within a closed competitive group.

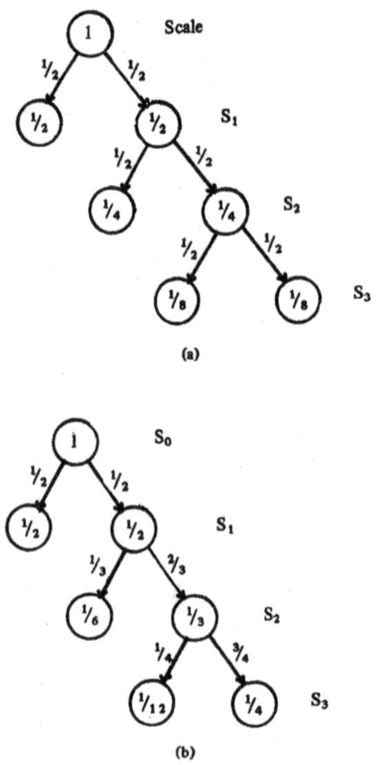


FIGURE 2. Similar diagrams for games played tournament style in which no step can be taken without success in the previous game. (a) shows the case of a constant even chance, as in a coin-tossing experiment where one is concerned with the probabilities that a continuous series of 0, 1, 2, 3, etc., heads will occur commencing with a given throw. (b) shows what happens if the game starts with even chances but with success improving with practice as in the case of the number of games one can get from a single coin with a pinball machine that gives free games with each skillful success in exceeding a standard score. In bibliometric phenomena the chance of an encore depends on the applause at the previous performance, and the applause grows (on the average) with the practice gained by each performance.

nothing of the life history of any particular individual. It is not that half of the original population is blighted by failure and refused permission to play again. That half consists of those who *post facto* at the end of the lifetime game have not exhibited another success.

The exponential falloff is necessarily much more rapid than all known distributions of publication and citation counts and severely underestimates the numbers of high scores. Any stacking of the odds by cumulating disadvantage in which chances of transition were decreased at each success would result in an even more rapid than exponential falloff. We therefore examine the simplest case of cumulating advantage which must increase transition probabilities at each success.

The result of starting from an even-chance transition and adding a red ball at each win [Fig. 2(b)] is very simply that the proportion of population in the $n$th state is $1/n\,(n+1)$. For large $n$ this behaves as $1/n^2$ which is well known to be the approximate empirical law found by Lotka for author productivities; it is also the underlying principle from which Bradford's law results.

This $1/n\,(n+1)$ distribution refers, of course, to author productivities and citation counts for their entire and virtually infinite life histories. The purpose of the continuous model is not to take a small slice of time, but a small subsection of the population of individuals and their successes such as one gets in course of a single year or a less than total selection of source journals. I see no way around the somewhat difficult analysis which shows that all such distributions are governed by the Beta function and have inverse power laws as a set of good approximations. As I have shown they all agree rather well with the empirical data.

Kantor's last paragraph contains a set of quite different misunderstandings. There is a fundamental difference between the monotonically decreasing hyperbolic distributions which concern us here and those more common which contain some maximum frequency value between the extremes of score. Distributions with a maximum can be scaled up with similar shape for all sizes of total population. Two hyperbolic distributions of similar equation but different populations cannot be geometrically similar, and hence such properties as mean values and extrema are size dependent. This can be seen most readily by considering the $1/n\,(n+1)$ hyperbolic distribution [Fig. 2(b)]. If the population of players is $N$, the number with $n$ successes is $N/n\,(n+1)$ and this group contains a total of $N/(n+1)$ successes. I suppose Kantor's difficulty to be that this is the harmonic series, well known to be divergent. It cannot be summed from unity to infinite score, and the mean of this distribution is therefore also infinite. I have dealt with this by showing that in real examples the maximum score must be of order of $N$. For example, the most any paper could be cited is about once by every other paper in the population. The harmonic series, summed to $N$ terms, yields approximately log $N$ for average value, and that is why [1, p. 301] even for a population of one-hundred million papers, $R$ would not be anywhere near infinite, but only ca. 18 successes/individual.

## References

1. de Solla Price, D. "A general theory of bibliometric and other cumulative advantage processes." *Journal of the American Society for Information Science.* 27(2):292-307; 1976.

*Reprinted from the American Society for Information Science, 8th Mid-Year Meeting, May 16-19, 1979, Collected Papers.*

# The Citation Cycle

Derek de S. Price, Yale University
2036 Yale Station, New Haven, CT 06520

This paper had its origin in a chart, long resident on my office wall. Frequently revised, corrected and redrawn, it seems to have taken on a life of its own and some utility to colleagues and students who acquired copies at various stages during more than ten years. The basic idea is to exhibit an interlocking metabolic complex of bibliometric (and scientometric) parameters in a comprehensive and integrated structure after the manner of the Nitrogen Cycle and other such paraphernalia beloved of organic chemists and ecologists. The data for this cycle are those drawn from the largest collection we have of machine-handled and automatically counted bibliographic items — the *Science Citation Index* (SCI) which has been published by the Institute for Scientific Information (ISI) since its foundation by Eugene Garfield in 1961. In biblio- and sciento-metrics it is often fatal and invariably debilitating to do your own counting. Beyond the tedious work and expense there is a hidden danger that one might well falsify the investigation by artifacts of definition and selection, so it is far better to use unobtrusive indicators produced by people who didn't know you were going to use them thus.[1] Much of my research in this area has been fed by a steady diet from the cutting room floor of printouts produced by ISI partly in their direct function of producing what is not only primarily a bibliographical aid but also *the* chief bibliographical service for scientists. The other part has been composed of special printouts generated by their admirable curiosity about their own processes, for which I am truly grateful.

An incidental advantage of this parasitic nourishment of my work is that the data, most of which are now conveniently published on an annual basis in the preambles to the *Social Science Citation Index,* the *Science Citation Index,* and the *Who is Publishing in Science* volumes, cover a large range of that which is implicated in the available corpus of both bibliometric and scientometric research theories. The citation cycle therefore embodies many of the elements of theory which are treated in the scholarly literature in our fields,[2] and it thus provides a sort of overview and coherent conspectus of a framework for the theories.

A tour of the Citation Cycle begins (see Figure 1), as does the formation of a citation index, with the selection of the Source Journals and the Items (usually research papers, but the more general term is useful) which are contained in them. The *selection* of journals is crucial to the success of a citation index because it is a strategy quite different from the usual librarian's striving for completeness. Though one may well start from an attempt to include all significant journals within some definition from all countries and all fields as sources, the ultimate test is provided as feedback from the journals which are cited by such sources. For many years the list of cited journals has provided a higher criticism of which journals to accept and which to reject as sources. Some journals may be so esoteric or so local that the citations they receive are from themselves. Others may have purposes of news and current awareness rather than the communication of citable knowledge and be for that reason almost uncited even by themselves. Then again some of the most cited journals may be extinct or living under a new name, or they may use the archaic practice of incorporating references in the body of the text where it is too expensive to employ key-punchers to excavate them.

If ISI chose its ca. 2700 source journals at random they would be only about 6.7 percent of the (maybe) 40,000 scientific and technical journals extant in the world, and hence they would contain only a comparable fraction of the current source literature. If ISI were perfectly successful, as no doubt they are not quite, in skimming only cream, they would get as sources just those source journals which were the most cited. In that case one can apply the powerful principle of Bradford's approximation to the distribution law of cumulative advantage in journals;[3] cumulating citations from the most-cited journals downwards, the total of citations is proportional to the logarithm of the number of journals included. This is much more realistic and it has the advantage, as it should, that the result is not at all sensitive to the count of all the world's journals — a ball-park estimate will serve. The result of this estimate is that the SCI now includes $\log 2700/\log 40000 = 0.75$ of all cited papers. Thus although it is derived from only 1/15 of the source papers, it includes 3/4 of the cited literature. As a corollary we may now claim that if the data in our Citation Cycle are multiplied by 4/3 they will give the world data for the cited corpus.

The 2700 source journals did not come all at once. The first few numbers of annual publications were based on about 600 journals and then in 1964-67 there was a period of expansion and revision (see Figure 2). From 1969 onwards the number of journals has been expanding at an exponential growth of 2.76% a year (derived from a regression of the logarithm of the number). This is much smaller than estimates of the world growth of scientific literature, 6-7% a year, so we are dealing with a relatively unchanging core of journals. The number of source articles in these journals is now about 500,000 and it has been growing since 1969 at a rate of 4.14% a year; it follows that on the average the journals have become slightly fatter at a rate of 1.38% a year. Apart from this slow change we can say that although there is considerable variation in size between journals, on the average each contains about 162 ± 5 source items/year (see Figure 3). Note the sharp drop in average size during the 1964-68 expansion as smaller journals are added. This is an interesting size, for it is equal in magnitude to an average invisible college of co-workers, usually 100-200 people, each writing about one paper a year in any of the major subdisciplines into which science is divided.[4] One might conjecture that a journal comes into being to serve such an internally communicating group of researchers, and then in the normal process of aging as the invisible college grows and produces new groups by fission some of the journals survive as media for aggregates of the living subfields.

The next stage of the tour of the Citation Cycle connects the number of Source Items (we shall designate this as S henceforth) with the authors of those items. In the dim distant past of science, from the late seventeenth century when scientific journals began until about World War I, when collaborative authorship was a rather rare event, the norm was that an active researcher produced about one scientific paper per year.[5] Professionals tend to have a discretionary period in their life style which runs on an annual basis, and in harmony with our annual reporting of activity the normal life cycle of a project tends to be adjusted to this calendar cycle. What has happened since that period, and with great rapidity in the time since World War II, is that scientific authors collaborate increasingly so that in most scientific fields there is an average of two names or a little more per paper. What is happening is that the developing entrepreneurial tradition of channeling research support funding through a principal investigator permits that person to purchase subsidiary authors in effect. The result is that the number of authors per paper has become a rather good indicator of the extent of grant support in the field. Cancer and heart disease research is highly collaborative, pure mathematics much less so; it may be that in fields that need big team work the grants have to run high, but the effect may just as well be the other way round in causality. At all events, even though it now takes two authors to produce a paper, the output in papers has stayed constant, for now instead of each author getting out one paper per year, the team of two on the average produces two papers per year. The result is that the number of Source Authors is also S, and to be more precise there will be amongst them 0.55 S primary authors and 0.45 S secondary authors. Also to be a little more precise, there are now 2.13 authorships associated with each paper, across all fields. It should be noted that this group of statistics varies quite a lot from field to field, perhaps even from country to country. There are some fields like systematic taxonomy in natural history, or certain parts of organic chemistry where a paper may correspond to only a few weeks' work, and there are fields like astrophysics where an ordinary research contribution may be of two years' duration or longer to make a single paper—such goes the size of atoms of knowledge in various disciplines.

For the next stage in the tour we enter the domain of citations. Each paper includes a list of articles to which it refers. The references are usually at the end of the paper or footnotes on the page, and in the formation of the SCI these are key-punched into the computer record to be sorted into a citation index, alphabetic by cited author. Although the source items include everything from those totally devoid of references, e.g., news items and pontificating remarks, to those with hundreds or thousands of references in a bibliography, on the average there are about 14 references from each of the source items. In fact, cumulative advantage theory shows that what is really happening is not to be thought of as the new papers making reference back to the old; it is the old papers that are throwing off citations every year and thereby making occasion for the new literature. At all events, the average number of references in a paper is determined by the size of the available archive of literature in that field. Indeed the number of references per paper must be a small constant (less than one) plus the natural logarithm of the size of the archive. The natural logarithm of one million is about 14 and that is why the number of references is what it is.

For the Social Science Citation Index (SSCI) the corresponding number is about 11 references per paper, which is what would happen for an archive of about 60,000 papers in each field. Both in the SCI and in the SSCI, the number of references per paper has been increasing as the archive has grown. For the SCI there has been an increase of just less than half a reference per year (0.49) and for the SSCI the value is 0.62 per year. For the SCI the relative growth in number of references is about 3.5% a year and for the SSCI about 5.5%, corresponding to rates of growth of the archive at these values. Though both are lower than the traditional 7% per year growth rate of all scientific literature that we used to assume, they match the growth rate of source articles reasonably well. One must suppose that the ISI corpus is now growing at little more than half the historic long-term growth rate of the literature in the past century or so.

The references back from the source papers fall upon the available archive of papers already published. As we shall see, only about half of this archive is cited at all in any particular year, but of those papers that are cited a large majority, 72.8%, are cited once only. Of the remaining papers about half are cited just twice, and though the number of papers falls off very rapidly at about the inverse cube of the number of citations, there are still 1/400 of the items with more than 20 citations per year. Since some few heavily cited items with several thousand citations a year exist — the so-called Method Papers and Reference Books — this tail of the distribution may represent a highly significant part of the citation behavior. Cumulative advantage theory accounts very well for the observed distribution. A fundamental parameter is the number of citations per cited paper[6] which varies slowly, as does the number of references per source item, with the logarithm of the available archive. There are now about 1.92 citations per cited item, and this is increasing linearly at 0.026 per year (see Figure 4). The corresponding figure for the SSCI is 1.33 citations per item cited, but as yet any secular increase appears to be masked by the settling down of the source selection which is still in its first few years.

As a result of this multiplicity of citation, the 14.9 S references from the S source items fall upon 14.9 S/1.92 = 7.76 S cited items. For the SSCI the corresponding figure is 10.8 S/1.33 = 8.12 S cited items. It should be remembered that although all source items are from journals, the cited items include also a significant proportion of books, monographs, etc. Even so, the cited items could be only a minority of the archive available for citation, since at a growth rate of 7% the archive must be ca. 14 S, and for the empirical growth rate of 4.14% for source items the archive would be 24 S. Even at random, the probability of an archival item being cited at all should be in the range 0.33 to 0.57 and with a Poisson Distribution the citation hits per item cited would be in the range 1.18 -1.31. The significantly higher empirical figures show that cumulative advantage works very forcibly to increase the number of highly cited items beyond those that would occur with random events.

Since the cited items are sorted alphabetically by author it is easy to make a distribution of the number of citations per cited author, or better still, the average number of cited items per cited author. At present this parameter has a value of about 4.2 for the SCI and 2.8 for the SSCI. In the former case we have enough years of data to establish a trend (see Figure 5); there seems to have been considerable perturbation of the parameter during the 1964-68 reorganization, but since 1969 the parameter has been increasing about 1% a year probably due more to the secular increase in collaborativeness rather than to any real increase in productivity of paper producing. Since we have 7.76 S cited items in the SCI there will be 7.76 S/4.2 = 1.85 S cited authors, and for the SSCI there will be 8.12 S/2.8 = 2.90 S cited authors.

At this point in the tour of the Citation Cycle we may complete a loop by examining the relationship between the cited authors and the source authors. A collating of source and cited indexes shows that for both the SCI and the SSCI only about half of the source authors in any year are also cited. This doubtless corresponds to the fact that about half of the year's source authors are collaborating graduate students and junior faculty without a backlog of papers of which they are the first author available for citation. The 0.55 S first authors in the sources are therefore to be compared with the 1.85S that are cited in the SCI and the 2.90 cited in the SSCI. It follows that those active in the year are 30% of the SCI stock and 19% of the SSCI stock.

Another, more accurate way of looking at the relationship is to note that we know from an independent investigation of a small slice of the SCI for a long period[7] that only some of the collaborative authors are newcomers. In fact, of the S source authors, 70% are continuants who publish for an extended period, and 30% are newcomers. Further, for the continuants we know that in any year they have a probability of 0.7 of making a publication. It follows that the S source authors imply the existence of the same number S continuants together with 0.3 S newcomers. The S continuants may now be compared with the cited authors, and we derive immediately that for the SCI some 0.85/1.85 — 46%, and for the SSCI some 1.90/2.90 — 66%, of the cited authors must have become discontinued by the current date. Many of the authors who once published, particularly those who published only transiently, are no longer cited; only a few are retired or deceased. It is worth noting as an overall figure that the number of cited authors in the SCI is just under a million, and in the SSCI about 112,000.

Having made one circuit of the Citation Cycle by the comparison of source and cited authors we may make another from the comparison of source and cited items. They have already been compared above through the medium of considering the available accrued corpus. We now look at structural relationships of the network of references/citations which, as has long been evident,[8] knit the new layer of source papers to a small selection of highly active papers in the accrued corpus. Items that are cited only once in the index are, so to speak, only tacked on to the source item that cites them, and they cannot relate two source papers or be related to any other cited paper except through this. Multiple-cited papers are comparatively rare, constituting about 27.2% of those in an annual index. Since we have 7.76 S cited items in the SCI there must be 2.11 S multiple-cited items which are connected to the S source items by about 7.63 links of reference/citation; there are therefore 7.63 links per source item and 7.63/2.11 = 3.6 links per multiple-cited item. Going to next higher level of papers cited three or more times it turns out that the number of such papers is approximately equal to S, and the number of links at this level will be about 5.5 for each source *or* multiple-cited paper. For the SSCI there is less referencing, a small corpus, and hence a lower level of miltiple citation. For those papers cited twice or more we have about 1.3 S which are connected to the S source papers by 4.2 S links of reference/citation. These parameters enable us to establish the way in which the corpus of papers is knitted together by its links into a structure of source papers overlaying a similarly structured corpus of source papers.

A first visualization of the implied structure may be had by cutting out the very highly referencing bibliography-like sources and also the very highly cited method-like cited papers as well as those which are singly-cited and cannot therefore contribute more than a tacking-on process. In this case to a first crude approximation we may suppose there to be roughly equal numbers of source and multiple-cited papers connected by about four links to and from each respectively. We can visualize the source papers as lying on the intersections of a rectangular grid on a thin sheet which overlaps a similar grid of cited papers on a thick sheet representing several years of accretion of former sources (see Figure 6). Each point on the thin sheet is directly linked to the neighboring four on a complementary place of the thick sheet and vice versa. In this convention we may now see that the bibliography and method papers may be reinserted as extensive areas, rather than points, that each blanket a whole region in the other sheet (see Figure 7). Clearly the general form of this picture can be extended to include the moderately referencing and cited papers, too, and we may make the depiction dynamic by supposing the thick corpus of cited papers to be formed from an onion-like accretion of annual shells growing out from a nucleus laid down in the distant past.

As a next stage in this visualization we note that if there were exactly four links per item the pattern of linkage might be represented by making each intersection of a square lattice represent an item and the four lines running to it as the links. If each of the alternating source and cited items (denoted as S and C in Figure 8) had *exactly* four links the result would be a perfect lattice. If four is only a statistical mean, the corresponding lattice with various numbers of links would look rather like a very torn and deformable fishing net (see Figure 9), and if this is not envisaged in a three-dimensional analog the result must look rather like the structure that is built into the network linkage of the corpus of science.

This property of the corpus now makes it possible to model relational structure of what has been called "subject space."[9] It is this space that is approximately mapped by the Griffith and Small[10] technique of cocitation analysis or that of Kessler in his bibliographic linkage which corresponds to co-referencing structure. What is implied is that we have built into the Citation Cycle not only the quantitative modeling but also a structural scheme. In a strong sense this structure provides a natural and automatic "indexing" of the entire corpus of scientific literature, and it seems evident that many of the recall/relevance trade-off problems of actual indexing arise from a conflict between this built-in structure and that imposed by the arbitrary structure of the classifier. Not the least of the problems must be that an essentially two-dimensional skin of source papers, or a three-dimensional corpus of cited papers (with time as the extra dimension) must be traversed by a classification scheme which, like the telephone book or the Dewey decimal system is essentially a one-dimensional traversing of the map.

1. Another advantage: this paper acknowledges no support whatsoever from any agency or foundation, but then, no time wasted either from preparing and submitting proposals.

2. For a general survey of the bibliometrics of citation see: Narin, Francis. *Evaluative Bibliometrics.* Computer Horizons, Inc., Project No. 704R, March 31, 1976; and, Garfield, Eugene. *Citation Indexing: Its Theory and Application in Science, Technology, and Humanities.* New York, Wiley-Interscience, 1979; and, Hjerppe, Roland. *An Outline of Bibliometrics and Citation Analysis.* Stockholm, The Royal Institute of Technology Library, October 1978.

3. Price, D.de S. "A General Theory of Bibliometric and other Cumulative Advantage Processes," *Journal of the American Society for Information Science,* 27,5/6:292-306, 1976; and, Price, D. de S. "Cumulative Advantage Urn Games Explained: A Reply to Kantor," *Journal of the American Society for Information Science,* 29:4, 204-206, 1978. For a recent large-scale empirical test of the Bradford

approximation see: Drott, M. Carl and Belver C. Griffith. "An Empirical Examination of Bradford's Law and the Scattering of Scientific Literature," *Journal of the American Society for Information Science,* 29: 238-246, September 1978.

4. Price, D. de S. and Donald deB. Beaver. "Collaboration in an Invisible College," *American Psychologist,* 21:1011-1018, November 1966.

5. For a history of scientific collaboration see: Beaver, D. DeB. and R. Rosen, "Studies in Scientific Collaboration, Part I. The Professional Origins of Scientific Collaboration, Part I. The Professional Origins of Scientific Co-authorship," *Scientometrics,* 1: 65-84, 1978; Beaver, D. deB. and R. Rosen, "Studies in Scientific Collaboration, Part II. Scientific Co-authorship, Research Productivity and Visibility in the French Scientific Elite, 1799-1830," *Scientometrics,* 1:133-149, 1979; and Beaver, D. deB. and R. Rosen, "Studies in Scientific Collaboration, Part III. Professionalization and the Natural History of Modern Scientific Co-authorship," *Scientometrics* (in press).

6. Garfield, E. "Is the Ratio Between Number of Citations & Publications Cited a True Constant?" *Current Contents* 6:editorial, February 9, 1976.

7. Price, D. de S. and S. Gursey. "Studies in Scientometrics. Part I. Transience and Continuance in Scientific Authorship," *International Forum on Information and Documentation,* International Federation for Documentation, Moscow 1:2: 17-24, 1976; and Price, D. de S. and S. Gursey. "Studies in Scientometrics. Part II. The Relation Between Source Author and Cited Author Populations," *International Forum on Information and Documentation,* Moscow 1:3: 19-22, 1976.

8. Price, D. de S. "Networks of Scientific Papers," *Science* 149, 510-515, 1965.

9. Meincke, Peter P.M. and Pauline Atherton. "Knowledge Space: A Conceptual Basis for the Organization of Knowledge," *Journal of the American Society for Information Science,* 27: 18-24, Jan.-Feb. 1976 and, McGill, Michael J. "Knowledge and Information Spaces: Implications for Retrieval Systems," *Journal of the American Society for Information Science,* 27: 205-210, July-August 1976.

10. Small, H. and B.C. Griffith. "The Structure of Scientific Literatures I: Identifying and Graphing Specialties," *Science Studies,* 4:17-40, 1974;

Griffith, B.C. and H.G. Small. "The Structure of Scientific Literature II: The Macro- and Micro-Structure of Science," *Science Studies,* 4: 339-365; Small, H.G. "A Co-citation Model of a Scientific Specialty: A Longitudinal Study of Collagen Research," *Social Studies of Science,* 7:139-166, 1977; and, Small, H. and Edwin Greenlee. Citation Context Analysis of a Co-citation Cluster: Recombinant-DNA," (to be published).

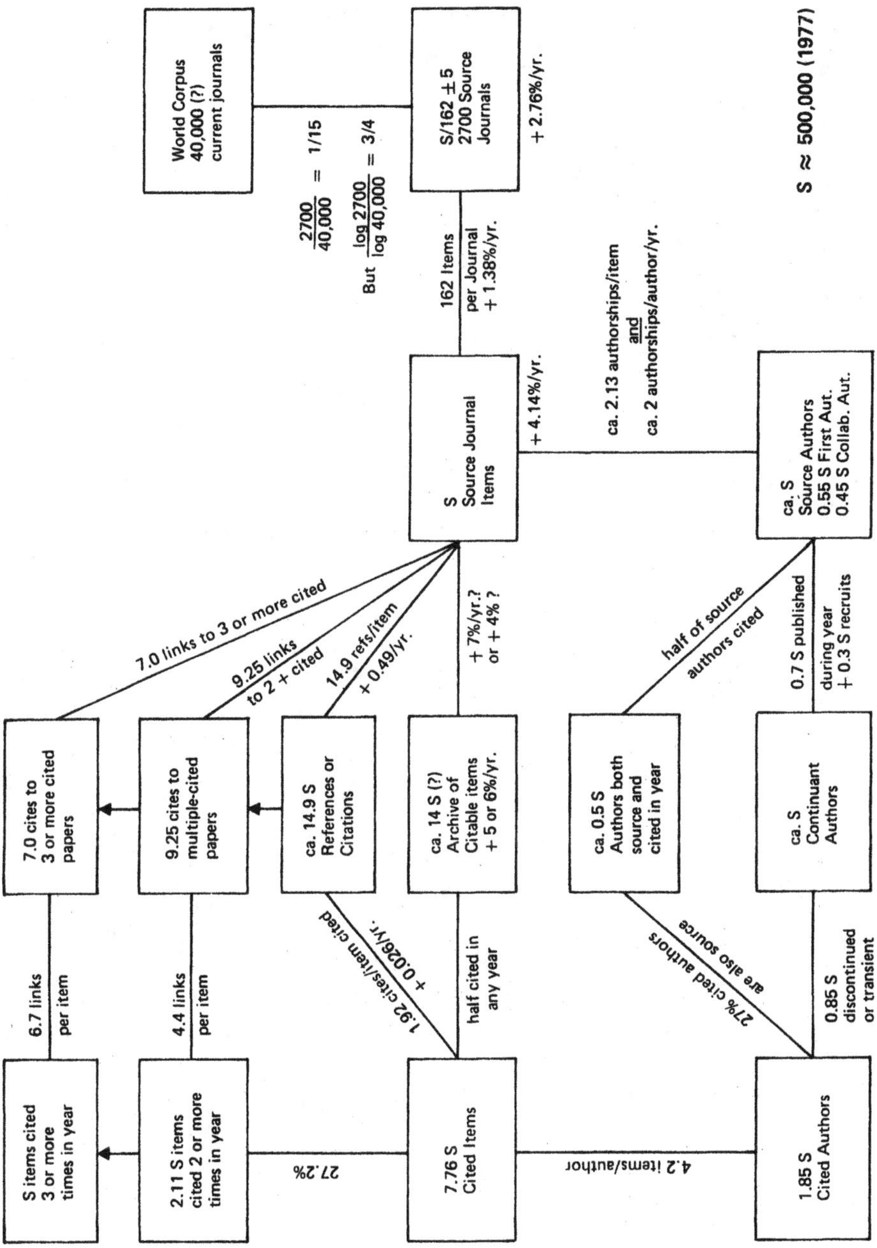


**Figure 1 The Citation Cycle**

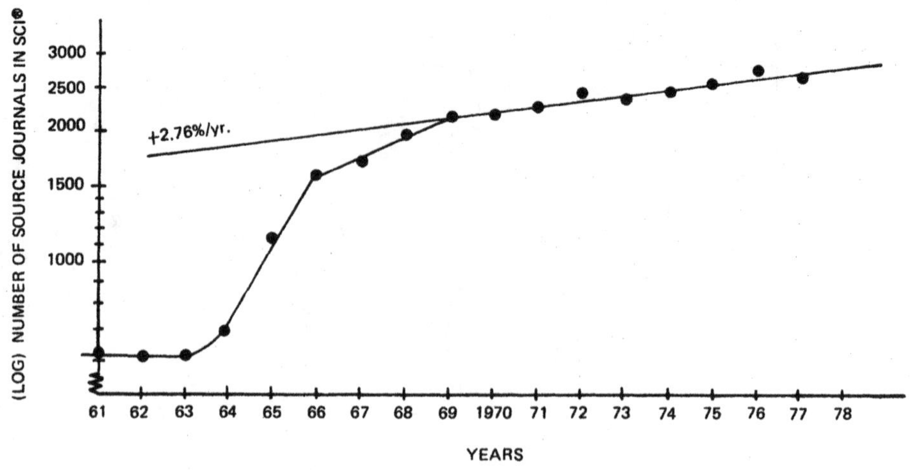


**Figure 2**

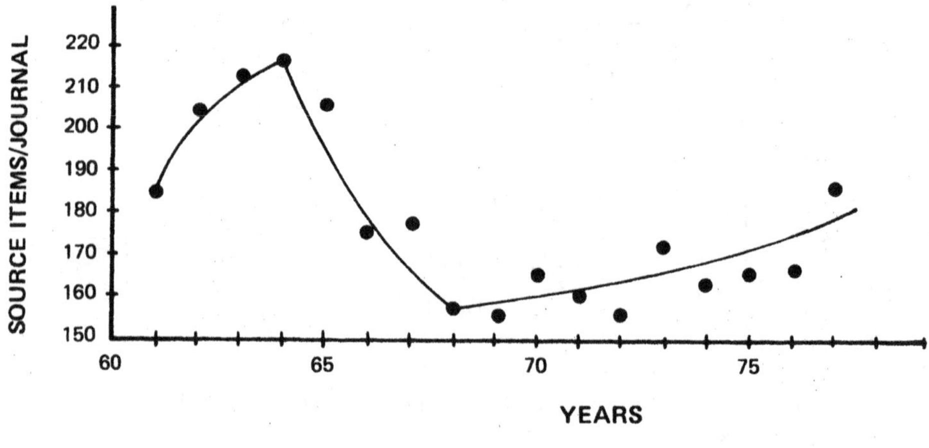


**Figure 3**

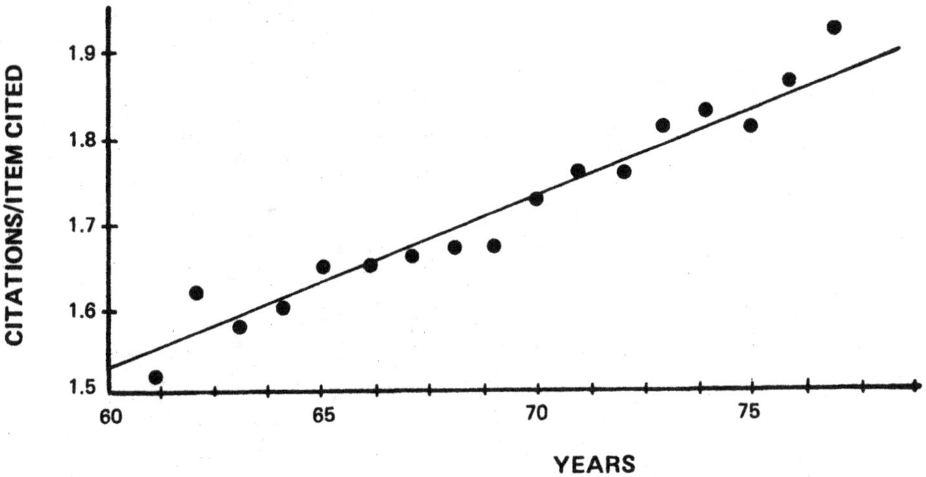


**Figure 4**

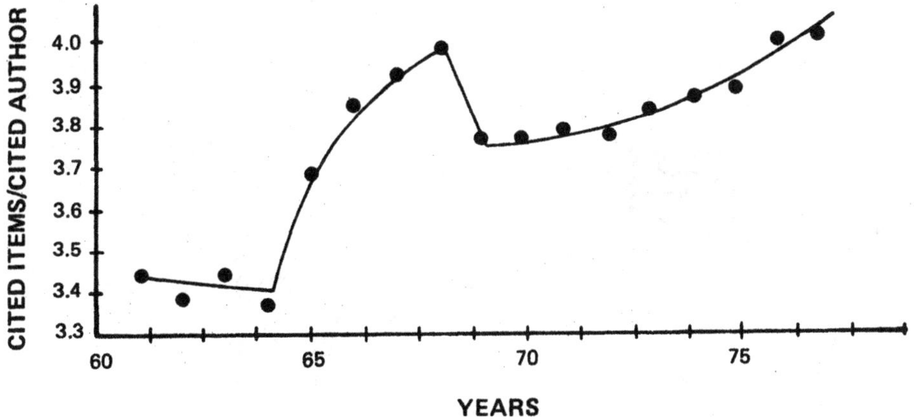


**Figure 5**

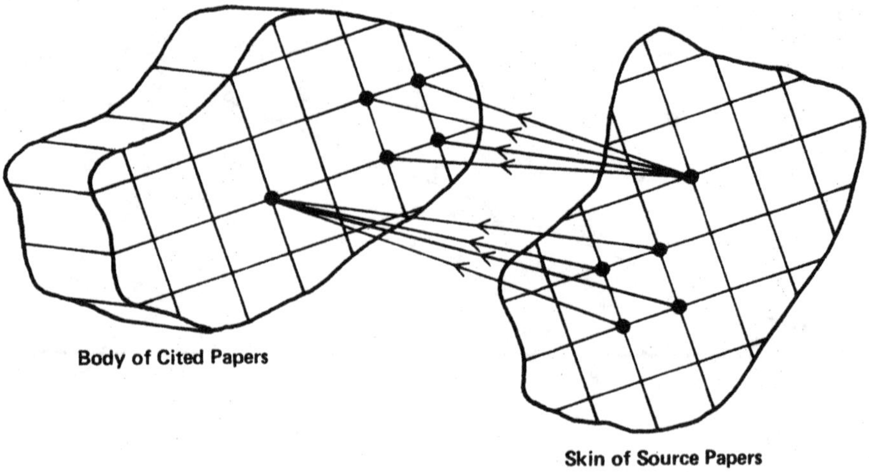


Figure 6

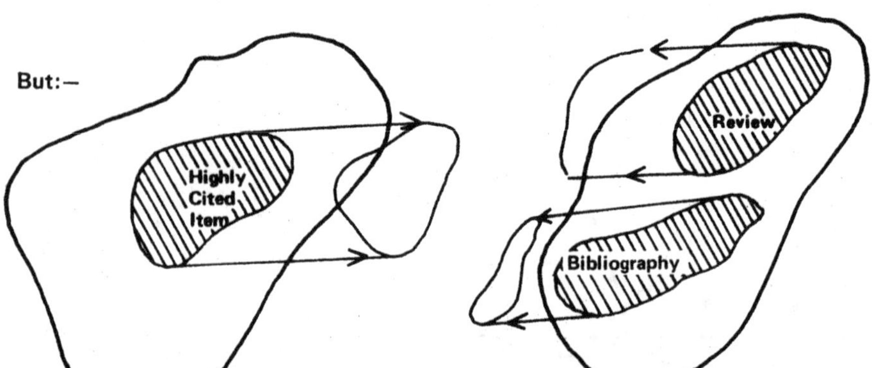


Figure 7

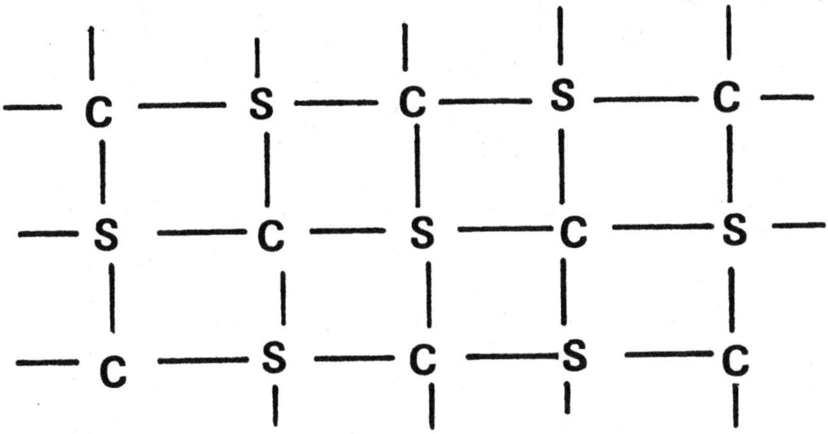


Figure 8

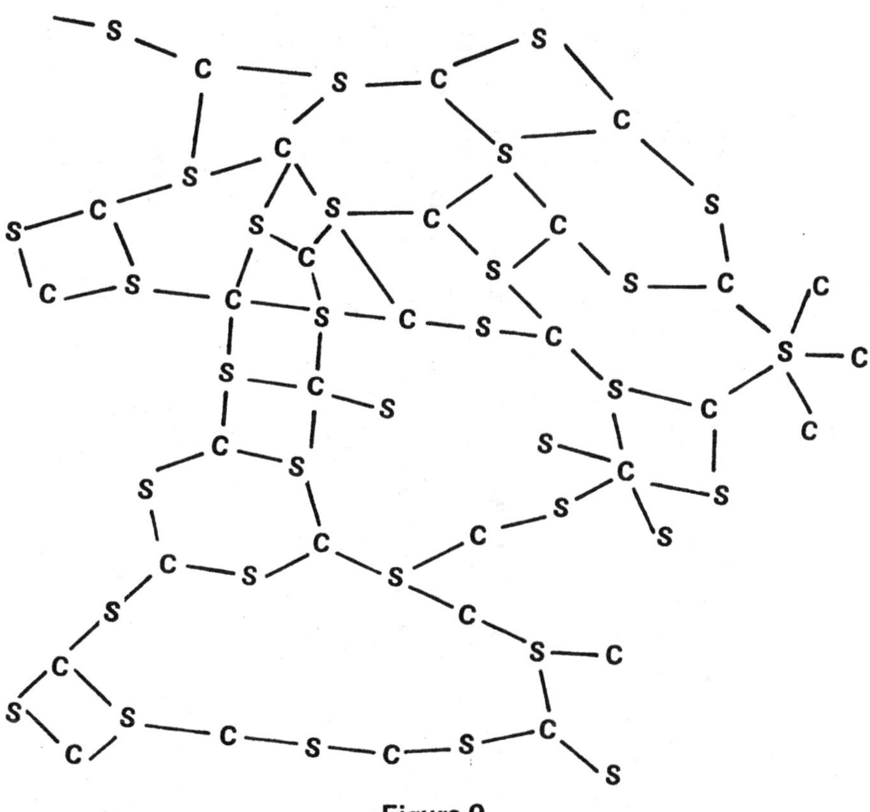

Figure 9

**SCIENCE CITATION INDEX®**

| | 1961 | 1962 | 1963 | 1964 | 1965 | 1966 | 1967 | 1968 | 1969 | 1970 | 1971 | 1972 | 1973 | 1974 | 1975 | 1976 | 1977 |
|---|---|---|---|---|---|---|---|---|---|---|---|---|---|---|---|---|---|
| Source Journals | 613 | 605 | 610 | 700 | 1146 | 1573 | 1711 | 1968 | 2180 | 2192 | 2277 | 2425 | 2364 | 2443 | 2540 | 2717 | 2655 |
| Source Items* | 113 | 124 | 129 | 152 | 236 | 274 | 304 | 309 | 341 | 362 | 364 | 378 | 407 | 401 | 419 | 451 | 495 |
| Refs/Cites* | 1370 | 1486 | 1558 | 1790 | 2925 | 3074 | 3387 | 3699 | 3850 | 4108 | 4380 | 4459 | 5017 | 5232 | 5536 | 6177 | 7398 |
| Items Cited* | 890 | 895 | 970 | 1092 | 1617 | 1821 | 1994 | 2139 | 2262 | 2340 | 2450 | 2597 | 2730 | 2818 | 3006 | 3246 | 3776 |
| Authors Cited* | 258 | 267 | 281 | 324 | 439 | 474 | 510 | 547 | 601 | 620 | 646 | 688 | 711 | 730 | 772 | 813 | 908 |
| Cites/Item Cited | 1.52 | 1.63 | 1.58 | 1.60 | 1.65 | 1.65 | 1.66 | 1.70 | 1.67 | 1.73 | 1.76 | 1.76 | 1.81 | 1.83 | 1.81 | 1.87 | 1.92 |
| Cites/Author Cited | 5.23 | 5.67 | 5.44 | 5.38 | 6.07 | 6.36 | 6.51 | 6.52 | 6.28 | 6.52 | 6.57 | 6.65 | 6.95 | 7.05 | 7.05 | 7.68 | 8.01 |
| Items/Author Cited | 3.44 | 3.36 | 3.44 | 3.36 | 3.68 | 3.85 | 3.92 | 3.91 | 3.76 | 3.77 | 3.79 | 3.78 | 3.84 | 3.85 | 3.90 | 4.00 | 4.17 |
| Refs/Source Item | 12.1 | 12.0 | 12.1 | 11.8 | 12.4 | 11.2 | 11.1 | 12.0 | 11.3 | 11.4 | 12.0 | 12.3 | 12.3 | 13.0 | 13.2 | 13.7 | 14.9 |

**SOCIAL SCIENCES CITATION INDEX®**

| | 1970 | 1971 | 1972 | 1973 | 1974 | 1975 | 1976 |
|---|---|---|---|---|---|---|---|
| Source Journals | 1000 | 1030 | 970 | 1052 | 1278 | 1232 | 1517 |
| Source Items* | 73 | 80 | 73 | 70 | 83 | 98 | 127 |
| Refs/Cites* | 618 | 644 | 604 | 633 | 872 | 1025 | 1372 |
| Items Cited* | 423 | 436 | 400 | 415 | 576 | 686 | 925 |
| Authors Cited* | 166 | 169 | 158 | 165 | 230 | 253 | 336 |
| Cites/Item Cited | 1.28 | 1.33 | 1.36 | 1.36 | 1.36 | 1.33 | 1.33 |
| Cites/Author Cited | 3.27 | 3.42 | 3.39 | 3.41 | 3.40 | 3.68 | 3.68 |
| Items/Author Cited | 2.55 | 2.57 | 2.53 | 2.51 | 2.50 | 2.71 | 2.77 |
| Refs/Source Item | 8.69 | 8.06 | 8.25 | 9.06 | 10.50 | 10.44 | 10.81 |

*Thousands

Data from prefaces of SCI® and SSCI™

**Figure 10**

*Reprinted from Social Studies of Science, Vol 7, 1977.*

# A Co-Citation Model of a Scientific Specialty: A Longitudinal Study of Collagen Research

Henry G. Small

The phenomenon of specialization in science is receiving increasing attention as it becomes clear that the 'specialty' is the principal mode of social and cognitive organization in modern science. Recently, there have been some attempts to formulate theories of specialty growth and change.[1] Before sufficient evidence can accumulate to confirm or refute these theories, it seems likely that systematic and consistent methodological frameworks must be developed. The specialty of collagen research is presented here as the vehicle for exploring the possibilities of one such methodology. Collagen research was selected because its recent history illustrates what is possibly an important type of specialty change – namely, that of rapid shift in research focus, or what might be loosely termed 'revolutionary' change.

In this paper I outline a general method for the study of specialty change, based upon citation data. The point of departure is a system which clusters highly cited documents, using their frequency of co-citation as a measure of association.[2] This system uses the magnetic tape version of the *Science Citation Index (SCI)* as its data base. The clusters obtained from the *SCI* have been found to correspond to narrow subject matter groupings and it has been suggested that these reflect the social and cognitive structures of research specialties. The collagen specialty was selected from roughly 1,000 clusters identified by applying this algorithm to the *SCI.*[3]

The methodology differs in a fundamental way from most other approaches to specialty development which use scientific literature as an integral part of the analysis. In many previous studies,[4] the first step is the creation of a bibliography extending over time for the specialty in question. Either an existing bibliography is used, or subject experts are called upon to comb the literature and select relevant items. The bibliography then becomes the data base for subsequent analyses of the specialty, including its growth and structural characteristics. To the extent that this approach is based upon subjective decisions of relevance by the individual(s) compiling the bibliography, the analysis is open to criticism for possible bias and lack of reproducibility. The principal difficulty with this approach is that it is almost impossible to establish precise criteria as to what should or should not be included within the boundaries of the subject, and the temptation is to apply present-day criteria to earlier literature. The method employed here, on the other hand, uses a clustering algorithm to establish these boundaries; it involves no subjective decisions on what is to be included or excluded from the specialty literature.

An important precursor study which used citiation data to examine the historical development of work on the genetic code was that of Garfield, Sher and Torpie.[5] Citations from key papers to earlier key papers led to the construction of what Garfield has called an 'historical map' for the field. The citation history was then compared with a conventional history of the events, as a means of validation. This study was perhaps the earliest to show the potential of citation analysis for reconstructing the history of scientific fields. But the methodology I use differs in some important respects. First, the means of linking papers is not by direct citation of one paper by another, but by the citing of papers together by later papers. The historical progression is then modeled, not as a flow chart of 'critical events', but as a changing cluster of such events. Second, Garfield, Sher and Torpie could compare their results with an already existing 'history' of the research area; but a study of the collagen specialty must rely on a survey of specialists for validation, since no such history is available.

The underlying assumption for a citation model of specialty development is that a shift in the cognitive and/or social state of a specialty is reflected in a shift in the citation patterns of the specialists. This seems plausible since the literature available to and cited by scientists is the result of many interlocking social and intellectual influences. In a different guise this hypothesis was mentioned in passing by Kuhn:

> . . . if I am right that each scientific revolution alters the historical perspective of the community that experiences it, then that change of perspective should affect the structure of post revolutionary textbooks and research publications. One such effect – a shift in the distribution of the technical literature cited in the footnotes to research reports – ought to be studied as a possible index to the occurrence of revolutions.[6]

Despite the extensive discussions of 'revolutions' in science by philosophers and historians, Kuhn's suggestion was not followed up. Most discussions of revolutions or conceptual shifts in science have relied on non-quantitative historical analysis. Citation data promise to provide a quantitative indicator of such events.[7]

## METHODOLOGY

The initial step in the clustering methodology is to select all documents cited 15 times or more in an annual *Science Citation Index (SCI)*. The threshold of 15 was selected primarily for convenience in computer processing, although, in practice, any threshold may be used. The assumption underlying this procedure is that highly cited papers are 'markers' or symbols of important concepts and methods in science and represent the current loci of consensus in the scientific community.

The next step is to find all the co-citations among the highly cited documents selected; that is, the number of times each has been cited together with the others. It is assumed that co-citation is a rough measure of association between concepts symbolized by the highly cited papers. Finally, the entire set of co-cited document pairs is input to a single-link clustering programme, and all clusters are extracted at a specified level of co-citation. In the present case, in order to be clustered together, documents had to be co-cited 11 times or more ('level 11'). Therefore, a cluster is complete when no other documents exist in the file which are co-cited 11 times with any document already in the cluster. This algorithm is one approach, and perhaps the simplest, to the discovery of local 'densities' in the citation network. Any threshold of co-citation may be used in practice, but what is appropriate for one specialty may not be appropriate for another. The threshold of 11 was used because it produces a large number of clusters, with the largest not exceeding about 100 documents. At level 11, an annual *SCI* yields roughly 900 clusters containing two or more highly cited documents, with a mean cluster size of about five documents.

The question of what is an 'appropriate' threshold for a specialty is a difficult one, since adequate significance tests for clusters have not yet been developed. Nevertheless, some heuristic guides are available. Ideally, I would like to vary the clustering level incrementally over a wide range, while observing a single cluster. If the cluster is a discrete area, it will add documents only gradually as the level is lowered. At some point there will be a sharp increase in cluster size corresponding to the level at which the specialty joins with other specialties to form a macrocluster. The ideal level for that specialty is just above this point. In practice, such 'fine tuning' of clusters is not economically feasible, and I have settled for a compromise level for all clusters. This is acceptable if none of the clusters in the file has reached the macrocluster stage. It means, however, that for some areas I err on the side of under-inclusion of documents, although the ones included are the most relevant (low recall, high precision). In the broadest sense, of course, the thresholds (and indeed the entire clustering procedure) should be regarded as a 'model' which requires rigorous testing.

For any cluster, a symmetric matrix of co-citations may be constructed showing how often any document in the cluster is co-cited with every other document. A further transformation can then be performed upon the co-citation frequencies which converts them into 'distances'. This procedure assigns to each highly cited document a normal probability 'hill' in two dimensions, whose volume is equal to the citation frequency of the document. The frequency of co-citation of two documents is then set equal to the volume of overlap between the two document hills.[8] The 'distance' between the documents is then given by the distance between the centres of the two hills. The distances between documents in a cluster are analyzed by a metric scaling algorithm[9] which assigns relative locations to the documents in two dimensional space. This configuration is plotted as a contour diagram.

The hypothesis explored in this paper is that the scaled configuration of highly cited and co-cited papers in a cluster is a concrete representation of the cognitive structure, 'subject space,' or current 'paradigm' of the specialty, and that the authors of the highly cited papers constitute the élite, or 'leading' scientists of the specialty. The authors of citing papers then comprise a subgroup of the current practitioners in the specialty. I will not be concerned with this latter group; rather, I will focus on how the cognitive structure of the specialty changes over time. Nor will I be concerned with the relationships of the collagen cluster to other clusters and specialties. Although such linkages exist and serve to place collagen in its context within the structure of biomedicine, the changes occurring within the specialty appear to be more significant (at least in this case) than the changes in its relationships with other biomedical specialties.

Change can be studied by carrying out the identical clustering procedure on successive annual cumulations of the *SCI*. The 1970, 1971, 1972, 1973, and 1974 files of the *SCI* were clustered at identical thresholds (that is, 15 citations per document per year, and 11 co-citations per document pair per year). By using the same thresholds each year the growth of the specialty can be gauged in terms of the growth of the cluster. The problem then is to match up the clusters obtained in successive years. A cluster is considered to have 'continued' if at least one of its highly cited documents is contained in a cluster the following year. In general, for any cluster in year 1 there are three possibilities in year 2:

1. None of the documents in the year 1 cluster are found in any cluster in year 2.
2. One or more of the documents in the cluster in year 1 are found in a single cluster in year 2.
3. The documents in the year 1 cluster may diffuse into two or more clusters in year 2.

Clearly, a mirror image of these possibilities exists for a cluster in year 2: it might be new; have continued in a simple fashion from a single cluster; or have formed from two or more earlier clusters. There are also degrees to which continuity can exist; from only one document being passed on to the next year's cluster, to all documents persisting to the next year. It is useful to introduce a 'Stability Index' (SI) to reflect the degree of continuity of clusters.[10] The SI of a continuous series of clusters over a period of N years is defined as

$$SI = \frac{\left| \bigcap_{i=1}^{N} C_i \right|}{\left| \bigcup_{i=1}^{N} C_i \right|}$$

where the numerator represents the number of documents which persist in the cluster over N years, and the denominator, the total number of distinct documents which appear in the sequence of clusters.[11]

For collagen, the sequence of clusters for 1970-74 is given in Figure 1. This pattern was obtained by application of the thresholds (15 citations and 11 co-citations) to each annual *SCI* (1970-74), and finding

**Figure 1. Collagen Clusters 1970-74**

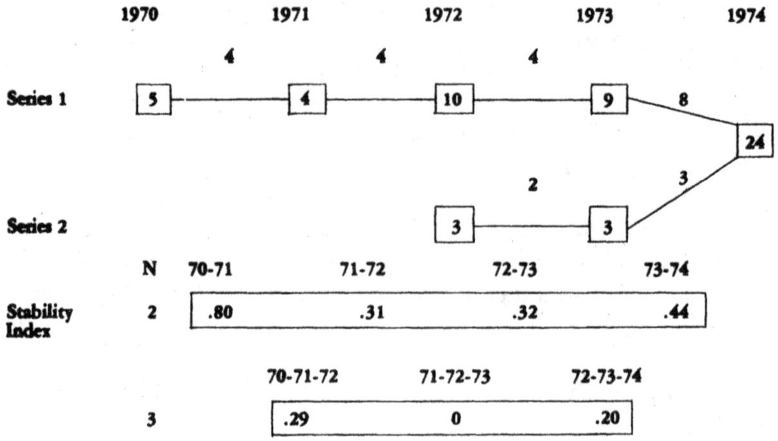


clusters with common cited documents in each successive year. Each box contains the number of cited documents in a cluster in a particular year; on the lines connecting the boxes are the numbers of documents common to clusters in adjacent years. Figure 1 shows that in 1974 two previously separate cluster series (series 1 and series 2) merge into a single large cluster with 24 documents. This pattern will later be interpreted as the joining of two lines of research on collagen.

Figure 1 presents SI values for the succession of collagen clusters, for both two and three year intervals (N=2 and 3). (Series 1 and 2 have been merged into a single strand for this calculation.) The maximum SI value is one, and as N increases (i.e. longer spans of time are taken) the SI value, in general, decreases. Note that the SI for the three years 1971-72-73 is zero; in other words, not one document continues in the cluster over those three years, although there are continuing documents from 1971 to 1972 and from 1972 to 1973. This finding will later be interpreted as a 'conceptual shift' in the specialty.

## HISTORICAL BACKGROUND

Before analyzing the citation maps, an account of recent events in collagen research is necessary. This account has been constructed from published papers and interviews with collagen researchers.

It is often argued that the importance of collagen lies in the abundance of this protein in the human body, where it is the major constitutent of connective tissue. In the 1920s and 1930s, the protein was studied by the technique of electron diffraction.[12] Later in the 1950s, electron microscopy was used to study the structure of the collagen fibre. Early studies centred on the question of structure (or, as one important pioneer expressed it, 'the molecular and macromolecular morphology') of collagen.[13] During the 1950s, X-ray diffraction suggested that the structure of collagen was a 'triple-stranded, coiled-coil'.[14] Before 1969, the typical collagen was thought to consist of two identical strands (both designated 'alpha 1') plus a third strand ('alpha 2'). Much of the work of the 1960s attempted to determine the structure of the alpha 1 and alpha 2 chains, including their amino acid sequences. The composition and nature of the cross linkages holding the helical chains together were also investigated. This work is still going on, and it is important to note that the structure of collagen is still not fully resolved.

Collagen investigators generally believe that biochemical methodologies have played a key, if not decisive, role in the advance of collagen research since World War II. In the 1960s, two critical methodologies were applied to collagen. The first was the use of cyanogen bromide (CNBr) to cleave the molecule into smaller protein sub-units;[15] the second was the use of the carboxymethyl cellulose chromatography column (CMC column) for separating the component molecular chains of collagen.[16] A major discovery was made by Miller in 1969,[17] when he found a genetic type of collagen consisting only of alpha 1 chains. The discovery stimulated the search for further types of collagen and several have been found to date.

The events of 1970-71 have been described as 'a great leap forward in our understanding of collagen'.[18] They began in 1970 with the presentation of results at a meeting of the Federation of American Societies of Experimental Biology by Layman, McGoodwin and Martin, from the National Institute for Dental Research.[19] A number of earlier researchers had postulated, on a theoretical basis, the existence of a soluble precursor molecule for collagen.[20] Martin's group provided the first clear evidence for a soluble precursor. Shortly after they had completed their work, Martin gave a seminar for the group under Paul Bornstein at the University of Washington in Seattle. There Martin learned of an independently obtained but related finding by the Bornstein group which provided further evidence for the precursor molecule. Bornstein called the substance 'procollagen', and presented his results in a paper[21] which appeared shortly after one by the Martin group,[22] in the spring of 1971. A simultaneous and, as it turned out, related discovery was made by researchers in Belgium,[23] where a new disease of cattle was characterized as a defect of collagen, causing a weakness of the skin called 'dermatosparaxis'. Karl Piez, also of the US National Institute of Dental Research, was visiting the Belgian laboratory at this time and was able to convey the news of the Martin and Bornstein work to the Belgian researchers. They concluded that their defective collagen in the skin of cattle was a form of procollagen.

A number of studies followed in quick succession during 1971, providing supporting evidence for the new substance, procollagen. The prompt acceptance of its discovery by the community was, perhaps, facilitated by the long history of theoretical speculations which predicted the existence of a soluble precursor. These discussions went back to at least 1960:[24] the most recent had been published almost simultaneously with the Martin discovery paper in 1971, although without knowledge of any of the new data.[25]

A number of social factors seem to be important in the development of the specialty, although no systematic effort has been made to collect such data. Gross has described the specialty as involving 'a small but intensely interested group of investigators'.[26] Specialists reported in interviews that very close informal communication exists between researchers in the field, and that there are frequent exchanges of personnel between a small number of 'key research centres'. A small 'core' of specialists is regarded as constituting the founders and intellectual forebears of the specialty. An example of a 'key research centre' is the National Institute for Dental Research (NIDR) in Bethesda, Maryland, which is one of the US National Institutes of Health. A veteran researcher on collagen at NIDR is Karl Piez. A large number of researchers have visited or received training in this laboratory. NIDR has, in a sense, played the role of a training centre for specialists in collagen research, who have later gone out to set up their own laboratories to work on collagen.

During the earlier period, the specialty was marked by what appears to be generally low esteem. Collagen was regarded as a rather inert and uninteresting molecule. Evidence of this attitude is provided by James Watson in his Nobel address.[27] When Watson was working on DNA at Cambridge he was worried that the structure of DNA might turn out to be as 'dull' and unexciting as that of collagen. Perhaps this 'dull' image discouraged new recruits to the specialty while, at the same time, it increased the dedication of those who were already committed to this research.

In the last few years (1970-74) the specialty has grown in size rather dramatically. It has become impossible, for example, for all active researchers to attend a single Gordon conference. One specialist reported that with the breakdown in the sense of a small community, there has also been an increase in competition among researchers. The image of collagen research has also improved. Recent advances, especially in methodology, have made possible a transfer of knowledge from basic biology to medical fields such as ageing, heart and lung disease, cancer and arthritis. Collagen has become a model system in biochemistry with far reaching implications for medicine.

## COLLAGEN MAPS: 1970-74

Figures 2 to 6 are contour maps of the series 1 collagen clusters from 1970 to 1974, derived according to the procedure outlined above. The configurations obtained from scaling in two dimensions are drawn as contour maps (increasing 'altitude' corresponds to increasing density of citation), taking care to convert all configurations to a common metric so that documents with the same citation frequency are equal in size.

The value of Kruskal's 'Stress II' is given on each plot and is a rough indicator of the goodness-of-fit of the input distances to the final configuration in two dimensions.[28] The 'Stress II' values obtained are rather high. There are three reasons why this is so. First, the hill model is constrained to two dimensional configurations: stress can be expected to be high when only two dimensions are used. Second, the metric scaling option of Kruskal's M-D-SCAL is used, which gives higher stress values than the non-metric option. Third, there is the imposed condition that the input distances fit the configuration distances as closely as possible. Technically, this means that a straight regression line passing through the origin is used to relate input to scaled distances. All of these conditions tend to increase stress. Furthermore, tests with the same data using the non-metric option of M-D-SCAL gave very similar configurations to those obtained with metric scaling. Therefore, it does not appear that the high stress values are evidence against the model. More important for evaluating the model is whether the relative positions of the documents in the configurations can be given some consistent interpretation, either in terms of the relationships of ideas or the social relations of authors. Therefore, each map will be examined in detail to see if such relations can be discerned.

## Figures 2-6: Collagen Maps, 1970-74

The following maps depict the collagen clusters for each of the years 1970-74. The metric scaling option of M-D-SCAL has been used to obtain two-dimensional configurations of the highly cited documents in the clusters, and the value of Kruskal's Stress II is given on each plot. The distance between two documents is determined by setting the citation frequency of each document equal to the volume of a normal probability hill and the co-citation frequency equal to the volume of overlap of the hills. Points on the maps indicate the tops of document hills and are labeled by the first author's last name and the year of publication. (See the Appendix for full bibliographic references.) On a given contour line the citation density is constant. The outermost contour corresponds to a density of one citation per unit area and increases by increments of one (going from the outermost to the innermost contour).

**Figure 2. Collagen 1970**

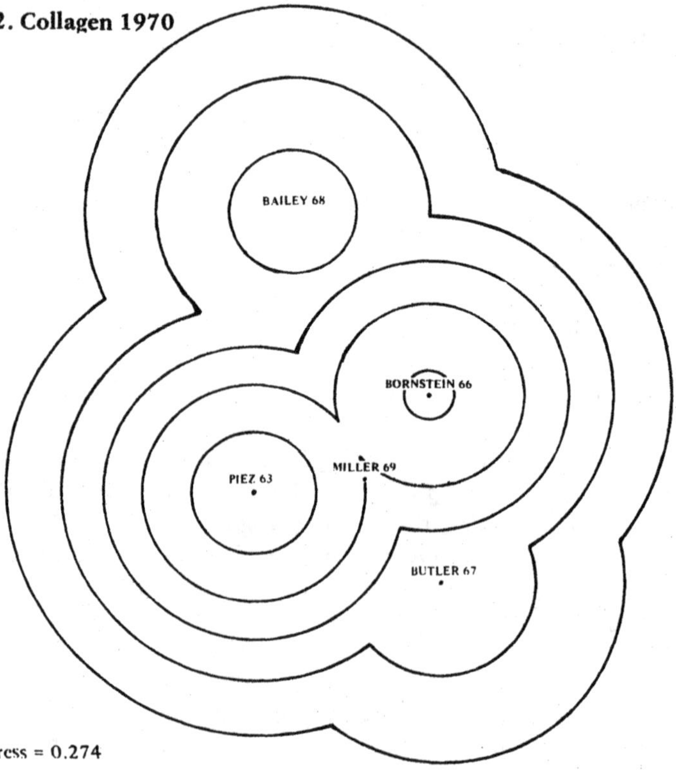


stress = 0.274

**Figure 3. Collagen 1971**

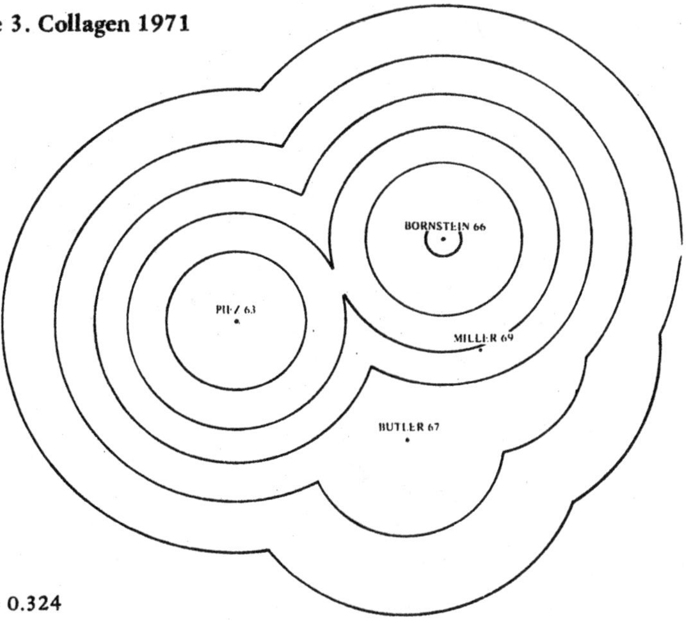


stress = 0.324

**Figure 4. Collagen 1972**

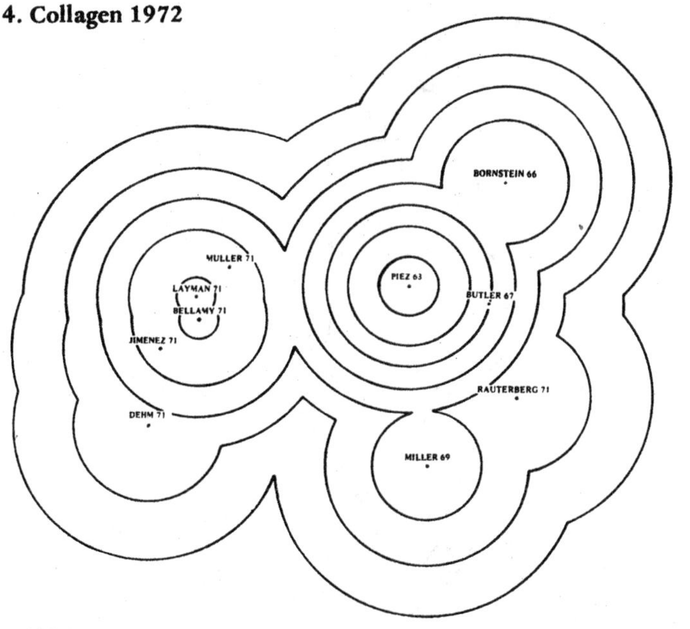


stress = 0.403

**Figure 5. Collagen 1973**

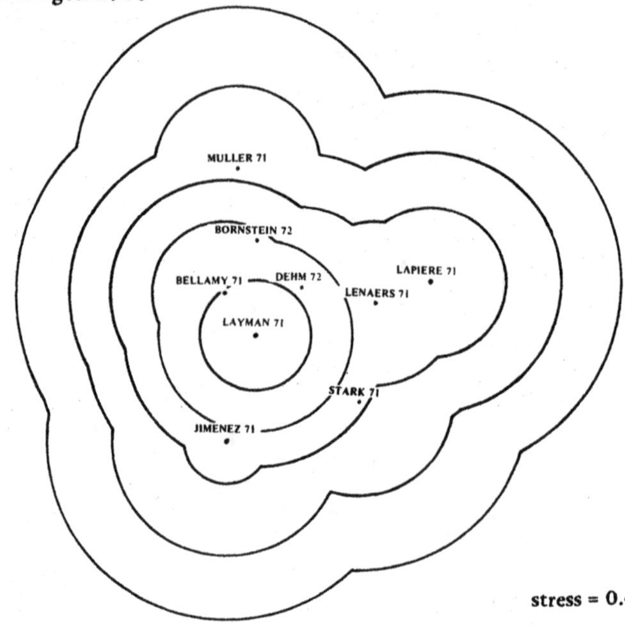


**Figure 6. Collagen 1974**

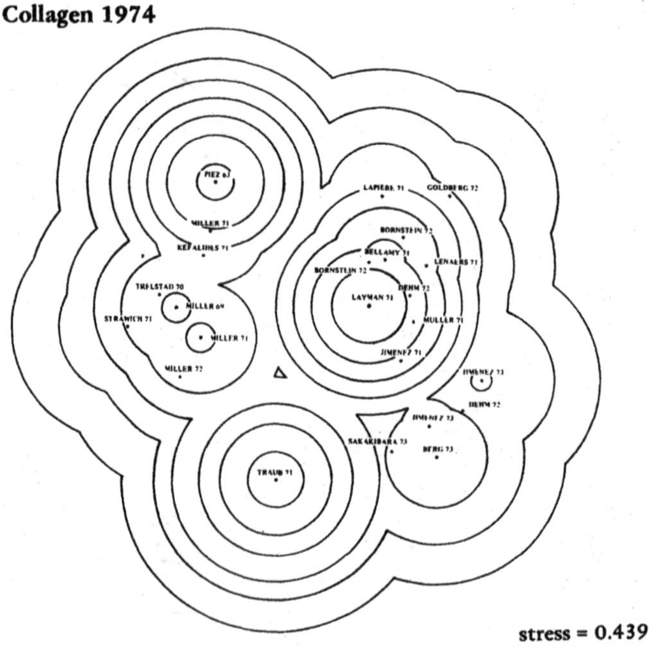

The 1970 map (Figure 2) shows a group of five documents. (The Appendix gives the full bibliographic reference for all documents appearing in this and all subsequent maps.) Of the five documents, Piez 63 is the most highly cited and also the oldest; this paper is important for its determination of the structure of the alpha 1 chain of collagen employing the CMC column method. The second most cited paper in the cluster is Bornstein 66, which was the first to elucidate the nature of the molecular cross linking between the collagen chains; this paper uses CNBr cleavage to reduce the collagen chains to a smaller number of peptides, but the paper's main contribution is toward a new conceptual understanding of collagen cross links. The Butler 67 and Miller 69 papers are both investigations into the structure of the alpha 1 chain of the collagen molecule, the prime difference between them being that one used collagen from bone and the other from skin; these papers are close to one another on the map, reflecting similarity of concern. The remaining paper, Bailey 68, is somewhat removed from the others. The objective of Bailey's work is different; it involves a cataloguing of amino acids on the collagen cross links. Bailey's paper drops out of the cluster the next year, and is never cited by any of the subsequent papers on our maps.

The factor which unifies all of the papers in the cluster in 1970 is their concern with the structure of the collagen molecule. The 1971 cluster (Figure 3) is identical in composition to the 1970 cluster, except for the absence of Bailey 68. Again, Miller 69 and Butler 67 are close to one another, and Piez 63 and Bornstein 66 are the most cited documents on the map.

A radically new situation is evident in 1972 (Figure 4). The map is clearly divided into two regions: one contains the old structural work which appeared in the cluster in 1970 and 1971, and the other is a group of new documents all dated 1971. A glance at these 1971 papers shows that they all discuss the newly discovered procollagen. First consider the older (right-hand) side of the 1972 cluster: the only new paper in this region is Rauterberg 71, which is a structural study of collagen using calf skin collagen, but otherwise similar to the work of Miller 69 and Butler 67. On the 72 map these three papers form a subgrouping on one side of the Piez 63 – Bornstein 66 axis. No major change in the configuration of the documents on this side of the map is evident.

Moving to the left side of the 1972 map, all documents are new to the cluster. Layman 71 first reported the discovery of what was later called procollagen, and the other papers appeared in very quick succession. Bellamy 71 was the first to call the new substance procollagen, and clearly established its role as the precursor to collagen. Muller 71, like Layman 71, was a product of the George Martin group; it is located on the map just above Layman 71, and was an attempt to show whether the formation of collagen from procollagen occurred inside or outside the cell. The Jimenez 71 and Dehm 71 papers were also the product of a single lab (University of Pennsylvania) and likewise fall on the same side of the discovery papers of Layman and Bellamy. Dehm 71 is important methodologically since it described the preparation of matrix-free cells for the study of collagen biosynthesis. Jimenez 71 used this method to obtain the first measurements of the molecular size of procollagen.

The 1972 map marks a transition in collagen research. It displays simultaneously the old concern with the static structure of collagen and the new concern with its dynamic character, the biosynthesis of collagen via procollagen. By 1973 the transition from old to new was complete. All documents on the right (or 'structural') side of the 1972 map dropped out in 1973 (Figure 5). What remained were the papers on procollagen from the 1972 cluster, plus new documents published in 1971 and 1972. On the 1973 map, Layman 71 is clearly at the centre, with Bellamy 71 not too far removed. Two new papers (Bornstein 72 and Dehm 72) fall close together above Layman 71 and are both concerned with showing that procollagen contains cystine. Muller 71 and Jimenez 71, both of which were on the 1972 map, are still on opposite sides of the discovery paper, but they have been displaced to the periphery by the entrance of the new 1972 papers. A second new group on the 1973 plot are papers by Stark, Lenaers and Lapiere, which form a sub-cluster to the right of Layman; all these came from the same laboratory in Belgium and deal with dermatosparaxis.

None of the papers in the 1973 cluster is more than two years old.[29] This remarkable 'currency' continues to some extent in 1974, where ten of the 24 papers in the cluster are less than two years old.

From 1973 to 1974, the cluster size more than doubles, from 9 to 24 documents. This reflects, in part, an increase in activity stimulated by the new discoveries, but it also reflects the merger of the two collagen clusters (series 1 & 2, see Figure 1). The 1974 cluster has a clear internal structure, consisting of three regions. The group of five documents, on the lower right, is a new addition to the cluster; four of the papers are only one year old. Its topic could be labelled 'stabilization of collagen by hydroxyproline' – in effect, a new discovery upon a new discovery, representing an attempt to understand collagen's stability biosynthetically. The central region on the map (around Layman 71) could be labelled 'collagen biosynthesis via procollagen', and is a continuation of the theme of the 1973 series 1 cluster; only three of the 10 documents from this second group are new to the cluster.

The group of papers at the left, and somewhat separate from the Layman 71 group, could be labelled 'genetic types of collagen'; this represents the merger of the previously separate collagen cluster (series 2) with the main collagen cluster (series 1). I have not discussed the structure of this sequence of series 2 clusters. It consists of three cited documents in 1972 and 1973, but the series was clearly dominated by Miller's work on genetic types of collagen. In 1969, Miller discovered that a cartilage collagen gave indications of having only alpha 1 chains, and he called this 'type II' collagen to distinguish it from 'type I' collagen, which has the usual two alpha 1 chains and one alpha 2 chain. Further work on identifying and characterizing other collagen 'types' was done by Trelstad 70, Strawich 71 and Kefalides 71. Merger of the two strands of collagen research may be interpreted as a strengthening of the link between genetic and procollagen related research.

A final feature of the 1974 map, the Piez 63 and Traub 71 papers, should be noted. Both papers are very highly cited, but somewhat removed from the main substantive areas on the map. Piez 63 appeared in the 70, 71 and 72 clusters, and reappears in 74; it is a landmark paper on collagen structure, and important methodologically for all the subspecialties. Traub 71 (with Piez as a second author) is a review paper which summed up knowledge in the whole field of collagen research. On the 74 map it borders on all three of the substantive regions, but does not belong to any of them. Its position reflects its broad importance for collagen research.

The most remarkable aspect of the development of collagen research is the rapidity with which the specialty was able to shift its concern from a structural and static conception of collagen to a concern with biosynthesis, and a dynamic conception of collagen. This is evident in the shift in the set of cited documents from 1971 to 1973, which, as pointed out earlier, resulted in a SI value of zero.

## QUESTIONNAIRE SURVEY

One of the most important and difficult problems in citation studies has been the proper form of validation. The data on collagen research contained in the succession of cluster maps present a plausible picture when viewed against the historical background of the specialty. Nevertheless, the historical sketch was not derived in a manner independent of the citation data, and it is qualitative in nature. What is needed is an independently derived picture which can be compared quantitatively with the citation picture. It was concluded that only by going to the specialists themselves could a direct test of validity be carried out. A questionnaire was therefore designed and sent to collagen specialists; it contained no mention of the citation data. The only assumption made was that the specialty of 'collagen research' existed and was properly named. The questionnaire was sent to 24 individuals, all of whom had published a paper on collagen in 1973; they were identified by having cited one or more papers in the collagen cluster in 1973. Eleven usable responses were received, with a generally high level of care and attention to detail given by the respondents. Although the sample was small, the unanimity and consistency of responses was so high that it is doubtful that a larger sample would have changed the results significantly.

The first question was: 'What are the most important scientific advances or developments in collagen research in the last five years?' Responses to this question are summarized in Table 1. There was a clear

**Table 1. Responses to Question 1:**

'What are the most important scientific advances or developments in collagen research in the last five years?'

| Advance or Development | Number of Responses |
|---|---|
| 1. procollagen, a biosynthetic precursor molecule | 11 (100%) |
| 2. genetic types of collagen | 10 |
| 3. sequencing of collagen chains | 5 |
| 4. genetic defects of collagen metabolism | 5 |
| 5. stabilization of collagen by hydroxyproline | 4 |
| 6. molecular packing of collagen | 2 |

consensus on the discovery of procollagen as a major advance, and a near consensus on the discovery of genetic types of collagen. These two advances, of course, match perfectly with the major strands of development embodied in the series 1 and 2 clusters, which finally converged in 1974. The next two ranked advances were mentioned by five respondents each. Item 3 (sequencing of collagen chains) corresponds to papers in series 1 clusters which were published before 1970; respondents were not adhering strictly to the five year limit. Item 4 (genetic defects) is not associated with any papers in the cluster, and thus represents an anomaly in the citation picture. Item 5 (stabilization by hydroxyproline), however, is clearly associated with the sub-cluster of papers appearing in the 1974 plot (Figure 6). Therefore, the citation data have accurately represented advances where there is near or complete unanimity, and in two of three cases, have reflected advances of a lesser degree of consensus.

The second question was: 'What papers were the first to describe the advances or developments mentioned in question 1?' The reponses to this question are summarized in Table 2, where they are compared with

**Table 2. Responses to Question 2:**

'What papers were the first to describe the advances or developments you mentioned in question 1?'

| Paper (First author, year) | No. of Mentions | Years in Cluster* 70 | 71 | 72 | 73 | 74 | Subject |
|---|---|---|---|---|---|---|---|
| 1. Layman 1971 | 7 | | | X | X | X | procollagen |
| 2. Bellamy 1971 | 7 | | | X | X | X | procollagen |
| 3. Miller 1969 | 6 | | | X | X | X | genetic types |
| 4. Jimenez 1973 | 3 | | | | | X | hydroxy-proline |
| 5. Berg 1973 | 3 | | | | | X | hydroxy-proline |
| 6. Jimenez 1971 | 2 | | | X | X | X | procollagen |
| 7. Miller 1971 | 2 | | | X | | X | genetic types |
| 8. Kefalides 1971 | 2 | | | | | X | genetic types |
| 9. Pinnell 1972 | 2 | | | | | | hereditary disease |

23 other papers received one mention. Six of these appeared in cluster.
*series 1 or 2 clusters.

the cluster data. Here it is possible to observe how accurately the citations have selected out the specific documents associated with the major advances in the specialty. Of the papers receiving two or more mentions, all but one (Pinnell 72) appear in the collagen clusters in one or more of the five years.

The Pinnell paper was associated with the 'genetic defects' advance (item 4 of Table 1). Why it was not included in the cluster requires a special explanation. This paper was cited 16 times in 1973 and 13 times in 1974. In 1974 it missed being included in the cluster formed at the threshold of 15 citations per year; in 1973 it exceeded this threshold, but failed to be cocited 11 times with any other of the collagen papers. The effect of thresholding was, in this case, to exclude an important and relevant item.

The two procollagen discovery papers (Layman 71 and Bellamy 71) received the greatest number of mentions – seven each. Miller 69, the discovery paper for genetic types of collagen, received six mentions. (This paper, of course, was not clustered with the procollagen work until 1974.) The next two papers received only three mentions each; both of them had to do with the stabilization of collagen by hydroxyproline, work which appears in the 1974 cluster. Finally, there are three papers receiving two mentions apiece: one on procollagen which supplied some early size measurements (Jimenez 71), and two more papers on genetic types of collagen.

In general, there is slightly less agreement on what papers were first to announce the discoveries and advances than on what the advances were. In all, 32 papers were nominated as reporting important advances; 31 papers appeared in the cluster over the five years; and 14 were both mentioned and in the cluster. A more important feature is that the frequently mentioned papers were consistently in the cluster; the three papers most often mentioned were each in the cluster for three straight years (1972-74). This is strong confirmation of the ability of citation data to identify key papers in the specialty.

The third question was: 'Whom do you regard as the leading investigators in collagen research?' Table 3 summarizes the responses and shows the number of authorships of highly cited clustered papers for each author mentioned two or more times. (In counting authorship, all authors listed on a paper were given equal credit.) All but three of the investigators mentioned two or more times had authorships of highly cited papers. The frequently named investigators generally have frequent authorships, but the inverse is not always true. Four investi-

Table 3. Responses to Question 3:

'Whom do you regard as the leading investigators in collagen research?'

| Investigator | No. of Mentions | No. of Authorships on Clustered Papers |
|---|---|---|
| 1. Bornstein | 11 | 5 |
| 2. Miller | 10 | 5 |
| 3. Prockop | 9 | 7 |
| 4. Piez | 9 | 6 |
| 5. Martin | 9 | 2 |
| 6. Kuhn | 7 | 2 |
| 7. Gross | 7 | 1 |
| 8. Viez | 3 | 0 |
| 9. Bailey | 2 | 1 |
| 10. Rosenbloom | 2 | 1 |
| 11. Trelstad | 2 | 1 |
| 12. Fessler | 2 | 0 |
| 13. Ballop | 2 | 0 |

11 other investigators received one mention. Five of these appeared in the cluster.

gators having three or more authorships on highly cited papers received fewer than two mentions (two had one mention and two had none). The clustered papers brought in more individuals than did the survey question. A total of 24 individuals were mentioned as leading investigators; there were 50 authors of the clustered papers; and 15 of the mentioned individuals were also cluster authors. Two effects may be at work here. First, because senior authors very often include assistants on their papers, the use of authorships to identify leading investigators will uncover a somewhat broader population, and in general, a young one. The second effect is that the up-and-coming young scientists may have many authorships to their credit, but are not yet recognized by their peers as leading investigators. Therefore, in one sense, the citation method for identifying important scientists may be a 'leading' rather than 'lagging' indicator of the peer method of nomination.

The last question was an attempt to measure the degree of perceived shift in the specialty. The question was: 'Has collagen research undergone a major change or conceptual shift in the last five years? Please explain.' Table 4 shows the outcome: ten respondents said 'yes'

**Table 4. Responses to Question 4:**

**'Has collagen research undergone a major change or conceptual shift in the last five years? Please explain.'**

| | Yes | No |
|---|---|---|
| | 10 | 1 |

| Reason for shift | Number of Responses |
|---|---|
| 1. Concern with collagen biosynthesis via procollagen | 9 |
| 2. Concern with genetically different collagens. | 5 |
| 3. Concern with genetic defects in collagen metabolism. | 2 |

and one said 'no'. The reasons given for the shift again paralleled responses on previous questions. Nine respondents indicated that the discovery of procollagen was the reason for the shift, and five said it was the findings on genetically different collagens. Two mentioned the genetic defects of collagen, which, as discussed earlier, did not appear in the cluster because of the severity of the thresholds. Again, on issues where agreement is substantial, the cluster data reflect the situation well. Procollagen and, to a somewhat lesser extent, genetic types of collagen clearly emerge as the key events in recent history (to 1974). The perceived shift in the specialty was reflected in the 1971-73 shift in the series 1 clusters (SI equal to zero), and the emergence in 1972 of the series 2 clusters devoted to work on genetic types of collagen, which eventually merged with the main cluster.

## CONCLUSIONS

In the validation I attempted to answer the question: Does the citation picture of this specialty's development match the perceptions of the specialists? The questionnaire survey demonstrated that the highly cited documents which clustered together were significant documents in the eyes of the specialists, and that the authors of these papers were, by and large, the leading researchers identified as such by their peers. The succession of cluster maps suggested that the specialty had undergone a rather radical shift in research focus. In this regard, too, the data reflected accurately the perceptions of the specialists. The citations provided, in effect, a physical and measurable manifestation of a collective mental switch from a static to a dynamic conception of collagen. Whether this example could be properly called a 'revolution' in Kuhn's sense is debatable. For example, there appear to be no 'incommensurable world views' involved on either side of the collagen shift. It seems likely, however, that a true Kuhnian paradigm switch, if one exists, would manifest itself through citation data in precisely the way exemplified by collagen.

Several specialists interviewed stressed the close knit character of their specialty: a few major centres of research, a small number of leading researchers, and a high level of informal communications among researchers. There seems to be little doubt that the co-citation clustering methodology has identified, at least in this case, a research specialty with all the characteristics ascribed to 'invisible colleges' — as, for example, those specialties described by Griffith and Mullins.[30] On the other hand, the collagen specialty differs in one important respect. There is no evidence in collagen of a self-conscious or deliberate revolutionary programme being carried out by a group of researchers when the specialty underwent its conceptual shift in the early 1970s. The developments, stimulated by simultaneous and serendipitous discovery, were taken up very quickly, and vigorously pursued, by the entire specialty. No single group controlled these developments (at least three groups played key roles).

The collagen case also suggests some hypotheses on specialty growth and change which should be tested in other cases. If Kuhn's theory is correct, and if the set of highly cited documents in a cluster is a representation of the paradigm for the specialty (high cited documents = exemplars), then, over several years, the SI should show periods of constancy alternating with sudden dips. This test would distinguish between a model of science which calls for sudden changes in research focus and a model which calls for gradual or evolutionary change, such as the one proposed by Toulmin.[31] In the latter case, the SI should remain fairly constant, showing only random fluctuations.

At a more detailed level of analysis, it should be possible to test the importance of discoveries and innovations for specialty change. In the case of collagen, the discoveries of 1971 appear to have precipitated the shift in research focus. An indicator of discovery appears to be the 'immediacy' or 'currency' of the cluster, and this, too, might display a cyclic behaviour over time.[32] The 1971 discovery papers formed a sub-cluster on the 1972 map consisting of papers all of which were only one year old. One hypothesis is that sudden shifts in a specialty are preceded by the emergence of a sub-cluster of very recent papers, and that one or all of these recent papers in the sub-cluster are perceived by the specialist as 'discovery' papers.

As Crane has observed,[33] exponential growth in the size of a specialty seems to follow rather than precede innovation, and this was true of collagen. The 1974 cluster represented the onset of rapid growth, three years after the publication of the discoveries. Also, the collagen specialty suggests that a discovery sub-group is attached to an older stable configuration containing methodologically important papers, and that the older group, by and large, disappears from the cluster as the shift is consolidated. There appears to be a tendency for methodological papers to persist as 'markers' for a specialty, even through a shift (e.g. Piez 63), while conceptual contributions are more quickly forgotten (e.g. Bornstein 66). Finally, the 1974 map shows considerable internal structure and may signal the beginning of further sub-specialization. Merger patterns may also mark specialties which are in periods of rapid growth.

In sum, the sequence of events suggested by the collagen case is: stability (1970-1971); discovery represented by a sub-cluster of recent papers attached to the older cluster (1972); a shift in research focus with the disappearance of the older cluster (1973); and rapid growth of the new cluster with a division into sub-specialties (1974). Only further work can determine whether this is a general pattern and part of the natural life-cycle of all specialties.

## APPENDIX

### Papers in the Collagen Clusters

**The following is a list (alphabetic by first author) of all papers appearing in the 1970-74 collagen clusters. The full bibliographic reference is preceded by the**

abbreviation of the item (last name of first author and year of publication) used in Figures 2-6. Below this abbreviation and in parentheses is the year(s) in which the paper has appeared in the cluster.


BAILEY 68 (70) : Allen J. Bailey and Catherine M. Peach, 'Isolation and Structural Identification of a Labile Intermolecular Crosslink in Collagen', Biochemical and Biophysical Research Communications, Vol. 33, No. 5 (1968), 812-19.

BELLAMY 71 (72, 73, 74) : Garland Bellamy and Paul Bornstein, 'Evidence for Procollagen, a Biosynthetic Precursor of Collagen', Proceedings of the National Academy of Sciences (USA), Vol. 68, No. 6 (June 1971), 1138-42.

BERG 73 (74) : Richard A. Berg and Darwin J. Prockop, 'The Thermal Transition of a Non-Hydroxylated Form of Collagen – Evidence for a Role for Hydroxyproline in Stabilizing the Triple-Helix of Collagen', Biochemical and Biophysical Research Communications, Vol. 52, No. 1 (1973), 115-20.

BORNSTEIN 66 (70, 71, 72) : Paul Bornstein and Karl A. Piez, 'The Nature of the Intramolecular Cross-Links in Collagen – the Separation and Characterization of Peptides from the Cross-Link Region of Rat Skin Collagen', Biochemistry, Vol. 5, No. 11 (November 1966), 3460-73.

BORNSTEIN 72 (74) : Paul Bornstein, H. Paul Ehrlich, and Anne W. Wyke, 'Procollagen: Conversion of the Precursor to Collagen by a Neutral Protease', Science, Vol. 175, (4 February 1972), 544-46.

BORNSTEIN 72 (73, 74) : Paul Bornstein, Klaus Von Der Mark, Anne W. Wyke, H. Paul Ehrlich, and Janet M. Monson, 'Characterization of the Pro- α1 Chain of Procollagen', The Journal of Biological Chemistry, Vol. 247, No. 9 (May 1972), 2808-13.

BUTLER 67 (70, 71, 72) : William T. Butler, Karl A. Piez, and Paul Bornstein, 'Isolation and Characterization of the Cyanogen Bromide Peptides from the α1 Chain of Rat Skin Collagen', Biochemistry, Vol. 6, No. 12 (December 1967), 3771-80.

DEHM 71 (72) : Peter Dehm and Darwin J. Prockop, 'Synthesis and Extrusion of Collagen by Freshly Isolated Cells from Chick Embryo Tendon', Biochemica et Biophysica Acta, Vol. 240 (1971), 358-69.

DEHM 72 (73, 74) : Peter Dehm, Sergio A. Jimenez, Bjorn R. Olsen, and Darwin J. Prockop, 'A Transport Form of Collagen from Embryonic Tendon: Electron Microscopic Demonstration of an $NH_2$ – Terminal Extension and Evidence Suggesting the Presence of Cystine in the Molecule', Proceedings of the National Academy of Sciences

(USA), Vol. 69, No. 1 (January 1972), 60-64.

DEHM 72 (73, 74) : Peter Dehm and Darwin J. Prockop, 'Time Lag in the Secretion of Collagen by Matrix-Free Tendon Cells and Inhibition of the Secretory Process of Colchicine and Vinblastine', Biochimica et Biophysica Acta, Vol. 264 (1972), 375-82.

GOLDBERG 72 (74) : Burton Goldberg, Ervin H. Epstein, Jr., and Charles J. Sherr, 'Precursors of Collagen Secreted by Cultured Human Fibroblasts', Proceedings of the National Academy of Sciences (USA), Vol. 69, No. 12 (December 1972), 3655-59.

JIMENEZ 73 (74) : Sergio A. Jimenez, Peter Dehm, Bjorn R. Olsen, and Darwin J. Prockop, 'Intracellular Collagen and Protocollagen from Embryonic Tendon Cells', The Journal of Biological Chemistry, Vol. 248, No. 2 (January (1973), 720-29.

JIMENEZ 71 (72, 73, 74) : Sergio A. Jimenez, Peter Dehm, and Darwin J. Prockop, 'Further Evidence for a Transport Form of Collagen – Its Extrusion and Extracellular Conversion to Tropocollagen in Embryonic Tendon', FEBS Letters, Vol. 17, No. 2 (October 1971), 245-48.

JIMENEZ 73 (74) : Sergio A. Jimenez, Margaret Harsch, and Joel Rosenbloom, 'Hydroxyproline Stabilizes the 'Triple Helix of Chick Tendon', Biochemical and Biophysical Research Communications, Vol. 52, No. 1 (1973), 106-14.

KEFALIDES 71 (74) : Nicholas Kefalides, 'Isolation of a Collagen from Basement Membranes containing Three Identical α-Chains', Biochemical and Biophysical Research Communications, Vol. 45, No. 1 (1971), 226-34.

LAPIERE 71 (73, 74) : Charles M. Lapiere, Albert Lenaers, and Leonard D. Kohn, 'Procollagen Peptides: An Enzyme Excising the Coordination Peptides of Procollagen', Proceedings of the National Academy of Sciences (USA), Vol. 68, No. 12 (December 1971), 3054-58.

LAYMAN 71 (72, 73, 74) : Don L. Layman, Ermona B. McGoodwin, and George R. Martin, 'The Nature of the Collagen Synthesized by Cultured Human Fibroblasts', Proceedings of the National Academy of Sciences (USA), Vol. 68, No. 2 (February 1971), 454-58.

LENAERS 71 (73, 74) : Albert Lenaers, Michel Ansay, Betty V. Nusgens, and Charles M. Lapiere, 'Collagen made of Extended α-Chains, Procollagen, in Genetically-Defective Dermatosparaxic Calves', European Journal of Biochemistry, Vol. 23, No. 3 (1971), 533-43.

MILLER 69 (70, 71, 72) : Edward J. Miller, Joseph M. Lane, and Karl A. Piez, 'Isolation and Characterization of the Peptides Derived from the α1 Chain of Chick Bone Collagen after Cyanogen Bromide Cleavage', Biochemistry, Vol. 8, No.

1 (January 1969), 30-39.

MILLER 69 (72, 73, 74) : Edward J. Miller and Victor J. Matukas, 'Chick Cartilage Collagen: a New Type of $\alpha 1$ Chain Not Present in Bone or Skin of the Species', Proceedings of the National Academy of Sciences (USA), Vol. 64, No. 4 (1969), 1264-68.

MILLER 71 (74) : Edward J. Miller, 'Isolation and Characterization of a Collagen from Chick Cartilage containing Three Identical $\alpha$ Chains', Biochemistry, Vol. 10, No. 9 (1971), 1652-59.

MILLER 71 (72, 74) : Edward J. Miller, Ervin H. Epstein Jr., and Karl A. Piez, 'Identification of Three Genetically Distinct Collagens by Cyanogen Bromide Cleavage of Insoluble Human Skin and Cartilage Collagen', Biochemical and Biophysical Research Communications, Vol. 42, No. 6 (1971), 1024-29.

MILLER 72 (74) : Edward J. Miller, 'Structural Studies on Cartilage Collagen Employing Limited Cleavage and Solubilization with Pepsin', Biochemistry, Vol. 11, No. 26 (1972), 4903-09.

MULLER 71 (72, 73, 74) : Peter K. Müller, Ermona McGoodwin, and George R. Martin, 'Studies on Protocollagen: Identification of a Precursor of Proto $\alpha 1$', Biochemical and Biophysical Research Communications, Vol. 44, No. 1 (1971), 110-17.

PIEZ 63 (70, 71, 72, 74) : Karl A. Piez, Elizabeth A. Eigner, and Marc S. Lewis, 'The Chromatographic Separation and Amino Acid Composition of the Subunits of Several Collagens', Biochemistry, Vol. 2 (1963), 58-66.

RAUTERBERG 71 (72) : Jurgen Rauterberg and Kalus Kühn, 'Acid Soluble Calf Skin Collagen -- Characterization of the Peptides Obtained by Cyanogen Bromide Cleavage of its $\alpha 1$-Chains', European Journal of Biochemistry, Vol. 19, No. 3 (1971), 398-407.

SAKAKIBARA 73 (74) : Shumpei Sakakibara, Katsuhiko Inouye, Keiko Shudo, Yasuo Kishida, Yuji Kobayashi, and Darwin J. Prockop, 'Synthesis of $(\text{Pro-Hyp-Gly})_n$ of Defined Molecular Weights – Evidence for the Stabilization of Collagen Triple Helix by Hydroxypyroline', Biochemica et Biophysica Acta, Vol. 303, No. 1 (1973), 198-202.

STARK 71 (73) : Marlies Stark, Albert Lenaers, Charles Lapiere, and Klaus Kühn, 'Electronoptical Studies of Procollagen from the Skin of Dermatosparaxic Calves', FEBS Letters, Vol. 18, No. 2 (November 1971), 225-27.

STRAWICH 71 (73, 74) : Elsa Strawich and Marcel E. Nimni, 'Properties of a Collagen Molecule containing Three Identical Components extracted from Bovine Articular Cartilage', Biochemistry, Vol. 10, No. 21 (1971), 3905-11.

TRAUB 71 (74) : Wolfie Traub and Karl A. Piez, 'The Chemistry and Structure of Collagen', Advances in Protein Chemistry,

Vol. 25 (1971), 243-352.

TRELSTAD 70 (72, 73, 74) : Robert L. Trelstad, Andew H. Kang, Shogo Igarashi, and Jerome Gross, 'Isolation of Two Distinct Collagens from Chick Cartilage', Biochemistry, Vol. 9, No. 25 (1970), 4993-98.

## NOTES

I am grateful to Karl Piez of the National Institute of Dental Research, who has provided much valuable information on the current state of collagen research, and to Belver C. Griffith of Drexel University for helpful comments. The research was supported by National Science Foundation grant SOC73-09096 A02 to the Institute for Scientific Information and National Library of Medicine grant 5-RO1 LM00911-02 to Drexel University.

1. M.J. Mulkay, G.N. Gilbert, and S. Woolgar, 'Problem Areas and Research Networks in Science', Sociology, Vol. 9 (1975), 187-203; E. Garfield, M.V. Malin, and H. Small, 'Citation Data as Science Indicators', in Y. Elkana, J. Lederberg, R.K. Merton, A. Thackray and H. Zuckerman (eds), Toward a Metric of Science (New York: John Wiley, forthcoming); N.C. Mullins, Theories and Theory Groups in Contemporary American Sociology (New York: Harper and Row, 1973).

2. H.G. Small and B.C. Griffith, 'The Structure of Scientific Literatures I: Identifying and Graphing Specialties', Science Studies, Vol. 4 (1974), 17-40; B.C. Griffith, H.G. Small, J.A. Stonehill and S. Dey, 'The Structure of Scientific Literature II: Toward a Macro- and Micro-Structure for Science', Science Studies, Vol. 4 (1974), 339-65.

3. H.G. Small and B.C. Griffith, 'Automatic Classification of Scientific Literature using Co-citation Clustering', Proceedings of the Twelfth Annual Allerton Conference on Circuit and System Theory (October 1974), 512-21.

4. J.R. Cole and H. Zuckerman, 'The Emergence of a Scientific Specialty: The Self-exemplifying Case of the Sociology of Science', in Louis A. Coser (ed.), The Idea of Social Structure: Papers in Honor of Robert K. Merton (New York: Harcourt, Brace, Jovanovich, 1975), 139-74; S. Cole, 'The Growth of Scientific Knowledge: Theories of Deviance as a Case Study', ibid., 175-220; D. Sullivan, D.H. White and E. Barboni, 'The State of a Science: Indicators in the Specialty of Weak Interactions', paper presented at the 70th Annual Meeting of the American Sociological Association, San Francisco, California (27 August 1975), and published in this issue of Social Studies of Science.

5. E. Garfield, I.H. Sher and R.J. Torpie, The Use of Citation Data for Writing the History of Science (Philadelphia: Institute for Scientific Information, 1964).

6. T.S Kuhn, The Structure of Scientific Revolutions (Chicago: University of Chicago Press, 1962), xi.

7. H.G. Small, 'A Citation Model for Scientific Specialties', Proceedings of the American Society for Information Science, Vol. 12 (1975), 34-35.

8. H.G. Small, 'Multiple Citation Patterns in Scientific Literature: The Circle and Hill Models', Information Storage and Retrieval, Vol. 10 (1974), 393-402.

9. Kruskal's M-D-SCAL is used: see J.B. Kruskal, 'Multidimensional Scaling by Optimizing Goodness-of-Fit to a Non-metric Hypothesis', Psychometrika, Vol. 29 (1964), 1-37.

10. In op. cit. note 4, Cole and Zuckerman use a similar measure for the degree of continuity of a specialty. See Garfield et al., op. cit. note 1, for further examples of the Stability Index for a sample of 30 specialties.

11. Strictly speaking, the numerator is the cardinality of the intersect of all cited document cluster sets ($C_i$), and the denominator is the cardinality of the union of the cluster sets.

12. R. Bear, 'The Structure of Collagen Fibrils', Advances in Protein Chemistry (New York: Academic Press, 1952), 69-160.

13. F.O. Schmitt, 'Ultra-structure of the Problem of Cellular Organization', The Harvey Lectures, 1944-45 (Lancaster, Pennsylvania: Science Press Printing Company, 1946), 249-68.

14. W. Traub and K.A. Piez, 'The Chemistry and Structure of Collagen', Advances in Protein Chemistry, Vol. 25 (1971), 243-352.

15. E. Gross and B. Witkop, 'Selective Cleavage of Methionyl Peptide Bonds in Ribonuclease with Cyanogen Bromide', Journal of the American Chemical Society, Vol. 83 (1961), 1510.

16. K.A. Piez, E.A. Eigner and M.S. Lewis, 'The Chromatographic Separation and Amino Acid of the subunits of Several Collagens', Biochemistry, Vol. 2 (1963), 58-66.

17. E.J. Miller and B.J. Matukas, 'Chick Cartilage Collagen: A New Type of α1 Chain Not Present in Bone or Skin of Species', Proceedings of the National Academy of Sciences (USA), Vol. 64 (1969), 1264-69.

18. J. Gross, 'Collagen Biology: Structure, Degradation, and Disease', The Harvey Lectures, 1972-73 (New York: Academic Press, 1974), 351-432.

19. D.L. Layman, E.B. McGoodwin and G.R. Martin, 'Nature of Collagen Produced by Cultured Human Fibroblasts', Federation Proceedings, Vol. 29 (March 1970), A668.

20. G.R. Martin, P.H. Byers and K.A. Piez, 'Procollagen', Advances in Enzymology, Vol. 42 (1975), 167-91.

21. G. Bellamy and P. Bornstein, 'Evidence for Procollagen, A Biosynthetic Precursor of Collagen', Proceedings of the National Academy of Sciences (USA), Vol. 68 (June 1971), 1138-42.

22. D.L. Layman, E.B. McGoodwin and G.R. Martin, 'The Nature of the Collagen Synthesized by Cultured Human Fibroblasts', Proceedings of the National Academy of Sciences (USA), Vol. 68 (February 1971), 454-58.

23. C.M. Lapiere, A. Lenaers and L.D. Kohn, 'Procollagen Peptidase: An Enzyme Excising the Coordination Peptides of Pro-collagen', Proceedings of the National Academy of Sciences (USA), Vol. 68 (1971), 3054-58.

24. F.O. Schmitt, 'Contribution of Molecular Biology to Medicine', Bulletin

of the New York Academy of Medicine, Vol. 36 (1960), 725-49.

25. P.T. Speakman, 'Proposed Mechanism for Biological Assembly of Collagen Triple Helix', Nature, Vol. 229 (22 January 1971), 241.

26. Gross, op. cit. note 18, 353.

27. J.D. Watson, 'The Involvement of RNA in the Synthesis of Protein', Nobel Lectures in Physiology or Medicine, 1942-1962 (Amsterdam: Elsevier, 1964), 784.

28. P.E. Green and F.J. Carmone, Multidimensional Scaling (Boston: Allyn Bacon, 1970), 38.

29. Price was one of the first to point out the importance of this 'immediacy effect' in the analysis of citations on the research front. D.J. de Solla Price, 'Citation Measures of Hard Science and Soft Science, Technology and Non-Science', in Carnot E. Nelson and Donald K. Pollak (eds), Communication Among Scientists and Engineers (Lexington, Mass.; Heath, 1970), 3-22. See also the paper by A.J. Meadows and J.G. O'Connor, note 32, below.

30. B.C. Griffith and N.C. Mullins, 'Coherent Social Groups in Scientific Change', Science, Vol. 177 (15 September 1972), 959-64.

31. S. Toulmin, Human Understanding: The Collective Use and Evolution of Concepts (Princeton, N.J.: Princeton University Press, 1972).

32. A.J. Meadows and J.G. O'Connor, 'Bibliographical Statistics as a Guide to Growth Points in Science', Science Studies, Vol. 1 (January 1971), 95-99. The 'citation half-life' discussed by Meadows and O'Connor as an indicator of new growth areas in science would correspond to the median year of publication of cited documents in our clusters.

33. D. Crane, Invisible Colleges: Diffusion of Knowledge in Scientific Communities (Chicago: University of Chicago Press, 1972), 67.

## PART IV: Information Retrieval and Analysis

This is, of course, a perennial topic within information science, and some would say it is the core of the discipline. The past few years, beginning with Swet's article, show this to be an area of increasing empirical difficulties. This critically important article is not included as an endorsement of his theoretical model, but rather as an indication of the difficulties in doing this research. In particular, one should note Swets' argument in identifying the best operating characteristic curve for information retrieval systems. Considering that argument, is there an absolute and quite low threshold for the effectiveness of these systems?

The important work of Swanson and Harter[2] on the Cranfield studies of information retrieval has not been included. These articles, which are so damaging to the original research in this area, mostly point to a truth which is now more obvious to all researchers, namely, that the identification of all relevant articles in an operating informaton system is incredibly difficult.

The papers which have been chosen discuss a variety of techniques, without any attempt to undertake overall empirical evaluation of retrieval performance as undertaken by Swets. The first area is the use of textual clues (either in title, abstract and full text or in indexing terms) to achieve improvements in information retrieval. These papers include those by Salton, Jardine, and Robertson. The other group of papers deals with the problem of evaluating the results of retrieval experiments. In particular they deal with the creation of measures which somehow characterize the "goodness" of a set of retrieved documents with respect to a specific query.

---

[2]These papers, not included in this volume, are: Stephen Harter, "The Cranfield II Relevance Assessments: A Critical Evaluation, *Library Quarterly,* 41 (July 1971) 229-243; Don Swanson, "Some Unexplained Aspects of the Cranfield Tests of Indexing Performance Factors," *Library Quarterly,* 41 (July 1971) 223-228.

# A Decision Theoretic Foundation for Indexing

**The indexing of a document is among the most crucial steps in preparing that document for retrieval. The adequacy of the indexing determines the ability of the system to respond to patron requests. This paper discusses this process, and document retrieval in general, on the basis of formal decision theory. The basic theoretical approach taken is illustrated by means of a model of word occurrences in documents in the context of a model information system; both models are fully defined in this paper. Though the main purpose of this paper is to provide insights into a very complex process, formulae are developed that may prove to be of value for an automated operating system. The paper concludes with an interpretation of recall and precision curves as seen from the point of view of decision theory.**

**Abraham Bookstein**
**Don R. Swanson**
*Graduate Library School*
*University of Chicago*
*Chicago, Illinois 60637*

## • Introduction

In this paper we shall examine indexing and, more generally, document retrieval, from a decision theoretic framework. More specifically, we shall explicitly regard the indexing of a document as part of the retrieval mechanism of an information system. Thus, the decision as to whether or not a particular index term ought to be applied to a particular document should be made with an understanding of its implications for the system's retrieval capability. In currently operating systems, the set of index terms applied to a document is the full representation of that document in the system; the choice of index terms completely determines the ability of the system to respond to requests made of it.

We recognize that perfect indexing is an unattainable ideal. Sometimes the inclusion of a word—however descriptive of a document—as part of that document's index record will cause that document to be inappropriately retrieved for some users. Similarly, omitting some terms will lose useful documents for some patrons. The approach we shall take attempts to balance the two errors on the basis of minimizing the implied costs to the system's patrons.

Some of the ideas developed below have been discussed in the earlier literature. Maron and Kuhns (*1*) have introduced the notion of probabilistic indexing, and have noted the relationship of a choice of index terms to the retrieval capability of a system. These authors suggest that index terms be chosen while keeping in mind the probability that a user wanting that document would choose those terms. Swets (*2*), while not discussing indexing directly, expressed Bayesian, or decision theoretic, ideas in an information system context. He considered documents as being classified into two groups on the basis of their "pertinence" to a particular topic, and that membership in a group influenced, in a probabilistic sense, the value of some parameter that can be evaluated for each document. Swets then made use of standard Bayesian theory to decide, with knowledge of the parameter's value, to which of the two groups a document should be assigned.

A similar problem was studied extensively by Mosteller and Wallace (*3*). These authors attempted to classify by author a number of the Federalist Papers whose authorship is in dispute. Among the techniques used were that of Bayesian Decision Theory. Closer to our own concerns, the variables examined were the number of occurrences of words in the documents. More recently, other researchers have advocated further use of decision theoretic techniques in the operation of an information system (*4, 5*).

In this paper we explore this approach in the context of a specific model of an information system and a model of word occurrence in documents. The models presented here are too elementary to be considered as descriptions of operating systems. However, we believe that an understanding of the concepts underlying these models does provide insights into the more complex cases, and that the models themselves are capable of generalization. Because of their simplified form these models allow us to rigorously calculate the fundamental properties of information systems, thereby giving some theoretical insight into these systems' behavior, and they provide a simple criterion for document retrieval that is founded on a concrete theoretical base.

## • Description of Model

In our model information system we have a collection of documents that are represented, for the purpose of manipulation, by records made up of index terms drawn from the documents. A user of our system expresses his information needs in the form of a request that is reduced to a single term. The system uses the request and the index records to decide, for each document, whether the document is to be retrieved. If the system is successful, documents that are desired by the patron will be concentrated in this set, while one would expect few documents not retrieved to be of value. Accordingly, the large collection of documents is reduced to a much smaller collection containing most of the desired documents. We shall afterwards consider an alternative approach, outside the indexing framework, that ranks documents according to their likelihood of satisfying the requester rather than simply retrieving them or not.

The retrieval of the documents is determined on the basis of a model of word occurrences. As the model is developed in detail elsewhere (*6*) we shall only describe it briefly here.

The development of the model begins with the observation that a reader's apprehension of a document's subject matter is determined by the words making up that document. In our model the process of subject recognition is assumed to be based on the statistical pattern of occurrences of words. A document is perceived as being about the subject symbolized by the word $w$ if $w$ occurs more frequently in that document than can be expected in a randomly chosen document; it is in this manner that words convey information as to what a document is about. If we have a set of documents, each of which is about $w$ to the same extent, then we expect that the occurrences of $w$ will be as if random within that set.

We shall assume that, for each term, $w$, our document corpus can be broken up into subsets, each subset being made up of documents that are "about" $w$ to the same degree; these subsets will be called "relevance classes." Because of this property, it is not possible to distinguish documents within a subset on the basis of how often $w$ occurs within a document. So far as that subset is concerned, $w$ seems to occur randomly, with the average number of occurrences per document being a characteristic of the subset. A distribution that represents such random occurrences is the Poisson. We can thus formally express our model, in its most general form, as follows:

1. The word, $w$, divides the corpus into subsets such that for the subset $S_i$, the probability, $P_i(k)$, that $w$ will occur $k$ times in a randomly chosen document is given by

$$P_i(k) = \frac{e^{-\lambda_i}\lambda_i^k}{k!} \qquad (1)$$

2. The probability that a randomly chosen document is in class $S_i$ is given by a parameter which we shall call $\pi_i$.
3. The probability that a document in $S_i$ will be perceived as relevant, that is, will be accepted by someone requesting documents "about $w$" is given by $r_i$.

This model assumes that it is possible to think of a document as being intrinsically about a term to some degree. In this regard our model bears a degree of similarity to that discussed by Swets. However, unlike Swets, we may have any number of relevance classes, including, possibly, a continuum. Furthermore, the model recognizes, with Maron and Kuhns, that the perception of relevance is probabilistic in essence. A document that is considered relevant by one person may be rejected by another person making the identical request. These fundamental notions are tied together in this paper by a model of word occurrences, whereby appearances of $w$ in a document gives information as to which of $w$'s relevance classes a document belongs, and thereby the probability of its being judged as relevant by a patron.

Although it is possible to proceed by using the model in its fullest generality, we shall continue with a special case for the purpose of simplicity. This model will assume two subclasses of documents, with $\pi$ and $1-\pi$ the probabilities of being in one or the other of the sets. The average number of terms, $w$, per document are $\lambda_1$ and $\lambda_2$ in the two sets. Finally, we assume $r_1 = 1$ and $r_2 = 0$; that is, documents in the first class will always satisfy patrons requesting items about $w$, while no item in the second class would satisfy such patrons; restricting $r$ in this manner produces a model similar to that of Swets.

This two-Poisson model is a three-parameter model; the parameters can be fitted purely on the basis of word occurrences and without assessments of relevance (*6, 7*). Once these parameters have been evaluated, it is then possible to use the model as a basis for the indexing and retrieval of documents.

## • Document Indexing and Retrieval

Let us ask, then, whether the term $w$ ought to be associated with a document as an index term. The basis of this decision, in our model information system, is the observation that we should apply $w$ to a document if, and only if, when someone asks for documents about $w$, we should give him that document. Suppose $w$ occurs $s$ times in a document, $d$; ought we, then, to give $d$ to the person initiating the request? If so, then $d$ should be indexed by $w$, at least so far as that particular request is concerned.

In the following we shall assume that for each request there is a cost associated with making a mistake; whether the cost is measured in dollars or patron displeasure need not concern us here. Suppose, in a given instance,

$c_1$ = cost of missing a relevant document, and

$c_2$ = cost of retrieving a non-revelant document.

In the following, the notation $P(A/B)$ will denote the probability of the event $A$ occurring provided the event $B$ occurs; the events of interest to us are:

$w$: a document is acceptable to a person requesting $w$;

$\overline{w}$: a document is not acceptable to such a person; and

$s$: a document has $s$ occurrences of $w$.

$P(A)$ will denote the unconditional probability of the event $A$ occurring. Then, in terms of this notation, our expected cost is smallest if we retrieve $d$ when

$$c_2 \, P(\overline{w}/s) < c_1 \, P(w/s), \qquad \text{or} \qquad (2)$$

$$\frac{P(w/s)}{P(\overline{w}/s)} > \frac{c_2}{c_1} \overset{def}{=} a_0 \qquad (3)$$

An application of Bayes' theorem to (1) yields

$$\frac{P(s/w)}{P(s/\overline{w})} \; \frac{P(w)}{P(\overline{w})} > a_0, \text{ or}$$

$$a \overset{def}{=} e^{-(\lambda_1 - \lambda_2)} \left(\frac{\lambda_1}{\lambda_2}\right)^s \frac{\pi}{1-\pi} > a_0, \qquad (4)$$

since $P(s/w)$ is given by (1).

If $\pi$, $\lambda_1$ and $\lambda_2$ were estimated from the distribution of occurences of $w$ throughout a corpus (7), $a$ for that word can be computed for each document. Since a document ought to be retrieved if $a > a_0$, such documents should be indexed by $w$ so far as the request with the above cost structure is concerned; once this is done, all documents indexed by $w$ would be retrieved in response to a request for $w$.

In fact we may expect a distribution of cost structures over our population of requests; let $f(c_1, c_2)$ be the joint probability distribution for these costs. Then the overall costs to the community of patrons due to useless documents being retrieved will have an expected value of $\int f(c_1, c_2) c_2 \, P(\overline{w} \mid s) \, dc_1 dc_2 = \overline{c}_2 \, P(\overline{w} \mid s)$, where $\overline{c}_2$ is the average value of $c_2$ over the population being considered. Similarly, the overall expected cost of not retrieving relevant documents is $\overline{c}_1 \; P(w \mid s)$. If it is overall expected cost that is to be reduced, then we can proceed as above, with $\overline{c}_1$ and $\overline{c}_2$ substituting for $c_1$ and $c_2$. This criterion would then be the basis of indexing in this system.

At this point we can make three observations:

1. If $\lambda_1 > \lambda_2$, an increase in the number of occurrences of $w$ increases the strength of the argument in favor of retrieving a document. $\left(\frac{\lambda_1}{\lambda_2}\right)^s$ shows the impact of the evidence "$s$" in the decision process; as $\frac{\lambda_1}{\lambda_2}$ increases, each additional occurrence of $w$ has greater impact. $e$ $(\lambda_1 - \lambda_2)$ indicates how disadvantageous the non-occurrence of $w$ is for retrieval.

2. $\frac{\pi}{1-\pi}$ gives the strength of the argument for retrieval if we are given no evidence. This is related only to the fraction of the documents that is relevant. The other factors give the effect of evidence in changing our decision.

3. The above discussion focuses on the costs to the user, treating all users as equal. Alternatively, the costs $c_1$ and $c_2$ may represent the *system's* concern over displeasing various classes of users, and $f(c_1, c_2)$ the distribution of requests over these classes of users. Thus the cost assessments acted upon by the system need not be identical to those perceived by the individual users of the system.

In summary, if we knew $a_0$ for each term, $w$, then we could index a document on the basis of the above formula, using average costs over the population of requests. Investigation of actual indexing practice might very well reveal a functional form $a_0$ $(\lambda_1, \lambda_2, \pi)$, or perhaps a workable conventional threshold value, $a_0$, thereby making the system complete. Such a system, however, is incapable of adjusting to individual variation among users in the threshold $a_0$. This limitation is true of all systems centered around the indexing of documents. To the extent these systems optimize indexing practice at all, it is in behalf of the average request.

However, if we are unable to assess $a_0$, we could still proceed as follows: for each document and each word, evaluate $a$ as given above. Then, if a patron requests documents about $w$, he could be presented with a list of documents ranked according to the values $a$ associated with $w$. For this simple model, this ranking is equivalent to ranking according to $s$, and provides theoretical justification for this practice. The user can then examine documents as far down the list as he sees fit; the value of $a$ for the last document he considers in effect estimates $a_0$ for that word for that user and for that request. Thus, even though the costs are not known, the assumption that they do in fact exist provides us with a basis for retrieving documents. Since the retrieval decision is based only on word occurrences, rather than on semantic considerations, it can potentially be implemented on a computer. We speculate that there may be some connection between the statistical distribution of occurrences of a word, and a reader's perception of that word as indicating the content of a text. Experience with the language may very well suggest, for each term, the likelihood that the term appears in a document without that document being relevant to the topic represented by that term (our parameters $\pi$, $\lambda_1$, $\lambda_2$) as well as the costs of mistakes.

It may be argued that other words convey information to the indexer as well. Currently models generalizing the above so as to include co-occurrence information are being developed for this purpose. We expect, however, that these more sophisticated models will modify rather than completely change the criterion formula given above. In any case, the philosophy and methodology developed above may very well be of interest to researchers in this field in connection with alternative models of word occurrence.

## • Selecting Content-Bearing Words

If the procedure described above were applied to every word, we would expect that those words that are not indicative of content would tend to retrieve every document. Users, intuitively noticing this, are not likely to use such words in their requests. For economic reasons, it is accordingly desirable to restrict the number of words for which the system carries out its calculations. One procedure for identifying the content-bearing words that is suggested by the model itself is as follows.

We would like to consider only those words that will produce good results, that is, result in least cost. Consider, once again, the word $w$. If we solve the inequality (4) for $s$, we find that there is a value, $s_0$, such that a document is retrieved if $s \geqslant s_0$.

If we adopt this approach, the expected cost to the user will be

$$\bar{c}_1\, P(w/s) \text{ if } s < s_0, \text{ and}$$
$$\bar{c}_2\, P(\bar{w}/s) \text{ if } s \geqslant s_0,$$

But, as is shown in (6), the model predicts that the probability of the $w$ occurring $s$ times in a document is given by

$$P(s) = \pi\, e^{-\lambda_1} \frac{\lambda_1{}^s}{s!} + (1\text{-}\pi)\, e^{-\lambda_2} \frac{\lambda_2{}^s}{s!} \qquad (5)$$

The expected cost, $C$, associated with $w$ is thus given by

$$C = \bar{c}_2 \sum_{s \geqslant s_0} P(s)\, P(\bar{w}/s) + \bar{c}_1 \sum_{s < s_0} P(s)\, P(w/s). \qquad (6a)$$

Expressing $P(w/s)$ as $\dfrac{P(w)\; P(s/w)}{P(s)}$ by use of Bayes' theorem, and using the corresponding expression for $P(\bar{w}/s)$, we find an alternative expression for $C$:

$$C = \bar{c}_2\, P(\bar{w}) \sum_{s \geqslant s_0} P(s/\bar{w}) + \bar{c}_1\, P(w) \sum_{s < s_0} P(s/w). \qquad (6b)$$

Finally, in terms of the two-Poisson model, $C$ becomes:

$$C = (1\text{-}\pi)\, \bar{c}_2\, e^{-\lambda_2} \sum_{s \geqslant s_0} \frac{\lambda_2{}^s}{s!} + \pi \bar{c}_1\, e^{-\lambda_1} \sum_{s < s_0} \frac{\lambda_1{}^s}{s!} \qquad (6c)$$

with $\lambda_1 > \lambda_2$.

Thus, having evaluated the parameters of the two-Poisson model, we can associate a cost with each request. Clearly we should then use as index terms those words with smallest expected costs, where $\bar{c}_1$ and $\bar{c}_2$ are values averaged over all requests. In practical terms, the system should effectively define a cutoff value $C_o$, and use as index terms those words for which $C \leqslant C_o$. This line of reasoning also provides some insight into the conventional measures of effectiveness of information systems.

The traditional measures of operating effectiveness for an information system are recall, precision, and the related measure, fallout. Since recall, $R$, is the probability that a relevant document be retrieved, it can be expressed in terms of our model as follows:

$$R\,(s_o) = \sum_{s \geqslant s_o} P\,(s/w).$$

Similarly, fallout, $F(s)$, which is the probability that a non-relevant document be retrieved, can be expressed as follows:

$$F(s_0) = \sum_{s \geqslant s_o} P(s/\bar{w}).$$

Thus each value $s_0$, defined in terms of the costs $\bar{c}_1$ and $\bar{c}_2$ and the parameters for $w$, determine an operating point on a recall-fallout curve.

For our development, it is more direct to define $N =$ 1-$R$ as "nonrecall" and to consider the nonrecall-fallout curve.

If $\bar{c}_2\; P(\bar{w}) \overset{def}{\equiv} \bar{\bar{c}}_2$ and $\bar{c}_1\; P(w) \overset{def}{\equiv} \bar{\bar{c}}_1$, then

$$C = \bar{\bar{c}}_2\, F + \bar{\bar{c}}_1 N.$$

Interpreted graphically, this means that the sets of all $N$-$F$ points of constant cost, that is, points of the system over which we are indifferent, are represented by lines on the $N$-$F$ plane. The slope of such a line is determined by the cost structure for the request in question, and the costs decrease as the line is shifted, parallel to itself, to the south-west.

But the system is not free to operate at any point on the $N$-$F$ plane. For a particular request, the system as described above is constrained to be on an operating curve of the system; each point on that curve represents a cut-off value of $s_0$, the number of occurrences of $w$ required for retrieving a document. For a particular request and cost structure, the optimal point at which to operate the system will thus be that point at which the indifference line of lowest cost, which will be the one tangent to the operating curve, meets the operating curve. Fig. 1 illustrates the above argument.

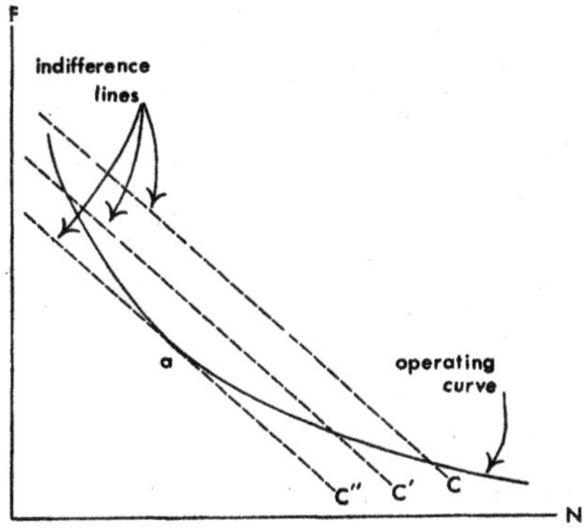


Fig. 1. *N-F* Operating curve and Indifference Lines, with $C'' < c' < c$. *A* Is Point on *N-F* Curve with Smallest Cost.

This development allows us to make precise our understanding of what constitutes a relatively good *N-F* curve. Generally, changing the cost structure $c_1$ and $c_2$ changes the slope of the indifference lines. A good curve, one belonging to a potential index term, is one for which the set of lines tangent to it tends to be the lower cost lines associated with commonly occurring cost structures. Such a curve lies closer to the origin than does a less desirable curve. Thus, in Fig. 2, curve *A* is better than curve *B*. We conclude that one can estimate which words will serve as index terms on the basis of their *N-F* curves, and these curves can be predicted by the model; it seems likely that a similar analysis can be carried out

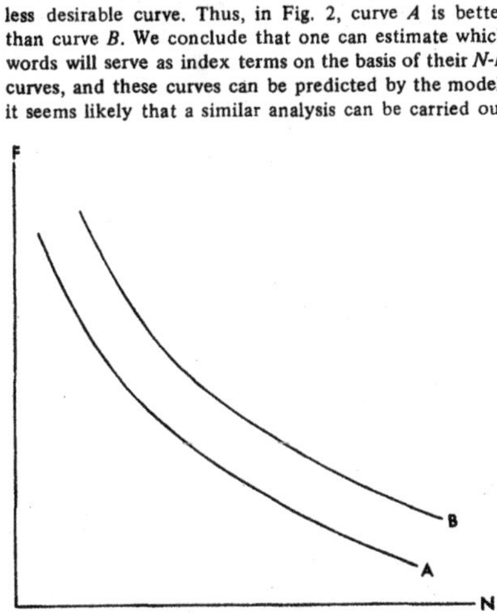


Fig. 2. Two Operating Curves in *N-F* Plane. The Term Belonging to Curve *A* Will Be Better As an Index Term Than That Belonging to Curve *B* For All Cost Structures.

in terms of the more conventional recall and precision curves. Such an analysis would offer a new interpretation of these curves and make precise in what sense some recall and precision curves are to be preferred to others.

The geometric picture introduced in this section also permits an alternative derivation of inequality (4). The value of $s$ at which the system ought to be operating corresponds to that point in Fig. 1 where the slope of the indifference line is the same as that of the system's operating curve. The slope of the indifference line is –

$$\frac{\bar{\bar{c}}_2}{\bar{\bar{c}}_1} = -\frac{(1-\pi)\ \bar{c}_2}{\pi\ \bar{c}_1}.$$

Since $N(s_o) = \sum_{s=o}^{s_o-1} P(s/w)$, if $s$ changes from $s_o$ to $s_o + 1$, $N(s_o)$ increases by $P(s_o/w)$. Similarly, $F(s_o) = \sum_{s=s_o}^{\infty} P(s/\bar{w})$. decreases by $P(s_o/\bar{w})$.

Thus, between $s_o$ and $s_o + 1$, the slope of the operating curve is $-\frac{P(s_o/w)}{P(s_o/\bar{w})} = -e^{-(\lambda_1-\lambda_2)} \frac{\lambda_1}{\lambda_2}^{s_o}$. For $s_o$ to be an optimal operating point we must have

$$-e^{-(\lambda_1-\lambda_2)} \left\{\frac{\lambda_1}{\lambda_2}\right\}^{s_o-1} \geqslant -\frac{\bar{c}_2\ (1-\pi)}{\bar{c}_2\ \pi} \geqslant -e^{-(\lambda_1-\lambda_2)} \left\{\frac{\lambda_1}{\lambda_2}\right\}^{s_o},$$

which is equivalent to (4).

## • Summary

Documents are indexed for the purpose of retrieval, and one can arrive at a theoretically well-founded procedure for indexing by being true to that purpose. We posited specific, though simplified, models of information retrieval systems and word occurrence distributions and showed how such models can be used to develop an indexing procedure. This procedure is self-contained in that it makes use only of word occurrence distribution counts within a corpus. On the basis of these counts the model can reveal which words are useful as index terms and how to rank documents according to relevance to each of these terms. The model developed here can also be used to predict the shape of recall and precision curves or their equivalents; the model provides a theoretical criterion for assessing the value of words as index terms on the basis of these curves.

The mathematical techniques used in this paper have a long history. The basic problem is how to decide, on the basis of evidence, in which of two classes an object belongs. An early analysis of this problem was made by R.A. Fisher while considering problems arising in biology (*8*). Since that time, these techniques have been greatly developed and have been applied to many fields. One such area of interest here is pattern recognition, and the reader can find an excellent exposition of this topic, as well as that of the mathematics used here, in reference

(*9*). Formally, the problem of information retrieval is similar to that of pattern recognition. The patterns studied are patterns of words occurring in text, and the variables considered are counts of words. On the basis of this "evidence," the patterns, or documents, are placed into classes, here relevance classes. Ultimately the decision as to which class a document is placed results in a decision as to whether that document should be retrieved in response to a request. Thus these two seemingly diverse fields are tied together by a shared body of mathematical techniques, and recognition of this overlap provides an interesting perspective as to the nature of information retrieval.


## • Acknowledgment

We are grateful to Stephen P. Harter for valuable discussions on the content of this paper. Mr. Harter has been carrying on research on related topics in preparation of a doctoral dissertation.


## References


1. **Maron, M.E.** and **J.L. Kuhns**, "On Relevance, Probabilistic Indexing and Information Retrieval," *Journal of the Association for Computing Machinery*, 7 (No. 3): 216-243 (1960).
2. **Swets, J.A.**, "Information Retrieval Systems," *Science*, 141: 245-250 (July 18, 1963).
3. **Mosteller, F.** and **D. Wallace**, *Inference and Disputed Authorship: The Federalist*, Reading, MA: Addison Weseley (1964).
4. **Kraft, D.H.**, "A Decision Theory View of the Information Retrieval Situation: An Operations Research Approach," *Journal of the American Society for Information Science* 24 (No. 5): 368-375 (1973).
5. **Tague, J.M.**, "A Bayesian Appraoch to Interactive Retrieval," *Information Storage and Retrieval* 9 (No. 3): 129-142 (1973).
6. **Bookstein, A.** and **D. Swanson**, "Probabilistic Models of Indexing," *Journal of the American Society for Information Science*, 25 (No. 5): 312-319 (1974).
7. **Harter, S.**, Doctoral Dissertation (in preparation), The University of Chicago.
8. **Fisher, R.A.**, "The User of Multiple Measurements in Taxonomic Problems." *Annals of Eugenics* 7, Part II: 179-188 (1936).
9. **Duda, R.O.** and **P.E. Hart**, *Pattern Classification and Scene Analysis*, New York: John Wiley and Sons (1973).

*Reprinted from Information Processing & Management, Vol. 13.*


# INCORPORATION OF THE AGE OF A DOCUMENT INTO THE RETRIEVAL PROCESS†

M. H. HEINE

Department of Librarianship and Information Science, Newcastle upon Tyne Polytechnic, Newcastle upon Tyne NEI 8ST, England

(*Received* 24 *June* 1976)

**Abstract**—A full treatment of the significance of a document for an enquirer should include a joint description of the similarity between the document and the enquiry in a linquistic sense, and the age of the document at the time of the enquiry. The basic variables are identified in terms of a signal detection model. The age variable is related to the phenomenon of obsolescence, which is treated as a perceived, signed attribute of relevant documents. Two retrieval methods that use both index terms and document age are described: one in which a set of documents, first selected by a term-intersection process, is reduced by applying a date of publication criterion (the "subset method"); and one in which a bivariate function attaches a single number to each document, and a retrieved set is defined by a single threshold value (the "bivariate weight method"). In the latter method, discriminant analysis is a useful aid. A model of the retrieval process, based on continuous variables, is described, and the effectiveness of each method is predicted, both in terms of the Precision-Recall graph and language measures. The model suggests that either method can improve retrieval performance but incorrect usage will depress it. The better choice of method will depend on the Recall/Precision mix required by the user, as well as the actual parameters of the distributions. A relationship is hypothesised between the growth rate of a data base and the underlying distributions defined by relevance iudgements.

## 1. INTRODUCTION

A conventional view of information retrieval is that it is largely concerned with "subject" relationships between documents and users' needs for documents. The proper portrayal of subject relationships in operational terms, it is understood, is through language, i.e. through words or coded representations of words being assigned to (a) documents (the "indexing process"), and (b) the user-enquiry of concern at the moment (the "profile construction process"). Retrieval algorithms are customarily based on assumptions about such relationships. Contemporary with this view is another, apparently separate view, in which "literature obsolescence" is seen as a phenomenon whereby users' preferences for documents (expressed via relevance judgements, document-seeking behaviour, citation practices, etc.) show a dependence on document age, and one moreover usually biased towards more recent documents. This paper is based on the view that our understanding of the importance of the information carried by a document to a user should incorporate both views in some coherent way, and that more effective retrieval algorithms can be designed using such understanding.

A model will be described which predicts the consequences of a systematic treatment of the two variables: linguistic similarity of document and enquiry, and document age at time of enquiry. Generalizations in respect of a multivariate theory of document significance and information retrieval are thereby suggested. The approach followed is fairly informal, in order that the results of the study are meaningful, and capable of generalization in recognised directions.

## 2. AN APPROACH TO THE JOINT TREATMENT OF LINGUISTIC SIMILARITY AND DOCUMENT AGE

Several present-day operational procedures support the view that users can effectively perceive attributes of relevance in documents, other than that of the index terms (or text or title words) which relevant documents carry. One such procedure involves the reduction of the output of a retrieval process, where the primary output has been based on retrieval using index terms. In this method, documents are rejected from a primary output when they do not meet additional criteria, such as: the document must be a journal paper, must be published after 1970, must be in French, etc. Such reduction methods can be seen to have two general characteristics: they are "subset" or end-on methods, in that successive criteria can only reduce (or maintain) the size of

†Work carried out in the Computing Laboratory, University of Newcastle upon Tyne.

the set; and they are *ad hoc* in that the procedures followed are not guided by a theory that would predict the worth of different operating strategies (in terms of their effect on the Precision-Recall graph, cost, etc.). A consequence of the first characteristic is that the Recall of each successive subset is less than or equal to that of its predecessor. It might be imagined that set-intersection methods involve a third characteristic: an increase in Precision—just as, it is sometimes said, the use of the Boolean "AND" operator between an existing profile and an additional term must increase the Precision. But neither statement is necessarily true since in casting out by secondary criteria, relevant documents acceptable by previous criteria may be rejected.

Another retrieval strategy is possible however, but is at present allowed in only a few operational systems. This involves ranking all documents in the data base by a single number attached to each document, where that number is determined jointly by two or more variables related to the types of attribute that can be taken by the enquirer to describe his perception of the relevant documents. When this is done it is possible to define a retrieved set by a single threshold value, rather than by a vector of such values as in the previous method.

The existence of the two general methods just described poses a variety of questions, such as:

(1) Are the two methods equivalent, or will they—for say a given Recall or Precision value—lead to different evaluations of the data base?

(2) Is there any systematic tendency for one method to be better than the other in different "areas of evaluation" (such as high or low Recall)?

(3) How should a theory be constructed to aid the practical management of retrieval procedures in respect of choosing between the two methods, and guiding the method chosen at the "tactical level"?

Answers to the above questions will be sought in respect of the two types of attribute indicated in the Introduction: linguistic similarity, and document age. The reasons for choosing the second of these are (i) it can be a strong indicator of document relevance, (ii) it is easily obtained in practice (i.e. readily extractable from record structures), and (iii) the variates it defines would appear to be highly independent, in a probabilistic sense, of those defined by the first attribute. (This assumption is clarified in Section 4.) These two types of attribute allow two weights to be assigned to each document, and thereby the possibility of forming a single weight from them jointly. There is an extensive literature on weights of the linguistic type, review papers having been contributed by SALTON and YANG[1], SPARCK JONES[2] and EVANS[3]. None of the latter authors discusses the possibility of bi- or multivariate weighting methods, suggesting that little or no attention has been given to such an approach. There are in fact papers by DIFONDI[4] and WILLIAMS[5] which describe the use of multivariate techniques in information retrieval: however neither author discusses the combination of attributes of fundamentally different type; only language based variables are considered.

## 3. LITERATURE OBSOLESCENCE

The term "literature obsolescence" has been ambiguously used to describe either or both of the following notions:

A. The information given in documents becomes less accurate or relevant, in some absolute sense, with increasing document age.

B. Document users behave as if "A" were true.

For recent analytical discussion of related theory and experiment see BROOKES[6] and MEADOWS[7], and for a comprehensive critical review see LINE and SANDISON[8]. The latter authors state, in agreement with the distinction made above:

> "It is most important... to be quite clear whether changes in library use... or in the value and interest of knowledge are being considered..." (p. 318)

In the following, it is assumed that "A" is meaningless in an objective sense, however meaningful it may be in subjective terms, and an amended form of "B" is taken as the basis for the objective description of the obsolescence involved in information retrieval

B′. Document users, through their behaviour, define a probability distribution on the ages of a set of documents the members of which they perceive to be relevant to their needs. (The behaviour is "asserting such relevance".) Obsolescence exists when the mean of such a distribution differs significantly from the mean of the distribution on the ages of a set of documents from which the relevant documents are drawn.

It is also noted that (1) the interest in obsolescence from an information retrieval standpoint is restricted to user behaviour of the "relevance-assessment type", and not to behaviour in the form of (say) requests for documents, or citations in documents; (2) as such, the interest is restricted to obsolescence of the "synchronous" type, to use Line's terminology; (3) the obsolescence of interest is *signed*: positive [negative] obsolescence being defined when the mean age of relevant documents is less [more] than the mean age of all documents; (4) in order for such obsolescence to be defined, a set of documents from which relevant documents are drawn is required to be defined at the time the enquiry is made.

Thus the philosophy adopted is that obsolescence in information retrieval is a dynamic observable entity, formally defined through probability distributions, and varying from enquiry to enquiry and user to user. Given behaviour in the form of an assertion as to the membership of a relevant set, the existence and sign of obsolescence would be readily found. However in an information retrieval situation the relevant set is only perceived by the enquirer. In that case the existence and sign of the obsolescence could form part of the user's search profile (just as the user's perception of the keywords assigned to relevant documents forms the main part of the profile). It is just this perception that is of concern.

A pivotal assumption in the model to be described is that the user is competent to estimate the mean age of relevant documents. This assumption is justified, in the author's view, by (i) the consideration that there is no difference in principle between users' perceptions of this type of attribute and perceptions of other types; and (ii) the observation that many information services implicitly recognise the usefulness of document age as an indicator of relevance. (For example the practice of presenting retrieval output in a form in which references are ranked by age; or the practice of limiting SDI to recent material.) Presumably the humanistic origins of such practices (which incidentally usually assume the existence of *positive* obsolescence in the enquirer's relevance judgements) lie in the tendency of newer documents to synthesise the information in order documents, the acceptability of the usefulness of the citation system for gaining access to older literature, and the "entropic" tendency for older documents to have been seen, or identified, previously by the enquirer, as well as the usefulness of date-of-publication as a convenient way of coping with natural redundancy in the literature.

Further complications that might be considered in building a complete theory based on index terms and document age jointly are: user/data base heuristics, the validity of the distributions assumed, and the consequences of users incorrectly estimating the true mean age of relevant documents. Obviously exploration of the last of these points would need to be accompanied by exploration of how accurately users choose words as attributes of the relevant documents which they seek.

## 4. THEORY

### (a) *The basic distributions*

Let us assume that to each document in a collection, two numbers are assigned by the retrieval process. One is a conventional linguistic or subject weight, $x$ say, based on the degree of agreement of the set of words or word codes attached to the document, with the set of words taken to represent the user's enquiry, e.g. the cosine correlation measure of Salton. The other number is the age of the document at the time of the enquiry. This "age weight" is denoted by $t$. A further convention is that the subscript $i$ attached to a quantity or variable relates that item to the set of relevant documents when $i = 1$, and to the non-relevant set when $i = 2$. The assumptions about the distributions are as follows.

First, following SWETS[9, 10] it is assumed that the random variables $X_i$ associated with $x$-values have probability mass functions that can be approximated† by Normal probability densities:

$$f_i(x) = (2\pi\sigma_i^2)^{-1/2} \exp(-(x-\mu_i)^2/2\sigma_i^2), \qquad x \in (-\infty, \infty). \tag{1}$$

†The approximation is actually between the CDFs of $f_i(x)$ where $x$ is continuous, and the CDFs of the discrete probability functions which are in fact observed. Note also that (1) relates to single enquiries, not to averaged data arising from many enquiries as considered by Swets (HEINE[11]).

Secondly, it is assumed that the random variables $T_i$ associated with the set of $t$-values for the entire set of documents in the discipline have mass functions that can be approximated by negative exponential densities:

$$g'_i(t) = \eta_i \exp(-\eta_i t), \qquad t \in [0, \infty). \tag{2'}$$

(Since it is only the broad effects of the two methods which are of interest, the "double-exponential" model favoured by some authors is ignored.) In view of the fact that some operational retrieval system do not allow users immediate access to all items in the data base, but only access to those with an age less than some specified date of incorporation in the data base, (2′) is rewritten so that this fact is reflected in the assumed densities for $T_1$ and $T_2$. If the ages of documents that can be retrieved, for the retrieval process of interest, fall in the interval $[0, A]$, then expressions (2′) become, after normalising:

$$\left.\begin{aligned} g_i(t) &= [\eta_i/(1-\exp(-\eta_i A))]\exp(-\eta_i t), \qquad A > 0, \qquad t \in [0, A] \\ &= 0, \qquad t \notin [0, A]. \end{aligned}\right\} \tag{2}$$

The mean values and variances of the $X_i$ are:

$$E(X_i) = \mu_i; \qquad V(X_i) = \sigma_i^2 \tag{3a}$$

and of the $T_i$ are:

$$\left.\begin{aligned} E(T_i) &= \frac{\exp(-\eta_i A)(A + (1/\eta_i)) - (1/\eta_i)}{\exp(-\eta_i A) - 1} \\ V(T_i) &= \left(\frac{A^2 \exp(-\eta_i A)}{\exp(-\eta_i A) - 1}\right) + E(T_i)\left(\frac{2}{\eta_i} - E(T_i)\right). \end{aligned}\right\} \tag{3b}$$

As a third and final assumption it is accepted that $X_1$ and $T_1$, and $X_2$ and $T_2$, are independent; i.e. that there is no systematic tendency for older documents to have less or more index terms in common with a question profile than newer documents. Since document age, and document subject (expressed by index terms), are such unlike concepts this seems plausible, notwithstanding that indexing terminology changes *slowly* with the development of knowledge.

Representing the joint densities of $X_i$ and $T_i$ by $h_i(x, t)$, we have, in view of the last assumption:

$$h_i(x, t) = f_i(x) g_i(t), \qquad (i = 1, 2).$$

The effect of ignoring the small amount of covariance between $X_i$ and $T_i$ which will exist in practice (due to the adaptation of language to changing human knowledge) will be that any theory building on this will describe an upper bound for retrieval effectiveness.

The functions $h_i(x, t)$ are illustrated in Fig. 1. The marginals are given by eqns (1) and (2). From an information science point of view, the separation of $h_1$ and $h_2$ might be taken as representing the user's propensity to create new (personal) knowledge, on the basis of the extant (public) knowledge represented in the data base. (The subjective notion of "relevance" might be identified with this propensity, but whereas relevance as such is not an observable, the variates $X_i$ and $T_i$—along with the formulation of the enquiry—are observables, and therefore subject to scientific investigation.) Since the new knowledge, or some fraction of it, is eventually contributed to the data base, this point of view allows the conjecture that the rate of advance of knowledge in an area defined by a data base and its users, is expressible as some function of the net propensities so identified. Accordingly the hypothesis is offered that if some experimental observable is taken as representing "knowledge" (e.g. the number of papers, $K$, in some specified data base), then its rate of growth can be expressed as a function of the enquiries put to it via:

$$\frac{\Delta K}{\Delta t} = \theta \frac{\sum_{u \in U(\Delta t)} M[h'_1(x, t), (h'_2)_u(x, t)]}{n(U)}. \tag{4}$$

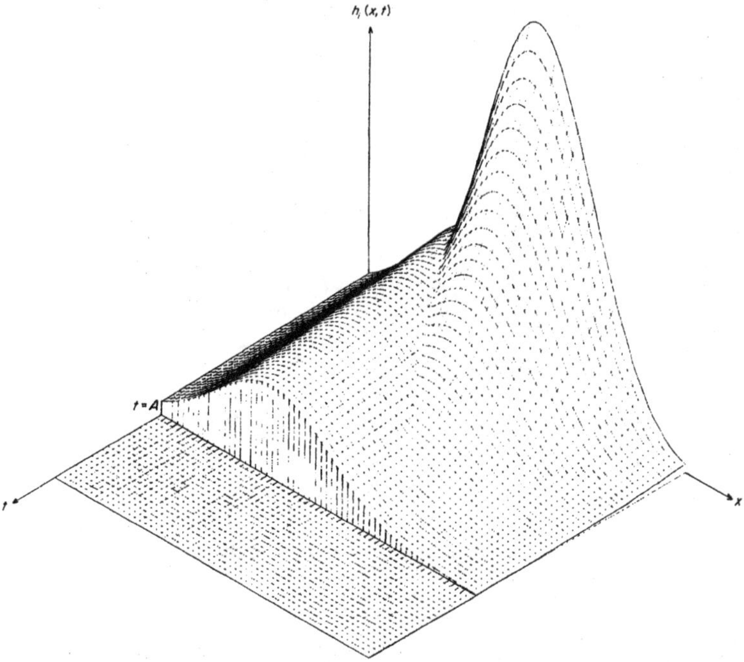


Fig. 1. The bivariate probability density functions $h_i(x, t)$, $(i = 1, 2)$, are shown for independent variates $X_i$ and $T_i$, and for the case where the obsolescence defined by the set of relevant documents is positive. The surface shown is in fact $\underline{max}$ $(h_1, h_2)$ with $h_1$ (pertaining to relevant documents) to the right. Each document corresponds to a point $\overline{(x, t)}$, the $x$-value indicating the document's linguistic weight vis-a-vis the enquiry, and the $t$-value indicating the age of the document at the time of the enquiry. The marginal density functions along the $x$-axis are the Swetsian Normal curves $f_i(x)$, and the marginals along the $t$-axis are truncated negative exponential functions, $g_i(t)$. The truncation point $t = A$ corresponds to the data base being available to users only for $t \leq A$, for the retrieval process of interest.

Here $U(\Delta t)$ is a set of enquiries put to the data base in an interval $\Delta t$, and $n(U)$ is the number of such enquiries; $M$ is a measure of the separation† of the functions $h'_1$ and $h'_2$ (where $h'_i = f_i g'_i \div f_i g_i = h_i$; $i = 1, 2$) and is an instance of a bivariate "language measure"[12]; and $\theta$ is a "knowledge constant" characteristic of at most $U$, $M$, and the data base. (A stronger hypothesis would make $\theta$ independent of the data base.) The change in language with knowledge could, as previously mentioned, be represented through the observables Cov $(X_i, T_i)$, $(i = 1, 2)$. A further refinement of (4) would be to introduce a factor $G_u$ in the summation, where $G_u$ is the Generality for query $u$.

(b) *Retrieval methods*

The two retrieval methods that we shall consider are:

(i) *The subset method.* Retrieve all documents having $x$-values exceeding some threshold $x_c$, and then extract from this set those documents which have $t$-values less than some threshold $t_c$. (Or these steps can be reversed.)

(ii) *The bivariate weight method.* Assign to each document a bivariate weight: $z = z(x, t)$, i.e. a single number $z$ which is a function of $x$ and $t$, and retrieve only those documents for which $z > z_c$. For example, $z$ could be chosen to have the linear form: $z = \lambda_1 x + \lambda_2 t$; $\lambda_1, \lambda_2$ constants.

The aim is to predict and compare retrieval effectiveness using these two methods. In the case of the bivariate weight method, $z$ is restricted to the linear form mentioned.

†$M$ is a measure of dissimilarity, rather than similarity, if it is true that highly-productive authors have stringent rather than lax relevance judgements.

For the "linguistic variable" $x$ we have, putting $R$ for Recall, $F$ for Fallout, and $G$ for Generality, the usual relations:

$$\left.\begin{aligned} R(x_c) &= \int_{x_c}^{\infty} f_1(x)\,\mathrm{d}x = \frac{1}{2}\operatorname{erfc}\left(\frac{x_c-\mu_1}{\sqrt{2}\,\sigma_1}\right) \\ F(x_c) &= \int_{x_c}^{\infty} f_2(x)\,\mathrm{d}x = \frac{1}{2}\operatorname{erfc}\left(\frac{x_c-\mu_2}{\sqrt{2}\,\sigma_2}\right) \end{aligned}\right\} \tag{5}$$

the Precision following from : $P(x_c) = GR(x_c)/[GR(x_c)+(1-G)F(x_c)]$. For the "age-of-document variable" $t$ we have, for *positive* obsolescence:

$$\left.\begin{aligned} R(t_c) &= \int_0^{t_c} g_1(t)\,\mathrm{d}t = \frac{\exp(-\eta_1 t_c)-1}{\exp(-\eta_1 A)-1} \\ F(t_c) &= \int_0^{t_c} g_2(t)\,\mathrm{d}t = \frac{\exp(-\eta_2 t_c)-1}{\exp(-\eta_2 A)-1} \end{aligned}\right\} \tag{6}$$

with $P$ again readily inferred. For *negative* obsolescence one would retrieve documents with $t$ values between $t_c$ and $A$, when the Recall and Fallout values would be obtained from (6) by : $R(t_c) := 1 - R(t_c)$, and $F(t_c) := 1 - F(t_c)$.

For the subset method the Recall will be, for positive obsolescence:

$$\begin{aligned} R(x_c, t_c) &= \iint_C h_1(x,t)\,\mathrm{d}x\,\mathrm{d}t, \qquad C = \{(x,t); x > x_c, t < t_c\} \\ &= \int_{x_c}^{\infty} f_1(x)\,\mathrm{d}x \int_0^{t_c} g_1(t)\,\mathrm{d}t \\ &= R(x_c)R(t_c) \\ &= \frac{1}{2}\operatorname{erfc}\left(\frac{x_c-\mu_1}{\sqrt{2}\,\sigma_1}\right)\left(\frac{\exp(-\eta_1 t_c)-1}{\exp(-\eta_1 A)-1}\right) \end{aligned} \tag{7a}$$

using the independence assumption, and (5) and (6). Similarly:

$$F(x_c, t_c) = \frac{1}{2}\operatorname{erfc}\left(\frac{x_c-\mu_2}{\sqrt{2}\,\sigma_2}\right)\left(\frac{\exp(-\eta_2 t_c)-1}{\exp(-\eta_2 A)-1}\right). \tag{7b}$$

Again, when negative obsolescence obtains, we write $1 - R(t_c)$ for $R(t_c)$ in (7a), and $1 - F(t_c)$ for $F(t_c)$ in (7b). Note that the same formulae for Recall and Fallout are given when the steps are reversed, i.e. when we first select documents by their $t$ values, and then select a subset by their $x$ values; a result that would not be true if $X_i$ and $T_i$ were not independent.

Turning to the bivariate weight method, it is seen that before the Recall and Fallout curves predicted by the distributions $h_i$ can be calculated, the forms of the probability density functions that describe the variation of random variables: $Z_i = \lambda_1 X_i + \lambda_2 T_i$, $(i = 1, 2)$ are required. The means and variances of the variates $Z_i$ can be calculated by substituting (3a, b) in:

$$\left.\begin{aligned} E(Z_i) &= \lambda_1 E(X_i) + \lambda_2 E(T_i) \\ V(Z_i) &= \lambda_1^2 V(X_i) + \lambda_2^2 V(T_i) + 0. \end{aligned}\right\} \tag{3c}$$

Call the density functions of the $Z_i$, $r_i(z)$. Then:

*either* $$r_i(z) = \int_{(z-\lambda_2 A)/\lambda_1}^{z/\lambda_1} h_i(x, s[x,z])\left|\frac{\partial s}{\partial z}\right|\mathrm{d}x, \quad \text{for} \quad \lambda_1, \lambda_2 > 0$$

*or* $$r_i(z) = \int_{z/\lambda_1}^{(z-\lambda_2 A)/\lambda_1} h_i(x, s[x,z])\left|\frac{\partial s}{\partial z}\right|\mathrm{d}x, \quad \text{for} \quad \lambda_1 > 0 > \lambda_2,$$

where $s(x, z) = t = (z - \lambda_1 x)/\lambda_2$; $|\partial s/\partial z| = |1/\lambda_2|$; and $h_i(x, s[x, z]) = f_i(x)g_i([z - \lambda_1 x])/\lambda_2)$. The limits of integration correspond to the range of $x$-values when $z$ = constant and $t$ varies over its range (i.e. $t \in [0, A]$). Note that $r_i(z)$[*first case*] $\neq -r_i(z)$[*second case*], as would be expected since such functions must be positive. To obtain more tractable integrals, the variable of integration is changed from $x$ to $u = x - (z/\lambda_1)$, giving:

for $\lambda_1, \lambda_2 > 0$:

$$r_i(z) = \int_{-\lambda_2 A/\lambda_1}^{0} f_i\left(u + \frac{z}{\lambda_1}\right) g_i\left(\frac{-\lambda_1 u}{\lambda_2}\right) \left|\frac{1}{\lambda_2}\right| du$$

$$= k_i \int_{-\lambda_2 A/\lambda_1}^{0} \exp\left(-\left(\frac{[u + (z/\lambda_1) - \mu_i]^2}{2\sigma_i^2}\right)\right) \exp\left(\frac{\eta_i \lambda_1 u}{\lambda_2}\right) du$$

where

$$k_i \equiv \frac{\eta_i}{(2\pi\sigma_i^2)^{1/2}|\lambda_2|(1 - \exp(-\eta_i A))};$$

or

$$r_i(z) = k_i \int_{-\lambda_2 A/\lambda_1}^{0} \exp[-(a_i u^2 + b_i u + c_i)] \, du, \qquad \lambda_1, \lambda_2 > 0, \qquad (i = 1, 2) \tag{8a}$$

where

$$a_i \equiv 1/2\sigma_i^2$$

$$b_i \equiv (\lambda_2 z - \mu_i \lambda_1 \lambda_2 - \sigma_i^2 \eta_i \lambda_1^2)/\lambda_1 \lambda_2 \sigma_i^2$$

$$c_i \equiv (z^2 - 2\mu_i \lambda_1 z + \mu_i^2 \lambda_1^2)/2\lambda_1^2 \sigma_i^2.$$

For the other case, where the age of the document is to be multiplied by a negative quantity, the densities are:

$$r_i(z) = k_i \int_{0}^{-\lambda_2 A/\lambda_1} \exp[-(a_i u^2 + b_i u + c_i)] \, du, \qquad \lambda_1 > 0 > \lambda_2, \qquad (i = 1, 2) \tag{8b}$$

with $a_i$, $b_i$, $c_i$, $k_i$ as above. When obsolescence is positive, the coefficients $\lambda_1$ and $\lambda_2$ should be chosen so that $\lambda_1 > 0 > \lambda_2$. In that event the effectiveness of retrieval using a weight $z = \lambda_1 x + \lambda_2 t$ is predicted using (8b). Conversely, when the user perceives negative obsolescence, both coefficients should be positive, and (8a) would be used. As can be seen from (8a) and (8b) it is the *ratio* of $\lambda_1$ to $\lambda_2$ that determines retrieval effectiveness, so that $\lambda_1$ can be conveniently put equal to 1. Since the values of $a_i$, $b_i$ and $c_i$ are in general not all positive, the integrals must be evaluated numerically. Once the variation of $r_i(z)$ with $z$ has been so obtained, further numerical integration yields the Recall and Fallout values according to:

$$R(z_c) = \int_{z_c}^{\infty} r_1(z) \, dz; \qquad F(z_c) = \int_{z_c}^{\infty} r_2(z) \, dz \tag{9}$$

for any specified threshold value $z_c$.

In contrast to the "paired measure" approach to system evaluation that has been given for each method, i.e. the usual "Precision–Recall" approach, two other types of effectiveness measure can be readily evaluated using the model. One type is the generalized *system* measure, defined as a function of Precision and Recall, and possibly other parameters. (A general measure of this type has been developed by Van Rijsbergen[13]; an instance of same is the Marczewski–Steinhaus metric, $D = (P + R - 2PR)/(P + R - PR)$[14].) System measures, whether simple or composite, depend on a value for the threshold being specified (equivalent to the retrieved set being defined)[11]. A rather more general concept of measurement is provided by the "language measure", which assess the separation of the mass functions of two variates, and thus describes indirectly the Precision-Recall graph defined by the variation of the threshold over its range. An instance of a language measure is Brookes's **S** measure[15], recently rediscussed by the author[12]. Swets's **E** measure provides another example. To evaluate language measures defined by the moments of the distributions involved, such as **E** and **S**, (3a–c) are substituted in the definition. For **S** we then have:

$$\mathbf{S}_X = \frac{E(X_1) - E(X_2)}{(V(X_1) + V(X_2))^{1/2}}; \qquad \mathbf{S}_T = \frac{E(T_1) - E(T_2)}{(V(T_1) + V(T_2))^{1/2}}; \qquad \mathbf{S}_Z = \frac{E(Z_1) - E(Z_2)}{(V(Z_1) + V(Z_2))^{1/2}}. \quad (10)$$

Brookes's measure, like Swets's measure, is a signed measure. For the usual linguistic weighting functions, both $\mathbf{S}_X$ and $\mathbf{S}_Z$ will be positive. However $\mathbf{S}_T < 0$ [>0] when positive [negative] obsolescence is perceived by the enquirer.†

## 5. THE APPLICATION OF LINEAR DISCRIMINANT ANALYSIS TO THE BIVARIATE WEIGHT METHOD

In Section 4, the Precision-Recall graph was derived for the bivariate weight method, for arbitrary coefficients $\lambda_1$ and $\lambda_2$. This left unanswered the question: "What are the optimim values for these coefficients?", a question equivalent to: "What is the optimum value for $\lambda$ in the weighting formula $z = x + \lambda t$?". (This was proved in the last section, but is in fact an instance of a more general result that a monotonic transformation of a weighting formula does not alter the Precision-Recall graph[12].) One method would be to use (8) and (9) for trial values of $\lambda_2/\lambda_1$, and then to identify the optimum value by (i) the "best graph" (according to some user-specified criterion), (ii) the minimum value of some general system measure, or (iii) the maximum value of a language measure. (In "(ii)" one seeks the "minimum of a minimum".) Of these, "(i)" is likely to prove most satisfactory.

A method related to the last of the criteria just given is linear discriminant analysis, a multivariate technique introduced by R. A. Fisher as a taxonomic aid in "separating" two populations of individuals, the members of which had been measured in different ways (see Hoel[16], for example). The L.D.A. technique is to derive such coefficients as a consequence of the maximization of some measure of separation of the populations; the measure being defined through the probability distributions on the set of values of a *multivariate attribute* of the two populations. The measure chosen by Fisher was:

$$\mathbf{G} = \frac{[E(Z_1) - E(Z_2)]^2}{\sum_{i=1}^{2} \sum_{j=1}^{n_i} [z_{ij} - E(Z_i)]^2}$$

where $n_i$ is the number of documents of type $i$, amd $j$ numbers the documents in each set. Note that **G** is the square of Brookes's measure **S**, and provides another example of a language measure. In order to indicate constancy in the Precision-Recall graph, **G** should be redefined on distributions over ***ranked*** attribute values[12], but this complication is not pursued here. **G** is adapted to the problem at hand by redefining the second summation as an integral (since the model used continuous variates), and although the matter is also not pursued here, it is noted that a deliberate "imbalance" between the two populations can be introduced to reflect the user's exclusive interest in only one of them: the relevant set. (In this regard, taxonomy and information retrieval follow different objectives.) Then:

$$\mathbf{G}(c) = \frac{[E(Z_1) - E(Z_2)]^2}{\sum_{i=1}^{2} k_i \int_{-\infty}^{\infty} [z - E(Z_i)]^2 \, dz}$$

where $k_1 = 2 - c$, $k_2 = c$ and $c$ is a constant between 0 and 2. The suggestion for the imbalance factors comes from Anderson and Bahadur[17], and has been taken up in the pattern-recognition

†It would be perfectly feasible to alter the convention, so that $\mathbf{S}_T$ is negative when obsolescence is negative, but this would go against our intuitive view that the usual form of obsolescence (embodied in the usage of the word) should be regarded as the "positive" one.

literature[18]. Fisher's technique then yields a value for $\lambda$ through:

$$\lambda = \lambda_2/\lambda_1 = \left(\frac{E(T_1) - E(T_2)}{k_1V(T_1) + k_2V(T_2)}\right) \Big/ \left(\frac{E(X_1) - E(X_2)}{k_1V(X_1) + k_2V(X_2)}\right\} \tag{11}$$

in which the values of the right-hand sides of (3a) and (3b) are to be substituted.

The advantage of the L.D.A. appraoch is that it indicates a value for $\lambda$ which is approximately optimum when $c = 1$, and an improved value for $\lambda$ for alternative values of $c$ suggested by experiment or simulation. However given the inevitability of errors in the user's estimates of relevant terms, $1/\eta_1$ and $G$, and in the system controller's estimates of $\mu_i$, $\sigma_i$ and $1/\eta_2$, as well as the general imperfection of the model, it might be sufficient in practice to provide the user with a table of $\lambda$ values generated by (11) with $c = 1$, which he would access through his estimates of $G$ and $E(T_1)$. Improvement beyond that could be through heuristics.

## 6. AN ILLUSTRATIVE EXAMPLE

Following Brookes's interpretation of sample Cranfield data[15],† it is assumed that $\mu_1 = 5.32$, $\mu_2 = 1.17$, $\sigma_1 = 2.00$, $\sigma_2 = 2.13$. These would be estimates by the system controller in practice. Suppose that the user has perceived the average age of relevant documents to be 6 months (i.e. $1/\eta_1 = 6.0$), and that the enquiry's Generality is estimated to be 0.001. The system controller knows, from direct measurement, that the average age of documents in the entire data base is $1/\eta_2 = 108$ months, and the value of $A$ determining that part of the data base that is immediately accessible is 36 months. Since $1/\eta_1 < 1/\eta_2$, the obsolescence perceived by the enquirer is positive.

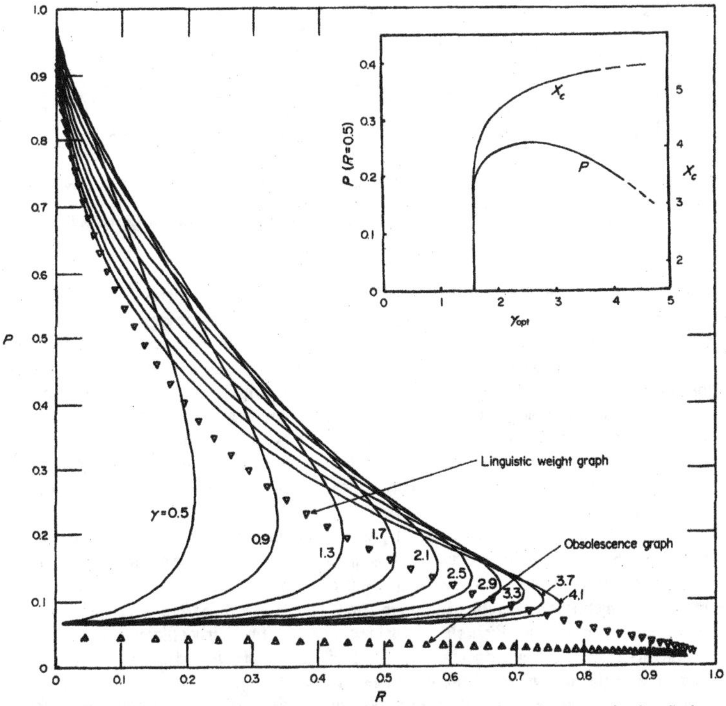


Fig. 2(a). Precision-Recall graphs for the "subset method" of document retrieval, for the enquiry described in the text. The thresholds $x_c$ and $t_c$ are related by $t_c/x_c = \gamma$ for each graph. For comparison, the graphs defined by the use of a linguistic weight alone, and an age-of-document weight alone, are superimposed. The inset shows the variation of Precision and $x_c$ with $\gamma$ for optimum retrieval at a Recall of 50%.

†The interpretation of linguistic weight here is simple level of coordination, so that $x \geq 0$.

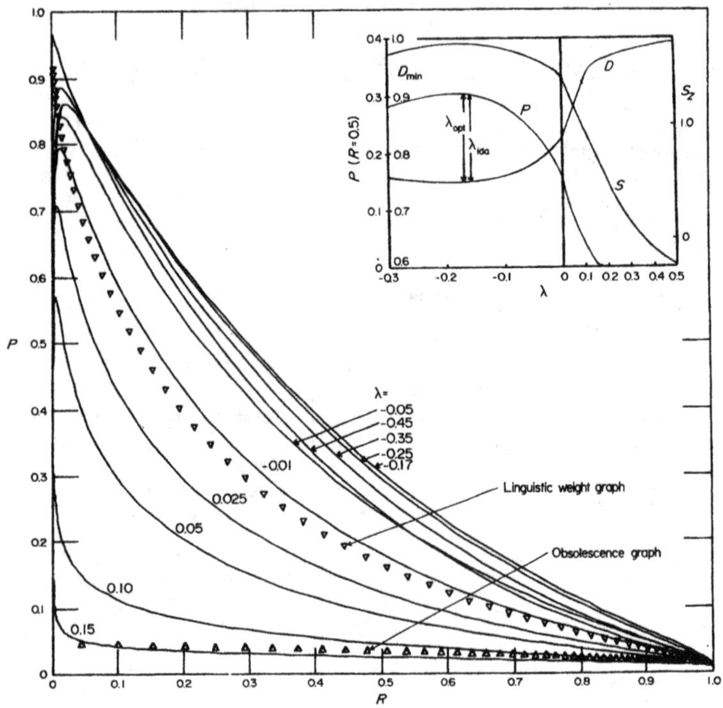


Fig. 2(b). Precision-Recall graphs for the "bivariate weight" method of retrieval. The curves are distinguished by different values for $\lambda$ in the document weighting formula $z = x + \lambda t$. The language and obsolescence graphs are again superimposed. The inset shows the variation of Precision ($R = 0.5$), $D_{min}$ and $S_z$ with $\lambda$.

Then the Precision-Recall graphs predicted by the model for various retrieval techniques can be found using computer simulation, and are as shown in the accompanying figures.

Figure 2(a) shows the Precision-Recall graphs for the subset method, with the joint criteria $x_c$ and $t_c$ related by $t_c = \gamma x_c$, and $\gamma$ has the values shown. As an inset is shown the approximate relation between Precision (at a Recall of 0.5), and $x_c$, and the optimum value for $\gamma$. Superimposed on the Precision-Recall graphs are those obtained using the linguistic weight alone (i.e. using $x$ plus a threshold $x_c$), and the age weight alone (i.e. $t$ with threshold $t_c$). It is clear that an unsystematic method for assigning values to the thresholds $x_c$ and $t_c$ (e.g. in the case where these are casually specified by the user) could easily depress retrieval performance below that achieved using $x$ and $x_c$ alone.

Figure 2(b) shows the Precision-Recall graphs obtained by applying the bivariate weight method. The curves vary with the value chosen for $\lambda \equiv \lambda_2/\lambda_1$, with optimum retrieval over a broad range of Recall values for the value $\lambda = -0.17$. The value of $\lambda$ determined by the method of Section 5 (i.e. by appropriate substitution in eqn (11)) is $\lambda = -0.16$ for $c = 1$, and $\lambda = -0.17$ for $c = 0.9$. In this particular case Fisher's original technique is thus fairly efficient. Inset in the figure are graphs of $\lambda$ vs (i) Precision (for $R = 0.5$), (ii) the minimum value of $D$, for all $(R, P)$ coordinates, and (iii) the value of the language measure $S_z$.

Figure 3 shows two other types of data relationship. In the right-hand column are the Relative-Operating-Characteristic graphs for the four retrieval methods. The distinctive "loop" is characteristic of the subset method when the two thresholds are chosen to be linearly related. (Such a relationship is therefore undesirable.) In the left-hand column are pairs of probability density curves for the variables $Z_i$, i.e. the functions $r_1$ and $r_2$. It can be seen that the

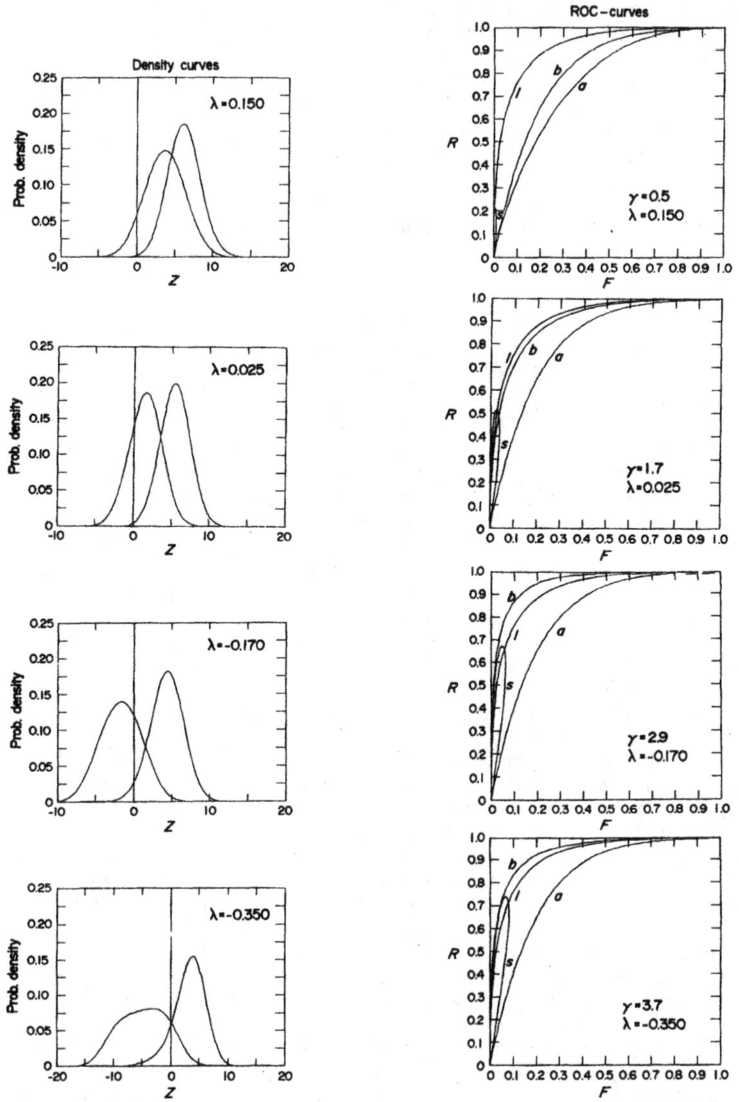


Fig. 3. The ROC-curves produced by the four retrieval processes mentioned in the text are described in the right-hand column. The curves are labelled: *s*-subset method, *b*-bivariate weight method, *l*-linguistic weight method, and *a*-age of document method. In the left-hand column are pairs of density graphs for the variates $Z_i$ ($i = 1, 2$) for different signs and values of $\lambda$.

transformation $z = x + \lambda t$ produces a distortion of the Normal curves for the variates $X_i$, the nature of the distortion depending on the sign and value of $\lambda$, as well as the parameters of the underlying distributions. The separation of these curves is measured by $S_Z$.

Without much more detailed data describing real-life system performance, it is impossible to be more than indicative about the likely effects of using the subset method and bivariate weight method in practice. With this reservation, the following conclusions are suggested:

A. Both retrieval methods can improve retrieval performance. Both can depress it if used unsystematically.

B. The shape of the Precision-Recall graph, for a given enquiry, will vary as between the subset method, with $t_c$ related to $x_c$ by $t_c = \gamma x_c$, and the bivariate weight method where the document weight is a linear function of $x$ and $t$.

C. Use of the subset method, in the manner indicated, renders an interval $[\alpha(\gamma), 1]$ of Recall inaccessible to the enquirer. Use of the bivariate weight method renders an interval $[\beta(\lambda), 1]$ of the Precision inaccessible.

D. L.D.A. yields a value for $\lambda$ in the bivariate weight method which is approximately optimum, but if the estimated errors in $\eta_i$, $\mu_i$, $\sigma_i$ and $G$ justify such an approach a better estimate is given through simulation.

## 7. FURTHER DISCUSSION

The approach adopted in this paper would appear to be only one instance of a general rationale of document retrieval, in which different types of document attribute $x_1, x_2, x_3, \ldots$ are recognised, each of which measures or characterises the relevance of a document to a query, and in which a choice is made between a retrieval method involving a vector of threshold values (and a sequence of subsets of the data base), and a method in which a multivariate document weight of the form: $z = \lambda_1 x_1 + \lambda_2 x_2 + \lambda_3 x_3 + \cdots$ is assigned to each document, and retrieval determined by a single threshold $z_c$. Other variables apart from linguistic weight and age-of-document weight are readily imagined: document language, provenance, or literary form (preprint, report, journal paper etc), for example, or possibly the rank of the source journal in the Bradford distribution defined by some previous set. Given the empirical finding by Fisher and Elchesen that title words and index terms are sufficiently independent to justify their joint use in retrieval[19], several of the attributes could possibly be taken as linguistic weights. Since the guiding principle behind the selection of useful attributes is that of independence, the multivariate weighting technique would appear to be especially appropriate to retrieval from a collection indexed by a faceted classification scheme.

Improvement in retrieval performance arising from a joint linguistic/obsolescence approach depends on the time scope of the accessible part of the data base, as expressed by the value of $A$. For positive obsolescence, the returns in improved effectiveness due to using either method will be small or large depending on whether $A$ is small or large, respectively. The setting of this value in existing information retrieval systems implicitly recognises the value of document age as an indicator of relevance (and also assumes that the obsolescence perceived will be positive), but does so in an *ad hoc* way. Finding the optimum value for $A$, or indeed finding the optimum partitioning of the data base by document age (and other types of document attribute), for a known pattern of user enquiries and relevance judgements, is a management problem which may be aided by the approach adopted here.

Finally, it is observed that (i) whereas the "effectiveness problem" in documentation has often been seen as rather a superfluity—as an area for analysis *after* retrieval has been carried out—both the choice of retrieval method, and the retrieval parameters (i.e. $(x_c, \gamma)$ or $\lambda$), can be made on the basis of a model of user/data base/effectiveness interaction, *prior* to retrieval being undertaken; (ii) the restriction on the $(R, P)$ coordinates accessible to an enquirer, with each retrieval method, suggests that there may be an analogy between documentation systems and classical thermodynamics which deserves exploration. Just as there are states which cannot be reached adiabatically by a thermal system, so an information retrieval system defined by a data base, a retrieval process and a set of relevant documents cannot reach certain states of efficiency without additional information input. The exact analogue of entropy remains a tantalising unknown.

*Acknowledgements*—I would like to thank Miss E. D. Barraclough and Dr. P. E. Lauer for helpful criticism. Mr. J. Chan suggested the use of, and advised on the implementation of, the "GINO" graph-plotting package. Any mathematical or conceptual errors are my own.

## REFERENCES

[1] G. Salton and C. S. Yang, On the specification of term values in automatic indexing. *J. Docum.* 1973, **29**, 351–372.
[2] K. Sparck Jones, Index term weighting. *Inf. Stor. Retr.* 1973, **9**, 619–633.

[3] L. EVANS, *Methods of Ranking SDI and IR Outputs. INSPEC(IEE)*, London, 1973. INSPEC Report R73/18; OSTI Report 5184.
[4] N. M. DIFONDI, *Statistical Information Retrieval System*. Rome Air Development Center, 1969. CFSTI Report AD-697403; the Center's Technical report RADC-TR-69-382.
[5] J. H. WILLIAMS, Results of classifying documents with multiple discriminant functions. In: *Statistical Association Methods for Mechanized Documentation* (Edited by M. E. STEVENS), pp. 217–224. National Bureau of Standards (1965).
[6] B. C. BROOKES, Obsolescence of special library periodicals: sampling errors and utility contours. *J. Am. Soc. Inform. Sci.* 1970, **21**, 320–329.
[7] A. J. MEADOWS, *Communication in Science*, Chap. 5. Butterworths, London (1974).
[8] M. B. LINE and A. SANDISON, "Obsolescence" and changes in the use of literature with time. *J. Docum.* 1974, **30**, 283–350.
[9] J. A. SWETS, Information retrieval systems. *Science* 1963, **241**, 245–250.
[10] J. A. SWETS, Effectiveness of information retrieval methods. *Am. Doc.* 1969, **20**, 72–89.
[11] M. H. HEINE, Design equations for retrieval systems based on the Swets model. *J. Am. Soc. Inform. Sci.* 1974, **25**, 183–198.
[12] M. H. HEINE, Measures of language effectiveness and the Swetsian hypotheses. *J. Docum.* 1975, **31**, 283–287.
[13] C. J. VAN RIJSBERGEN, Foundation of evaluation. *J. Docum.* 1974, **30**, 365–373.
[14] M. H. HEINE, Distance between sets as an objective measure of retrieval effectiveness. *Inf. Stor. Retr.* 1973, **9**, 181–198.
[15] B. C. BROOKES, The measures of information retrieval effectiveness proposed by Swets. *J. Docum.* 1968, **24**, 41–54.
[16] P. G. HOEL, *Introduction to Mathematical Statistics*. 4th Edn, pp. 181–186. Wiley, New York (1971).
[17] T. W. ANDERSON and X. X. BAHADUR, Classification into two multivariate normal distributions with different covariance matrices. *Ann. Math. Stat.* 1962, **33**, 420–431.
[18] D. H. FOLEY and J. W. SAMMON, An optimal set of discriminant vectors. *IEEE Trans. Comput.* 1975, C-**24**, 281–289.
[19] H. L. FISHER and D. R. ELCHESEN, Effectiveness of combining title words and index terms in machine retrieval searches. *Nature* 1972, **238**, 109–110.

# THE USE OF HIERARCHIC CLUSTERING IN INFORMATION RETRIEVAL

N. JARDINE and C. J. VAN RIJSBERGEN

King's College Research Centre, Cambridge

**Summary**—We introduce information retrieval strategies which are based on automatic hierarchic clustering of documents. We discuss the evaluation of retrieval strategies and show, using a subset of the Cranfield Aeronautics document collection, that cluster-based retrieval strategies can be devised which are as effective as linear associative retrieval strategies and much more efficient. Finally, we outline how cluster-based retrieval may be extended to large growing document collections and indicate some ways in which the effectiveness of cluster-based retrieval strategies may be improved.

WE CONSIDER very simple conditions for experimental document retrieval. Each of a collection of documents is described by presence or absence of each of a set of index terms. Each of a set of test requests consists of a subset of the index terms which describe the documents. Both documents and requests can therefore be specified by indexed binary strings. A 1 in the $i$th position of the string indicates presence of the $i$th index term in the document or request, and a 0 indicates its absence. The binary strings we shall call the *representatives* of documents and requests; although where the sense is obvious we shall for brevity often write of comparison of documents with documents, and the comparison of requests with documents, where strictly we ought to write of their representatives. Similarly, where the sense is obvious, we shall write of retrieval of documents by automatic retrieval strategies when in fact document references are retrieved.

It has been determined in advance whether each document is relevant or non-relevant to each request. In response to each request a *retrieval strategy* produces a set of documents. The proportion of the relevant documents in the collection which are retrieved is called *recall*. The proportion of the retrieved documents which are relevant is called *precision*. In practice it turns out that attempts to achieve high recall tend to produce low precision and vice versa. Retrieval strategies are therefore sought which trade precision against recall in some optimal manner. The performance of a retrieval strategy measured in terms of precision and recall we call its *effectiveness*. Effectiveness is not, however, the only criterion which guides us in our choice of a retrieval strategy. Some strategies are more costly than others in terms of computer store and time. This aspect of retrieval strategies we call *efficiency*. In the first section we describe how effectiveness and efficiency of certain retrieval strategies may be compared.

Often it may be sensible to consider more complicated experimental systems than that outlined above. For example, relative frequencies of incidence of index terms may be taken into account in representing documents; differential weighting of terms may be allowed in requests; retrieval for a single request may be carried out more than once, the retrieval strategy being modified in the light of the user's response to the first set of documents obtained; requests may be processed in batches; relevance may be measured on an ordinal or numerical scale; and so on. We have focused attention on a very simple system for two reasons. Firstly, the data-base on which we have carried out our experiments is in this simple form. Secondly, the retrieval strategies which we describe are most readily evaluated and compared with other strategies using a simple experimental system.

The majority of the automatic document retrieval experiments which have been described in the literature depend on comparison of requests with individual documents. The experimental strategy generally called *linear associative retrieval* proceeds as follows. A measure of association between request representatives and document representatives is defined. Associations between each request and each document are calculated. The documents are then ranked in order of decreasing association with each request. Rank positions $i > j > \ldots > n$ are selected, and for each request precision and recall values are calculated for the $i$ most highly associated documents; the $j$ most highly associated documents; and so on. The precision and recall values at each rank position averaged over all requests may be plotted as a precision/recall graph (as in Fig. 4). Some workers have chosen instead of rank positions particular thresholds of the association measure.

As it stands, linear associative retrieval is not a complete retrieval strategy. In order to obtain a retrieval strategy from it we must decide for each request the rank position or association measure threshold at which to select a set of documents. This is the *cut-off* problem. Choice of a cut-off position or threshold may be based on learning from past effectiveness at various rank positions or thresholds. It may involve evaluation by a user of an initial set of documents, or of a sequence of sets of documents, retrieved in response to his request (interactive retrieval). Surprisingly little attention has been paid to this aspect of linear associative retrieval strategies.

Calculation of association values between each request and each document is laborious, and so is the subsequent ranking of documents in order of decreasing association. If the document collection is of size $n$, the procedure has a dependence of order $(n + n \log n)$. Clustering of documents has been used by several workers to increase the efficiency of linear associative retrieval without serious loss of effectiveness. Association values between pairs of document representatives are calculated. On the basis of these values documents are assigned to clusters. Each cluster is then represented in some way, for example by a typical document or by a centroid. A request is first matched with the representatives of each cluster and the best matching cluster is selected. Linear associative searching is applied to the documents in the best matching cluster and may be extended to the next best matching cluster, and so on. In section (iii) we review briefly some of the cluster methods which have been used for this purpose.

The use of automatic clustering of documents which we shall investigate involves a complete break with linear associative retrieval. A hierarchic system of document clusters is constructed and retrieval strategies are devised which match requests with representatives of clusters at successively lower levels in the hierarchy. The cluster with which the best match is achieved is the set of documents retrieved by the strategy.

It is obvious that such strategies will be much faster than any strategy based on linear associative searching. Consider a collection of $n$ documents. Order $n^2$ work is used to construct a hierarchic clustering, and there are ways of reducing this for large collections. We show that in return for this initial investment the retrieval of documents in response to each request is reduced from the order $(n + n \log n)$ dependence of a linear associative search to order $(\log n)$.

However, it is at first sight surprising that cluster-based retrieval can equal, let alone improve on, the effectiveness of linear associative retrieval. Before describing in detail the setting up and operation of cluster-based retrieval strategies and investigating their effectiveness experimentally, we indicate informally (and without rigour) reasons for supposing that document clustering can in principle improve retrieval effectiveness. It is intuitively plausible that the associations between documents convey information about the relevance of documents to requests. This hypothesis, which we call the *cluster hypothesis*, can easily be checked on a particular document collection. For each request we calculate the associations between all pairs of documents both of which are relevant, and the associations between all pairs of documents one of which is relevant and the other non-relevant. The distributions of the two sets of association values may then be compared as in Fig. 1.

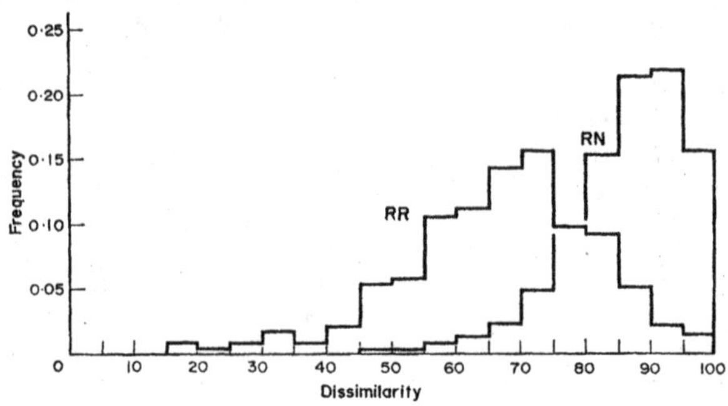


**Fig. 1. Comparison of the distribution of association values between pairs of documents relevant to the same request (RR), and the distribution of association values between pairs of documents one of which is relevant and the other non-relevant to a request (RN). The association coefficient used is described in section (ii).**

Each of the clusters of documents used in cluster-based retrieval consists of a set of documents which are relatively isolated from documents not in the cluster. The clusters are arranged in a hierarchic system in which clusters of highly associated documents are nested within clusters of less highly associated documents (see Fig. 7). The retrieval strategies first match a request with clusters at the top of the hierarchy and choose the best matching cluster *C*. They then match the request with representatives of the clusters immediately included in *C*, and so on, working down the hierarchy until an optimal match is achieved. The effectiveness of this procedure depends on the fact that closely associated documents tend both to belong to the same clusters and (as suggested by Fig. 1) to be relevant to the same requests.

We now outline the layout of the paper. We first discuss the evaluation and comparison of effectiveness and efficiency of document retrieval strategies. Sections (ii–iv) which are fairly technical describe the measurement of association between documents, methods for clustering document collections, the algorithm devised by C. J. van Rijsbergen for implementing hierarchic document clustering, and ways of representing document clusters and setting up search strategies. In section (v) we report the results of some cluster-based strategies on the Cranfield data-base, and in section (vi) we suggest ways in which the effectiveness of our cluster-based retrieval strategies could be improved, and ways in which cluster-based retrieval can be extended to large growing document collections.

The data-base which we used is derived from the Cranfield Aeronautics document collection. It was made available to us by Dr K. Spärck Jones, and full details of it have been published in SPÄRCK JONES and JACKSON [1]. Full details of the Cranfield Aeronautics document collection from which our data-base is derived are given in CLEVERDON, MILLS and KEEN [2]. Its vital statistics are as follows:

| | |
|---|---|
| Number of documents: | 200 |
| Number of requests: | 42 |
| Number of terms: | 712 |
| Average number of index terms per document: | 31 |
| Average number of index terms per request: | 6 |
| Average number of relevant documents per request: | 4 |

The technical symbols used in the following sections are:

$|\ |$ for the number of elements in a set,
$\cap$ for the intersection of sets,
$\cup$ for the union of sets,
$\Delta$ for the symmetric difference of sets.

(i) *Evaluation and comparison of information retrieval strategies*

(a) *Effectiveness.* We denote the set of documents relevant to a request by $A$ and the set of documents retrieved by a retrieval strategy by $B$. *Precision* is the proportion of the retrieved documents which are relevant, that is

$$\frac{|A \cap B|}{|B|}.$$

*Recall* is the proportion of relevant documents which are retrieved, that is

$$\frac{|A \cap B|}{|A|}.$$

When linear associative retrieval is used experimentally it is usual, after ranking the documents in order of decreasing association with each request, to calculate precision and recall values achieved for each request at selected rank positions. The values of precision and recall at each rank position are then averaged over requests and displayed by a precision/recall graph (see Fig. 4). Other effectiveness measures for experimental systems based on precision and recall have been discussed by KEEN [3]. Effectiveness measures of other kinds have been described by SWETS [4] and ROBERTSON [5]. Some of the problems which arise in evaluating effectiveness of operational retrieval systems have been discussed by LANCASTER [6] and CLEVERDON [7].

Cluster-based retrieval strategies have built into them a process analogous to choice of a cut-off position in linear associative retrieval, so that only a single set of documents is produced in response to each request. Precision/recall graphs cannot, therefore, be used to evaluate their effectiveness. It is necessary to find a more general evaluation method which can be used to measure and compare the effectiveness of retrieval strategies.

We seek a measure of effectiveness $F$ which takes real values on sets of retrieved documents. For convenience we bound $F$ between 0 and 1. Denoting precision $P$ and recall $R$, the following conditions on $F$ are self-explanatory:

(i) $F$ is a function of $P$ and $R$
(ii) $F=0$ if $R=0$ (note that if $R=0$ then $P=0$)
(iii) $F=1$ if $R=1$ and $P=1$
(iv) if $P'>P''$ and $R'=R''$ then $F'>F''$
(v) if $R'>R''$ and $P'=P''$ then $F'>F''$.

If $F$ is to be used to measure the effectiveness of retrieval strategies for a user we require it also to be a function of the relative importance which is attached by the user to recall and precision. There are many ways in which we might define "relative importance" in this context. One way of defining it is as follows. We stipulate that a user who attaches *equal* importance to recall and precision is one who when $P=R$ is prepared to trade a given increment in recall for an equal loss of precision. In this case $F$ must satisfy the condition

$$\text{if } R/P = 1 \text{ then } (\partial F/\partial P)_R = (\partial F/\partial R)_P.$$

We define the relative importance $\beta$ attached to recall and precision by a user as the recall/precision ratio at which he is prepared to trade a given increment in recall for an equal loss of precision. In general therefore, we require the function $F$ to satisfy the condition:

$$\text{(vi) if } R/P = \beta \text{ then } (\partial F/\partial P)_R = (\partial F/\partial R)_P.$$

A function $F$ which satisfies conditions (i)–(vi) is

$$\frac{(\beta^2+1)PR}{\beta^2 P+R}.$$

In practice we have used $E=1-F$ as a measure of effectiveness. In case $\beta=1$, $E$ reduces to

$$\frac{|A \Delta B|}{|A|+|B|}$$

which is a normalized symmetric difference of $A$ (the set of relevant documents) and $B$ (the set of retrieved documents). The behaviour of the function $E$ for selected values of $\beta$ as recall and precision are varied is shown in Fig. 2.

Effectiveness of a retrieval strategy is investigated by calculating values of $E$ (for selected values of $\beta$) achieved on the sets of documents retrieved in response to test requests. In practice we usually first calculate $E$ for $\beta=1{\cdot}0$. Corresponding values of $E$ for $\beta=0{\cdot}5$ and $\beta=2{\cdot}0$ can be seen on Fig. 2.

Values of $E$ achieved in response to a test set of requests can be used in various ways to compare effectiveness of retrieval strategies. In this paper we have plotted for each retrieval strategy the cumulative frequency distribution of values of $E$ (see Fig. 3). Alternative presentations include frequency distributions in histogram form and scatter diagrams. It is difficult to find an adequate single measure of overall effectiveness for comparison of search strategies on a test set of requests. The standardized difference between the mean values of $E$ achieved on a test set of requests is not in general a satisfactory measure of difference in overall effectiveness, because there is no reason to suppose that values of $E$ will have distributions of any simple form. The variation distance

$$\int |p_1(x)-p_2(x)|\, dx$$

where $p_1$, $p_2$ are distributions of values of $E$, may be a more satisfactory measure.

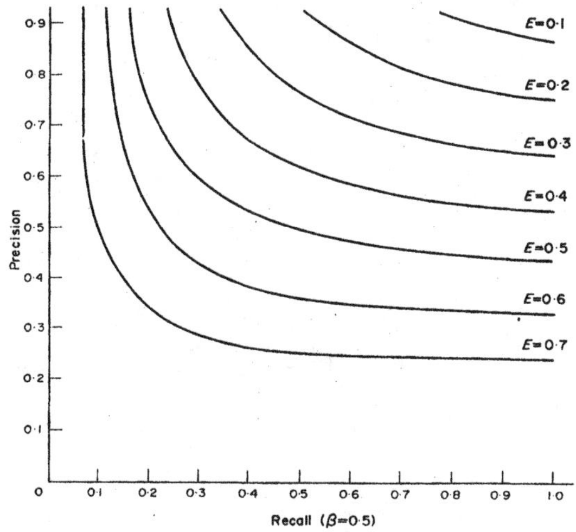

E=0·1
E=0·2
E=0·3
E=0·4
E=0·5
E=0·6
E=0·7
Precision
0·9
0·8
0·7
0·6
0·5
0·4
0·3
0·2
0·1
0
0·1
0·2
0·3
0·4
0·5
0·6
0·7
0·8
0·9
1·0
Recall (β=0·5)


Fig. 2 (a).

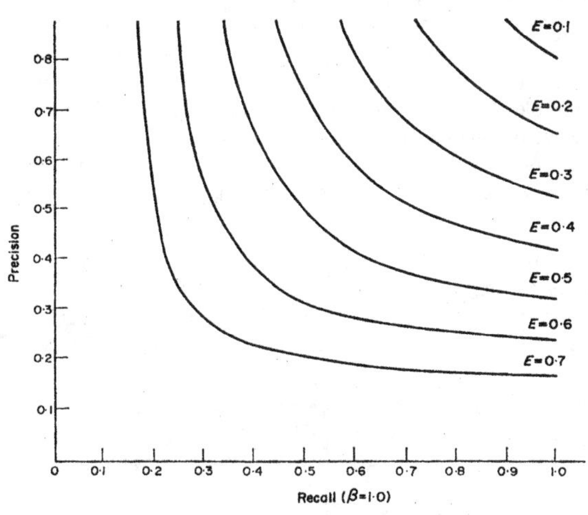

E=0·1
E=0·2
E=0·3
E=0·4
E=0·5
E=0·6
E=0·7
Precision
0·8
0·7
0·6
0·5
0·4
0·3
0·2
0·1
0
0·1
0·2
0·3
0·4
0·5
0·6
0·7
0·8
0·9
1·0
Recall (β=1·0)


Fig. 2 (b).

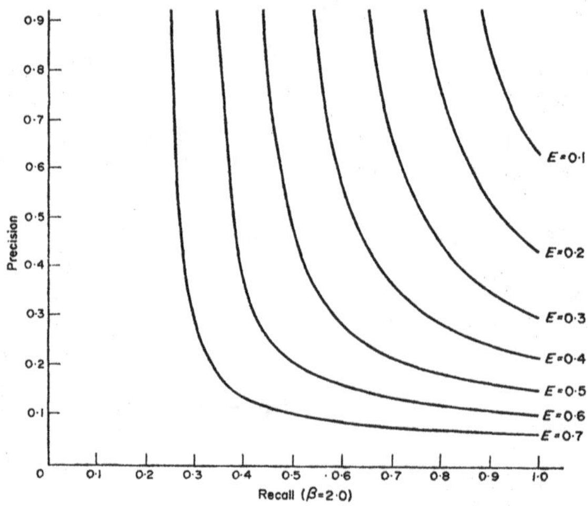


FIG. 2 (c).

FIG. 2. Behaviour of the effectiveness measure $E$ for selected values of $\beta$ as recall and precision are varied. (a), $\beta=0{\cdot}5$. (b), $\beta=1{\cdot}0$. (c), $\beta=2{\cdot}0$. See text for fuller explanation.

It is likewise difficult to find appropriate tests for significance of difference in overall effectiveness of retrieval strategies. Parametric tests are inappropriate because of our ignorance about the form of distributions of values of $E$. Non-parametric tests such as the sign test and the Kolmogorov–Smirnov test may be more appropriate (see SIEGEL [8]). However, it is reasonable to doubt whether any statistical significance test is appropriate. The test requests are unlikely to be independent and it is probably unreasonable to regard them as random samples from a population of requests. The same difficulties arise in comparing precision/recall graphs (see SALTON [9] p. 311).

In order to obtain *benchmarks* against which to compare experimentally the effectiveness of cluster-based retrieval strategies we carried out the following evaluations using the Cranfield data-base:

*MK*1. *Measurement of the maximum effectiveness which is theoretically attainable by a cluster-based retrieval strategy which selects a single cluster in response to each request.* For each request the cluster of documents is selected which yields the least value of $E$ (for chosen values of $\beta$). The method used to generate document clusters is described in section (iii).

*MK*2. *Measurement of the maximum effectiveness which is theoretically attainable using linear associative retrieval at a single rank position.* The single rank position is selected at which the sets of documents retrieved yield the least average value of $E$ (for chosen values of $\beta$).

*MK*3. *Measurement of the maximum effectiveness which is theoretically attainable using a linear associative retrieval strategy.* For each request the rank position at which the set of documents retrieved gives the least value of $E$ (for chosen values of $\beta$) is selected.

The cumulative frequency distributions of values of $E$ achieved by the "ideal" strategies $MK1$, $MK2$ and $MK3$ on the Cranfield data-base are plotted for $\beta = 0{\cdot}5$, $\beta = 1{\cdot}0$ and $\beta = 2{\cdot}0$ in Fig. 3.

It is evident that when equal importance is attached to precision and recall the effectiveness of $MK1$, the ideal cluster-based retrieval strategy, is substantially greater than the effectiveness of the ideal linear associative retrieval strategies, $MK2$ and $MK3$. When more importance is attached to precision than to recall, the effectiveness of the ideal cluster-based strategy relative to that of the ideal linear associative retrieval strategies is increased. However, as progressively more importance is attached to recall than to precision, the relative effectiveness of the ideal linear associative retrieval strategies approaches that of the ideal cluster-based strategy.

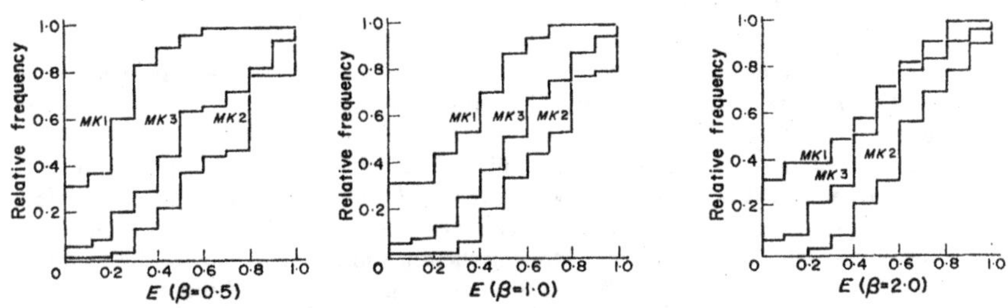


FIG. 3. Comparison of the maximum effectiveness theoretically attainable by two kinds of linear associative retrieval strategy and the maximum effectiveness theoretically attainable by a cluster-based strategy. See text for fuller explanation.

It should be noted that the cumulative frequencies of values of $E$ plotted in Fig. 3 are benchmarks. They set upper bounds to the effectiveness of certain kinds of retrieval strategies. In order to achieve the effectiveness of $MK3$ in practice, a linear associative strategy would have to incorporate an infallible method for learning the optimal threshold at which to retrieve documents for each request. It is very difficult to envisage such a learning procedure. In order to achieve the effectiveness of $MK2$ in practice, a linear associative strategy would have to incorporate an infallible method for learning the threshold which is on average optimal for requests. $MK2$ is a more realistic estimate than $MK3$ of the effectiveness which may be achievable in practice by a linear associative strategy, because it is possible to envisage appropriate learning techniques. In order to achieve the effectiveness of $MK1$, a cluster-based retrieval strategy would have to search the hierarchy of clusters in a way which infallibly finds the optimal cluster.

(b) *Efficiency*. The primary motive in considering cluster-based retrieval strategies is to improve *efficiency* in document retrieval so as to make effective retrieval a feasible proposition for large collections. Cluster-based strategies need substantial initial investment of computer time to construct the system of document clusters. This initial investment pays dividends in reduction in the effort involved at search time in retrieving documents in response to each request or batch of requests.

In Table 1 we contrast the efficiency of linear associative retrieval based on a document file with the efficiency of hierarchic cluster-based retrieval. We have given only rough

TABLE 1. COMPARISON OF EFFICIENCY OF LINEAR ASSOCIATIVE RETRIEVAL AND HIERARCHIC CLUSTER-BASED RETRIEVAL

| | Linear associative retrieval | Hierarchic cluster-based retrieval |
|---|---|---|
| Computer time for generation of data-structure | | order ($n^2$) [this can be greatly reduced for large collections; see text] |
| Computer store for data-structure | order ($n$) | order ($n$) |
| Search time for each request | order ($n+n \log n$) | order ($\log n$) |

estimates of efficiency, because there are many factors affecting the efficiency of an operational retrieval strategy which we cannot easily anticipate from consideration of experimental strategies.

Some of the estimates given in Table 1 require comment. The effort needed to construct a hierarchic clustering is order $n^2$. However, in the final section we show how it is possible to reduce this greatly for large document collections by constructing a hierarchic clustering of a small subset of a collection and allocating the remaining documents to this by a fast allocation procedure. If the total collection is of size $n$ and the clustered subset is of size $m$, the dependence of this method is order $(m^2+(n-m) \log m)$. The storage requirements are self-explanatory (for hierarchic clustering note that the number of distinct clusters in a hierarchy on $n$ objects is order $n$).

Search of a document file requires $n$ operations to compare a request with each document and $n \log n$ operations to rank documents in order of decreasing association with a request. Under certain circumstances the efficiency of linear associative retrieval can be increased by combining a document file with an inverted file (in which documents in which each index term occurs are listed). A single scan of an inverted file can eliminate all documents which share no index terms with a request, and a linear associative search can be applied to the remaining documents using a document file. But, of course, the combined files require much more store. The retrieval time for a hierarchic document clustering using the simple downward search strategies described in section (iv) is of order $\log n$ (see WINDLEY [10] for details of search efficiency for hierarchic structures).

(ii) *Measures of association*

Both document and request representatives are binary strings in which a 1 in the $i$th position indicates occurrence of the $i$th index term, and a 0 indicates its absence.

Numerous coefficients of association between binary strings have been described. See, for example, GOODMAN and KRUSKAL [11, 12], KUHNS [13], SOKAL and SNEATH [14] and CORMACK [15]. We give only a brief guide to the selection of an appropriate coefficient.

Let $X$ and $Y$ be the sets of index terms occurring in two document (or request) representatives. The simplest of all association coefficients is

$$\text{(i)} \quad |X \cap Y|$$

which is the number of shared index terms. This coefficient does not take all the information contained in $X$ and $Y$ into account. The following coefficients which have been used in document retrieval take account of all the information contained in $X$ and $Y$:

(ii) $\frac{2|X \cap Y|}{|X|+|Y|}$ Dice's coefficient

(iii) $\frac{|X \cap Y|}{|X \cup Y|}$ Jaccard's coefficient

(iv) $\frac{|X \cap Y|}{|X| \times |Y|}$ Cosine coefficient, SALTON [9]

(v) $\frac{|X \cap Y|}{\min(|X|, |Y|)}$

Overlap coefficient, SALTON [9].

These may all be considered as normalized versions of (i). In Fig. 4 we give precision/recall graphs for linear associative retrieval on the Cranfield data-base using (i) and (ii) to show the effect of normalization.

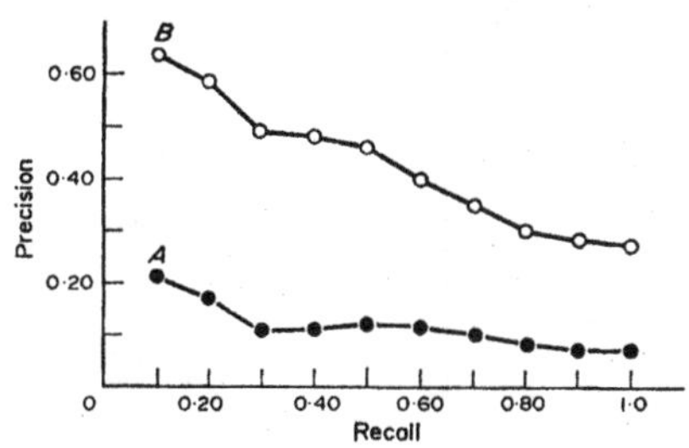


FIG. 4. Precision/recall graphs showing the effect of normalization of the association coefficient on the effectiveness of linear associative retrieval. A, not normalized. B, normalized.

Failure to normalize the association coefficient has an equally drastic effect on cluster-based retrieval. If (i) is used as an association coefficient, documents described by relatively large numbers of index terms tend to form a single cluster.

Some workers have based their choice of an association measure on a model for requests and document representatives. Thus SALTON [9] considered requests and document representatives as vectors imbedded in a $k$-dimensional Euclidean space, where $k$ is the total number of index terms. (iv) above, then has an interpretation as the cosine of the angular separation of two vectors (see also SWITZER [16]). He showed that in linear associative searching, (iv) is more effective than (v). This is probably because $\min(|X|, |Y|)$ is an inappropriate normalization. Other workers have sought to measure association in terms of deviation from independence in the occurrence of index terms in two representative strings [17, 13, 18]. Most of the measures proposed have taken as a null hypothesis independence and equal probability of occurrence of the terms in each string. This is obviously unrealistic. Unfortunately if the unequal probabilities of occurrence of terms and the statistical dependences between terms were taken into account any such measure would be computationally formidable.

The cluster method which we shall apply to measures of association between document representatives depends only on the rank-ordering of association values. Measures (ii) and (iii) are monotone, so that the clusters obtained are unaffected by choice between them. Because of its (slightly) greater computational convenience we have used Dice's coefficient subtracted from 1.

$$1-\frac{2|X\cap Y|}{|X|+|Y|}=\frac{|X\,\Delta\,Y|}{|X|+|Y|}$$

which is a normalized symmetric difference of $X$ and $Y$.

(iii) *Document clustering*

Just as many measures of association have been proposed, so numerous methods of automatic classification have been described. For surveys see SOKAL and SNEATH [14], BALL [19], HARRISON [20], JARDINE and SIBSON [21], SPÄRCK JONES [22] and CORMACK [15].

In Fig. 5 we show some of the kinds of classification which may be obtained from an association or dissimilarity coefficient on a set of documents.

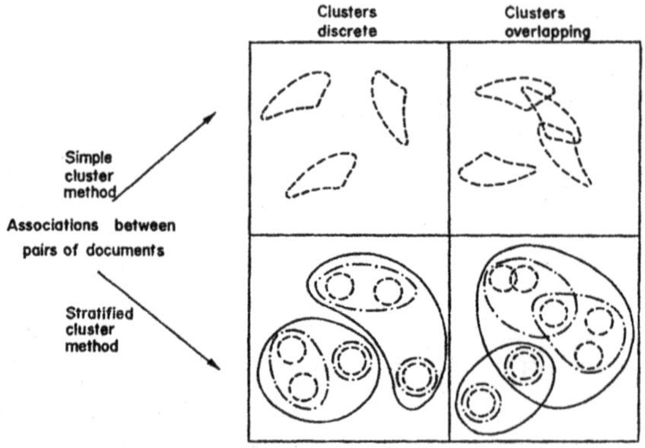


FIG. 5. Kinds of classification derivable from an association coefficient on a set of documents.

FAIRTHORNE [23] and GOOD [24] were amongst the first to suggest that automatic classification might prove useful in document retrieval. Several workers have used simple cluster methods in order to reduce the extent of linear associative searches [9 Ch. 7] [25]. Simple cluster methods have also been used for clustering of index terms in automatic thesaurus construction [26, 1, 27]. Two approaches to simple clustering have been suggested. One approach starts by generating an initial set of clusters and then seeks to improve the clustering by reallocation of objects. The methods of ROCCHIO [28] and NEEDHAM [29] are of this kind. Both methods lead to clusters which satisfy a homogeneity criterion, and Rocchio's method allows initial specification of the number of clusters and bounds on their sizes. DATTOLA'S [30] method starts with an initial partition of the documents and reallocates documents using comparison of document representatives with the frequency distribution of index terms in each initial cluster (the cluster profiles). The algorithm is of interest because of its efficiency. It has an order $n \log n$ dependence whereas cluster algorithms which operate on an association measure have dependence of at best order $n^2$. The results obtained by these methods are not independent of starting point. The other approach uses algorithms which find all clusters which satisfy a cluster definition. The graph-theoretic methods of GOTLIEB and KUMAR [31], AUGUSTSON and MINKER [32, 33] and VASWANI [34] are of this kind. The results obtained by these methods are independent of starting point. BONNER'S [35] method forms initial clusters by the second approach and then allows reallocation of documents so as to adjust the sizes of clusters. BORKO and BERNICK [36] applied factor analysis to index terms and used the factor-loadings of the documents as a basis for construction of simple clusterings.

The cluster methods which are appropriate for retrieval strategies based entirely on matching of requests with clusters are very different from those which are appropriate for term clustering or for document clustering to limit the extent of search in linear associative retrieval. *Stratified* systems of clusters are appropriate because the level of a cluster can be used as a parameter in retrieval strategies analogous to rank position or association measure threshold in linear associative retrieval. Retrieval of a cluster at a low level in the hierarchy which matches a request well tends to produce high precision but low recall; just as cut-off at a low rank position in linear associative retrieval tends to yield high precision but low recall. Similarly, retrieval of a cluster at a high level in the hierarchy which matches a request well tends to produce high recall but low precision and this is analogous to cut-off at a high rank position in linear associative retrieval. *Hierarchic* systems of clusters are appropriate for two reasons. First, very efficient strategies can be devised to search a hierarchic clustering. Secondly, construction of hierarchic systems is much more efficient than construction of non-hierarchic systems of clusters (see JARDINE and SIBSON [21], appendices 3, 4 and 5).

DOYLE [37] and LITOFSKY [38, 39] have described and applied methods for hierarchic document classification. Doyle used a method due to WARD [40] which, like the single-link method described below, operates on an association coefficient on documents, and is independent of starting point. He considered document classification as a technique for organizing and indexing a document collection, rather than specifically as a basis for automatic document retrieval. Litofsky's method operates directly on document representatives without calculation of an association coefficient. The algorithm used by Litofsky seeks to minimize the average number of distinct index terms which occur in the documents in a cluster at the lowest level of the hierarchy. Each cluster in the hierarchy is then represented by the index terms which are common to all its members and which are not common to all members of the cluster immediately containing it. Litofsky applied the method to a collection of 45,000 documents, and showed that the representation obtained is useful for browsing, and could be used to limit the sets of documents searched in response to requests. The method appears inappropriate for retrieval based entirely on matching of requests with clusters.

The single-link method of hierarchic clustering was selected for the following reasons:

1. The clustering obtained by single-link depends only on the rank-ordering of values of the association coefficient on the documents.

2. The single-link method is stable in the sense that small errors in values of the association coefficient lead to correspondingly small changes in the system of clusters.

3. A set of documents in which all pairs are linked at some value $\theta$ of the association coefficient (a *completely linked set*) is never assigned to more than one cluster at level $\theta$.

4. The single-link method produces a clustering which is unlikely to be altered drastically when further documents are incorporated. A new document is assigned to a cluster at level $\theta$ if it has association value $\theta$ or more with any document in the cluster. If a document is assigned to two or more clusters at level $\theta$ they are amalgamated. If it is assigned to no cluster at level $\theta$ it generates a new cluster at level $\theta$.

A full account of the properties of the single-link method and other hierarchic cluster methods is given in JARDINE and SIBSON [21, 41].

The first property is important because absolute numerical values and ratios of values of an association coefficient are rarely significant. There is usually no statistical justification for using the particular values obtained rather than, for example, their logarithms or square-roots. The second property is important because it ensures that the document clustering obtained by single-link cannot be greatly affected by minor errors in compilation of index terms or by minor computational errors in calculation of an association coefficient or in the subsequent clustering. The effects of errors in indexing on values of association coefficients have been discussed in detail by JACKSON [42]. The third property is important because if the cluster hypothesis is correct, completely linked sets of documents are likely to be relevant to the same requests; so that a cluster method which breaks up completely linked sets would not serve as a basis for effective retrieval. The fourth property is important, because it makes it relatively easy to update the system of clusters obtained by the single-link method when representatives of new documents in a growing collection are considered.

The way in which single-link clusters are related to an association coefficient on a set of documents can be pictured as follows. Suppose we select a threshold $\theta$ of the association coefficient. We may then draw a graph with vertices representing documents and edges joining just those pairs of documents with association $\theta$ or more. The single-link clusters at level $\theta$ are the connected components of the graph. (See Fig. 6.)

A hierarchic system of single-link clusters can be displayed geometrically as in Fig. 7. This kind of representation of a hierarchic system of clusters is generally called a *dendrogram*. The level at which a cluster last appears as one moves down the hierarchy is called its

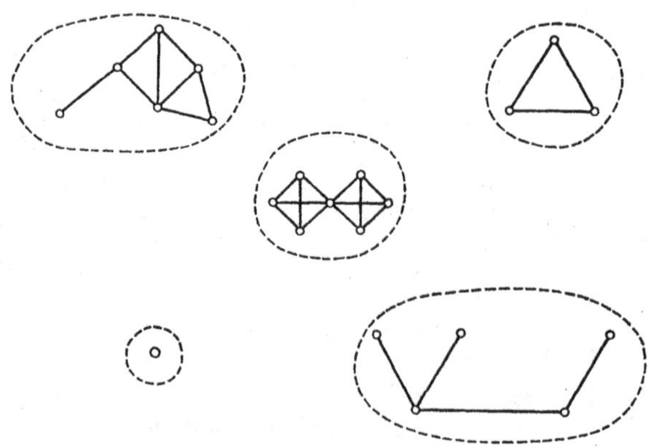

FIG. 6. Single-link clusters at level $\theta$ in a hierarchic clustering displayed on a graph which represents an association coefficient thresholded at level $\theta$. See text for fuller explanation.

*splitting-level.* Alternatively, we may display a single-link clustering as a tree in which each node represents a cluster at its splitting-level. (See Fig. 7.) A tree description is useful both for visualizing the data-structure which is used to store a single-link clustering in the computer, and in formulating search strategies. The clusters which are immediately included in a cluster $C$ constitute the *filial set* of $C$; conversely, $C$ is the *parent* of each cluster in its filial set.

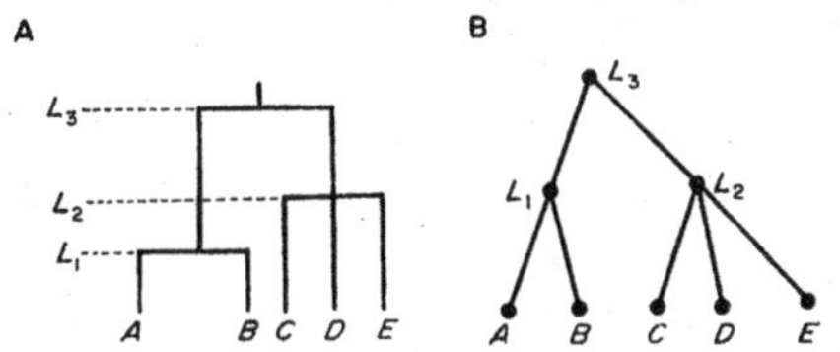


FIG. 7. **A**, a hierarchic system of clusters displayed as a dendrogram. **B**, the same system of clusters displayed as a tree in which nodes represent clusters at their splitting-levels.

In the data-structure (described in Appendix 1) two kinds of information about clusters are stored. The positions of clusters in the system of clusters are indicated by their parents and filial sets. This information is needed for the search strategies described in the next section. The information needed for computing values of a matching function between clusters and requests is also stored.

The DYNALINK algorithm which constructs this data-structure was described by VAN RIJSBERGEN [43]. We given here only an informal sketch of its operation. The values of the association coefficient are considered in a single scan in arbitrary order. At each stage of the operation of the algorithm (except the last) the association values already considered constitute a subset of the entire set of association values. At each stage the algorithm constructs a provisional representation of a single-link hierarchy which is consistent with the subset of the association values considered so far. As new association values are considered, the provisional representation is updated until finally the representation of the single-link hierarchy based on the entire set of association values is obtained.

When a large document collection is clustered, substantial computer store can be saved by implementing single-link in this way. Storage of the entire association coefficient can be eliminated by calculating association values sequentially and inputting them directly to the algorithm. Updating of the system of clusters as new documents are considered is readily carried out by the algorithm.

(iv) *Cluster representation and cluster search strategies*

Hierarchic cluster-based retrieval strategies produce in response to each request a single set of documents which constitute a cluster at some level in the hierarchy. In section (i) we defined a function $F$ which evaluates retrieved sets of documents in terms of recall, precision, and a parameter $\beta$ which measures the relative importance attached to recall and precision. Given a choice of value for $\beta$ we may define the cluster *optimal* with respect to a request as the cluster on which $F$ achieves a maximum value (and $E = 1 - F$, a minimum value). The ideal cluster-based search strategy is that which always finds the optimal cluster. In section (i) we showed that on the Cranfield data-base the effectiveness of an ideal cluster-based strategy is substantially greater than is attainable by any linear associative strategy. In constructing real cluster-based retrieval strategies we aim to approximate to this ideal.

Cluster search strategies are based on matching functions between requests and clusters. A *global* cluster search strategy calculates a matching value between a request and each cluster and selects the cluster on which the highest matching value is achieved. Global cluster searches are very inefficient: substantially less efficient than linear associative searches. The most efficient cluster search strategies are *simple downward searches*. A request is first matched with each of the clusters at the top of the hierarchy (or at some selected starting level) and the best matching cluster is selected. The request is then matched with each of the clusters which are immediately included in the best matching cluster (its filial set), and again the best matching cluster is selected, and so on. The *simple stopping rule* terminates the search when at some stage the best match which is currently achieved is worse than the best match achieved at the preceding stage. The operation of a simple downward search with the simple stopping rule is illustrated in Fig. 8.

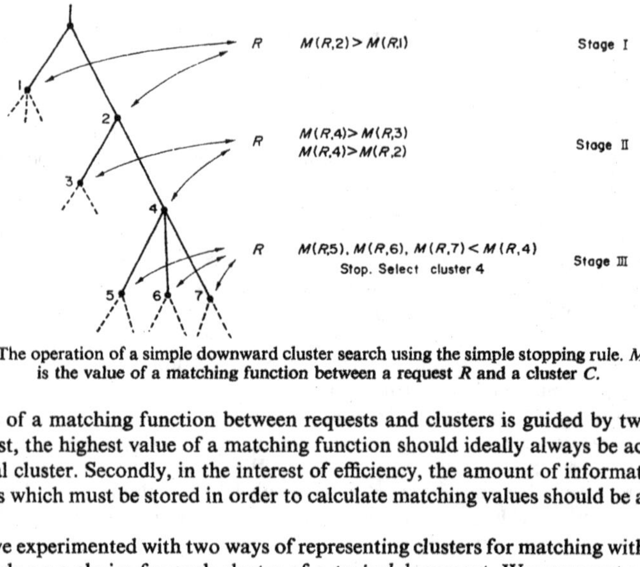


FIG. 8. The operation of a simple downward cluster search using the simple stopping rule. $M(R, C)$ is the value of a matching function between a request $R$ and a cluster $C$.

Choice of a matching function between requests and clusters is guided by two requirements. First, the highest value of a matching function should ideally always be achieved on the optimal cluster. Secondly, in the interest of efficiency, the amount of information about the clusters which must be stored in order to calculate matching values should be as small as possible.

We have experimented with two ways of representing clusters for matching with requests. One depends on a choice for each cluster of a *typical* document. We represent a cluster at level $\theta$ in the hierarchy by the representative of a maximally linked document; that is, a document which is linked to a maximum number of other documents at a threshold $\theta$ of the association measure (see VAN RIJSBERGEN [43]). Where there are two or more maximally linked documents an arbitrary choice is made. (See Fig. 9.) Other ways of selecting a typical member as representative of a cluster have been described by HYVARINEN [44] and by SILVESTRI *et al.* [45] (in the context of choice of a typical specimen to represent a group of organisms). In the other approach the representative of each cluster is some function of the representatives of its component documents. It may also be a function of such parameters of the cluster as its size. The latter approach requires storage of more information about clusters and their members in the data-structure, but in our experiments on the Cranfield data-base it led to more effective retrieval.

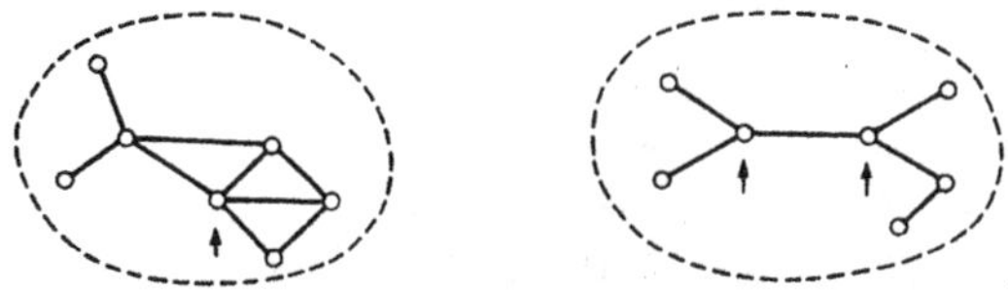

FIG. 9. Selection of maximally linked documents to typify clusters. In the graph vertices represent documents and edges join pairs of documents with association value $\theta$ or more, whether $\theta$ is the splitting-level of a cluster. In cluster *A* there is a unique maximally linked document. In cluster *B* there are two maximally linked documents and an arbitrary choice has to be made.

(v) *Experimental evaluation of some cluster-based strategies*

The data-structure used in our experiments is described in Appendix 1. Our initial experiments using the entire single-link hierarchy achieved very poor effectiveness. At the highest levels in the hierarchy, the majority of the clusters obtained on the Cranfield database consist of single aberrant documents which are closely associated with no other documents. In many cases a downward search strategy retrieved a single one of these documents in response to a request, when all the relevant documents were to be found in a cluster at a much lower level in the hierarchy. The problem of aberrant individuals which form small isolated clusters arises in many classification problems. Such individuals are sometimes assigned to a separate "garbage" cluster (RUBIN [46]). In the following experiments we deal with aberrant documents by truncating the hierarchy at a high level and searching only clusters below this level. Our evaluations of effectiveness are therefore conservative since for each experiment we evaluate retrieval effectiveness for the whole collection, not just for the subset which is searched. The effect can be seen in Fig. 10 which shows the effectiveness of one of the search strategies both for the whole collection and for the subset which was searched. In practice it appears that the best way to deal with aberrant documents may be to reallocate each of them to the cluster below the truncation level which it matches best. We have not done this in the following experiments because there is some doubt whether

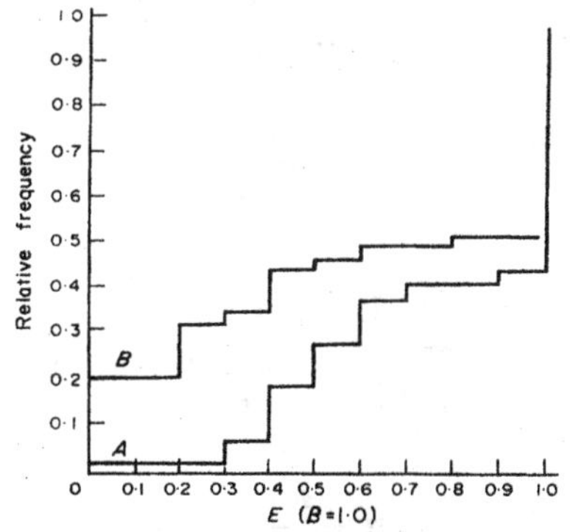


FIG. 10. Cumulative frequency of values of *E* achieved by the cluster-based strategy *E*3. A, evaluated on the entire document collection. B, evaluated on the subset of the document collection which remains when aberrant documents have been rejected by truncating the hierarchy of document clusters.

this would be the best way to deal with aberrant documents for document collections which show different patterns of clustering. On the Cranfield data-base, reallocation of aberrant documents would yield a substantial improvement in the effectiveness of retrieval, but it is dangerous to attach too much significance to improvement in effectiveness achieved by *ad hoc* measures applied to a single document collection.

The cluster representatives used in the retrieval experiments were as follows:

A. By a binary string in which a 1 in the $i$th position indicates occurrence of the $i$th index term in a maximally linked document of the cluster;

B. By a binary string in which a 1 in the $i$th position indicates presence of the $i$th index term in more than one document in the cluster;

C. By a binary string in which a 1 in the $i$th position indicates presence of the $i$th index term in more than $\log_2 |C|$ documents, where $|C|$ is the number of documents in the cluster.

The matching function used with criteria A, B and C is

$$\frac{|X \Delta Y|}{|X| + |Y|}$$

where $X$ is the set of index terms in the cluster representative and $Y$ is the set of index terms in the request representative.

The cumulative frequency distributions of values of $E$ achieved by simple downward searches using matching functions based on criteria A–C are shown in Figs. 11–13, respectively. In Fig. 14 we show the results achieved by a global cluster search using criterion C for cluster representation.

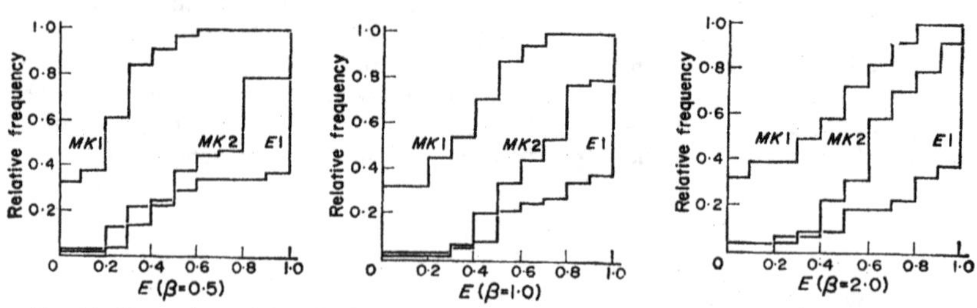


FIG. 11. Comparison of the effectiveness of the simple downward cluster search strategy using criterion A for cluster representation ($E1$) and the ideal strategies $MK1$ and $MK2$.

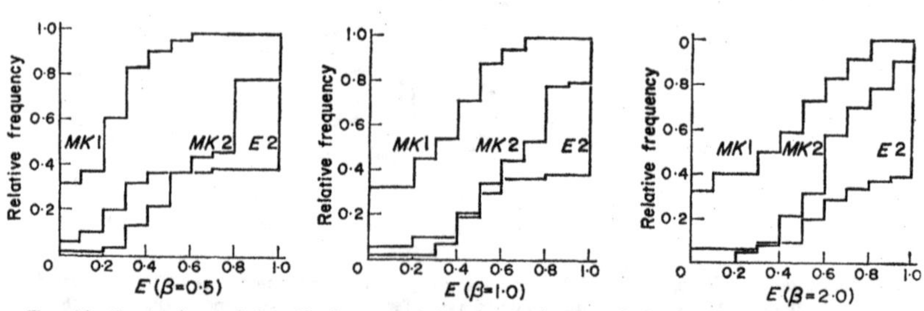


FIG. 12. Comparison of the effectiveness of the simple downward cluster search strategy using criterion B for cluster representation ($E2$) and the ideal strategies $MK1$ and $MK2$.

17

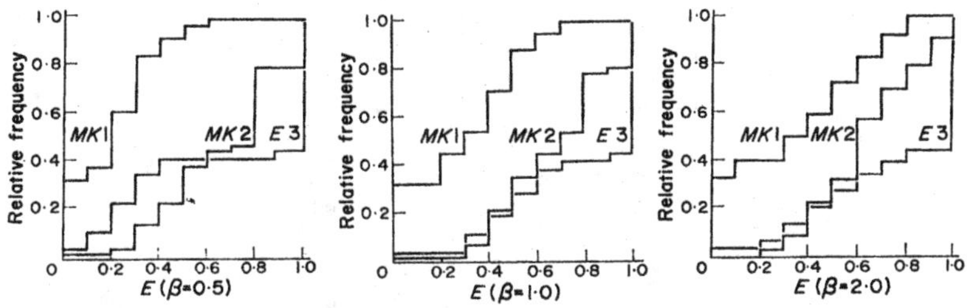


FIG. 13. Comparison of the effectiveness of the simple downward cluster search strategy using criterion C for cluster representation (*E*3) and the ideal strategies *MK*1 and *MK*2.

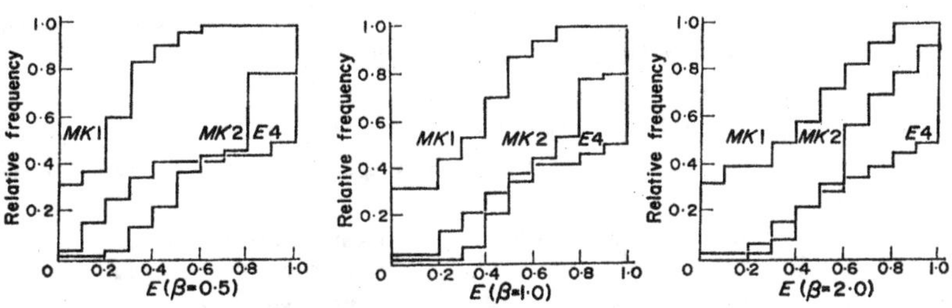


FIG. 14. Comparison of the effectiveness of the global cluster search strategy (*E*4) and the ideal strategies *MK*1 and *MK*2.

In each figure two of the benchmarks described in section (ii) are shown. The benchmark labelled *MK*1 is the ideal effectiveness attainable by retrieval of the optimal cluster in response to each request. The benchmark labelled *MK*2 is the ideal effectiveness attainable by linear associative retrieval with cut-off at an optimal single rank position. To approach the effectiveness of *MK*2 in practice an associative retrieval strategy would have to include some procedure for learning the optimal cut-off position. We have chosen *MK*2 as a benchmark rather than the ideal effectiveness attainable by linear associative retrieval with choice of an optimal cut-off for each request (*MK*3 shown in Fig. 3), because as indicated in section (i) it appears to be a fairer estimate of what is likely to be attainable in practice by a linear associative strategy. In Table 2 we give the mean values of *E* achieved by the various strategies.

The following tentative conclusions can be drawn from the results shown in Figs. 11–14 and Table 2:

1. A simple downward search using criterion C for cluster representation proved to be more effective than the other two simple downward search strategies. This is not surprising because criterion C takes account of more information about each cluster than criterion A or criterion B.

2. Global search using criterion C for cluster representation proved to be scarcely more effective than a simple downward search using the same criterion. The result is, at first sight, surprising, but it is also encouraging. It suggests that the highly efficient simple downward search strategies are appropriate for cluster-based retrieval, and that improvement in effectiveness is best sought by experimenting with more sophisticated cluster representatives

TABLE 2. MEAN VALUES OF $E$ ACHIEVED BY THE IDEAL STRATEGIES $MK1$ AND $MK2$ AND THE EXPERIMENTAL STRATEGIES $E1$–4

| | $\beta=0\cdot5$ | $\beta=1\cdot0$ | $\beta=2\cdot0$ |
|---|---|---|---|
| $MK1$ | 0·16 | 0·25 | 0·29 |
| $MK2$ | 0·63 | 0·64 | 0·58 |
| $E1$ | 0·74 | 0·79 | 0·81 |
| $E2$ | 0·68 | 0·73 | 0·77 |
| $E3$ | 0·64 | 0·70 | 0·73 |
| $E4$ | 0·63 | 0·68 | 0·71 |

and matching functions. This is encouraging because simple downward search strategies are the most efficient possible. Choice of alternative cluster representatives and matching functions can lead only to relatively slight loss of efficiency.

3. All the cluster-based retrieval strategies show greater effectiveness the greater the relative importance attached to precision (i.e. the *smaller* the value of $\beta$).

4. None of the cluster-based retrieval strategies approaches the effectiveness of the ideal cluster-based retrieval strategy $MK1$.

5. The global cluster search using criterion C for cluster representation approaches the effectiveness of the ideal linear associative strategy $MK2$ except when more importance is attached to recall than to precision (i.e. when $\beta$ is greater than 1).

6. The simple downward search using criterion C for cluster representation approaches the effectiveness of the ideal linear associative strategy $MK2$, except when more importance is attached to recall than to precision.

(vi) *Developments of cluster-based retrieval*

We outline briefly some of the ways in which we intend to develop cluster-based retrieval strategies to improve their efficiency and effectiveness.

*Extension to large document collections.* The DYNALINK algorithm described by VAN RIJSBERGEN [43] cannot be applied to collections of more than about 2000 documents, because computation time shows an order $n^2$ dependence. It is, however, possible to construct a hierarchic clustering much more efficiently using a modification of this approach. The single-link cluster method is applied to a sample of the document collection to construct a *core* clustering. The remaining documents are then allocated to clusters in the core clustering as follows. A matching function is defined between core clusters and documents. Each document is then assigned to a cluster using a simple downward search. The efficiency of this method is estimated in section (i). The effectiveness of retrieval strategies based on hierarchic clustering of this kind depends on the adequacy with which the core clustering represents the structure of the entire collection.

The time taken by the DYNALINK algorithm to update the single-link clustering on a set of documents when an additional set of documents is incorporated is a measure of the extent to which the clustering has been modified. If many new clusters are created and many existing clusters are amalgamated, the updating is relatively slow; if the new documents fit readily into existing clusters updating is relatively fast. We may use this fact to find out how large a random sample of a document collection need be clustered to provide an adequate core clustering. Suppose that we select $n$ documents at random from a collection, cluster them using DYNALINK, and then incorporate into the resultant system of clusters successive increments of $n$ randomly selected documents. If the relative extent of modification falls steadily and at the $i$th increment falls below some chosen low threshold, it is reasonable to infer that the clustering obtained when the $i$th set of documents is incorporated is an adequate core clustering. On the Cranfield collection, for example, we have found that a core clustering of 50 documents closely approximates the cluster structure of the entire collection.

Using this approach it would be possible to generate a hierarchic clustering on at least 50,000 documents provided that a core clustering on a random sample of size 500 proved to be adequate.

*Generalization of the cluster search strategy.* Particularly when high importance is attached to recall it may be profitable, despite the loss in efficiency, to use a search strategy which inspects more clusters than does the simple downward search [described in section (iv)].

The simple downward search may be generalized by allowing the selection of a cluster at each stage to be determined by the highest matching value which would be achieved at the $n$ subsequent stages *if* it were selected. Informally speaking, the search strategy looks several stages ahead before making a decision. The simple stopping rule can be generalized by causing the search to terminate only when the best matching value achieved at each of the $n$ preceding stages is greater than that achieved at the $n+1$'th preceding stage. Informally speaking, the stopping rule looks back several stages before making a decision. The fact that on the Cranfield collection a global cluster search did not improve on the effectiveness of a simple downward search casts some doubt on the likely effectiveness of these generalizations.

A different, and perhaps more promising, generalization of the simple downward search strategy allows the search to proceed down more than one branch of the hierarchy whenever at some stage the match between a request and the best matching cluster is only slightly better than its match with another cluster. With this strategy it would be appropriate to retrieve more than one cluster if the highest matching value eventually achieved were approximated by matching values achieved by clusters on other branches of the hierarchy.

*Request expansion.* Automatic classification of index terms based on statistical measures of concurrence of terms in document representatives has been used to generate thesauri. Several workers, notably STILES [47] and SPÄRCK JONES [26, 1], have attempted to improve recall by request expansion based on an automatically generated thesaurus. Some or all of the index terms which occur in the same categories of the thesaurus as the terms in the request are added to the request.

As pointed out by DOYLE [37], a term classification can be generated indirectly *via* a hierarchic document clustering. Each term cluster consists of terms which occur in more than some specified proportion of the documents in a single document cluster. Expansion of requests using a term clustering generated in this way is an appropriate adjunct to cluster-based retrieval and involves relatively little extra computation at search time.

*Improvement of matching functions.* The cluster representatives which we have used as a basis for calculation of matching values between requests and clusters are somewhat arbitrary. Intuition is probably a poor guide in seeking a matching function which will achieve a maximum value in a downward search on the optimal document cluster.

It is probable that the efficiency of simple downward search strategies can be improved by using matching functions which allow numerical weighting of the index terms in document cluster representatives. At each stage in a simple downward search a single cluster is selected from a set of clusters with the same parent (see Fig. 8). Let $C_1 \ldots C_n$ be a set of clusters with the same parent. If $f_{ij}$ is the frequency of the $i$th index term in the $j$th cluster

$$W_{ij} = \frac{f_{ij}}{\sum_{j=1 \ldots n} f_{ij}}$$

is a measure of the *evidence* for selecting $C_j$ from $C_1 \ldots C_n$ given by the occurrence of the $i$th index term in a request. It is difficult to find appropriate ways of combining evidence weights in calculating matching values between requests and clusters, because index terms are not statistically independent.

An alternative way of obtaining index term weights is to use learning strategies which seek an assignment of weights which optimizes the effectiveness of a cluster-based retrieval strategy on test sets of requests.

*Summary of results*

1. Hierarchic cluster-based document retrieval strategies are substantially more *efficient* than linear associative strategies, and theoretical reasons are given for believing that their *effectiveness* in terms of recall and precision can equal, or improve on, the effectiveness of linear associative strategies.

2. A new approach to the comparison of effectiveness of experimental document retrieval strategies is suggested and is related to existing evaluation methods.

3. It is shown that on the Cranfield data-base the theoretical upper bound to retrieval effectiveness achievable by a hierarchic cluster-based strategy is substantially better than the theoretical upper bound to retrieval effectiveness achievable by a linear associative strategy.

4. When applied to the Cranfield data-base, one of the hierarchic cluster-based strategies tested proved to approach in effectiveness the theoretical upper bound to effectiveness of linear associative retrieval at a single cut-off; but all cluster-based strategies tested fell far short of the theoretical upper bound to hierarchic cluster-based retrieval.

5. The DYNALINK algorithm which constructs hierarchic clusterings for use in cluster-based retrieval can be applied to collections of up to about 2000 documents. It can handle document representatives sequentially and hence can be applied to growing document collections. We describe a modification of this approach which could be used to cluster much larger document collections.

6. We outline ways in which the relatively crude cluster-based retrieval strategies which we have tested may be improved in the quest for greater effectiveness without substantial loss of efficiency.

Finally, we conclude that the results reported in this paper should be regarded with caution until they have been substantiated on other data-bases. It is difficult to decide whether experimental evaluations of effectiveness and efficiency of retrieval strategies on a particular data-base reflect properties of the retrieval strategies or peculiarities of the data-base.

*Acknowledgements*—The authors thank Dr Karen Spärck Jones, Dr J. K. M. Moody and Dr P. L. Holmes for many stimulating discussions. The Cranfield data-base was generously made available by Dr Spärck Jones. The work was supported by an OSTI Research Grant and was carried out during the tenure of a Royal Society Scientific Information Research Fellowship by N. Jardine. Facilities were kindly provided by the King's College Research Centre, Cambridge and the Cambridge University Computer Laboratory. We thank Mrs Norma Sober who drew the figures.

## REFERENCES

[1] K. SPÄRCK JONES and D. M. JACKSON: *Inform. Stor. Retr.* 1970, **5**, 175–207.

[2] C. CLEVERDON, J. MILLS and M. KEEN: *Factors Determining the Performance of Indexing Systems*, 2 Vols., 1966, College of Aeronautics, Cranfield.

[3] E. M. KEEN: Evaluation parameters, Report ISR 13 to the National Science Foundation, 1967, Cornell University, Department of Computer Science, Chap. II.

[4] J. A. SWETS: Effectiveness of information retrieval methods, Bolt Beranek and Newman, Rept. 47CAFCRL-67-0412, 1967, Cambridge, Mass.

[5] S. E. ROBERTSON: *J. Docum.* 1969, **25**, 1–27.

[6] F. W. LANCASTER: *Information Retrieval Systems: Characteristics, Testing and Evaluation*, John Wiley, New York (1968).

[7] C. CLEVERDON: *J. Docum.* 1970, **25**, 55–67.

[8] S. SIEGEL: *Nonparametric Statistics for the Behavioral Sciences*, McGraw-Hill, New York (1956).

[9] G. SALTON: *Automatic Information Organisation and Retrieval*, McGraw-Hill, New York (1968).

[10] P. F. WINDLEY: *Comput. J.* 1960, **3**, 84–88.

[11] L. GOODMAN and W. KRUSKAL: *J. Am. statist. Ass.* 1954, **49**, 732–764.

[12] L. GOODMAN and W. KRUSKAL: *J. Am. statist. Ass.* 1959, **54**, 123–163.

[13] J. L. KUHNS: In: *Statistical Association Methods for Mechanised Documentation* (Eds. M. E. STEVENS, V. E. GUILIANO and L. B. HEILPRIN), pp. 33–39, U.S. Department of Commerce, Washington D.C. (1965).

[14] R. R. SOKAL and P. H. A. SNEATH: *Principles of Numerical Taxonomy*, W. H. Freeman, San Francisco, (1963).

[15] R. M. CORMACK: *Jl R. statist. Soc. B*, (in press).

[16] P. SWITZER: In: *Statistical Association Methods for Mechanised Documentation* (Eds. M. E. STEVENS, V. E. GUILIANO and L. B. HEILPRIN), pp. 163–171, U.S. Department of Commerce, Washington D.C. (1965).

[17] V. E. GUILIANO: In: *Statistical Association Methods for Mechanised Documentation* (Eds. M. E. STEVENS, V. E. GUILIANO and L. B. HEILPRIN), pp. 25–32, U.S. Department of Commerce, Washington D.C. (1965).

[18] M. E. MARON and J. L. KUHNS: *J. ACM*, 1960, **7**, 216–244.

[19] G. H. BALL: *Proc. Fall jt. comput. Conf.* 1966, **27**, 533–559.

[20] I. HARRISON: *Metra* 1968, **7**, 513–528.

[21] N. JARDINE and R. SIBSON: *Mathematical Taxonomy*, John Wiley, New York (1971).

[22] K. SPÄRCK JONES: *J. Docum.* 1970, **26**, 89–107.

[23] R. A. FAIRTHORNE: *Proc. Brit. Soc. Int. Bibl.* 1947, **9**, 35.

[24] I. J. GOOD: Speculations concerning information retrieval, Research Report RC-78, 1958, IBM Research Centre, Yorktown Heights, New York.

[25] J. D. BROFFIT, H. L. MORGAN and J. V. SODEN: On some clustering techniques for information retrieval, Report ISR 11 to the National Science Foundation, Sect. IX, 1966, Cornell University, Department of Computer Science.

[26] K. SPÄRCK JONES: *Proc. IFIP Congress* 1968, Booklet G, 5–9.

[27] R. M. NEEDHAM and K. SPÄRCK JONES: *J. Docum.* 1964, **20**, 3–15.

[28] J. J. ROCCHIO: *Document Retrieval Systems—Optimisation and Evaluation*, Report ISR 10 to the National Science Foundation, 1966, Harvard University Computer Laboratory, Chap 4.

[29] R. M. NEEDHAM: The theory of clumps. II. Rept. ML 139, 1961, Cambridge Language Research Unit.

[30] R. T. DATTOLA: A test algorithm for automatic classification, Report ISR 14 to the National Science Foundation, 1968, Cornell University, Department of Computer Science.

[31] C. C. GOTLIEB and S. KUMAR: *J. ACM* 1968, **15**, 493–513.

[32] J. G. AUGUSTSON and J. MINKER: *J. ACM* 1970, **17**, 571–588.

[33] J. G. AUGUSTSON and J. MINKER: *Jl Am. Soc. inf. Sci.* 1970, **21**, 101–111.

[34] P. K. T. VASWANI and J. B. CAMERON: The National Physical Laboratory experiments in statistical word associations and their use in document indexing and retrieval, National Physical Laboratory, Division of Computer Science, 1970, Publ. 42.

[35] R. E. BONNER: *IBM Jl Res. Dev.* 1964, **8**, 22–32.

[36] H. BORKO and M. BERNICK: *J. ACM* 1963, **10**, 151–162.

[37] L. B. DOYLE: In: *Statistical Association Methods for Mechanised Documentation* (Eds. M. E. STEVENS, V. E. GUILIANO and L. B. HEILPRIN), pp. 15–24, U.S. Department of Commerce, Washington D.C. (1965).

[38] H. LITOFSKY: *Utility of Automatic Classification Systems for Information Storage and Retrieval*, Doctoral Dissertation, 1969, University of Pennsylvania.

[39] N. S. PRYWES and H. LITOFSKY: *Proc. Spring jt. comput. Conf.* 1970, 323–331.

[40] J. H. WARD: *J. Am. statist. Ass.* 1963, **58**, 236–244.
[41] N. JARDINE and R. SIBSON: *Comput. J.* 1968, **11**, 177–184.
[42] D. M. JACKSON: *Automatic Classification and Information Retrieval*, Doctoral Dissertation, 1969, University of Cambridge, England.
[43] C. J. VAN RIJSBERGEN: *Comput. J.* 1971 (in press).
[44] L. HYVARINEN: *Nord. Tidskr. Inf.-Behandl.* 1968, **2**, 83–89.
[45] L. SILVESTRI, M. TURRI, L. R. HILL and E. GILARDI: In: *Microbial Classification* (Eds. G. C. AINSWORTH and P. H. A. SNEATH), pp. 333–360, Cambridge University Press (1967).
[46] J. RUBIN: *J. theor. Biol.* 1967, **15**, 103–144.
[47] H. E. STILES: *J. ACM* 1961, **8**, 271–279.

## APPENDIX

### *A data-structure for experimental cluster-based document retrieval*

The data-structure used in our experiments on hierarchic cluster-based retrieval is shown diagrammatically in Fig. 15. The tree represents a hierarchic clustering of the set of objects $\{A, B, C, D, E, F\}$. Each node represents a cluster at its splitting-level in the hierarchy and corresponds to a cell in the data-structure. Each cell is divided into four fields. The first field contains the level of the corresponding node. The third and fourth fields contain pointers which indicate the parent and filial set of each node. These pointers make it possible to move around the data-structure systematically. Only these three fields are used in generating the clustering (see VAN RIJSBERGEN [43]). Note that the level of a terminal node is set to $-1$ to allow clustering at level 0.

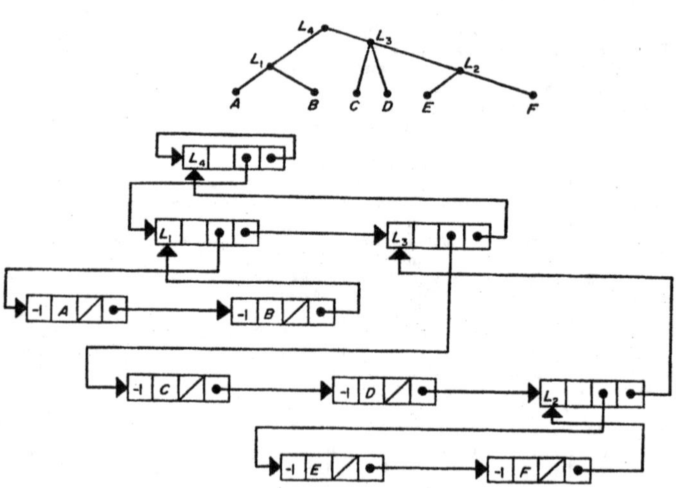


FIG. 15. A data-structure for experimental cluster-based document retrieval.

The second field is used during retrieval experiments. It contains a pointer to the information required to compute a matching value between a request and the node. This information varies in complexity. In the simplest case the information is the binary string representing a document chosen to typify the cluster. More complicated cases arise when the information consists of a cluster representative which is a function both of the representatives of the documents in the cluster and of such parameters of clusters as their size. In such cases rather than compute a chosen representative before an experiment, it is computed at search time. This entails storing the representatives of the documents which belong to each cluster. The pointer in field two now points to a list of cluster members and to any cluster parameters needed to compute the matching function.

We emphasize that this data-structure is designed for experimental purposes. Flexibility in the system is obtained at the cost of extra storage and loss in efficiency. In an operational situation the chosen cluster representatives would be computed in advance rather than at search time. Field two of a cell in the data-structure would contain a pointer to the cluster representative and both the list of cluster members and the dictionary of document representatives would be eliminated.

*Reprinted from* <u>*Science*</u>*, Vol. 168, pp. 335-343, April 17, 1970.*

# Automatic Text Analysis

## Automatic document indexing and classification methods are examined and their effectiveness is assessed.

G. Salton



Over the years, linguists and philosophers of language have deplored the fact that no adequate theory exists to account for many of the important phenomena connected with the natural language. The lack of such a theory has in particular made it impossible to construct linguistic models which would completely and accurately represent the structure of the natural language, and this in turn has led to predictions that computers, which must rely on some model specifying the processing rules, would have only a relatively minor role in the analysis of written texts (*1*).

While remarks concerning the lack of appropriate linguistic theories and models are entirely justified, the many experiments conducted over the last few years in the general area of automatic text processing, including automatic document indexing and classification and automatic text analysis, provide evidence that computer-based text processing is practicable and useful for many kinds of applications. In fact, the indication is that some of the automatic content analysis and text processing methods not only are relatively easy to implement but can be used in an automatic information storage and retrieval environment to produce a retrieval effectiveness at least equal to that obtained by the conventional, mostly manual procedures used in the past.

In this article the principal experiments in automatic text analysis are briefly reviewed, and an indication is given of developments to be expected in the future.

### General Methodology

The first serious work in automatic text analysis dates back to the middle and late 1950's, when Luhn argued that the vocabulary contained in individual document texts would necessarily have to constitute the basis for a useful content analysis and classification (*2, 3*). Several possible indexing methods were proposed by Luhn, including, for example, the following (*2*, p. 315):

> . . . a notion occurring at least twice in the same paragraph would be considered a major notion; a notion which occurs also in the immediately preceding or succeeding paragraph would be considered a major notion even though it appears only once in the paragraph under consideration; notations for major notions would then be listed in some standard order.

Luhn further suggested that the inquirer's "document" (that is, the search request) be encoded in exactly the same manner as the documents of the collection, so that queries and documents could appropriately be matched.

These early ideas were not universally appreciated, partly because they could not be applied uniformly to all query and document texts—many counterexamples were produced to show that a given methodology would not operate under certain circumstances—and partly because the automatic procedures were never adequately tested. Nevertheless, a good deal of work has been done to refine and expand the original ideas, and several operational automatic content analysis systems are now in existence. The following types of operations are often used.

1) Expressions are first chosen from the document or query texts; often this implies the identification or generation of words, word stems, noun phrases, prepositional phrases, or other content units, with certain specified properties.

2) A weight may be assigned each expression on the basis of the frequency of occurrence of the given expression, or the position of the expression in the document, or the type of entity.

3) Expressions originally assigned to documents may be replaced by new expressions, or new expressions may be added to those originally available, thereby "expanding" the set of content identifiers; such an expansion may be based on information contained in a stored dictionary, or, alternatively, it may be based on statistical co-occurrence characteristics between the terms in a document collection, or on syntactical relations between words.

4) Additional relational indicators between expressions may be supplied to express syntactical, or functional, or logical relationships between the entities available for content identification.

The result of such an automatic indexing process is then similar to that outlined by Luhn in the sense that each document or search request is identified by a set of terms. However, these terms may consist of complete phrases which do not necessarily originate in the document to which they are assigned; moreover, each term may carry a weight reflecting its presumed importance for purposes of content analysis.

It is impossible in a brief article such as this to discuss the many strategies that have been proposed for automatic indexing (*4*). Instead, the experimental evidence derived from many of the recent studies in automatic indexing and text analysis is examined, and conclusions are drawn concerning the effectiveness of the various techniques.

### Indexing Experiments

Most of the early experiments in automatic indexing did not include any kind of retrieval test but consisted principally of a comparison between automatically derived index terms and preestablished manually assigned subject categories. Typically, a manually indexed document collection would be taken, and an attempt would be made to duplicate by automatic means as many of the preassigned terms as possible. Three types of studies may be distinguished, depending on the testing device actually used: (i) title word studies, (ii) studies involving comparisons of automatically generated and manually assigned terms, and (iii) studies based on automatic assignment to known subject classes.

The title word studies use as a criterion the similarity between entries derived from document titles and from manually assigned subject headings. Montgomery and Swanson (*5*) used an issue of *Index Medicus* containing title

The author is professor of computer science, Cornell University, Ithaca, New York.

citations in biomedicine cross-filed under the various manually derived subject headings and concluded that, for 86 percent of almost 5000 titles, a correlation existed between the subject heading assigned in *Index Medicus* and the document title ("Correlation" was defined as an actual match between word stems, or a match between rather loosely defined synonymous terms). In a somewhat related study based on use of the chemical literature, Ruhl (*6*) found that 57 percent of the titles examined contained all the important concepts (or their equivalents) listed for these documents in the subject index of *Chemical Abstracts*, while only 12 percent of the titles missed three or more important subject headings. Similar results were found by Kraft (*7*) for the legal literature: only about 10 percent of the document titles examined did not contain any key words useful for indexing purposes, while 64 percent of the title entries contained one or more of the subject heading words included in the *Index to Legal Periodicals*, and an additional 25 percent of the titles contained "logical equivalents" of the subject headings.

While results of this type are not directly usable, particularly in the absence of tests in a retrieval environment, the evidence nevertheless suggests that simple automatic word-extracting methods are not necessarily worthless. Furthermore, the counter-evidence cited by O'Connor (*8*), who finds a correlation between assigned subject headings and title words ranging from a low of only 13 percent to a high of only 68 percent, was produced with a very strict definition of synonymy (that is, the terms were required to be strictly synonymous in order to be considered equivalent) which is not necessarily desirable either for indexing or for retrieval (*8*).

The next set of experiments consists of a comparison between automatically generated and manually assigned sets of index terms. Such term set comparisons are often performed by matching a set of automatically generated index terms with the available manually assigned terms. An evaluation coefficient such as $q$ may be used to measure the amount of overlap between vocabularies, where

$$q = \frac{c}{a + m - c}$$

[Here $c$ represents the number of common term assignments, $a$ is the number of automatically derived terms, and $m$ is the number of manually assigned terms (*9*).]

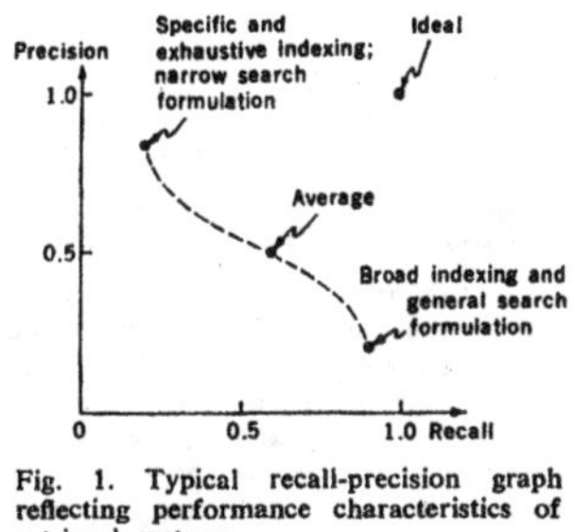


Fig. 1. Typical recall-precision graph reflecting performance characteristics of retrieval systems.

Various tests of this general type have been performed (*10, 11*), and the consensus is that about 60 percent agreement between manually and automatically produced terms is obtainable. In one test involving the automatic assignment of phrases to documents, as many as 86 percent of the automatically assigned phrases were found by human judges to be acceptable subject heads, the "overassignment" (that is, the assignment of extraneous phrases) being of the order of 14 percent, and the "underassignment" (that is, proper content indicators not recognized by the machine) being of the order of 11 percent (*12*). A related approach, consisting of a comparison between automatically derived document affinities based on similarities in the bibliographic citations attached to the documents with document affinities based on overlapping sets of manually assigned subject headings, also indicates a considerable amount of agreement between the automatic and manual procedures (*13*).

The last set of experiments (apart from tests in a retrieval environment) involves automatic classification of documents into subject categories (rather than assignment of index terms to documents) (*14*). This is often accomplished as follows. A *test* collection is used manually to classify documents into subject categories and to compute similarity parameters between a given subject category and the vocabularies of documents contained in that category. These parameters are then used automatically to classify a *control* collection consisting of new, incoming documents (*15, 16*). It is found that, for the original test documents, an automatic assignment to subject categories is about 80 to 90 percent effective (that is, the correct category is chosen in about 80 to 90 percent of the cases). For control items—documents not used in deriving the test parameters—the effectiveness of the automatic classification based on document vocabularies drops down to about 50 percent.

O'Connor (*16*) remarks that the percentage of correctly classified documents increases when more refined classification parameters are used (from 76 percent when key words alone are used to 92 percent when certain relationships between key words are also utilized); at the same time, the number of incorrectly classified items which are wrongly included in a category also increases from 13 to 18 percent. This tradeoff between the number of correct and incorrect responses—as the first goes up, the second goes up also—is characteristic of retrieval system performance.

**Retrieval Experiments**

The indexing experiments described above were not performed within a normal retrieval situation, and involved reliance on criteria supplied by human experts for purposes of evaluation. In a retrieval environment, on the other hand, it is possible to use as a criterion of system effectiveness the ability of the system to satisfy the user's need for information by retrieving wanted material and rejecting unwanted items. Two measures have been widely used for this purpose, known as "recall" and "precision," and representing, respectively, the proportion of relevant material actually retrieved and the proportion of retrieved material actually relevant. Ideally, all relevant items should be retrieved and all nonrelevant items should be rejected; such a situation is reflected in perfect recall and precision values, equal to 1.

It should be noted that both the recall and the precision figures achievable by a given system are adjustable, in the sense that a relaxation of search criteria (a broader search formulation) often leads to high recall, while a tightening of search criteria (a narrower search formulation) leads to high precision. Unhappily, experience has shown that, on the average, recall and precision tend to vary inversely: the retrieval of a greater number of relevant items normally also leads to the retrieval of a greater number of irrelevant ones. When recall and precision are plotted against each other, a monotonically decreasing curve of the type shown in Fig. 1 reflects the average performance characteristic of a retrieval system.

In practice, a compromise is usually made, and a performance level is chosen such that much of the relevant material is retrieved while the number of nonrelevant items also retrieved is kept within tolerable limits. Thus, in what is probably the most exhaustive evaluation of an operating retrieval system involving the use of manually indexed documents (in this case the Medlars system at the National Library of Medicine), Lancaster (*17*) reports an average recall of 0.577 and an average precision of 0.504 (*18*). Additional evaluation results are to be found in the extensive literature dealing with the evaluation of operating, manually based retrieval systems (*19*).

The first comparison of conventional retrieval (retrieval of manually indexed documents) with automatic text processing systems appears to be the one made by Swanson in the late 1950's, using 100 documents and 50 queries (*20*). Three indexing and analysis systems were used: (i) conventional retrieval based on a subject heading index; (ii) retrieval based on specifications provided by words and phrases automatically extracted from the document texts; and (iii) retrieval based on use of a thesaurus in addition to the words obtained from the documents. A measure similar to the "recall-precision" measure was used to evaluate system performance; it varied directly with the relevance weight of the retrieved items and included in addition a penalty factor for retrieval of irrelevant material.

The test results indicated that the average retrieval performance of a system based on automatic text analysis was superior to the performance of the standard system based on manual indexing. Since Swanson provides the first of a long series of results all tending to prove the same point, it is worth quoting from his report (*20*):

> The first conspicuous implication of the result is that the proportion of relevant information retrieved under any circumstances is rather low.
>
> The second implication of the data is the apparent superiority of machine-retrieval techniques over conventional retrieval within the famework of our model. Conventional retrieval was carried out under the favorable conditions of a highly detailed and specific subject-heading list, tailored to a sample library. . . .
>
> It is expected that the relative superiority of machine text searching to conventional retrieval will become greater with subsequent experimentation as retrieval aids for text searching are improved, whereas no clear procedure is in evidence which will guarantee improvement of the conventional system. . . . Thus even though machines may never enjoy more than a partial success in library indexing, a small suspicion might justifiably be entertained that people are even less promising.

In view of the test results produced by far more extensive experimentation reported below, these prophesies appear to have been remarkably accurate.

Swanson's original results were confirmed in an extension of the test in which, for the first time, natural-language queries were used (instead of manually constructed query formulations) (*21*). Documents were retrieved in decreasing order of similarity to the queries, the similarity score for an article being computed by summing the weights of those words in the article which coincided with the query words. With such a ranked list of retrieved documents, it is then possible to compute recall and precision values following the retrieval of each document (or each *n*th document); this produces a sequence of recall-precision pairs which can be plotted as a curve similar to that of Fig. 1. Swanson concludes his study by stating (*21*):

> . . . though these results [that automatic text processing using an automatic thesaurus is more accurate than the human process of assigning appropriate subject index terms to documents and queries] may violate one's sense of intuition, there is no good theoretical reason to believe that they ought to have come out differently.

Various later studies also included elements of automatic text analysis, including full text search (*22*), the use of phrase dictionaries and syntactic analysis procedures (*23, 24*), statistical term associations (*25, 26*), and automatically constructed term groupings (thesauri) (*27*). In each case the intent is to show that one or another of the proposed automatic language analysis methods operates more successfully than either a manual indexing process or an automatic process based on a less sophisticated approach. In general, the case is made that the use of manually constructed thesauri or of automatic term associations or term groups is useful in a retrieval environment. [In the one case where an automatic phrase-matching procedure appeared not to produce reasonable results, the test conditions were peculiar, since the texts processed in the experiment were not the same as those used to determine the relevance of a given document to a query (*24*); furthermore, retrieval appears to have been based on the presence, or absence, of a single matching phrase or sentence fragment, so the test results are difficult to interpret effectively.]

Most of these studies are somewhat fragmentary, and a detailed report of their findings is not given here. Instead, the test environment and results of the Aslib-Cranfield and SMART retrieval experiments, both of which include a large range of automatic text analysis methods, are described in some detail in the next section.

## Retrieval System Evaluation

The work described above generally consists in implementing a particular type of text analysis process, and in testing it through use of a sample document collection and a set of sample queries. Both the Cranfield experiments, undertaken in England by Cleverdon and his associates, and the SMART project, based at Cornell and Harvard universities, have gone beyond that in the sense that a whole range of automatic text analysis methods were systematically tested, and that, at least in the case of SMART, the experimentation was extended to many different document collections in diverse fields, including documentation, computer engineering, aerodynamics, and medicine.

The Cranfield II experiments [not to be confused with the earlier Cranfield I tests designed to compare four conventional systems based on manual indexing (*28*)] were designed to measure a large variety of index-language "devices" that are potentially useful in the representation of document content. These devices include the use of synonym dictionaries, hierarchical subject classifications, phrase assignment methods, and many others. All the indexing tasks were performed manually by trained indexers, starting with the simple "single term" methods and proceeding to more complex methods involving use of a controlled vocabulary and various types of dictionaries. The indexing rules were carefully specified in each case, and were always based initially on the text of the documents or of the queries; the indexers were therefore simulating potential machine operations, and the evaluation results may thus be applicable to automatic indexing procedures.

A collection of 1400 documents in aerodynamics was available (the Cranfield collection) together with 279 search requests prepared by aerody-

Table 1. Order of effectiveness of three types of indexing languages. [Adapted from Cleverdon and Keen (*31*, fig. 8.1 T, p. 253)]

| Type of indexing language | Rank orders for methods using indexing language | Average score for language |
|---|---|---|
| Single terms: content words manually chosen from full document | 1, 2, 3, 4, 5, 6, 7, 12 | 64.15 |
| Controlled terms: single terms modified by look-up in manually constructed thesaurus or authority list | 10, 11, 15, 17, 18, 19 | 60.34 |
| Simple concepts: single terms concatenated into standard noun phrases reflective of document content | 8, 9, 21, 22, 23, 24, 25, 26, 27, 28, 29, 30, 31, 32, 33 | 54.55 |

namicists. Three main indexing languages were tested, known respectively as "single terms," "controlled terms," and "simple concepts." The single terms are content words chosen from document texts; controlled terms are single terms modified by "look-up" in a manually constructed subject authority list; and simple concepts are terms concatenated to form phrases. The test consisted in determining the retrieval effectiveness of these languages when used with the indexing devices referred to above. It was expected that some linguistic devices (the "recall devices"), including synonym dictionaries, concept associations, and term hierarchies, would broaden document and query identifications, thereby improving recall, while others (the "precision devices"), such as the assignment of term weights and the specification of relational indicators between terms, would narrow the content identifications, or make them more specific, thereby improving precision.

The evaluation process was based on a computation of recall and precision measures at various "coordination levels" (*29*)—that is, for various degrees of matching between queries and documents—followed by an averaging of results over all the search requests used. The output was then presented as a set of recall-precision tables and graphs. In addition, a global "normalized recall" measure, consisting, for each system, of a single value, computed in a manner somewhat analogous to computation of the "normalized" measures used in the SMART system (*30*), was used to rank the various systems in decreasing order of effectiveness. The detailed retrieval results (*31, 32*) cannot be reproduced here. However, a summary of the main results is contained in Table 1 where the three language types are arranged in decreasing order of effectiveness according to the average normalized recall score obtained.

It may be seen from Table 1 that the simple, uncontrolled indexing language involving single terms produces the best retrieval performance, while the controlled vocabulary and the phrases (simple concepts) furnish increasingly worse results. To quote from Cleverdon and Keen (*31*):

> . . . quite the most astonishing and seemingly inexplicable conclusion that arises from the project is that the single term index languages are superior to any other type . . .
>
> . . . of the six controlled term index language; . . . on the other hand, the single gave the best performance . . . as narrower, broader, or related terms are brought in, ranking orders . . . decrease . . .
>
> . . . the conceptual terms of the simple concept (phrase) index languages were over-specific when used in natural language; . . . on the other hand, the single terms appear to have been near the correct level of specificity; only to the relatively small extent of grouping true synonyms (using a synonym dictionary) and word forms (using a suffix cut-off process to generate word stems) could any improvement in performance be obtained. . . .

In other words, the surprising conclusion is that, on the average, the simplest indexing procedures which identify a given document or query by a set of terms, weighted or unweighted, obtained from document or query texts are also the most effective. Of the many procedures tried in an attempt to increase recall or precision, only the use of a synonym dictionary which groups related terms into concept classes produces a better performance than the original, unmodified terms. It goes without saying that single term indexing is easier to implement automatically than the more sophisticated, seemingly less effective alternatives.

One might be tempted to dismiss the Cranfield results by ascribing them to some peculiar test conditions were it not for the fact that the extensive evaluation work carried out for some years with the SMART system points in the same direction (*33, 34*). The SMART system is an experimental, fully automatic document retrieval system, operating with an IBM 7094 and a 360/65 computer. Unlike most other computer-based retrieval systems, the SMART system does not rely on manually assigned key words or index terms for the identification of documents and search requests, nor does it use primarily the frequency of occurrence of certain words or phrases included in the texts of documents. Instead, an attempt is made to go beyond simple word-matching procedures by using various intellectual aids in the form of synonym dictionaries, hierarchical arrangements of subject identifiers, statistical and syntactic phrase-generation methods, and the like, in order to obtain the content identifications useful for the retrieval process.

The following facilities incorporated into the SMART system for document analysis appear of principal interest.

1) A system for separating English words into stems and affixes (the so-called suffix "s" and stem thesaurus methods) used to construct document identifications consisting of the stems of words contained in the documents. Such a stem analysis is, preferably, applied only to those words whose frequency of occurrence in a given document is unexpectedly high, as compared with their frequency of occurrence in the literature at large (*10, 25*).

2) A synonym dictionary, or thesaurus, which can be used to recognize synonyms by replacing each word stem by one or more "concept" numbers; these concept numbers then serve as content identifiers, instead of the original word stem.

3) A hierarchical arrangement of the concepts included in the thesaurus which makes it possible, given any concept number, to find its "parents" in the hierarchy, its "sons," its "brothers," and any of a set of possible cross references. The hierarchy can be used to obtain more general content identifiers than the ones originally given (by going *up* in the hierarchy), more specific ones (by going *down*), and a set of related ones (by picking up brothers and cross-references) (*33*).

4) Statistical association procedures which use similarity coefficients based on term co-occurrences within the sentences of a document, or within the documents of a collection, to determine the "associated" terms. Such association methods then produce for each term a "profile" of associated terms, from which in turn a second-order profile containing still further associations

can be obtained, and so on (*35*); the original terms and their associations may then be used for content identification.

5) Syntactic analysis methods which make it possible to compare the syntactically analyzed sentences of documents and search requests. The syntactic analysis used to identify the phrases or sentence structures to be matched may be formal in the sense that it is based on a complete phrase structure or transformational grammar of the language, or the analysis may be of an ad hoc nature, based principally on recognition of certain function words from which prepositional and other phrases are then derivable (*36*).

6) Statistical phrase-matching methods which operate like the syntactic phrase procedures—that is, through use of a dictionary to identify phrases used as content identifiers. However, no syntactic analysis is performed in this case, and phrases are defined as equivalent if the phrase components match, regardless of the syntactic relationships between components.

7) A dictionary system, designed to revise the several dictionaries included in the system, such as the word stem dictionary, the word suffix dictionary, the common word dictionary (for terms to be deleted during analysis), the thesaurus (synonym dictionary), and the statistical and syntactic phrase dictionaries.

8) An automatic document classification system which groups documents with similar content identifiers into document clusters in such a way that a given file search can be confined to certain document clusters instead of being extended to the complete file.

9) A user feedback system which modifies document and query identifiers, on the basis of information supplied by the customers during the search process (*37*).

Stored documents and search requests are processed by the SMART system, without any prior manual analysis, by one of several dozen combinations of these and other automatic content analysis methods, and those documents which most nearly match a given search request are extracted from the document file in answer to each request.

In Table 2, a sample analysis produced by the SMART system, with a thesaurus process, is shown for query Q 13 B. The original query text is given, together with the resulting set of weighted (*38*) concept numbers (terms). Listed opposite each concept number is a sample of the terms appearing in the thesaurus under that concept category.

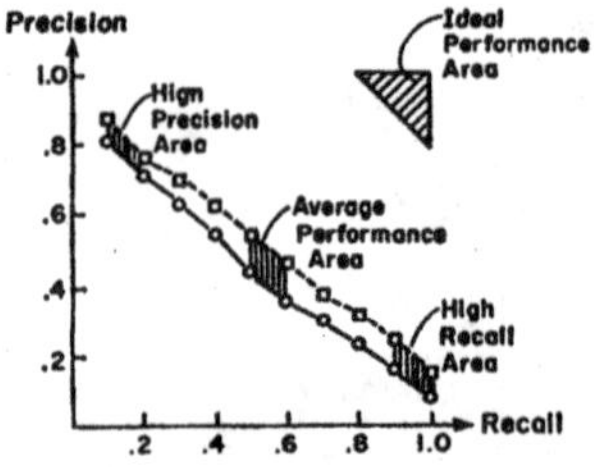


Fig. 2. Recall-precision graph illustrating word stem and thesaurus performance (averages for 780 Institute of Radio Engineers documents). (Circles) Word stem; (squares) thesaurus-3.

The SMART system organization makes it possible to evaluate the effectiveness of the various processing methods by comparing the output obtained from a number of different runs. This is achieved by processing the same search requests against the same document collections several times, while making selected changes in the analysis procedures between runs. By comparing the performance of the search requests under different processing conditions, it is possible to determine the relative effectiveness of the various analysis methods. The evaluation is then performed by averaging performance over many search requests and plotting recall-precision graphs of the type shown in Fig. 1. The effectiveness of a given method is reflected by the nearness of the corresponding curve to the upper right-hand corner of the graph, where both recall and precision are high.

Extensive evaluation results obtained with the SMART system have been published for collections in computer engineering, medicine, documentation, and aerodynamics (*33, 39, 40*). In each case, recall-precision graphs are drawn for the performance of two or more analysis and search procedures, averaged over many search requests, and the statistical significance of the differences in performance for any two methods is computed. A typical example, showing differences in performance for an antomatic word stem analysis and an analysis involving use of a stored synonym dictionary (or thesaurus) to transform weighted word stems into weighted thesaurus classes is shown in Fig. 2. It may be seen that, for the collection of 780 documents in computer engineering used with 35 search requests, the synonym recognition afforded by the thesaurus produces an increase in precision of about 10 percent for any given recall point.

Table 2. Thesaurus analysis for English query Q 13 B: "In what ways are computer systems being applied to research in the field of the belles lettres? Has machine analysis of language proved useful, for instance, in determining probable authorship of anonymous works or in compiling concordances?"

| Concept Nos. | Weight | Sample terms in thesaurus category |
|---|---|---|
| 3 | 12 | Computer, processor |
| 19 | 12 | Automatic, semiautomatic |
| 33 | 12 | Analyze, analysis, etc. |
| 49 | 12 | Compendium, compile |
| 65 | 12 | Authorship, originator |
| 147 | 12 | Discourse, language |
| 207 | 12 | Area, branch, field |
| 267 | 12 | Concordance, KWIC† |
| 345 | 12 | Bell |
| * | | Anonymous, lettres |

*Query terms not found in thesaurus. †KWIC, "Key Word in Context."

It is not possible to reproduce here in detail the evaluation results obtained for many hundreds of runs. A few quotations from the published conclusions (slightly paraphrased to avoid introducing new terms not otherwise needed) may suffice (*40*, pp. 33–34).

> The order of merit is generally the same for all three collections [that is, computer engineering, aerodynamics, and documentation].
>
> The use of unweighted terms [weights restricted to 1 for terms that are present, and 0 for those that are absent] is always less effective than the use of weighted terms.
>
> The use of document titles alone is always less effective for content analysis purposes than the use of full document abstracts.
>
> The thesaurus process involving synonym recognition always performs more effectively than the word stem methods where synonyms and other word relations are not recognized.
>
> The thesaurus and statistical phrase methods are substantially equivalent in performance; other dictionaries, including term hierarchies and syntactic phrases, perform less well.

These results indicate that, in automatic content analysis systems, weighted terms should be used, derived from document excerpts whose length is at least equivalent to that of a document abstract. Furthermore, synonym dictionaries should be incorporated whereever they are available. The principal conclusions reached by the Cranfield project are also borne out by the SMART studies: that phrase languages are not substantially superior to single terms as indexing devices, and that sophisticated analysis tools are less effective than had been expected.

## Comparison of Automatic and Manual Indexing

The evaluation results described in the preceding section appear to raise as many questions as they answer. (i) What is the explanation for the finding, the reverse of what intuition leads one to expect, that simple automatic term extraction, combined with weighting and dictionary "look-up" methods, apparently produces a higher retrieval effectiveness than more sophisticated, semantically more complete, content analysis procedures such as complete word recognition, identification of pronoun referents, and analysis across sentence boundaries? (ii) How do the simple automatic indexing methods compare with conventional methods based on manual term assignment? (iii) How can the automatic procedures be improved (given that the performance range exemplified by the output of Fig. 2 is not as high as one would hope)? (iv) How would the automatic indexing process cope with the practical problems of automatic document input and of foreign language processing? (v) What is likely to be the future of automatic document processing? These questions are now treated in order.

The problem of rationalizing research results different from those one intuitively expects is always a difficult one. In the present case, however, some reasonable arguments are readily available.

First, it must be remembered that the problem of automatic documentation is not comparable to automatic translation or to automatic question answering, in that a retrieval system is designed only to lead a user to items likely to be related to the subject in which he is interested. A somewhat gross rendition of document content, consisting mostly of the more salient features, may therefore be perfectly adequate, in place of the line-by-line type of analysis needed, for example, for translation.

Second, a retrieval system is designed to serve a large, sometimes heterogeneous user population. Since users may have different needs and aims, and since their search requests may range from survey or tutorial type questions to very detailed analytical queries, an excessively specific analysis may be too specialized for most users.

Finally, in the evaluation procedures used to judge retrieval effectiveness, a performance criterion averaged over many search requests is used. This implies that analysis methods whose overall performance is moderately successful are given preference over possibly more sophisticated procedures which may operate excellently for certain queries but far less well for others. In practice, it may turn out that, for each query, a specific type of sophisticated analysis will be optimal, whereas, for the average query, the simpler type of indexing is best.

In explaining the test results, one might also argue that the evaluation results are inherently untrustworthy, first because they were obtained with small collections, often outside an accepted user environment and, second, because the recall and precision results are unreliable since they are based on subjective judgments of the relevance of the documents to the queries. Concerning the first point, it can be said that, although the tests were in fact conducted with collections of small size (less than 1500 documents each), the evaluation results are remarkably consistent over many collections in diverse subject areas; furthermore, the total test environment has included several thousand documents and several hundred queries. There is therefore no likelihood that such consistent results could have occurred by chance.

The second point appears, on the surface, more serious. It is a fact that recall and precision measures require a prior determination of relevance; that is, for each query it is necessary first to identify the set of relevant and nonrelevant items before the evaluation measures can be generated. Relevance assessments must be made by human subjects—preferably by the requester himself—and they will vary from one assessor to another. Studies of the relevance assessment process have indicated that the overall agreement between assessors may not be greater than about 30 percent (*41, 42*). Nevertheless, the conclusion that the recall and precision values are therefore unreliable is unwarranted. In fact, a recent study performed with four different sets of relevance assessments and a collection of 1200 documents in library science has shown that the average recall and precision curves are almost identical, even though the relevance sets are completely dissimilar. The explanation is that, for those documents which are most similar to the queries and which are therefore retrieved early in the search, the assessments are in almost perfect agreement; these documents are also the ones which principally determine the shape of the recall-precision curves in the nonzero regions, and which are therefore responsible for the relative invariance of the test results (*42*).

It appears, then, that reasonable arguments can be furnished to support the principal test conclusions, and that

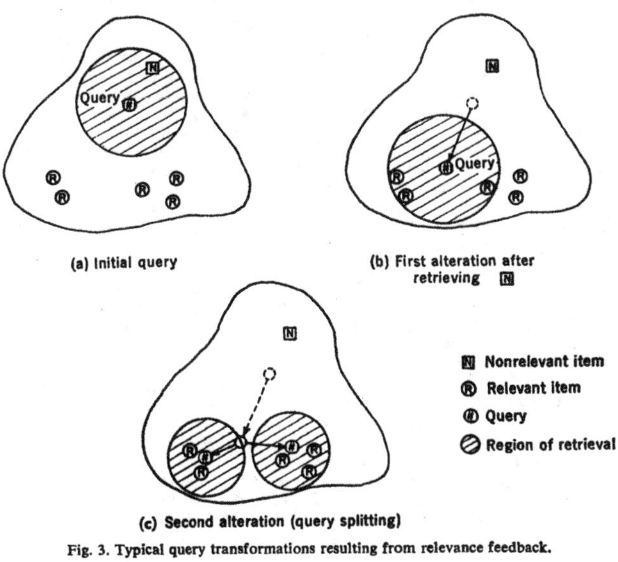


Fig. 3. Typical query transformations resulting from relevance feedback.

appropriate answers can be made in response to the more obvious objections. Finally, one must examine any counterevidence that may be available. Although systematic tests of automatic indexing procedures have not been made outside of the SMART and Cranfield environments, some data are available which appear not to be in agreement with the results reported above. For example, Saracevic reports that, in a test involving the use of 2600 documents in biomedicine and 124 queries, use of a thesaurus for term expansion was found not to be effective (*43*). It is not clear whether the fault, in this case, lay with the type of thesaurus [the SMART results apply only to certain types of thesauri, constructed in accordance with a specific set of principles (*33, 40*)] or with the type of analysis (a different analysis process was used for documents on the one hand and for queries on the other). Furthermore, because the results were cumulated for five different analysis procedures instead of being individually displayed, the output is not strictly comparable to the SMART or Cranfield data, and the results are difficult to assess.

The same is true of the test results obtained by Jones and his associates (*12*) using 22 queries each specified by a single phrase (or "content-bearing unit"). Here, a very high search precision (0.84) is reported for the phrase-matching process, but no recall values are given; the cited performance may thus correspond to a system operating at the left-hand end of a normal recall-precision curve. Furthermore, the queries, each consisting of a single two-word phrase, are probably not typical of queries normally received in information centers, and are in any case not comparable to the natural-language queries processed by SMART and Cranfield.

To summarize, there is no obvious evidence for distrusting the main results of the automatic indexing studies outlined above.

In some of the early text processing experiments it was seen that the automatic document search procedures were producing retrieval results at least equivalent to those obtained with conventional manual indexing (*20, 21*). Furthermore, the later tests conducted in an automatic retrieval environment indicate that the simple, single-term methods, which are easiest to implement on a computer, are also the most effective. It is interesting to try to determine under these circumstances how

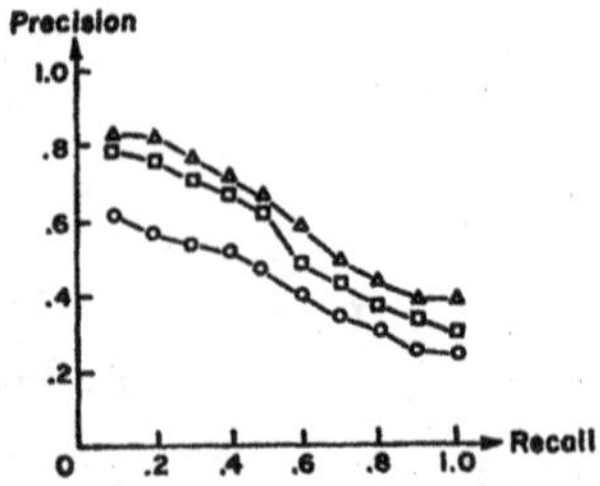


Fig. 4. Recall-precision graph illustrating the performance of abstract display and relevance feedback. (Circles) Original queries (word stem); (triangles) relevance feedback (word stem), one iteration; (squares) abstract display (word stem).

the automatic SMART procedures compare with standard manual indexing methods. The evidence here is not wholly conclusive, since the SMART processing is necessarily performed with small document collections. However, whatever evidence exists shows that the automatic indexing procedures are not inferior to what is now achieved by conventional, manual means.

For example, an initial comparison between the manual indexing used at Cranfield and the automatic processing of abstracts performed by SMART shows that the results obtained by the two systems are not statistically different (*31, 40*). To check these results, a comparison was made between the test results obtained by Lancaster for the manually based Medlars system (*17*) and the results for the SMART system. Specifically, for 18 of the Medlars queries used earlier by Lancaster, document abstracts were keypunched, and the retrieval process was repeated by means of the automatic text searching methods incorporated in SMART (*44*). The results indicate that, for that subcollection, a slightly higher average recall is obtained by SMART (0.69 as compared with 0.64 for Medlars), whereas Medlars achieves a somewhat higher precision (0.61 for SMART and 0.62 for Medlars). In any case, the intuitive feeling that the conventional indexing would necessarily be superior is again not confirmed.

One might interpret the results of the SMART-Medlars comparison by saying that the conventional and the automatic indexing procedures produce equally poor results (a recall and precision performance between 0.55 and 0.65, as compared with a possible maximum of 1). The reasons for the relatively poor performance of the automatic methods are clear when one considers the simplicity of the content analysis procedures used. For the manual indexing process, Lancaster reports the following main sources of failure (*17*): (i) index language problems (lack of specific terms or false coordination of terms); (ii) search formulation (query formulation too exhaustive or too specific); (iii) document indexing (document indexing insufficiently exhaustive, or too exhaustive, or important terms omitted); and (iv) lack of user-system interaction during the search process. The first three sources of failure all have to do with the query or document indexing process. The last inadequacy, however, appears to be one that can be remedied immediately.

For this reason, interactive search procedures have been incorporated into several recently implemented retrieval systems. The SMART system, in particular, attempts to meet the user problem by performing multiple rather than single searches. Thus, instead of submitting a search request and obtaining in return a final set of relevant items, a partial search is first made and, on the basis of the preliminary output obtained, the search parameters are adjusted before a second, more refined search is attempted. The adjustments made may differ from user to user, depending on individual needs, and the search process may be repeated as often as desired.

Various strategies are available for improving the results of a search by means of user feedback procedures (*37, 45, 46*). The first is based on a selective printout of stored information to be brought to the user's attention during the search process. For example, a set of additional, possible search terms related to those initially used by the requester may be extracted from the stored dictionary and presented to the user. The user may then be asked to reformulate the original query after selecting those new associated terms which appear to him most helpful in improving the search results. Typically, the statistical term associations discussed above can be used to obtain the set of related terms, or the sets of associated thesaurus classes can be taken from the thesaurus. This "search optimization" procedure is straightforward, but leaves the burden of rephrasing the query to the user (*45*).

A second strategy consists in automatically modifying a search request by using the partial results from a previous search. The user is asked to examine the documents retrieved by an initial search, and to designate some of them as either relevant (R) or irrelevant (N) to his needs. Concepts from the documents termed relevant can then be added to the original search request if they are not already present, or, if they are, their importance can be increased through a suitable adjustment of weights; contrariwise, terms from documents designated irrelevant can be deleted or given a lower weight (*37, 45–47*). An illustration of such a "relevance feedback" process is shown in Fig. 3, where a query first retrieves a document identified as nonrelevant (Fig. 3a). The query-updating process which follows then shifts the query in such a way that a new search operation retrieves some relevant documents (Fig. 3b). These documents, in turn, are used to generate two subqueries, which are then successful in retrieving all relevant items (Fig. 3c).

| | | |
|---|---|---|
| 230 | ART | ARCHITEKTUR |
| 231 | INDEPEND | SELBSTAENDIG<br>UNABHAENGIG |
| 232 | ASSOCIATIVE | |
| 233 | DIVIDE | |
| 234 | ACTIVE<br>ACTIVITY<br>USAGE | AKTIV<br>AKTIVITAET<br>TAETIGKEIT |
| 235 | CATHODE<br>CRT<br>DIODE<br>FLYING–SPOT<br>RAY<br>RELAIS<br>RELAY<br>SCANNER<br>TUBE | DIODE<br>VERZWEIGER |
| 236 | REDUNDANCY<br>REDUNDANT | |
| 237 | CHARGE<br>ENTER<br>ENTRY<br>INSERT<br>POST | EINGANG<br>EINGEGANGEN<br>EINGEGEBEN<br>EINSATZ<br>EINSTELLEN<br>EINTRAGUNG |
| 238 | MULTI–LEVEL<br>MULTILEVEL | |
| 239 | INTELLECT<br>INTELLECTUAL<br>INTELLIG<br>MENTAL<br>MIND<br>NON–INTELLECTUAL | GEISTIG |
| 240 | ACTUAL<br>PRACTICE<br>REAL | PRAXIS |

Fig. 5. Excerpt from multilingual English-German thesaurus.

A good deal of work has been done to improve this type of feedback operation, and evaluation results indicate that the process is considerably more effective than the standard one-pass search process. Figure 4 is a typical feedback evaluation graph showing averages for 200 documents and 42 queries in aerodynamics. Here an initial one-step search process based on a word stem analysis is compared with a feedback procedure based on the display of abstracts of previously retrieved documents; such a display is then used for manual updating of queries. The results of such manual updating are in turn compared with one iteration of the automatic relevance feedback process. It may be seen in Fig. 4 that the automatic updating procedure is more effective than the manual one, and that an improvement of about 20 percent in precision is obtained through the feedback procedure. Moreover, this type of improvement in retrieval effectiveness has been duplicated for all collections so far processed (*45–47*).

Two other practical points—document input and foreign language processing—require discussion, since it is sometimes claimed that no automatic indexing process would be viable without consideration of these questions. The input problem is particularly acute in an environment which includes automatic indexing, since document excerpts of at least abstract length should be available for analysis. Obviously, if all the material contained in an abstract (or, possibly, in the full text) requires manual keypunching, the main benefits of the automatic analysis procedure may be lost. No overall solution appears immediately available. However, the use of automatic character recognition equipment and of automatic typesetting processes is becoming more widespread, with the result that document input products that can be automatically read may well become generally available with each document before long.

Concerning the foreign language problem, the situation is less difficult than might appear to be the case. It is true that, in certain subject areas, up to 50 percent of the pertinent documents are not written in English [this is true of the documents in biomedicine processed at the National Library of Medicine (*17*)]. The English-language analysis methods will obviously not be applicable for these documents. However, it is also true that 90 percent of these documents are in one of only six or seven languages, most of them being in French, German, and Russian.

Table 3. Thesaurus analysis for German query Q 13 B: *"Inwieweit werden Computersysteme zur Forschung auf dem Gebiet der schönen Literatur verwendet? Hat sich maschinelle Sprachenanalyse als hilfreich erwiesen, um z. B. die vermutliche Autorenschaft bei anonymen Werken zu bestimmen oder um Konkordanzen zusammenzustellen?"**

| Concept Nos. | Weight | Sample terms in thesaurus category |
|---|---|---|
| 19† | 12 | Computer, Datenverarbeitung |
| 3† | 12 | Automatisch, Kybernetik |
| 21 | 4 | Artikel, Presse, Zeitschrift |
| 33† | 6 | Analyse, Sprachenanalyse |
| 45 | 4 | Herausgabe, Publikation |
| 64 | 4 | Buch, Heft, Werk |
| 65† | 12 | Autor, Verfasser |
| 68 | 12 | Literatur |
| 147† | 6 | Linguistik, Sprache |
| 207† | 12 | Arbeitsgebiet, Fach |
| 267† | 12 | Konkordanz, KWIC |
| ‡ | | schönen, hilfreich, vermutlich, anonymen, zusammenzustellen |

*For translation, see Table 2. †Common concepts with English query. ‡Query terms not found in thesaurus.

Some experiments were recently conducted with the SMART system and a collection of about 500 German documents in the field of library science. A multilingual thesaurus (Fig. 5) was prepared manually by translating the English version of an existing thesaurus into German. From Fig. 5 it may be seen that the same concept-class number represents both an English word class and the corresponding German class. The translation test performed consisted in processing a set of original English language queries against both the English and the German document collections; the test was then repeated by processing the English queries manually translated into German against the same two collections (English and German). The test results indicate that no significant loss in performance results from the process of query translation (*48*).

A sample German query processed through the German thesaurus is shown in Table 3. A comparison with Table 2 shows that a large number of "English" concepts are also present in the German analysis, and this accounts for the fact that the thesaurus translation is successful. The foreign language problem appears not to present a major roadblock to development of an automatic document processing system.

## Summary

A large number of automatic text analysis and indexing experiments have been examined. All the available evidence indicates that the presently known text analysis procedures are at least as effective as more conventional manual indexing methods. Furthermore, a simple indexing process based on the assignment of weighted terms to documents and search requests produces better retrieval results than a more sophisticated content analysis based on syntactic analysis or hierarchical term expansion. Such a simple automatic indexing procedure is easily implemented on present-day computers, and there are no obvious technical reasons why manual document analysis methods should not be replaced by automatic ones.

While automatic document analyses appear, therefore, to be at least as efficient as presently used manual methods, it is unfortunately the case that all known indexing procedures—whether manual or automatic—produce relatively mediocre results. One of the most fruitful ways of upgrading retrieval performance consists in using multiple searches based on user feedback information furnished during the search process. Interactive search methods should then lead to a retrieval effectiveness approaching a recall and precision of about 0.70 instead of the present 0.50 to 0.60. Some tentative extrapolations appear to indicate that an increased sophistication in indexing and search methodology may eventually lead to "optimal" systems for which the average recall and precision values would approach 0.80 (*42, 49*).

No obvious advances leading to additional large-scale improvements in retrieval effectiveness are likely to be made soon. For this reason, the known automatic document analysis and search procedures described in this article may well become the standard tools in most mechanized information systems of the future.

### References and Notes


1. Y. Bar Hillel, in *Digitale Informationswandler*, W. Hoffman, Ed. (Vieweg, Brunswick, Germany, 1962).
2. H. P. Luhn, *IBM J. Res. Develop.* **1**, No. 4 1957).
3. ———, "Potentialities of Auto-Encoding of Scientific Literature," *IBM Res. Cent. Rep. No. RC-101* (1959).
4. J. O'Connor, *J. Ass. Comput. Mach.* **11**, 437 (1964); M. E. Stevens, "Automatic Indexing: A State of the Art Report," *U.S. Nat. Bur. Stand. Monogr. 91* (1965); ———, V. E. Giuliano, L. B. Heilprin, Eds., "Statistical Association Methods for Mechanized Documentation," *U.S. Nat. Bur. Stand. Monogr. 269* (1965).
5. C. Montgomery and D. R. Swanson, *Amer. Doc.* **13**, 359 (1962).
6. M. J. Ruhl, *Amer. Doc.* **15**, 136 (1964).
7. D. H. Kraft, *Amer. Doc.* **15**, 48 (1964).
8. J. O'Connor, *Amer. Doc.* **15**, 96 (1964).
9. H. Fangmeyer and G. Lustig, "The Euratom automatic indexing project," paper presented before IFIP [International Federation for Information Processing] Congress 68, Edinburgh (1968).
10. F. J. Damerau, "An Experiment in Automatic Indexing," *IBM. Res. Cent. Rep. No. RC-894* (1963).
11. M. E. Stevens and G. H. Urban, in *Proceedings, Spring Joint Computer Conference* (Spartan, Washington, D.C., 1964), pp. 563–575; T. N. Shaw and H. Rothman, *J. Doc.* **24**, No. 3 (1968).
12. P. E. Jones, V. E. Giuliano, R. M. Curtice, "Papers on Automatic Language Processing—Development of String Indexing Techniques," *Arthur D. Little* (*Cambridge, Mass.*) *Rep. ESD-TR-67-202* (1967), vol. 3.
13. M. M. Kessler, *Amer. Doc.* **16**, 223 (1965).
14. R. M. Needham, *Mech. Transl.* **8**, Nos. 3 and 4 (June–Oct. 1965); L. B. Doyle, *J. Ass. Comput. Mach.* **12**, No. 4 (1965); H. Borko and M. D. Bernick, *J. Ass. Comput. Mach.* **10**, No. 2 (1963).
15. M. E. Maron, *J. Ass. Comput. Mach.* **8**, 404 (1961).
16. J. O'Connor, *J. Ass. Comput. Mach.* **12**, 490 (1965).
17. F. W. Lancaster, "Evaluation of the Operating Efficiency of Medlars," *Nat. Libr. Med. Final Rep.* (1968).
18. These figures imply that an average search processed by Medlars manages to retrieve almost 60 percent of what is wanted, while only half the retrieved items are not relevant; in view of the large document file being processed—over 600,000 items—this is a remarkable achievement.
19. P. Atherton, D. W. King, R. R. Freeman, "Evaluation of the Retrieval of Nuclear Science Document References Using UDC as the Indexing Language for a Computer Based System," *Amer. Inst. Phys. Rep. AIP-UDC 8* (1968); F. H. Barker and D. C. Veal, "The Evaluation of a Current Awareness Service for Chemists," *Chem. Soc. Res. Unit Inform. Dissemination Retrieval Rep.* (1968); C. D. Gull, in *Coordinate Indexing*, M. Taube *et al.*, Eds. (Documentation, Inc., Washington, D.C., 1963); L. B. Heilprin and S. S. Crutchfield, in *Proceedings, 1964 Annual Meeting of ADI* [*American Documentation Institute*] (Spartan, Washington, D.C., 1964); M. R. Hyslop, *ibid.*; W. F. Johanningsmeier and F. W. Lancaster, "Project SHARP Information Storage and Retrieval System: Evaluation of Indexing Procedures and Retrieval Effectiveness," *U.S. Bur. Ships Rep. NAVSHIPS 250-210-3* (1964); D. W. King, *J. Chem. Doc.* **5**, 96 (1965); D. B. McCarn and C. R. Stein, in *Electronic Handling of Information: Testing and Evaluation*, A. Kent *et al.*, Eds. (Thompson, Washington, D.C., 1967), pp. 110-122; E. Miller, D. Ballard, J. Kingston, M. Taube, in *Proceedings, International Conference on Scientific Information* (National Academy of Sciences-National Research Council, Washington, D.C., 1959), vol. 1, pp. 671–685; B. A. Montague, *Amer. Doc.* **16**, 201 (1965); National Academy of Sciences Ad-Hoc Committee of the Office of Documentation, "The Metallurgical Searching Service of the American Society of Metals—Western Reserve University: An Evaluation," *Nat. Acad. Sci. Nat. Res. Counc. Publ. 1148* (1964); J. A. Schuller, *Aslib Proc.* **12**, 372 (1960); J. Tague, *Effectiveness of a Pilot Information Service for Educational Research Materials* (Center for Documentation and Communication Research, Western Reserve University, Cleveland, 1963).
20. D. R. Swanson, *Science* **132**, 1099 (1960).
21. ———, in *Proceedings IFIP* [*International Federation for Information Processing*] *Congress 62*, C. Popplewell, Ed. (North Holland, Amsterdam, 1963), pp. 288–293.
22. E. M. Fels, *Amer. Doc.* **14**, No. 1 (1963).
23. B. Altmann, *Amer. Doc.* **18**, No. 1 (1967).
24. J. S. Melton, "Automatic Processing of Metallurgical Abstracts for the Purpose of Information Retrieval," *Center for Communication and Documentation Research, Case Western Reserve University, Cleveland, Final Rep. NSF-4* (1967).
25. S. F. Dennis, in *Information Retrieval—a Critical View*, G. Schechter, Ed. (Thompson, Washington, D.C., 1967).
26. V. E. Giuliano and P. E. Jones, "Study and Test of a Methodology for Laboratory Evaluation of Message Retrieval Systems," *Arthur D. Little* [*Cambridge, Mass.*] *Rep. ESD-TR-66-405* (1966).
27. K. Sparck Jones and D. M. Jackson, "The Use of Automatically Obtained Keyword Classifications for Information Retrieval," *Cambridge* [*England*] *Language Research Unit Final Rep. ML 211* (1969).
28. C. W. Cleverdon, in *Proceedings, International Conference on Scientific Information* (National Academy of Sciences–National Research Council, Washington, D.C., 1959), vol. 1, pp. 687–698; ———, "Testing and Analysis of an Investigation into the Comparative Efficiency of Indexing Systems," *Cranfield* (*England*) *Res. Proj. Rep.* (1962).
29. A document exhibiting *n* terms in common with a given query is said to be retrieved at coordination level *n*.
30. G. Salton, in *Proceedings, FID Congress 1965* (Spartan, Washington, D.C., 1966).
31. C. W. Cleverdon and E. M. Keen, "Factors Determining the Performance of Indexing Systems," *Aslib Cranfield* (*England*) *Res. Proj. Rep.* (1966), vols. 1 and 2.
32. C. W. Cleverdon, *Aslib Proc.* **19**, No. 6 (1967).
33. G. Salton, *Automatic Information Organization and Retrieval* (McGraw-Hill, New York, 1968).
34. ——— and M. E. Lesk, *Commun. Ass. Comput. Mach.* **8**, No. 6 (1965); G. Salton, *IEEE* (*Inst. Elec. Electron. Eng.*) *Spectrum* **2**, No. 8 (1965).
35. H. E. Stiles, paper presented at the 3rd Institute on Information Storage and Retrieval, American University, Washington, D.C., 1961.
36. P. B. Baxendale, *IBM J. Res. Develop.* **4**, No. 2 (1958); D. J. Hillman and A. J. Kasarda, in *Proceedings AFIPS Spring Joint Computer Conference* (AFIPS Press, Montvale, N.J., 1969).
37. G. Salton, in *Proceedings IFIP* [*International Federation for Information Processing*] *Congress 68* (North-Holland, Amsterdam, 1969).
38. In the SMART system the term weights are based on the frequency of occurrence of each term in a document, as well as on individual term charateristics derived from the word stem or from thesaurus dictionaries.
39. G. Salton, *Amer. Doc.* **16**, 209 (1965); ——— *et al.*, "Information Storage and Retrieval," *Dep. Computer Sci. Cornell Univ. Rep. Nos. ISR-11, ISR-12, ISR-13, ISR-14, and ISR-16 to Nat. Sci. Found.* (1966–1969).
40. G. Salton and M. E. Lesk, *J. Ass. Comput. Mach.* **15**, 8 (1968).
41. C. A. Cuadra and R. V. Katter, *J. Doc.* **23**, No. 4 (1967); A. M. Rees and D. G. Schultz, "A Field Experimental Approach to the Study of Relevance Assessments in Relation to Document Searching," *Cent. Doc. Commun. Res. Case Western Reserve Univ. Final Rep. to Nat. Sci. Found.* (1967).
42. M. E. Lesk and G. Salton, *Inform. Storage Retrieval* **4**, No. 4 (1968).
43. T. Saracevic, "The Effect of Question Analysis and Searching Strategy in Performance of Retrieval Systems: Selected Results from an Experimental Study," *Comp. Syst. Lab. Rep. No. CSL:TR:5, Cent. Doc. Commun. Res. Case Western Reserve Univ. Cleveland* (1968).
44. G. Salton, *Amer. Doc.* **20**, No. 1 (1969).
45. M. E. Lesk and G. Salton, in *Proceedings AFIPS Spring Joint Computer Conference* (AFIPS Press, Montvale, N.J., 1969).
46. E. Ide, "Relevance Feedback in an Automatic Document Retrieval System," *Dep. Computer Sci. Cornell Univ. Rep. No. ISR-15 to Nat. Sci. Found.* (1969).
47. G. Salton, in *Mechanized Information Storage, Retrieval and Dissemination*, K. Samuelson, Ed. (North-Holland, Amsterdam, 1968), pp. 73–107.
48. ———, "Automatic processing of foreign language documents," *J. ASIS* [*Amer. Soc. Inf. Sci.*], in press.
49. C. W. Cleverdon, "The Methodology of Evaluation of Operational Information Retrieval Systems based on the Test of Medlars," *Cranfield (England) Res. Proj. Rep.* (1968).


50 This study was supported in part by the National Science Foundation under grant GN-750.

*Reprinted from the Journal of the American Society for Information Science, Vol. 26, No. 1, 1975.* 

# A Theory of Term Importance in Automatic Text Analysis

**A good deal of work has been done over the years in an attempt to use statistical or probabilistic techniques as a basis for automatic indexing and content analysis. (1-10) Unfortunately, many of these methods are lacking in effectiveness, and the more refined procedures are computationally unattractive.**

**A new technique, known as discrimination value analysis, ranks the text words in accordance with how well they are able to discriminate the documents of a collection from each other; that is, the value of a term depends on how much the average separation between individual documents changes when the given term is assigned for content identification. The best words are those which achieve the greatest separation.**

**The discrimination value analysis is computationally simple, and it assigns a specific role in content analysis to single words, juxtaposed words and phrases, and word groups or thesaurus categories. Experimental results are given showing the effectiveness of the technique.**

**G. Salton,**
**C.S. Yang**
*Department of Computer Science*
*Cornell University*
*Ithaca, New York 14853*

**C.T. Yu**
*Department of Computing Science*
*University of Alberta*
*Edmonton, Alberta, Canada*

## • Document Space Configuration

Consider a collection of entities D (documents) represented by weighted properties $w$. In particular, let

$$D_i = (w_{i1}, w_{i2}, \ldots, w_{it}) \quad (1)$$

where $w_{ij}$ represents the weight of term $j$ in the vector corresponding to the $i$th document. Given two documents $D_i$ and $D_j$, it is possible to define a measure of relatedness $s(D_i, D_j)$ between the documents depending on the similarity of their respective term vectors. In three dimensions (when only three terms identify the documents), the situation may be represented by the configuration of Fig. 1, where the similarity between any two of the document vectors may be assumed to be a function inversely related to the angle between them. That is, when two document vectors are exactly the same, the corresponding vectors are superimposed and the angle between them is zero.

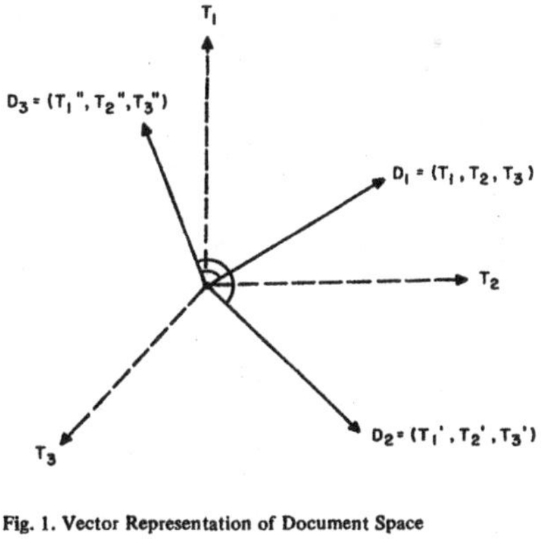


Fig. 1. Vector Representation of Document Space

When the dimensionality of the space exceeds three, that is when more than three terms are used to identify a given document, the envelope of the vector space may be used to represent the collection as in the example of Fig. 2. Here only the tips of the document vectors are shown represented by $x$'s, the size of the vectors is normalized to some common length, and the distance between two $x$'s is inversely related to the similarity between the corresponding document vectors—the smaller the distance between $x$'s, the smaller will be the angle between the vectors, and thus the more similar the term assignment.

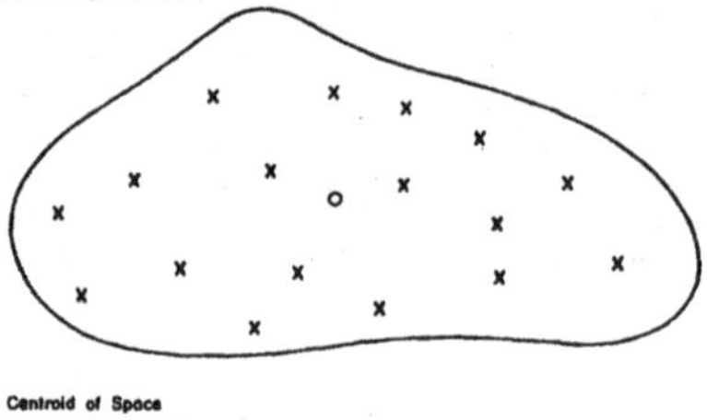


Fig. 2. Multidimensional Document Space

A central document, or centroid $C$, may be introduced, located in the center of the document space, which for certain purposes may represent the whole collection. The $i$th vector element $c_i$ of the centroid can simply be defined as the average of the $i$th term $w_{ij}$ across the $n$ documents of the collection; that is

$$c_i = \frac{1}{n} \sum_{j=1}^{n} w_{ij}.$$

It is clear that a particular document space configuration, such as that of Fig. 2, reflects directly the details of the indexing chosen for the identification of the documents. This raises the question about the choice of an optimum indexing process, or alternatively, about an effective document space configuration. A number of studies, carried out over the last few years, indicate that a good document space is one which maximizes the average separation between pairs of documents (*10-11*). In particular, the document space will be maximally separated, when the average angular distance between each document and the space centroid is maximized, that is, when

$$Q = \sum_{i=1}^{n} s(C, D_i) \qquad (2)$$

is minimum.* Obviously, in such a case, it may be easy to retrieve each given document without also necessarily retrieving its neighbors. This insures a high precision output, since the retrieval of a given relevant item will then not also entail the retrieval of many nonrelevant items in its vicinity. Furthermore, when the relevant documents are located in the same general area of the space, high recall may also be obtainable, since many relevant items may then be correctly retrieved, and many nonrelevant ones correctly rejected.†

A particular indexing system, known as the discrimination value model, assigns the highest weight, or value, to those terms which cause the maximum possible separation between the documents of a collection. This model is described and analyzed in the remainder of this study.

## • The Discrimination Value Model.

The *discrimination value* of a term is a measure of the changes in space separation which occur when a given term is assigned to a collection of documents. A good discriminator is one which, when assigned as an index term, will render the documents less similar to each other; that is, its assignment decreases the space density. Contrariwise, a poor discriminator increases the density of the space. By computing the space densities both before and after assignment of each term, it is possible to rank the terms in decreasing order of their discrimination values.

In particular, consider a measure of the space sparseness, or inverse space density, such as the $Q$ value given in equation (2), and let $Q_k$ represent the density $Q$ with the $k$th term removed from all document (and from the centroid) vectors. The discrimination value of term $k$ may then be defined as

$$DV_k = Q_k - Q. \qquad (3)$$

Obviously, if term $k$ is a good discriminator, then its removal will cause a compression in the document space (an increase in space density), because its assignment would have resulted in an increase in space separation. Thus for good discriminators $Q_k > Q$ and $DV_k$ is positive. The reverse is true for poor discriminators whose removal causes a decrease in space density, leading to negative discrimination values. A vast majority of the terms may be expected to produce neither increase nor decrease in space density; in such a case a discrimination value near zero is obtained. The operations of a good discriminator are illustrated in the simplified drawing of Fig. 3.

In the retrieval experiments conducted earlier with three collections in aerodynamics (Cranfield collection, 424 documents comprising 2651 distinct terms), medicine (Medlars collection, 450 documents comprising 4726 terms), and world affairs (*Time* collection, 425

*As stated earlier, the similarity measure $s$ between two vectors may be assumed to be an inverse function of the angle between them. A typical measure of this type is the cosine function.

†Retrieval performance is often measured by parameters such as *recall* and *precision*, reflecting the ratio of relevant items actually retrieved, and of retrieved items actually relevant.

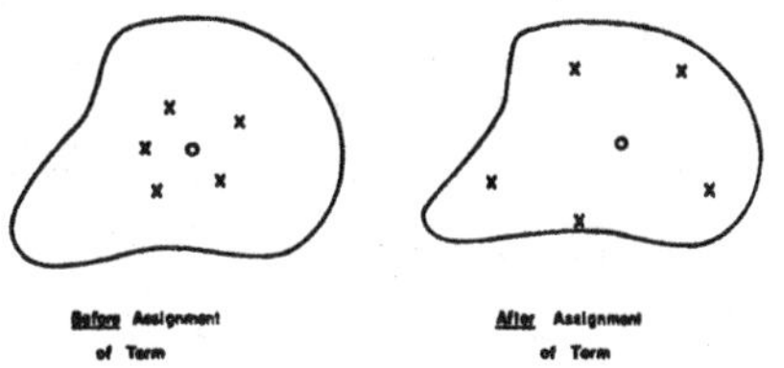


Fig. 3. Operation of Good Discriminating Term

documents comprising 14,098 terms), the discrimination value model produced excellent retrieval results (*10*). In particular, a term weighting system which assigns to each term $k$ a value $w_{kj}$ consisting of the product of its frequency of occurrence in document $j$ ($f_{kj}$) multiplied by its discrimination value $DV_k$,

$$w_{kj} = f_{kj} \cdot DV_k, \tag{4}$$

produces recall and precision improvements of about ten percent over methods where only the term frequencies $f_{kj}$ are taken into account.*

It may be of interest to inquire what kind of terms are favored by a weighting system such as that of expression (4), and what accounts for the value of the discrimination model. Some experimental evidence relating the discrimination values to certain frequency characteristics of the terms in the document collections is presented in the next section. This, in turn, leads to an indexing theory to be examined in the remainder of this study.

## • Discrimination Values and Document Frequencies

Consider any term $k$ assigned to a collection of documents, and let $d_k$ be its document frequency ($DF$), defined as the number of documents in the collection in which term $k$ appears. More specifically,

$$d_k = \sum_{j=1}^{n} b_{kj}$$

where $b_{kj} = 1$ whenever $f_{kj} \geq 1$, and $b_{kj} = 0$ otherwise. Consider the set of terms assigned to a given document collection in increasing document frequency order, that is, first all the terms of document frequency 1, followed by those with document frequency 2, and so on up. For each set of terms exhibiting a common document frequency, consider the average rank in decreasing discrimination value order of the corresponding terms, thereby relating the document frequencies of terms and the corresponding discrimination values.*

A plot giving the average discrimination value rank for the terms exhibiting certain document frequency ranges is shown in Figs. 4(a), (b) and (c) for the collections in aerodynamics, medicine and world affairs (Cranfield, Medlars and *Time*) respectively. It may be seen that a U shaped curve is obtained in each case, with the following interpretations:

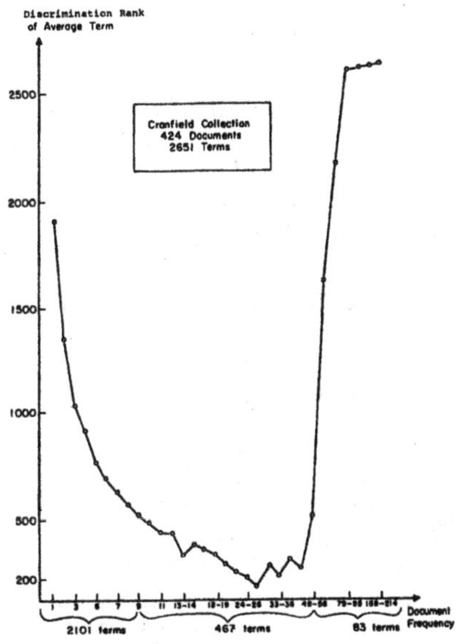


Fig. 4(a). Average Discrimination Value Rank of Terms

a. the terms with very low document frequencies, located on the left-hand side of Fig. 4, are poor discriminators, with average discrimination value ranks in excess of $t/2$ for $t$ terms;
b. the terms with high document frequencies exceeding $n/10$, located on the right-hand side of Fig. 4, are the worst discriminators, with average discrimination value ranks near $t$;
c. the best discriminators are those whose document frequency is neither too high nor too low—with document frequencies between $n/100$ and $n/10$ for $n$ documents; their average discrimination value ranks are generally below $t/5$.

*Terms receiving high weights according to expression (4) are those which exhibit high occurrence frequencies in certain specified documents, and at the same time can distinguish these documents from the remainder of the collection.

*For a set of $t$ terms, the discrimination value rank ranges from 1 for the best discriminator to $t$ for the worst.

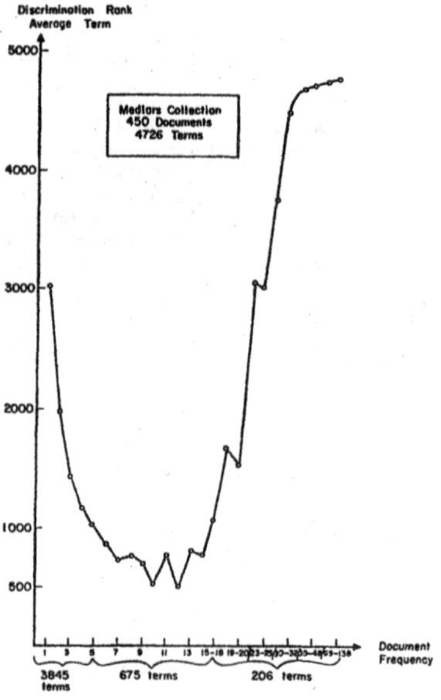


Fig. 4(b). Average Discrimination Value Rank of Terms

The output of Fig. 4 shows average discrimination value ranks only. Before deciding that all terms with low and high document frequencies can automatically be disregarded, it is useful to determine whether any good discriminators are in fact included in the corresponding low frequency and high frequency term sets. Figs. 5(a) and 5(b) show sets of low frequency terms for the Medlars and *Time* collections respectively, together with the number of good discriminators—those with discrimination ranks between 1 and 100—included in each set. Fig. 5 exhibits overlapping term sets, consisting of all terms with document frequency equal to 1, 1 and 2, 1 to 3, etc., together with the percentage figures of the total number of terms represented by the corresponding sets.

Thus when 70% of the terms are taken in increasing document frequency order—corresponding in the Medlars collection to about 3200 terms out of 4700 with document frequencies of 1 or 2, and in the *Time* collection to 9900 terms out of 14,000 with document frequencies 1 to 3—it is seen that only about 15 good discriminators are included for Medlars, and about 12 for *Time*. When the proportion of terms increases to 80% in increasing document frequency order, including 3800 Medlars terms, or 11,300 *Time* terms, ranging in document frequency from 1 to 6, the number of good discriminators rises to 30 for Medlars and to 35 for *Time*. When so few good discriminators are included among the mass of low frequency terms, it is obvious that special provisions must be made in any indexing process for the utilization of these terms.

Consider, now, the very high frequency terms—those which according to the output of Fig. 4 exhibit the lowest discrimination values. While the number of such terms is not large, each of the terms accounts for a substantial portion of the total term assignments to the documents of a collection because of the high document frequency involved.

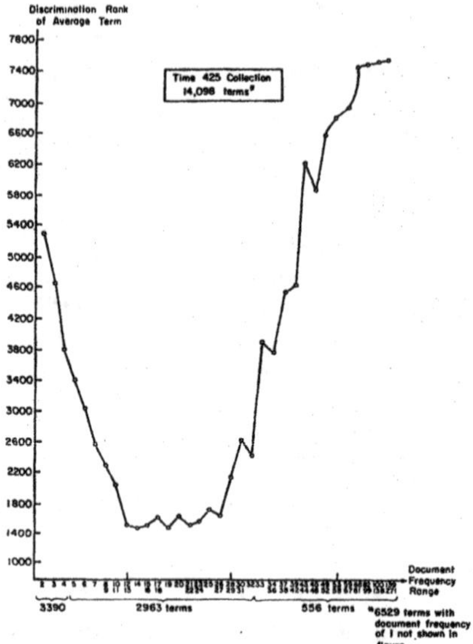


Fig. 4(c). Average Discrimination Value Rank of Terms

The output of Fig. 6(a) for Medlars and 6(b) for *Time* shows that about four percent of the high-frequency terms present in a document collection, accounts for 40% to 50% of all term assignments, when the terms are taken in decreasing document frequency order. The absolute number of distinct terms is 200 approximately for the Medlars collection and about 500 for *Time*. In each case, less than 15 of these terms are classified as good discriminators. When the proportion of terms taken in high frequency order increases to six percent, accounting for 46% of the term assignments in Medlars, and 57% for *Time*, the number of good discriminators increases to about 20 in each case.

The information included in Figs. 5 and 6 is summarized in Table 1. In each case, certain cutoff percentages are given for terms taken either in low document frequency or in high document frequency order. For each such percentage, the number of good discriminators included in the corresponding term set is stated for each of the three test collections. Thus when 60% of the terms are taken in increasing document frequency order, not a single good discriminator is included among the 1668 terms for the Cranfield collection; only five of the top 50 terms, or 16 of the top 100, are present among the 3238 Medlars terms; finally, for *Time* one out of the top 50 or 11 of the top 100 are included among the first 8916 low frequency terms.

The number of good discriminators included among the high frequency terms for the three collections is similarly low, as shown in the bottom half of Table 1.

The conclusion to be reached from the data of Figs. 5 and 6 and of Table 1 is that very few good discriminators are included among the bottom 70%, or among the top four percent when the terms included in a collection of documents are taken in increasing document frequency order. This fact is used to construct an indexing strategy in the remainder of this study.

## • A Strategy for Automatic Indexing

Consider the graph of Fig. 7 in which the terms are once again arranged in increasing document frequency order. If the assumption is correct that the best terms for indexing purposes are concentrated among the good discriminators whose document frequency is neither too high nor too low—the frequency being approximately between $n/100$ and $n/10$—then the following term transformation should be undertaken:

a. Terms whose document frequency lies between $n/100$ and $n/10$ should be used for indexing purposes directly without any transformation; these terms include the vast majority of the good discriminators.

b. Terms whose document frequency is too high—above $n/10$—comprise the worst discriminators. These terms are too general in nature, or too broad, to permit proper discrimination among the documents; hence their use produces an unacceptable precision loss (it leads to the retrieval of too many items that are extraneous). These terms should be transformed into lower frequency terms—right-to-left on the graph of Fig. 7—thereby enhancing the precision performance.

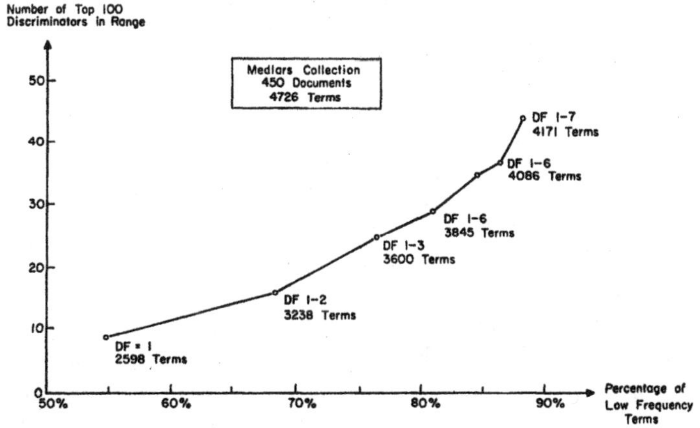


Fig. 5(a). Number of Good Discriminators Among Low Frequency Terms

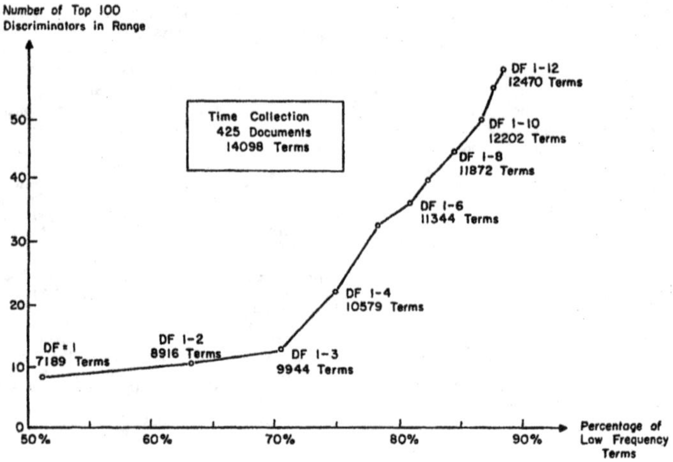


Fig. 5(b). Number of Good Discriminators Among Low Frequency Terms

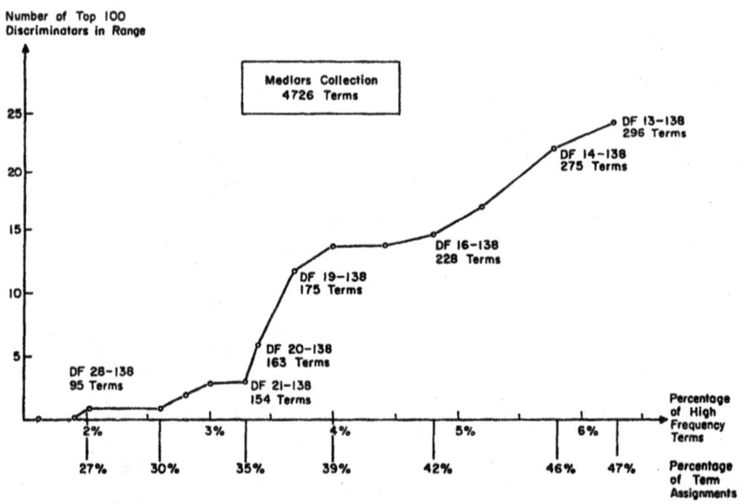


Fig. 6(a). Number of Good Discriminators Among High Frequency Terms

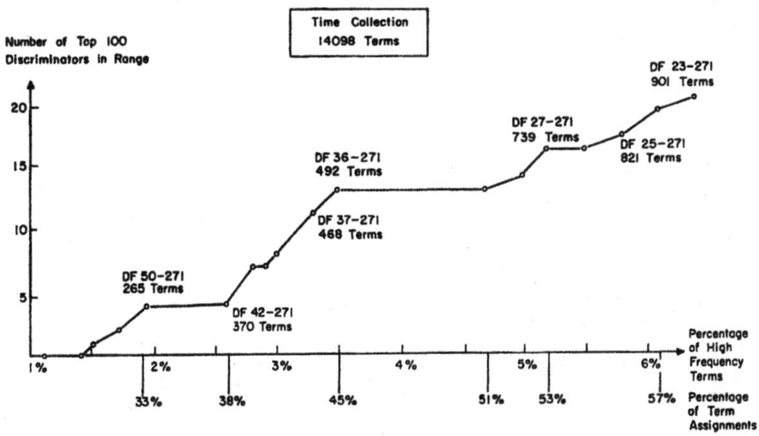


Fig. 6(b). Number of Good Discriminators Among High Frequency Terms

| Type of Terms | Fraction of Terms Covered (Fraction of Term Assignments) | Number of Terms | | Document Frequency of Terms | Number of Good Discriminators | |
|---|---|---|---|---|---|---|
| | | | | | From Top 50 | From Top 100 |
| Low Frequency | 60% | CRAN | 1668 | 1-3 | 0 | 0 |
| | | MED | 3238 | 1-2 | 5 | 16 |
| | | *TIME* | 8916 | 1-2 | 1 | 11 |
| | 70% | CRAN | 1899 | 1-4 | 0 | 4 |
| | | MED | 3600 | 1-3 | 8 | 25 |
| | | *TIME* | 9944 | 1-3 | 2 | 13 |
| | 80% | CRAN | 2153 | 1-9 | 5 | 14 |
| | | MED | 3845 | 1-4 | 8 | 29 |
| | | *TIME* | 11344 | 1-6 | 12 | 36 |
| High Frequency | (42%) | CRAN | 91 | 54-214 | 5 | 11 |
| | 3.5% (36%) | MED | 163 | 20-138 | 5 | 6 |
| | (45%) | *TIME* | 492 | 36-271 | 8 | 13 |
| | (45%) | CRAN | 105 | 48-214 | 7 | 15 |
| | 4.0% (39%) | MED | 192 | 18-138 | 10 | 14 |
| | (47%) | *TIME* | 555 | 33-271 | 8 | 13 |
| | (47%) | CRAN | 115 | 44-214 | 9 | 17 |
| | 4.5% (40%) | MED | 206 | 17-138 | 10 | 14 |
| | (51%) | *TIME* | 660 | 29-271 | 8 | 13 |

Table 1. Number of Good Discriminators for Various Deletion Percentages of Low and High Frequency Terms

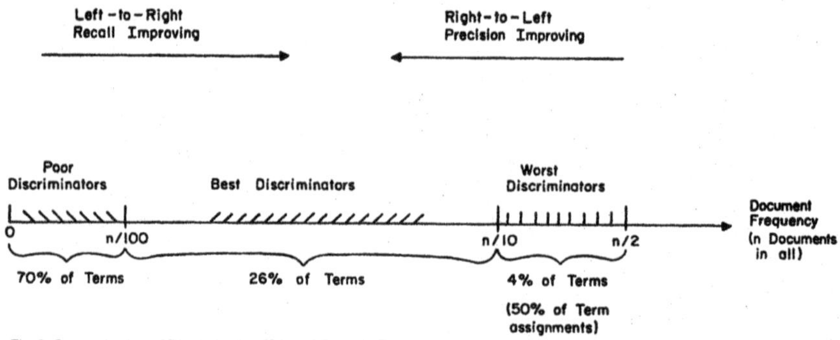


Fig. 7. Summarization of Discrimination Value of Terms in Frequency Ranges

c. Terms whose document frequency is too low—below $n/100$—are so rare and specific that they cannot retrieve an acceptable proportion of the documents relevant to a given query; hence their use depresses the recall performance. These terms should be transformed into higher frequency terms—left-to-right on the graph of Fig. 7—thereby enhancing the recall performance.

It remains to describe the right-to-left and left-to-right transformations that may be used to generate useful indexing vocabularies. The obvious way of transforming the high frequency terms into lower frequency entities is to combine them into *indexing phrases.* In general, a phrase such as "programming language" exhibits a lower assignment frequency than either of the high frequency components "language" or "program." The summary of Fig. 7 then indicates that:

> *Indexing phrases should be constructed from high frequency single term components in order to enhance the precision performance of the retrieval system.*

The other left-to-right transformation which is required for recall enhancing purposes is now equally obvious. Low frequency terms with somewhat similar properties, or meanings, can be combined into term classes, normally specified by a thesaurus of related terms, or a synonym dictionary. When a single term is replaced for indexing purposes by a thesaurus class consisting of several terms, the assignment frequency of the thesaurus class will in general exceed that of any of the components included in the class. Thus:

> *The main virtue of a thesaurus is its ability to group a number of low frequency terms into thesaurus classes, thereby enhancing the recall performance.*

A large number of different strategies is available for the generation of indexing phrases and term thesauri. Consider first the criteria used for the formation of phrases. A phrase might be created whenever two or more components co-occur in the same document or query; or when they co-occur in the same paragraph or sentence of a document; or when they occur in certain specified positions within the same sentences; or, finally, when they co-occur in certain specified positions in a text while exhibiting certain predetermined syntactical relationships. The methods needed to identify the indexing phrases attached to a given document or query may then range from quite simple (any pair of noncommon terms co-occurring in a document may represent a phrase) to quite complex (the various phrase components must exhibit appropriate syntactical relationships, and these relationships must be ascertained) (*12*).

For present purposes, a compromise position is adopted which bypasses an expensive syntactic analysis system in favor of the following procedure:

a. phrases are defined by using query texts;
b. common function words are removed and a suffix deletion method is used to reduce the remaining query words to word stems;
c. the remaining word stems are taken in pairs, and each pair defines a phrase provided that the distance in the text between the two phrase components does not exceed two (at most one intervening word occurs between components), and provided that at least one of the components of each phrase is a high frequency term;
d. phrases for which both components are identical are eliminated;
e. duplicate phrases, where all components match an already existing phrase, are eliminated.

The texts of all documents are checked for the presence of any phrase thus defined from the query statements, and appropriate weights are assigned.

The phrase formation process is illustrated in Fig. 8 for a query dealing with world affairs. It is seen that this query gives rise to eight distinct phrases with adjacent

| QUERY: | COALITION GOVERNMENT TO BE FORMED ITALY BY THE LEFT-WING SOCIALISTS, THE REPUBLICANS, SOCIAL DEMOCRATS, AND CHRISTIAN DEMOCRATS. |
|---|---|

DELETE COMMON WORDS AND ELIMINATE SUFFIXES:

COALI GOVERN FORM ITALY LEFT–W SOCIAL REPUBLIC SOCIAL DEMOCRAT CHRIST DEMOCRAT

PHRASES:

| ADJACENT COMPONENTS | ONE INTERVENING WORD |
|---|---|
| COALI GOVERN, | COALIFORM, |
| GOVERN FORM, | GOVERN ITALY, |
| FORMITALY, | FORM LEFT–W, |
| ITALY LEFT–W, | ITALY SOCIAL, |
| LEFT–W SOCIAL, | LEFT–W REPUBLIC, |
| SOCIAL REPUBLIC, | ~~SOCIAL SOCIAL~~,† |
| ~~REPUBLIC SOCIAL~~*, | REPUBLIC DEMOCRAT, |
| SOCIAL DEMOCRAT, | SOCIAL CHRIST, |
| DEMOCRAT CHRIST, | ~~DEMOCRAT DEMOCRAT~~† |
| ~~CHRIST DEMOCRAT~~* | |

*Duplicate Phrases Eliminated
†Identical Components Elminated Word Order Immaterial

Fig. 8. Sample Phrase Formation Process

components, plus seven additional phrases for which the components are separated by one intervening word in the reduced query text.

It remains to determine an appropriate weight to be assigned to each phrase created by the foregoing process. Thus if terms $p$ and $q$ exhibit weights $w_{ip}$ and $w_{iq}$, respectively in document $i$, corresponding, for example, to the frequencies of occurrence of the respective terms in the document, the phrase consisting of components $p$ and $q$ might be assigned weight $w_{ipq}$ defined as

$$w_{ipq} = \frac{w_{ip} + w_{iq}}{2}. \qquad (5)$$

A somewhat more refined weighting method uses $w_{ipq}$ in conjunction with an "inverse document frequency" (*IDF*) factor which gives higher weights to phrases that occur comparatively rarely in the collection. The original inverse document frequency (*IDF*) factor, introduced by Sparck Jones, was defined as (*3*):

$$IDF_k = \lceil \log_2 n \rceil - \lceil \log_2 d_k \rceil + 1,$$

where $IDF_k$ is the *IDF* factor for term $k$, and $d_k$ is the document frequency of term $k$ in a collection of $n$ documents. Clearly $IDF_k$ is large when $d_k$ is small, and becomes small as $d_k$ approaches $n$.

By analogy, a phrase *IDF* factor may be defined as:

$$IDF_{pq} = (\log n - \frac{\log d_p + \log d_q}{2}), \qquad (6)$$

where $d_p$ and $d_q$ are the respective document frequencies of phrase components $p$ and $q$.

In conformity with the composite weighting system of equation (4), which uses the product of term frequencies and discrimination values, a composite phrase weight $\underline{W}_{ipq}$ for phrase $pq$ in document $i$ may then be defined as the product of the *IDF* factor and the average component weight (equations (5) and (6)):

$$W_{ipq} = \left[\log n - \frac{\log d_p + \log d_q}{2}\right] \cdot \left[\frac{w_{ip} + w_{iq}}{2}\right]. ^{*} \qquad (7)$$

In a retrieval environment, the high frequency phrases defined by the foregoing procedure may be used to replace the original phrase components—that is, the original components may be removed from the document and query vectors before the phrase identifiers are added. Alternatively, phrase components may be used in addition to the single term components. For the experiments described in the next section, the former policy was used in that phrases are introduced replacing the original component terms.

Consider now the converse to the right-to-left phrase formation process, namely the left-to-right thesaurus construction method. Here the idea is to use low frequency terms and to assemble them into classes of terms replacing the original vector components. If $d_p$ and $d_q$ are the document frequencies of terms $p$ and $q$ respectively, the document frequency of the class which includes both $p$ and $q$ may be defined as

$$D_{pq} = d_p + d_q - d_{pq}.$$

$D_{pq}$ then represents the number of documents in which either term $p$ appears, or term $q$, or both $p$ and $q$. In general $D_{pq}$ may be expected to be larger than either $d_p$ or $d_q$ individually. When $m$ terms are included in a given term class, the document frequency of the class is defined simply as the number of documents in which at least one term assigned to that class appears.

Term classes are often defined by a thesaurus, and a given thesaurus class normally includes terms that are sufficiently similar in meaning, or context, to make it reasonable to ignore their differences for indexing purposes. A great many thesaurus construction procedures have been described in the literature including manual term grouping as well as fully automatic methods (*13-16*). Among the latter are the so-called *associative indexing* procedures, where statistically associated terms are jointly assigned to the documents of a collection, and a variety of *term clustering* methods designed to group into a common class those terms which exhibit similar term assignments to documents of a collection.

For experimental purposes it may be sufficient to use existing manually constructed thesauri for the three test collections, and restrict the thesaurus to include only classes whose document frequency does not exceed a stated maximum. Such a thesaurus then effectively

*As before, the weighting system of expression (7) assigns high weights to phrases with highly weighted components in individual documents but with relatively low overall document frequency in the collection.

limits the number of high frequency terms that can appear in any class, and provides the left-to-right frequency transformation specified by the model of Fig. 7. The weight with which a thesaurus class is assigned to a document or query vector may again be defined as a function of the weights of the component terms originally present in that vector.

A frequency-restricted thesaurus such as the one described above may not specify classes that are completely identical with the term classes obtainable by initially using only the low frequency terms for a separate term clustering process; however the experimental recall-precision results may be expected to be close to those produced by an original thesaurus construction method.

The recall-precision results obtained from the operation modelled in Fig. 7 are examined in the next section.

## • Experimental Results

The right-to-left phrase formation process is designed to produce lower frequency entities from high frequency components, and vice versa for the left-to-right thesaurus grouping process. The data of Table 2 prove that the required frequency alterations are in fact obtained by the two transformations for the test collection in use.

Table 2(a) shows that the document frequency of the phrases is only about one-third as large as the frequency of the individual components entering the phrase formation process. In Table 2(b) the reverse is seen to be the case for the thesaurus concepts whose document frequency is one-and-a-half times that of the individual thesaurus entries. If the model of Fig. 7 specifying ideal frequency characteristics for index terms is appropriate, considerably better recall and precision output should be obtainable with the transformed terms (phrases and thesaurus classes) than the originals.

Detailed recall-precision output is contained in Tables 3 and 4, and in the summary in Table 5 for the various

| | Minimum Document Frequency needed for High-Frequency Component | Average Document Frequency | |
|---|---|---|---|
| | | Single Terms Entering Phrase Process | Phrases |
| CRANFIELD | (45) | 106 | 39 |
| MEDLARS | (22) | 40 | 7 |
| TIME | (49) | 101 | 38 |

Table 2(a). Average Document Frequency for Phrases

| | Maximum Document Frequency needed for Thesaurus Class to Insure Inclusion | Average Document Frequency | |
|---|---|---|---|
| | | Single Terms Entering Thesaurus Process | Thesaurus Classes |
| CRANFIELD | (60) | 24 | 32 |
| MEDLARS | (40) | 10 | 16 |
| TIME | (60) | 17 | 31 |

Table 2(b). Average Document Frequency for Thesaurus Classes

| | CRAN 424 | | | MED 450 | | | TIME 425 | | |
|---|---|---|---|---|---|---|---|---|---|
| | Standard Term Frequency | Phrase Assignment | Advantage | Standard Term Frequency | Phrase Assignment | Advantage | Standard Term Frequency | Phrase Assignment | Advantage |
| .1 | .6844 | .8793 | +28% | .7891 | .8811 | +12% | .7496 | .8488 | +13% |
| .2 | .5303 | .7344 | +38% | .6750 | .8149 | +21% | .7071 | .8419 | +19% |
| .3 | .4689 | .6013 | +28% | .5481 | .6992 | +28% | .6710 | .7998 | +19% |
| .4 | .3482 | .5205 | +49% | .4807 | .6481 | +35% | .6452 | .7729 | +20% |
| .5 | .3134 | .4150 | +32% | .4384 | .5930 | +35% | .6351 | .7025 | +11% |
| .6 | .2556 | .3623 | +42% | .3721 | .5450 | +46% | .5866 | .6800 | +16% |
| .7 | .1989 | .3017 | +52% | .3357 | .4867 | +45% | .5413 | .6331 | +17% |
| .8 | .1631 | .1953 | +20% | .2195 | .3263 | +49% | .5004 | .5895 | +18% |
| .9 | .1265 | .1463 | +16% | .1768 | .2767 | +56% | .3865 | .4618 | +19% |
| 1.0 | .1176 | .1314 | +12% | .1230 | .1969 | +60% | .3721 | .4529 | +22% |
| | | Average | +32% | | Average | +39% | | Average | +17% |

Table 3. Average Precision Values at Ten Recall Points (Phrase Process vs. Standard)

Table 4. Average Precision Values at Ten Recall Points (Thesaurus and Phrases vs. Standard)

| | CRAN 424 | | | MED 450 | | | TIME 425 | | |
|---|---|---|---|---|---|---|---|---|---|
| | Standard Term Frequency | Thesaurus Plus Phrases | Advantage | Standard Term Frequency | Thesaurus Plus Phrases | Advantage | Standard Term Frequency | Thesaurus Plus Phrases | Advantage |
| .1 | .6844 | .8745 | 27.8% | .7891 | .8919 | 13.0% | .7496 | .8339 | 11.2% |
| .2 | .5303 | .7908 | 49.1% | .6750 | .8331 | 23.4% | .7071 | .8138 | 15.0% |
| .3 | .4689 | .6387 | 36.2% | .5481 | .7057 | 28.8% | .6710 | .7812 | 16.4% |
| .4 | .3482 | .5401 | 55.1% | .4807 | .6443 | .340% | .6452 | .7681 | 19.0% |
| .5 | .3134 | .4516 | 44.1% | .4384 | .6099 | 39.1% | .6351 | .7006 | 10.3% |
| .6 | .2556 | .3718 | 45.5% | .3721 | .5548 | 49.1% | .5866 | .6882 | 17.3% |
| .7 | .1989 | .2979 | 49.8% | .3357 | .5179 | 54.3% | .5413 | .6389 | 18.0% |
| .8 | .1631 | .2019 | 23.8% | .2195 | .3949 | 79.9% | .5004 | .5915 | 18.2% |
| .9 | .1265 | .1556 | 23.0% | .1768 | .3505 | 98.2% | .3865 | .4842 | 25.3% |
| 1.0 | .1176 | .1375 | 16.9% | .1230 | .2484 | 101.9% | .3721 | .4790 | 28.7% |
| | | Average | +37% | | Average | +52% | | Average | +18% |
| | | Average (Phrases) | +32% | | Average (Phrases) | +39% | | Average (Phrases) | +17% |
| | | | + 5% | | | +13% | | | + 1% |

indexing methods applied to the three test collections in aerodynamics, medicine, and world affairs. Performance figures comparing the standard term frequency weighting ($f_{ki}$) for single terms $k$ in documents $i$ with the phrase process are shown in Table 3. The phrase procedure uses the normal single terms in addition to indexing phrases weighted in accordance with the formula of expression (7).

Table 3 contains precision figures averaged over 24 user queries for each of the test collections at ten specified recall levels ranging in magnitude from 0.1 to 1.0 in steps of 0.1. The percentage improvement in precision for the phrase process over the standard is also given at each recall level, together with an average improvement ranging from a high of 39% for the Medlars collection to a low of 17% for *Time.*

Table 4 contains output similar to that already shown in Table 3. However the data in Table 4 apply to an indexing system using both left-to-right (thesaurus) and right-to-left (phrase) transformations. It is seen from Table 4 that the thesaurus transformation adds an additional average improvement of 13% in precision for the Medlars collection; additional advantages are also obtained for the Cranfield and *Time* collections.

The evaluation results are summarized in Table 5. It is seen that average precision values of approximately 0.70, 0.40, and 0.20 at high, medium, and low precision are transformed into average figures of 0.90, 0.60 and 0.30 approximately when the discrimination properties of the terms are optimized. The retrieval results displayed in Tables 3, 4 and 5 have not been surpassed by any manual or automatic indexing procedures previously tried with sample document collections and user queries. Furthermore, because of the high average precision values produced by the indexing theories described in this study, it is not likely that additional drastic improvements in retrieval effectiveness are obtainable in the foreseeable future.

Table 5. Summary of Recall-Precision Evaluation (Three Collections)

| CRAN 424 | MED 450 | TIME 425 |
|---|---|---|
| Automatic Phrases vs. Standard Term Frequency +32% | Automatic Phrases vs. Standard Term Frequency +39% | Automatic Phrases vs. Standard Term Frequency +17% |
| Automatic Phrases Plus Thesaurus vs. Standard Run +37% | Automatic Phrases Plus Thesaurus vs. Standard Run +52% | Automatic Phrases Plus Thesaurus vs. Standard Run +18% |
| Best Precision Low Recall 0.89 Medium Recall 0.43 High Recall 0.13 | Best Precision Low Recall 0.88 Medium Recall 0.61 High Recall 0.23 | Best Precision Low Recall 0.85 Medium Recall 0.70 High Recall 0.45 |

## References


1. **Luhn, H.P.**, "A Statistical Approach to Mechanized Encoding and Searching of Literary Information," *IBM Journal of Research and Development*, 1 (No. 4): 309-317 (1957).
2. **Damerau, F.J.**, "An Experiment in Automatic Indexing," *American Documentation*, 16 (No. 4): 283-289 (1965).
3. **Sparck Jones, K.**, "A Statistical Interpretation of Term Specificity and its Application in Retrieval," *Journal of Documentation*, 28 (No. 1): 11-21 (1972).
4. **Dennis, S.F.**, "The Design and Testing of a Fully Automatic Indexing-Searching System for Documents Consisting of Expository Text," (in) *Information Retrieval—A Critical Review*, G. Schecter (ed.), Washington, DC: Thompson Book Co., 67-94 (1967).
5. **Bookstein, A.**, and **D.R. Swanson**, "Probabilistic Models for Automatic Indexing," *Journal of the American Society for Information Science*, 25 (No. 5): 312-318 (1974).
6. **Giuliano, V.E.**, and **P.E. Jones**, "Linear Associative Information Retrieval," (in) *Vistas (in) Information Handling*, **P. Howerton**, (ed.), Washington, DC: Spartan Books, Inc. (1963).
7. **Doyle, L.B.**, "Indexing and Abstracting by Association," *American Documentation*, 13 (No. 4): 378-390 (1962).
8. **Maron, M.E.**, and **J.L. Kuhns**, "On Relevance, Probabilistic Indexing and Information Retrieval," Journal of the Association for Computing Machinery, 7 (No. 3): 216-244 (1960).
9. ————————, "Automatic Indexing: An Experimental Inquiry," *Journal of the Association for Computing Machinery*, 8 (No. 3): 404-417 (1961).
10. **Salton, G.** and **C.S. Yang**, "On the Specification of Term Values in Automatic Indexing," *Journal of Documentation*, 29 (No. 4): 351-372 (1973).
11. ————————, **A. Wong** and **C.S. Yang**, *A Vector Space Model for Automatic Indexing*, Technical Report No. 74-208, Department of Computer Science, Cornell University, Ithaca, N.Y. (July 1974).
12. ————————, and **M.E. Lesk**, "Computer Evaluation of Indexing and Text Processing," *Journal of the Association for Computing Machinery*, 15(No. 1): 8-36 (1968).
13. **Sparck Jones, K.**, *Automatic Keyword Classifications*, London: Butterworths (1971).
14. **Gotlieb, C.C.** and **S. Kumar**, "Semantic Clustering of Index Terms," *Journal of the Association for Computing Machinery*, 15 (No. 4): 493-513. (1968).
15. **Salton, G.**, "Experiments in Automatic Thesaurus Construction for Information Retrieval," *Information Processing 71*, Amsterdam: North Holland Publishing Co., 115-123 (1972).
16. **Salton, G.**, **C.S. Yang** and **C.T. Yu**, "Contributions to the Theory of Indexing, *"Information Processing 74*, Amsterdam: North Holland Publishing Co., 584-590 (1974).

*Reprinted from* Journal of Documentation, *Vol. 28, No. 1, 1972.*

# A STATISTICAL INTERPRETATION OF TERM SPECIFICITY AND ITS APPLICATION IN RETRIEVAL

KAREN SPARCK JONES

*University of Cambridge Computer Laboratory*

The exhaustivity of document descriptions and the specificity of index terms are usually regarded as independent. It is suggested that specificity should be interpreted statistically, as a function of term use rather than of term meaning. The effects on retrieval of variations in term specificity are examined, experiments with three test collections showing in particular that frequently-occurring terms are required for good overall performance. It is argued that terms should be weighted according to collection frequency, so that matches on less frequent, more specific, terms are of greater value than matches on frequent terms. Results for the test collections show that considerable improvements in performance are obtained with this very simple procedure.

## EXHAUSTIVITY AND SPECIFICITY

WE ARE FAMILIAR with the notions of exhaustivity and specificity: exhaustivity is a property of index descriptions, and specificity one of index terms. They are most clearly illustrated by a simple keyword or descriptor system. In this case the exhaustivity of a document description is the coverage of its various topics given by the terms assigned to it; and the specificity of an individual term is the level of detail at which a given concept is represented.

These features of a document retrieval system have been discussed by Cleverdon *et al.*[4] and Lancaster,[6] for example, and the effects of variation in either have been noted. For instance, if the exhaustivity of a document description is increased by the assignment of more terms, when the number of terms in the indexing vocabulary is constant, the chance of the document matching a request is increased. The idea of an optimum level of indexing exhaustivity for a given document collection then follows: the average number of descriptors per document should be adjusted so that, hopefully, the chances of requests matching relevant documents are maximized, while too many false drops are avoided. Exhaustivity obviously applies to requests too, and one function of a search strategy is to vary request exhaustivity. I shall be mainly concerned here, however, with document descriptions.

Specificity as characterized above is a semantic property of index terms: a term is more or less specific as its meaning is more or less detailed and precise. This is a natural view for anyone concerned with the construction of an entire indexing vocabulary. Some decision has to be made about the discriminating power of individual terms in addition to their descriptive propriety. For example, the index term 'beverage' may be as properly used for documents about tea, coffee, and cocoa as the terms 'tea', 'coffee', and 'cocoa'. Whether the more general term 'beverage' only is incorporated in the vocabulary, or whether 'tea', 'coffee', and 'cocoa' are adopted, depends on judgements about the retrieval utility of distinctions between documents made by the latter but not the former. It is also predicted that the more general term would be applied to more documents than the separate terms 'tea', 'coffee', and 'cocoa', so the less specific term would have a larger collection distribution than the more specific ones.

It is of course assumed here that such choices when a vocabulary is constructed are exclusive: we may either have 'beverage' or 'tea', 'coffee', and 'cocoa'. What happens if we have all four terms is a different matter. We may then either interpret 'beverage' to mean 'other beverages' or explicitly treat it as a related broader term. I shall, however, disregard these alternatives here.

In setting up an index vocabulary the specificity of index terms is looked at from one point of view: we are concerned with the probable effects on document description, and hence retrieval, of choosing particular terms, or rather of adopting a certain set of terms. For our decisions will in part be influenced by relations between terms, and how the set of chosen terms will collectively characterize the set of documents. But throughout we assume some level of indexing exhaustivity. We are concerned with obtaining an effective vocabulary for a collection of documents of some broadly known subject matter and size, where a given level of indexing exhaustivity is believed to be sufficient to represent the content of individual documents adequately, and distinguish one document from another.

Index term specificity must, however, be looked at from another point of view. What happens when a given index vocabulary is actually used? We predict when we opt for 'beverage', for example, that it will be used more than 'cocoa'. But we do not have much idea of how many documents there will be to which 'beverage' may appropriately be assigned. This is not simply determined even when some level of exhaustivity is assumed. There will be some documents which cry out for 'beverage', so to speak, and we may have some idea of what proportion of the collection this is likely to be. There will also be documents to which 'beverage' cannot justifiably be assigned, and this proportion may also be estimated. But there is unfortunately liable to be some number of documents to which 'beverage' may or may not be assigned, in either case quite plausibly. In general, therefore, the actual use of a descriptor may diverge considerably from the predicted use. The proportions of a collection to which a term does and does not belong can only be estimated very roughly; and there may be enough intermediate documents for the way the term is assigned to these to affect its overall distribution considerably. Over a long period the character of the collection as a whole may also change, with further effects on term distribution.

This is where the level of exhaustivity of description matters. As a collection grows maintaining a certain level of exhaustivity may mean that the descriptions of different documents are not sufficiently distinguished, while some terms are very heavily used. More generally, great variation in term distribution is likely to appear. It may thus be the case that a particular term becomes less effective as a means of retrieval, whatever its actual meaning. This is because it is not discriminating. It may be properly assigned to documents, in the sense that their content justifies the assignment; but it may no longer be sufficiently useful in itself as a device for distinguishing the typically small class of documents relevant to a request from the remainder of the collection. A frequently used term thus functions in retrieval as a non-specific term, even though its meaning may be quite specific in the ordinary sense.

### STATISTICAL SPECIFICITY

It is not enough, in other words, to think of index term specificity solely in setting up an index vocabulary, as having to do with accuracy of concept representation. We should think of specificity as a function of term use. It should be interpreted as a statistical rather than semantic property of index terms. In general we may expect vaguer terms to be used more often, but the behaviour of individual terms will be unpredictable. We can thus redefine exhaustivity and specificity for simple term systems: the exhaustivity of a document description is the number of terms it contains, and the specificity of a term is the number of documents to which it pertains. The relation between the two is then clear, and we can see, for instance, that a change in the exhaustivity of descriptions will affect term specificity: if descriptions are longer, terms will be used more often. This is inevitable for a controlled vocabulary, but also applies if extracted keywords are used, particularly in stem form. The incidence of words new to the keyword vocabulary does not simply parallel the number of documents indexed, and the extraction of more keywords per document is more likely to increase the frequency of current keywords than to generate new ones.

Once this statistical interpretation of specificity, and the relation between it and exhaustivity, are recognized, it is natural to attempt a more formal approach to seeking an optimum level of specificity in a vocabulary and an optimum level of exhaustivity in indexing, for a given collection. Within the broad limits imposed by having sensible terms, i.e. ones which can be reached from requests and applied to documents, we may try to set up a vocabulary with the statistical properties which are hopefully optimal for retrieval. Purely formal calculations may suggest the correct number of terms, and of terms per document, for a certain degree of document discrimination. Work on these lines has been done by Zunde and Slamecka,[10] for instance. More informally, the suggestion that descriptors should be designed to have approximately the same distribution, made by Salton for example, is motivated by respect for the retrieval effects of purely statistical features of term use.

Unfortunately abstract calculations do not select actual terms. Nor are document collections static. More importantly, it is difficult to control requests. One may characterize documents with a view to distinguishing them nicely and then find that users do not provide requests utilizing these distinctions. We may therefore be forced to accept a de facto non-optimal situation with terms of varying specificity and at least some disagreeably non-specific terms. There will be some terms which, whatever the original intention, retrieve a large number of documents, of which only a small proportion can be expected to be relevant to a request. Such terms are on the whole more of a nuisance than rare, over-specific terms which fail to retrieve documents.

These features of term behaviour can be illustrated by examples from three well-known test collections, obtained from the Aslib Cranfield, INSPEC, and College of Librarianship Wales projects. In fact in these the vocabulary consists of extracted keyword stems, which may be expected to show more variation than controlled terms. But there is no reason to suppose that the situation is essentially different. Full descriptions of the collections are given in Cleverdon *et al*,[4] Aitchison *et al*,[1] and Keen (forthcoming). Relevant characteristics of the collections are given in Section A of Table 1. The INSPEC Collection, for instance, has 541 documents in-

TABLE I

| | *Cranfield* | *INSPEC* | *Keen* |
|---|---|---|---|
| A. Number of documents | 200 | 541 | 797 |
| Number of terms | 712 | 1,341 | 939 |
| Number of terms per document | 32 | 12·2 | 7·9 |
| Number of documents per term | 9 | 4·9 | 6·1 |
| B. Number of requests | 42 | 97 | 63 |
| Number of terms represented | 166 | 248 | 183 |
| Number of terms per request | 6·9 | 5·6 | 5·3 |
| Number of documents per request term | 31·6 | 11·5 | 44·8 |
| C. Number of retrieving terms per request | 5 | 3·2 | 3·3 |
| Number of retrieving terms per document | 1·8 | 1·2 | 1·2 |
| Number of retrieving terms per relevant document | 3·6 | 2 | 1·8 |
| D. Number of frequent terms | 96 | 73 | 50 |
| Number of frequent terms per request | 4 | 2·5 | 2·3 |

dexed by 1,341 terms. In all the collections, there are some very frequently occurring terms: for example in the Cranfield collection, one term occurs in 144 out of 200 documents; in the INSPEC one term occurs in 112 out of 541, and in the Keen collection one term occurs in 199 out of 797 documents. The terms concerned do not necessarily represent concepts central to the subject areas of the collections, and they are not always general terms. In the Keen collection, which is about information science, the most frequent term is 'index–', and other frequent ones include 'librar–', 'inform–', and 'comput–'. In the INSPEC collection the most frequent is 'theor–', followed by 'measur–' and 'method–'. And in the Cranfield collection the most frequent is 'flow–', followed by 'pressur–', 'distribut–' and 'bound–' (boundary). The rarer terms are a fine mixed bag including 'purchas–', and 'xerograph–' for Keen, 'parallel–' and 'silver–' for INSPEC, and 'logarithm–' and 'seri–' (series) for Cranfield.

## SPECIFICITY AND MATCHING

How should one cope with variable term specificity, and especially with insufficiently specific terms, when these occur in requests? The untoward effects of frequent term use can in principle be dealt with very naturally, through term combinations. For instance, though the three terms 'bound–', 'layer–', and 'flow–' occur in 73, 62, and 144 documents each in the Cranfield collection, there are only fifty documents indexed by all three terms together. Relying on term conjunction is quite straightforward. It is in particular a way of overcoming the untoward consequences of the fact that requests tend to be formulated in better known, and hence generally more frequent, terms. It is unfortunate, but not surprising, that requests tend to be presented in terms with an average frequency much above that for the indexing vocabulary as a whole. This holds for all three test collections, as appears in Section B of Table 1. For the Cranfield collection, for example, the average number of postings for the terms in the vocabulary is nine, while the average for the terms used in the requests is 31·6; for Keen the figures are 6·1 and 44·8.

But relying on term combination to reduce false drops is well-known to be risky. It is true that the more terms in common between a document and a request, the more likely it is that the document is relevant to the request. Unfortunately, it just happens to be difficult to match term conjunctions. This is well exhibited by the term matching behaviour of the three collections, as shown in Section C of Table 1. The average number of starting terms per request ranges from 5·3 for Keen to 6·9 for Cranfield. But the average number of retrieving terms per request, i.e. the average of the highest matching scores, ranges from 3·2 to 5·0. More importantly, the average number of matching terms for the relevant documents retrieved ranges from only 1·8 for Keen to 3·6 for Cranfield, though fortunately the average for all documents retrieved, which are predominantly non-relevant, ranges from a mere 1·2 to 1·8.

Clearly, one solution to this problem is to provide for more matching terms in some way. This may be achieved either by providing alternative substitutes for given terms, through a classification; or by increasing the exhaustivity of document or request specifications, say by adding statistically associated terms. But either approach involves effort, perhaps considerable effort, since the sets of terms related to individual terms must be identified. The question naturally arises as to whether better use of existing term descriptions can be made which does not involve such effort.

As very frequently occurring terms are responsible for noise in retrieval, one possible course is simply to remove them from requests. The fact that this will reduce the number of terms available for conjoined matching may be offset by the fact that fewer non-relevant documents will be retrieved. Unfortunately, while frequent terms cause noise, they are also required for reasonably high recall. For all three test collections, the deletion of very frequent terms by the application of a suitable threshold leads to a decline in overall performance. For the INSPEC collection, for example, the threshold was set to delete terms occurring in twenty or more documents, so that seventy-three terms out of the total vocabulary of 1,341 were removed. The effect in retrieval performance is illustrated by the recall/precision graph of Figure 1 for the Cranfield collection. Matching is by simple term

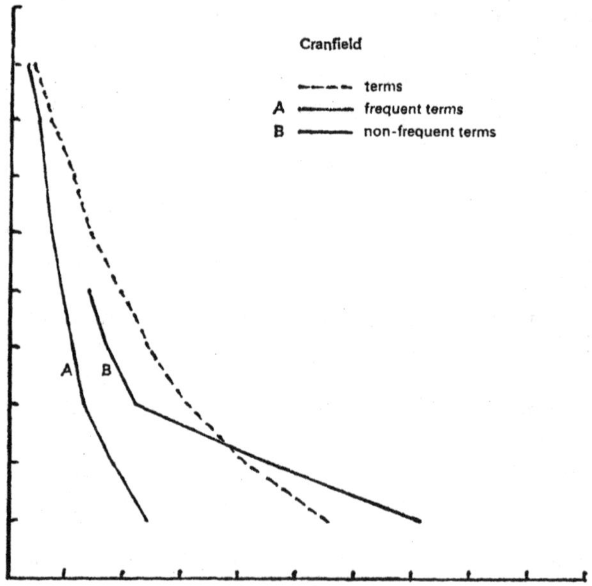


FIG. 1

co-ordination levels, and averaging over the set of requests is by straightforward average of numbers. Precision at ten standard recall values is then interpolated. The same relationship between full term matching and this restricted matching with non-frequent terms only is exhibited by the other collections: the recall ceiling is lowered by at least 30%, and indeed for the Keen collection is reduced from 75% to 25%, though precision is maintained.

Inspection of the requests shows why this result is obtained. Not merely is request term frequency much above average collection frequency; the comparatively small number of very frequent terms plays a large part in request formulation. 'Flow–' for example, appears in twelve Cranfield requests out of forty-two, and in general for all three collections about half the terms in a request are very frequent ones, as shown in Section D of Table 1. Throwing very frequent terms away is throwing the baby out with the bath water, since they are required for the retrieval of many relevant documents. The combination of non-frequent terms is discriminating, but no more than that of frequent and non-frequent terms. The value of the non-frequent terms is clearly seen, on the other hand, when matching using frequent terms only is compared with full matching, also shown in Figure 1. Matching levels for total and relevant documents are nearly as high as for all terms, but the non-frequent terms in the latter raise the relevant matching level about 1.

These features of term retrieval suggest that to improve on the initial full term performance we need to exploit the good features of very frequent and non-frequent terms, while minimizing their bad ones. We should allow some merit in frequent term matches, while allowing rather more in non-frequent ones. In any case we wish to maximize the number of matching terms.

## WEIGHTING BY SPECIFICITY

This clearly suggests a weighting scheme. In normal term co-ordination matches, if a request and document have a frequent term in common, this counts for as much as a non-frequent one; so if a request and document share three common terms, the document is retrieved at the same level as another one sharing three rare terms with the request. But it seems we should treat matches on non-frequent terms as more valuable than ones on frequent terms, without disregarding the latter altogether. The natural solution is to correlate a term's matching value with its collection frequency. At this stage the division of terms into frequent and non-frequent is arbitrary and probably not optimal: the elegant and almost certainly better approach is to relate matching value more closely to relative frequency. The appropriate way of doing this is suggested by the term distribution curve for the vocabulary, which has the familiar Zipf shape. Let $f(n) = m$ such that $2^{m-1} < n \leqslant 2^m$. Then where there are $N$ documents in the collection, the weight of a term which occurs $n$ times is $f(N) - f(n) + 1$. For the Cranfield collection with 200 documents, for example, this means that a term occurring ninety times has weight 2, while one occurring three times has weight 7.

The matching value of a term is thus correlated with its specificity and the retrieval level of a document is determined by the sum of the values of its matching terms. Simple co-ordination levels are replaced by a more sophisticated quasi-ranking. The effect can be illustrated by the different retrieval levels at which two documents matching a request on the same number of relatively frequent and relatively non-frequent terms respectively. With the Cranfield range of values, a document matching on two terms with frequencies 15 and 43 will be retrieved at level $5 + 3 = 8$, while one matching on terms with frequencies 3 and 7 will be retrieved at level $7 + 6 = 13$. Clearly, as the range of levels is 'stretched', more discrimination is possible.

The idea of term weighting is not new. But it is typically related to the presumed importance of a term with respect to a document in itself. For instance, if a document is mainly about paint and only mentions varnish in passing, we may utilize some simple weighting scale to assign a weight of 2 to the term 'paint' and 1 to 'varnish'. More informally, in putting a request, we may state that during searching term x must be retained, but term y may be dropped. More systematic weighting on a statistical base may be adopted if the necessary information is available. If the actual frequency of occurrence of terms in a document (or abstract) is known, this may be used to generate weights. Artandi and Wolfe[2] report the use of frequency to select a weight from a three-point scale, while Salton[7] more wholeheartedly uses the frequency of occurrence as a weight. In a range of experiments Salton has demonstrated that weighting terms in this way leads to a noticeable improvement in performance over that obtained for unweighted terms.

Weighting by collection frequency as opposed to document frequency is quite different. It places greater emphasis on the value of a term as a means of distinguishing one document from another than on its value as an indication of the content of the document itself. The relation between the two forms of weighting is not obvious. In some cases a term may be common in a document and rare in the collection, so that it would be heavily weighted in both schemes. But the reverse may also apply. It is really that the emphasis is on different properties of terms.

The treatment of term collection frequency in connection with term matching does not seem to have been systematically investigated. The effect of term frequency on statistical associations has been studied, for example by Lesk, but this is a different matter. The fact that a given term is likely to retrieve a large number of documents may be informally exploited in setting up searches, in particular in the context of on-line retrieval as described by Borko[6] for example. More whole-hearted approaches are probably hampered by the lack of the necessary information. Such a procedure as the one described is also much more suited to automatic than manual searching. It is of interest, therefore, that term frequencies have been exploited in the general manner indicated within an operational interactive retrieval system for internal reports implemented at A. D. Little (Curtice and Jones[5]). In this system indexing keywords are extracted automatically from text, and the weighting is therefore associated with a changing vocabulary and collection. However, no systematic experiments are reported.

## EXPERIMENTAL RESULTS

The term weighting system described was tried on the three collections. As noted, these are very different in character, with different sizes of vocabulary, document description, and request specification, as indicated in Table 1. In all cases, however, matching with term weighting led to a substantial improvement in performance over simple term matching. The results presented in the form mentioned earlier, are given in Figure 2. A simple significance test based on the difference in area enclosed by the curves shows that the improvement given by weighted terms is fully significant, the difference being well above the required minimum.

These results are of interest for two reasons. All three collections have been used for a whole range of experiments with different index languages,

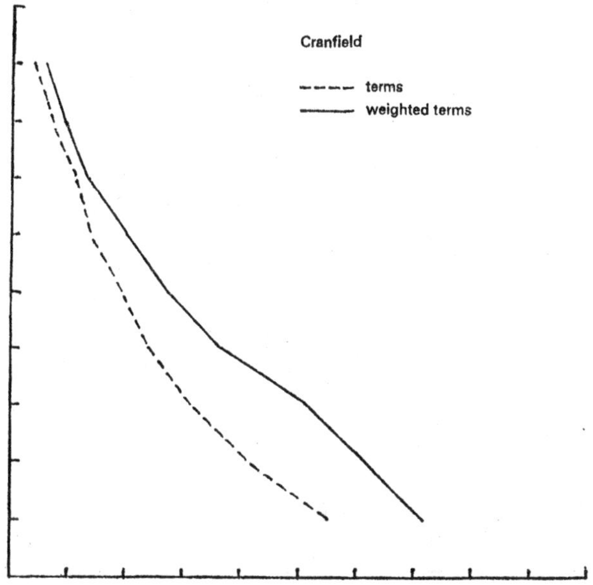


FIG. 2a

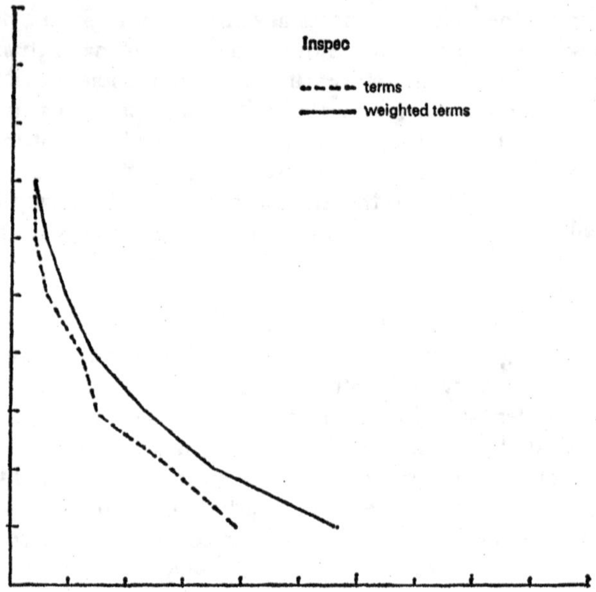


FIG. 2*b*

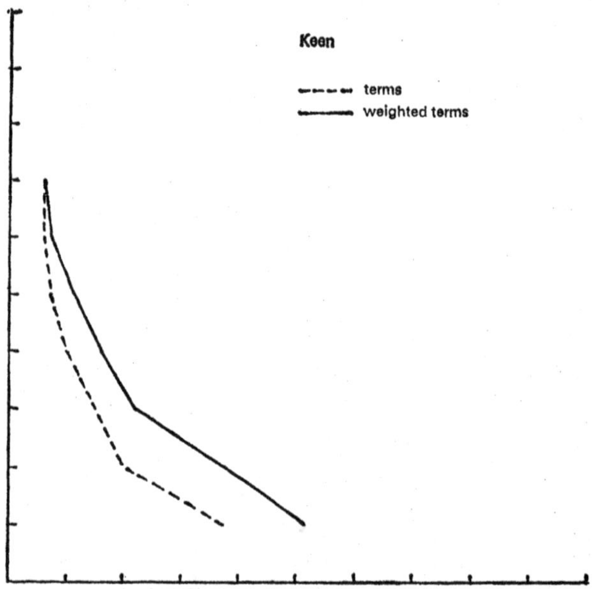


FIG. 2*c*

search techniques, and so on: see Cleverdon *et al*,[4] Salton,[7] Salton and Lesk,[8] and Sparck Jones;[9] Aitchison *et al*[1] and Keen (forthcoming). The performance improvement obtained here nevertheless represents as good an improvement over simple unweighted keyword stem matching as has been obtained by any other means, including carefully constructed thesauri: Salton's iterative search methods are not comparable. The details of the way these experimental results are presented varies, so rigorous comparisons are impossible: but the general picture is clear. Indeed, in so far as anything can be called a solid result in information retrieval research, this is one. The second point about the present results is that the improvement in performance is obtained by extremely simple means. It is compatible with an initially plain method of indexing, namely the use of extracted keywords, which may be reduced to stems automatically; it is readily implemented given an automatic term-matching procedure, since all that is required is a term frequency list and this is easily obtained; and it has the merit that the weight assigned to terms is naturally adjusted to follow the growth of and changes in a collection. Experiments with very much larger collections than those used here are clearly desirable; they will hopefully not be long delayed.

## REFERENCES


1. AITCHISON, T. M., HALL, A. M., LAVELLE, K. H., *and* TRACY, J. M. *Comparative evaluation of index languages, Part II; Results*, Project INSPEC, Institute of Electrical Engineers, London, 1970.
2. ARTANDI, S. *and* WOLF, E. H. The effectiveness of automatically-generated weights and links, *American Documentation*, vol. 20, 1969, p. 198–202.
3. BORKO, H. Interactive document storage and retrieval systems—design concepts, *Mechanised information storage, retrieval and dissemination* (ed. Samuleson), Amsterdam, North-Holland, 1968, p. 591–99.
4. CLEVERDON, C. W., MILLS, J., *and* KEEN, E. M. *Factors determining the performance of indexing systems*, 2 vols. Cranfield, 1966.
5. CURTICE, R. M. *and* JONES, P. E. An operational interactive retrieval system. Cambridge, Mass., Arthur D. Little Inc., 1969.
6. LANCASTER, F. W., *Information retrieval systems: characteristics, testing and evaluation*, New York, Wiley, 1968.
7. SALTON, G. *Automatic information organization and retrieval*, New York, McGraw-Hill, 1968.
8. SALTON, G. *and* LESK, M. E. Computer evaluation of indexing and text processing, *Journal of the ACM*, vol. 15, 1968, p. 8–36.
9. SPARCK JONES, K. *Automatic keyword classification for information retrieval*, London, Butterworths, 1971.
10. ZUNDE, P. *and* SLAMECKA, V. Distribution of indexing terms for maximum efficiency of information transmission, *American Documentation*, vol. 18, 1967, p. 104–8.

*Reprinted from Information Processing & Management, Vol. 15.*


# EXPERIMENTS IN RELEVANCE WEIGHTING OF SEARCH TERMS

K. SPARCK JONES

Computer Laboratory, University of Cambridge, Corn Exchange Street, Cambridge, England

(*Received* 15 *September* 1978)

**Abstract**—Following successful initial tests of theoretically-based schemes for relevance weighting of search terms, further experiments were undertaken to validate these results. The experiments were designed to investigate weighting for a large document set, poor matching conditions, heterogeneous data, and limited relevance information, i.e. the use of weighting in more realistic conditions than the initial ones. The results confirm the earlier ones: very striking improvements in retrieval performance were obtained, especially for the theoretically best-founded weighting formula. The experiments illustrate a much more promising application of statistical methods to indexing and searching than any studied hitherto.

This paper describes large scale experiments to test the value of index term weighting based on relevance information, and presents results showing that weighting leads to remarkable improvements in retrieval performance.

## RELEVANCE WEIGHTING

ROBERTSON and SPARCK JONES[1] discussed the use of relevance weights for index terms, i.e. term weights derived from information about the occurrences of request terms in known relevant documents; presented a statistically-based approach to the computation of such weights; and, with reference to relatively limited experiments, showed (a) that substantial improvements in retrieval performance could be obtained through the use of these weights, and (b) that formulae with certain specific bases work better than others.

This paper describes experiments designed to investigate these methods of relevance weighting more fully. In particular, since it can be proved (see YU and SALTON[2], ROBERTSON[3]) that relevance information in given circumstances must improve retrieval performance in simple term matching, the experiments attempted to show whether favourable conditions are likely to be encountered in practice. It might indeed be argued, though somewhat tentatively, that if the experimental material is sufficiently varied, the tests can be regarded as falsifying rather than confirming ones.

The theoretical basis of our approach to weighting is fully described in [1], and so is simply summarised for convenience here. Specifically, we assume simple binary term document and request characterisations, with the terms treated independently in matching. The information available for weighting a given request term (assuming some documents are known to be relevant to the request) is expressed in the following contingency table:

| | | relevant + | relevant − | |
|---|---|---|---|---|
| indexed | + | $r$ | $n-r$ | $n$ |
| indexed | − | $R-r$ | $N-n-R+r$ | $N-n$ |
| | | $R$ | $N-R$ | $N$ |

where for term $t$ in request $q$: $n$ = the number of documents containing $t$, $r$ = the number of relevant documents containing $t$, $N$ = the number of documents in the collection, and $R$ = the number of relevant documents for $q$.

The exploitation of this information in a probabilistic weighting formula is determined by a choice of an underlying Independence Assumption about the data and an Ordering Principle for the search output. There are two possible Assumptions I1 and I2, as follows: I1, the distribution of terms in relevant documents is independent, and their distribution in all documents is independent; I2, the distribution of terms in relevant documents is independent, and their distribution in non-relevant documents is independent; and two possible Principles 01 and 02, as follows: 01, that probable relevance is based only on the presence of search terms in documents; 02, that probable relevance is based on both the presence of search terms in documents and their absence from documents. Assumptions and Principles may be combined in four ways giving four weighting formulae F1–F4:

| | I1 | I2 |
|---|---|---|
| 01 | F1 | F2 |
| 02 | F3 | F4 |

Thus the formulae define the weight of an index term as follows:

$$w = \log \frac{\left(\frac{r}{R}\right)}{\left(\frac{n}{N}\right)} \qquad \text{(F1)}$$

$$w = \log \frac{\left(\frac{r}{R}\right)}{\left(\frac{n-r}{N-R}\right)} \qquad \text{(F2)}$$

$$w = \log \frac{\left(\frac{r}{R-r}\right)}{\left(\frac{n}{N-n}\right)} \qquad \text{(F3)}$$

$$w = \log \frac{\left(\frac{r}{R-r}\right)}{\left(\frac{n-r}{N-n-R+r}\right)} \qquad \text{(F4)}$$

The development of these formulae is outlined in the Appendix to [1]. It was argued in [1] that theoretically F4 should perform best, and this was borne out by experiment in that the other formulae either performed less well, or no better. F1, which is closest to relevance formulae used in other work (see MILLER[4], BARKER *et al.*[5] and ROBSON and LONGMAN[6]) performed least well. Results for F2 were similar to those for F1 and F3 to F4. Since F1 and F4 represent the most strongly contrasted formulae, subsequent work has been confined to them.

In searching, documents are ordered by their sum of weights score, but only documents with positive scores are deemed retrieved.† Performance is evaluated using recall and precision: specific results are obtained by averaging by numbers at matching value levels, with subsequent linear interpolation to obtain precision at ten standard recall levels.

It is evident that the primary use of relevance information is in predictive weighting, i.e. in the derivation of weights from given data for use in new searches. In the experiments reported in [1] the value of predictive weighting was shown by the application of weights derived from half of a test collection, the even-numbered documents, in searching the other, odd-numbered half. Thus for 225 requests and 700 out of 1400 documents characterised by relatively long, manually-obtained term lists, requests with relevance weights performed substantially better than unweighted requests; relevance weighting was also much superior to simple weighting by (inverse) term collection frequency alone, itself superior to unweighted matching. For prediction the weighting formulae are modified to allow for uncertainty by the addition of 0.5 to the contingency table components. Thus F1 and F4 respectively become

†F4 requires a scaling constant: see [1].

$$w = \log \frac{\left(\frac{r+0.5}{R+1.0}\right)}{\left(\frac{n+1.0}{N+2.0}\right)} \quad \text{and} \quad w = \log \frac{\left(\frac{r+0.5}{R-r+0.5}\right)}{\left(\frac{n-r+0.5}{N-n-R+r+0.5}\right)}.$$

The formula for collection frequency weighting is the simple one

$$w = -\log\left(\frac{n}{N}\right),$$

implemented as

$$w = -\log\left(\frac{n}{\max n}\right). \qquad \text{(F0)}$$

This formula is not directly related formally to the relevance formulae, but is clearly based on a similar statistical approach.

Relevance weights may, however, also be applied retrospectively to establish optimal performance for the weighting formulae used, and hence a performance yardstick. The retrospective weighting tests also reported in [1] showed that for the relatively small collections used, a high level of performance is possible. SPARCK JONES[7] suggested that such yardsticks have a wider utility in the evaluation of indexing and searching experiments generally. The retrospective application of the relevance weighting formulae requires special treatment of limiting cases where components = 0. These are fully detailed in [1]. Unfortunately retrieval runs with special cases are expensive, so to simplify matters weights computed with the predictive formulae may be applied retrospectively: the performance obtained is still useful as a yardstick, though it tends to be lower than that given by the "pure" formulae.

## EXPERIMENTAL OBJECTIVES

The object of the present series of experiments was to test relevance weighting more adequately. They were designed (a) to test our initial results with new data for (i) the performance of relevance weighted terms compared with collection frequency weighted terms (F0), (ii) the performance of relevance weighted terms compared with unweighted terms, and (iii) the performance of terms relevance weighted by F4 compared with terms weighted by F1; and (b), more importantly, to establish the possible practical limits on the utility of relevance weighting. In fact, tests appropriate to (b) would cover (a) as well.

Specifically, tests for the utility of relevance weighting should provide answers for the following questions:

(1) is relevance weighting impervious to scale effects, i.e. is it effective for the large collections encountered in real life?

(2) is relevance weighting useful in poor matching conditions, i.e. when few index keys are available for requests and documents?

(3) is relevance weighting helpful for heterogeneous collections, i.e. where the document files consist of only partly-related subject groupings?

(4) is relevance weighting effective even where little relevance information is available?

Ideally, such questions should be answered for the stringent conditions of modern on-line search systems where files are large and heterogeneous, a search specification may be filled out only slowly, and few documents may be evaluated on each search iteration. But there are many methodological and practical difficulties about adequate, controlled, on-line search experiments, and we thought it would be more useful to start by investigating relevance weighting in less stringent but more realistic conditions than those of our first experiments. The tests reported here therefore model SDI operations, with real data. Their limitations and the direction of future experiments are considered in the conclusion.

## EVALUATION PROBLEMS

The main problem about conducting any experiments designed to answer questions (1)–(4) is of obtaining adequate test data. The tests described in (1) used a small collection with requests and documents indexed in an appropriate way by natural language word stem lists, and for which exhaustive relevance assessments were available. Weighting was therefore simply a natural extension of the coordination searching used in other experiments with the collection (see for example CLEVERDON *et al.*[8] and SPARCK JONES and BATES[9]), and the calculation of weights and evaluation of output presented no problems since the relevance status of every document in the collection was known.

Limited relevance information makes evaluation difficult when new search methods retrieve unassessed documents. If evaluation is geared to previously assessed output a completely false picture of performance for the new methods may be obtained; thus if the assessed output is associated with a specific search method, characterising performance for a new strategy only by its failures compared with the other's successes, and not vice versa, is evidently unfair. The difficulty is compounded, for weighting experiments, if the assessed output is that of Boolean searches. As the objective of weighting is to order output, it is most appropriately compared only with other indexing and searching strategies designed to produce similar output; if unordered output is in question, some neutral method is required of fixing a cutoff to select the highest ranking documents as the output set. Since operational systems tend to produce retrieved sets meeting Boolean specifications, comparing unconventional relevance weight searching with their conventional searching clearly presents problems. MILLER[4] approached this problem by setting the cutoff for the weighted search to give approximately the number of documents retrieved in the earlier Boolean searches, but this technique clearly introduces bias. A similar technique, noted as not wholly satisfactory, was used by EVANS[10]. Abandoning the ordering given by weighting is in any case only plausible if it is so small that ordering within it is unimportant; applying a cutoff to obtain a set for comparison with a large Boolean output is throwing away an advantage of weighting.

These evaluation difficulties are liable to arise when any attempt is made to conduct large scale experiments relevant to operational systems, and in particular to exploit any available test data derived from such systems, since this is typically restricted in some "undesirable" way. It may be possible with such data to carry out some experiments of interest, for example to compare the performance of F1 and F4; but for the reasons just mentioned it may not be possible to relate performance for the relevance weighting techniques with which we are concerned to conventional performance for the systems from which the data was derived, in a systematic and reliable way.

This point has been laboured to ensure that our experimental results are not misinterpreted. The tests reported in this paper are primarily ones designed to provide more information about the value of relevance weighting for search contexts to which it is appropriate, and only secondarily, given the limitations of the available data, to allow some estimates to the extent to which relevance weighting could compete with conventional search techniques.

## TEST DATA

The only conveniently available data meeting the requirements imposed by the test questions was that derived from the UKCIS project (BARKER *et al.*[5] and also [11]).† This consists of 27361 documents taken from Chemical Abstracts Condensates and 75 standard Boolean profiles intended for SDI use. The documents are represented by titles, while the profiles are of an exhaustive kind involving words or word strings, with front and/or back truncation. Relevance assessments are for the pooled output of UKCIS searches on different document fields and with different profile formulations, representing an average of 195.6 documents assessed per profile. For the relevance weighting tests the Boolean profile structure was abandoned, and in addition NOT terms were rejected. This gave simple term (fragment, word or string) lists for the profiles, averaging 18.3 terms.

It will be evident that the material is subject to the limitations discussed earlier in providing only limited relevance information, and those relating to Boolean search performance. It is, however, adequate for direct studies of relevance weighting, and specifically, meets the requirements of our initial questions. Thus the document set is large, if not enormous. (The request set is also a respectable size, meeting a general experimental requirement.) The

†Made available by courtesy of UKCIS.

document set size means that predictive experiments on an acceptable scale can be conducted, in an attempt to answer question 1. As the set is large, subsets of varying sizes and predictive merit can be extracted for tests to answer question 4. Further, the document set consists of two major blocks of items from CAC, representing two major subject area groupings of CA: this provides material for question 3. (The file size is in any case large enough for considerable topic variation.) Finally, the original user need statements are available for use in answering question 2: when processed "straight" they provide an average of 5.7 search terms per question, for comparison with the much fuller profiles. Obtaining test data without any limitations is outside the scope of the individual project: the UKCIS material meets the essential test requirements, and is also derived from an operational service. It is therefore adequate for the purpose of validating past experiments and of beginning to relate them to operational environments. Details of the test data are given in Table 1.

## EXPERIMENTS

The general pattern of the tests was as follows. In each case two parts of the document set were used: the first, the weight generation subset, provided the information for computing the term relevance weights; the second, the weight application subset, was searched using the weights for the request terms derived from the documents in the first subset. In the artificial conditions of the experiment it was assumed that the entire weight generation subset was evaluated to provide relevance information: i.e. all the known relevant documents in the subset were deemed identified relevant. This treatment of the collection allows the following performance comparisons:

(a) between relevance weighted term searching and simple unweighted term searching for the application set;

(b) between relevance searching and collection frequency weighted searching for the application set;

(c) between relevance weighted term searching based on different formulae, i.e. F1 and F4; and

(d) between the predictive relevance weighted searching and the corresponding retrospective relevance weighted searching, the latter using the application set as generation set.

In a given test, therefore, the range of comparisons is over terms, collection frequency weights, predictive relevance weights using F1 and the same using F4, and retrospective relevance weights. As indicated earlier, performance is represented by recall/precision figures giving a conventional graph. As significance tests are not easily applied to such results, it is assumed, crudely, that an area difference of 5% is significant. In earlier papers a difference of more than 5% was labelled noticeable, and one of more than 10% material. We are dealing here with rather larger performance differences, and also with a wide range of performance comparisons, while we may attach more importance to a smaller percentage improvement at high precision than a larger one at low because the absolute performance improvement is greater. We can accordingly only characterise performance differences informally, and will use three degrees of difference, saying (a) is better than (b), or much better, or strikingly better, than (b), and defining these degrees ostensively by reference to the test recall/precision results. A convenient notation for the degrees of difference is '⟩', '⟩⟩' and '⟩⟩⟩', while the forms of searching may be named T (terms), C (collection frequency weights), R (relevance weights), hence R1 and R4 and Y (yardstick), hence Y1 and Y4, or Y1p and Y4p if the predictive formula is applied retrospectively. Our experimental objective may therefore be summarised as being to show that in four defined contexts, at least R4⟩R1⟩C⟩T.

The individual tests were as follows.

### *Experiment* 1: *scale effects*

Following the model of the experiments reported in (1), the document set was divided into even and odd-numbered subsets. The Even set was used for generation and the Odd for application. Relevant data details are given in Table 1. The recall and precision results obtained for the different runs are given in Table 2.1 and illustrated in Fig. 1. They cover terms, T, collection weights, C, predictive relevance weights R1 and R4, yardstick "pure" retrospective relevance weights for both formulae, i.e. Y1 and Y4, and Y1p and Y4p. Comparison across the

Table 1. Data details.

| | | | |
|---|---|---|---|
| No. profiles | | 75 | |
| Av. terms per profile | | 18.3 | |
| No. documents | | 27361 | |
| No. word stems in titles | | 17537 | |
| Av. stems per document | | 6.6 | |
| No. different documents relevant to some profile | | 3380 | |
| No. relevant postings | | 3739 | |
| Av. relevant per profile | | 49.9 | |
| Av. documents assessed per profile by UKCIS | | 195.6 | |
| **Experiment 1** | | | |
| No. documents | | Even | 13680 |
| | | Odd | 13681 |
| No. relevant postings | | Even | 1837 |
| | | Odd | 1902 |
| Av. relevant per profile | | Even | 24.5 |
| | | Odd | 25.4 |
| **Experiment 2** | | | |
| Av. word stems per request | | | 5.7 |
| Documents as Experiment 1 | | | |
| Relevant " " " | | | |
| **Experiment 3** | | | |
| No. documents (CAC-1) | | First | 11613 |
| (CAC-2) | | Last | 15748 |
| No. relevant postings | | First | 1444 |
| | | Last | 2295 |
| Av. relevant per profile | | First | 19.3 |
| | | Last | 30.6 |
| **Experiment 4** | | | |
| No. documents | | Sixteenth | 1711 |
| | | Eighth | 3421 |
| | | Quarter | 6841 |
| | | Half | 13681 |
| | Search | Quarter | 6840 |
| No. relevant postings (estimated as percent whole collection for generation sets) | | Sixteenth | 234 |
| | | Eighth | 467 |
| | | Quarter | 935 |
| | | Half | 1870 |
| | Search | Quarter | 902 |
| Av. relevant per profile | | Sixteenth | 3.1 |
| | | Eighth | 6.2 |
| | | Quarter | 12.5 |
| | | Half | 24.9 |
| | Search | Quarter | 12.0 |

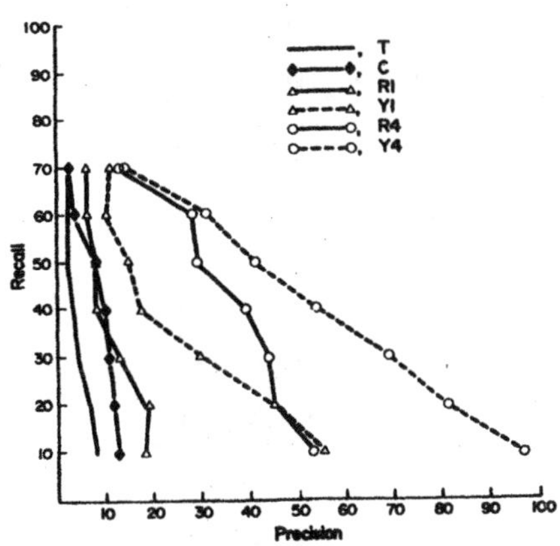


Fig. 1. Experiment 1.

**Table 2. Retrieval performance.**

| | | PRECISION | | | | | | | | | | |
|---|---|---|---|---|---|---|---|---|---|---|---|---|
| 2.1 | G | - | - | Even | Even | Odd | Odd | Odd | Odd | | | |
| Experiment 1 | A | Odd | Odd | Odd | Odd | Odd | Odd | Odd | Odd | | | |
| | | T | C | R1 | R4 | Y1 | Y4 | Y1p | Y4p | | | |
| RECALL | 100 | 0 | 0 | 0 | 0 | 0 | 0 | 0 | 0 | | | |
| | 90 | 0 | 0 | 0 | 0 | 0 | 0 | 0 | 0 | | | |
| | 80 | 0 | 0 | 0 | 0 | 0 | 0 | 0 | 0 | | | |
| | 70 | 2 | 2 | 6 | 13 | 11 | 14 | 6 | 14 | | | |
| | 60 | 2 | 3 | 6 | 28 | 10 | 31 | 6 | 28 | | | |
| | 50 | 2 | 8 | 8 | 29 | 15 | 42 | 8 | 36 | | | |
| | 40 | 3 | 10 | 8 | 39 | 17 | 54 | 9 | 42 | | | |
| | 30 | 4 | 11 | 13 | 44 | 30 | 69 | 15 | 54 | | | |
| | 20 | 7 | 12 | 19 | 45 | 45 | 81 | 22 | 60 | | | |
| | 10 | 8 | 13 | 18 | 53 | 55 | 97 | 23 | 62 | | | |
| 2.2 | G | - | - | Even | Even | Odd | Odd | Odd | Odd | | | |
| Experiment 2 | A | Odd | Odd | Odd | Odd | Odd | Odd | Odd | Odd | | | |
| | | T | C | R1 | R4 | Y1 | Y4 | Y1p | Y4p | | | |
| RECALL | 100 | 0 | 0 | 0 | 0 | 0 | 0 | 0 | 0 | | | |
| | 90 | 0 | 0 | 0 | 0 | 0 | 0 | 0 | 0 | | | |
| | 80 | 0 | 0 | 0 | 0 | 0 | 0 | 0 | 0 | | | |
| | 70 | 0 | 0 | 0 | 0 | 0 | 0 | 0 | 0 | | | |
| | 60 | 0 | 0 | 0 | 0 | 0 | 0 | 0 | 0 | | | |
| | 50 | 0 | 0 | 0 | 0 | 0 | 0 | 0 | 0 | | | |
| | 40 | 0 | 0 | 0 | 0 | 0 | 0 | 0 | 0 | | | |
| | 30 | 1 | 2 | 2 | 4 | 5 | 8 | 2 | 6 | | | |
| | 20 | 1 | 6 | 8 | 16 | 13 | 29 | 8 | 22 | | | |
| | 10 | 5 | 14 | 14 | 30 | 38 | 58 | 19 | 46 | | | |
| 2.3 | G | - | - | First | First | Last | Last | Last | Last | | | |
| Experiment 3 | A | Last | Last | Last | Last | Last | Last | Last | Last | | | |
| | | T | C | R1 | R4 | Y1 | Y4 | Y1p | Y4p | | | |
| RECALL | 100 | 0 | 0 | 0 | 0 | 0 | 0 | 0 | 0 | | | |
| | 90 | 0 | 0 | 0 | 0 | 0 | 0 | 0 | 0 | | | |
| | 80 | 0 | 0 | 0 | 0 | 0 | 0 | 0 | 0 | | | |
| | 70 | 2 | 2 | 3 | 0 | 6 | 8 | 3 | 7 | | | |
| | 60 | 2 | 4 | 3 | 16 | 12 | 43 | 7 | 41 | | | |
| | 50 | 2 | 7 | 6 | 20 | 12 | 52 | 7 | 46 | | | |
| | 40 | 3 | 10 | 6 | 23 | 11 | 56 | 6 | 51 | | | |
| | 30 | 3 | 12 | 7 | 23 | 20 | 65 | 9 | 57 | | | |
| | 20 | 6 | 13 | 8 | 36 | 42 | 79 | 18 | 62 | | | |
| | 10 | 7 | 13 | 12 | 41 | 51 | 92 | 20 | 70 | | | |
| 2.4 | G | - | - | Six. | Ei. | Quar. | Half | Se.Q. | Se.Q. | Ei. | Se.Q. | Se.Q. |
| Experiment 4 | A | Se.Q. | Se.Q. | Se.Q. | Se.Q. | Se.Q. | Se.Q. | Se.Q. | Se.Q. | Se.Q. | Se.Q. | Se.Q. |
| | | T | C | R4 | R4 | R4 | R4 | Y4 | Y4p | R1 | Y1 | Y1p |
| RECALL | 100 | 0 | 0 | 0 | 0 | 0 | 0 | 0 | 0 | 0 | 0 | 0 |
| | 90 | 0 | 0 | 0 | 0 | 0 | 0 | 0 | 0 | 0 | 0 | 0 |
| | 80 | 0 | 0 | 0 | 0 | 0 | 0 | 0 | 0 | 0 | 0 | 0 |
| | 70 | 2 | 3 | 0 | 8 | 12 | 13 | 24 | 18 | 4 | 12 | 6 |
| | 60 | 2 | 5 | 13 | 27 | 31 | 26 | 36 | 34 | 5 | 13 | 6 |
| | 50 | 2 | 7 | 37 | 32 | 33 | 33 | 54 | 43 | 6 | 17 | 7 |
| | 40 | 3 | 11 | 38 | 37 | 41 | 43 | 63 | 50 | 7 | 24 | 10 |
| | 30 | 4 | 12 | 45 | 47 | 46 | 45 | 74 | 51 | 10 | 35 | 15 |
| | 20 | 7 | 12 | 48 | 48 | 51 | 49 | 87 | 59 | 13 | 51 | 20 |
| | 10 | 8 | 15 | 53 | 46 | 51 | 52 | 98 | 62 | 13 | 61 | 22 |

**Key**

Indexing :

- T = terms
- C = collection frequency weights
- R1 = predictive use of relevance weights, formula F1
- R4 = " " " " " " " formula F4
- Y1 = yardstick retrospective use of relevance weights, formula F1
- Y4 = " " " " " " " " " formula F4
- Y1p = yardstick using predictive form of formula F1
- Y4p = " " " " " " " formula F4

Document sets :

- G = generation set for relevance weights
- A = application set for searching

strategies finds R4 strikingly superior to R1, the latter the same as C, with C much better than T, i.e. R4⟩⟩⟩R1 = C⟩⟩T. We note also that Y4⟩⟩R4 and Y1⟩⟩R1, but interestingly that R4⟩⟩Y1, i.e. that predictive relevance weighting by formula F4 is much better than yardstick formula F1. Table 2.1 also shows that when the yardsticks are set by the predictive versions of the formulae they are inferior to the "pure" ones, and indeed that Y1p is much the same as R1.

*Experiment 2: poor matching*

For this test the initial need statement texts were processed to give request statements analogous to those represented by the profiles, but much briefer. As noted earlier, the profiles are long and carefully worked out, and so provide high-class matching material even when treated as term lists rather than Boolean formulations. The alternative brief requests were obtained by simple automatic processing: stop words were eliminated from the texts, and the remaining words replaced by word stems defined by a stem dictionary derived from the document title texts. Some of the characteristic fragmentation of the profiles is thus repeated, but less full profiles are obtained indirectly rather than directly: hand reduction of the original profiles to obtain a strictly comparable poorer version for matching proved too difficult. The content of the original statements and profiles is, however, fundamentally the same, so the use of the text-derived requests for this experiment seems acceptable. They are detailed in Table 1. Weighting and searching are based on the even and odd-numbered document sets, as in Experiment 1. The results are given in Table 2.2 and illustrated in Fig. 2. The strategy comparison here shows essentially the same pattern as Experiment 1, i.e. R4⟩⟩R1 = C⟩⟩T, though absolute levels of performance are much lower. The weighting improves precision noticeably, though the recall ceiling is low and overall performance is poor. Again the yardsticks define much better performance than prediction achieves; but in this case predictive weighting using formula 4 is the same as yardstick F1. The relationship between the forms of yardstick is as in Experiment 1.

*Experiment 3: heterogeneous documents*

Here the regular profiles were used but the documents were divided into First and Last sets representing the major division of CAC by subject groupings. In general the documents known to be relevant to a request fall predominantly into one set, but most profiles have some relevant documents in the other. Predictive weighting from one set to the other should therefore constitute a rather stronger test than the even/odd case. The experiment should properly be done both ways round, but the effort involved would be considerable and it was thought adequate to predict from the first set of documents 1-11613 (CAC-1) to the last documents 11614-27361 (CAC-2). Data details again appear in Table 1, and retrieval results in Table 2.3 and Fig. 3. Comparative performance in this experiment is similar to that of Experiment 1;

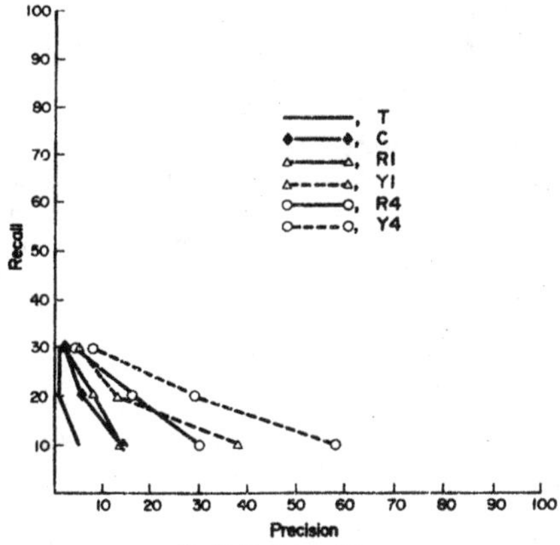


Fig. 2. Experiment 2.

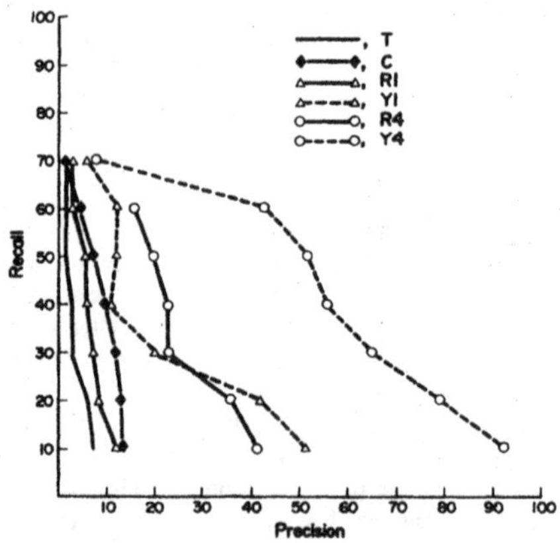


Fig. 3. Experiment 3.

specifically R4⟩⟩R1 = C⟩⟩T. Yardstick performance is again much better than predictive, while R4 is in this case the same as Y1. Absolutely, R4 performance in Experiment 1 is better than in Experiment 3.

*Experiment* 4: *little information*

For this experiment the generation document set was progressively reduced. The application set, called Search Quarter, contained every fourth document, 4,8,12,16, etc.† The largest generation set, called Half, contained 1,2,5,6,9,10, etc.; this was divided to obtain Quarter, containing 1,5,9, etc. Quarter was divided to form Eighth, containing 1,9, etc. and Eighth was divided to obtain Sixteenth, containing 1,17, etc. The implication of this reduction for the amount of relevance information input to weight computation is indicated in Table 1 by the average number of relevant documents per request (figures estimated from the whole collection). Thus we see that for Sixteenth only 3–4 relevant documents are available. Relevance weighting for this experiment was confined to formula F4 for all the sets, with F1 only for Eighth. Performance is shown in Table 2.4 and Figs. 4a and 4b, leading to the conclusion that the reduction in source has no effect on precision and only lowers the recall ceiling slightly. Fig. 4a shows R4 for Sixteenth and Half virtually the same. The overall picture otherwise is as for Experiment 1, i.e. R4⟩⟩⟩C⟩⟩T, while comparisons for generating set Eighth including predictive weighting using formula F1 give the same result as Experiment 1, with R1 = C. Predictive formula F4 is better than retrospective F1, while the "pure" yardsticks are much better than the predictive formula versions.

## SUMMARY OF RESULTS

The results for Experiment 1 show the same relative picture, but for a much larger file, as the original tests of (1). They show relevance weighting clearly superior to simple term or collection weight matching; F4 strikingly better than F1, indeed predictive F4 comparable to retrospective F1; and predictive F4 achieving a remarkable improvement in performance. In Experiment 2 the same relative results are obtained, though the absolute level of performance is much lower. Since the average number of plain matching terms per relevant document is a mere 1.3, the weighting is doing a great deal of work. Performance for the relevance weights in Experiment 3 is inferior to that for Experiment 1, but still improves performance very considerably. The results for Experiment 4 are very interesting: performance does not decline as the size of the generation set is reduced, so the improvement over term matching even for Sixteenth is very marked: i.e. relevance information, even when very limited, is of great value.

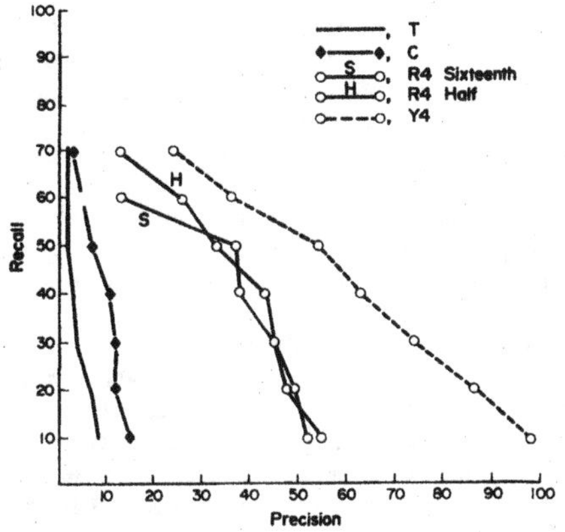


Fig. 4(a). Experiment 4.

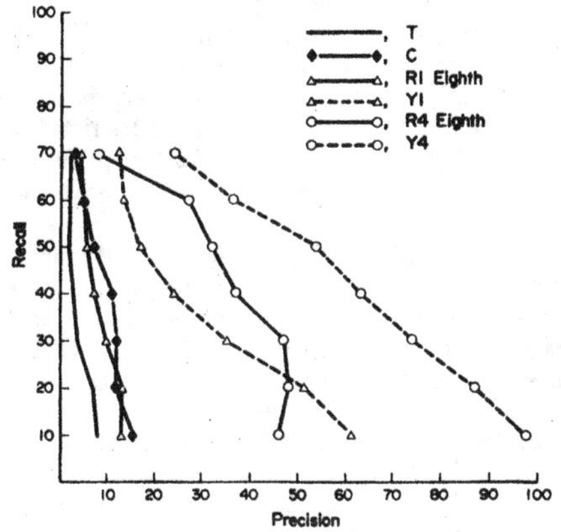


Fig. 4(b). Experiment 4.

## DISCUSSION

### (a) *Straightforward performance of relevance weights*

All the tests show that relevance weighting in a coordination matching environment is very effective, much more effective than previously investigated statistical indexing/searching techniques. Tests with other, though smaller collections, confirm the general picture: for example with 39 profiles and 2542 documents used for a variety of coordination and weighting tests by Evans[10]. One question which may be asked about the testing procedure is whether results would be different if another evaluation technique was adopted. For example, what happens if ranking is explicit and averaging across requests is by matching ranks rather than matching scores? Ranking experiments are very expensive, present methodological problems, and are perhaps of doubtful operational relevance, so some trials only have been conducted. A test with the even and odd-numbered Cranfield documents used for the original experiments of (1) shows overall results similar to those reported above, but much smaller absolute performance differences (a 15–20% improvement in precision for predictive formula 4) and no difference between F1 and F4. Further work in this area is needed.

### (b) *Operational implications of relevance weights*

(i) Comparison with conventional Boolean search performance is very difficult for the reasons discussed earlier. The output of the original UKCIS alternative Boolean searches was all assessed, and recall relative to the pooled output of all the searches obtained. The UKCIS workers estimated absolute recall for Boolean searches on titles at about 40% as opposed to the relative value of about 60%[11]. The problem for comparing our coordination output with the Boolean is first, what proportion of the hypothetical total relevant documents be deemed retrieved in the much larger output of the coordination searches, and second, what distribution over the levels should be assumed for the extra relevant documents. Various plausible totals of "real" relevant retrieved can be suggested under the first head, but the second problem is much more intractable. For unweighted terms distributing the extra documents in parallel with the known ones is a possibility, but with relevance weighting negative weights make the situation too complicated. Only a very limited comparison between our test results and the original UKCIS operational ones can therefore be made. Specifically, we adjust the given Boolean search point to its estimated real value, i.e. reduce recall from 60% to 40%. A worst assumption adjustment of coordination searching would add extra documents at the lowest level only, raising the recall ceiling but not affecting recall/precision graph shape. The net result for the even/odd case would be very similar precision at 40% recall. Thus the original relative recall of 64% and precision of 44% become recall 40% and precision 44%, compared with 39% precision at recall 40% for predictive relevance weights with formula F4. Precision at recall 40% for F4 weights derived from the Sixteenth generation set in Experiment 4 is 38%.

Such games should be treated with some reserve: they are intended chiefly to suggest that a proper experimental comparison between unconventional weighting techniques and conventional searching would show the former competitive with the latter. In the meantime it cannot be stressed too strongly that the performance figures obtained in our experiments are not absolute, and are likely to be in some degree affected by the restricted relevance information available for evaluation. It should also be noted that the Boolean profiles used by UKCIS were finely honed on the basis of experience over searches, and therefore present an unusually high standard for comparison.

The performance of relevance weights must be influenced by the number and quality of the given search terms. The experiments reported were to some extent unrealistic since it is not surprising that relatively good performance can be obtained with a long and carefully formulated term list. From this point of view the substitution of weights for Boolean structure does not represent much effort saving. On the other hand, we must reckon on many searches with far less carefully developed input. If coordination performance here is not very good, neither is Boolean (see, for example, Aitchison *et al.*[12]). The important point here, as Experiment 2 shows, is that relevance weights improve poor coordination performance considerably, though how competitively with poor Boolean searching our data cannot show.† Miller's relatively limited experiments[4, 13] show even weighting by F1 competitive, so F4 would presumably be superior to Boolean. It is hoped that tests can be carried out to compare relevance weights with simple Boolean searches, or subsearches, preferably in an on-line environment. This would allow better estimates of the value of relevance weights, balancing their contribution to performance against the effort required to generate them, in relation to the relative contribution to conventional Boolean performance of term choice and request structure. As some effort is involved in choosing terms, in providing structure, and in deriving weights, we need to know how they are most efficiently combined for best performance with least effort.

(ii) The tests reported assume that all the documents in the generation set are scanned for relevance. This is clearly unrealistic. Even Sixteenth generation set in Experiment 4 represents some 1711 documents. The question is how much would be lost, in input information for relevance weight computation, if data for far fewer documents was available. Or rather, since the crux is relevance information, how few documents scanned provide enough relevance information. As the experiments in input reduction show, 3–4 relevant documents provide valuable information. It appears, using Search Quarter of Experiment 4 as an example, that simple term matching retrieves 2.7 relevant documents for 39.3 scanned (at matching level 2), while collection weighting retrieves 3.0 relevant for 24.2 scanned (at level 9) or 4.6 for 37.7 scanned (at level 8). We may thus hope to obtain enough relevance information from a far smaller number of documents inspected than the whole set, in this case 6840. In itself, the proportion of relevant thus obtained is small (though bearing in mind the data properties, it is probably misleadingly small) but as the means to a future large return it looks quite different. At any rate, such figures show that obtained productive relevance information would not be the effort the experimental design assumed.

This point is clearly relevant to current on-line search procedures where relatively few documents may be inspected to provide relevance information. Tests are currently under way to evaluate relevance weighting in a simulation of such an environment.

## CONCLUSION

As noted earlier, though the tests reported here are confined to one collection, similar performance patterns have been obtained with other data. The questions asked initially have been satisfactorily answered for the test environment. The results show quite clearly that relevance weighting, expecially formula F4, is very useful, leading to really substantial performance improvements over simple term matching. The levels of performance attained are higher than those achieved by other statistical techniques applied to term coordination matching; and they are comparable with those achieved by conventional Boolean searches, and perhaps can be obtained with less effort.

## REFERENCES


[1] S. E. Robertson and K. Sparck Jones, Relevance weighting of search terms. *J. ASIS* 1976, 27, 129–146.

[2] C. T. Yu and G. Salton, Precision weighting—an effective automatic indexing method. *J. ACM* 1976, 23, 76–88.

[3] S. E. Robertson, *A Theoretical Model of the Retrieval Characteristics of Information Retrieval Systems*, Ph.D. Thesis, University of London, 1976.

[4] W. L. Miller, A probabilistic search strategy for MEDLARS. *J. Docum.* 1971, 27, 254–266.

[5] F. H. Barker, D. C. Veal and B. K. Wyatt, Towards automatic profile construction. *J. Docum.* 1972, 28, 44–55.

[6] A. Robson and J. S. Longman, Automatic aids to profile construction. *J ASIS* 1976, 27, 213–223.

[7] K. Sparck Jones, A performance yardstick for test collections. *J. Docum.* 1975, 31, 266–272.

[8] C. W. Cleverdon, J. Mills and M. Keen, *Factors Determining the Performance of Indexing Systems*, 2 vols., College of Aeronautics, Cranfield, 1966.

[9] L. Sparck Jones and R. G. Bates, *Research on Automatic Indexing* 1974–76, 2 vols., Computer Laboratory, University of Cambridge, 1977.

[10] L. Evans, *Search Strategy Variations in SDI profiles*, Report No. 75/21, Institute of Electrical Engineers, London, 1975.

[11] F. H. Barker, D. C. Veal and B. K. Wyatt, *Retrieval Experiments Based on Chemical Abstracts Condensates*, Research Report No. 2, UKCIS, Nottingham, 1974.

[12] T. M. Aitchison, A. M. Hall, K. H. Lavelle and J. M. Tracy, *Comparative Evaluation of Indexing Languages, Part II: Results*. Project Inspec, Institute of Electrical Engineers, London, 1970.

[13] W. L. Miller, *The Evaluation of Large Information Retrieval Systems with Application to MEDLARS*, Ph.D. Thesis, University of Newcastle, 1970.

*Reprinted from Library Quarterly, Vol. 47, No. 2, 1977 by permission of The University of Chicago.*

# INFORMATION RETRIEVAL AS A TRIAL-AND-ERROR PROCESS[1]

Don R. Swanson

Recognition of the essential role of trial and error in access to scientific literature may point the way toward improved information services and may illuminate inconsistencies that have beset many retrieval experiments. This paper examines three important and well-known information retrieval experiments, with a focus on certain internal inconsistencies and on the high variability of search results. In these experiments, retrieval systems are evaluated in terms of their ability to select relevant documents and reject those that are irrelevant. It is suggested that this criterion is inadequate because of ambiguities inherent in the concept of relevance and that closer attention to trial-and-error processes may be helpful in developing better criteria. Specific examples of how one might improve document retrieval, library use, and citation indexing are offered.

---

The great quantity of published literature on any topic makes compelling a need for better methods of selecting what to read. The following summary of this article illustrates one of the aids to such selection that the article itself recommends. In the space of about one-eighth of the complete article I attempt to offer readers a substantive basis for deciding whether the rest of the article is likely to meet their own needs or interests.

## Summary

Information retrieval systems are usually evaluated on the basis of their ability to select relevant documents and reject those that are irrelevant. However, insufficient attention has been given to the meaning of relevance itself. I shall examine here what might be certain consequences of this failure in the context of several important retrieval experiments of the past decade. In each of the experiments to be examined, a collection of documents was searched in response to a number of test questions. The search was aided by one or more indexing methods under test. A central problem in all experiments was that of determining how many relevant documents had been missed in any search.

In the Cranfield II project [1], an attempt was made, prior to any retrieval tests, to identify all possibly relevant documents in an experimental collection by directly

1. This paper, in substantially the present form, was presented on February 26, 1976, at a meeting of the Argonne chapter of Sigma Xi.

examining every document with respect to each question. It has been shown [2] that this method very likely missed about 90 percent of the relevant documents. Some new perspectives on this mystery are offered; difficulties with the concept of relevance are almost certainly implicated.

Lancaster's tests of MEDLARS (Medical Literature Analysis and Retrieval System) [3] involved a method for determining "recall" (the percent of relevant documents retrieved) that could be misleading. He estimated recall by the percent of documents retrieved from a sample of documents previously judged relevant by the requester. However, that sample was constructed in part from documents screened in advance, that is, chosen as possibly relevant, by someone other than the requester. Such documents might be easier to recognize as relevant, and so perhaps easier to index and retrieve, than relevant documents not subjected to prior screening.

Using experimental collections of a few hundred documents, Salton compared MEDLARS with a fully automatic system for searching the text of abstracts and inferred that such automatic systems should replace those that depend on manual indexing [4, 5]. It is pointed out here that there is as yet no evidence to support an inference of this kind for very large document collections. Putting aside for the moment the above objections to Lancaster's tests, these tests imply that the MEDLARS system is capable of selecting a few dozen relevant documents while rejecting on the order of 800,000 that are irrelevant. One cannot establish by experimenting with collections as small as those used by Salton that any competing system is capable of so high a degree of discrimination.

The relevance of a document to a request in all of these experiments ostensibly was defined in terms of the requester's judgment alone. Yet in each experiment the judgment of relevance was implicitly delegated to someone else in a preliminary screening process. This inconsistency prompts a closer examination of the concept of relevance.

I consider in some detail two quite different meanings of relevance. First, it may be seen as a creative, subjective mental act by the requester, expressing whether a document fulfills whatever information need prompted his request. Second, it may reflect a requester's judgment that a document is "on the same topic" as his stated request, but not necessarily whether that document fulfills his underlying information need. In the second case, but not in the first, the requester's judgment might at least to some extent be predicted by someone else. Recognition of these two viewpoints in the interpretation of retrieval experiments, as we shall see, may illuminate some of the difficulties under discussion.

It is a matter of common experience that document retrieval is a trial-and-error process. I suggest that a more systematic application of this idea is needed. A request is no more than a guess about the attributes a desired document is expected to have. In general, the response of the system to the request is then used to correct the initial guess for another try. We may take as a model Popper's description of the acquisition and growth of scientific knowledge [6]. It follows that retrieval systems should be designed to achieve maximum flexibility and rapid response in the trial-and-error process itself. Three specific practical measures for achieving such flexibility are suggested.

The first is aimed at extending and improving the dialogue between user and retrieval system. Computerized interactive systems are capable of providing a bibliographic reference (author and title) to a document within seconds. Subsequent delivery of the complete document, however, may take days or weeks. What seems to be needed is an intermediate capability—such as a system which delivers summaries like this in access times on the order of minutes. An ability rapidly to retrieve and reject titles, abstracts, summaries, "suggestive fragments," and finally the articles themselves would be an invaluable aid in correcting and revising requests.

The second suggestion concerns the browsability of libraries. Browsing in a library is a familiar example of a trial-and-error information system, but it is impeded by the failure to adopt rational circulation policies. Present policies tend to insure that the most used, and so possibly the most valuable, material is not available on the shelves. The browsability and hence the usefulness of libraries can be improved by establishing loan periods which depend on the expected frequency of use of a book. Within certain limits, shorter loan periods would be assigned to materials with high use frequencies. Such policies have been tried experimentally with some success at the University of Lancaster.

The third suggestion is addressed to improving citation-based procedures. To enhance trial-and-error retrieval in any process which makes use of the references cited in a scientific paper, authors might identify more clearly their reasons for citing each reference. The references at the end of this paper illustrate one means of implementing this suggestion. Each reference is annotated to indicate the specific relationship which the cited work bears to this paper.

## Measures of Retrieval Effectiveness

The problem of information retrieval is usually posed in the following way. We suppose that bibliographic records for a collection of documents, books, journal articles, and reports are to be searched in response to a request for material on a specified topic or subject. The output may be a list of references, abstracts, or possibly the documents or articles themselves. The term "information retrieval," though in common use for such a process, is not accurate. "Document retrieval," "reference retrieval," or "abstract retrieval" are preferable terms. In this article a "document" will be taken as a generic term covering technical reports, journal articles, and books. I shall not be dealing here with question-answering or other systems which might more literally provide items of "information" as an output.

The search procedure may involve the use of an index, a system of subject headings, or a classification scheme. No index, however, has proved so thorough, no search method so effective, as to assure a high degree of success in this attempt. Thus the problem of developing measures of performance of indexing and retrieval systems to permit comparing one system with another has been given considerable attention. One commonly used measure is a pair of variables called "recall" and "precision." With respect to any given request, a particular document is assumed to be either relevant or nonrelevant, and either retrieved or not retrieved. Recall is the percent retrieved of the total number of relevant documents; precision is the percent relevant of the number of retrieved documents. Precision can be directly measured, since the quantity of retrieved material usually is small enough so that it can be submitted to the requester for an evaluation of the relevance of each item retrieved. To measure recall on the other hand depends on knowing in addition which nonretrieved documents are relevant. Often such measurements are made in the context of experimental collections sufficiently small to permit examining each document in the collection one by one.

A central problem of document retrieval experiments is that of making valid inferences about indexing and searching large collections based on small-scale experiments. To understand more clearly the nature of this problem, it may be helpful to mention one more retrieval measure, called "fallout." Fallout is defined for a given request as the percent retrieved of the total number of irrelevant documents. Recall and fallout can also be seen as conditional probabilities. Recall is the probability that a document will be retrieved given that it is relevant. Fallout is the probability that a document will be retrieved given that it is irrelevant. Indexing and search techniques designed to increase the material retrieved tend to increase both recall and fallout, that is, both the amount of relevant and nonrelevant material; those that narrow a search decrease these two quantities. In general, recall and fallout tend to be covariant and so cannot be used independently to evaluate retrieval systems. For similar reasons, recall and precision cannot be used independently. At least some of the problems of designing retrieval experiments involve constructing suitable samples of relevant and nonrelevant documents selected from large collections.

I have selected for comment three experiments which are valuable, influential, and well publicized. I shall describe these experiments only to the extent necessary to illuminate certain aspects that are inconsistent or questionable.

*The Cranfield Tests of Indexing Performance Factors*

In 1966 an important series of experiments to test specific features of indexing systems was carried out at the Cranfield Aeronautical Laboratories in England [1, 7]. This project is usually referred to as "Cranfield II." Results of the Cranfield II tests have been widely cited, and data from the project have been used by a number of other investigators. As a preparation for measuring recall, an attempt was made—prior to any retrieval tests—to determine which documents in an experimental collection were relevant to each search question by examining each document in the collection with respect to each question. Knowing all relevant documents in advance, it could then be determined which ones the retrieval system failed to find in any subsequent test. I have shown in an earlier critique [2] that this preparatory procedure in all likelihood must have missed something like 92 percent of the relevant documents. My argument was essentially as follows.

The experimental collection consisted initially of 1,200 documents on aerodynamics. A total of 280 questions related to aerodynamics was formulated by authors of papers on aerodynamics, that is, by experts in the field who could be presumed to represent the type of user the collection was intended to serve. The intent was then to test the efficacy of different indexing methods in finding documents relevant to each of the 280 questions. Whether a document was or was not relevant to a request was to be decided by the author, that is, the requester. However, in order to know which relevant documents were missed by any system tested, it was necessary in principle to examine beforehand each document in the experimental collection with respect to each question. This would have required that over 300,000 separate document-question pairs be judged for relevance. Because so large a task was not feasible for the authors of the questions, five postgraduate students in aeronautical engineering were hired to screen out all question-document pairs that seemed clearly nonrelevant. Those pairs not screened out (about 1,000) were then submitted to the authors for a judgment of relevance. About 60 percent were accepted as relevant. Several other methods of locating potentially relevant documents were also used. One of these methods, which was apparently altogether independent of the screening process by the students, led to the identification of 129 relevant document-question matches. Of these 129, the students had located only ten. The investigators noted that this number was curiously small, but drew no inferences concerning the effectiveness of the students' screening process. Had the screening process been 100 percent effective it would have led to the students' identifying all 129 instead of only ten. Assuming the above-remarked independence to hold, then, one may infer from this sample of 129 that the students were only 8 percent effective in finding relevant documents. Since the students actually located 592 relevant document-question matches, they must have missed another 7,600 or so. (The 7,600 is a "maximum likelihood" estimate; it is subject to a sampling uncertainty of about 3,000.) The Cranfield investigators proceeded with the project as though the 1,900 relevant document-question matches which had been located through the several methods which they used was a complete set. They failed to use a statistical argument to infer, from the degree of overlap of apparently independent methods, how many cases must have been missed. It was essentially this failure that occasioned my critical review [2]. Harter [8] subsequently established more directly that many relevant documents had been missed and examined some of the implications for the results claimed by the Cranfield II project.

The question of why the students missed so many relevant documents has never been satisfactorily answered. I shall return to it after discussing a few not entirely dissimilar mysteries that arise in connection with other well-known retrieval experiments.

### *The MEDLARS Tests*

During the period 1960–72, the National Library of Medicine developed and operated a large-scale system called MEDLARS (Medical Literature Analysis and Retrieval System) which manually indexed the journal literature of medicine, biomedicine, and related sciences and which provided two methods of access for searching the index. The first and most important product of MEDLARS is its printed and widely distributed publication called the *Index Medicus*. The second, which has now been essentially replaced by MEDLINE, is a computerized searching system based on manually assigned index terms. The number of index terms per article in the mechanized data base was several times greater than the number of "print" terms appearing in the *Index Medicus.*

The effectiveness of MEDLARS in responding to subject-oriented requests for medical journal articles was tested by Lancaster in 1967. Actual questions submitted by users of the system from many medical institutions were tested. The requesters themselves were asked to assist in the test only after they had submitted a question and so were unaware at the time of formulating the question for a MEDLARS search that it was to be used in a test of the system. Few other retrieval experiments have operated in so realistic a fashion. Each question was cast originally as a sentence or phrase expressing certain relationships among a set of topics, for example, "neurological complications of kidney disease," or "effect of radiation on infectivity and structure of viruses." Over 800,000 journal articles were in the system at the time, so the method often used in small-scale experiments of examining each document against each question in advance of retrieval tests in order to measure recall was unfeasible. Instead, Lancaster established what he called a "recall base" for each question consisting of a sample of documents judged relevant by the requester and contained in the MEDLARS system, but located by some means independent of MEDLARS. The proportion of these documents retrieved in a subsequent search was then taken as an estimate of recall for that search. The published results [9, p. 123] indicated an average recall of about 58 percent and average precision of about 50 percent. The averages were taken over 302 search questions.

These averages are often quoted and well known. Less often remarked is their extraordinarily high variability. Lancaster's more detailed report [3, p. 129] showed a scatter diagram with a recall/precision point plotted for each question searched. The variability from question to question was enormous. Sampling error could be expected to be rather large, but taken alone probably could not have accounted for so high a variability. Recall/precision points were almost uniformly scattered throughout the rectangle representing the full range of 0–100 percent recall and 0–100 percent precision. Thus the test results had little predictive value for the result of any specific subsequent search. One pair of values for recall/precision was about as likely as any other pair. Although an extensive and helpful analysis was carried out of the sources of recall and precision failures, one nevertheless must conclude that the huge variability in results for different questions has not been explained in terms of any illuminating generalizations.

The validity of the results of these tests hinges on the supposition that the recall base for each question represented in effect a random sample of all documents relevant to that question. This assumption bears further examination. In part the recall base consisted of documents found by conducting searches at the National Library of Medicine using indexes and bibliographic tools *other* than MEDLARS or the MEDLARS-based *Index Medicus.* We might notice, however, that such a procedure potentially involves a systematic bias toward selecting articles for the recall base that are inherently easier to index. Moreover, insofar as different bibliographical services do not take an approach to indexing substantially different from one another, the notion that the tools used were independent of MEDLARS may be illusory.

There is an even more serious objection to this procedure. The search for potentially relevant documents necessarily involved rejection of many that were judged not to be potentially relevant. But this judgment was not made by the requester, and the rejected documents were never submitted to the requester. There is no way of knowing, then, if those who were doing the screening were not systematically excluding certain classes or types of documents that might have been judged relevant by the requester. The nature and extent of the bias is unknown, but it is plausible to describe those excluded as being "not recognizable as relevant by someone other than the requester." The recall base then became those that *were* "recognizable as relevant by someone other than the requester." I shall comment further on this "fallacy of delegation," but we may note at this point the similarity to Cranfield II. In both cases the screening out of possibly relevant documents was delegated to someone other than the requester.

Another contribution to the recall base consisted of relevant articles supplied by the requester, which he found presumably by means other than a search of the *Index Medicus*. Just how he came to know about such articles was not investigated, however, so it seems questionable to assume that they were free of bias.

Our present state of knowledge of the effectiveness of indexing and retrieval systems for large collections is, so far as I know, essentially what it was at the time of completion of the MEDLARS tests. The degree of success of any one search is largely unpredictable, and the average over many searches of 58 percent recall and 50 percent precision is probably optimistic. Furthermore, few other literature search tools are as powerful as MEDLARS (in terms of thoroughness of indexing and versatility of search), so other disciplines are not likely to be substantially better off than medicine.

Is there hope of major improvement in subject access to the literature by means of systems that substitute machine procedures for human judgment in indexing? Certain claims related to this question have been advanced which are worth exploring briefly.

### *The SMART-MEDLARS Comparison*

Salton [4, 5, 10] has reviewed and evaluated a number of experiments on automatic indexing and has concluded that fully automatic information retrieval systems should replace those which depend on human judgment in any aspect of indexing or searching. The strongest evidence which he advances in support of this conclusion is based on his own experiments comparing SMART with MEDLARS.

SMART is a system developed by Salton for searching the natural language text of abstracts by computer. The abstracts and the original requests are processed by computer without introducing human judgment at any point. Thus the system is fully mechanized, in contrast to MEDLARS which utilizes manual indexing.

Two sets of experiments were reported, each based on a small collection of journal articles held by the MEDLARS system. One set of experiments was based on 273 articles, the other on 450 articles. These experiments yielded values of recall and precision for the SMART system that were close to those of the MEDLARS system. Salton argues that a fully automatic text analysis system is preferable because of its greater potential for improvement and because "all the available evidence" indicates that such procedures are "at least as effective as more conventional manual indexing methods" [10, p. 343]. It is important to note that the comparable performance of SMART and MEDLARS on a collection as small as 450 documents, together with all other available evidence from experiments with small document collections, does not justify an inference that fully automatic systems should replace large-scale operational indexing and retrieval systems such as MEDLARS. Salton does not make any direct claim that the results of his small-scale tests imply that SMART could perform as well as MEDLARS on the full MEDLARS data base of over 800,000 documents. He confines himself to the claim that there is no evidence to the contrary, but on this basis advocates fully automatic systems. It is no doubt true that there is no evidence to the contrary, but no tests have yet been performed, to my knowledge, which could have yielded such evidence. A simple statistical argument will show that tests on collections of a few hundred documents are not sufficiently sensitive to permit even rough estimates of performance on very large collections of hundreds of thousands of documents. A typical MEDLARS search might retrieve anywhere from a few dozen to a few hundred articles out of the 800,000 in the data base. Thus fallout (fraction of irrelevant retrieved) must be extremely small—on the order of one article in 8,000 or so. (We shall assume here that all articles in the data base are accessible to the MEDLARS system and that they all have about the same a priori probability of being retrieved. This latter supposition is not quite accurate, however, since about one-third of the articles were indexed to an average depth of ten terms per article, while the rest were indexed to an average depth of about four terms per article. The following very rough argument ignores this distinction.)

To establish that any competing system has comparably low fallout, one would have to experiment with a collection which included on the order of 8,000 or so randomly selected irrelevant documents, preferably several times that amount. Salton's two sets of experiments [4, 5] on experimental collections of 273 documents and 450 documents, respectively, could not possibly have yielded evidence that fallout was as small as one in 8,000. Even if fallout were ten times that value, or one in 800, such value corresponds to less than one irrelevant retrieved document per search question, and so would be difficult to distinguish from zero.

The retrieval of many irrelevant documents from the small data bases used by Salton does not necessarily imply a large fallout, since those data bases were not randomly selected from the full MEDLARS collection. Rather they were selected in such a way as to be particularly rich in documents with a high probability of being relevant. Thus they probably do not offer any basis for estimating what fallout would have been for the SMART system operating on the full MEDLARS collection. Salton does not attempt such an estimate, but at the same time he fails to add the qualification that his conclusions are valid only for very small document collections. For estimating the performance of SMART on very large document collections, it is not helpful to establish that the SMART system yields about the same recall as MEDLARS if it is not known whether the comparison is made at even roughly the same values of fallout. As noted earlier, recall and fallout cannot be used independently. The fallout for SMART, if SMART were applied to the complete MEDLARS collection, could differ from that for MEDLARS by approximately an order of magnitude (factor of 10) without Salton's tests having detected the fact.

It should be noted that the first of Salton's experiments [4] is subject to the same objections as the Lancaster MEDLARS tests, since Salton used Lancaster's recall-base data. This point, however, is of significance only with respect to the absolute performance of SMART, not to its performance relative to MEDLARS.

One might make a strong case for fully automatic text-processing techniques on the grounds that they offer a more flexible trial-and-error capability than do systems based on manual indexing, since all text (or abstract) words are available as search terms. Thus Salton's advocacy of fully automatic systems may be quite justified on this basis.

## A Misconception of Relevance

I have outlined no more than a small sample of the numerous difficulties that have characterized information retrieval experiments, difficulties so numerous in fact that one is tempted to suppose either that something is wrong with the idea of evaluating retrieval systems on the basis of their ability to deliver relevant documents or that there is a serious problem with the notion of relevance itself.

Most researchers in this field have taken the sensible position that a document is relevant to a request if the requester says that it is relevant. I think that this idea is not taken seriously enough, that its implications have not been sufficiently explored, and that, by itself, it leaves excessive room for varying interpretations by the requester himself. The fact that the Cranfield II researchers hired students to screen for potentially relevant documents violated their own criterion that relevance should be judged only by the requester. It is reasonable to assume that the students missed those documents whose relationship to the question was less apparent than the documents which they chose. This bias is similar to that described for the MEDLARS recall base. In the MEDLARS tests, Lancaster's entire design was based on the notion that relevance reflects nothing but the opinion of the requester, but then, as noted, he constructed the recall base in part by using the judgment of others as to which documents could be excluded. Salton, in the second of the two SMART-MEDLARS tests [5], used search questions from Lancaster's tests but then hired a medical student to make relevance judgments instead of using the requesters themselves.

Understanding what even a requester means by relevance cannot be taken for granted, as we shall see. The word "relevance" has been used as though it were a property, jointly, of a document and a request. I suggest now that this idea may be seriously mistaken.

## The Questioning of "Relevance" by Others

This paper is not the first to question "relevance" as a basis for evaluating retrieval systems. One early and very cogent statement is that of Lauren Doyle [11]. He argues that retrieval systems should be evaluated on the basis of their exploratory capabilities, since it is essentially impossible to measure their ability to deliver documents relevant to an actual information need. The last sentence of Doyle's brief article must hold some kind of record for multiple fulfillment of a prophecy: "The gradually increasing awareness of a human's incapability of stating his true need in simple form will tend to pull the rug out from under many IR system evaluation studies which will have been done in the meanwhile" [11, p. 200]. Doyle refers to a number of writers during that period who emphasized the importance of a multistage man-machine dialogue. Taylor notes, "When the system has answered a question, the process has just begun for the inquirer. His need for information is not at an end; it has only changed" [12]. Bar-Hillel clarified the relative roles of man and machine in reference-providing systems and stressed that question reformulation in a man-machine conversation must depend on human judgment [13]. Saracevic, in a valuable review of work on the concept of relevance, however, concludes: "It seems that no other effectiveness criterion than relevance was or is being seriously contemplated, or at least none exists that has caught some general attention" [14].

This is not to say that the concept of relevance has gone unexamined. Indeed several extensive studies have been carried out (notably by Cuadra and Katter [15] and by Rees and Schultz [16]) in which a large number of factors have been systematically varied in order to determine their effect on the judgment of the relevance of documents to topics. All of this concern, however, has not resulted in any basic change in the practice of using relevance judgment as the foundation of retrieval system evaluation.

A number of writers have suggested that the word "relevance" is troublesome and should be replaced by something like "usefulness." I am inclined to agree, since this tends more to emphasize the idiosyncratic nature of the judgment. However, the conditions under which "utility" terms have been used in practice invite suspicion that the change has invariably been more one of form than of substance. Accordingly I shall continue to use the word "relevance" in the ensuing discussion, but I contend that similar arguments could be made about "usefulness," at least as the concept has actually been employed.

## Scientific Research as a Trial-and-Error, Problem-oriented Process; Analogy to Information Retrieval

Karl Popper [6, esp. chap. 1] has discussed the acquisition and growth of scientific knowledge in a framework that we might profitably adopt as a model for document retrieval. How do human beings acquire knowledge of the world? Popper argues that we have a propensity to expect regularities and that such expectation must be logically prior to any experience with regularity. If it were not prior to experience, that is, innate, we would not be able to interpret two similar events as a repitition. All recognition of similarity involves an interpretation, since no two events are ever identical. We jump to conclusions first, then test our conclusions against experience. Popper describes scientific theory building in the same way. Creative scientific research does not begin with a "topic" but with a problem—a researcher must be puzzled, curious, in a sense "bothered" about something. Even this is not enough—some initial conjecture as to at least the nature of a possible solution to the problem must also be present. Theories are not synthesized from observations. Quite the contrary; one cannot gather data or make an observation without having a theory first. Thus new observations can lead to a theory only by correcting or modifying an earlier version of the theory. Theories are inventions or conjectures put forward and then subject to refutation. Knowledge grows by a process of trial and error.

Analogously, we might look upon the process of information retrieval as a trial or a conjecture, guided by some idea of what one is seeking. The principal value of the process lies not so much in the direct use of the retrieved documents but rather in the indirect function which they serve of stimulating a reformulation of the request. A request is only an imperfect description by the requester of the attributes he thinks a relevant document might have or might be assigned in the process of indexing or cataloging. It is a conjecture, which he tests by examining the retrieved documents. I presume here that the requester is engaged in creative scientific research and seeks journal articles that could help him extend his knowledge of the problem he is trying to solve. Each article that is found should be considered principally as a stimulus to a new trial in what may be a quest having no absolute criterion for successful termination. Because each responding document contributes, in general, to the shaping of a new request, one learns through making (and correcting) mistakes—and perhaps only in this way. The retrieval of irrelevant documents may therefore sometimes play as significant a role in stimulating research as does the retrieval of relevant documents. Errors or mistakes are not to be thought of in a pejorative sense, but rather as essential components of the research process. My thesis here is that trial and error is central to the process of document retrieval, particularly when such retrieval is used in support of creative scientific research. This point may possibly be obvious, but its significance seems to have been largely disregarded in the design and evaluation of information systems.

It will be helpful now to subdivide what is usually referred to as "relevance" into two frames of reference, not in a quest for precision of definition, which in any case is unattainable, but rather to illuminate problems in the design and evaluation of information retrieval systems. I shall then go on to examine the way in which information systems and services, and information retrieval experiments, might change if the trial-and-error nature of retrieval processes were taken seriously.

## Frame of Reference 1—Relevance Judgment as Creation of New Knowledge

The "relevance" of a document is here taken to be a piece of new knowledge constructed by the requester in the light of some information need or deficit. This knowledge can be described only as a subjective experience of the requester. In this sense, relevance is not something already present which is to be measured or judged; it is created. It is not and cannot be a property of a document and a request. To assign the determination of relevance in information retrieval experiments to anyone other than the requester is therefore a serious error. This assignment may be referred to as the "fallacy of delegation," and I have noted that it was deeply implicated in each of the major retrieval experiments outlined earlier.

Such a view of relevance as is put forward here suggests that the connection between Popperian philosophy and trial-and-error processes in document retrieval may be seen as more than an analogy. To say that relevance is created or constructed by the requester is to make a statement about how knowledge is acquired. It implies that relevance itself is a conjecture for which a trial document has served as stimulus.

We infer therefore that a consensus as to whether a particular document is relevant to some request is meaningless, for this notion of relevance has meaning only in the mind of the one person whose information need gave rise to the request. Yet when a consensus is sought, often it can be obtained. Is this not evidence that some property of the document and the request must exist that we can call relevance? If so, how can we suppose that each of several people is engaged in an independent creative act? I believe that a consensus of this kind is usually about something other than relevance to the underlying research problem or information need. It refers instead to "relevance to a topic." I shall enlarge on this idea in the next section.

## Frame of Reference 2—"Relevant" Meaning "On the Same Topic"

By a "topic" here I mean to include the more general notion of a combination of topics, such as "jet engines for supersonic transport aircraft" or "neurological complications of kidney disease." I have extended the notion of topic perhaps beyond conventional use to include syntactic relationships among individual subtopics. In most retrieval experiments a request is topic oriented and the retrieved information is then submitted to the requester for a judgment of relevance. All this seems at first sight clear, but I am inclined to suspect that in fact a source of limitless confusion lies hidden in the instructions given to the requester (and in his perception of those instructions) to make a judgment of relevance. How can one be sure that the requester himself is doing anything other than noting whether the document and the request are on the same topic? I suspect that very often what is thought to represent the ineffable quality of relevance to an underlying information need is instead a judgment by the requester that a given document does deal with the topic that he requested, that it fits the description of the topic given in his request. This does not mean, however, that this document necessarily fulfills his original need for information.

One might point out to the requester several possible frames of reference for considering the idea of relevance and ask him to classify his response accordingly. Cuadra and Katter [15] have investigated what might seem to be just this problem. They devised fourteen frames of reference for judging relevance and then studied how the imposition of a frame of reference influenced the judgment. Their fourteen categories all seem to be topic oriented and so lead to a relevance judgment appropriate to the frame of reference being discussed here. In other words, the study concerns fourteen different implicit-use contexts for answering the question, "Is this document on the topic indicated in the stated information requirement?" Their categories 8 ("stimulative value") and 9 ("practical use") may not fit this description and possibly are related to my frame of reference 1.

Experiments on the selective dissemination of biomedical information which I and my colleagues carried out some years ago [17] tend to confirm the suspicion that even requesters often take relevance to mean no more than "on the topic requested." A "statement of research interests" from each recipient of the dissemination service constituted the request; that is, it defined the field and the general class of problems which the recipient was investigating. All available indexing and abstracting services covering biomedicine and related fields were regularly searched and, periodically, a bibliography of articles potentially of current interest to the recipient was sent to him. From this bibliography, the recipient selected articles which he considered relevant (or "useful"—though in practice the distinction turned out to be inconsequential) and for which he wished to receive the full text copy. About 80 percent of the disseminated bibliographic entries were judged by the recipients to be at least slightly related to their research interests, and for about half of these the full texts were requested. Of the delivered full-text articles, 90 percent were then judged by the recipients to be at least moderately related to the stated research interests. It is noteworthy that each recipient requested and was sent a very large number of full-text articles per year (about 600)—many more than could have been thoroughly studied. In fact, for the most part they were not read but were simply glanced at, then squirreled away into a private file. Estimates made a year after the project terminated suggested that probably not even 10 percent of these articles had been carefully read or studied.

It seems plausible that only a few articles could be considered relevant in the sense of frame of reference 1 (relevance as a creative construction of new knowledge), whereas all other articles were being evaluated in terms more like topic relatedness—that is, in frame of reference 2. The lesson here is that the number of articles a requester judges relevant can vary by a factor of 10 or more, depending on how he interprets the task of making a relevance judgment. This represents a much greater variation than Cuadra and Katter found among their fourteen categories.

Four points are particularly worth emphasizing. First, the two frames of reference for relevance can lead to widely different values for recall for any given set of retrieved documents. Second, the distinction between the two has apparently never been made in retrieval tests. Third, anyone other than the requester who attempts to select relevant documents almost certainly must take a topic-oriented view of relevance (framework 2). Fourth, to say that a document and a stated request are on the same topic (framework 2) is not to imply that the document necessarily fulfills the underlying need for information that prompted the request.

One cannot of course dismiss the significance of a document's being on the same topic as a request. At any one stage of a dialogue, a retrieval system can give the requester only what he asks for—whether it is or is not what he really needs or wants—and often the stated request is topic oriented. Topic-oriented retrieval may be regarded as one technique among many for finding documents which the requester is more likely to judge as relevant (in framework 1) to his underlying need than would be the case for a randomly selected document.

I do not imply that relevance in frame of reference 2 is an objective property of a document and a request. It is still a matter of opinion, but there is no doubt greater potential for common agreement here than is the case for frame of reference 1. Thus it can make sense to speak of a consensus within frame of reference 2, but not in frame of reference 1.

In the light of the preceding discussion, both the high variability of the MEDLARS results and the failure of the student searching in Cranfield II seem more understandable. In the case of Cranfield II we might surmise that the students reacted only to conspicuous evidence, perhaps in the title of a document, for highly specific topics or subjects, whereas the authors of the questions may have taken a more liberal (but still topic-oriented) viewpoint, much as did the recipients in the dissemination experiment.

## Implication of a Trial-and-Error Approach for Retrieval Systems Design

I suggest that frame of reference 1 reflects the more important and fundamental view of relevance, while frame of reference 2 reflects a subordinate and intermediate role for relevance. The distinction between the two frames of reference is particularly cogent in the context of trial-and-error retrieval processes. The quest for a document by means of trial and error is ultimately satisfied (if at all) only by one or more creative acts in which a relationship (framework 1) is constructed between the document and the underlying need for information which triggered the quest. Many documents "on the same topic" (that is, relevant in framework 2) but not necessarily relevant in framework 1 might be found as intermediate steps in the quest.

If we take seriously the idea that only by trial and error can a relevant (framework 1) document be found, the implications for designing information systems and services are clear. The design should facilitate the trial-and-error process itself, as a means of enhancing the correctability of the request. The number of documents that must be seen and rejected in the quest for relevant material is unpredictable but may be very large. It is likely that the reject ratio is typically very high. Thus we need a rapid-response capability for delivering enough information about a document to permit the requester to reject it rapidly. "Enough information" may in some cases mean title, in some cases title and abstract, and in other cases the full document; the choice of which to receive should be the requester's. Certain existing systems offer access to titles—and in some cases to abstracts—within a matter of seconds or minutes. Systems for interrogating on-line mechanized bibliographic data bases at least hold the potential for supporting a flexible trial-and-error process insofar as one can reject a document on the basis of its title or abstract. The response time for delivering the full document, however, even for brief inspection and rejection, is often a matter of hours, days, or weeks; herein lies the main weakness of existing systems for supporting trial-and-error retrieval.

I suggest that an intermediate stage between abstracts and full documents may be needed. Perhaps a condensed article several times as long as most abstracts or suggestive fragments of the full article, or both, could be provided by the author and recorded in a form that permits access times of a few minutes. The "Summary" at the beginning of this article is one example of such a condensed article. Microform technology may eventually make practical very large local holdings of both summaries and complete documents able to fulfill the hypothetical need I have described for successive stages of rapid selection, inspection, and rejection.

However implemented, there is a need to support a rapid-response dialogue in which the requester can ask for and receive progressively increasing amounts of information about a document. At each stage of the dialogue, the response of the system is put to the test. The indexing and classification system operative should be hospitable to a wide range of conjectures on the part of the requester. An important class of conjectures of course deals with subjects or topics. Thus, clearly, indexing to considerable depth is called for. It is not enough to confine an index to central themes of a document, for the peripheral themes might be central to the requester; the chance of identifying suggestive or stimulating portions of an article should be maximized.

These ideas imply that new performance criteria and measures of effectiveness based on flexibility and response time should be accorded a role of central importance. Moreover, recall and precision can be seen now to be more complex than they are usually taken to be. One must specify, for example, whether such measures are taken at one stage of a dialogue or as cumulative over many stages and whether they are taken in frame of reference 1 or 2. Even for processes not usually evaluated by measuring recall and precision, the notion of trial-and-error searching has some important implications. Two of these processes, library browsing and reference citation, will be explored briefly.

## Implications of a Trial-and-Error Approach for Libraries

An appreciation of the significance of trial and error in the process of finding the right book in a library can lead to some new views of more familiar operations.

A good example of a rapid-response trial-and-error information retrieval process familiar to almost everyone is browsing in the book stacks. If the stacks are open to users and organized by some kind of classification scheme, then books bearing at least some common subject attributes will be found together on the shelves and can be rapidly examined and rejected until something relevant (in the sense of framework 1) to the problem at hand is found. Thus libraries are in part organized around the principle of trial and error. Regrettably, however, effective browsing is as a rule unintentionally but greatly obstructed in most libraries by certain policies. This point is worth more detailed exploration. I shall assume here that the context for such exploration is a large university or other research library in which the bookstacks are open to the users of the library. To close the stacks to users is to misunderstand, or deny, one of the important purposes which most such libraries ought to fulfill.

It is characteristic of all collections that a large part of the circulation and use is consistently concentrated in a relatively small part of the collection which thus tends to be heavily used. Because it is heavily used, it is seldom available to any one user. A book that is out 90 percent of the time is probably failing to serve on the order of 90 percent of its potential users. This percentage is quite sensitive to the loan period. Within certain limits, a book can be made more available by shortening its loan period. Clearly a circulation policy designed to maximize the availability of books to users would assign shorter loan periods to the more popular books. (The loan period, however, must not be so short that effective use of the book is precluded.) The University of Lancaster Library [18] was, so far as I know, the first library to experiment systematically with this very sensible approach to circulation policies. Today even in the largest of research libraries there is a marked tendency in many disciplines for the particular book that one wants to use to be checked out to someone else. It is not implausible to assume that the books most valuable for browsing are often those most in demand for circulation—it follows then that these are the ones most likely to be unavailable to a browser, as Buckland points out. Effective browsing is thus obstructed first of all by the almost universal failure to develop rational policies for loan period and for procuring multiple copies of books.

In some university libraries the faculty bestows upon itself the privilege of an unlimited loan period, subject, usually, to recall by another borrower. A browser, however, cannot recall a book of whose existence he is unaware. One might plausibly suppose, too, that faculty members tend to use the more important books. It is difficult to imagine a policy more effectively designed to frustrate the trial-and-error process I have described, nor one more efficiently designed to keep the most desirable material off the shelf. So far as loan policies are concerned, this can only be described as whatever is the opposite of optimum—perhaps "pessimum."

If unlimited borrowing by faculty, together with the absence of any policy to reduce normal circulation interference by means of a variable loan and duplication policy, does not completely subvert effective trial-and-error browsing; the coup de grâce is delivered by the reserve system. Whatever popular or important materials are not imprisoned in faculty offices are removed en masse from the shelves to be placed in a usually nonbrowsable (closed-stack) reserve system for an entire quarter or semester.

Some genuine conflicts of interest among library users are not easy to resolve, but their nature should at least be identified. The heart of the matter

I think is this. It is not simply that three different users need the same book at the same time, say, but rather that the first needs to use it intensively for a full week, the second would like it instantly available for several weeks so that he can spend a few hours with it at some unpredictable time, and the third needs only a five-minute look at it in order to reject it.

Perhaps in the future we can expect a better exploitation of technology in order to resolve at least some of these conflicting interests. A library book that is checked out or on reserve should also be accessible for at least partial browsing. This might be accomplished, for example, by providing rapid access to "suggestive fragments" of a book, such as title page, table of contents, index, summary, first page of each chapter, etc., all recorded either in machine language or in microform and callable on demand by any user of the library.

I do not imply, however, that we should await any breakthrough in technology itself. The question is whether we can get well enough organized to take advantage of technology already available. Rapid response information systems are costly, but even so there is a prior problem. We are, I think, caught up in a web of mistaken ideas on the best mechanism of paying for information services. Even when there is a user willing to pay a price for some kind of extra service and a system which could provide the service if only someone would pay, nothing happens. The problem lies in the area of management, planning, and organization. More services should be able to evolve by means of a trial-and-error process. The test of the marketplace is a reasonable mechanism for evaluating information services. A greater range of options for a price is needed.

One commercial venture offering an extraordinary service for a price is the *Science Citation Index*, published by the Institute for Scientific Information. It is worthwhile commenting on this service both because of its importance and its limitations. This service is a printed quarterly and annual index, by author, to both cited and citing articles; it covers about 2,500 journal titles on a current and continuing basis.

The importance of the *Science Citation Index* lies in the fact that it captures the link that an author of a journal article establishes when he cites, that is, makes reference to, some other article. By so doing the author indicates that he has constructed some kind of a relevance bridge (at least occasionally in the sense of frame of reference 1) between his own and the cited article. Thus he has left a trail that in part describes the end result of his own trial-and-error adventures in using the scientific literature. Such trails are central to the process of scientific communication and so would seem to be a good point of departure for developing better information services. However, what is lacking in present systems is any convenient and rapid method for discovering the *nature* of the relevance link which the citing author has established. This can be discerned only by studying the citing article. We might imagine a future citation-based system which provides rapid access to just those portions of the citing article which reveal the nature of its relationship to the cited article. Here would be one important class of the "suggestive fragments" mentioned earlier. If the cooperation of authors could be enlisted (or coerced) in the process, citation practices might be considerably improved by making more explicit the reasons for citing and by utilizing more stringent criteria as a basis for citing.

I have illustrated a possibly desirable practice in the following list of references. Each reference is accompanied by a brief description of the relationship which it bears to this article. My criteria for citing are restricted; I could have appended a bibliography of several hundred articles related to the evaluation of retrieval systems, to the study of relevance, to interactive systems, and to citation indexing. I suggest that such bibliographies of articles "on the same topic" clutter the reference/citation system to no useful purpose. A new art of trail marking needs to spring up among authors of scientific articles.

## REFERENCES

(*Denotes article of more central importance to this paper.)

1. *Cleverdon, Cyril; Mills, J.; and Keen, Michael. *ASLIB Cranfield Research Project: Factors Determining the Performance of Indexing Systems*. Vol. 1. *Test Design*. Cranfield, Bedfordshire: College of Aeronautics, 1966.

   This project is one of three major tests of retrieval systems which are here noted as having certain limitations or inconsistencies that may reflect difficulties with all evaluation methods based on the concept of relevance (see also [7]).

2. *Swanson, Don R. "Some Unexplained Aspects of the Cranfield Tests of Indexing Performance Factors." *Library Quarterly* 41 (July 1971): 223–28.

   This article includes a criticism of the method that was used in the Cranfield II project to locate, prior to retrieval tests, all relevant documents for each request, and demonstrates from the Cranfield data itself that probably 90 percent or so of the relevant document-question matches were missed. The mystery of why so many were missed has apparently never been explained. It is conjectured now that basic difficulties with the concept of relevance may be at the heart of the matter (see also [7]).

3. *Lancaster, F. W. *Evaluation of the MEDLARS Demand Search Service*. Washington, D.C.: National Library of Medicine, U.S. Department of Health, Education, and Welfare, 1968.

   Attention is called to the large variability of retrieval results for different requests, as shown in the graph on p. 129. It is suggested that this variability might be related to basic difficulties with the concept of relevance. Other reasons for citing this project are given in [9].

4. *Salton, Gerard. "A Comparison between Manual and Automatic Indexing Methods." *American Documentation* 20 (January 1969): 61–71.

   This project is one of three major tests of retrieval systems which are here noted as having certain limitations that may reflect difficulties with all evaluation methods based on the concept of relevance. This experiment utilizes Lancaster's recall-base data and so is subject to its limitations (see [9]). The project is valuable for illuminating the comparative performance of the SMART and MEDLARS systems applied to small document collections, but does not permit inferences concerning the performance of SMART on very large collections.

5. *Salton, Gerard. "A New Comparison between Conventional Indexing (MEDLARS) and Automatic Text Processing (SMART)." *Journal of the American Society for Information Science* 23 (1972): 75–84.

   See comments for [4]. The claim that fully automatic document systems should replace manual systems is restated. The new comparison is based on a collection size of 450 abstracts, still far too small to permit any inference to be drawn concerning "fallout" (percent of irrelevant retrieved) in large collections. I comment on the delegation of relevance judgment, in the above project, to someone other than the requester.

6. *Popper, Karl R. *Conjectures and Refutations: The Growth of Scientific Knowledge.* New York: Harper Torchbooks, 1968.

   Popper's philosophy, especially as expressed in chap. 1 (pp. 33–59), provides stimulus for viewing information retrieval as a trial-and-error process and so furnishes a foundation for the main theme of this paper.

7. *Cleverdon, Cyril. "Cranfield Tests on Index Languages Devices." *ASLIB Proceedings* 19 (1967): 173–93.

   See [1]. Of particular interest here is the method of locating, prior to any retrieval tests, all relevant documents for each request. I have criticized this method in [2] and discuss further implications of it in the present article.

8. Harter, Stephen P. "The Cranfield II Relevance Assessments: A Critical Evaluation." *Library Quarterly* 41 (July 1971): 229–43.

   This article is mentioned as carrying a more fully developed critique of the Cranfield II Project than appears in [2].

9. *Lancaster, F. W. "MEDLARS: Report on the Evaluation of Its Operating Efficiency." *American Documentation* 20 (April 1969): 119–42.

   This project is one of three major tests of retrieval systems which are here noted as having certain limitations or inconsistencies that may reflect difficulties with all evaluation methods based on the concept of relevance. The method of constructing the "recall base" is criticized. The implied delegation of the judgment of relevance to someone other than the requester is objectionable in that the recall base is then biased toward articles that can be most easily recognized as relevant. Such articles might be easier to index and retrieve than randomly selected relevant articles.

10. *Salton, Gerard. "Automatic Text Analysis." *Science* 168 (April 17, 1970): 335–43.

    This article makes certain claims that fully automatic indexing and retrieval systems should replace those that depend on manual techniques. One of the most important experiments cited as evidence is [4] (see comments on [4]).

11. Doyle, Lauren B. "Is Relevance an Adequate Criterion in Retrieval System Evaluation?" In *Automation and Scientific Communication: Short Papers Contributed to the Theme Sessions of the 26th Annual Meeting of the American Documentation Institute*, edited by H. P. Luhn. Washington, D.C.: American Documentation Institute, 1963.

This paper is cited, and quoted, because it is an early and lucid statement which questions relevance and suggests exploratory efficiency as a basis for evaluating retrieval systems.

12. Taylor, Robert S. "The Process of Asking Questions." *American Documentation* 13 (1962): 391–96.

    A passage is quoted to the effect that the response of a system changes rather than fulfills the inquirer's information need—an idea much in harmony with the present paper.

13. Bar-Hillel, Yehoshua. *Some Theoretical Aspects of the Mechanization of Literature Searching.* U.S. Office of Naval Research Technical Report no. 3. Washington, D.C.: Office of Technical Services, U.S. Department of Commerce, 1960.

    This report is mentioned as one of the earliest which clarifies a number of basic issues bearing on the concept of relevance.

14. Saracevic, Tefko. "The Concept of 'Relevance' in Information Science: A Historical Review." In *Introduction to Information Science*, edited by Tefko Saracevic. New York: R. R. Bowker Co., 1970.

    A valuable review of work up to 1970 on the concept of relevance, cited as background.

15. Cuadra, Carlos A., and Katter, Robert V. "Opening the Black Box of Relevance." *Journal of Documentation* 23 (1967): 291–303.

    This study is mentioned as related background. The authors have carried out an important series of experiments which include tests of fourteen categories that serve as frames of reference for interpreting the concept of relevance. A few comments are made on the topic orientation of those frames of reference and on their relatively small impact.

16. Rees, Alan M., and Schultz, Douglas G. *A Field Experimental Approach to the Study of Relevance Assessments in Relation to Document Searching.* 2 vols. Cleveland: Center for Documentation and Communication Research, Case Western Reserve University, 1967.

    This project is mentioned as background; it is one of the few extensive studies of the factors involved in relevance testing.

17. *Swanson, Don R. "Selective Dissemination of Biomedical Information: A Series of Studies and a Model System." *Library Quarterly* 44 (July 1974): 189–205.

    This paper is cited and discussed as additional evidence for difficulties with the concept of relevance. The notion of relevance in the above experiments can be interpreted as meaning essentially "on the same topic." Results of experiments of this type are probably very sensitive to the instructions given to the recipients for judging relevance.

18. Buckland, Michael K. "An Operations Research Study of a Variable Loan and Duplication Policy at the University of Lancaster." *Library Quarterly* 42 (January 1972): 97–106.

    This project is cited as one of the very few which have recognized and studied the effect of circulation policies on the browsability of a library. Browsing is of particular interest as a trial-and-error information process.

Reprinted from AMERICAN DOCUMENTATION
January 1969, Vol. 20, No. 1

# Effectiveness of Information Retrieval Methods*

**Results of some 50 different retrieval methods applied in three experimental retrieval systems were subjected to the analysis suggested by statistical decision theory. The analysis validates a previously-proposed measure of effectiveness and demonstrates its several desirable properties. The examination of a wide range of data in relation to this one metric provides a clear and general assessment of the current state of the retrieval art.**

JOHN A. SWETS

*Bolt Beranek and Newman Inc.*
*Cambridge, Massachusetts*

A desirable measure of retrieval performance would have the following properties. First, it would express solely the ability of a retrieval system to distinguish between wanted and unwanted items—that is, it would be a measure of "effectiveness" only, leaving for separate consideration factors related to cost or "efficiency." Second, the desired measure would not be confounded by the relative willingness of the system to emit items—it would express discrimination power independent of any "acceptance criterion" employed, whether the criterion is characteristic of the system or adjusted by the user. Third, the measure would be a single number—in preference, for example, to a pair of numbers which may covary in a loosely specified way, or a curve representing a table of several pairs of numbers—so that it could be transmitted simply and apprehended immediately. Fourth, and finally, the measure would allow complete ordering of different performances, indicate the amount of difference separating any two performances, and assess the performance of any one system in absolute terms—that is, the metric would be a scale with a unit, a true zero, and a maximum value. Given a measure with these properties, we could be confident of having a pure and valid index of how well a retrieval system (or method) was performing the function it was primarily designed to accomplish, and we could reasonably ask questions of the form, "Shall we pay $X$ dollars for $Y$ units of effectiveness?"

* This work was supported by the Advanced Research Projects Agency under ARPA Order No. 627, Amendment 2, and under Contract No. AF19(628)-5065 with the Air Force Cambridge Research Laboratories.

In a previous article I reviewed 10 measures that had been suggested prior to 1963, and proposed another (*1*). None of the 10 measures, and none that has come to my attention since then, has more than two of the properties just listed. Some of them, including those most widely used, have the first two properties, and some of the others have the last two properties. The measure I proposed, one drawn from statistical decision theory, has the potential to satisfy all four desiderata. At the time it was proposed, however, the decision-theory measure had not been applied to any empirical retrieval results, so that its assumptions about the form of retrieval data had not been tested. In the present paper we examine this measure in relation to test results obtained from three experimental retrieval systems with some 50 different retrieval methods. With minor qualifications, the data are uniformly consistent with the assumptions of the decision-theory measure and quite clearly demonstrate its usefulness. A substantive outcome of the extensive analysis in terms of this measure is a clear appraisal of the current state of the retrieval art. The analysis shows in precise terms how much room for improvement is left by current retrieval techniques. The room for improvement, as we shall see, is large.

Before proceeding to a review of the decision-theory measure and to an examination of the data, let us consider briefly the domain of the measure and a disclaimer about the scope of this paper.

The measure is most clearly applicable to retrieval systems that deal in documents or messages, and it is applied here to systems of this type. Less clearly perhaps, but as well, the measure can be applied to information systems that handle facts or give answers to ordinary English questions. In both cases queries are addressed to a system and the system's responses to the queries must be evaluated. Whether the response is a set of documents or a fact selected or deduced from a collection of writings is immaterial. Appropriate text must be isolated in either case, to constitute the response or to supply the base from which the response is drawn. The data represented by the decision-theory measure are entries in a two-by-two contingency table: Just as documents suited or unsuited to a need may be retrieved or not retrieved, so facts that correctly or incorrectly answer questions may be presented or withheld. For some relatively simple fact systems, of course, such as airline-reservation systems, discrimination or correctness is not a problem; the reference here is to fact systems in which the facts to be retrieved are not all neatly isolated and in which the questions are not all anticipated in detail.

This measure, like those used most often in the past, is most directly applicable when the entire information store is known and when, in particular, the number of items appropriate as responses to each query is known. This condition is frequently satisfied in experimental systems, which usually contain no more than a few thousand items. If the measure is to be applied to stores large enough to make impractical a complete knowledge of them, three alternatives exist for estimating the required number. One is to select, by some heuristic process or by fiat, that subset of the full store likely to contain almost all of the items appropriate to a given set of queries, and to examine the subset in detail. A second alternative, used in one instance in the following, is simply to sample the large store and to extrapolate from the sample. A third alternative, used in another instance in the following, is to preselect certain items from the store and to design test queries specifically to retrieve those items.

Application of the decision-theory measure assumes that the "relevance" of any item in the store to a given query or user's need can be determined. As the reader will know, or can imagine, the definition of relevance is generally regarded in the retrieval field as a very thorny problem, and even the concept itself has at times come under attack. However that may be, the definition of relevance is an issue separate from the measure under consideration, and is not discussed here. Nor is the concept defended here; I take it for granted that it is essential to the evaluation of retrieval performance and that sooner or later we shall come to terms with it. For our present purposes, we can accept the definitions of relevance adopted by the investigators who collected the data we shall examine, just as we accept for the present purposes other experimental procedures they have followed. It will become clear, by the way, that the decision-theory measure can be applied when judges use several, rather than two, categories of relevance, and that it uses to full advantage the output of a system that ranks or otherwise scales all items in the store according to their degree of relevance to the query at hand.

## • Decision-Theory Measure

A good way to begin in reviewing the decision-theory measure is to consider a measure more familiar in the retrieval context and to note the differences between the two. The measure used far more than any other (*2*) consists of two quantities termed the "recall ratio" and the "precision ratio." Like other measures that attempt to assess only retrieval effectiveness, this measure can be described by reference to the relevance-retrieval contingency table shown in Fig. 1.

The recall ratio is defined as $a/a+c$, the number of items both relevant and retrieved divided by the number of items relevant. This ratio, then, is the proportion of relevant items retrieved, and it may be taken as an estimate of the conditional probability that an item will be retrieved given that it is relevant. The precision ratio (formerly called the "relevance ratio") is defined as $a/a+b$, the number of items both relevant and retrieved divided by the number of items retrieved. This ratio is the proportion of retrieved items deemed relevant, and an estimate of the conditional probability that an item will be relevant given that it is retrieved.

Now, if a system's effectiveness is characterized by two numbers, a value of the recall ratio and a value of the precision ratio, we know relatively little about the system, for one reason because we don't know how the two quantities relate to each other. What does it mean, for example, to say that a system yielded a recall ratio of 0.70 and a precision ratio of 0.50? If System A performs this way, and System B yields a recall ratio of 0.90 and a precision ratio of 0.40, is System B more or less discriminating than System A? That is, is a gain of 0.20 in recall and a loss of 0.10 in precision good or bad? Of course, should System B show a gain in both recall and

| | $r$ | $\bar{r}$ | |
|---|---|---|---|
| $R$ | $a$ | $b$ | $a+b$ |
| $\bar{R}$ | $c$ | $d$ | $c+d$ |
| | $a+c$ | $b+d$ | $a+b+c+d$ |

FIG. 1. The relevance-retrieval contingency table: $r$ and $\bar{r}$ denote, respectively, relevant and irrelevant items; $R$ and $\bar{R}$ denote, respectively, retrieved and unretrieved items; $a$, $b$, $c$, and $d$ represent frequencies of occurrence of the four conjunctions.

precision over System A, we know B's effectiveness is superior to A's, but, in general, the measure consisting of this pair of quantities will give only a partial ordering of different systems or of different methods employed by one system.

The problem here is that System A's recall of 0.70 and precision of 0.50 represents only one of the many balances between the two ratios that it can achieve. This balance might have occurred when an item had to satisfy five descriptors specified in a query in order to be retrieved. If this requirement is changed, so that now an item has only to satisfy any two of the query's five descriptors, it is very likely that more items will be retrieved, and that recall will go up and precision will go down. But we must know exactly how recall and precision will covary, along with variation in the acceptance criterion, if uncertainties are to be avoided in attempting to rank different systems or methods.

A solution to this problem, one that is sometimes adopted, is to test each system with several acceptance criteria and to present as the measure of a system's effectiveness the empirical curve so generated. Extensive tests have shown (*3*) that the empirical curve will resemble in form the curve shown in Fig. 2. If System A yields the curve shown while System B yields another curve everywhere above and to the right of the one shown, it is clear that B is superior to A.

However, these curves do not tell us, in general terms, by how many units B is superior to A. (We can determine that B's precision is greater than A's by some specific percentage at some specific value of recall, but this number varies widely as a function of the value of recall selected.) Nor can we tell from the curves how good either system is in absolute terms. And, of course, it is

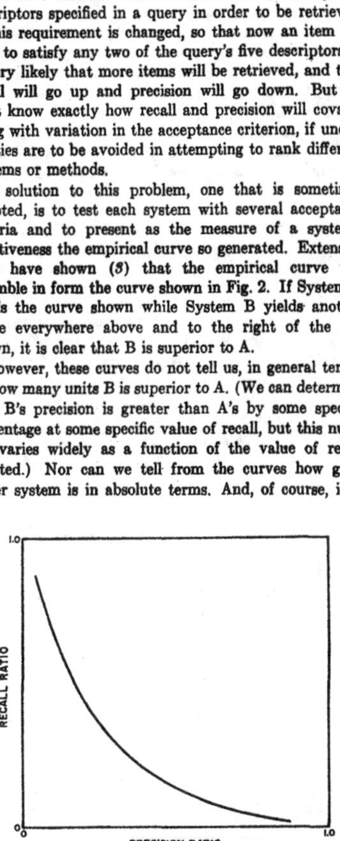


FIG. 2. Idealized example of an empirical recall-precision curve, fanned out by varying the acceptance criterion. For lenient criteria, recall is high and precision is low. Progressively more stringent acceptance criteria increase precision at the expense of recall.

relatively awkward (We might say that a large "bandwidth" is required) to transmit and receive a full curve.

A measure that retains the basic information inherent in the recall-precision curve, and at the same time overcomes the drawbacks of using a curve as a measure, would be attained if there is a way to represent completely an empirical curve of this general sort by a single number on a scale with a unit, a true zero, and a maximum. The thrust of my earlier article was that statistical decision theory offers a way—indeed, several ways. Whether or not we can take advantage of one of them, or to what extent, depends upon the form of retrieval data when analyzed by decision-theory techniques, and that form is the concern of this paper.

Though a way might be found to completely characterize any empirical recall-precision curve by a single number on the type of scale desired, decision theory suggests using the curve that results when another variable is substituted for precision. The variable to be substituted, in the terms of Fig. 1, is $b/b+d$. This quantity is the number of items both irrelevant and retrieved divided by the number of items irrelevant, or the proportion of irrelevant items retrieved, and is an estimate of the conditional probability that an item will be retrieved given that it is irrelevant.

As in my earlier article (*1*), I refer to the retrieval of an irrelevant item as a "false drop." Also for consistency, the retrieval of a relevant item is termed a "hit," so instead of the term "recall ratio" I use "the conditional probability of a hit." Some of the notation used here differs from that of the previous article. Here, as seen in Fig. 1, lower-case letters, $r$ and $\bar{r}$, designate relevant and irrelevant items, while upper-case letters, $R$ and $\bar{R}$, designate retrieved and unretrieved items. The two conditional probabilities of principal interest are here denoted $P(R|r)$ and $P(R|\bar{r})$. In the present notation, the curve we shall consider has $a/a+c$ or $P(R|r)$ on the ordinate and $b/b+d$ or $P(R|\bar{r})$ on the abscissa. This curve is a comparison of two "operating characteristics," as the term is used in statistics, and is called here the "relative operating characteristic," or "*ROC*."

One consideration in choosing the two variables used in decision theory, which are derived from the two columns of the relevance-retrieval contingency table, is that they contain all the information in the table; the remaining quantities of the table ("misses" and "correct rejections") are, respectively, their complements. The recall and precision ratios are derived from a column and a row of the table and do not serve to specify the remainder of the table.

A related, but more salient, consideration is that using the two variables of decision theory permits us to draw upon several models of the retrieval process which stipulate different forms that empirical *ROC* curves may take. That is, each of several available models developed within decision theory precisely specifies a given form for a theoretical *ROC* curve. Or rather, each model specifies a family of *ROC* curves having an index of effectiveness as the parameter. Conveniently, the *ROC* curves of all but one of the models devised to date are straight lines or very nearly straight lines when plotted on linear normal-deviate, or "probability," scales. A single number is adequate as an index of effectiveness, because it is sufficient to generate the entire curve, under those models that assume some fixed relationship between the degree of effectiveness and the slope of the curve. Generality is gained at the cost of a second parameter in one model that permits a variable relationship between effectiveness and slope. Still another model gives a one-parameter fit to data without regard to the slope, or, for that matter, without regard to the general form of the *ROC* curve, but this number is not sufficient to regenerate the curve from which it is taken. We turn now to a description of these alternative models, and then to the retrieval data that will enable us to choose from among them the one or ones that will be useful.

### The General Decision Model

Though the assumption is not essential to their application, I shall assume in describing the alternative decision-theory models that for each query submitted to a system, the system in some manner assigns an index value (call it $z$) to each item in the store to represent the degree of relevance of the item to the query. Plotting separately for irrelevant and relevant items the probability of assignment of each value of $z$ yields two probability density functions. One form the two density functions might have is depicted in Fig. 3. The left-hand function is associated with irrelevant items, $f(z|\bar{r})$, and the right-hand function is associated with relevant items, $f(z|r)$.

If, as suggested in the figure, any given value of $z$ might be assigned by the system to an item that is relevant or to an item that is irrelevant (as judged by a user or other umpire), then, as shown, some criterion value of $z$, denoted $z_c$, should be adopted, such that items assigned values greater than $z_c$ are retrieved while items assigned values less than $z_c$ are not retrieved. The areas under the two density functions to the right of $z_c$ represent the probabilities of retrieving irrelevant and relevant items. They are the coordinates of the *ROC* curve, $P(R|\bar{r})$ and $P(R|r)$.

Any given separation between the two density functions represents a stable retrieval system, with some particular capacity to distinguish between relevant and irrelevant items or some particular degree of effectiveness. For a fixed separation between the density functions, variation in the acceptance criterion $z_c$ will result in a particular *ROC* curve. Another system or method, with greater or lesser ability to discriminate relevant and irrelevant items, will yield a different *ROC* curve as the acceptance criterion is varied.

The exact form of an *ROC* curve, it is clear, depends upon the shapes of the density functions that underlie it. Various measurement models are generated by hypothesizing density functions of different shapes.

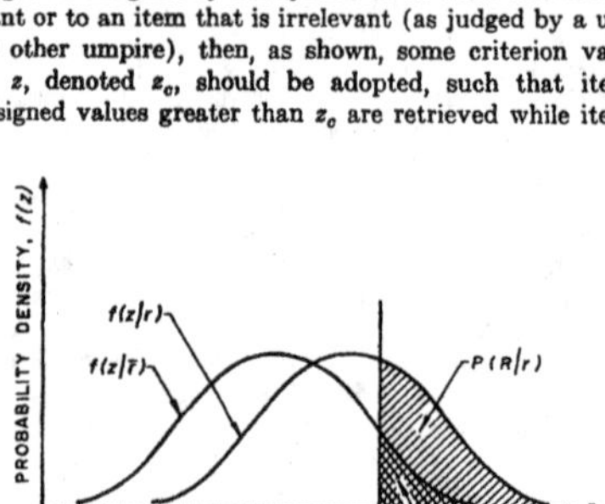


Fig. 3. One possible representation of the density functions for relevant and irrelevant items. The abscissa is the index of relevance, $z$, assigned by the system to each item. An acceptance criterion is labeled $z_c$.

### Gaussian, Equal-variance Model

The density functions shown in Fig. 3 are Gaussian and of equal variance. Given the separation shown, variation in the acceptance criterion will trace the *ROC* curve labeled $E=1$ in Fig. 4. The measure $E$ is defined as the difference between the means of the two density functions divided by their common standard deviation. If the separation is increased so that the difference between the means is twice as great as that shown in Fig. 3, then criterion variation will produce the *ROC* curve labeled $E=2$ in Fig. 4.

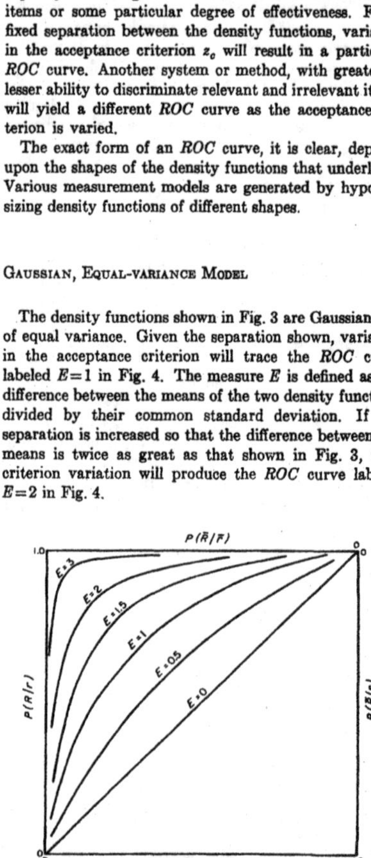


Fig. 4. A family of relative-operating-characteristic curves, based on Gaussian density functions of equal variance, with values of the parameter $E$. Labels on the upper and right-hand scales indicate that the full relevance-retrieval contingency table can be recovered from the plot.

We see that empirical data obtained from a test of a retrieval system could be plotted in the space of Fig. 4. If the data points followed the contour of one of the curves shown, or one of the intermediate curves not shown, the label on that curve would completely describe the effectiveness of the system: Knowing the single number permits reconstruction of the entire curve.

It is more convenient to plot data fitted by the *ROC* curves of Fig. 4 on probability scales, that is, on axes scaled linearly for the normal deviate, for then these *ROC* curves are straight lines with unit slope, as shown in Fig. 5. The measure *E* for any curve can be read from the normal-deviate scales; one simply subtracts the value on the right-hand scale from the value on the top scale corresponding to any point on the curve. In Fig. 5, *E* is also scaled along the negative diagonal.

It can be seen that for practical purposes *E* has a maximum of approximately 5.0; though the axes could be extended to show higher values of *E*, effectiveness is not really at issue for retrieval systems yielding a hit probability greater than 0.99 and, simultaneously, a false-drop probability less than 0.01. There is the additional fact that reliable estimation of such extreme probabilities demands a sample of excessive size.

### Gaussian, Unequal-variance Model

If the density functions are Gaussian, but of unequal variance, the *ROC* curves on the scales of Fig. 5 will be linear with slopes other than unity. In particular, the slope of the *ROC* curve is equal to the ratio of the standard deviation of $f(z|\bar{r})$ to the standard deviation of $f(z|r)$.

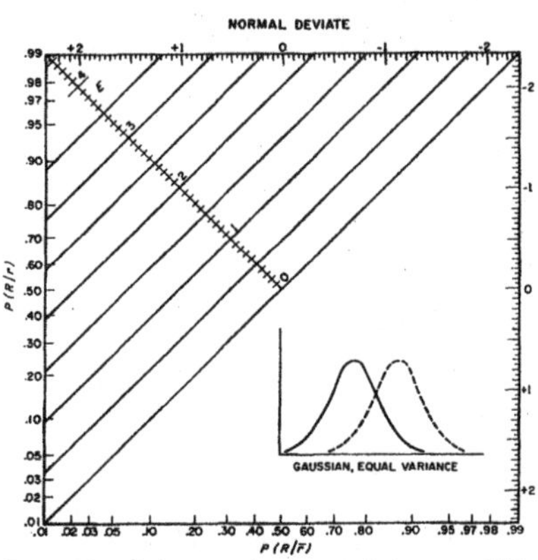


Fig. 5. The relative-operating-characteristic curves of Fig. 4 on probability scales, that is, on axes scaled linearly for the normal deviate. Density functions inserted at lower right identify the basis of these *ROC* curves in Gaussian, equal-variance density functions.

For density functions of unequal variance, *E* must be redefined, for it was previously defined in terms of a standard deviation common to the two functions. Note that for *ROC* curves of non-unit slope, the value of *E* obtained by subtracting a normal-deviate value on the right scale from one on the top scale is not constant along the curve. The definition adopted here consists in normalizing the difference between the means of the two density functions by their average standard deviation; this definition is reflected by measuring *E* at the intersection of the *ROC* curve and the negative diagonal of the *ROC* space.

Now, at least two alternatives are open to us. If we find that the slopes of empirical *ROC* curves vary without regard to *E* (measured at the intercept of the negative diagonal), two parameters will be needed to fit the curve. Reconstruction of the curve will require reporting the value of the slope, *s*, in addition to the value of *E*. It could turn out, on the other hand, that *s* bears some fixed relation to *E*, for example, that *s* increases regularly as *E* increases. This would be the case if the ratio of the increment in the mean of $f(z|r)$ to a decrement in its standard deviation were a constant. If this constant were a stable property of a given retrieval system, it could be reported once, and then the single value of *E* would be sufficient to describe the various curves the system produces as a result of changes in one or another independent variable.

### Exponential Model

Simply as an illustration of further modelling possibilities, consider hypothesizing that the density functions are exponential in form, as shown at the lower right in Fig. 6. Then, again, the *ROC* curve is essentially linear on probability scales and can be described by a single parameter. The parameter $K=\sqrt{k}$ is defined in the figure; for $k>1.0$, the *ROC* curves have the property that *s* decreases regularly as the effectiveness (*K*) increases.

### Distribution-free Model

If, after looking at data, hypothesizing some particular form of the density functions, and hence of the *ROC* curve, seems too strong a procedure, we can resort to a measurement scheme that leaves these forms unspecified and free to vary. We can take as the measure of effectiveness the percentage of the area of the *ROC* space that falls beneath any empirical *ROC* curve, when plotted on linear scales (as in Fig. 4). This measure, call it *A*, will vary from 50% for a curve that follows the positive diagonal, representing equal hit and false-drop proportions or no discrimination, to 100% for a curve that follows the extreme left and top coordinates of the graph, representing a hit proportion of 1.0 at a false-drop proportion of 0.0 or perfect discrimination. The measure

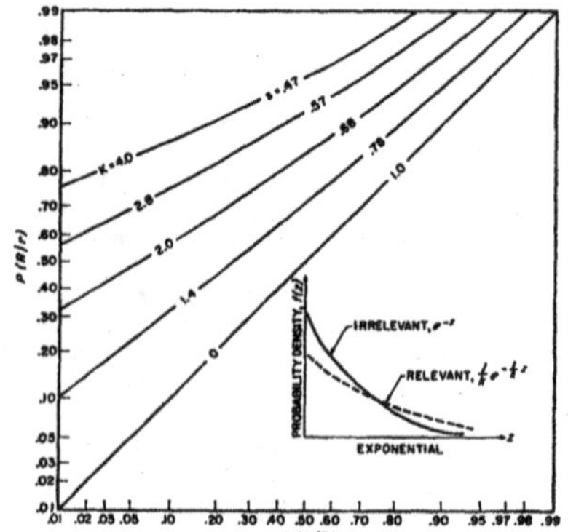


FIG. 6. A family of *ROC* curves based on exponential density functions, plotted on probability scales.

*A*, though a simple summary measure of effectiveness, does not permit reconstruction of the empirical curve from which it is drawn. It has the property useful for conceptual purposes that the value of *A* is equal to the percentage of correct choices a system will make when attempting to select from a pair of items, one drawn at random from the irrelevant set and one drawn at random from the relevant set, the item that is relevant. As demonstrated elsewhere (*4*) this equality holds for *ROC* curves of any form.

## • Data

The three sets of data we shall examine were collected, respectively, at the Computation Laboratory of Harvard University by Gerard Salton ( now at Cornell University) and Michael Lesk; under the Aslib project at Cranfield, England, by Cyril Cleverdon and Michael Keen; and at Arthur D. Little, Inc., by Vincent E. Giuliano and Paul E. Jones. These data were originally presented in technical reports published in late 1966 (*3, 5, 6*).

Salton and Lesk and Giuliano and Jones kindly made their raw data available to me so that I could calculate the hit and false-drop proportions. Cleverdon and Keen presented these quantities in their report. Though they are not responsible for the outcome, one or more of the authors of each report discussed with me the problem of measurement and commented on a draft of this paper. Their cooperation was essential, and I am pleased to acknowledge their very helpful advice and criticism.

Plots of data following are identified by the various terms for independent variables used in the original reports, to make possible cross references, but the terms are not defined here. Similarly, our present purposes do not require a description of the procedures of the three sets of experiments. However, a brief characterization of the scopes of the studies will be helpful in evaluating the general conclusions drawn here.

At Harvard, the questions asked experimentally include these: "Can automatic text processing methods be used effectively to replace a manual content analysis; if so, what parts of the documents [titles, abstracts, full text] are most appropriate for incorporation into the analysis? Is it necessary to provide vocabulary normalization methods to eliminate linguistic ambiguities; should such normalization be handled by means of specially constructed dictionaries, or is it possible to replace thesauruses by statistical word association methods? What dictionaries can be used most effectively for vocabulary normalization? Is it important to provide hierarchical subject arrangements, as is done in library classification systems; alternatively, should syntactical relations between subject identifiers be preserved? Does the user have an important role to fulfill in controlling the search procedure?" (*5*, pp. I-3, I-4). The experimental retrieval system, which operated on an IBM 7094 computer, was fully automatic in most applications; content-analysis procedures incorporated into the system processed documents and queries in natural language with no prior manual analysis. Stores of items used consisted of four collections of documents in three subject fields: documentation, aerodynamics, and computer sciences.

Experiments at Cranfield were based on manual analysis of documents. They were conducted to examine several different index languages (some languages using single terms, others based on concepts, and others based on a thesaurus); the exhaustivity of indexing; the level of specificity of index terms; a gradation of relevance assessments; and the amount of intelligence applied in formulating search rules. Two collections used consisted of documents in aerodynamics and aircraft structures.

The experiments at Arthur D. Little, Inc., evaluated manual and automatic indexing; length of the query; coordinate retrieval methods; and retrieval methods based on statistical word associations, with and without human intervention. The system operated on an IBM 1401 computer, with fully automatic indexing in most applications. All items in the file were abstracts of reports in the aerospace field.

Data from the three sources lead to the same conclusions about the usefulness of a decision-theory measure, so the analyses of the three sets of data will be presented with little evaluative comment prior to a general discussion of results. Each of the *ROC* plots is made on probability scales. Most of the plots summarize the results of one method of retrieval used with a given system; a few of them summarize the results of a single query used with a given method. The first question we ask is whether or not the plots of data are adequately fitted by straight lines. If they are, then we are interested in the slopes of the lines.

## Harvard-Cornell Data

All of the data I obtained from the Harvard-Cornell project are presented here; this set includes almost all of the data collected under the project before June of 1966, the major exception being some collected toward the end of that time in tests permitting iterative searches under the user's control.

The system at Harvard, called "SMART," assesses the relevance of each item in the store to each query addressed to the system. Print-outs of data containing the relevance index for each item are, of course, extensive, and are not usually obtained; therefore we can not examine directly the shapes of the density functions. The standard print-out lists, for each query, the code number of every item relevant to it and the rank value of each of these items in a list ordered (by the system) according to degree of relevance. Data in this form permit adopting, for purposes of analysis, each of several arbitrary acceptance criteria according to the total number of items considered as retrieved. That is, $P(R|r)$ and $P(R|\bar{r})$ are calculated in turn, for example, for the 5 items ranked highest, the 10 items ranked highest, the 15 items ranked highest, and so forth, terminating at an arbitrary point.

To gain a relatively stable sample, results are combined for all queries used with a single method. One can pool results before calculating $P(R|r)$ *and* $P(R|\bar{r})$, or alternatively, can calculate these quantities for each query and take their average. The first of these procedures was followed in the analyses reported here.

Figure 7 shows the results for the collection of items in the subject field of documentation (called the ADI collection), under each of six retrieval methods. As in subsequent figures, in order to conserve space, only a portion of the *ROC* space is shown for each plot; the last panel in the figure reproduces the lines of the previous panels on the full *ROC* space. These lines, in all cases, were fitted to the data by eye.

The data are quite adequately fitted by straight lines in every instance. Indeed, according to standards acquired through experience in other fields (for example, human signal detection and recognition memory) where the decision-theory measure has proved to be useful (*4*), the fits are very good.

A small staircase effect can be discerned in the data. This effect may be the result of having a relatively small sample (containing an average of five relevant items for 35 questions); the procedure used in analysis for defining acceptance criteria forces each successive point a certain distance to the right, and a low density of relevant items would produce irregular upward movement. In any case, the effect is not large enough to be of much concern. We can see also some variation in the slopes of the lines; we shall consider the significance of this variation after all the data have been examined.

Figure 8 shows the results of seven retrieval methods applied to a collection of items on aerodynamics borrowed by the Harvard-Cornell group from the Cranfield project. Again, the straight-line fits exceed reasonable aspirations, and a variation in slopes appears.

Figure 9 represents one of two collections in the subject area of computer science, called IRE 1, and six retrieval methods. Figure 10 shows the second IRE collection and 10 methods. Figure 11 shows the second IRE collection with a different set of 10 methods.

With the IRE collection we notice a tendency, at higher values of $E$, for the slopes to be greater than unity. The slopes in Fig. 9 range from 0.95 to 1.12, in Fig. 10 from 0.98 to 1.40, and in Fig. 11 from 1.20 to 1.56. With the ADI collection (Fig. 7) the slopes range from 0.83 to 0.99, and with the Cranfield collection (Fig. 8), from 0.76 to 1.00.

We can't help but observe the substantive result of this analysis that the differences in effectiveness among the various methods are small relative to the differences among collections. The range in $E$ for the six methods applied to the ADI collection is 0.20 (from 0.90 to 1.10); for the seven methods used with the Cranfield collection, 0.35 (from 1.45 to 1.80); for the six methods used with the IRE 1 collection, 0.40 (from 2.00 to 2.40); for the first 10 methods used with the IRE 2 collection, 0.55 (from 1.95 to 2.50); and for the second group of 10 methods used with the IRE 2 collection, 0.30 (from 2.10 to 2.40). These ranges, on the order of 0.50 or less, can be compared with the range over all collections of 1.60, keeping in mind the scale range of about 5.00 from chance performance to very good performance. The Harvard-Cornell and Cranfield investigators are inclined to believe that the dependency of effectiveness on the collection results both from differences in the "hardness" of the vocabularies of the three subject fields and from the use of different procedures with the three collections for establishing relevance (*7*).

## Cranfield Data

The study at Cranfield has been actively pursued for several years, and the last report contains an enormous amount of data. I have plotted only a fraction of the results; however, I am not aware of any particular bias in my casual sampling, and all the plots prepared are included here.

The Cranfield data are distinguished from the Harvard data in being based on a larger file (in most cases 1,400 items, as compared with the largest Harvard collection of about 400 items), and on more questions (approximately 220, as compared with the Harvard maximum of about 40). One consequence is the appearance of lower false-drop proportions, proportions that fall off the graph paper (Codex Graph Sheet No. 41,453) used in the preceding figures. So we use another graph paper (Keuffel and Esser Co. No. 47 8062) that ranges down to a proportion of 0.0001. Though the graphs have on them scales of the normal deviate, these scales, unfortunately, are not given on the Keuffel and Esser paper available commercially.

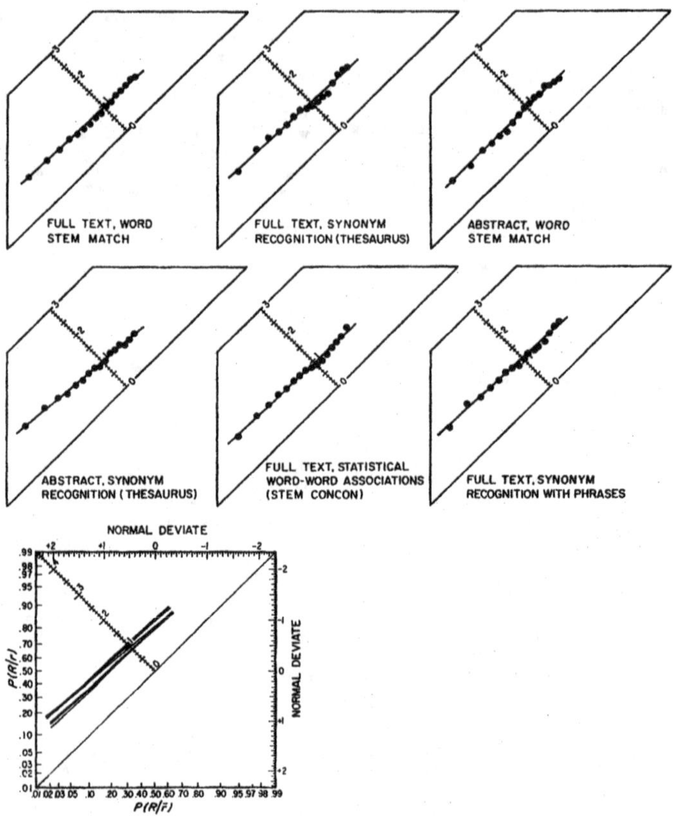


FIG. 7. ADI collection: 6 methods. 82 items, 35 queries. 170 relevant + 2,700 irrelevant = 2,870 total. Criteria: 3, 6, 9, . . ., 47 retrievals. Harvard-Cornell: Salton and Lesk.

In the Cranfield system, a manual one, the relevance of every item to every query is determined by judges, but the system itself does not rank items according to their degree of relevance to the query. Various acceptance criteria are obtained by establishing different "levels of coordination," that is, by varying the requirements on the number of query terms an item must satisfy in order to be retrieved.

Figure 12 shows the results of five retrieval methods that vary in the "recall device" they employ. The slopes are quite uniform, slightly greater than unity, and not many of the points fall off the fitted lines. Essentially the same comments apply to Fig. 13, which shows two levels of indexing exhaustivity for two sets of recall devices. Likewise for Fig. 14, which illustrates the effects of requiring different degrees of relevance for retrieval to be effected. The left panel results when all four categories of judged relevance satisfy the retrieval criterion; moving to the right, the relevance requirement is strengthened, so that in the last panel we have the results when only those items with the highest degree of relevance are retrieved. Figure 15 shows some results obtained with a smaller collection when retrieval is based on only titles

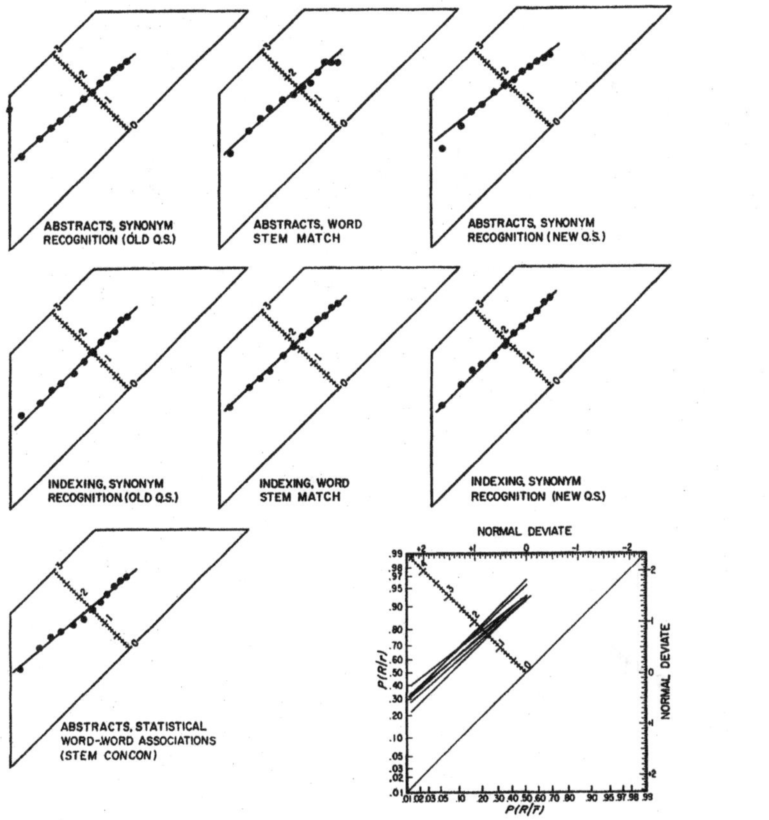


FIG. 8. Cranfield collection: 7 methods. 200 items, 42 queries. 198 relevant + 8,202 irrelevant = 8,400 total. Criteria: 5, 10, 15, 20, 30, 40, . . ., 100 retrievals. Harvard-Cornell: Salton and Lesk.

and abstracts, or on titles only, and the fits are about as good as before.

In Fig. 15 values of $E$ range from 1.33 to 1.70, and values of the slope range from 0.80 to 0.95. In the three figures preceding, $E$ ranges from 1.58 to 1.86, and $s$ lies between 1.08 and 1.18.

ARTHUR D. LITTLE, INC., DATA

Like the Harvard system, the system constructed at Arthur D. Little, Inc. (ADL) assigns an index value to each item according to its relevance for each query. Again, however, the system did not produce a print-out of data in full enough form to enable us to look directly at the density functions supposed to underlie the *ROC* curves.

The ADL system was used with a still larger store, effectively 4,000 items. I have based arbitrary acceptance criteria, again, on the number of items considered as retrieved. The terminal criterion, in this case, was determined by the ADL investigators; they proceeded through the items according to their rank to judge the relevance of each, and stopped when it seemed that relevant items were turning up on a random basis. In order to determine the recall ratio, or hit proportion, the total number

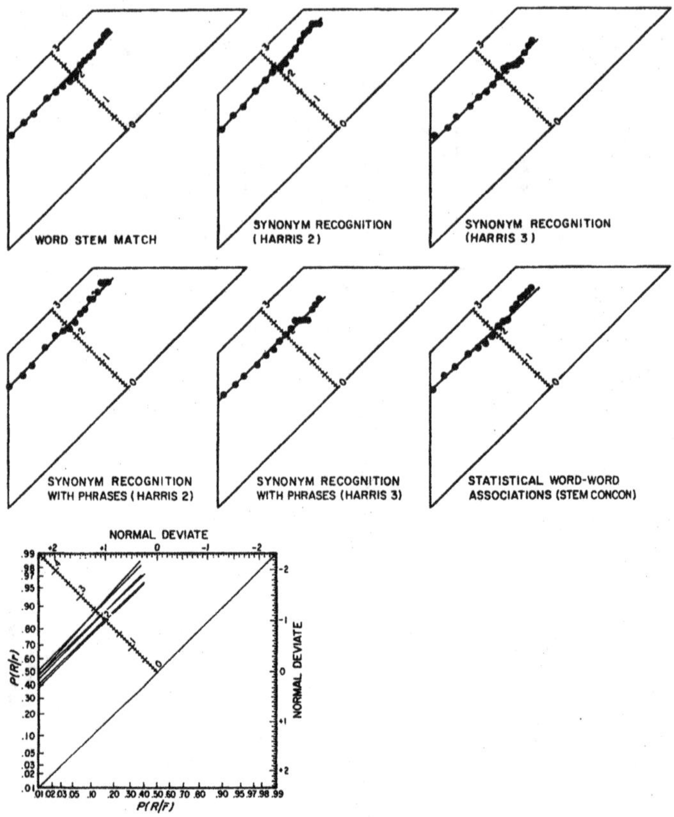


FIG. 9. IRE 1 collection: 6 methods. 405 items, 17 queries. 186 relevant + 6,699 irrelevant = 6,885 total. Criteria: 10, 15, 20, 30, 40, . . ., 150 retrievals. Harvard-Cornell: Salton and Lesk.

of relevant items for each query had to be established. These numbers were estimated at ADL from a sample of 400 items drawn from the store of 4,000 items.

Included in the following figures are almost all the data, and all the major data, collected at Arthur D. Little, Inc. A difference between these and foregoing plots is that most of these are based on single queries. The data points, surprisingly, do not show much greater scatter about a line, but substantially greater variation in the slopes is evident.

Figure 16 shows the associative retrieval method applied to four queries which consisted of abstracts ("full text queries"). Also shown is the same method applied to briefer forms of the same queries. In the latter case ("CBU queries") the queries consisted of critical word strings selected from the abstracts, designated as "content-bearing units." The full *ROC* plots show the pooled results for queries 1, 3, and 4 for each type of query. Query 2 was excluded from the pooled results because the range of acceptance criteria available for it was relatively limited, and various means of pooling queries with different ranges of acceptance criteria proved unsatisfactory. If the curves of the last two plots are extrapolated to the negative diagonal, values of $E$ are obtained (ap-

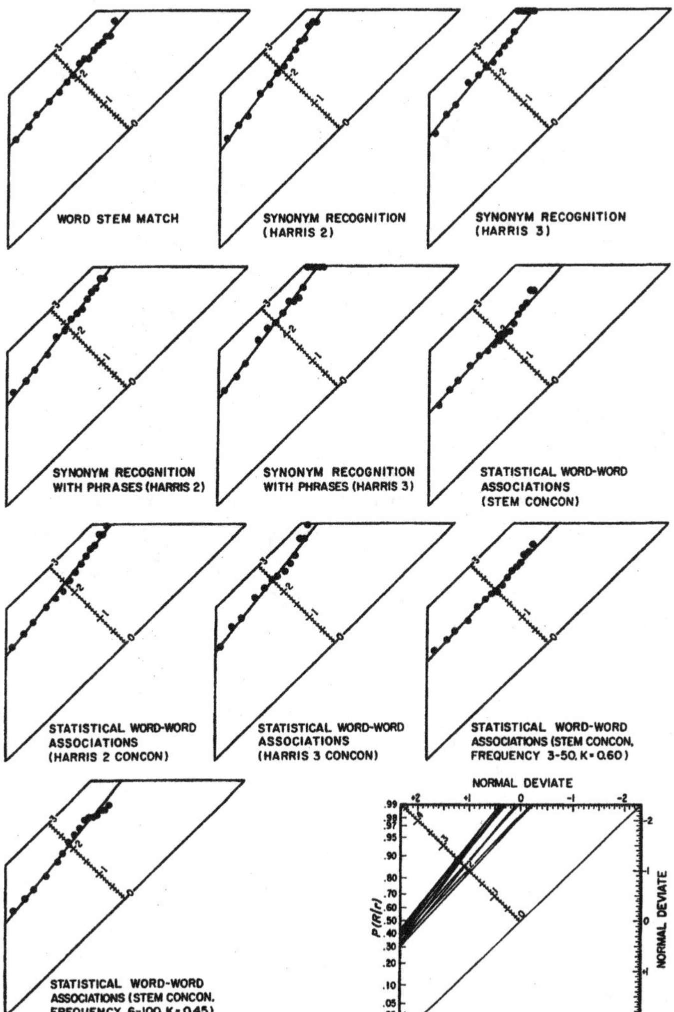


FIG. 10. IRE 2 collection: first set of 10 methods. 380 items, 17 queries. 181 relevant + 6,279 irrelevant = 6,460 total Criteria: 10, 15, 20, 30, 40, . . ., 150 retrievals. Harvard-Cornell: Salton and Lesk.

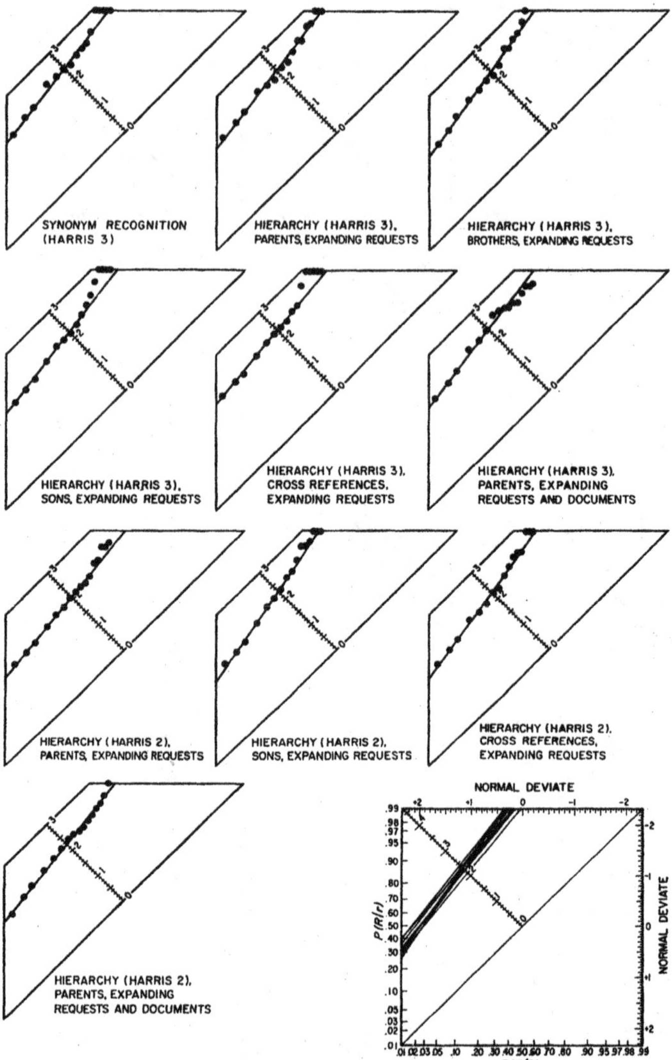


FIG. 11. IRE 2 collection, second set of 10 methods. 380 items, 17 queries. 178 relevant + 6,282 irrelevant = 6,460 total. Criteria: 10, 15, 20, 30, 40, . . ., 150 retrievals. Harvard-Cornell: Salton and Lesk.

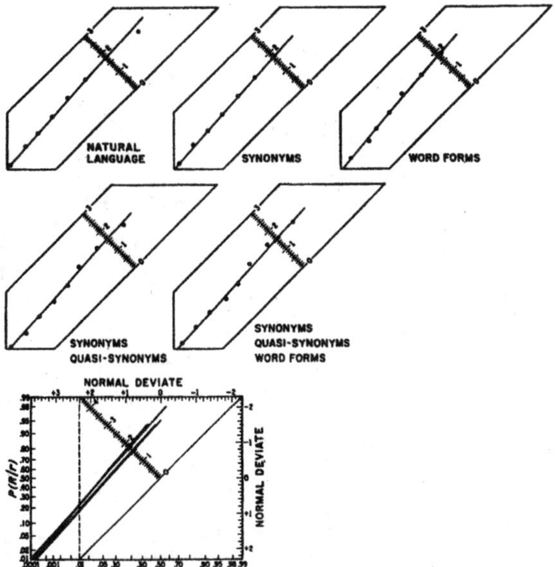


FIG. 12. Recall devices, single-term index language: 5 methods. 1,400 items, 221 queries. 1,590 relevant + 307,810 irrelevant = 309,400 total. Criteria: levels of coordination. Cranfield: Cleverdon and Keen.

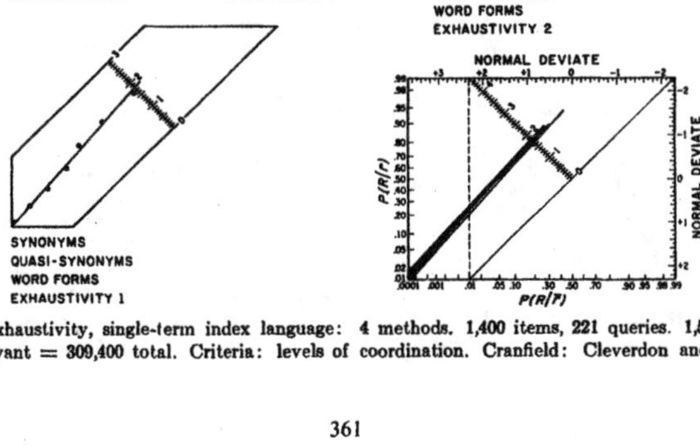


FIG. 13. Indexing exhaustivity, single-term index language: 4 methods. 1,400 items, 221 queries. 1,590 relevant + 307,810 irrelevant = 309,400 total. Criteria: levels of coordination. Cranfield: Cleverdon and Keen.

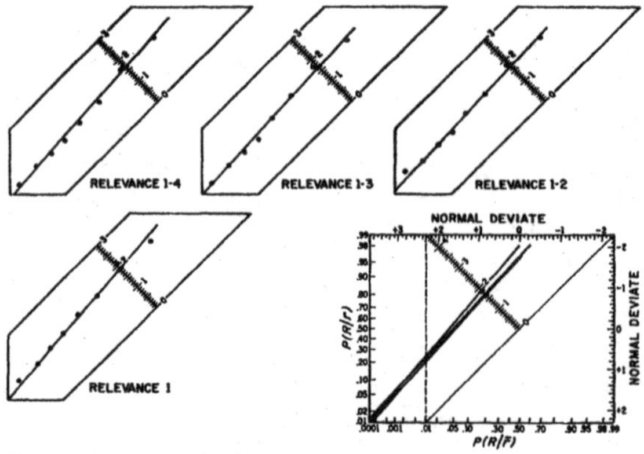


FIG. 14. Document relevance, single-term index language, natural language: 4 methods. 1,400 items, 50 queries.
Relevance 1–4: 361 relevant + 69,639 irrelevant = 70,000 total.
Relevance 1–3: 297 relevant + 69,703 irrelevant = 70,000 total.
Relevance 1–2: 155 relevant + 69,845 irrelevant = 70,000 total.
Relevance 1: 95 relevant + 69,905 irrelevant = 70,000 total.
Criteria: levels of coordination. Cranfield: Cleverdon and Keen.

proximately 1.30 and 2.20) that lie in the range of empirical values noted earlier. The slopes of the lines (approximately 1.00 and 1.50) are also in the range of empirical values noted earlier.

Figure 17 shows three different retrieval methods used with the short queries. Figure 18 shows another method and reproduces the fitted lines for the four methods of Figs. 17 and 18 for each query. There is a tendency for the slopes to depend more upon the query than the method. Averaging over methods, the slopes range from about 1.00 for query 4, through approximately 1.45 for queries 2 and 3, to about 1.75 for query 1. Average slopes for the four methods lie between 1.28 and 1.52. The average values of $E$ associated with the four methods, by extrapolation, range from 1.60 to 2.10.

We may note that the highest value of $E$, 2.10, is obtained with the method called "selected associations," shown in panels (i) through (l) of Fig. 17. It can be seen that, in fitting straight lines to the data obtained with that method, data points falling below the line at the lower false-drop probabilities were virtually ignored in the case of two queries (queries 1 and 4). Clearly, if we were to restrict our interest to low false-drop probabilities—say, if we were to consider only the left-most half-dozen or so points—then the slopes for that method would be steeper, and the values of $E$ estimated would be higher. In fact, if the four queries are pooled with only the left-most nine points included, the resulting value of $E$ is close to 3.0 (and the resulting slope is about 1.8). The "selected-associations" method is one of two methods tried at ADL with user intervention between iterative searches. The other method in which adjustments were made between iterations is the one called "reweighted associative," shown in Fig. 18; in that case all the data points are quite well taken into account in fitting lines, and an $E = 1.90$ is obtained.

## • Conclusions

The consistent linearity of the empirical relative-operating-characteristic curves confirms that a decision-theory measure can be used to reflect solely the effectiveness of a retrieval system, and effectiveness unconfounded by variation in the acceptance criterion. The apparently irregular variation in the slopes of the curves presents a slight complication relative to achieving a measure that is a single number, but not enough of a complication to impair seriously the usefulness of a decision-theory measure.

Two numbers—$E$ measured at the negative diagonal of the *ROC* space, and the slope, $s$—give an accurate description of the curve representing constant retrieval effectiveness over varying acceptance criteria. Two numbers are not as convenient as one, but these particular two give a considerably more economical description of the performance curve than available previously and can be reported in cases where conveying information about the full curve is desirable.

The data at hand indicate, however, that for most purposes conclusions about effectiveness can be drawn from

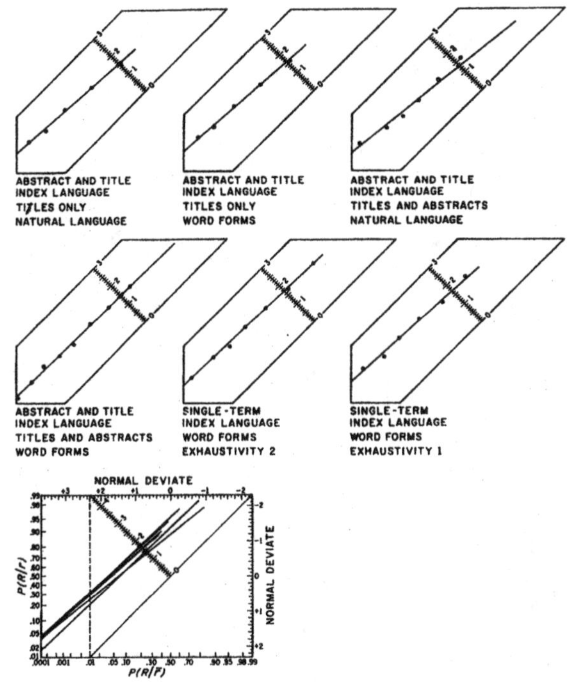


FIG. 15. Abstracts and titles: 6 methods. 200 items, 42 queries. 198 relevant + 8,202 irrelevant = 8,400 total. Criteria: levels of coordination. Cranfield: Cleverdon and Keen.

the value of $E$ alone, without regard to $s$. In short, there is little point in concern over small differences in $s$ when differences in $E$ are small. We have seen that when values of $s$ are based on more than a few queries they do not vary enough to obscure a substantial difference in $E$.

What constitutes a "substantial difference" in $E$, or a difference of practical significance? An approximate answer derived from the present data is that a difference in $E$ in the neighborhood of 0.30 to 0.50 is a reasonably significant one. Thus, for example, in the Harvard data based on the IRE collections (Figs. 9, 10, 11), a difference between two methods of that magnitude corresponds to a factor of about two in the false-drop probability. (By way of illustration, it can be seen in Fig. 9 that at a hit probability of 0.90 the extreme methods show false-drop probabilities of approximately 0.25 and 0.13; at a hit probability of 0.70 the extreme false-drop probabilities are about 0.13 and 0.07; at a hit probability of 0.50 the extreme false-drop probabilities are about 0.02 and 0.01.) It seems unlikely that a smaller experimental difference would have much practical import.

As discussed earlier, if it should seem worthwhile to have a measure that is both a single number and sensitive to variation in slope, the distribution-free measure $A$ could be used. Let us use the measure $A$ now to get a different view of the observed differences among methods in the present sample, a view that will help us judge how small a difference in $E$ is practically significant. $A$, it will be recalled, is the proportion of the area of the *ROC* space that lies beneath an *ROC* curve plotted on linear scales (as in Fig. 4), and is equal to the probability of choosing between two items, one drawn at random from the relevant set and the other drawn at random from the irrelevant set, the item that is relevant. Assume for the purpose at hand that all of the *ROC* curves in our sample are of unit slope; this approximation introduces a distortion that is negligible relative to the point of interest here, and permits a conversion from $E$ to $A$ by

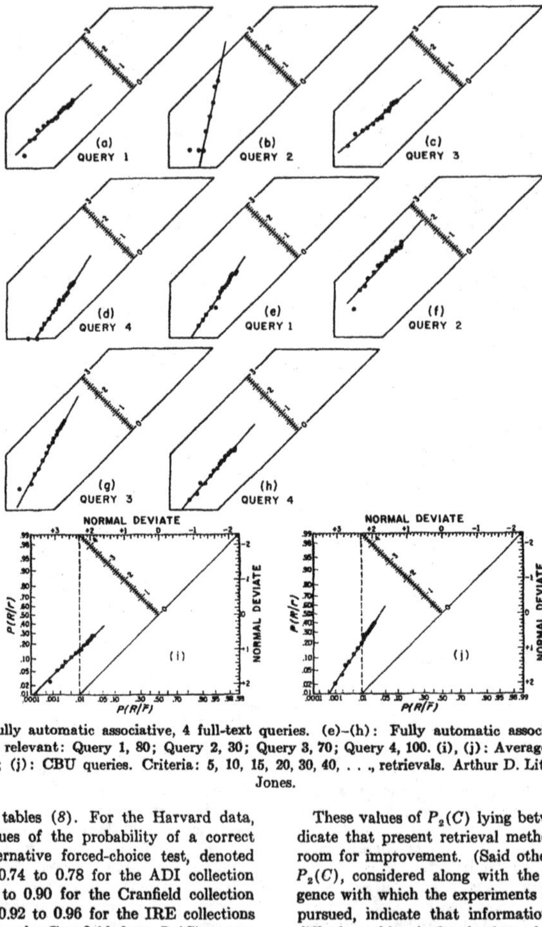

FIG. 16. (a)–(d): Fully automatic associative, 4 full-text queries. (e)–(h): Fully automatic associative, 4 CBU queries. 4,000 items. Number relevant: Query 1, 80; Query 2, 30; Query 3, 70; Query 4, 100. (i), (j): Average of Queries 1, 3, and 4. (i): full-text queries; (j): CBU queries. Criteria: 5, 10, 15, 20, 30, 40, . . ., retrievals. Arthur D. Little, Inc.: Giuliano and Jones.

means of published tables (*8*). For the Harvard data, values of *A*, or values of the probability of a correct choice in a two-alternative forced-choice test, denoted $P_2(C)$, range from 0.74 to 0.78 for the ADI collection (Fig. 7), from 0.85 to 0.90 for the Cranfield collection (Fig. 8), and from 0.92 to 0.96 for the IRE collections (Figs. 9, 10, 11). For the Cranfield data, $P_2(C)$ ranges from 0.87 to 0.91 for the large collection (Figs. 12, 13, 14) and from 0.83 to 0.89 for the small collection (Fig. 15). For the data collected at Arthur D. Little, Inc., the range of the four "CBU" methods (Figs. 17, 18), averaged over the four queries, is from 0.87 to 0.93. It might be argued, again, that the differences between extreme methods for any collection, of 0.04 to 0.06, are real differences, but it seems unlikely that differences of less than 0.04 in $P_2(C)$ have material implications.

These values of $P_2(C)$ lying between 0.74 and 0.96 indicate that present retrieval methods leave considerable room for improvement. (Said otherwise, these values of $P_2(C)$, considered along with the competence and diligence with which the experiments here represented were pursued, indicate that information retrieval is a very difficult problem.) On the face of it, choosing the single relevant item from a collection of two items is not a demanding task, and we should hope that our retrieval systems would make the correct choice almost every time, say, with a probability of 0.99 or greater. A more compelling impression, however, of the current state of the retrieval art is gained by taking pairs of hit and false-drop probabilities from the empirical *ROC* curves and converting these probabilities to raw numbers.

Consider an *ROC* curve with $E=2.5$ and $s=1.3$. This

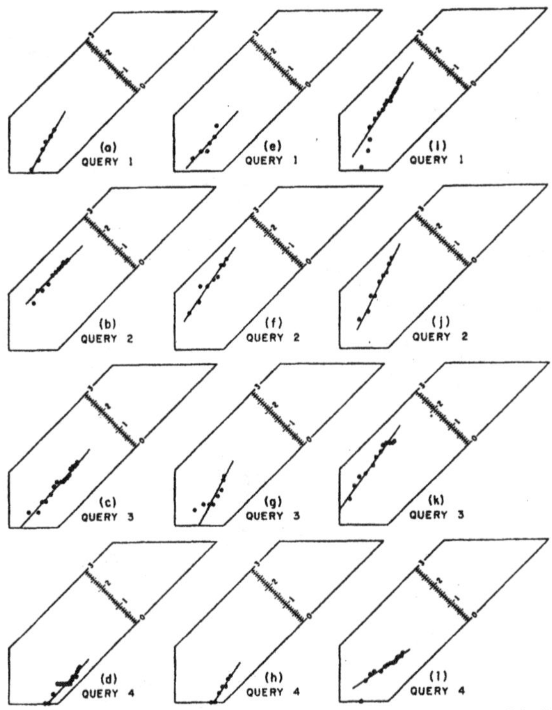


FIG. 17. CBU queries: 3 methods. (a)–(d): Modified coordinate. (e)–(h): Frequency-weighted coordinate. (i)–(l): Selected associations. Number of items, number relevant per query, and criteria as in Fig. 16. Arthur D. Little, Inc.: Giuliano and Jones.

curve is close to the best of the curves seen in the foregoing, and exceeded by none of them. It passes through the points $P(R|\bar{r})$ and $P(R|r)$ having coordinate values of (0.001, 0.12), (0.01, 0.42), and (0.10, 0.88). Assume a file of 3,000 items and a group of queries to each of which 10 of the 3,000 items are relevant. Now, if we will settle for retrieving, on the average, only 1 of the 10 relevant items per query, we will also receive 3 false drops each time. If we desire 4 of 10 relevant items, we will have to winnow the 4 from 30 irrelevant items. If we should aspire to 9 of 10 relevant items, we would have to examine more than 300 items in response to each query to find the 9.

These noise-to-signal ratios are dramatically large. The ratio mounts rapidly even for a file as small as 3,000 items: from 3 to 7 to 33 for the three acceptance criteria of the example. For a file of 10,000 items the corresponding noise-to-signal ratios are 10, 25, and 100 plus. It is with these ratios in mind that I earlier suggested dismissing small differences in $E$ and ignoring small variations in $s$.

The decision-theory analysis can be seen to set the stage clearly for identifying an important advance in retrieval technique. The best of the performances sampled here, in the vicinity of $E=2.5$ and $s=1.3$, gives a false-drop probability of approximately 0.10 for a hit probability of 0.90. Assuming the same slope, and taking the same hit probability, an $E=3.0$ corresponds to a false-drop probability of 0.05, and an $E=3.8$ corresponds to a false-drop probability of 0.01. An $E=4.0$ means a false-drop probability of 0.005, or reception of 15 unwanted items along with 9 of the 10 wanted items from a file of 3,000. An $E=4.5$ means a false-drop probability of 0.001, or reception of 3 unwanted items along with 9 of the 10 wanted items from a file of 3,000.

A belief of several people working in the retrieval field is that a very significant advance in retrieval effectiveness will be achieved in the near future by "on-line" systems,

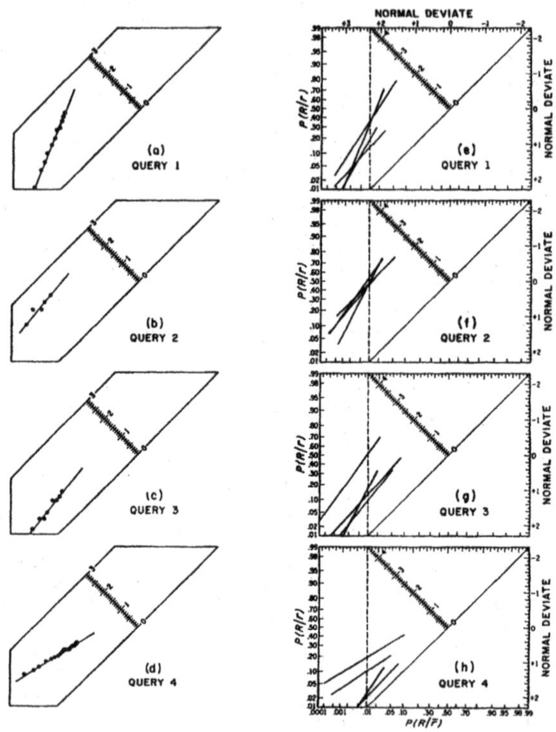


FIG. 18. CBU queries: a fourth method, and summaries of it and the 3 methods of Fig. 17. (a)–(d): Reweighted associative. (e)–(h): results of 4 methods for each query. Number of items, number relevant per query, and criteria as in Fig. 16. Arthur D. Little, Inc.: Giuliano and Jones.

in which the user is given immediate feedback and enabled to progressively refine the search prescription over successive trial searches. It will be informative to apply the decision-theory analysis in experiments on on-line procedures. Will we see values of $E$ in the vicinity of 3.0, or 3.5? Might we even find values of $E$ about 4.0—or will present knowledge of language forms impose a barrier at a lower level of effectiveness?

## References

1. SWETS, J. A., Information Retrieval Systems, *Science*, 141:245–250 (1963).
2. BOURNE, C. P., *Annual Review of Information Science and Technology*, Interscience, New York, 1966, Chapter 7, pp. 176–179.
3. CLEVERDON, C., and M. KEEN, *Factors Determining the Performance of Indexing Systems*, vol. 2, *Test Results*, Association of Special Libraries and Information Bureaux, Cranfield, England, 1966.
4. GREEN, D. M., and J. A. SWETS, *Signal Detection Theory and Psychophysics*, John Wiley, New York, 1966, pp. 45–51.
5. SALTON, G., M. LESK, et al., *Information Storage and Retrieval*, Scientific Report No. ISR-11, Department of Computer Science, Cornell University, 1966.
6. GIULIANO, V. E., and P. E. JONES, *Study and Test of a Methodology for Laboratory Evaluation of Message Retrieval Systems*, Interim Report, Arthur D. Little, Inc., Cambridge, Mass., 1966.
7. LESK, M., and M. KEEN, Personal communications, 1967.
8. SWETS, J. A. (Ed.), *Signal Detection and Recognition by Human Observers*, John Wiley, New York, 1964, pp. 682–683.

# Part V: Tools and Ideas

This is a miscellany which extends and/or explodes basic theory in the field, and the inclusion of these papers is intended to give a broader perspective to information science. There are quite good things which lie nearly beyond the fringe, generally applying a technique to the analysis of a problem in librarianship.

*Reprinted from the Journal of the American Society for Information Science, Vol. 27, No. 5, 1976.* 

# Availability Analysis

**A recently proposed technique for determining the availability of items in a circulating collection is expanded and applied. We present a discussion of the theoretical justification and a careful analysis of the sources of error and the reliability of the results. We report the results of a new longitudinal study using this technique and apply it retrospectively to a number of previous studies to which it is applicable. The resulting data indicate certain striking regularities in the performance of large university libraries, as well as significant differences.**

**The implications of this tool, both for management and for the scientific analysis of various aspects of library performance, are discussed.**

**Paul B. Kantor**
*School of Library Science*
*Case Western Reserve University*
*Cleveland, OH 44106*

## • Introduction

In evaluating the effectiveness of an information service, there are important quantitative and qualitative aspects to the meaning of the phrase "service to the users." The quantitative aspects have been discussed at some length in an earlier paper (*1*) where we have argued that the *Total Contact Time* is probably the best single quantitative measure of service rendered in the specific field of book circulation and in-library use.

The present work is directed to the analysis of the qualitative aspects of service.

There are three important qualitative dimensions to the service rendered: relevance, accessibility and availability. The last of these factors is particularly amenable to mathematical analysis. In particular, the probability of satisfaction (on author-title searches) can be resolved into several conditional probabilities which are separately meaningful and which respond essentially independently to changes in policy.

The outline of this paper is as follows. In Section 1, we review the basic ideas of this type of availability analysis. In Section 2, we present some new data on a "before and after" study conducted at Case Western Reserve University. In Section 3, we essay a retrospective analysis of a number of important frustration studies which have been carried out by other authors prior to the development of this analytical tool. In Section 4, we assemble the various results, comment and look toward the future.

## • Availability Analysis

Let us suppose for the moment, that there is only one reason preventing library users from finding the titles they seek. Specifically, we assume that either the book is circulating or the user will be satisfied. If we denote the number of inquiries by $W$, the number of Dissatisfactions which are caused by Circulation by $DC$ and the number of user Satisfactions by $S$ we have:

$$W = S + DC$$

For example, if $W = 100$ and $DC = 20$, then $S = 80$. We can also say that the probability that a book is not circulating, $p_C$, is 80 percent.

Now let us make a more realistic assumption. Even if the book is not circulating, the user does not necessarily find it. Suppose, to be specific, that 10 of the 80 items not in circulation have been misshelved (Dissatisfaction caused by Library Performance). Thus, the number of satisfactions is reduced to 70. However, performance at the level of circulation remains 80 percent. To describe the additional dissatisfaction we introduce a second performance factor $p_L$, which measures the probability that a book which is *in* is also correctly shelved. Thus $p_L$ = 70/80 = 87.5 percent. Of course, we could also define the fraction of all books sought which are correctly shelved, which is 70 percent. Let us see why that does not make sense.

Suppose for some reason (a change in circulation policy) a new study shows that (on the average) 12 out of 100 books are circulating. Then of each 100 books, there are now 88 which are in the library. Presumably the eight additional books are no easier or harder to shelve than the other 80, and so (on the average) 7/8 X 8 = 7 of them will be in the correct place, while one of them will be out of place. Thus the second performance factor becomes 77/88 = 7/8, which is the same. Of course, if we were comparing the number of satisfactions to the number of inquiries we would now have 77 percent instead of 70 percent.

Obviously the correct way to look at it is that there are two factors $p_C$ and $p_L$, and one of them can remain constant while the other one changes:

Before: 8/10 X 7/8 = 70%

After: 88/100 X 7/8 = 77%.

Finally, there could be a change in the accuracy of reshelving, without a change in circulation. Suppose it rises to 90 percent. Then the overall satisfaction is given approximately by the product

$$8/10 \times 9/10 = 72\%.$$

If we think about it more carefully, we see that a change in the accuracy of the reshelving will produce some change in the probability $p_C$. Roughly, if more books are reshelved correctly all the time, then more of them will have been found by previous borrowers and will be circulating at the time of the study. Detailed analysis shows that this effect is, in general, less than a 1 percent in $p_C$. Thus, for *practical purposes* $p_C$ and $p_L$ are independent.

Now that the principle is clear we can easily see how to deal with the four principal categories of dissatisfaction:

*DA* = dissatisfaction due to the books never having been acquired.

*DC* = dissatisfaction due to the books having been in circulation.

*DL* = dissatisfaction due to the books having been misshelved, lost, etc.

*DU* = dissatisfaction due to the user's error.

An actual frustration study (*1, 2*) results in six numbers, the number of inquiries (*W*); the number of satisfactions (*S*); and *DA, DC, DL, DU.*

The corresponding performance measures are denoted by $p_A$, $p_C$, $p_L$ and $p_U$. They are calculated using the branching diagram shown in Fig. 1:

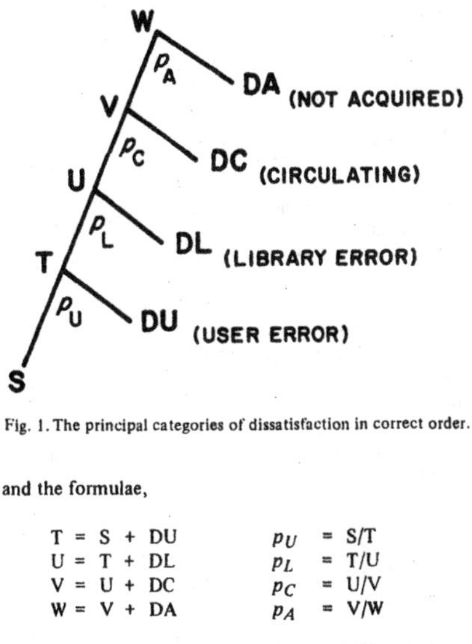


Fig. 1. The principal categories of dissatisfaction in correct order.

and the formulae,

$$\begin{aligned} T &= S + DU \qquad & p_U &= S/T \\ U &= T + DL & p_L &= T/U \\ V &= U + DC & p_C &= U/V \\ W &= V + DA & p_A &= V/W \end{aligned}$$

The performance measures combine multiplicatively to determine the total probability of satisfaction $p_S$:

$$p_S = p_A \, p_C \, p_L \, p_U$$

We have discussed elsewhere (*1*) the relevance of such an analysis for deciding how to improve library procedures. That discussion can be summed up by a rule of thumb: attack the lowest factor first, and improve it until it is no longer the lowest.

## • A Longitudinal Study of Availability

The techniques described here have been applied to a pair of studies at the Freiberger Library of Case Western

Reserve University, a nontechnical library containing about 1,000,000 items. In fact, the analysis technique was developed between the occurrence of the two studies, so that the earlier data represents a retrospective analysis of data collected by students under the guidance of Professor Tefko Saracevic. The later data were collected by students studying the technique of availability analysis.

The study itself uses two instruments. One is a form (Fig. 2) handed to each user as he approaches the author-title catalogue. It is designed to obtain the information which *we* need (author, title, and call number) in a mode which actually facilitates the user's search, by providing him with "scratch paper." It has a column marked "can't find", a column for reporting the "cause code", and some additional columns related to a subproject not reported here.

With the form, the following statement is made to the user: "We are studying how well this library satisfies its users. Would you use this as 'scratch paper' and put a check in this column (point to it) for each book that you can't find? Just drop it off here when you leave. Thank you." (The study was aided by the fact that one person can easily monitor the A–T catalogue and also the exit, to remind participants to drop off the forms when leaving.) The data requested at the bottom of the form can be used for a differential study, but it requires a larger sample.

The second instrument is a check list* to guide the investigators in tracking down the books which the user is unable to find. The major headings are:

C1. Not owned by the library,
C2. Incorrect call number,
C3. Book located in a special area identified on catalog card,
C4. Book properly shelved,
C5. Book misshelved,
C6 Book recently used or in use in library,
C7 Book in preshelving,
C8 Book located in (or listed in) an area not identified on card catalog,
C9 Book circulating,
C10. Other.

The specific subheadings should be drawn up by someone familiar with the specific library being studied. At least two investigators are required since one continues to monitor the catalogue and exit, while the other(s) immediately investigate those books which the user could not find.

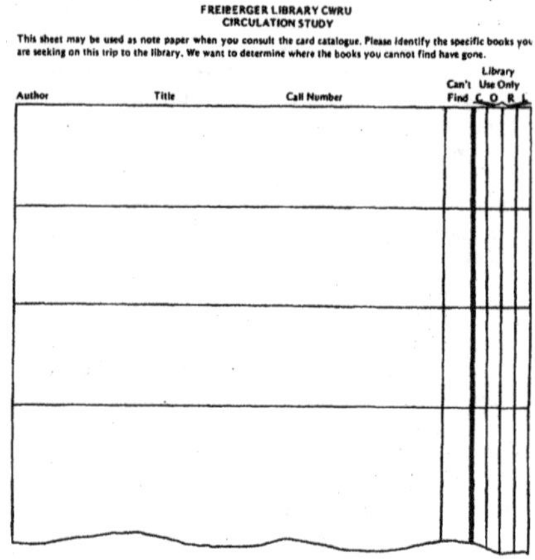
FREIBERGER LIBRARY CWRU
CIRCULATION STUDY

This sheet may be used as note paper when you consult the card catalogue. Please identify the specific books you are seeking on this trip to the library. We want to determine where the books you cannot find have gone.

| Author | Title | Call Number | Can't Find | Library Use Only C | O | R | L |
|---|---|---|---|---|---|---|---|
| | | | | | | | |
| | | | | | | | |
| | | | | | | | |
| | | | | | | | |

Fig. 2. The data collection form handed to patrons.

It took about 12 hours (24 person hours) to collect data on 312 titles during April 1975. The categories C1–C10 were assigned to the four performance categories in the following fashion:

$$DA = C1$$
$$DU = C3 + C4 + C2$$
$$DL = C5 + C7 + C8 + C10$$
$$DC = C9 + C6$$

Multiple copies were treated as follows. If there are two copies, one in each of two different categories, we counted 1/2 a dissatisfaction in each. This results in logically consistent counting in all cases.

The numbers were:

$$S = 203$$

| | | | | |
|---|---|---|---|---|
| C1 - 30 | C2 - 4 | C3 - 0 | C4 - 8 | C5 - 4 |
| C6 - 6 | C7 - 5 | C8 - 7 1/2 | C9 - 18 1/2 | C10- 26 |

Thus:

$DA = 30 \quad DC = 24\ 1/2 \quad DL = 42\ 1/2 \quad DU = 12$

These are summarized by the branching diagram shown in Fig. 3.

When using these performance measures as a guide in policy planning, it is important to be aware of the limits

*We are indebted to Dr. William Shaw for preparing the list.

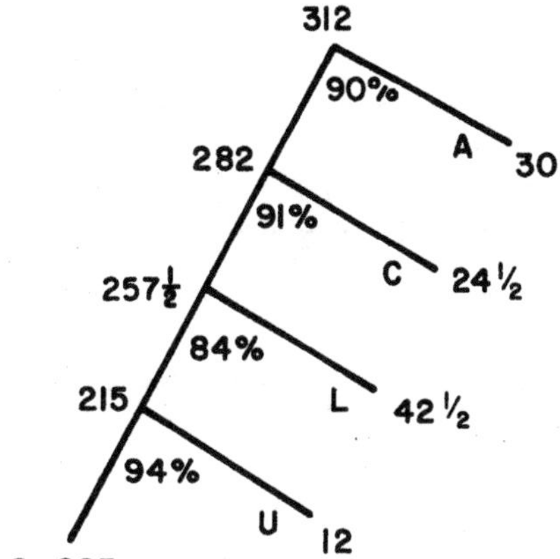


Fig. 3. Results of the April 1975 study at Freiberger Library.

of significance of the figures obtained. Small variations with time, or differences between institutions, are not likely to be significant, while large ones can be very meaningful. To explain what we mean by "small" and "large" we must discuss the sources of error and uncertainty.

There are basically two sources of uncertainty, which we will refer to as statistical error and systematic error.

Statistical error arises because we do not determine the fate of every item search which is made at the library. We use a sample, and there are well understood procedures for determining the probable deviation of the sample value from the true value. We quote the standard error, determined on the assumption that the branches of the diagram are independent and that individual searches are uncorrelated Bernoulli trials. This results in the simple formula

$$\delta p = [p(1-p)/N]^{1/2}$$

$N$ = the number of cases to which $p$ applies.

The systematic error arises from two sources. The first is simply mistakes in counting the number of dissatisfactions. These errors are minimized by being as careful as we can and double checking all cases in which no positive identification could be made. We believe that the remaining errors of this type are negligible.

The second source of systematic error arises from the difficulty of assigning the observed categories C1. . . .C10 to the theoretical categories *DA*. . . .*DU*. In most cases there is no problem, but there are some points which cannot be resolved by theory alone.

One example will serve to illustrate this idea. Reserve books are somewhere in limbo between library error and "not in the collection." However, they cannot be circulating, so they cannot be entered on the branching diagram at an intermediate position. If a great many reserve books are encountered in the study, it is probably best to treat them as a separate collection as we have done below in analyzing the data collected by Meier. Even in that case, however, the library may be frustrating the reader by *concealing* the true location of the book. For this reason, unless the number of such items is very large we simply include them in the category *DL*.

Systematic uncertainties can be of the order of 2 to 3 percent.

Our experience shows that data can be collected at a rate somewhere between 8 and 20 items per person-hour. This depends, of course, on the rate at which requests arrive, the size of the library, its performance factors and so on. However, these represent reasonable limits. The task of checking up on causes cannot be done much faster than about ten items per hour. Remember that more than 50 percent of the items are found and do not require further work. If the rate at which requests arrive is too low, it becomes inefficient to use this study tool at all.

If it is important to know more about the details of the performance picture (for example, in order to make improvements in policy), it becomes necessary at this point to attack the problem from the other direction. For example, suppose it has been determined that library procedures are the limiting performance factor. The next step is not *statistical* analysis of the categories (C) involved, it is *management* analysis of policies, working procedures and perhaps personnel. Usually such analysis will point up inconsistencies or bottlenecks which have grown up in the system, perhaps over the years, that can be eliminated by establishing new procedures or (sometimes) simply by following, rather than ignoring, old ones. The function of availability analysis in this example is to tell us that library procedures (rather than collection size, user skills, or circulation policy) are what need to be studied further. As always, analytical techniques can serve to guide the study of policy, but they cannot replace it.

In our tabulated results only the statistical error is quoted. By the reasoning outlined above we estimate that systematic uncertainty is of the order of 2 to 3 percent. Combining these we conclude that the results of our availability analysis are reliable to within about

4 or 5 percent. Thus, a change or difference of more than 5 percent is to be regarded as significant, while a smaller change in any particular performance measure may simply be due to the effects of systematic and statistical uncertainties.

The statistical formula can be used to estimate the sample size needed. For example, to achieve the value $\delta = 2\%$ for a (typical) value of $p = 85\%$ requires a sample of size

$$N = (85\%) \times (15\%) / (2\%)^2 = 320$$

## • Comparison With Previous Performance

An earlier study done at the same library, in the Spring of 1973 (*3*) can now be analyzed in exactly the same fashion. The principal features of that analysis are shown in Fig. 4:

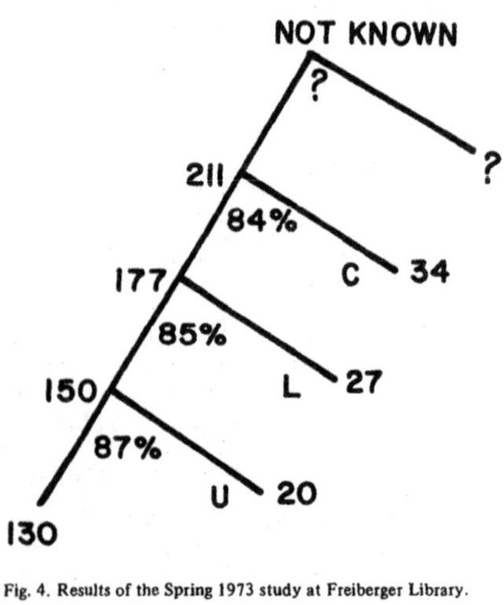


Fig. 4. Results of the Spring 1973 study at Freiberger Library.

The statistical errors can be calculated in the same fashion. The results are summarized in Table 1.

We note that two of the three performance measures, for which a change might be observed, show significant change. The crucial question to ask is: "Can we identify policy changes which would account for this?"

Table 1.

| Category | Performance 1973 | 1975 | |
|---|---|---|---|
| A | not known | 90 ± 1.7% | |
| C | 84% ± 2.5% | 91.3 ± 1.4% | * |
| L | 85 ± 2.7% | 83.5 ± 2.4% | |
| U | 87 ± 2.7% | 94 ± 1.6% | * |

With regard to circulation the answer is definitely yes. Between the two studies the library changed from a semester loan policy to a four week loan policy. This should, of course, decrease the dissatisfactions caused by circulation. In fact, using very reasonable approximations we can account not only for the existence of the change, but also for its magnitude.*

With regard to the *user* performance, $p_U$, we cannot be so certain. There has in fact been an orientation program introduced between the two studies. We do not have a mathematical means of predicting the effect of such a program, nor at the present time do we have any other "before-and-after" studies on such programs. The sign of the change is certainly as we would expect. But, in all honesty, we cannot say whether the observed 7 percent increase can be reasonably attributed to the orientation program.

In summary, the data presented here provides encouraging support for the hypothesis stated in Section 1, that the parameters described will characterize the availability aspect of library performance and will respond independently to changes in policy. This is the second such longitudinal study to be reported. The first was done at the Sears (Technical) Library of Case Western Reserve University by Saracevic, Shaw and the author and has been described in some detail elsewhere (2). The results of that study are also in agree-

*If requests arrive uniformly through the semester at a rate $r$, then the probability that a book is *not* out ($p$) is determined by the average loan period ($t$) (in the one copy approximation) by the formula $p = 1/(1 + rt)$. We do not precisely know $t$, but a good estimate is $t = 50$ days for semester loan and $t = 20$ days for 4 week loan (*1*). For technical reasons discussed elsewhere, (*1*) this $p$ cannot be compared directly with $p_C$, but must be compared with an adjusted figure defined by

$$p = S/(S + C9),$$

whose value is 79% (1973) and 92% (1975).

Assuming that there was no significant change in the average demand, the theoretical result would predict a rise from 79 percent (given) to 90.4 percent (calculated). This is obviously in excellent agreement with the 92 percent actually observed.

ment with the hypothesis of this analysis, and are summarized in the third and fourth columns of Table 2.

## • Retrospective Analyses

A variety of studies have been carried out over the past 20 years, each of which tells something about the availability of library materials. Some are amenable to retrospective analysis using the branching diagram technique. The crucial ingredient is obviously a record of the *number of satisfactions,* as well as an analysis of the number of failures or dissatisfactions attributable to each cause. Those studies which did not record the number of satisfactions cannot be analyzed in our terms. The point is that the apportionment of the dissatisfactions to the various causes is not a set of independent parameters and, if any one of them changes, all the rest will change also. That is why the additional effort required to record the number of satisfactions is a justified expense.

The earliest study we found which is amenable to this type of analysis is one conducted by Meier and reported in 1957 (*4*). He studied the closed stack library of a large university, and thus the category of "user error" does not apply. Since the study began with the receipt of filled out book slips, no items were included unless they were listed in the card catalogue. This means that the category *DA*, and the corresponding measure $p_A$ are not included in this study. An enormous number of requests (4614) were analyzed, of which 58 percent were delivered immediately (*S*). The remaining 42 percent were divided as follows: 12 percent elsewhere (that is, located in other parts of the university library system); 24 percent were in the reserve collection; 32 percent were circulating; and 32 percent were "not found." Finally, of those which were not found, a portion (about 2/3rds) were looked for, and 82 percent of them were located. From this array of data we can conclude the value of $p_C$ without ambiguity. The value of $p_L$ (which in some sense represents all the remaining dissatisfactions) invites further analysis.

The category of items which were "not found" presumably corresponds to two sources of dissatisfaction: (1) books or items which the library has lost track of; or (2) items which were in or near their proper place but were missed by the staff members who looked for them. This human source of error corresponds to the kind of user errors which we have defined, and gives us some idea of how well the users might be expected to perform by comparing them with library staff. We can analyze this possibility by supposing that the 84 percent figure (Fig. 5) represents items which could be located in their proper places. This results in a lower bound on the human performance factor of the library staff. The numerical results are obtained from the diagram shown in Fig. 5.

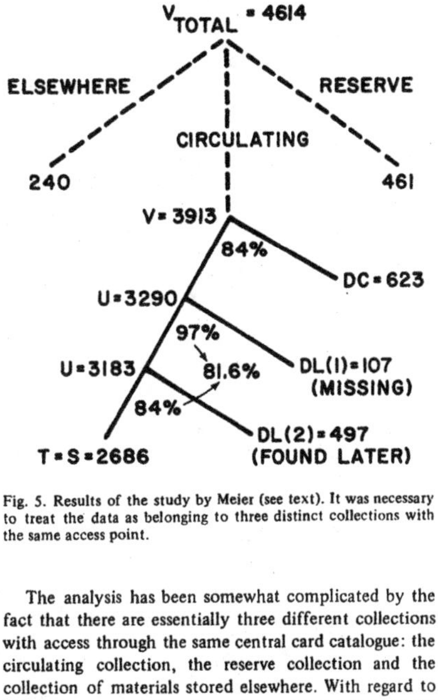


Fig. 5. Results of the study by Meier (see text). It was necessary to treat the data as belonging to three distinct collections with the same access point.

The analysis has been somewhat complicated by the fact that there are essentially three different collections with access through the same central card catalogue: the circulating collection, the reserve collection and the collection of materials stored elsewhere. With regard to the first, we can define the performance measures in the usual fashion. With regard to the other two, we do not have enough additional information to consider them.

In the present retrospective study, we must content ourselves with an analysis of the circulating collection alone. The results are: $p_C = 84$ percent, $p_L = 81.6$ percent and a lower bound on the human error of 84 percent. The "missing books" performance factor is 97 percent, reflecting the enormous advantages, *in this regard,* of a closed stack system.

A second study amenable to the present availability analysis was conducted by Buckland and colleagues at the University of Lancaster Library (*5*). They identified 18 distinct causes of failure. A total of 188 items were obtained, and 132 were identified but not obtained. We have assigned the 18 causes of failure as follows:

*DA* = not owned or on order.
*DA* = on loan, second copy also on loan.

*DL* = missing, missing and on order, binding, awaiting photocopy, awaiting binding, temporarily removed.

*DU* = on shelves, on short loan shelves, in stack, kept at service desk.

The resulting analysis yields the branching diagram of Fig. 6. (In the case of double copies, we count each single item as contributing 1/2 dissatisfaction, etc.) The analysis in this case is complicated slightly by the fact that, with the type of questionnaires which were used, there were 32 cases of dissatisfaction in which they could not identify the item sought. Therefore, only 132 of the 165 dissatisfactions could be analyzed. We dealt with this by assuming that the other 33 were also item searches, and they would have been distributed in the same way as the cases which were analyzed. This means that for each branch of the diagram, the analyzed cases represent only 132/165ths (which equals 4/5ths) of the true number of dissatisfactions. They are corrected by multiplying by 5/4ths, as shown in Fig. 6.

Urquhart and Schofield (*6*) report on a study in which users were asked to place slips on the shelves where the books they were looking for should have been. They did not directly measure the number of satisfactions.

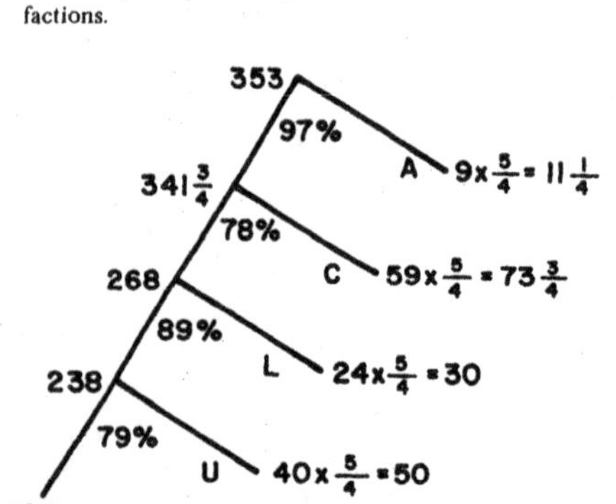


Fig. 6. Results of the study by Buckland (see text). The correction factor 5/4 has been applied because only 4/5ths of the cases in that study were analyzed in detail.

When information about the number of inquiries is not available at any corner of the branching diagram (that is, *W* or *V* or *U* or *T*), it is not possible to calculate any of the performance measures. Thus the data which these authors obtain cannot be used to provide performance measures.

A similar study by Seymour and Schofield (*7*), in which detailed information was reported on the type of user and the source of his information, also could not be analyzed because the number of satisfactions is not reported.

N.K. Kaske (*8*) collected data for the University of Oklahoma Library of a related type under the heading "Collection Status Report." His sample of volumes was drawn in a significantly different fashion. To determine all factors except misshelving he used a random sample drawn from the shelf list. This means there was no user participation (hence no *DU* category) and inactive volumes are included more often then they would be in a study of actual users. Thus the value called $p_C$ in what follows is probably an overestimate of the actual $p_C$ as experienced by users. The number of misshelved volumes was determined directly, that is, the shelves were sampled to determine what fraction of all volumes are shelved out of sequence. The results shown in Fig. 7 are for his first study, December 3, 1972.

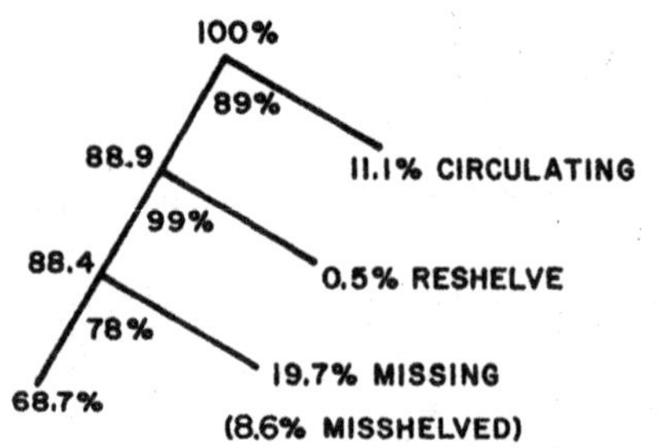


Fig. 7. Results of the study by Kaske (see text) done on December 3, 1972. Books in the reshelving areas were counted separately.

Roughly speaking, the 78 percent is a library performance figure and the 89 percent is an upper bound for the circulation performance. Sample size is about 600 volumes.

The Kaske study was repeated at two later dates, January 14, 1973 and April 15, 1973, with results summarized in Table 2. As Kaske points out, the circulation factor responds to changes in academic activity. The high value (94 percent) was measured during the first week in a term. We are also able to see that the library performance factor remains essentially constant at 79 ± 2%. (The "significant differences" which Kaske noted are due to circulation or to the change in the number of

Table 2. Performance Measures

| | Case Western Reserve University FREIBERGER | | SEARS | | MEIER | BUCKLAND | KASKE | | |
|---|---|---|---|---|---|---|---|---|---|
| | '73 | '75 | '72 | '74 | 1961 | | I | II | III |
| $p_A$ | --- | 90 | 88 | 91 | ---- | 97 | --- | --- | --- |
| $p_C$ | 84 | 91 | 77 | 87 | 84 | 78 | <89 | <94 | <89 |
| $p_L$ | 85 | 84 | 89 | 86 | 81.6 | 89 | 78 | 81 | 79 |
| $p_U$ | 87 | 94 | 80 | 82 | ---- | 79 | ---- | ---- | ---- |
| $p_S$ | ~56* | 64 | 48 | 56 | ---- | 53 | ---- | ---- | ---- |

*assuming $p_A$ = 90%

volumes misshelved. From the *users* point of view there is no significant change in library performance.)

Additional studies, partially amenable to analysis in that they present the product of several performance factors together, have been presented by Tagliocozzo and Kochen (*9*). In connection with a study of catalogue use, they studied the probability that users would find books in the stacks. This corresponds to the product $p_C p_L p_U$ and yielded results of 58 percent at the University of Michigan Medical Library and 69 percent at the Undergraduate Library. If these are combined with a typical figure of 90 percent for the performance of acquisition, we would arrive at satisfaction probabilities of 52 percent and 62 percent respectively.

Their studies of the card catalogue failure rate provide a direct measure of the single parameter $p_A$. This was determined at four libraries: the University of Michigan Undergraduate Library, the General Library, the Medical Library and the Ann Arbor Public Library. The results, together with the approximate size of the collection in each library, are summarized in Table 3.

Table 3. Values of $p_A$ Obtained From Catalog Use Studies

| | Tagliocozzo and Kochen | | | | Lipetz |
|---|---|---|---|---|---|
| | Gen. Lib.* | Undergrad.* | Medical* | Ann Arbor Pub. Lib. | Yale |
| $p_A$ | 93.9% | 72.5% | 89.6% | 65.2% | 90% |
| Size of Lib. | 1.6M | 156K | 175K | 155K | 4M |

*Libraries at the University of Michigan included in the study.

Finally, the large study by Lipetz (*10*) of the Yale Library catalogue yields the value of $p_A$ for that library directly. He found that in 10 percent of all searches "the document definitely or probably exists, but was not in the catalogue at the time of the search". This leads directly to the value $p_A$ = 90 percent recorded here in Table 3.

## • Summary and Conclusions

All of our numerical results are summarized in Tables 2 and 3. In particular, the changes observed in those libraries which were studied twice correlate well with the known changes in policy. This provides important inductive verification for our hypothesis, originally presented on the basis of deductive arguments, that these parameters tend to remain constant unless they are altered by specific changes in policy.

With regard to the Table 2 as a whole, the first observation to make is that the numbers are generally similar to each other (all but one lie in the range of 75 percent to 95 percent). Since the libraries also have many common characteristics—all are large libraries associated with universities in English language nations—we venture the hypothesis that this range of parameter values is indeed typical for such institutions.

Taking 87 percent as a typical value for any entry in the Table 2, we can say that "typically" the probability of satisfaction (that is, the availability of items) is given by

$$p_S = 87\% \times 87\% \times 87\% \times 87\% = 57\%.$$

If, on the other hand, there is no circulation whatever, the availability is given by

$$p_S = 87\% \times 100\% \times 87\% \times 87\% = 66\%.$$

That is to say, even if circulation is completely removed as a source of dissatisfaction, only about two-thirds of the items sought will be promptly found at a "typical" library.

Having noted that there is a general similarity, we then note that there are variations which lie well outside the range of experimental uncertainties. This fact, combined with the two longitudinal studies, suggests that the variations are caused by significant differences in policy.

Thus, three directions for future study are opened.

1. Studies of this kind should be performed at a variety of libraries—such as special and technical libraries, public libraries and reference libraries. These studies will determine what range of values of performance measures is typical of the corresponding class of libraries.

2. The existence of statistically significant differences should be used as the starting point in the search for general relations between policy and effectiveness and, ultimately, guidelines for the selection of cost-effective (optimal) policies.

3. The use of this technique provides a quantitative method for answering a host of troublesome questions, such as "How much does an orientation program really improve user performance?" "Do users have more trouble with the Dewey or Library of Congress classification?" "How much does a change in loan period affect availability?"; etc.

## Acknowledgments

This work grew out of studies done at the Complex Systems Institute of Case Western Reserve University, directed by William Goffman. I am indebted to T. Saracevic for making the results of his earlier study available; to the students in LS 509 (O. Mansur, T. Murthy, T. Kochtanek, M. Kinnucan and A. Quijano) for data collection; and to W. Shaw for numerous discussions and criticisms which have led, among other things, to the discussion of the limits of this technique, given in Section 2. The enlightened cooperation and interest of Ann Drain (Head Librarian at the Freiberger Library) and James Jones (Director of the University Libraries at Case Western Reserve University) were essential to the work described here.

At the suggestion of the editor and referees, this paper was condensed from a more detailed manuscript in which several troublesome points dealing with the logical foundations, the mathematical interrelations and the sources of error in Availability Analysis are examined. The complete paper is available from the author upon request.

## References

1. **Kantor, P.B.** 1976. "The Library as an Information Utility in the University Context: Evolution and Measurement of Service." *Journal of the American Society for Information Science.* 1976; 27:100-112.
2. **Saracevic, T.; Shaw, W.; Kantor, P.B.** "Causes and Dynamics of User Satisfaction in an Academic Library." *College and Research Libraries.* (to be published).
3. **Saracevic, T.** Personal communication.
4. **Meier, R.L.** 1963. "Information Input Overload: Features of Growth in Communications—Oriented Institution." *Libri.* 1963; 13: 1-44.
5. **Buckland, M.K.; Hindle, A.; Mackenzie, A.G.; Woodburn, I.** 1970. *Systems Analysis of a University Library; Final Report on a Research Project.* University of Lancaster Library Occasional Papers, No. 4. 1970.
6. **Urquhart, J.A.; Schofield, J.L.** 1971. "Measuring Readers' Failure at the Shelf." *Journal of Documentation.* 1971 December; 27: 273-286.
7. **Seymour, C.A.; Schofield, J.L.** 1973. "Measuring Reader Failure at the Catalog." *Library Resources and Technical Services.* 1973; 17(1): 6-24.
8. **Kaske, N.K.** 1973. "Effectiveness of Library Operations: A Management Information Systems Approach and Application." Library Science Dissertation. The University of Oklahoma. 1973.
9. **Tagliocozzo, R.; Kochen, M.** 1970. "Information Seeking Behavior of Catalog Users." *Information Storage and Retrieval.* 1970 December; 6(5), 363-381.
10. **Lipetz, B.** 1972. "Catalog Use in a Large Research Library." *Library Quarterly.* 1972 January; 42: (1) 129-139.

*Reprinted from* The American Political Science Review, *Vol. 63, No. 3, September 1969.*

# TOWARD A RATIONAL THEORY OF DECENTRALIZATION: SOME IMPLICATIONS OF A MATHEMATICAL APPROACH

MANFRED KOCHEN
*University of Michigan*

KARL W. DEUTSCH
*Harvard University*

This paper seeks to open for exploration the field of decentralization in politics and organizational design. As a first approach, it examines conditions under which decentralization is preferable from the viewpoint of rationality or cost-effectiveness. Our normative statements as to what would be best, or what should be done, are formulated first from the viewpoint of the subjects or clients, but they are expected to include the interest of the community in ensuring adequate service at low cost, and they also include the interest of the rulers, insofar as their power in the long run depends on their capacity to respond to the demands made upon them quickly enough and adequately enough to retain their political support.

The political theory underlying our study assumes that modern governments retain "their just powers by the consent of the governed," and hence that both their legitimacy and their power will depend at least in significant part on their ability to respond adequately to the popular demands made upon them. We do not deal in this study with other important criteria of preference, such as the psychological value which some of those who take the role of powerholders may put upon centralized control, or the contrary value which some of those who identify with their subjects may put upon power sharing and decentralization. We do hope to suggest, however, which side to the centralization-decentralization controversy is likely to be favored by the pressure of cost-effectiveness considerations, and under what conditions.

At this stage, we also assume ethnic, linguistic, cultural and social uniformity, as the conditions most likely to favor centralization. According to traditional theory, at least, strong centralization under non-uniform conditions usually would be more difficult.

We consider a situation where several identical and equally spaced facilities for decision making, information processing, or other operations perform services in response to requests from sources that are uniformly distributed in time and across varying distances. Such distances could be measured in terms of intervening decision points, switching points, waiting lines, or simple geographic space. As the simplest first approximation, we have analyzed this last type—service through communication and/or transport along a long thin spatial strip.

In the simplest models, the focus is on *costs*: the number of duplicated facilities is determined by setting the marginal increase in fixed costs equal to the marginal decrease in the costs of communication and transportation due to decentralization. In later models, the utility of *time* gained by more rapid service in response to requests is taken into account, and attention is given to the more dependable availability of service that comes with decentralization involving duplication of facilities. Throughout all these models the total *volume* of requests, and its ratio to the speed of communication and transport, turn out to be crucial.

As far as they go, the results of the present analysis suggest that the social, political and economic changes, which influence the rising volume of requests, may outweigh in many cases the effects of the technological changes that have speeded up communication and transport, and that societies which adopt the technological changes are likely to be societies that increase also—or even more—the volume of requests for service or responses. Where these conditions apply, current and future social, political and technical developments may increase, rather than decrease, conditions favoring decentralization.

More extended mathematical derivations and discussions are presented elsewhere.[1]

The present paper is the first of a projected series which is to investigate problems of centralization and decentralization by means of a series of models intended to be increasingly close to the actual variables and problems encountered in the practice of governments and other organizations. Problems of uneven distributions of messages or service requests, in space and time, questions of hierarchies among service or decision centers, and questions of lateral communications or interference among multiple facilities among several centers at the same level, will have to be investigated in such later papers.

[1] M. Kochen and K. W. Deutsch, "A Mathematical Model for a Study of Political Decentralization," submitted to *Operations Research*, September 1968.

## I. DECENTRALIZATION AS A GENERAL PROBLEM

When the director of a research institute in which there are several independent investigators plans to provide computer-based information services, a choice presents itself. Should he provide each independent investigator with his own small computer? Should he install a large computer system everyone must share? Should he provide some mix of these two extremes?

When an architect plans a low-income housing project on a fixed budget, he faces a somewhat analogous choice. Should he provide one bathroom for each family but no swimming pool plus bathhouse for the project (assuming that the budget does not stretch to cover both) or should he provide 50% fewer bathrooms than families, thus making every two families share one, but providing a swimming pool plus bathhouse for use by all as well?

A university library system may comprise over a dozen branches plus departmental and special libraries. In planning the construction of new buildings and ordering library materials, should the university librarian favor the creation of branches and special libraries wherever they are wanted, supplying each with duplicate copies and each with a separate bibliographic control system? Or should he favor the creation of a central custodial unit where responsibility for bibliographic control is concentrated?

A school system may concentrate most of the effective control in the hands of a single board of education for an entire metropolitan area with several million inhabitants, or it may decentralize much or most of this control down to about three dozen neighborhood school boards, each serving a community of between 100,000 and 200,000 people. Apart from group demands and local power contests, which arrangement would be more rational? In what respects and on what grounds?

To what extent should the commander-in-chief delegate various battlefield responsibilities to local commanders and platoon sergeants? What are the consequences of too much or too little autonomy for the junior managers and foremen of a 100,000-employee industrial organization, as distinct from rigid control by a strong chief executive?

Are the customers of an industry better served by a single firm, or a single decision-making unit within a firm, or by several firms or several decision-making units?

Is the population of a territory best served by a single nation-state or government or a single administrative center within a nation, or by several states, governments, or administrative centers?

All these questions have a common core. It is the concept of the "degree of decentralization" of an organization or institution and its relation to the "performance" of the latter. The performance of every human organization includes crucially its *responses* to information received from its environment. Service organization, such as governmental housing or other public or private service agencies, health services, libraries, or computing centers, often appear passive in that they wait for requests from their potential clients or users, to which they then respond. Other public or private agencies appear more active in that they often initiate a sequence or transaction between themselves and some members of the public. Thus tax collection agencies, draft boards, truant officers, public health departments, and private sales organizations often take some initiative in this sense; and some organizations, such as legislatures, general administrative agencies, and police departments play a mixed role, initiating some transactions and also responding to messages from the outside.

Human organizations of all kinds, however, depend critically on the *feedback* of information from their environment in order to discover the results of their actions and to correct their errors.[2] It is in regard to this exchange of information, and often also of things and persons, with their environment, that the performance of more or less centralized or decentralized organizations is to be compared here, in a series of preliminary steps toward a theory of decentralization.

The approach proposed here would go somewhat deeper, therefore, than the familiar view that centralization is a matter of power—that the strong tend to centralize in their own hands as much power as they can, and concede to the weak only as much decentralization as they must. It is quite true that a powerful person, group or office often can concentrate a great many flows of information and of decision making responsibilities in their own hands, but it does not necessarily follow that they will be able to use this information effectively to produce timely and adequate responses.

The relation between power and communi-

[2] On the concept of feedback, see Norbert Wiener, *The Human Use of Human Beings*, (New York: Avon Books, 1967), ch. 1; K. W. Deutsch, *The Nerves of Government*, (2nd ed.; New York: Free Press, 1966), with references; and Robert A. Rosenthal and Robert S. Weiss, "Problems of Organizational Feedback Processes," in *Social Indicators*, Raymond A. Bauer (ed.), (Cambridge: M.I.T. Press, 1966), pp. 302–340.

cation is thus not a one-way process. Power can command communication, but communication and information-processing capacity may increase power or reduce it to the point of paralysis. Where power originally produced centralization, delays or failures in information-processing or responsiveness may then tend to shift both loyalties and power away from the centralized but unresponsive offices or places of command. The operational effectiveness of centralized or decentralized information-processing or decision-making centers, governmental agencies, business organizations and service facilities, is thus in each case a question intellectually distinct from the question of power, and worth considering in its own right.

Much of the well-known political and social theory on centralization and decentralization implies that centralization is preferable on the grounds of efficiency, and that modern technology, with its jet aircraft and electronic communication, has increased the pressures toward centralization.[3] Some theories also assert, however, that decentralization is better suited to protect the values of democracy, liberty, and popular participation in decision-making.[4] Some theorists point our that these different views balance to some extent, and that the optimal point on some more or less continuous centralization-decentralization scale must be discovered in each case; but they give little further indication as to how these discoveries are to be made.

For a start, we shall try to make explicit a few of the basic notions involved, leaving other aspects of the problem for later work. Thus we shall start from the feedbacks and transactions with the outside world, postponing for later analysis elsewhere the internal decision processes of organizations and their possible overloads which play such a large role in much of current organization theory.[5]

We stress in this paper the concern of the person with primary responsibility for the institutional organization rather than the concerns of the members of that organization. Further, we stress what he *should* be concerned with in terms of purposive rationality, rather than what may actually concern him most for personal, psychological, or sociological reasons. By "what he should be concerned with" we mean norms, related to the basic functions and the survival of the institution for which he is responsible; these norms are determined environmentally in terms of feedback processes that are decisive about the survival of the institution. Not that these neglected subjective aspects are unimportant. Far from it. They may well be the salient features of a viable theory of decentralization. So much more reason to treat them thoroughly, but separately, at a later stage.

There is surprisingly little published literature on which to base a formal explication of the decentralization concept.[6] Some of the

[3] See, e.g., Herbert A. Simon, Donald W. Smithburg, and Victor A. Thompson, *Public Administration* (New York: Knopf, 1956), pp. 272–279. For a related argument in international relations, see Albert Wohlstetter, "Illusions of Distance," *Foreign Affairs*, 46 (January 1968), p. 250.

[4] A qualified emphasis on decentralization is found in Joseph A. Litterer, *The Analysis of Organizations* (New York: John Wiley & Sons, 1965), pp. 378–393; and John M. Pfiffner and Frank P. Sherwood, *Administrative Organizations*, (Englewood Cliffs, N.J.: Prentice-Hall, 1960), pp. 440–462.

[5] For some important general approaches, see Herbert Kaufman, "Organization Theory and Political Theory," this REVIEW, 58 (1964), 5–14, esp. 7–8, 13–14; Mason Haire, *Organization Theory in Industrial Practice* (New York: John Wiley & Sons, Inc., 1962), pp. 6–7; Albert H. Rubenstein and Chadwick J. Haberstroh, *Some Theories of Organization* (Homewood, Illinois: Irwin and Dorsey, 1966).

[6] For examples of discussions of the political and social aspects of decentralization and the size of political units or areas, see Bernard H. Baum, *Decentralization in a Democracy*, (Englewood Cliffs, N.J.: Prentice Hall, 1961); Robert A. Dahl, "The City in the Future of Democracy," this REVIEW, 61 (1967), 953–970; James W. Fesler, *Area and Administration* (University, Ala.: University of Alabama Press, 1942); S. W. Hess, *et. al.*, "Non-Partisan Political Redistricting by Computer," *Operations Research*, 13 (1965), 998–1006; Philip Jacob and James V. Toscano (eds.), *The Integration of Political Communities*, (Philadelphia: Lippincott, 1964); Arthur W. Macmahon, *Delegation and Autonomy* (New York: Asia Publications and Taplinger, 1967); E.A.G. Robinson (ed.), *Economic Consequences of the Size of Nations* (New York: St. Martins Press, 1963). General studies of decentralization are relatively rare in political science. *The Cumulative Index to the American Political Science Review* (1906–1963) (ed.), (Evanston, Ill: Northwestern University Press, 1964) lists only one article for the 57 years covered, S. G. Lowrie's "Centralization versus Decentralization (Federalism)", which appeared in the REVIEW in 1922. During the same 57 years, three articles referring to their titles to the delegation of legislative powers appeared in 1908, 1926, and 1947, respectively.

operations research literature dealing with warehouse allocation problems[7] is relevant, as is some of the applied mathematical statistics literature on problems for determining the optimum number of machines or service facilities.[8] Generally, however, customers are assumed to arrive at the service facility, and the time for requests to pass from the customer's site to the facility and for responses to pass back to the customer is not taken into account. The conventional "warehouse-location" problem is to locate a specified number of warehouses and assign customers to each warehouse so that the sum of the squared distances between each customer and the warehouse closest to him is minimized. Actually, distance may not be best represented by its second power;[9] and the present paper will treat the best number of warehouses not as given but as to be computed. It is primarily in the analysis of information systems that such problems are encountered, and relatively little analytical study has been devoted to these.

In this paper we analyze the simplest of these mathematical problems which are, nonetheless, quite generic to a large class of situations in which centralization vs. decentralization is an issue.

## II. MOVING PEOPLE, THINGS AND INFORMATION: THE LOGISTICS OF ORGANIZATION

Decentralization depends in large part on logistics, and all social organizations have problems of logistics. All of them must move messages from one place to another; many of them also must move people, such as field representatives, investigators, fire truck crews, riot squads, case workers or other agents of various kinds; and many must also move material objects, ranging from small samples or mail order items to bulky goods in mass production. Yet some organizations mostly depend in their functioning on the inflow and outflow of messages, as do telephone exchanges, while others depend most critically on the movement of material goods, as do factories. Still other organizations depend primarily on receiving information, such as orders or requests, and on responding to these by moving material objects or people, as do mail order houses and at higher rates of speed also fire departments and ambulance services.

The agencies of government and politics overlap these various types. Public school systems depend upon the movement both of people and of information. The long-run recruitment and maintenance of an army depends upon the movement of persons and supplies, but the short-run intervention of some of its forces may occur in response to an order or message. A law court requires the physical presence of the parties or their representatives, and a prison insists on the physical presence of its inmates. Administrative decisions, on the other hand, often are sent out as control signals or messages in response to information that was received at some earlier stage. Legislation consists from this point of view in a special class of messages issued in response not only to earlier messages but also in response to the physical movement of various spokesmen for interest groups at formal hearings, or more informally of lobbyists, and to the bodily movement of legislators and constituents between their respective constituencies and the capital.

A simple overview of such organizations classified into basic logistic types is shown in Table 1.

[7] See Hess, *et. al.*, *op. cit.*; W. J. Baumol and P. Wolfe, "A Warehouse Location Problem," *Operations Research*, 6 (1958), 252–263; L. Hurwicz, *Decentralized Resource Allocation*, Cowles Commission Discussion Paper No. 2112, 1955; T. C. Koopmans and M. J. Beckmann, "Assignment Problems and the Location of Economic Activities," *Econometrica*, 25 (1957), 53–76; A. A. Kuehn and M. J. Hamburger, "A Heuristic Program for Locating Warehouses," *Management Science*, 9 (1963), 643–666; Alan S. Manne, "Plant Location under Economies-of-Scale—Decentralization and Computation," *Management Science*, 11 (1964), 213–235.

[8] J. P. Anderson, *et. al.*, "D825—A Multiple Computer System for Command and Control," in *AFIPS Conference Proceedings*, Volume 22, (Washington, DC: Spartan Books, 1962), pp. 86–96; K. J. Arrow and L. Hurwicz, "Decentralization and Computation in Resource Allocation," in R. W. Pfouts (ed.), *Essays in Economics and Econometrics* (Chapel Hill: University of North Carolina Press, 1960), pp. 34–104; Information Dynamics Corporation, *A Methodology for the Analysis of Information Systems*, Final Report to the National Science Foundation, NSF-C-370, (1965); J. R. Jackson, "Networks of Waiting Lines," *Management Sciences Research Project Research Report No. 53* (Los Angeles: University of California, mimeographed, 1957); Z. S. Wurtele, "A Criterion for Determining the Number of Identical Machines to be Installed at a Machine Center," *Management Sciences Research Project Discussion Paper No. 78* (Los Angeles: University of California, mimeographed, 1961); Edgar M. Hoover, *The Location of Economic Activity*, (New York: McGraw Hill, 1948).

[9] K. W. Deutsch and W. Isard, "A Note on a Generalized Concept of Distance," *Behavioral Science*, 6 (1961), 308–311.

TABLE 1. SOME EXAMPLES OF LOGISTIC TYPES OF ORGANIZATION

| | | OUTGOING | |
|---|---|---|---|
| | | Matter | Information |
| INCOMING | Matter* | Army<br>Law Court<br>Prison<br>Repair Shop<br>Hospital<br>Medical Examination<br>Factory or Plant<br>Legitimate Theater | Quality Control Stations<br>Analytical Laboratory<br>Movie Studio<br>Live Television<br><br>Museum, Gallery, Archives |
| | Information | Military Task Force<br>Police<br>Fire Department<br>Ambulance<br>Relief Supplies<br>Mail Order House | Decision-making and Control Centers (governmental and private)<br>Telephone Switching Nets<br>Data Centers<br>Reference Services<br>Computer Facilities |

* Material objects and/or human bodies

Each entry in any cell in Table 1 refers to either a task to be performed ("medical examination and treatment") or to an institution which performs some task or tasks (e.g., "army," "hospital"). In some cases, such a task is performed only by relatively large institutions, while other tasks can be decentralized in their performance to the level of individual clients. Government and defense usually are concentrated in such larger institutions, but some physicians still visit patients in their homes. Even governments and armies, however, can decentralize their functions to a greater or lesser degree.

For a functional theory of decentralization, toward which the present paper is directed, the social tasks to be performed are more important than the historical institutions which currently happen to perform them. Though institutions have a great deal of persistence and tend to protect their own survival, they nonetheless do change. Some of these changes tend toward greater or lesser decentralization, and a functional analysis of the level of decentralization most appropriate to their chief task is essential in order to evaluate rationally the actual changes which occur in response to technological or political pressures.

We emphasize the distinction between the movement and storage of persons and materials on the one hand, and the transmission and storage of information on the other hand as most important from the viewpoint of logistics. Messages move more quickly by several orders of magnitude than do persons and materials, and unlike persons and materials they can be duplicated at low cost. All information, of course, depends on some material carrier or marker which bears it, much as a book depends on printer's ink and paper, but the ratio of amount of information to mass of carrier, say in bits per pound per hour, is very high and on a computer display terminal (e.g., teletypewriter or display screen), it is still higher. Our analysis will show that transmission speed is often critical for determining the optimum level of decentralization of a network of facilities and we may expect, therefore, to get different answers for systems depending primarily upon transport as against those depending primarily upon communication.

A simple exercise may illustrate these points. Here we idealize a special but prototypical problem to such an extent that we can analyze it mathematically. Our prototype model will deal with the supply of services from one or several storage facilities. This is not irrelevant. For politics and administration, government, administrative agencies, and law courts all can be thought of as storage places for memories, recorded in their files or carried in the minds of their specialized personnel, and as suppliers of decisions to their clients or constituents. The mathematical analysis of this simplified model may give us insights that a purely verbal analysis does not provide. Building on such a more precise and explicit foundation, we hope then to make some progress toward an edifice of theory that explicates the core problems and proves helpful in explaining the success of various organizations and possibly also in advising decision-makers.

## III. A PROTOTYPE MODEL

Imagine an institution existing to supply objects of value, e.g., books or mail-order items, to customers located in an elongated region from Boston to San Francisco in which the north-south dimension is treated as negligible.

Let $D$ be the east-west distance of this region in miles or in terms of relay stations, traffic intersections, intervening opportunities or other conditions affecting the probability and costs of transmission or transport (Definition 1). Let us make the further assumption that the demand for these valuable objects is spread uniformly over the length of this strip. For example, suppose that ten requests per month originate from each mile along the strip.

Let $L$ denote the total load, in requests per month (Definition 2). The total load, $L$, resulting from this demand requiring service, then would be $L = 10D$ requests per month. Assume that we can control the way the institution is organized, and we wish to explore the consequences of various degrees of decentralization.

By the most centralized organization we mean a single service facility, say a warehouse, which maintains a large enough stock of the valuable objects to clear the demand at all times. (At this first stage of the analysis we assume that the time to forward and process requests is negligible.) It is obvious that the best location for this warehouse is in the middle of our stretched-out region, as shown in Figure 1.

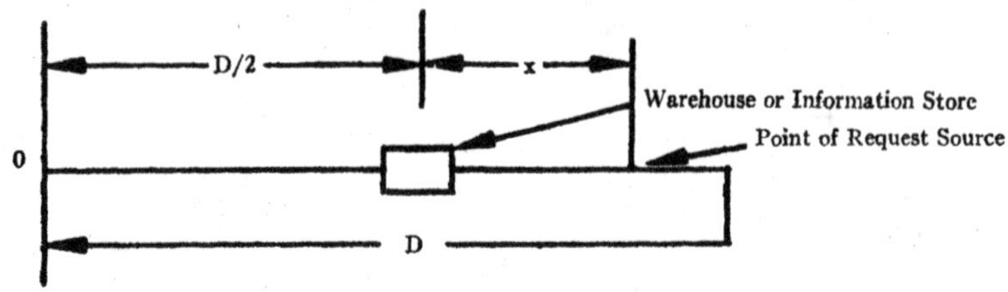


FIG. 1. A Centralized Organization

The manager of the organization is uncertain about the exact distance x between the service facility and the site from which a request (for an object) originates at any moment. When such a request is made, the manager must find the wanted object in the warehouse and transport it to that location.

We assume having a transportation medium which transports at a uniform speed of $v$ miles per hour (Definition 3).

Then the delivery time to a point at a distance of $x$ from the warehouse is $x/v$. Because the sites of requests are assumed to be uniformly distributed over the length D, the average distance between the site of a randomly selected request and the warehouse at the midpoint is D/4. Hence, the average delivery time for a request is D/4v.

By a slightly less centralized organization we mean two warehouses, with identical inventories (each containing a copy of each valuable object), located at the quarter points of our elongated region (see Figure 2).

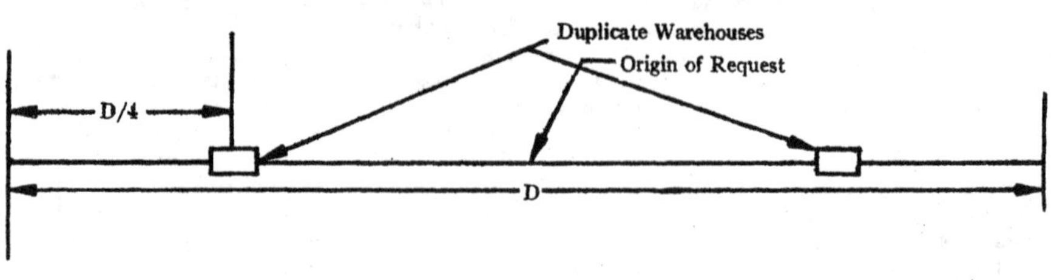


FIG. 2. A Two-Facility Organization

A request originating at any point is serviced by the warehouse nearest to it; requests from points equidistant from two facilities are serviced at random by either.

While for the single facility shown in Figure 1, the delivery time, averaged over many randomly originating requests, was D/4v, it is half of that, or D/8v, for the two facilities shown in Figure 2.

Let the dollar costs of operating a warehouse be $C per month (Definition 4).

Then the fixed cost of operating the single repository organization of Figure 1 is $C$ (including interest and amortization on its cost of installation) while that of the duplicated service in Figure 1 is 2C.

Let the dollar cost of delivering objects be $c$ dollars per hour (Definition 5).

Then the total demand is L requests per month (with L/2 for each of the two warehouses in the organization of Figure 2), and the average delivery cost is cDL/4v dollars per month for Figure 1 and cDL/8v for Figure 2.

If we used three warehouses, we would arrange them as shown in Figure 3.

quests per unit of time, has no effect on the transmission speed $v$, and that it has no effect on the throughput rate of the system.

The maximum throughput rate of the system is defined as its capacity, called here $M$ for objects and $B$ for information, respectively (Definition 7).

If the system were partially obstructed, the speed $v$ of transport or transmission would decline with rising input loads; if the system were *overloaded*, its throughput rate would decline with increasing inputs, and it would fall increasingly below the system's capacities $M$ or $B$. In reality, there often is an extended range of traffic loads L over which the speed $v$ remains substantially unchanged. In the present prototype example, however, we are assuming that this range extends all the way to the maximum capacity point and beyond it, so that $v$ is treated as independent from $L$ at all times. More realistic congestion effects and other complicating possibilities must be left for later treatment.

Suppose time were of no value to users, and only costs mattered to them. Then it would

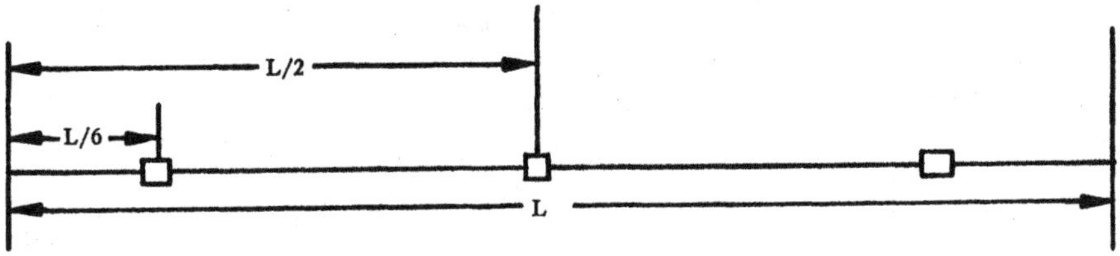


FIG. 3

The most primitive index of decentralization is $n$, the number of duplicate warehouses (Definition 6).

We would, in the general case, place the left-most warehouse at distance $D/2n$ miles from the left, and space $n-1$ warehouses $D/n$ miles apart, the right-most warehouse being $D/2n$ miles from the right end. Each warehouse meets requests issuing from a distance of $D/n$ or fewer miles to its right or left. Since a request, on the average, should originate $\frac{1}{2}$ $(D/2n)$ miles to the right or left of the warehouse, the average transport distance is $D/4n$. The average delivery time (in hours) is the average distance divided by transport speed (miles per hour) or $D/4vn$.

This first approximation neglects the internal cost of processing and servicing each request within each facility. It also neglects congestion effects and instead assumes *unobstructed* channels of transport and communication. That is, it assumes that the input load $L$, in re-

pay to increase the number, $n$, of facilities until the marginal increase in fixed costs is equal to the marginal decrease in delivery costs.

Let $C_n$ be the cost of operating an organization with $n$ warehouses. Let us assume that $C_n = nC$, namely that it costs simply $n$ times as much to operate an $n$-warehouse organization as it does to operate a single repository. That is, the marginal increase in fixed costs is $C_n + 1 - C_n$ or just $(n+1-n).C$; that is, it is simply equal to $C$ and remains therefore constant.

We have shown earlier that the average delivery cost per month for a system of n facilities is $cDL/4vn$. An increase by 1 in the number of facilities reduces this cost to $cDL/4v(n+1)$, by a difference of

$$\frac{cDL}{4v}\left(\frac{1}{n} - \frac{1}{n+1}\right)$$

which is

$$\frac{cDL}{4v} \frac{1}{n(+1)}.$$

There is a point, therefore, where the savings from lower delivery costs will be just equal to or less than $C$, the increase in capital costs, and where it will no longer pay to increase n, the number of facilities, any further. We set $C$ equal to

$$\frac{cDL}{4v}\,\frac{1}{n(n+1)}$$

and solve for $n$. The best number $n$ of decentralized facilities thus would be the integer just larger than:

$$1/2\left(\sqrt{1+\frac{cDL}{Cv}}-1\right) \qquad (1)$$

The average service cost per request, $S$, of this optimal service is given by:

$$s = \frac{nC}{L} + \frac{cD}{4nv} \qquad (2)$$

Even these simple formulas have some interesting implications. Let us suppose the following possibilities, as in Table 2:

TABLE 2. SOME EXAMPLES OF OPTIMAL DECENTRALIZATION LEVELS

| | Low Load, Low Delivery Cost | | High Load, High Delivery Cost | |
|---|---|---|---|---|
| | low capital cost, low speed | high capital cost, medium speed | high capital cost, high speed | very high capital cost, very high speed |
| | A | B | C | D |
| 1. Distance D (miles) | 3,000 | 3,000 | $3\times10^3$ | $3\times10^3$ |
| 2. Load (requests per month) L | $3\times10^4$ | $3\times10^4$ | $3\times10^6$ | $3\times10^6$ |
| 3. Costs of delivery c ($ per hour) | 0.10 | 0.10 | 10.– | 10.– |
| 4. Capital cost C ($ per month) | $10^2$ | $10^4$ | $10^4$ | $10^5$ |
| 5. Velocity of transport v (miles per hour) | 10 | $10^2$ | $10^3$ | $10^4$ |
| cDL | $9\times10^6$ | $9\times10^6$ | $9\times10^{10}$ | $9\times10^{10}$ |
| Hence Cv | $10^3$ | $10^6$ | $10^7$ | $10^9$ |
| Then optimum number of facilities N | 47 | 1 | 47 | 5 |
| Distance among facilities | 64 | — | 64 | 600 |
| Cost of service, S, in dollars per request | .32 | 1.08 | .32 | .32 |

This simple exercise demonstrates—as does, of course, the formula

$$\frac{1}{2}\left(\sqrt{1+\frac{cDL}{Cv}}-1\right)$$

given earlier—that this simple model is equally sensitive over a wide range to proportionate changes in $c$, $D$, $L$, $C$ and $v$, but is more sensitive to changes in $C$ and $v$ where these values are very small. The table also shows that decentralization may decline as capital costs and/or delivery speeds increase, but that it may increase again at high levels of capital cost and delivery speeds, if the load of service requests and the costs of delivery have risen faster.

This result tends to modify the suggestion of Herbert Simon and his associates, that the introduction of long-distance or intercontinental telephones makes it "unnecessary" for governments "to allow (their) representatives much discretion in the choice of decisional premises." Generally, they stress that "improved methods of communication have made a much greater degree of centralization possible."[10] If we are to judge what is probable or rational, in addition to what is merely possible, we now may consider that a society which produces telephones also produces higher request rates, service demands, and decision loads for public and pri-

[10] Simon, Smithburg, & Thompson, *op. cit.*, pp. 275, 279. Simon's thoughtful comments on the various tendencies making for actual, rather than merely possible, centralization are wholly compatible with our analysis. The latter merely adds some emphasis on several no less real tendencies which may work in the opposite direction.

vate agencies, and that they may become more affluent in regard to capital costs, so that the optimum degree of decentralized facilities may increase.

The optimum level of decentralization emerges as a systems property in response to changes, not in one parameter, but in the configuration of several critical parameters. Such a configuration may favor the excellent telephone service and considerable political decentralization of present-day Switzerland rather than the slow messenger service and the much greater political centralization of ancient Egypt or Tokugawa Japan.[11] Even under the simplified assumptions of our prototype model, growth of the capitalization and performance of service organizations of all kinds, including governments, may rationally lead to decentralization or to centralization, depending on which of the relevant parameters grow at a greater rate.

### IV. TRANSPORTATION VS. TRANSMISSION: THE BULK OF OBJECTS AND THE LENGTH OF MESSAGES

Whether or not to service requests with a centralized or decentralized deployment of facilities depends to some extent on what is being requested: materials or information. Both are transmitted through channels in which they would move at characteristic primary speeds if the channels were unobstructed. In each case, however, these channels have limited capacities. They can, and usually do, become overloaded and obstructed with a resulting decline in the effective rate of flow. Thus, congested roads may cut the effective speed of traffic flow from 60 to 15 miles per hour; congested airports may cut the effective speed of downtown-to-downtown jet air travel from 600 miles per hour to 300 miles per hour for airport-to-airport speed and 100 m.p.h. for downtown-to-downtown speeds. Similarly, overloaded switchboards and relays reduce the effective speed of electronic transmission from the theoretical limit of the speed of light (186,000 miles per second, or over .67 billion miles per hour, making light from the sun take about nine minutes to reach the earth) to an average effective speed varying from 1,000 to 10,000 miles per hour. Even when delayed in this manner, however, electronically-optically transmitted information will tend to move on the average about 100 times as fast as would bulky material objects. Communication thus differs from transport by several orders of magnitude in regard to the degree of centralization or decentralization which it makes relatively optimal.

At this point it becomes desirable to consider the bulk or weight of objects, measured in pounds or tons, and the length of messages, measured in bits of information. (Actually, we shall be more concerned here with orders of magnitude than with precise measurements.) The cost variable previously introduced measured the cost of "delivering an object" in response to a request, in dollars per hour. But $c$ depends not only on the speed but on the nature of the object as well. It costs more to deliver a massive object than a light one. It costs more to deliver a voluminous message that requires wider and costlier communication channels than to deliver a brief message.

As to the average volume of transmission per request, we shall call it $m$ for material objects and measure it in pounds or tons; and we shall call it $b$ when referring to the transmission of information, which is measured conventionally in "bits." (A bit is a single yes-or-no decision, such as the on-or-off position of a switch, or a dot or dash in the Morse code, or a black or white point on a television screen. A single digit number corresponds to about four bits, a teletype letter six bits, an average English word about thirty bits, a printed page in a book about 10,000 bits, a 300-page book three megabits, i.e., three million bits, and over twenty megabits for one second's picture on a normal television screen.) The capacity of a transportation channel then is the amount of mass $M$ it can move times the velocity $v$ (i.e., distance/time) at which it can do so under the best traffic conditions. The formula for this is $Mv$ for the overall capacity of the channel and $mv$ for its effective capacity in regard to the size and speed of transmitting and/or servicing the average request. Both $Mv$ and $mv$ are formally analogous to the concept of momentum in mechanics. As it takes force to change momentum in mechanics, so it takes innovation—in the form of visible investment in capital equipment and/or invisible investment in new technology—to change capacity in a

[11] On centralization and communication at earlier levels of technology, Lewis Mumford comments: "Action at a distance, through scribes and swift messengers, was one of the identifying marks of the new megamachine (the centralized state) . . . 'The scribe, he directeth every work that is in this land,' an Egyptian New Kingdom composition tells us . . . They made possible the constant 'report to political headquarters' essential for a centralized organization": *The Myth of the Machine* (New York: Harcourt Brace, 1967), p. 192. Cf. also Harold A. Innis, *Empire and Communication*, (Oxford: Oxford University Press, 1950).

transport channel (e.g., to a supersonic transport aircraft). The change in capacity $Mv$ is then a possible measure of the effect (or "force") of innovation in respect to the overall capacity of a channel, and the change in $mv$ similarly would measure its effect in regard to the servicing of average sized requests.

Decentralization often depends critically on the effective service capacities of the available transport and communication channels, and changes in the optimum level of decentralization for a given organization, government or service.

The following table may clarify some of the relations between capacities, rates and the different conditions examined so far.

munication, though, of course, the cost differs. These channels differ mainly in their capacity, in how many bits, or $bv$, similar to $v$ per second of information, $mv$ for materials. In the communication processes, therefore, the number of duplicated facilities does not depend very much on geography with respect to saving message delivery time. The distribution of overall channel capacities, $B$ (bits per second), and data transmission rates $B'$, in place of $bv$ (i.e., message speed times message length), plays a much more central role in this regard. A low value of $B$ is about 2,000 bits per second for voice-grade telephone lines, and a high value about 200,000 bits per second for wireless transmission, such as radio telephony or tele-

TABLE 3. SUMMARY OF KEY VARIABLES

*3a. Basic Variables*

- $D$ = length of strip, in miles, typically 3,000 for a big country, 300 for little one
- $L$ = total load, in requests per month, about 30,000 for heavy demand, 3,000 for low demand
- $C$ = fixed cost for one facility, in dollars per month, about 10,000 for an expensive facility and 100 for a cheap one
- $v$ = average transport speed under actual traffic conditions, in miles per hour, about 1,000 for jet speeds and 10 to 100 for ground passenger speeds
- $m$ = mass or bulk of items to be transported in response to requests, in pounds, about 100 for massive objects to 1 for light ones
- $b$ = amount of information in an average message delivered in response to a request, in bits, from 10 megabits for a second's worth of TV to 10,000 for a printed page's worth
- $B'$ = rates of information transmission under channel conditions, in bits/second, from $10^7$ for video to 2,000 for digital telephone

| *3b. Parameters* | *Unit Transport Cost* | *Average Cost To Service Request* | *Assumption* |
|---|---|---|---|
| Simplest Model ($m=0$) | $c_v$, dollars per hour, for transport at a speed-capacity of $v$ miles per hour | $c_v \cdot \frac{D}{4nv}$ | $v = V$ |
| Bulk Taken Into Account | $c_{MV}'$, dollars per pound per hour, for transport characterized by speed-bulk capacity of $MV$ pound-miles per hour | $c_{MV}' \cdot m \frac{D}{4nv}$ | $mv = MV$ |
| Digital | $c_B''$, dollars per mile per hour, for communication characterized by a capacity of $B$ bits per second | $c_B'' \frac{D}{4n} \frac{1}{3600} \cdot \frac{b}{B'}$ | $B' = B$ |

Actual rather than maximum transmission speeds, however, are very nearly the same for a person-to-person call over a distance of thirty miles than over a distance of 3,000 miles and what really counts is not the velocity in miles per hour but the capacity in bits per second. The value of $v$ for telephone, telegraph, wireless via radio or television, etc., is substantially the same for local as for long-distance communication graphy, and at least one hundred times this amount for television.

These considerations permit us to make our notion of current transport costs somewhat more realistic. Let us begin with the case of bulk movements, such as mail, freight, or personnel. We have previously considered $c$, or more precisely, $c_V$, as the transport cost in dollars per hour depending only on speed capacity, but regardless of the bulk to be moved. Now let us consider, instead, $c'MV$ as the transport cost in dollars per pound transported per hour for a carrier with capacity $MV$. Here it costs more to move the same bulk of freight more quickly, as airmail and airfreight cost more than do slower services, but it also still costs more to move a larger number of pounds at unchanged speeds. The average transport cost per request is simply $c'MV$ times m times $D/v$. The optimal number of facilities can therefore be calculated with these refined assumptions by the formula:

$$\frac{1}{2}\left(\sqrt{1+\frac{c'_{MV}DLm}{Cv}}-1\right) \qquad (3)$$

The average cost of service $S'$ per request of average shipment weight $m$ then becomes:

$$S' = \frac{nC}{L} + \frac{c'Dm}{4nv} \qquad (4)$$

and the total cost of service $S'' = S'L$ (Formula 4a).

In order to take into account in these formulas the weight of the average shipment, we had to replace $c/C$ by $c'/C$ and $D/v$ by $mD/v$, while the total load of requests, $L$, has remained unchanged. If $c'_{MV} = m$, the cost of transporting the shipments of average weight m, equals $c_V$, the average transport cost of filling a request, then the weight of the average shipment would make no difference for the optimum level of decentralization, and the results of Table 2 would remain unchanged. If, however, an increase in the average weight of shipment would bring about an increase in the transport cost, then the optimum number of facilities would increase, in proportion to the square root of the change: a 100-fold increase in average shipment weight (and cost) would then require approximately a 10-fold increase in the most efficient number of facilities.

Let us assume that an administrative agency has to consult a file on each case on which it has to make a decision. Servicing a case would then require either transporting, on the average, one pound of documents from the repository to the site of the request, or else transmitting the information in those documents over a long distance computer channel. The file to be transmitted is assumed to contain the equivalent of a 200-page book, that is, about 4 million bits, or 4 megabits.[12] According to formula (3), the optimal number of facilities for electronic transmission under the above assumptions is now sixteen. This is more than three times as many as in the earlier case presented in column D of Table 2, where the transmission costs depended only on speeds and not on the amount of information being transmitted to service the average request.

Had we sent our four megabits by express messenger service at the rate of $c' = \$.04$ per pound-hour, then the optimal number of facilities, according to formula (2), would be three. In other words, *under the assumptions of our example, a slower service based on messengers or mail delivery could be much more highly centralized than a fast service based on a computer-based or satellite-based communication net.*

It might be interesting to compare the total costs for these two kinds of service. Let us recall that each of them would have to cope with 3 million requests per month, each request requiring transmission of four megabits. The cost of servicing requests by digital telephone—called "dataphone"—transmission would be \$1.05 per request, compared with \$.20 per request for service by mail or express messenger. *The five-fold increase in cost*, however, *here would buy a sixty-fold increase in speed.* The dataphone replies would be available within little more than half an hour, in contrast to the thirty hours response time required for the more highly centralized service based on messengers or mail.

The situation is similar in some respects to the transmission of messages through communication channels. Here $c_B''$ is the cost of transmission for a channel with a capacity (maximum rate) of B bits per second, in dollars per hour per mile. The average cost of servicing a request would then be $c_B''/3600 \cdot b/B \cdot D/4n$, because $D/4n$ is the average distance from a request to its nearest service facility when there are n such facilities. The actual cost of telephone transmission does not increase in *direct* proportion to distance; it increases by less for large distances than it does for small distances, but this will be neglected for the purpose of this paper. The cost $c_B''$ for long distance telephone is about \$.02 per mile per hour for ordinary long-distance transmission. (This would amount to \$3.00 for a three-minute business-hour call from Boston to San Francisco and \$1.00 for a similar Boston-

[12] This calculation assumes roughly the usual average of 6 bits per character, 80 characters per line, and 42 lines per page. For further discussion, see Manfred Kochen (ed.), *The Growth of Knowledge* (New York: John Wiley & Sons, Inc., 1967); also Manfred Kochen, "Newer Techniques for Processing Bibliographic Information," in F. Kilgour (ed.), *Proceedings of the Symposium on Data Processing in University Libraries* (Philadelphia: Drexel Institute of Technology, 1968).

Chicago call.) Such a channel is characterized by a capacity of $B=2000$ bits per second.

The formula for computing the optimal number of facilities in this case is therefore

$$\frac{1}{2}\left(\sqrt{1+\frac{c_B''}{C}\cdot\frac{1}{3600}\cdot\frac{b}{B}\cdot D\cdot L}-1\right). \qquad (5)$$

Note that we have replaced $c/C$ and $D/v$ in formula (1), or $c'/C$ and $Dm/v$ in formula (2) by $c_B''/C$ and $1/3600\cdot b/B$ respectively.

### V. THE VALUE OF TIME: A FIRST APPROACH THROUGH OPTIMIZATION

In the primitive model treated so far, no value was assigned to time. Users were assumed not to care how long they had to wait for service. In fact, however, users find service with smaller delivery time more valuable than service with high delivery time. Similarly, clients or constituents of a governmental agency often request decisions which are to be acceptable to them in substance but which are valued more highly if they are prompt in time. In some other studies, the probability that a government, or a governmental agency, will produce within an acceptable time an acceptable response to the average demand upon it has been called the *responsiveness* of that agency.[13] Responsiveness and mean response time thus may be included among the highly relevant performance indicators of governments and their agencies. This section of our inquiry will attempt to make explicit some possible relationships between response time, the utility of time to the average user, and the degree of decentralization.

As a first step, let us assume a single "representative user" with the properties of both the average and the median users of the service, who are assumed to be identical. (We assume at this point uniform distribution of locations and utilities for all users.)

The net worth, $W$, of the institution is its utility to the user minus the cost to operate it. Figure 4 shows a possible relation between utility and communication speed, compared with approximate current rates for sending a brief message across 1000 miles in the United States.

It is difficult to infer even very roughly the shape of the demand curve of the American people for speed of transmission of their messages. It is illuminating, however, to plot the rates for the transmission of messages by telephone, telegraph, and mail (air and regular). All these rates have been set by complex processes. These are at least partially responsive to the political demand generated by the population in their roles as interest groups and citizens. Since these rates have remained relatively stable and have not aroused intense opposition, they can serve as indicators of acceptability. Fitting a curve to these data suggests a monotonically decreasing function of rate versus delivery time such as shown in this figure.

Let us first consider the case of a society which can afford to back up its utilities completely with actual purchasing power representing all the required resources. Such a society might then consider increasing the number of decentralized facilities $n$ so long as this increases the net worth to the society. It would stop increasing only when the marginal increase in net worth with n duplicated centers is zero. This enables us to derive a formula for n, which depends on the utility of time. The higher the utility of time, the more we shall be willing to pay for higher speeds of response or of service.

The utility of time will be large in a society that has urgent needs to save time or that puts great cultural value on speed (which some critics of contemporary Western culture might call impatience), or whose members have many attractive alternative opportunities for occupying, so that the opportunity cost of time to them is raised sometimes to an oppressive degree.[14] Our $R$ may reflect a combination of all these pressures. The same cultural factors of urgency and impatience would be reflected to an even greater extent in the shape of a curve describing the variation of utility with response time. The greater the society's concern with speed, the steeper the curve will be.

In the case just presented, the optimal degree of decentralization would be to make n as large as possible if the value of time is larger than the increase in total cost. If the opposite condition

[13] On the concept of responsiveness, see K. W. Deutsch, S. A. Burrell, *et. al.*, *Political Community and the North Atlantic Area*, (Princeton: Princeton University Press, 1957, 1968), pp. 40–41, 199–200; Bruce M. Russett, *Community and Contention: Britain and America in the Twentieth Century*, (Cambridge: M.I.T. Press, 1963), pp. 29–30; Dean Y. Pruitt, "Definition of the Situation as a Determinant of International Action," in Herbert C. Kelman (ed.), *International Behavior: A Social-Psychological Analysis* (New York: Holt, Rinehart and Winston, 1965), pp. 397–399.

[14] On the general problem of the "quality of life," which is connected with our growing lack of and need for time, compare John Kenneth Galbraith, *The Affluent Society* (New York: Houghton-Mifflin, 1958) and *The New Industrial State* (New York: Houghton-Mifflin, 1967).

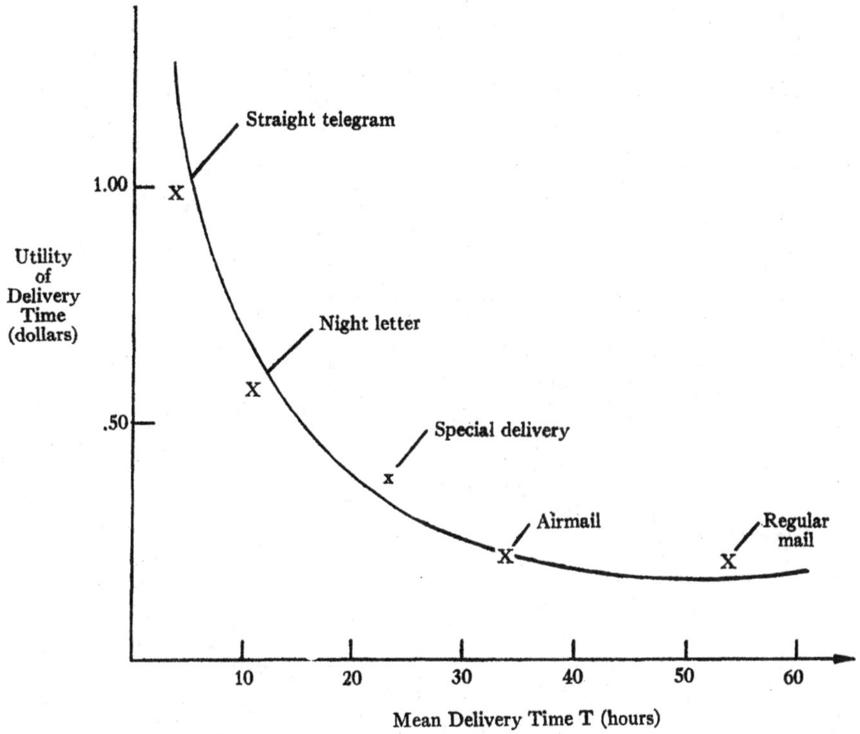


FIGURE 4

holds and increases in the speed of response on service are valued less highly than the increases in cost resulting from increases in decentralization, then the optimum number for n is 1; that is, complete centralization. A society as rich and as pressed for time, therefore, as we assumed it to be in this example would tend to go to one extreme or the other: complete centralization or decentralization. The tendencies toward substituting in many parts of the United States individual transportation by personal automobile instead of public transportation may resemble in some ways the second of these trends—up to the point, at least, where mutual interference among automobiles on congested streets and highways becomes critical.

#### MORE REFINED MODELS: REDUNDANCY AND FLUCTUATIONS IN DEMAND

*Using multiple facilities for more dependable service.* In the models analyzed so far, we assumed that if there are n duplicated facilities any one of which could have serviced all the $L$ requests per month, then each facility is used only $1/n$th of the time. Each is to some degree redundant, therefore, for each now services only $L/n$ requests per month. For a decentralized organization, with large n, the utilization percentage is quite low and redundancy is high. If low response time has very high utility —i.e., the value of $R$ is high—and transmission costs are high but fixed costs are not too high, then such low utilization is tolerable. The unused portion of the time, however, has considerable potential value in:

(a) insurance against the effects of breakdown;
(b) smoothing losses due to fluctuating demands and busy local facilities;
(c) control of errors.

Clearly this average delivery time increases with the probability of breakdown in one particular facility, but in proportion to $n$. As we decentralize, we gain more side benefits in reduced mean time loss due to failure. The greater the transmission speed $v$, the greater the effect of this time saving. Technical progress may confront designers with a choice between increasing the speed or the reliability of their equipment. Decentralization and redundancy, at higher cost but at the same level of technology, may permit them to have both.

*Total response time and fluctuations in demand.* Instead of mean delivery time $\bar{T}_n$, it would be more realistic to consider the total response time $Q_n$. This is the total time lapse between the epoch the request originates and the epoch the information or item requested is received by the requestor at the site where it originated. It is this turn-around time which matters to the originator of a request. This is the sum of three terms:

$$Q_n = F_n + S_n + T_n \qquad (6)$$

Here $F_n$ is the time to transmit and forward the request from its source to the nearest station able to service it.

It is the run-around time, which the customer does not notice, apart from the turn-around time.

Next, we let $Sn$ be the time it takes to service the request at that station, including the time at the other stations which had to decide whether to pass it on and to do so.

Finally, $T_n$ is the time to transmit or transport the results back to the source, as defined before.

Since we can calculate $\bar{T}_n$, we can do likewise for $\bar{F}_n$ and $\bar{S}_n$. The latter term, the internal service time $S_n$, includes the time needed for decision-making and the possible delays resulting from the overloading of the decision-making and the possible delays resulting from the overloading of the decision-making capabilities of the service organization or bureaucratic agency. This aspect of the problem has received a good deal of attention in the literature of organization theory and management science.[15]

If the total demand is $L'$ requests per hour, then each of n stations has to service $L'/n$ requests per hour under the assumption of uniformity over length D of the strip. If we assume $10\times30$ or 300 hours per month, then $L = 300\ L'$ where $L$ is the load in requests per month, as previously defined. If one service could handle the total demand, its service time must be $S=1/L'$ hours per request. Thus n replicated facilities offering this service could handle n times this total demand or each be utilized only a fraction $1/n$ of the time. On the other hand, slower services, with service time $S_n=n/L'$, could be used to handle the same demand, and these would be utilized one-hundred-per-cent.

Of course, the cost of such a slower service with service time $n/L'$ hours per request should not be $C$, the cost of a service with $S=1/L'$ hours per request; it should be lower. Since many identical such services are required, their fixed cost $C_n$ might be lowered still further, at least in regard to those components that could be produced in quantity.

If the demand is not constant in time, but fluctuates randomly, and if the capacity of each facility is only equal to the average demand, then there will be times when a request cannot be serviced by the nearest server because it is busy. In that event, the request is forwarded according to the same pattern used for routing when the nearest server was down. If the request has to be rerouted several times, $\bar{F}_n$ becomes a "run-around time," comparable to the possibly longer or shorter waiting time in a queue or single centralized facility. In either case, the effective waiting time may exceed the waiting capacity or tolerance of the client, as in the case of emergency patients for hospitals, or of emergency responses in military or police systems, or in urgent local or national political decisions.

The formulas and calculations involved even in this simplified model would permit us to derive conditions on $R$ and optimal $n$ in many additional pages of more complex mathematics. For this reason, as well as for reason of the greater flexibility in modeling more realistic systems, it seems desirable for future work to obtain these quantities by computer, either by evaluating complex formulas or by Monte-Carlo simulation.

In this more realistic and complex analysis, we suppose that the service time, $s$, per server varies with the percentage $u$ "he" is utilized. That is, $u$ is the percentage of time a facility is utilized.

If $u$ is small, $s(u)$ is high. He is slow because he is out of practice, because start-up time causes delays, etc. If $u$ is close to 100%, $s(u)$ is also high. He is slow again, this time because he is overloaded. Some services don't get done at all if the server is too overloaded, and this may be far more costly than under-utilizing him; this is especially true when the value of the service is high, as in cases where the server is a highly paid executive. For intermediate values of $u$, $s(u)$ is moderate. A curve like $s(u)=s_0$

[15] See references in notes 2–6, above.

$(u-u_0)^2+s_{00}$ might represent the general shape of the curve.

### VII. SOME IMPLICATIONS FOR ORGANIZATION THEORY AND POLITICS: SOME SECULAR CHANGES IN KEY VARIABLES

Our crude models suggested that a greater number of multiple service facilities, $n$, and hence a higher degree of decentralization, becomes rational with an increase in the load or volume of services demanded. Also, a higher degree of decentralization becomes desirable with an increase in the value of time, and in those portions of service costs which are related to time and/or distance.

Our models further suggested that this optimal degree of decentralization increases with a decrease in the proportion of the fixed capital costs of the service among its total costs; and they suggest that the optimum degree of decentralization also increases with any decrease in the margins of error and of breakdown that are considered acceptable in the performance of the service.

All these decentralization-promoting conditions will tend to increase with economic growth and technological development. Let us first consider changes in direct costs. If other things remain equal, then the optimal number of decentralized facilities for a service increases in proportion to the square root of the ratio of its time-distance costs $c$ to its capital costs $C$. Secular trends toward highly advanced levels of economic and technological development make human labor more expensive, and they make capital goods relatively cheaper. Thus they may tend to increase this ratio, and hence the desirable degree of decentralization. Some economic data suggest that this may have happened, both in Communist and non-Communist countries. An increase in real wages normally represents an increase in the price of labor relative to the price of goods, including capital goods, and hence also an increase in the $c/C$ ratio. In many advanced countries of the world during recent decades, real wages have tended to grow on the average at about three per cent per year, thus doubling every twenty-three years. If real wages should grow fourfold in the course of a half-century, while capital costs would not, then at the end of such a period the optimal number of decentralized facilities for a wide variety of services may well have as much as doubled during the same time. If capital costs should grow somewhat but less than real wages, there would still be a net tendency toward some decentralization, albeit to a lesser extent.

Demographic, economic and technological growth in many countries in recent decades, very roughly speaking, has proceeded at annual rates of about 2 per cent and 3 per cent, respectively, adding up to about annual 5 per cent increase in the demands for many services, and doubling about every 14 years the load upon many of the public or private centers that have to supply them. Such increases in loads include the volume of demands for many political, administrative, judicial and quasi-judicial decisions and responses, as well as for many services and for the communication and transportation they imply.[16] Moreover, as

[16] In the 1950s, the average rate of per capita income growth in 68 countries, comprising 86 per cent of the world's population, was about 3 per cent, while the average rate of population growth in 111 countries, with 97 per cent of mankind was 2.3 per cent. (B. M. Russett, *et. al.*, *World Handbook of Political and Social Indicators*, New Haven: Yale University Press, 1964, pp. 46–48, 160–161.) More recently, in 1960–66, world population increased at an annual rate of 1.9 per cent. During the last two decades, total GNP in many countries may have been rising, therefore, at about 5 per cent per year, and thus doubling every 14 years. Request loads and service loads in many fields, including governments may have grown at about the same rate as GNP. *United Nations Demographic Yearbook*, 1966 (New York: 1967), p. 95. During the same years, 1960–66, the population of the United States increased at the rate of 1.4 per cent, while its gross national product in constant 1958 prices grew at 4.8 per cent. Murders and non-negligent homicides grew at 2.3 per cent, all accidents at 2.8 per cent, domestic mail at 3.5 per cent, and daily telephone conversations at 5.0 per cent, and automobile thefts at about 7 per cent. In contrast to this, the average speed of motor vehicles increased only at 1.4 per cent a year, and about the same low rate held for the 1945–66 period. The average speed of aircraft on scheduled domestic air carrier routes increased at about 3.5 per cent for 1950–67 period, but rose more quickly, at 5.0 per cent, during the years 1960–67, and the speed of aircraft on international flights in 1960–67 increased at about 7 per cent per year. (Approximate rates, computed from data in the *Statistical Abstract of the United States 1967*, pp. 58, 86, 505, 508–509, 561 and 586; and *ibid.*, 1968, pp. 6, 550 and 573; and *Uniform Crime Reports for the United States*, 1960, p. 2, and *ibid.*, 1965, p. 3.) These figures exclude, however, the delays caused by getting to and from the airports, and the delays by traffic congestion on the ground, and in the air above many airports. If these delays are taken into account, it seems plausible that many activities,

technological progress speeds up transport and communication, it increases the opportunity cost of time, since more things now could be done or experienced in each unit of time than had been the case earlier. Finally, highly modernized and automated technologies may require higher levels of accuracy and reliability of service. Thus they may need more redundancy of facilities as an insurance against error and breakdown.

Perhaps most importantly, the growing need for greater precision and adaptability of responses to the increasingly complex, diverse and changing needs of people will require in many cases more frequent dialogs and feedback cycles of back-and-forth communication between service centers and customers, agencies and clients, administrators and constituents, the rulers and the ruled. This will multiply the effective distance $D$ (regardless of whether it is measured in rules, switching points, or intervening obstacles or opportunities); it will multiply it by the average number of feedback cycles of communication, travel or transport required to ensure an acceptable fit between each specific demand and the particular response to it. The current demands for more popular participation, initiative and communication "from below," if heeded, would have similar effects: it would increase the average number of feedback cycles needed, and hence often the importance of distance and proximity. Each of these changes makes for an increase in the degree of desirable decentralization.

Under the assumptions of our models it seems quite possible, therefore, that many of the highly modernized and automated societies and nations which we may find by the end of this century will by then require a much greater degree of decentralization in public and private services than the one to which we are accustomed now. Doubtless some of these assumptions will have to be replaced by more realistic ones. In particular, refining our simple concept of decentralization, introducing the notion of hierarchies of facilities, and revising the assumption of uniform distribution of demand in space and time, all may well modify some of our findings. The present paper already may suggest, however, that the naive images of a future of ever increasing centralization in business organizations, public services, national governments, and the international political systems may have to be revised.

---

calling for public service, now may be growing faster than does our effective speed in moving persons and goods in daily practice. Something similar may apply to telephone communications: a telephone call from Washington to San Francisco during business hours does not get through much more quickly to the individual we want to reach in a busy office than it did in 1945.

# CATALOG USE IN A LARGE RESEARCH LIBRARY

BEN-AMI LIPETZ

ABSTRACT

Concern with the questions of when and how best to computerize the catalog of a large research library, and how to improve an existing conventional catalog, motivated a study of the utilization of the main catalog of the Yale University Library. The study was carefully designed to provide a representative sample of catalog use. Traffic through the catalog area was observed over a period of more than a year. A schedule of interviews with catalog users was based on observed traffic volume by hour of day, day of week, and time of year. More than 2,000 interviews were completed, using nonleading interviewing technique. Information was derived on the catalog user's objective, starting clues, and university affiliation. Search success was determined. Follow-up studies were performed on the catalog cards and the actual books identified in successful searches. Reasons for search failure were determined for known-item searches. Availability and accuracy of different categories of search clues were ascertained. Published algorithms for searching computerized bibliographic files were evaluated. Attention was given to the feasibility of automatic construction of computerized catalogs. Some of the available results are presented and discussed.

## INTRODUCTION: GENERAL OBJECTIVES

This paper summarizes a study of catalog use that was carried out at the main library of Yale University. The study was carefully designed to produce valid information on a variety of topics related to catalog use, including volume of catalog use, nature of the user population, types of catalog searches attempted, responsiveness of the catalog, and potential responsiveness of the catalog.

The primary motivation for this study was a twofold conviction: First, that computerization of the catalogs of all or most large libraries is inevitable sooner or later. Second, that knowledge to guide library managers in determining when the time for conversion has arrived and how it should properly be accomplished is lacking. A secondary motivation, of course, was interest in the immediate possibility of improving the conventional card catalog while it remains in use.

The foregoing statements about computerization of catalogs should not be construed as indicating that library catalogs have never been computerized. Indeed, some have—but not the catalogs of the very large research libraries that we are concerned with here. To the multimillion-book library, the automation projects that have been carried out on the catalogs of smallish collections are only interesting and suggestive experiments, not mandates to emulate.

On the other side of the issue, there are some obvious and powerful arguments to keep the large libraries from plunging into catalog computerization right away. One is the high cost of equipment—the gigantic fast computer memory required for storage of the text already in the large card catalogs has barely been developed yet and would be prohibitively expensive for libraries. Then, too, there is the huge cost of retrospective conversion of existing catalogs to machine-readable form. Optimistically, these two problems will be resolved: the first by technological advances that will lower the cost of computers and related equipment; the second through sharing of data conversion efforts by means of standardization and distribution projects such as MARC.

But even when computerization of the large library catalog becomes technically and economically possible, there will still be the valid problem of determining how to design the computerized catalog to do its job most efficiently. Merely trying to put into a computer all of the features of a conventional card catalog would tend to preserve any drawbacks that are inherent in the physical nature of conventional catalogs and would tend to overlook possible improvements.

To solve this design problem rationally, one must know what library users really want from catalogs. But available knowledge on this matter of catalog use is woefully inadequate. The study reported here was undertaken to help fill the void.

Catalog-use studies are not a novelty. Quite a large number (mostly projects for masters' degrees) have been reported in the literature. But all of the older studies seemed to have flaws in their design which made their reported results suspect or unusable. Very commonly they were based on exceedingly small samples of catalog users, casting grave suspicion on any findings. Often they were based on highly incomplete returns of questionnaires, raising the question of whether nonrespondents constituted a set of users systematically ignored by the findings. In many studies, use of questionnaires distributed to catalog users some time after a catalog search raises doubts regarding the reliability of human recall of the details of their search activity. And in studies using questionnaires or interviews there was frequently evidence or the strong possibility of questions being asked in such a way as to bias the results. The present study was designed to avoid all of these methodological weaknesses.

The study was conducted over a three-year period ending in late 1970. It was supported by a grant from the U.S. Office of Education. An extensive report on the work has been published [1], and the results reported here are largely a selection from that report. Credit is due to Frederick G. Kilgour for the original suggestion of the need for a research study of this kind and to Peter Stangl, who was primarily responsible for the implementation of the research design and the preliminary reduction of data.

## SPECIFIC OBJECTIVES: DESIGN OF THE STUDY

The study was concerned specifically with utilization of the public card catalog of the Yale University Library. This catalog is located in the main hall of the Sterling Memorial Library building. It is a single-alphabet catalog, containing some 7 million cards in some 7,000 drawers. It contains full sets of catalog cards for the more than 3 million volumes housed in Sterling Memorial Library, and at least main-entry cards for the more than 2 million volumes housed in the other sixty or so libraries of Yale University. (Catalogs in the branch libraries contain full sets of cards for their respective holdings.) The main catalog is open to the public. The stacks of Sterling Memorial Library are open to Yale students and faculty and to many authorized outside users. The catalog area is a scene of constant activity, with people entering to make searches of various kinds and durations, then leaving with different degrees of satisfaction and edification.

Basically, every catalog search is a word-matching exercise in which the user attempts to match some known clue (for example, a name, or a title, or a subject term) against the filing terms in the catalog—in the hope of finding some useful associated information on the catalog card, such as a call number or a complete bibliographic description of a work. The success or failure of a catalog search depends on several factors: whether or not the desired material is in the library to start with; the clues which the catalog user brings to a search; how he applies them; and the file terms and associated data provided in the catalog. The study was designed to cast light on all of these factors.

A crucial consideration was the establishment of a clearly representative sample of catalog searches to study. There are several hundred thousand searches made every year, roughly 1,000 each day. Sampling was essential in order to hold study costs and annoyance of catalog users to reasonable levels. The desired representative sample was obtained by making very careful observations of traffic in the catalog area, then purely on the basis of observed traffic selecting a sample of specific searches to study. The observation of traffic consisted of counting the number of people entering the catalog area (through several entries) during various hours of the day, portions of the hour, and days of the week, for more than a year. (Actually, several other kinds of traffic statistics were obtained at the same time; all of these traffic measurements contribute to understanding of demand patterns for catalog facilities.) After the first ten weeks of observation, a profile of catalog-use rates was constructed; using this, an interview schedule was constructed that would yield approximately a 1 percent sample of catalog searches, completely representative of the observed traffic profile. Interviews with catalog users were carried out for a full year using this schedule. Throughout this period, observations of catalog traffic were continued in order to check on the consistency of the original observations and to provide a basis for appropriate weighting of interview results for periods in which any significant change in traffic pattern was observed.

Interviews were conducted by several staff members, each with a rigid, predetermined schedule to follow. The interviewer was required to be at a particular entrance to the catalog area at a specified time and on a specified day, and was to interview the first person to enter and begin to use the catalog within a specified number of minutes. The purpose of the interview was to learn as much as possible about the objective of the search about to be performed and the clues available to the catalog user. Interviewers were carefully trained to avoid leading questions; they used a standard set of questions which started off deliberately vague ("What were you about to do here at the catalog when I interrupted you?") and became more specific only if full details were not elicited with the vague questions. Information was sought on the type of search to be performed, on the motivation for the search, on the clues which the catalog user had in his mind (spellings were requested of author names and uncommon terms), on the clues which the catalog user had available in written notes or printed matter (these were photocopied), on his intended search approach, on the nature and length of his association with Yale University, and on the frequency of his use of the library system. The refusal rate among catalog users who were approached for interviews was less than 1 percent; most interviewees were delighted to be asked about their searches. The average interview took only a few minutes to complete. In all, more than 2,100 interviews were completed during the study year.

After an interview, the user was permitted to complete the catalog search but was kept in view from a distance until leaving the catalog area. He was then approached a second time and asked whether his search had been successful, what call numbers he had identified to satisfy his requirement, and how many terms he had looked up during his search. If he was uncertain about the success of the search but was going elsewhere in the library to continue it (for example, to the stacks to look over some possibly useful books), he was given a simple follow-up form on which to report results afterward.

A third type of data gathered in this study (in addition to catalog traffic observations and interviews with catalog users) was on matching and potential matching of users' search clues to catalog filing terms. In the case of successful searches, call numbers of desired books were obtained from the catalog users. With these numbers it was possible later to obtain photocopies of the corresponding catalog cards from the shelf-list file. It was also possible to borrow the actual books at a later date and to photocopy those portions of the front matter and back matter which could potentially be used for creating catalog-file terms under a highly formalized, possibly automated, cataloging procedure; candidate portions of the book included title pages, contents, preface, and indexes. These photocopied cards and book pages were appended to the respective interview records for purposes of comparison.

Partial analysis of the data amassed in this study was accomplished through the use of computers and statistical techniques. The traffic observations were easily transcribed on punched cards for machine analysis. Interview and follow-up data were more difficult to transcribe; too much detail was available about users and catalog cards and books. However, by inventing abbreviated codes and formats, it was possible to record on punched cards whether or not a given category of data was available from an interview and, if so, the range of values or alternatives in which it fell. It should be understood that the selection of categories of data to record in this manner is largely subjective; there is ample possibility for further analysis of the collected data. In this study, about forty variables were identified.

By computer, the co-occurrence of each variable with each other variable was calculated. From the results, it was possible to identify pairs of variables that are linked to each other in some way that is probably no coincidence. For these pairs of variables, detailed matrixes were printed out for more careful scrutiny. These matrixes included tables of actual data values, row percentages, and column percentages.

For some of the questions investigated in this study, purely manual data analysis methods were used.

RESULTS

Traffic observations permitted the plotting of a number of graphs showing the pattern of demand on catalog facilities. For example, figure 1 shows how catalog use varies from hour to hour during the day (in half-hour intervals); it can be used in assigning librarians to the catalog area to provide a consistent level of reference service throughout the day.

Variations in catalog use from week to week throughout the year are plotted in figure 2 in terms of both users per week and users per hour of library open time. (Open hours are usually reduced during recess periods and holidays.) The graphs clearly indicate the difference in activity level between the academic year and the summer vacation period. Also indicated is the tendency for catalog use to drop below normal at the beginning of a holiday or recess and then rise above normal at the end of that interval.

Superimposed on the graph of catalog users per week in figure 2 is the plot of books per week circulated from Sterling Memorial Library over the same period of time. The two curves match almost perfectly, indicating that a measurement of the profile of either parameter can be used by librarians for predicting the other parameter. It is not suggested that every use of the catalog results in the borrowing of exactly one book; that degree of match

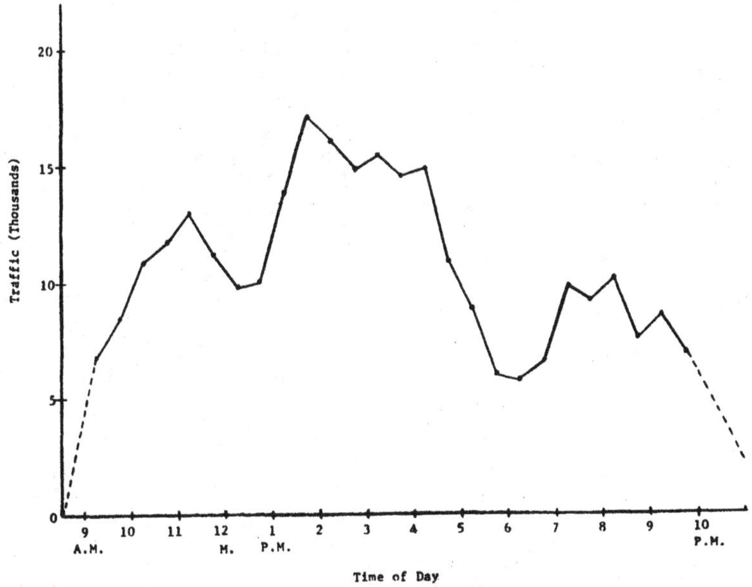


FIG. 1.—Yearly weekday catalog traffic by half-hour of the day

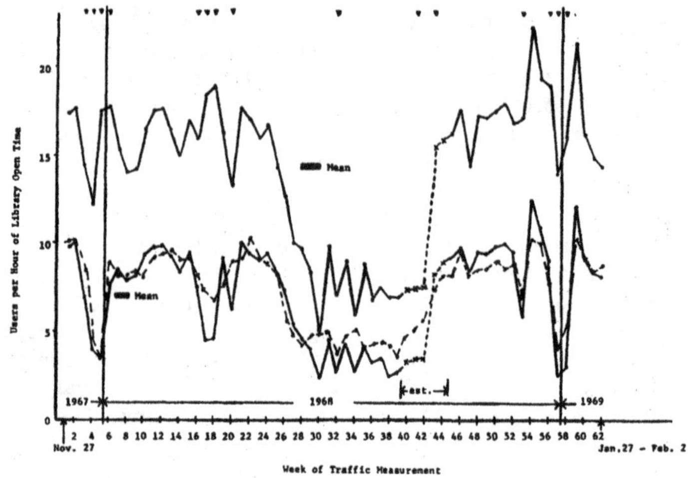


FIG. 2.—Weekly catalog traffic and weekly book circulation. ▼ = weeks with shortened library hours; - - - = users in week in thousands; —— = circulation per week in thousands.

in figure 2 is probably coincidental. Many books are selected for borrowing by shelf browsing without using the catalog. Many catalog searches result in failure, or in the selection of more than one book. Still, in aggregate, all of these possibilities tend to add up throughout the entire year to a consistent pattern in which catalog use and book borrowing are always in the same proportion.

Throughout the week, there is variation in catalog use from day to day (table 1). Monday, Tuesday, and

TABLE 1

VARIATION IN CATALOG ATTENDANCE BY DAY OF WEEK

| Day | Entrants per Hour | Percent of Yearly Average |
|---|---|---|
| Monday | 100.4 | 104.7 |
| Tuesday | 106.5 | 111.1 |
| Wednesday | 102.0 | 106.4 |
| Thursday | 95.0 | 99.1 |
| Friday | 92.6 | 96.6 |
| Saturday | 81.7 | 85.2 |
| Sunday | 82.5 | 86.0 |
| Yearly average | 95.9 | 100.0 |

Wednesday traffic is above average; the other days, below. There is a steady decline in traffic after the peak on Tuesday.

Interview data yielded valuable information on the nature of the catalog-user population and on the relative activity of different user groups throughout the year (table 2). Graduate students are the heaviest users. Their relative use of the catalog remains constant through the year (although absolute use of the catalog drops to half in the summer period). Undergraduates are the next heaviest users; their use is concentrated in the academic year and is lower for freshmen than for other undergraduates in terms of the number of potential users. Faculty and staff show up as comparatively light users of the catalog (but this does not necessarily indicate their comparative level of use of books in the library). About one-fifth of catalog use throughout the year is by persons not actively affiliated with the

TABLE 2

ACADEMIC STATUS OF CATALOG USERS BY SEASON

| Status | Approximate Eligible Population | Catalog Use (%) | | |
|---|---|---|---|---|
| | | Full Year | Academic Year | Summer |
| Yale freshmen | 1,600 | 7.0 | 8.3 | 12.3 (freshmen and other undergraduates combined) |
| Other Yale undergraduates | 2,900 | 24.9 | 27.7 | |
| Graduate, postgraduate students | 4,700 | 35.5 | 35.6 | 34.9 |
| Yale faculty | 5,000 (faculty and staff combined) | 8.8 | 7.3 | 16.0 |
| Yale staff | | 3.3 | 2.9 | 5.0 |
| Non-Yale students | ? | 9.5 | 9.9 | 7.6 |
| Non-Yale faculty | ? | 3.2 | 2.8 | 5.3 |
| Yale faculty family | 5,000 | 1.5 | 1.1 | 3.3 |
| Visitors, retirees, others | ? | 6.3 | 4.3 | 15.7 |
| Total | ... | 100.0 | 99.9 | 100.1 |

university; this use is relatively much greater during the summer period.

Determination of the distribution of catalog-search objectives was among the most interesting results of the study (table 3). Four general search objectives were identified. The objective of a "document search" is to determine whether and where the library holds a work that the user already knows to exist. This is the most prevalent type of search. A "subject search" is for pertinent works on a known topic. An "author search" is to determine what works if any are available from some known author or publishing body; selection of specific works may or may not follow from this determination. A "bibliographic search," like a document search, is for a known work, but the objective is to make use of data from the catalog card and not to locate or borrow the book.

TABLE 3

DISTRIBUTION OF SEARCH OBJECTIVES

| Search Type | Immediate | Underlying (%) |
|---|---|---|
| Document | 73 | 56 |
| Subject | 16 | 33 |
| Author | 6 | 6 |
| Bibliographic | 5 | 5 |
| Total | 100 | 100 |

In terms of immediate intent at the time of interview, almost three-fourths of the catalog users are interested in document searches. However, when these users were asked at the end of their interviews about what they would do in the case of an unsuccessful search, a very substantial number stated that there were other ways to get the needed information. This indicated clearly that the underlying objective was to find information on a particular topic (that is, to perform a subject search), and that looking up a known book on the subject was only an expedient approach. In terms of underlying motivation, about one-third of catalog searches are subject searches, but half of these are sublimated to document searches in using the existing library catalog.

The rate of success in document searches was 84 percent (table 4), and about the same in other types of searches. Success rates did not vary much among different groups of users. Evidence of a library frustration factor among newcomers to Yale (which would be indicated by decreasing use of the catalog throughout the year

TABLE 4

SUCCESS AND FAILURE OF ATTEMPTED DOCUMENT SEARCHES

| Result of Search | % |
|---|---|
| Document in catalog, located by user ..... | 84 |
| Document in catalog, not located by user but found by research staff through user's starting clues .................. | 5 |
| Document definitely or probably exists but was not in catalog at time of user's search ............................ | 10* |
| Document possibly in catalog, user's clues inadequate or grossly inaccurate ....... | 1 |
| Total .............................. | 100 |

* One-fifth of this group of documents were added to the catalog from one to twelve months after the user's unsuccessful search.

studied) could not be found. There was evidence that undergraduates occasionally try to use search clues that are not necessarily filed in the catalog (for example, title of an analytic, name of a translator, title of a publisher's series) but tend to abandon them after a year or two.

The reasons for failure of document searches were determined by having the project staff repeat the searches at a later time, using the clues available at the time of the original search. Also, standard bibliographic tools were employed to help verify the existence of the desired works. Of the sixteen (of 100) searches that ended in failure, ten failed because the desired books were not in the collection at the time of the search (but two were added soon afterward). Another five searches should not have failed; the user did not use all of the clues available to him or did not use them correctly. In one search out of 100 it was impossible to determine whether the failure was user fault, catalog deficiency, or absence of the desired work. There is apparently far more to be gained from increasing collection size and improving catalog users' orientation than there is from attempting to increase the complexity of the existing catalog. Indeed, it is conceivable that reinvesting the savings from somewhat reduced cataloging effort could actually increase search success rates. However, this conclusion could be negated if evidence is adduced to suggest that increased complexity would attract many new users or uses.

In a document search, the intended approach (table 5) is usually through

TABLE 5

INTENDED APPROACH TO DOCUMENT SEARCHES

| Approach | % |
|---|---|
| Author name (personal or corporate) .... | 62.0 |
| Title of monograph or periodical ........ | 28.5 |
| Subject term .......................... | 4.5 |
| Editor name .......................... | 4.0 |
| Author or title of portion of work (analytic) .......................... | 0.5 |
| Series title .......................... | 0.2 |
| Other (publisher, translator, geographic location, etc.) ....................... | 0.3 |
| Total .............................. | 100.0 |

the author of the desired work. (This makes particularly good sense in the catalog studied, since the author approach is the only one provided for many of the works represented in the catalog.) A sampling of the records of actual successful searches (table 6) shows that two or more look-ups are required in about 15 percent of the searches because of errors in either clues or approaches. The availability and accuracy of author clues and title clues are compared in table 7; there is very little basis for favoring one approach over the other when both are available. The availability and accuracy of catalog users' knowledge of publishing date are shown in table 8;

TABLE 6

INTENDED AND ACTUAL APPROACHES FOR 126 SUCCESSFUL KNOWN-ITEM SEARCHES

| Approach Intended | Item Found Under | Number of Look-Ups Required 1 | 2 | 3 | 4 | 5 |
|---|---|---|---|---|---|---|
| Author | Author | 73 | 5 | ... | ... | 1 |
| Author | Title | ... | 1 | ... | ... | ... |
| Author | Added title | ... | 1 | ... | ... | ... |
| Title | Title | 23 | 3 | 2 | 1 | ... |
| Title | Author | ... | ... | 1 | ... | ... |
| Title | Added author | ... | 1 | ... | ... | ... |
| Added author | Added author | 4 | 1 | ... | ... | ... |
| Added title | Added title | 2 | ... | ... | ... | ... |
| Subject | Subject | 5 | 1 | 1 | ... | ... |
| Total | ... | 107 | 13 | 4 | 1 | 1 |

TABLE 7

AUTHOR AND TITLE DATA IN DOCUMENT SEARCHES
(%)

| Result of Search | Author Data | Title Data | Title Data × 82% |
|---|---|---|---|
| 1. Applicability to desired documents | 82 | 100 | 82 |
| 2. Availability in search clues (right or wrong). Sum of 3–7 | 77 | 97 | 79.5 |
| 3. Available, complete, and accurate in search clues | 42.3 | 61.5 | 50.4 |
| 4. Available in search clues, but only partially complete and accurate (last name, first corporate level, or first title word correct and in place) | 23.2 | 15.0 | 12.3 |
| 5. Available in search clues, inaccurate | 10.5 | 15.5 | 12.7 |
| 6. Available and accurate in search clues, appears in catalog card but not designated as a file entry | 0.7 | 1.6 | 1.3 |
| 7. Available in search clues but not on catalog card, accuracy not determined | 0.3 | 3.4 | 2.8 |

NOTE.—Third column percentages normalized to facilitate comparison of title data with author data since the latter apply to only 82% of document searches.

date of publication would clearly not be a productive primary approach of the catalog.

The availability of both users' author and title clues and the correct bibliographic data (from the actual books or their catalog cards) made it possible to evaluate, by manual simulation, two published algorithms [2, 3, pp. 133–36] for effecting computer retrieval from author-title files despite inaccurate clues. One algorithm uses word compression before matching; the other uses word truncation before matching. Results of these evaluations were published previously [4, 5, pp. 125–27]. Both algorithms yielded 70 percent computer retrieval in a test group of 126 searches which had been 100 percent successful by the manual approach.

TABLE 8

AVAILABILITY AND ACCURACY OF PUBLICATION DATE INFORMATION IN DOCUMENT SEARCHES

| Result of Search | % |
|---|---|
| "No information" on date | 41 |
| Information more than five years wrong | 12 |
| Information two to five years wrong | 18 |
| Information one year wrong | 10 |
| Correct year | 19 |

It is unlikely that any single computer algorithm will match human performance in manual-file searches. However, it does seem likely that using a combination of algorithms could give much better retrieval than a single algorithm. Combining the two algorithms that were tested, for example, would raise the success rate to about 75 percent. However, each algorithm retrieves false drops along with valid references, and the number of false retrievals increases with file size and with the number of algorithms employed. The key to effective suppression of false retrievals is in the use of exclusion criteria along with selection criteria (for example, "published after 1945 and before 1960," or "must deal with biology"). Although the temptation is strong to strip computerized bibliographic files down to the categories of author, title, and call number in the interest of economy, there is good reason to believe that a file so stripped cannot possibly give adequate retrieval performance.

The possibility of automatic construction of adequate computerized catalogs was considered through examination of front and back matter in retrieved works and comparison of this material with user clues. The examination hypothesized use of a machine that would transcribe specified portions of a book into machine-readable form followed by identification and alphabetization of nontrivial terms. It seems possible that a catalog adequate for document searches could be constructed by this method, even if little or no human interpretation of the data were incorporated. For subject searches, however, a very large amount of human intervention and interpretation seems indispensable until such time as computers are able to cope with synonyms and distinguish key portions of text from trivia.

## CONCLUSION

This study provided, at best, only a few pieces of the answer to the original question of when and how to computerize a large library catalog and to the secondary question of how to improve a conventional card catalog. However, it is a start. It should be remembered that the results reported here pertain specifically to the catalog at Yale and are not necessarily applicable to other libraries. Other recent studies [6, 7] have shown general agreement with these findings; but more research is needed. The data collected for this study have been only partially analyzed so far. Further results will be reported as they become available.

## REFERENCES

1. Lipetz, Ben-Ami. *User Requirements in Identifying Desired Works in a Large Library*. New Haven, Conn.: Yale University Library, 1970.
2. Ruecking, Frederick H., Jr. "Bibliographic Retrieval from Bibliographic Input: The Hypothesis and Construction of a Test." *Journal of Library Automation* 1, no. 4 (December 1968): 227–38.
3. Kilgour, Frederick G. "Retrieval of Single Entries from a Computerized Catalog File." In *American Society for Information Science, Proceedings*. Vol. 5, *Annual Meeting, October 20–24, 1968, Columbus, Ohio*. Westport, Conn.: Greenwood Press, 1969.
4. Lipetz, Ben-Ami; Stangl, Peter; and Taylor, Kathryn F. "Performance of Ruecking's Word-compression Method When Applied

to Machine Retrieval from a Library Catalog." *Journal of Library Automation* 2 (December 1969): 266–71.

5. Stangl, Peter; Lipetz, Ben-Ami; and Taylor, Kathryn F. "Performance of Kilgour's Truncation Algorithm When Applied to Bibliographic Retrieval from a Library Catalog." In *American Society for Information Science, Proceedings*. Vol. 6, *Annual Meeting, October 1–4, 1969, San Francisco*. Westport, Conn.: Greenwood Press, 1970.
6. Tagliacozzo, Renata; Rosenberg, Lawrence; and Kochen, Manfred. *Access and Recognition: From User's Data to Catalog Entries*. Communication no. 257. Ann Arbor: University of Michigan, Mental Health Research Institute, 1970.
7. Palmer, Richard P. "User Requirements of a University Library Card Catalog." Doctoral thesis, University of Michigan, 1970.

Reprinted from the Journal of the American Society for Information Science, Vol. 25, No. 3, 1974. 

# Densities of Use, and Absence of Obsolescence, in Physics Journals at M I T

**Chen's data for the raw frequency of use of 138 physics journals in the science library at M I T are re-examined and converted to densities of use-per-metre of shelf. Other units of size for obtaining densities, and their measurement, are discussed. There is no evidence for synchronous obsolescence in the 1955 to 1968 volumes of these journals: instead there is some statistically significant evidence of greater density of use with greater age. Similar evidence elsewhere is cited. The ranking order for heaviness of use is also radically altered by converting raw frequencies to densities of use.**

**It is suggested that, for comparing the relative values of different journals, or age groups, in library use or citation studies, analyses of raw frequencies are valueless, and indeed potentially dangerously misleading, until they are converted to allow for the numbers of available items in each group examined.**

**Alexander Sandison**
*Science Reference Library*
*London*
*England W2 4DE*

## • Introduction

In a recent paper, Professor Chen (*1*) reported some extremely interesting data for the use of 138 physics journals in the science library at M I T Over a three-and-a-half-month period in 1971, she had recorded the items left out to be reshelved by library staff. This data was used to construct a ranked list of journals in the order of the number of times each was used and to prepare diagrams of the relation between that use and the year of publication, showing the usual rapid decrease in frequency of use with increasing age, but also showing wide differences of pattern between individual journals.

In interpreting her data Chen adopted the conventional approach that raw frequency of use is a measure of heaviness of use, capable of revealing obsolescence, and of distinguishing the core journals from those less in demand suitable for remote storage, discard or cancellation. But she added that her detailed findings should be used very cautiously. This was wise, for the conventional approach ignores the warnings in the literature, *e.g.*, by Raisig in 1962 (*2*), Garfield in 1972 (*3*), and others, that some adjustment must be made to raw frequencies to relate the numbers of items used to the numbers available for use. These warnings were sounded in relation to citation studies, but they are equally valid for library use. The situation is perhaps comparable to that of attempting to assess the value of materials for use as ballast in a boat by comparing two samples (*e.g.*, a pillow and a pin) by their weights instead of by their densities. Raisig proposed, as an "index of use," dividing the number of articles cited by the number originally published and multiplying by 1,000. Garfield used the term "impact factor." Line (*4*) suggested correcting obsolescence rates by a factor derived from the growth rate.

In an analysis of the use of scientific literature at the National Reference Library of Science and Invention (now the Science Reference Library [SRL]) (*5*), I suggested the term "item-consultations" for the raw frequency divided by an estimate of the number of available items, and that this indicates the relative probability that each item would be consulted. The same concept can be described as the density of use. Both the terms probability and density help to clarify the real meaning of heaviness of use in practical terms. When Chen's use frequencies are re-examined in this way the results appear rather different from those given in her paper.

## • Estimating Available Literature

To calculate any estimate of density of use, the size of the available literature must be estimated or measured. There is not, unfortunately, any generally accepted measure, and none of the possible units are entirely satisfactory. Theoretically the size should be measured in identical units to those in which the frequency is counted. This is not now possible for the M.I.T. data for several reasons. In a survey lasting over three-and-a-half months, the number of bound and unbound items in the library is altering daily as new ones arrive, others are removed for binding and yet others are returned as a smaller number of bound volumes. For most of the individual titles Chen did not distinguish between parts and volumes, and of course the use of one volume may represent the use of several of its parts. Furthermore, the number of volumes in any library is a product of its binding policies over the years and can be accurately estimated only by counting volumes in the library surveyed. This is a very large task: there must be some 5,000 volumes of the 138 titles recorded by Chen.

Other potential units of measurement for any one journal include the numbers of years it has been in publication, of the papers, pages or words it has included, or the length of shelf it occupies. The first of these (title-years) is the easiest to estimate, for it can be done at a desk from catalog or *World List* entries. The similar concept of the number of titles publishing in any year was used for most of the SRL study already mentioned (*5*) with the comment that it probably underestimated growth rates. Raisig (*2*) had sounded a similar warning. Title-years are even less satisfactory for comparing individual journals, as one title may publish from 0 to 25,000 pages a year.

For comparison with citation studies, the numbers of papers published would be a very valuable figure, but in practice it means finding each contents page and adding the entries. It is less time consuming to note the number on the last page of each nominal volume and this has been done for each of the ten most frequently used journals for which Chen gave a full age analysis of use. Page and type size changes tend to distort these results for comparative purposes, but probably not seriously. Editorial policies on the lengths of individual contributions could distort between-journal comparisons in citation analyses, but this is irrelevant to records of use of volumes.

Less time consuming, again, to measure is the length of shelf occupied, for volumes do not have to be moved to be measured. Changes in the thicknesses of paper and in numbers and thicknesses of binding boards introduce minor distortions. But indeed, from the librarians' point of view, many of the costs of holding a journal are directly related to shelf occupation, so that any measure of the density of literature use in terms of shelf length is directly relevant to cost-effectiveness studies. Shelf length is very closely correlated to numbers of pages and was used in most of this present study because it is so much easier to measure.

Boutry (*6*) made a monumental estimate of words published in 13 of the main physics journals. The exponential annual increase for 1950-64 of 1.09 is the same as that for their shelf-length (1.09).

Having decided to use shelf-length as the main measure of the literature, a number of the M I T journals were measured individually at SRL, in the age groups adopted by Chen for her analysis of use by age. The science librarian at M I T very kindly provided details of those titles mentioned by Chen for which their holdings are not complete, so that the measurements could be directly related to M.I.T stock and therefore be relevant to the use frequencies observed there.

Some 68 titles (a 48% sample) were measured, selected on several criteria. First, 28 represented a 20% random sample of Chen's titles (indicated in the Appendix in bold italics); then the rest of the ten most frequently, and the ten English least frequently, used; and finally, a number of others which it was convenient to measure for another purpose. The exponential growth rates for the random sample and for the other 40 titles are virtually identical, as is the plot of cumulated title-years, so that the data from the full sample can be considered representative.

## • Growth of Literature at M I T

From data on available literature collected for this study it was possible to calculate growth rates for the physics journals at M I T. Growth had been remarkably uniform since W.W. II. For the 68 journals measured, regression constants were calculated for age by the log of either the numbers of title-years or of the length of shelf occupied. The resulting exponential growth factors are shown in Table 1, and it will be noted that title-years considerably underestimate new shelf occupation. The total holdings and new titles were growing over the period 1945-68 at about 5-6% per year compound and doubling every 11.5 years: the extra shelving required each year was increasing by about 10.5% per year compound. Only a small part of this growth was due to the acquisition of new titles several years after first publication.

Table 1. Growth Rates for Physics Journals at M I T: 1945-68

| | Exponential annual growth factor |
|---|---|
| Net numbers of new titles each year | 1.059 |
| Length of additional items each year | 1.104 |
| Total numbers of title-years | 1.065 |
| Total length of occupied shelf | 1.053 |

## • Relation between Use and Age

Chen gave an age distribution of the total frequencies of use recorded, and also details for the ten most frequently used titles individually. Table 2 shows her

Table 2. Densities of Use of Physics Journals at M I T (Densities as Use-per-page x $10^4$ except +)

| Year of publication / Ages | 1970 / 1 | 1969 / 2 | 1968 / 3 | 67-66 / 4-5 | 65-64 / 6-7 | 63-62 / 8-9 | 61-60 / 10-11 | 59-55 / 12-16 | Annual increase over ages 3-16 | Confidence limits (P=0.05) |
|---|---|---|---|---|---|---|---|---|---|---|
| All 138 journals+ | 60.6 | 60.1 | 43.1 | 46.8 | 46.2 | 47.0 | 42.6 | 43.8 | -0.13 | +.28 to -.55 |
| *Phys. Rev.* | 27.3 | 30.3 | 20.6 | 16.3 | 22.8 | 21.0 | 29.5 | 25.4 | +0.79 | +1.56 to +0.03 |
| *J. Chem. Phys.* | 42.0 | 43.0 | 36.5 | 45.5 | 47.2 | 48.8 | 47.8 | 63.9 | +1.99* | +2.88 to +1.10 |
| *J. Appd. Phys.* | 27.4 | 37.0 | 27.1 | 29.0 | 39.9 | 32.7 | 47.7 | 42.9 | +1.62 | +2.82 to +0.43 |
| *J. Ac. Soc. Am.* | 62.6 | 40.0 | 38.6 | 36.1 | 40.6 | 49.9 | 38.2 | 57.9 | +1.60 | +2.94 to +0.26 |
| *Phil. Mag.* | 26.7 | 30.3 | 30.1 | 32.1 | 22.6 | 32.6 | 20.8 | 18.7 | -1.10 | -0.07 to -2.13 |
| *Phys. Fluids.* | 38.8 | 34.5 | 25.0 | 35.7 | 38.1 | 23.0 | 38.0 | 70.4 | +3.18 | +5.88 to +0.48 |
| *J. Opt. Soc. Am.* | 11.5 | 5.8 | 41.0 | 29.3 | 39.8 | 30.1 | 44.0 | 35.0 | +0.05 | +1.51 to -1.41 |
| *J. Fluid Mech.* | 34.9 | 4.0 | 24.0 | 34.0 | 15.9 | 26.0 | 28.1 | 20.5 | -0.39 | -0.02 to -0.76 |
| These 8: | 32.2 | 31.2 | 27.3 | 28.8 | 32.6 | 32.3 | 36.7 | 37.1 | +0.94** | +1.36 to +0.51 |
| *Phys. Rev. Let.* | 71.5 | 79.0 | 28.9 | 61.6 | 71.5 | 50.3 | 28.2 | 24.4 | | |
| *Phys. Letters.* | 42.5 | 27.9 | 13.9 | 32.5 | 34.2 | 11.6 | – | – | | |
| These 2: | 54.8 | 44.0 | 21.2 | 46.1 | 52.0 | 29.4 | 28.2 | 24.4 | | |

*+ as relative use-per-metre*
** correlation coefficient probably significant ($P < 0.05$)*
*** correlation coefficient significant ($P < 0.01$)*

figures converted to densities of use, as relative frequencies-per-metre for the group as a whole and as frequencies-per-page for the ten individual titles and two subgroups among them. The figures for annual increase are the calculated regression constants for the changes in density with age for items published 1968–1955. These data are also presented as histograms with the regression lines as solid lines and with broken lines for the raw frequency-of-use curves presented in Chen's diagrams. The data for the older (pre-1955) literature have not been included because it is kept in the basements at M I T and only the items brought upstairs to be read were recorded. This must, as Chen points out, have underestimated the use, which is in any case liable to be reduced by the relative inaccessibility of the items.

It is clear from these histograms that, for what have been described as "basic searches" in these physics journals from three to 16 years old, there is no evidence for any obsolescence at M I T. This is the more surprising, because physics literature is always reputed to have a particularly high obsolescence rate. For the collected data for all 138 journals (Fig. 1) the correlation between age and density of use is nowhere near significant (r = 0.23 when densities are based on the sample of 68 titles, or r = -0.004 when based on the random sample of 28 titles).

Considering the ten most frequently used titles individually, there are eight conventional journals and two of advance publication letters. As can be seen, these two groups show different patterns of use over ages three to 16 years. For the "Letters" (Fig. 3) there is a peak of use when they are six to seven years old. Most of the eight conventional journals over two years old (Fig. 2) show an increasing density of use with increasing age: this increase gives a probably significant ($P < 0.05$) correlation (r = 0.91) in the case of *Journal of Chemical Physics*, and, when the eight journals are taken together, the correlation is significant ($P < 0.01$: r = 0.94). Only for *Philosophical Magazine* does the correlation (r = -0.72) approach a probably significant level (P = 0.05, r = -0.81) of obsolescence represented by decreasing density of use with age.

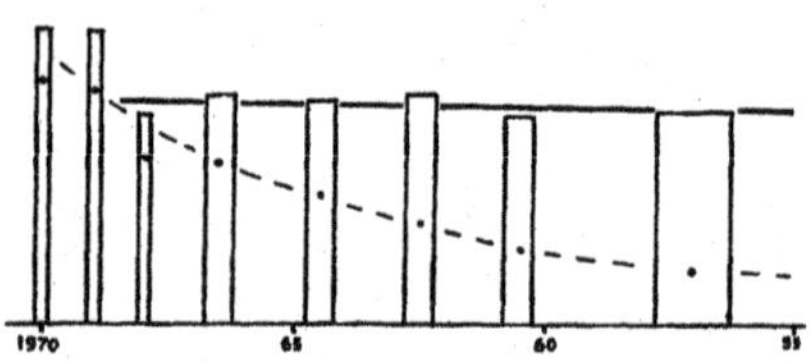

Fig. 1. Relation between density of use-per-metre and age since publication for 138 physics journals.
Solid line is the calculated regression line: broken line is that for raw frequencies of use as presented by Chen.

The discussion so far has ignored the youngest literature published after 1968. The histograms show some evidence for a genuine obsolescence in the short age group of one to three years, which I attributed (*5*) at SRL to "updating searches" in literature becoming available since a previous search. For this period the

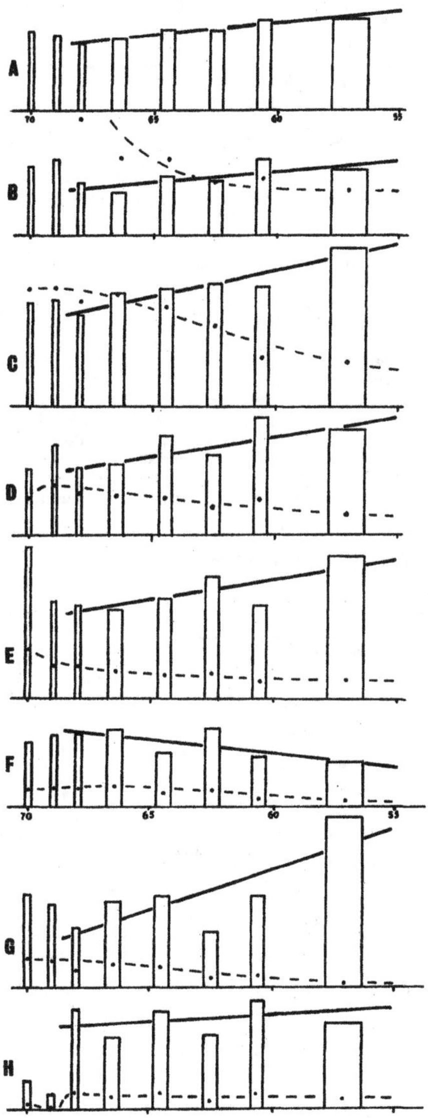


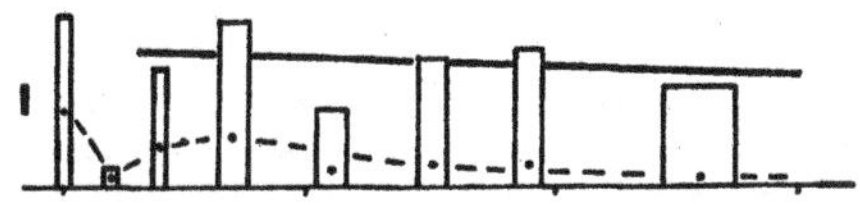


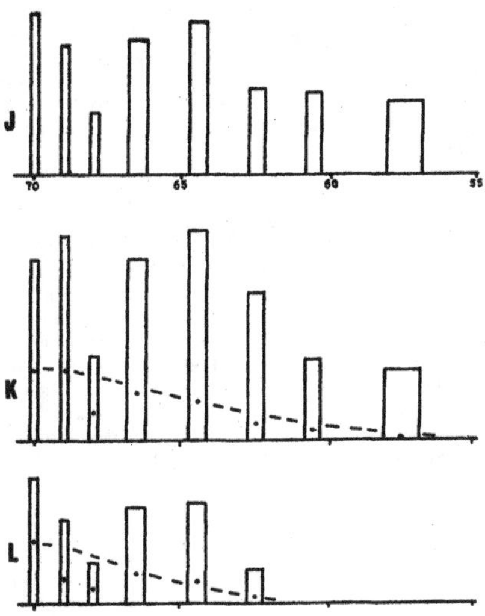


Fig. 3. Above. Relation between density of use-per-page and age since publication for the two most frequently used 'letters' type journals.
Solid line is the calculated regression line: broken line is that for raw frequencies of use as presented by Chen.

J. Both journals together.
K. Physical Review Letters.
L. Physics Letters.

interpretation of the data is complicated by the effects of counting some items as parts and some as bound volumes, and by the absence at the bindery of some which could not be taken into account in estimating occupied shelf-length for "available" items.

Fig. 2. Left. Relation between density of use-per-page and age since publication for the eight most frequently used conventional type journals.
Broken line is that for raw frequencies of use as presented by Chen.

A. All eight journals.
B. Physical Review.
C. Journal of Chemical Physics.
D. Journal of Applied Physics.
E. Journal of the Acoustical Society of America.
F. Philosophical Magazine.
G. Physics of Fluids.
H. Journal of the Optical Society of America.
I. Journal of Fluid Mechanics.

- **Data from NLL and SCI**

This paper was prepared in 1972. More recently I have had the opportunity of considering data from other sources for the eight conventional titles most frequently used in Chen's data. First the British Library Lending Division has supplied figures for loans for seven of those titles during six months in 1969 from the then National Lending Library of Science and Technology. When these are converted to loans-per-metre of shelf, the results show similar general patterns to Chen's data from M I T

Table 2a. shows the calculated regression constants for the individual titles, and gives the M I T data for comparison as well as data for citations-per-cm. These came from *Science Citation Index* (*12*) in their analysis of the 1,000 titles most frequently cited.

Table 2a. demonstrates that, in broad terms, the pattern of use of these particular journals is similar in two very different types of library, one an American teaching and research institution, and the other for interlibrary lending for the whole of Britain. There is no evidence here for any "law of obsolescence" and statistically strong evidence that, for some types of journals and library, it could be the reverse of the truth.

The citation data is of equal interest. Despite the large samples, only one individual title shows probably significant citation–density decay over an eight-year period. For the eight titles combined the decay is significant at a rate of about 2.5% per annum.

It should be mentioned that all these results fit simple regression lines as well, or as badly, as they do exponential ones. Badly may be the operative word. Variances are so high that the safest conclusions are that obsolescence in library use is unproven (if it exists it is too unreliable to form a basis for forecasting) and citations do not provide reliable evidence either.

- **Identification of "Core" Journals**

The arguments for relating frequency of use to journal size apply to attempts to identify the individual, most heavily used titles with even more force than they do to the study of the relation with age. The lengths of holdings among the 138 titles at M I T vary from one to 172 years (*Annalen der Physik*), to which must be added the wide variability in the annual size of each title. Chen's Appendix I ranked the 138 journals in order of raw frequency of use. The 68 journals I have measured are shown in my Appendix in the order of density of use as frequency-per-metre. For comparison the densities

Table 2a. Relation between Density of Use (Or Citation) and Age
b= regression constant y = a + bx;
r= correlation coefficient
n= total uses or citations

| Source / Date of survey / Units / Age range considered | M I T 1970 Use-per-metre 3 to 16 | | | N L L S T 1969 Loans-per-metre 5 to 30 | | | S C I 1970 Citations-per-cm. 2 to 10 | | |
|---|---|---|---|---|---|---|---|---|---|
| | b | r | n | b | r | n | b | r | n |
| *Phys. Rev.* | +0.79 | +0.71 | 355 | +2.92 | +0.94** | 230 | -0.60 | -0.72* | 13,583 |
| *J. Chem. Phys.* | +1.99 | +0.91* | 412 | +6.60 | +0.96*** | 319 | -0.21 | -0.41 | 9,260 |
| *J. Appl. Phys.* | +1.62 | +0.80 | 169 | +3.09 | +0.58 | 325 | -0.41 | -0.55 | 3,905 |
| *J. Acoust. Soc. Am* | +1.60 | +0.76 | 131 | -1.57 | -0.42 | 247 | -0.18 | -0.39 | 799 |
| *Phil. Mag.* | -1.10 | -0.72 | 69 | -0.78 | -0.89** | 75 | -0.24 | -0.62 | 1,077 |
| *Phys. of Fluids* | +3.18 | +0.76 | 70 | -3.45 | -0.73 | 27 | -0.79 | -0.81 | 1,149 |
| *J. Opt. Soc. Am.* | +0.05 | +0.04 | 72 | -2.36 | -0.18 | 269 | -1.12 | -0.91 | 993 |
| *J. Fluid Mech.* | -0.39 | -0.25 | 62 | Not available | | | +0.04 | +0.09 | 767 |
| All 8 titles | +0.94 | +0.95** | 1340 | – | – | – | -0.51 | -0.84** | 31,533 |
| 7 titles (excl. *J. Fluid Mech.*) | +2.09 | +0.98*** | 1278 | +2.71 | +0.92** | 1492 | – | – | – |
| Degrees of freedom | 4 | | | 5 | | | 9 | | |

*Correlation probably significant ($P < .05$)
**Correlation significant ($P < .01$)
***Correlation highly significant ($P < .001$)

and ranks as frequency-per-year in publication, and as the raw frequencies in Chen's appendix, are also shown. I had suggested in an earlier note (*7*) that the number of years in publication must be taken into account when ranking journals in order of use. This study makes it evident that the comment, though valid, is inadequate and that variations in size between journals in any one year must also be allowed for. The following Table (3) brings this home, by showing the corresponding ranking orders of the top ten journals from the columns for Chen's raw frequency, for frequency-per-year in publication, and for frequency-per-metre.

This paper is intended mainly as a contribution to methodology, and I therefore make no attempt to reinterpret Chen's comments on subscription costs-per-title, policy on duplicates, etc. I would, however, emphasise the need to check that any ranking order is consistent from year to year in view of evidence (*7, 8*) of considerable variations.

One point made by Chen, however, that foreign language journals were little used, is amply confirmed in my Appendix.

In considering the details in that Appendix, the high variance of the figures should be borne in mind. In the three-and-one-half months of the survey, 24 titles were used once only and 82 not at all. Which particular title fell into each category is best considered as a matter of chance. Furthermore, in measuring shelf-lengths, the variations due to page, type, paper and binding size have already been mentioned: to these must be added experimental errors in measurement, some of which may arise from gaps in the holdings not immediately apparent at the shelf. Density of use figures therefore contain potential variations of several percent so that small differences in ranking order are meaningless, particularly among the less frequently used items where the difference between being used once, twice or not at all can double or halve the density.

The recognition of the "core" journals is therefore much more difficult than is sometimes suggested (*e.g.*, *9*). Ranked orders of titles must be based on comparable figures allowing for variations in the sizes of the groups recorded. The orders must be interpreted with full regard for the extremely high variability both from one sample to another, and within every sample, due to such factors as experimental error, the differences between updating and basic searching, and other points mentioned in the footnote to the appendix. I have been told that "few physicists would agree with your 'core' journals." This is probably true, but their judgment is largely subjective and biased by the vast bulk of the 20 metres of *Physical Review* which so easily obscures the relatively greater density of use of the one-and-one-half metres of *Reviews of Modern Physics*. But I would not go so far as to suggest that the order in my Appendix accurately identifies the "core" journals in physics. It can do no more than present some of the evidence in terms of more practical value to cost-conscious librarians than raw frequency figures.

## • Conclusions

This study of densities of journal use at M I T challenges several of the generally accepted tenets of librarians. It seems that, for basic searches of literature in libraries, the concept of obsolescence may perhaps be no more than a myth. There is now positive evidence for no reduction in, or increasing, use with increasing age for physics journals at M I T : for periodicals from 1850 to 1930 in reserve in the SRL (*5*); and for literature published between 1450 and 1900 in the British Museum (*5*). The statement (*10*) that similar numbers of books had been requested from each decade 1550 to 1800 at Yale shows a similar situation there. Vickery (*11*) commented on loan figures for *Liebig's Annalen* that "useful papers appear to be scattered at random over the years" 1942-1885. At SRL the growth of literature in reserve had been estimated by counting volumes: that on open access, where some obsolescence was found, had been underestimated as title-years. If the M I T growth rate for the occupation of physics shelves is valid for the full range of subjects in SRL, and is used to correct for that underestimate, then the evidence for obsolescence in basic searches in periodicals on open access there disappears.

The widespread practice of attempting to identify "core" journals from a single ranked order of raw frequencies is also challenged. Ranks based on holdings of abnormally few, or abnormally many, years are particularly suspect, even when calculated as densities.

It does not seem to be an exaggeration to suggest that it is worthless to try and compare journals, either as individual titles or as of different age groups, from analyses of raw frequencies, without correcting for the numbers or sizes of available items. Uncorrected analyses can in fact be dangerously misleading, and this is just as true for citation studies as it is for those of library use. As a basis for useful analyses, there is an urgent need for reliable figures of the sizes of the annual outputs of individual journals in some convenient unit, be it numbers of papers or of pages, or shelf occupation. The

| Raw frequency | 1 | 2 | 3 | 4 | 5 | 6 | 7 | 8 | 9 | 10= | 10= | 30= | 16 | 23 | 12 | 54= | 42= |
|---|---|---|---|---|---|---|---|---|---|---|---|---|---|---|---|---|---|
| Frequency/year | 4 | 1 | 8 | 13 | 2 | 17 | 5 | 24 | 3 | 12 | 26= | 6= | 6= | 9 | 10 | 30= | 16 |
| Frequency/metre | 23= | 8 | 11 | 10 | 6 | 19= | 9 | 23= | 12 | 22 | 41= | 1 | 3 | 2 | 4 | 5 | 7 |

Table 3. Corresponding Ranking Orders for the Top Ten Sets of Titles

first could perhaps be a valuable by-product of the computerized activities of *Science Citation Index*. The other two could be recorded by national libraries when their volumes return from the binderies and the resulting data could be made available to those who need it. They would also, of course, be invaluable to the libraries themselves in planning shelving policy and in extrapolating growth rates to estimate future needs. The details obtained for individual physics journals mentioned in this paper, and some others, can be supplied to anyone interested.

For library use studies the base of "available" literature is precisely identifiable, but the use frequency data should be collected in such a way that it is possible to observe the differences between updating and basic searches, and any effects on use of different categories of accessibility—*e.g.*, between open and closed access. But for citation studies, the pool of items within a literature available for citation is nebulous and how it can best be identified is a very open question deserving serious study.

That so many former comparative use studies are almost valueless does nothing to discount the need for and the importance of such studies. If it is true that obsolescence is a myth so far as it relates to library use of journals, the policies, so widely adopted, of relegating, or outhousing, older volumes need re-examination. How far does such relegation, by discouraging use, prevent genuine need for and interest in older literature from being revealed in use figures? And if, for citations, reduced density with increasing age does prove significant (*e.g.*, *8*), how far is this a valid indication that older literature should be, or is, less read, or how far is it due to the effect of chain citation, whereby both author and readers rely on one recent reference to lead to earlier ones? These are questions of fundamental importance which need an answer. But reliable data is needed on the annual outputs of individual journals. To measure these is a laborious and tedious task, but it is so essential to profitable study of vital problems that it should be undertaken by national services.

## • Disclaimer

*I should make it clear that the opinions I have* expressed in this paper are my own and not necessarily those of the SRL, of the British Museum or of the British Library of which the SRL has become a part.

## References

1. **Chen, C. C.**, "The Use Patterns of Physics Journals in a Large Academic Research Library," *Journal of the American Society for Information Science*, 23(No. 3):254-70 (1972).
2. **Raisig, L. M.**, "Statistical Bibliography in the Health Services," *Bulletin of the Medical Libraries Association*, 5:454 (1962).
3. **Garfield, E.**, "Citations-to Divided by Items-Published Gives Journal Impact Factor;... *Current Contents*, 15 (No. 8): 6-7 (1972).
4. **Line, M. B.**, "The Half-Life of Periodical Literature—Apparent and Real Obsolescence, "*Journal of Documentation*, 26 (No. 1): 46-52 (1970).
5. **Sandison, A.**, "The Use of Older Literature and its Obsolescence," *Journal of Documentation*, 17 (No. 3): 184-99 (1971).
6. **Boutry, G. A.** "*L'Evolution des Publications Scientifiques Primaires—Etudes Statistiques,*" *Bulletin de Bibliothèques de France*, 14: 431-61 (1969).
7. **Sandison, A.** "Library optimum." *Nature (London)*, 234 (No. 5328): 368-9 (1971).
8. **Line, M. B., A. Sandison** and **J. MacGregor**, *Patterns of citations to articles within journals: a preliminary test of scatter, concentration and obsolescence.* Bath (England): Bath University Library, Bath/Lib/2. (1972).
9. **Brookes, B. C.** Optimum P% Library of Scientific Periodicals, *Nature (London)*, 232 (No. 5311): 458-61 (1971).
10. **Ash, L.** *Yale's Selective Book Retirement Program.* Shoestring Press (1963) (quoted in) **Seymour, C. A.** "Weeding the Collection: A Review of Research on Identifying Obsolete Stock," Part 1: Monographs. *Libri.* 23 (No. 2): 141 (1971).
11. **Vickery, B. C.**, "Periodical Sets: What Should You Buy?" *Aslib Proceedings*, 5 (No. 2): 72 (1953).
12. Institute for Scientific Information. *ISI Journal Citation Reports*, Philadelphia: ISI (1973).

# Appendix Density of Use of Physics Journals in Science Library at M.I.T.

| Journal | Use per metre | Rank | Use per Year in publ'n | Rank | Use Freq'y (raw) | Rank | Country of Publ'n | Language |
|---|---|---|---|---|---|---|---|---|
| *Optics Communications: 1969–* | 229 | 1 | 7.0 | 6= | 14 | 30= | Neth | E, F, G |
| *IEEE J. of Quantum[ Electronics:* 1965– | 131 | 2 | 6.0 | 9 | 36 | 23 | USA | E |
| *Applied Physics Letters:* 1962– | 112 | 3 | 7.0 | 6= | 63 | 16 | USA | E |
| *J. of Molecular Spectroscopy:* 1957– | 80 | 4 | 5.7 | 10 | 80 | 12 | USA | E |
| *Review of Physics in Technology:* 1970– | 77 | 5 | 1.0 | 30 | 1 | 54= | GB | E |
| *Physical Review Letters:* 1958– | 76 | 6 | 11.9 | 2 | 155 | 5 | USA | E |
| *CRC Critical Reviews in Solid State Sciences:* 1970– | 75 | 7 | 4.0 | 16 | 4 | 42 | USA | E |
| *J. of Chemical Physics:* 1933– | 74 | 8 | 14.7 | 1 | 560 | 2 | USA | E |
| *Physics of* Fluids: 1958– | 70 | 9 | 7.5 | 5 | 97 | 7 | USA | E |
| *Acoustical Society of America Journal:* 1929– | 59 | 10 | 4.6 | 13 | 192 | 4 | USA | E |
| *J. of Applied Physics:* 1937– | 56 | 11 | 6.7 | 8 | 227 | 3 | USA | E |
| *Physics Letters:* 1962– | 52 | 12 | 9.6 | 3 | 86 | 9 | GB | E |
| *Physics Today:* 1948– | 46 | 13 | 2.0 | 23 | 45 | 21 | USA | E |
| *Reviews of Modern Physics:* 1929– | 45 | 14 | 1.6 | 25 | 66 | 14 | USA | E |
| *Applied Optics:* 1962– | 44 | 15 | 5.6 | 11 | 50 | 20 | USA | E |
| *Molecular Physics:* 1958– | 42 | 16 | 2.9 | 19 | 38 | 22 | GB | E |
| *British J. of Applied Physics:* 1955-67 | 39 | 17 | 2.4 | 21 | 31 | 22 | GB | E |
| *Ferroelectrics:* 1970– | 38 | 18 | 1.0 | 30= | 1 | 54= | GB | E |

| | | | | | | | | |
|---|---|---|---|---|---|---|---|---|
| ***J. of Nuclear Materials:*** 1959- | 37 | 19= | 2.9 | 20 | 35 | 24 | Neth | *E*, F, G |
| *Comments on Solid State Physics:* 1968– | 37 | 19= | 0.7 | 35 | 2 | 45= | GB | E |
| *Philosophical Magazine:* 1945– | 37 | 19= | 3.9 | 17 | 101 | 6 | GB | E |
| *J. of Fluid Mechanics:* 1956– | 33 | 22 | 5.4 | 12 | 81 | 10= | GB | E |
| *Annals of Physics:* 1957– | 30 | 23= | 4.3 | 14 | 60 | 18 | USA | E |
| *Physical Review:* 1893– | 30 | 23= | 7.7 | 4 | 597 | 1 | USA | E |
| *Optical Society of America: Journal:* 1917– | 30 | 23= | 1.7 | 24 | 92 | 8 | USA | E |
| ***Comments on Atomic and Molecular Physics:*** 1969– | 28 | 26 | 0.5 | 39= | 1 | 54= | GB | E |
| *Review of Scientific Instruments:* 1930– | 27 | 27= | 1.5 | 26= | 63 | 16= | USA | E |
| *Comments on Nuclear and Particle Physics:* 1967– | 27 | 27= | 0.5 | 39= | 2 | 45= | GB | E |
| *Canadian J. of Physics:* 1961– | 27 | 27= | 3.8 | 18 | 75 | 13 | Can | E |
| *Optics and Spectroscopy:* 1959– | 26 | 30 | 2.0 | 22 | 24 | 26 | USSR | E(t) |
| *Infrared Physics:* 1961– | 25 | 31 | 0.5 | 39= | 5 | 39= | GB | E |
| *Soviet Physics: J.E.T.P.:* 1955– | 22 | 32 | 4.1 | 15 | 65 | 15 | USSR | E(t) |
| ***J. of Applied Spectroscopy:*** 1965– | 20 | 33 | 0.7 | 35= | 4 | 42= | USSR | E(t) |
| *Soviet Physics: Uspekhi:* 1956– | 18 | 34 | 0.9 | 32 | 14 | 30= | USSR | E(t) |
| *Physica:* 1933– | 17 | 35 | 1.4 | 28 | 53 | 19 | Neth | E |
| *Communications in Mathematical Physics:* 1965– | 15 | 36= | 1.3 | 29 | 8 | 35 | Germ'y | E |
| *Contemporary Physics:* 1959– | 15 | 36= | 0.6 | 37= | 7 | 36= | GB | E |
| *Optica Acta:* 1954– | 14 | 38= | 0.4 | 42= | 6 | 38 | GB | *E*, F, G |

| | | | | | | | | |
|---|---|---|---|---|---|---|---|---|
| *Czechoslovak J. of Physics:* 1952– | 14 | 38= | 0.8 | 33= | 15 | 29 | Czech | *E*, F, G |
| *Plasma Physics:* 1959– | 12 | 40 | 0.8 | 33= | 9 | 32= | GB | E |
| *Indian J. of Pure and Applied Physics:* 1963– | 11 | 41= | 0.6 | 37= | 5 | 39= | India | E |
| *Nuovo Cimento:* 1918– | 11 | 41= | 1.5 | 26= | 81 | 10= | Italy | *E*, F, G |
| *Acta Physica Austriaca:* 1947– | 11 | 41= | 0.4 | 42= | 9 | 32= | Austria | *E*, F, G |
| *Astrophysics:* 1965-69 | 11 | 41= | 0.2 | 51= | 1 | 54= | USSR | E(t) |
| *Spectroscopy Letters:* 1968– | 10 | 45= | 0.3 | 46= | 1 | 54= | USA | E |
| *J. of Scientific Instruments:* 1922-68 | 10 | 45= | 0.4 | 42= | 17 | 27= | GB | E |
| *Arkiv for Fysik:* 1949– | 7 | 47= | 0.4 | 42= | 9 | 32= | Sweden | *E*, F |
| *Revue de Physique Appliquee:* 1967– | 7 | 47= | 0.3 | 46= | 1 | 54= | France | F |
| *Beitrage aus der Plasmaphysik:* 1960– | 7 | 47= | 0.2 | 51= | 2 | 45= | Germ'y | G |
| *Chinese J. of Physics:* 1965-67 | 6 | 50 | 0.3 | 46= | 1 | 54= | China | E |
| *Zeitscrift fur Angewandte Physik:* 1948– | 5 | 51 | 0.2 | 51= | 5 | 39= | Germ'y | G |
| *Paris: Institut Henri Poincare: Annales: A:* 1964– | 4 | 52= | 0.3 | 46= | 2 | 45= | France | F |
| *Cosmic Research:* 1964– | 4 | 52= | 0.3 | 46= | 2 | 45= | USSR | E(t) |
| *Astrofizika:* 1965– | 4 | 52= | 0.2 | 51= | 1 | 54= | USSR | R |
| *Cahiers de Physique:* 1960-68 | 4 | 52= | 0.1 | 58= | 1 | 54= | France | F |
| *Archiv fur Technisches Messen:* 1931-40 | 4 | 52= | 0.1 | 58= | 1 | 54= | Germ'y | G |
| *Zhurnal Tekhnicheskoi Fiziki:* 1931– | 2 | 47= | 0.2 | 51= | 7 | 36= | USSR | R |

| | | | | | | | | |
|---|---|---|---|---|---|---|---|---|
| ***Zurnal Eksperimental' Noi i Teoreticheskoi Fiziki: Pisma v Redaktsiiu:*** 1965– | 2 | 57= | 0.2 | 51= | 1 | 54= | USSR | R |
| ***International J. of Solids and Structures:*** 1965– | 2 | 57= | 0.2 | 51= | 1 | 54= | GB | E |
| *Akademie van Wetenschappen, Amsterdam: Proceedings: B.* 1951– | 2 | 57= | 0.1 | 58= | 2 | 45= | Neth | *E*, F |
| *Bulletin of the Atomic Scientists:* 1946– | 2 | 57= | 0.05 | 65= | 1 | 54= | USA | E |
| ***Ukrainskii Fizychnyi Zhurnal:*** 1957– | 2 | 57= | 0.1 | 58 | 2 | 45= | Ukr. | R |
| ***Isvestiia Vysshikh Uchebnykh Zavedenii: Fizika:*** 1963– | 1 | 63= | 0.1 | 58= | 1 | 54= | USSR | R |
| ***Acta Physica (Hungarica):*** 1951– | 1 | 63= | 0.05 | 65= | 1 | 54= | Hung'y | *E*, F, G R |
| *Annalen der Physik:* 1799– | 1 | 63= | 0.1 | 58= | 17 | 27= | Germ'y | *G*, E |
| *Zhurnal Eksperimental' Noi i Teoreticheskoi Fiziki:* 1944– | 1 | 63= | 0.1 | 58= | 3 | 44= | USSR | R |
| *British H. of Radiology:* 1925– | 1 | 63= | 0.05 | 65= | 2 | 45= | GB | E |
| ***American J. of Roentgenology and Radium Therapy:*** 1918-51 | 0.2 | 68= | 0.05 | 65= | 1 | 54= | USA | E |

**Notes**

1. Titles in bold italics are a random sample.
2. The ranking orders of titles for which holdings start before 1955 are probably too low because the use of the pre-1955 volumes in the basements was underestimated.
3. The ranking orders of titles which started publication recently are uncertain: the effects of updating searches and of counting unbound parts make the ranking orders too high, whereas the non-arrival at M I T of any overdue parts would make the orders too low.

# APPENDIX

This appendix uses a variety of citation retrieval strategies to identify recent publications based upon papers in the present volume. The retrieval was done by Patricia N. Servi with the assistance of the Editor and Howard D. White, and frequently employs White's author-intersection method of retrieval. The basis of retrieval is indicated in each case, customarily with Boolean operators (in all capitals). The creation of this appendix was supported by PHS grant from the National Library of Medicine, #R01-LM00911-07.

The Structure and Dynamics of Science Information Flow

List 1: The result of an author search, Crane AND Griffith AND Mullins, intended to restrict a burgeoning body of literature on informal communication in science. The "Crane" term casts a broad net, restricted to science by the "Mullins" term, and hopefully, to scientific communication by the "Griffith" term. The strategy should eliminate documents making casual mention of "invisible colleges" and find more technical works.

Small, H. G. and Crane, D. "Specialties and Disciplines in Science and Social-Science--Examination of Their Structure Using Citation Indexes." Scientometrics. 1(5-6): 445-461; 1979.

Lancaster, F. W. and Smith, L. C. "Science, Scholarship and the Communication of Knowledge." Library Trends. 27(3): 367-388; 1979.

Chubin, D. E. and Studer, K. E. "Knowledge and Structures of Scientific Growth--Measurement of a Cancer Problem Domain." Scientometrics. 1(2): 171-193; 1979.

Friedkin, N. E. "University Social-Structure and Social Networks Among Scientists." American Journal of Sociology. 83(6): 1444-1465; 1978.

Narin, F. and Moll, J. K. "Bibliometrics." Annual Review of Information Science and Technology. 12: 35-58; 1977.

Mullins, N. C., Hargens, L. L., Hecht, P. K., and Kick, E. L. "Group Structure of Co-citation Clusters--Comparative-Study." American Sociological Review. 42(4): 552-562; 1977.

Orand, A. M. "Professional Standing and Peer Consultation Status Among Biological Scientists at a Summer Research Laboratory." Social Forces. 55(4): 921-937; 1977.

Sullivan, D., White, D. H., and Barboni, E. J. "State of a Science--Indicators in Specialty of Weak Interactions." Social Studies of Science. 7(2): 167-200; 1977.

Small, H. G. "Co-citation Model of a Scientific Specialty--Longitudinal-Study of Collagen Research." Social Studies of Science. 7(2): 139-166; 1977.

Kadushin, C. "Networks and Circles in Production of Culture." American Behavioral Scientist. 19(6): 769-784; 1976.

Zimmerman, D. H. "Two Methods in Search of Substance--Reply." American Sociologist. 11(1): 4-13; 1976.

Brieger, R. L. "Career Attributes and Network Structure--Blockmodel Study of a Biomedical-Research Specialty." American Sociological Review. 41(1): 117-135; 1976.

Mullins, N. C. "New Causal Theory--Elite Specialty in Social-Science." History of Political Economy. 7(4): 499-529; 1975.

Groeneveld, L., Koller, N., and Mullins, N. C. "Advisers of United-States National-Science-Foundation." Social Studies of Science. 5(3): 343-354; 1975.

Chubin, D. "Journal as a Primary Data Source in Sociology of Science--With Some Observations from Sociology." Social Science Information. 14(1): 157-168; 1975.

Wolek, F. W. and Griffith, B. C. "Policy and Informal Communications in Applied Science and Technology." Science Studies. 4(4): 411-240; 1974.

Hagstrom, W. O. "Competition in Science." American Sociological Review. 39(1): 1-18; 1974.

Mullins, N. C. "Development of Specialties in Social Science--Case of Ethnomethodology." Science Studies. 3(3): 245-273; 1973.

Gilbert, G. N. "Measuring the Growth of Science--Review of Indicators of Scientific Growth." Scientometrics. 1(1): 9-34; 1978.

Reskin, B. F. "Sex Differentiation and the Social-Organization of Science." Sociological Inquiry. 48(3-4): 6-37; 1978.

Chubin, D. E. "Conceptualization of Scientific Specialties. Sociological Quarterly. 17(4): 448-476; 1976.

Chubin, D. E. "Trusted Assessorship in Science--Relation in Need of Data." Social Studies of Science. 5(3): 362-368; 1975.

Lecuyer, B. P. "Evaluation and Perspectives of Sociology of Science in Western Countries." Archives Europeennes de Sociologie. 19(2): 257-336; 1978.

Ben David, J. "Emergence of National Traditions in the Sociology of Science--United-States and Great-Britain." Sociological Inquiry. 48(3-4): 197-218; 1978.

Hargens, L. "Theory and Method in the Sociology of Science." Sociological Inquiry. 48(3-4): 121-139; 1978.

List 2: The result of an author search, Garvey AND Crane, in which the "Garvey" term picks up informatin processing through disciplines and the "Crane" term eliminates Garvey's psychological work.

Griffith, B. D. "Social and Behavioral-Sciences Literature." Proceedings of the American Society for

Information Science." 16: 254-262; 1979.

Hiltz, S. R. "Impact of a Computerized Conferencing System Upon Scientific-Research Specialties." Journal of Research Communication Studies. 1(2): 111-124; 1978.

Gottfredson, S. D. "Evaluating Psychological-Research Reports--Dimensions, Reliability, and Correlates of Quality Judgments." American Psychologist. 33(10): 920-934; 1978.

Hurt, C. D. "Correlation Study of Journal Article Productivity of Environmental Scientists." Information Processing & Management. 13(5): 305-309; 1977.

Groves, D. L., and Wolensky, R. "Applied Recreation Research--Missing Link Between Theoretical Research and Practitioner." Journal of Environmental Systems. 7(1): 59-98; 1977.

Markusova, V. A. "Some Aspects of Study of Information Links Among Scientists (A Review of Research Outside USSR)." Nauchno-Tekhnicheskaya Informatsiya Seriya 1-Organizatsiya I Metodika Informatsionnoi Raboty. 1977(5): 17-21; 1977.

Embry, D. D. "Disseminating Research Findings--Blueprint for Affecting Educational-Research and Practice." Educational Technology. 19(3): 25-29; 1979.

Orand, A. M. "Professional Standing and Peer Consultation Status Among Biological Scientists at a Summer Research Laboratory." Social Forces. 55(4): 921-937; 1977.

Mitroff, I. and Kilmann, R. H. "Systematic Knowledge--Toward an Integrated Theory of Science." Theory and Society. 4(1): 103-129; 1977.

Meadows, A. J. "Diffusion of Information Across Sciences." Interdisciplinary Science Reviews. 1(3): 259-267; 1976.

Mulkay, M. "Mediating Role of Scientific Elite." Social Studies of Science. 6(3-4): 445-470; 1976.

Hagstrom, W. O. "Production of Culture in Science." American Behavioral Scientist. 19(6): 753-768; 1976.

Mulkay, M. J. "3 Models of Scientific Development." Sociological Review. 23(3): 509-526; 1975.

Peters, E. B. "International Scientific and Technical Meetings--Why Go--Who Profits." R & D Management. 5(2): 139-147; 1975.

Mulkay, M. J., Gilbert, G. N., and Woolgar, S. "Problem Areas and Research Networks in Science." Sociology. The Journal of the British Sociological Association. 9(2): 187-203; 1975.

Wolek, F. W. and Griffith, B. C. "Policy and Informal Communications in Applied Science and Technology." Science Studies. 4(4): 411-420; 1974.

Covitch, S. C. S., Fallon, L. F., and Rothenberg, D. H. "Informal Communication in an Academic Community." Proceedings of the American Society for Information Science. 11: 264-267; 1974.

Lin, N. "Stratification of Formal Communication System in American Sociology." American Sociologist. 9(4): 199-206; 1974.

Mulkay, M. "Conceptual Displacement and Migration in Science--Prefatory Paper." Science Studies. 4(3): 205-234; 1974.

Kochen, M. and Taglioco, R. "Matching Authors and Readers of Scientific Papers." Information Storage and Retrieval. 10(5-6): 197-210; 1974.

Lofthous, S. "Thoughts on Publish or Perish." Higher Education. 3(1): 59-79; 1974.

Hood, P. D. "How Research and Development on Educational Roles and Institutional Structures can Facilitate Communication." Journal of Research and Development in Education. 6(4): 96-113; 1973.

Short, E. C. "Knowledge Production and Utilization in Curriculum--Special Case of General Phenomenon." Review of Educational Research. 43(3): 237-301; 1973.

Oromaner, M. "Career Contingencies and Fate of Sociological Research." Social Science Information. 12(2): 97-111; 1973.

Gustin, B. H. "Charisma, Recognition, and Motivation of Scientists." American Journal of Sociology. 78(5): 1119-1134; 1973.

Zaltman, G. and Kohler, B. M. "Dissemination of Task and Socioemotional Information in an International Community of Scientists." Journal of the American Society for Information Science. 23(4): 225; 1972.

Bowen, D. D., Perloff, R., and Jacoby, J. "Improving Manuscript Evaluation Procedures." American Psychologist. 27(3): 221, 1972.

Lin, N. and Garvey, W. D. "Information Needs and Uses." Annual Review of Information Science and Technology. 7: 5-37; 1972.

Okazawa, K. "Invisible College--Diffusion of Knowledge Among Political Scientists in Japan." Library and Information Science. 1978(16): 19-48; 1978.

Zuckerman, H. "Theory Choice and Problem Choice in Science." Sociological Inquiry. 48(3-4): 65-95; 1978.

Tsuda, Y. "Research Activities on Informal Communication Among Research Workers in Japan." Library and Information Science. 1977(15): 15-27; 1977.

Chubin, D. E. "Trusted Assessorship in Science--Relation in Need of Data." Social Studies of Science. 5(3): 362-368; 1975.

Mulkay, M. J. "3 Models of Scientific Development." Kolner Zeitschrift Fur Soziologie und Sozial Psychologie. 1975(18): 48-61; 1975.

Gieryn, T. F. "Problem Retention and Problem Change in Science." Sociological Inquiry. 48(3-4): 96-115; 1978.

Reskin, B. F. "Sex Differentiation and the Social Organization of Science." Sociological Inquiry. 48(3-4): 6-37; 1978.

Chubin, D. E. "Conceptualization of Scientific Specialties." Sociological Quarterly. 17(4): 448-476; 1976.

Alemann, H. V. "Organizational Factors in Knowledge Transfer--Exploratory Study on Situation in Social Sciences." Kolner Zeitschrift Fur Soziologie und Sozial Psychologie. 1975(18): 254-286; 1975.

The Structure of Literature and Documents

List 3: The results of an author search, Price AND Brookes, which retrieves work citing both these central writers, but eliminating documents citing their work in other fields. (This strategy is perhaps, a bit too restrictive.)

Hubert, J. J. "Bibliometric Models for Journal Productivity." Social Indicators Research. 4(4): 441-473; 1977.

Bottle, R. T. and Rees, M. K. "Liquid-Crystal Literature--Novel Growth-Pattern." Journal of Information Science. 1(2): 117-119; 1979.

Avramescu, A. "Actuality and Obsolescence of Scientific Literature." Journal of the American Society for Information Science. 30(5): 296-303; 1979.

Braun, T. and Bujdoso, E. "Growth of a Journal Reflects Trends in the Literature of Nuclear Analytical Methods." Journal of Radioanalytical Chemistry. 50(1-2): 9-31; 1979.

Sandor, P. and Imre, R. "Use of Scientometry for the Survey of Branches of Science Investigation of the Hungarian Literature of Coordination Chemistry (1934-1976)." Kemiai Kozlemenyek. 51(3-4): 345-358; 1979.

Drott, M. C., Mancall, J. C., and Griffith, B. C. "Bradfords Law and Libraries--Present Applications--Potential Promise." ASLIB Proceedings. 31(6): 296-304; 1979.

Vlachy, J. "Publication Output of European Physics." Czechoslovak Journal of Physics Section B. 29(2): 237-244; 1979.

Worthen, D. B. "Short-Lived Technical Literatures--Bibliometric Analysis." Methods of Information in Medicine. 17(3): 190-198; 1978.

Fjodorov, V. T. "Ranking of Publications on a Fundamental Scientific and Technical Problem." Nauchno-Tekhnicheskaya Informatsiya Seriya 2-Informatsionnye Protsessy I Sistemy. 1978(2): 15-16; 1978.

Dwinell, L. D. "Advances in Information Systems and Services for Forestry Community." Journal of Forestry. 76(2): 80-83; 1978.

Narin, F. and Moll, J. K. "Bibliometrics." Annual Review of Information Science and Technology. 12: 35-58; 1977.

Stern, B. T. "Evaluation and Design of Bibliographic Data-Bases." Annual Review of Information Science and Technology. 12: 3-30; 1977.

Rawski, C. H. "Scientific Study of Subject Literatures." Visible Language. 11(1): 5-23; 1977.

Goffman, W. and Saracevic, T. "Structure and Behavior of Subject Literatures as Base for Forecasting in Scientific Communication." International Forum on Information and Documentation. 2(1): 17-19; 1977.

Harte, N. B. "Trends in Publications on Economic and

Social History of Great Britain and Ireland, 1925-74." Economic History Review. 30(1): 20-39; 1977.

Aiyepeku, W. O. "Productivity of Geographical Authors--Case Study from Nigeria." Journal of Documentation. 32(2): 105-117; 1976.

Saracevic, T. "Relevance--Review of and a Framework for Thinking on Notion in Information Science." Journal of the American Society for Information Science. 26(6): 321-343; 1975.

Lawani, S. M. "Obsolescence of American and French Agronomic Literatures." Journal of Librarianship. 7(1): 12-30; 1975.

Kraft, D. H. and Polacsek, R. A. "Biomedical Literature Dynamics." Methods of Information in Medicine. 13(4): 242-248; 1974.

Line, M. B. and Sandison, A. "Progress in Documentation--Obsolescence and Changes in Use of Literature with Time." Journal of Documentation. 30(3): 283-350; 1974.

Kohut, J. J. "Comparative Analysis of Obsolescence Patterns of U.S. Geoscience Literature." Journal of the American Society for Information Science. 25(4): 242-251; 1974.

Gilbert, G. N. and Woolgar, S. "Quantitative Study of Science Examination of Literature." Science Studies. 4(3): 279-294; 1974.

Turkeli, A. "Doctoral Training Environment and Post-Doctorate Productivity Among Turkish Physicists." Science Studies. 3(3): 311-318; 1973.

Buckland, M. K. "Are Obsolescence and Scattering Related." Journal of Documentation. 28(3): 242; 1972.

Donohue, J. C. "Bibliometric Analysis of Certain Information Science Literature." Journal of the American Society for Information Science. 23(5): 313; 1972.

Braga, G. M. "Some Aspects of the Bradford Distribution." Proceedings of the American Society for Information Science. 15: 51-54; 1978.

Buckland, M. K. "10 Years Progress in Quantitative Research on Libraries." Socio-Economic Planning Sciences. 12(6): 333-339; 1978.

Price, D. D. S. "General Theory of Bibliometric and Other Cumulative Advantage Processes." Journal of the American Society for Information Science. 27(5-6): 292-306; 1976.

Avramescu, A. "Modeling Scientific Information Transfer." International Forum on Information and Documentation. 1(1): 13-19; 1975.

List 4: The results of a document search retrieving papers that cite Price's "cumulative advantage" paper, Journal of the American Society for Information Science 27, pp. 292-306, 1976. The paper, and a couple others in the collection, were judged as so distinctive as to warrant a separate list of recent citing papers.

Simonton, D. K. "Multiple Discovery and Invention--Zeitgeist, Genius, or Chance." Journal of Personality and Social Psychology. 37(9): 1603-1616; 1979.

Jones, W. T. and Chiaraviglio, L. "Is Science an Adaptive System." Behavioral Science. 24(5): 325-333; 1979.

Sandor, P. and Imre, R. "Use of Scientometry for the Survey of Branches of Science. 3. Investigation of the Hungarian Literature of Coordination Chemistry (1934-1976)." Kemiai Kozlemenyek. 51(3-4): 345-358; 1979.

Narin, F. and Moll, J. K. "Bibliometrics." Annual Review of Information Science and Technology. 12: 35-58; 1977.

Salton, G. "Mathematics and Information Retrieval." Journal of Documentation. 35(1): 1-29; 1979.

Drott, M. C., Mancall, J. C., and Griffith, B. C. "Bradfords Law and Libraries--Present Applications--Potential Promise." ASLIB Proceedings. 31(6): 296-304; 1979.

Small, H. G. "Cited Documents as Concept Symbols." Social Studies of Science. 8(3): 327-340; 1978.

Braga, G. M. "Some Aspects of the Bradford Distribution." Proceedings of the American Society for Information Science. 15: 51-54; 1978.

List 5: The results of two searches, Small AND Narin, to find new papers focusing on the use of citations in evaluation and policy, and Small AND Griffith, to find papers focusing on structure. The searches were combined to reduce unnecessary duplication.

Small AND Narin


Koenig, M. E. D. "Online Serials Collection Analysis." Journal of the American Society for Information Science. 30(3): 148-153; 1979.

Garfield, E. "Is Citation Analysis a Legitimate Evaluation Tool." Scientometrics. 1(4): 359-375; 1979.

Rabkin, Y. M. and Lafittehoussat, J. J. "Cooperative Research in Petroleum Chemistry." Scientometrics. 1(4): 327-338; 1979.

Small, H. G. and Koenig, M. E. D. "Journal Clustering Using a Bibliographic Coupling Method." Information Processing & Management. 13(5): 227-288; 1977.

Narin, F. and Moll, J. K. "Bibliometrics." Annual Review of Information Science and Technology. 12: 35-58; 1977.

Studer, K. E. and Chubin, D. E. "Ethics and Unintended Consequences of Social Research--Perspective from Sociology of Science." Policy Sciences. 8(2): 111-124; 1977.

Narin, F., Pinski, G., and Gee, H. H. "Structure of Biomedical Literature." Journal of the American Society for Information Science. 27(1): 25-45; 1976.

Ben David, J. and Sullivan, T. A. "Sociology of Science." Annual Review of Sociology. 1: 203-222; 1975.

Small, H. and Griffith, B. C. "Structure of Scientific Literatures. 1. Identifying and Graphing Specialties." Science Studies. 4(1): 17-40; 1974.

Narin, F. "Objectivity Versus Relevance in Studies of Scientific Advance." Scientometrics. 1(1): 35-41; 1978.

Gilbert, G. N. "Measuring the Growth of Science--Review of Indicators of Scientific Growth." Scientometrics. 1(1): 9-34; 1978.

Lecuyer, B. P. "Evaluation and Perspectives of Sociology of Science in Western Countries." Archives Europeennes de Sociologie. 19(2): 257-336; 1978.

Hargens, L. "Theory and Method in the Sociology of Science." Sociological Inquiry. 48(3-4): 121-139; 1978.

Chubin, D. E. "Conceptualization of Scientific Specialties." Sociological Quarterly. 17(4): 448-476; 1976.

Moravcsik, M. J. "Progress Report on Quantification of Science." Journal of Scientific & Industrial Research. 36(5): 195-203; 1977.

Small AND Griffith

Sullivan, D., Koester, D., White, D. H., and Kern, R. "Understanding Rapid Theoretical Change in Particle Physics--Month-by-Month Co-citation Analysis." Proceedings of the American Society for Information Science. 16: 276-285; 1979.

Griffith, B. D. "Science Literature--How Faulty a Mirror of Science." ASLIB Proceedings. 31(8): 381-391; 1979.

Shearer, E. and Moravcsik, M. J. "Citation Patterns in Little Science and Big Science." Scientometrics. 1(5-6): 463-474; 1979.

Crawford, S. "Identification of Problem Domains in Psychiatry." Proceedings of the American Society for Information Science. 16: 263-269; 1979.

Griffith, B. C. "Social and Behavioral Sciences Literature." Proceedings of the American Society for Information Science. 16: 254-262; 1979.

Price, D. D. S. "Revolution in Mapping of Science." Proceedings of the American Society for Information Science. 16: 249-253; 1979.

Small, H. G. "Co-citation Context Analysis--Relationship between Bibliometric Structure and Knowledge." Proceedings of the American Society for Information Science. 16: 270-275; 1979.

Small, H. G. and Crane, D. "Specialties and Disciplines in Science and Social Science--Examination of Their Structure using Citation Indexes." Scientometrics. 1(5-6): 445-461; 1979.

Krauze, T. K. and McGinnis, R. "Matrix Analysis of Scientific Specialties and Careers in Science." Scientometrics. 1(5-6): 419-444; 1979.

Chubin, D. E. and Studer, K. E. "Knowledge and Structures of Scientific Growth--Measurement of a Cancer Problem Domain." Scientometrics. 1(2): 171-193; 1979.

Drott, M. C. and Griffith, B. C. "Empirical Examination of Bradford Law and Scattering of Scientific Literature." Journal of the American Society for Information Science. 29(5): 238-246; 1978.

Mendez, A. "Some Considerations on Retrieval of Literature Based on Citations." _Information Scientist_. 12(2): 67-71; 1978.

Mullins, N. C., Hargens, L. L., Hecht, P. K., and Kick, E. L. "Group Structure of Co-citation Clusters--Comparative Study." _American Sociological Review_. 42(4): 552-562; 1977.

Cawkell, A. E. "Science Perceived Through Science Citation Index." _Endeavor_. 1(2): 57-62; 1977.

Sullivan, D., White, D. H., and Barboni, E. J. "Co-citation Analyses of Science--Evaluation." _Social Studies of Science_. 7(2): 223-240; 1977.

Sullivan, D., White, D. H., Barboni, E. J. "State of a Science--Indicators in Specialty of Weak Interactions." _Social Studies of Science_. 7(2): 167-200; 1977.

Small, H. G. "Co-citation Model of a Scientific Specialty--Longitudinal Study of Collagen Research." _Social Studies of Science_. 7(2): 139-166; 1977.

Arabie, P. "Clustering Representations of Group Overlap." _Journal of Mathematical Sociology_. 5(1): 113-128; 1977.

Gilbert, G. N. "Referencing as Persuasion." _Social Studies of Science_. 7(1): 113-122; 1977.

Small, H. G. "Structural Dynamics of Scientific Literature." _International Classification_. 3(2): 67-74; 1976.

Belkin, N. J. and Robertson, S. E. "Information Science and Phenomenon of Information." _Journal of the American Society for Information Science_. 27(4): 197-204; 1976.

Garfield, E. "Literature of Social Sciences and Usage and Effectiveness of Social Sciences Citation Index." _Current Contents_. 1976(34): 5-10; 1976.

Garfield, E. "Keeping up with Science May be Difficult but Understanding it is even more so." _Current Contents_. 1976(33): 5-13; 1976.

Garfield, E. "There's More than One Way to Search Chemical Literature." _Current Contents_. 1976(29): 5-10; 1976.

Cawkell, A. E. "Understanding Science by Analyzing its Literature." _Information Scientist_. 10(1): 3-10; 1976.

Mullins, N. C. "New Causal Theory--Elite Specialty in Social Science." _History of Political Economy_. 7(4): 499-529; 1975.

Martyn, J. "Citation Analysis. _Journal of Documentation_. 31(4): 290-297; 1975.

Mullins, N. C. "Development of Science Disciplines--Internal and External Origins of Change." Sociologie et Societes. 7(1): 133-142; 1975.

Moravcsik, M. J. and Murugesa, P. "Some Results on Function and Quality of Citations." Social Studies of Science. 5(1): 86-92; 1975.

Small, H. G. "Multiple Citation Patterns in Scientific Literature--Circle and Hill Models." Information Storage and Retrieval. 10(11-1): 393-402; 1974.

Cawkell, A. E. and Ovshinsky, S. R. "Search Strategy, Construction and Use of Citation Networks, with a Socio-Scientific Example--Amorphous Semi-Conductors." Journal of the American Society for Information Science. 25(2): 123-130; 1974.

Griffith, B. C., Small, H. G., Stonehill, J. A., and Dey, S. "Structure of Scientific Literatures. 2. Toward a Macro-structure and Microstructure for Science." Science Studies. 4(4): 339-365; 1974.

Ben David, J. "Emergence of National Traditions in the Sociology of Science--United States and Great Britain." Sociological Inquiry. 48(3-4): 197-218; 1978.

Chubin, D. E. "Trusted Assessorship in Science--Relation in Need of Data." Social Studies of Science. 5(3): 362-368; 1975.

Garfield, E. and Cawkell, A. E. "Citation Analysis Studies." Science. 189(4200): 397; 1975.

Information in Innovation: Required Flows of Knowledge

List 6: The results of a document search, on Allen's review paper, ASLIB Proceedings 20, pp. 433-453, 1968. Note that all lists in this section are relatively short; generally this appears to be a relatively underdeveloped area. (Several major journals have recently appeared dealing with innovation and the diffusion of technology; it is uncertain as to how and whether the information profession and science will relate to those developments.)

Allen, T. S. "Information in Innovation." ASLIB Proceedings. 20: 433-453; 1968.

Lancaster, F. W. and Smith, L. C. "Science, Scholarship and the Communication of Knowledge." Library Trends. 27(3): 367-388; 1979.

Bellardo, T. and Waldhart, T. J. "Marketing Products and Services in Academic-Libraries." Libri. 27(3): 181-194; 1977.

Shapiro, E. L. "Complementarity of Formal and Informal Communications." Nauchno-Tekhnicheskaya Informatsiya Seriya 1-Organizatsiya I Metodika Informatsionnoi Raboty 1976(3): 3-6; 1976.

Kemp, D. A. "Relevance, Pertinence and Information System Development." Information Storage and Retrieval. 10(2): 37-47; 1974.

Johnston, J. "Survey of Construction Industry Libraries." ASLIB Proceedings. 27(10): 401-413; 1975.

Blagden, J. "Communication--Key Library Management Problem." ASLIB Proceedings. 27(8): 319-326; 1975.

Thomas, M. D. and Leheron, R. B. "Perspectives on Technological Change and Process of Diffusion in Manufacturing Sector." Economic Geography. 51(3): 231-251; 1975.

Waldhart, T. J. "Utility of Scientific Research--Engineers Use of Products of Science." IEEE Transactions on Professional Communication. 17(2): 33-35; 1974.

Kenning, T. D. "Local Government Information Services." Journal of Librarianship. 6(1): 1-9; 1974.

List 7: The results of an author search, the term being "F. Wolek." His work has been closely focused on the policy aspects of innovation in high technology.

Campbell, R. J. "Evaluation of Need for New Information Technology to Support Branch Operations." Journal of Risk and Insurance. 45(3): 401-412; 1978.

Chagnon, M., Audette, L. M., Lebrun, L., and Tilquin, C. "Patient Classification System by Level of Nursing Care Requirements." Nursing Research. 27(2): 107-113; 1978.

Ginzberg, M. J. "Steps Towards More Effective Implementation of MS and MIS." *Interfaces*. 8(3): 57-63; 1978.

Wolek, F. W. "Uses and Benefits of Technical Information Systems." *Research Management*. 20(5): 37-41; 1977.

Ford, G. "Progress in Documentation--Research in User Behaviour in University Libraries." *Journal of Documentation*. 29(1): 85-106; 1973.

Priest, W. C. "Restructuring Communication in Science and Technology." *IEEE Transactions on Professional Communications*. 15(2): 20; 1972.

Daellenbach, H. G. "Implementation is 1st Phase of an or Project." *New Zealand Operational Research*. 6(1): 1-12; 1978.

Wolek, F. W. and Griffith, B. C. "Policy and Informal Communications in Applied Science and Technology." *Science Studies*. 4(4): 411-420; 1974.

Fox, J. G. "Ergonomics and Information Systems." *ASLIB Proceedings*. 24(3): 178; 1972.

Wolek, F. W. "Engineering Roles in Development Projects." *IEEE Transactions on Engineering Management*. 19(2): 53; 1972.

List 8: The results of a document search utilizing Glaser and Taylor's excellent *American Psychologist* article (28, pp. 140-146, 1973). This article summarizes an early and well-executed study of innovation in the behavioral sciences.

Glaser, E. M. and Taylor, S. E. "Innovation in Information." *American Psychologist*. 28(2): 140-146; 1973.

Bartunek, J. M. and Keys, C. B. "Participation in School Decision-Making." *Urban Education*. 14(1): 52-75; 1979.

Keys, C. B. and Bartunek, J. M. "Organization-Development in Schools--Goal Agreement, Process Skills, and Diffusion of Change." *Journal of Applied Behavioral Science*. 15(1): 61-78; 1979.

Roos, L. L., Roos, N. P., and McKinley, B. "Inplementing Randomization." *Policy Analysis*. 3(4): 547-559; 1977.

Cox, G. B. "Managerial Style--Implications for Utilization of Program-Evaluation Information." Evaluation Quarterly. 1(3): 499-508; 1977.

Glaser, E. M. "Consultation in Institutions for Child Development." Journal of Applied Behavioral Science. 13(1): 89-109; 1977.

Nickels, J. B., Harvey, D., and Ledger, J. "Interdisciplinary Approach to Scientific Research on Quality of Life in Canadian North." Center for Settlement Studies. Research Reports. University of Manitoba. 2(25): 1; 1976.

Silverman, W. H., Beech, R. P., Fiester, A. R. "Community Psychologist as Researcher--Hidden and Unhidden Agenda." Professional Psychology. 7(2): 141-146; 1976.

Klein, M. W. "Collaboration between Practitioners and Researchers--Relevant Knowledge in Corrections." Federal Probation. 37(4): 42-46; 1973.

Perloff, R., Perloff, E., and Sussna, E. "Program Evaluation." Annual Review of Psychology. 27: 569-594; 1976.

McNamara, J. R. "Ways by Which Outcome Measures Influence Outcomes in Classroom Behavior--Modification Research." Journal of School Psychology. 13(2): 104-113; 1975.

Miller, G. and Willer, B. "Proposal for Development of Provincial Mental Health Evaluation Resource Centers." Canada's Mental Health. 23(2): 6-10; 1975.

Bolton, B. "Research Utilization of R and D Project Results with Severely Handicapped Deaf Clients." Journal of Rehabilitation of the Deaf. 8(1): 87-94; 1974.

Information Retrieval and Analysis

List 9: The results of an author search, Salton AND Spark Jones, which seeks documents citing two central writers in this area. This is quite a rather restrictive serach which probably identifies integrative pieces within the literature.

Crawford, R. G. "Automatic Thesaurus Construction Based on Term Centroids." Canadian Journal of Information Science. 4(May): 124-136; 1979.

Sparck Jones, K. "Search Term Relevance Weighting Given Little Relevance Information." Journal of Documentation. 35(1): 30-48; 1979.

Salton, G. "Mathematics and Information Retrieval." Journal of Documentation. 35(1): 1-29; 1979.

Pao, M. L. "Automatic Text Analysis Based on Transition Phenomena of Word Occurrence." Journal of the American Society for Information Science. 29(3): 121-124; 1978.

Yu, C. T., Salton, G., and Siu, M. K. "Effective Automatic Indexing Using Term Addition and Deletion." Journal of the Association for Computing Machinery. 25(2): 210-225; 1978.

Attar, R., Choueka, Y., Dershowitz, N., and Fraenkel, A. S. "Kedma--Linguistic Tools for Retrieval Systems." Journal of the Association for Computing Machinery. 25(1): 52-66; 1978.

Liston, D. M. and Howder, M. L. "Subject Analysis." Annual Review of Information Science and Technology. 12: 81-118; 1977.

Ghose, A. and Dhawle, A. S. "Problems of Thesaurus Construction." Journal of the American Society for Information Science. 28(4): 211-217; 1977.

Robertson, S. E. "Theories and Models in Information Retrieval." Journal of Documentation. 33(2): 126-148; 1977.

Attar, R. and Fraenkel, A. S. "Local Feedback in Full-Text Retrieval Systems." Journal of the Association for Computing Machinery. 24(3): 397-417, 1977.

Bookstein, A. and Cooper, W. "General Mathematical Model for Information Retrieval Systems." Library Quarterly. 46(2): 153-167; 1976.

Yu, C. T. and Salton G. "Precision Weighting--Effective Automatic Indexing Method." Journal of the Association for Computing Machinery. 23(1): 76-88; 1976.

Harter, S. P. "Probabilistic Approach to Automatic Keyword Indexing. 2. Algorithm for Probabilistic Indexing." Journal of the American Society for Information Science. 26(5): 280-289; 1975.

Field, B. J. "Towards Automatic Indexing--Automatic Assignment of Controlled Language Indexing and Classification From Free Indexing." Journal of Documentation. 31(4): 246-265; 1975.

VanRijsbergen, C. J. and Croft, W. B. "Document Clustering--Evaluation of Some Experiments with Cranfield 1400 Collection." Information Processing & Management. 11(5-7): 171-182; 1975.

Hirschman, L., Grishman, R., and Sager, N. "Grammatically-Based Automatic Word Class Formation." Information Processing & Management. 11(1-2): 39-57; 1975.

Salton, G., Yang, C. S., and Yu, C. T. "Theory of Term Importance in Automatic Text Analysis." Journal of the American Society for Information Science. 26(1): 33-44; 1975.

Summit, R. K. and Firschei, O. "Document Retrieval Systems and Techniques." Annual Review of Information Science and Technology. 9: 285-331; 1974.

Sparck Jones, K. "Progress in Documentation--Automatic Indexing." Journal of Documentation. 30(4): 393-432; 1974.

Iker, H. P. "Historical Note on Use of Word-Frequency Contiguities in Content Analysis." Computers and the Humanities. 8(2): 93-98; 1974.

Tell, B. V. "Towards Automated Multi-Disciplinary Information Retrieval." Journal of Documentation. 30(2): 216-223; 1974.

Salton, G. and Yang, C. S. "Specification of Term Values in Automatic Indexing." Journal of Documentation. 29(4): 351-372; 1973.

Preece, S. E. "Clustering as an Output Option." Proceedings of the American Society for Information Science. 10: 189-190; 1973.

Batten, W. E. "Document Description and Representation." Annual Review of Information Science and Technology. 8: 43-68; 1973.

Adamson, G. W. and Bush, J. A. "Method for Automatic Classification of Chemical Structures." Information Storage and Retrieval. 9(10): 561-568; 1973.

Sparck Jones, K. "Collection Properties Influencing Automatic Term Classification Performance." Information Storage and Retrieval. 9(9): 499-513; 1973.

Minker, J., Peltola, E., and Wilson, G. A. "Document Retrieval Experiments Using Cluster Analysis." Journal of the American Society for Information Science. 24(4): 246-260; 1973.

Sparck Jones, K. "Statistical Interpretation of Term Specificity and Its Application in Retrieval." Journal of Documentation. 28(1): 11, 1972.

Brandhor, W. T. and Eckert, P. F. "Document Retrieval and

Dissemination Systems." Annual Review of Information Science and Technology. 7: 379-437; 1972.

Prywes, N. S. and Smith, D. P. "Organization of Information." Annual Review of Information Science and Technology. 7: 103-158; 1972.

Vernimb, C. "Automatic Query Adjustment in Document Retrieval." Information Processing & Management. 13(6): 339-353; 1977.

Sager, W. K. H. and Lockemann, P. C. "Classification of Ranking Algorithms." International Forum on Information and Documentation. 1(4): 12-25; 1976.

Barraclough, E. D. "Online Searching in Information Retrieval." Journal of Documentation. 33(3): 220-238; 1977.

Klingbiel, P. H. and Rinker, C. C. "Evaluation of Machine-Aided Indexing." Information Processing & Management. 12(6): 351-366; 1976.

Garfield, E., Malin, M. V., and Small, H. "System for Automatic Classification of Scientific Literature." Journal of the Indian Institute of Science. 57(2): 61-74; 1975.

List 10: The results of a document search identifying work citing Swets' "signal detection" approach to retrieval evaluation (Journal of the American Society for Information Science 20, pp. 72-89, 1969). This list was developed because of the distinctiveness of this approach.

Salton, G. "Mathematics and Information Retrieval." Journal of Documentation. 35(1): 1-29; 1979.

Sloggem, J. "Drug Information Systems for Hospital Pharmacists." Journal of Clinical Pharmacy. 2(4): 239-245; 1978.

Swets, J. A. "Information Retrieval and Analysis." American Documentation. 20(1): 72-89; 1969.

Hubert, J. J. "Bibliometric Models for Journal Productivity." Social Indicators Research. 4(4): 441-473; 1977.

Kraft, D. H. and Bookstein, A. "Evaluation of Information Retrieval Systems--Decision-Theory Approach." Journal of the American Society for Information Science. 29(1): 31-40; 1978.

Robertson, S. E. "Theories and Models in Information Retrieval." Journal of Documentation. 33(2): 126-148; 1977.

Heine, M. H. "Incorporation of Age of a Document into Retrieval Process." Information Processing & Management. 13(1): 35-47; 1977.

Heine, M. H. "Measures of Language Effectiveness and Swetsian Hypotheses." Journal of Documentation. 31(4): 283-287; 1975.

Cawkell, A. E. "Measure of Efficiency Factor--Communication Theory Applied to Document Selection Systems." Information Processing & Management. 11(8-12): 243-248; 1975.

Heine, M. H. "Inverse Relationship of Precision and Recall in Terms of Swets Model." Journal of Documentation. 29(1): 81-84; 1973.

Heine, M. H. "Distance Between Sets as an Objective Measure of Retrieval Effectiveness." Information Storage and Retrieval. 9(3): 181-198; 1973.

Robertson, S. E. and Teather, D. "Statistical Analysis of Retrieval Tests--Bayesian Approach." Journal of Documentation. 30(3): 273-282; 1974.

Farradan, J. "Evaluation of Information Retrieval Systems." Journal of Documentation. 30(2): 195-209; 1974.

Heine, M. H. "Design Equations for Retrieval Systems Based on Swets Model." Journal of the American Society for Information Science. 25(3): 183-198; 1974.

Carmon, J. L. "Discriminant Function Index for Information System Evaluation." Journal of the American Society for Information Science. 25(2): 118-122; 1974.

Thompson, C. W. "Functions of Abstracts in Initial Screening of Technical Documents by User." Journal of the American Society for Information Science. 24(4): 270-276; 1973.

Herner, S. and Snapper, K. J. "Application of Multiple Criteria Utility Theory to Evaluation of Information Systems." Journal of the American Society for Information Science. 29(6): 289-296; 1978.

Bookstein, A. "When Most Pertinent Document Should Not Be Retrieved--Analysis of Swets Model." Information Processing & Management. 13(6): 377-383; 1977.

*Tools and Ideas: The Interface of Information Science and Librarianship.*

List 11: Results of a document search retrieving papers citing Kochen and Deutsch. "Toward a Rational Theory of Decentralization: Some Implications of a Mathematical Approach." *American Political Science Review.* 63: 734-749; 1969.

Kochen, M. and Deutsch, K. W. "Delegation and Control in Organizations with Varying Degrees of Decentralization." *Behavioral Science.* 22(4): 258-269; 1977.

Giertz, J. R. "Decentralization at State and Local Level--Empirical Analysis." *National Tax Journal.* 29(2): 201-209; 1976.

Park, S. J. "Planning and Political Process in Developing Countries." *Zeitschrift Fur Politik.* 23(1): 16-29; 1976.

Porter, D. O. and Olsen, E. A. "Some Critical Issues in Government Centralization and Decentralization." *Public Administration Review.* 36(1): 72-84; 1976.

Brown, L. A. "Market and Infrastructure Context of Adoption--Spatial Perspective on Diffusion of Innovation." *Economic Geography.* 51(3): 185-216; 1975.

Furniss, N. "Northern Ireland as a Case Study of Decentralization in Unitary States." *World Politics.* 27(3): 387-404; 1975.

Furniss, N. "Practical Significance of Decentralization." *Journal of Politics.* 36(4): 958-982; 1974.

Kochen, M. and Deutsch, K. W. "Note on Hierarchy and Coordination--Aspect of Decentralization." *Management Science Series A. Theory.* 21(1): 106-114; 1974.

Kochen, M. and Deutsch, K. W. "Decentralization by Function and Location." *Management Science Series B. Application.* 19(8): 841-856; 1973.

Kochen, M. "Directory Design for Networks of Information and Referral Centers." *Library Quarterly.* 42(1): 59; 1972.

Hart, D. K. "Theories of Government Related to Decentralization and Citizen Participation." *Public Administration Review.* 32(Oct.): 603-622; 1972.

Schmandt, H. J. "Municipal Decentralization--Overview." *Public Administration Review.* 32(Oct.): 571-588; 1972.

Park, S. J. "Planning and Political Process in Developing

Countries." Law and State. 16: 30-47; 1977.

List 12: Results of a document search retrieving papers citing Lipetz. "Catalog Use in a Large Research Library." Library Quarterly. 42: 129-139; 1972.

Fussler, H. H. and Kocher, K. "Contemporary Issues in Bibliographic Control." Library Quarterly. 47(3): 237-252; 1977.

Saracevic, T., Shaw, W. M., and Kantor, P. B. "Causes and Dynamics of User Frustration in an Academic Library." College & Research Libraries. 38(1): 17-18; 1977.

Grady, A. M. "Divided Catalogs--Selected Bibliography." Library Resources & Technical Services. 20(2): 131-142; 1976.

Weintraub, S., Robinson, H. M., Smith, H. K., and Plessas, G. P. "Summary of Investigations Relating to Reading, July 1, 1971, to June 30, 1972." Reading Research Quarterly. 8(3): 247-439; 1973.

Simmons, P. "Library Automation." Annual Review of Information Science and Technology. 8: 167-201; 1973.

Batten, W. E. "Document Description And Representation." Annual Review of Information Science and Technology. 8: 43-68; 1973.

Minder, T. "Application of Systems Analysis in Designing a New System." Library Trends. 21(4): 553-564; 1973.

Seymour, C. A. and Schofield, J. L. "Measuring Reader Failure at Catalogue." Library Resources and Technical Services. 17(1): 6-24; 1973.

Richmond, P. A. "Document Description and Representation." Annual Review of Information Science and Technology. 7: 73-102; 1972.

Kantor, P. B. "Availability Analysis." Journal of the American Society for Information Science. 27(5-6): 311-319; 1976.

List 13: Results of a document search retrieving papers citing Kantor. "Availability Analysis." Journal of the American Society for Information Science. 27(5): 311-319; 1976.

Kantor, P. B. "QUBMIS--Quantitatively Based Management Information System for Libraries." Proceedings of the American Society for Information Science. 15: 174-176; 1978.

Wulff, Y. "Book Availability in University of Minnesota Bio-Medical Library." Bulletin of the Medical Library Association. 66(3): 349-350; 1978.

Buckland, M. K. "10 Years Progress in Quantitative Research on Libraries." Socio-Economic Planning Sciences. 12(6): 333-339; 1978.

List 14: Results of a document search retrieving papers citing Sandison. "Densities of Use, and Absence of Obsolescence, in Physics Journals at MIT." Journal of the American Society for Information Science. 25(3): 172-182; 1974.

Maxin, J. A. "Periodical Use and Collection Development." College & Research Libraries. 40(3): 248-253; 1979.

Bastille, J. D. and Mankin, C. J. "Report on Subsequent Demand for Journal Titles Dropped in 1975." Bulletin of the Medical Library Association. 66(3): 346-349; 1978.

Sinha, B. K. and Clelland, R. C. "Modeling Library Collections--Reply." Management Science. 24(1): 115-117; 1977.

Sandison, A. "Modeling Library Collections." Management Science. 24(1): 113-114; 1977.

Perk, L. J. and VanPulis, N. "Periodical Usage in an Education-Psychology Library." College & Research Libraries. 38(4): 204-208; 1977.

Piternick, A. B. "Effects of Binding Policy and Other Factors on Availability of Journal Issues." Bulletin of the Medical Library Association. 64(3): 284-292; 1976.

Cho, Y. J. "Citation Characteristics of Periodical Literature in Veterinary Science." American Journal of Veterinary Research. 38(1): 131-133; 1977.

Piternick, A. B. "Derivation of a Sample of Journal Issues for Tests of Availability and Use." Journal of the American Society for Information Science. 26(5): 269-270; 1975.

Bourne, C. P. and Gregor, D. "Planning Serials Cancellations and Cooperative Collection Development in Health Sciences--Methodology and Background Information." Bulletin of the Medical Library Association. 63(4): 366-377; 1975.

Line, M. B. and Sandison, A. "Practical Interpretation of Citation and Library Use Studies." College & Research Libraries. 36(5): 393-396; 1975.

Sandison, A. "References--Citations in Study of Knowledge." Journal of Documentation. 31(3): 195-198; 1975.

Subramanyam, K. "Criteria for Journal Selection." Special Libraries 66(8): 367-371; 1975.

Sandison, A. "Sampling Library Use." Bulletin of the Medical Library Association. 63(2): 234; 1975.

Bailey, M. J. "Densities of Use and Absence of Obsolescence in Physics Journals at MIT." Journal of the American Society for Information Science. 25(6): 383; 1974.

Line, M. B. and Sandison, A. "Progress in Documentation--Obsolescence and Changes in Use of Literature with Time." Journal of Documentation. 30(3): 283-350; 1974.

Rouse, W. B. "Circulation Dynamics--Planning Model." Journal of the American Society for Information Science. 25(6): 358-363; 1974.

Bailey, M. J. "Selecting Materials for Interdisciplinary Programs." Special Libraries. 69(12): 468-474; 1978.

Vlacky, J. "Czechoslovak Journal of Physics in World Physics Literature. Czechoslovak Journal of Physics Section B. 27(12): 1417-1424; 1977.

Wenger, C. B. and Childress, J. "Journal Evaluation in a Large Research Library." Journal of the American Society for Information Science. 28(5): 293-299; 1977.

Singleton, A. "Journal Ranking and Selection--Review in Physics." Journal of Documentation. 32(4): 258-289; 1976.

Sinha, B. K. and Clelland, R. C. "Application of a Collection Control Model for Scientific Libraries." Journal of the American Society for Information Science. 27(5-6): 320-328; 1976.

Vlacky, J. "Europhysics Journals Size, Cost, Authors, Collaborativeness, Citations." Czechoslovak Journal of Physics Section B. 26(12): 1395-1406; 1976.

List 15: Results of a document search retrieving papers citing Trueswell. "Two Characteristics of Circulation and Their Effect on the Implementation of Mechanized Circulation Control Systems."

College and Research Libraries. 25: 285-291; 1964.

Line, M. B. and Sandison, A. "Progress in Documentation--Obsolescence and Changes in Use of Literature with Time." Journal of Documentation. 30(3): 283-350; 1974.

Morse, P. M. "Measures of Library Effectiveness." Library Quarterly. 42(1): 15; 1972.

www.ingramcontent.com/pod-product-compliance
Lightning Source LLC
LaVergne TN
LVHW011903200926
848484LV00002B/511
* 9 7 8 0 3 1 3 2 5 7 7 7 3 *